Understanding Computers and Data Processing: Today and Tomorrow with BASIC

Second Edition

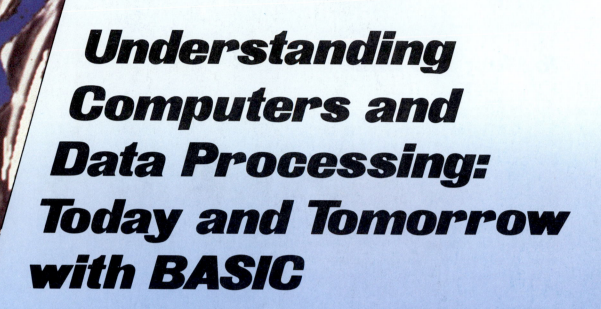

Understanding Computers and Data Processing: Today and Tomorrow with BASIC

Second Edition

Charles S. Parker

The College of Santa Fe
Santa Fe, New Mexico

The Colorado College
Colorado Springs, Colorado

Holt, Rinehart and Winston,
New York   Chicago   San Francisco   Philadelphia
Montreal   Toronto   London   Sydney   Tokyo
Mexico City   Rio de Janeiro   Madrid

To Mom and Dad

Publisher: Ted Buchholz
Associate Editor: David Chodoff
Production Manager: Paul Nardi
Production Coordinator: Lila M. Gardner, Cobb/Dunlop Publisher Services, Inc.
Interior Design and Color Sections: Marsha Cohen/Parallelogram
Cover Design: Steven Bliss
Illustrations: Scientific Illustrators
Composition: Science Press
Printing and Binding: Von Hoffman Press

Library of Congress Cataloging in Publication Data

Parker, Charles S., 1945–
  Understanding computers and data processing.

  Includes index.
  1. Electronic digital computers. I. Title.
QA76.5.P318   1987   004   86-18424

ISBN 0-03-008119-X

Printed in the United States of America
Published simultaneously in Canada

 8 9 0   032   9 8 7 6 5 4

CBS COLLEGE PUBLISHING
Holt, Rinehart and Winston
The Dryden Press
Saunders College Publishing

Brief Contents

For detailed contents see page vii

The Windows

Detailed Contents

Module B Hardware   91

Preface

Three years passed between the publication of the first edition of *Understanding Computers and Data Processing: Today and Tomorrow* and the arrival of this second edition. In many fields, not much changes in three years. The study of computers and the world of information, however, is not like most other fields. Brand new technologies emerge almost overnight. Older technologies that were on the cutting edge quickly become history. Where computers are involved, constant change is one of the few certainties.

My greatest challenge in preparing the second edition of this textbook was to keep pace with this rapidly changing environment without sacrificing the qualities that made the first edition so successful. This second edition, I feel, meets today's classroom needs while retaining the readability, the depth of coverage, and the useful instructional tools that characterized its predecessor.

The textbook is but one component of a complete and flexible instructional package—one that can easily be adapted to virtually any classroom format. Supplementing the textbook, which is available in two versions—one with an appendix on BASIC programming and one without—is a comprehensive set of student and teacher support materials.

THE TEXTBOOK

Understanding Computers and Data Processing: Today and Tomorrow, second edition, is designed for students taking a first course in computers and data processing. The text meets the requirements proposed for the first course in computing by the Data Processing Management Association (DPMA). It provides a thorough introduction to the world of computers, but it is not overly technical. Coverage is given to both commercial and personal applications of computers.

What's New: Changes from the First Edition

Among the most noteworthy differences between the first and second editions are the following:

✘ The book now has two full chapters on productivity software. These chapters—12 and 13—discuss word processing, spreadsheets, presentation graphics, file managers, database management systems, and integrated software packages.

✘ A special productivity software manual, *A Beginner's Guide to WordStar,*® *1-2-3,*® *and dBASE,*® comes packaged with both versions of the text. The *Guide* provides easy-to-follow, hands-on instruction designed to get students performing useful work with these popular software packages as quickly as possible.

Microcomputers and microcomputer-based computer systems receive increased coverage in the second edition, reflecting their increased importance in the marketplace. In expanding the book in this manner, I took great care to avoid the trap of excluding minicomputers and mainframes from their well-deserved coverage.

Chapter 14 in the first edition—which is now Chapter 15 (Business Systems)—has been reworked completely to provide a general introduction to business computer systems.

Chapter 15 (Systems Development I) and 16 (Systems Development II) in the first edition have been combined into a single chapter, 16 (Systems Development), in the second edition. This chapter now includes a section on prototyping.

Chapter 18 (Computers in Our Lives: The Costs and the Benefits) has been expanded to include coverage of state-of-the-art applications in such fields as education, art, sports, medicine, and science.

The programming chapters and (for the "with BASIC" version of this text) the appendix on BASIC reflect an increased emphasis on the use of structured techniques. Several features relating to developing and debugging BASIC programs have also been added to the appendix.

Coverage of number systems has been expanded and moved from Chapter 4 (The Central Processing Unit) to a separate appendix.

Key Features of the Text

Like the first edition, the second edition of *Understanding Computers and Data Processing: Today and Tomorrow* is both current and comprehensive. It offers a flexible teaching organization and a readable and engaging presentation. Learning tools in each chapter help students master important concepts. Tomorrow boxes and other boxed features provide extra insight on major issues. The seven thematic "Windows," each of which highlights some major aspect of data processing, bring the world of computers to life. A glossary at the end of the book gives concise definitions of important terms. The appendix on BASIC, for those who adopt the version of the text that contains it, provides a comprehensive introduction to BASIC in a style students will find easy to read.

CURRENCY.   The state-of-the-art content of this book reflects both current trends and current needs. Take a look, for example, at the materials on display devices and printers in Chapter 6; at the chapters on teleprocessing (7), productivity software packages (12 and 13), and microcomputers (14). Glance at the Tomorrow boxes in each chapter, which give students a sense of the direction of change in the world of computers. And look at the array of technologies and applications illustrated in the seven full-color "Windows" that appear throughout the book.

COMPREHENSIVENESS AND DEPTH.   Before work began on the second edition of this book, the publisher conducted several extensive studies to determine the selection of topics, degree of depth, and other features that instructors of introductory data processing courses most want to see in a textbook of this type. As the manuscript developed, instructors at a variety of institutions around the country—including those who used the first edition and those who did not—were asked to review it. The resulting textbook accommodates a wide range of teaching preferences. It not only covers traditional topics thoroughly, but it also includes the facts your students should know about today's "hot" topics, such as teleprocessing, productivity software packages, interactive terminal use, microcomputer systems and their components, office technologies, CAD/CAM, and structured practices in software and systems development.

FLEXIBLE ORGANIZATION.   A textbook locked into a rigid organization, no matter how thorough, will inevitably find its uses limite . In order to appeal to a wide audience, I have continued to keep this book flexible. Its eighteen chapters are grouped into five modules: Introduction (Chapters 1–3), Hardware (Chapters 4–7), Software (Chapters 8–13), Computer Systems (Chapters 14–16), and Computers in Society (Chapters 17 and 18). Every effort was made to have each chapter as self-contained as possible, making it easy for you to skip chapters or teach them in a sequence other than the one followed in the book. And each chapter is organized into well-defined sections, so you can assign only parts of a chapter if the whole provides more depth than you need.

READABILITY.   We remember more about a subject if it is presented in an organized, straightforward way and made interesting and exciting. This book is written in a conversational, down-to-earth style—a manner designed to be accurate without being intimidating. Concepts are explained clearly and simply without use of confusing terminology. And technical points are made vivid with realistic examples from everyday life.

CHAPTER LEARNING TOOLS.   Each chapter contains a number of learning tools to help students master the materials.

- *Chapter Outline*   An outline of the headings in the chapter shows the major topics to be discussed.

- *Chapter Objectives*   A list of learning objectives is provided for the student to keep in mind while reading the chapter.

- *Overview*   Each chapter starts with an overview that puts the subject matter of the chapter in perspective and helps students organize the material they will be reading.

- *Boldfaced Key Terms*   Important terms appear in boldface type as they are introduced in the chapter. These terms are also defined in the glossary.

✕ *Tomorrow Boxes*   These special features (there's one in each chapter) provide students with a look at possible future developments in the world of computers and serve as a focus for class discussion.

✕ *Other Boxed Features*   Each chapter has one or more additional features with supplementary information designed to stimulate class discussion.

✕ *Photographs and Diagrams*   Instructive, full-color photographs and diagrams appear throughout the book to help illustrate important concepts. The use of color in the diagrams has been carefully controlled to be a functional part of the book.

✕ *Summary and Key Terms*   This is a concise summary of the main points in the chapter. Every boldfaced key term in the chapter also appears in boldface type in the summary. Students will find this summary a valuable tool for study and review.

✕ *Review Exercises*   Every chapter ends with a collection of fill-in, matching, and short-answer discussion questions.

WINDOWS.   The book contains seven full-color photo essays. Each of these "Windows" on the world of computers is organized around a major text theme (see page vi for details).

GLOSSARY.   The glossary at the end of the book defines 532 important computer terms mentioned in the text, including all the boldfaced key terms. Each glossary item has a page reference indicating where it is boldfaced or where it first appears in the text.

APPENDIX A: NUMBER SYSTEMS.   This appendix covers the binary, octal, decimal, and hexadecimal numbering systems, including rules for converting numbers from one system into another.

APPENDIX B: A BEGINNER'S GUIDE TO BASIC.   The "with BASIC" version of this book contains an appendix that provides a comprehensive, 112-page introduction to that language. It is not just a list of rules and procedures, but an engaging, easy-to-read tutorial that encourages students to begin creating programs immediately. Systematic program development and the honing of debugging skills are also an integral part of the presentation.

STUDENT AND TEACHER SUPPORT MATERIAL

Understanding Computers and Data Processing: Today and Tomorrow comes with a complete package of support materials for instructors and students. These include a student *Study Guide,* an *Instructor's Manual, Transparency Acetates,* a *Test Bank,* instructional software to accompany the appendix on BASIC, and a productivity software manual entitled *A Beginner's Guide to WordStar, 1-2-3, and dBASE.*

Study Guide

The *Study Guide* is designed to help students master the material in the text through self-testing. For each of the eighteen chapters in the text the Study Guide provides:

❌ A list of **Chapter Objectives.**

❌ A **Pretest** that lets students test their knowledge of the chapter before they begin to study it intensively.

❌ An **Overview** that puts the subject matter of the chapter in perspective.

❌ A **Summary** of the chapter, written in narrative form. This summary is more detailed than the end-of-chapter summary in the text.

❌ A **Boxed Feature** that explores in greater detail one or more of the chapter topics.

❌ A list of the **Key Terms** in the chapter, with page references indicating where each is boldfaced.

❌ A **Crossword Puzzle** using chapter key terms.

❌ Five types of **self-testing questions:** matching, true/false, multiple-choice, fill-in, and short answer.

❌ A set of especially challenging questions and projects.

❌ An **Answer Key.**

The *Study Guide* also covers the number systems appendix and the appendix on BASIC programming. For each section of the BASIC appendix, the *Study Guide* provides a brief summary, a review of BASIC commands, multiple-choice questions, and new programming problems.

Instructor's Manual

In the *Instructor's Manual* I draw on my own teaching experience to provide instructors with practical suggestions for enhancing classroom presentation. The *Instructor's Manual* also contains suggestions for adapting this textbook to various course schedules, including one-quarter, two-quarter, one-semester, two-semester, and night courses. For each of the eighteen chapters of the text the *Instructor's Manual* provides:

❌ A list of **Chapter Objectives.**

❌ A **Summary,** oriented to the instructor, with teaching suggestions.

❌ A list of the **Key Terms** in the chapter, with a page reference indicating where each is boldfaced.

❌ A **Teaching Outline** that gives a detailed breakdown of the chapter, with all headings and subheadings as well as points to cover under each. References to the *Transparency Acetates* are keyed into this outline.

✖ **Activity Notes,** with recommended topics for class discussion, suggestions for using the windows and boxes, important points to discuss on the transparency acetates, and mention of additional instructor resources.

✖ **Answers** to the end-of-chapter Discussion Questions. Some chapters contain additional discussion questions and answers to them.

The *Instructor's Manual* also covers the number systems appendix, the appendix on BASIC programming, and the productivity software manual, *A Beginners Guide to WordStar, 1-2-3, and dBASE.*

Transparency Acetates

A set of 105 ready-to-show *Transparency Acetates* for use with an overhead projector is available to help instructors explain key points. The figures are derived from selected text diagrams. The Teaching Outlines of the *Instructor's Manual* indicate when to show the acetates, and the Activity Notes lists points to make about them.

Test Bank

The *Test Bank* contains over 3200 test items in various formats, including true/false, multiple-choice, fill-in, short-answer, and matching questions. The *Test Bank* is also available in computerized form for the IBM PC and the Apple II family of computers.

Software for the BASIC Appendix

Instructors who adopt the "with BASIC" version of this book will receive self-documenting, interactive tutorial software to accompany it. The software is available on disks for the IBM PC and the Apple II family of computers.

Productivity Software Guide

The productivity software supplement, *A Beginner's Guide to WordStar, 1-2-3, and dBASE,* has been prepared to enable students to quickly learn and use WordStar, 1-2-3, and dBASE II, III, or III Plus in a PC-DOS or MS-DOS-based computing environment. The *Guide* uses an easy-to-follow, tutorial-style format that allows students to pick up the basics of each of these packages quickly. It also covers such basics of microcomputer operation as keyboard use, working with floppy disks and their drives, and interfacing with PC-DOS or MS-DOS. This makes the supplement a complete learning package for microcomputer-based instruction on one or more of these productivity software packages.

Full-powered Productivity Software

CBS College Publishing and THORN EMI, the distributor of Perfect Software, have signed an agreement that allows Holt, Rinehart and Winston to license the use of Perfect Writer,® Perfect Calc,® and Perfect Filer® at your school if you adopt this text. Perfect Writer is a sophisticated word-processing package with state-of-the-art editing and search functions; Perfect Calc is a powerful spreadsheet program; and Perfect Filer provides a comprehensive assortment of data management facilities. For details, call collect, (212) 872-2247 or contact your Holt sales representative.

ACKNOWLEDGMENTS

I could never have completed a project of this scope alone. I owe a special word of thanks first to the many people who reviewed the text—those whose extensive comments on the first edition helped define the second, those whose comments on drafts of the second edition helped mold it into its final form, and those who reviewed parts of the instructional package:

Richard Batt	Saint Louis Community College at Meremec
James Buxton	Tidewater Community College, Virginia
Vernon Clodfelter	Rowan Technical College, North Carolina
Robert H. Dependahl, Jr.	Santa Barbara City College, California
Eugene T. Dolan	University of the District of Columbia
J. Patrick Fenton	West Valley Community College, California
William C. Fink	Lewis and Clark Community College, Illinois
George P. Grill	University of North Carolina, Greensboro
David W. Green	Nashville State Technical Institute, Tennessee
Dennis Guster	Saint Louis Community College at Meremec
L. D. Harber	Volunteer State Community College, Tennessee
Sharon A. Hill	Prince Georges Community College, Maryland
J. William Howorth	Seneca College, Ontario, Canada
Richard Kerns	East Carolina University, North Carolina
Gordon C. Kimbell	Everett Community College, Washington
James G. Kriz	Cuyahoga Community College, Ohio
Alden Lorents	Northern Arizona University
James McMahon	Community College of Rhode Island
Don B. Medley	California State Polytechnic University
Marilyn D. Moore	Indiana University Northwest
Kenneth R. Ruhrup	Saint Petersburg Junior College, Florida
Sandra Swanson	Lewis and Clark Community College, Illinois
Joyce V. Walton	Seneca College, Ontario, Canada

A special word of thanks must go to Lila Gardner of Cobb/Dunlop Publisher Services, who oversaw the design and production of the project and assured its timely publication. I would also like to thank Marsha Cohen, who outdid herself on the handsome book design, and Steven Bliss for an inviting cover design, and Shelly Langman, for her helpful comments on the BASIC appendix and the productivity software guide.

David Chodoff, Associate Editor at Holt, Rinehart and Winston provided valuable editorial direction. Paul Nardi, production manager at Holt, provided valuable help on design. Also to be thanked at Holt are Bob Woodbury and Howard Weiner.

Charles S. Parker

Understanding Computers and Data Processing: Today and Tomorrow with BASIC

Second Edition

Module A

INTRODUCTION

We are living in an age of computers. Businesses, government agencies, and other organizations use computers extensively to handle tedious paperwork, to provide better service, and to assist in decision making. As the cost of computers and computing resources continues to decrease relative to the price of everything else, computer technology will become even more widespread in our society. It is therefore essential to know something about it.

The chapters that follow are an introduction to computers and some of their uses. Chapters 1 and 2 orient you to what computer systems are, how they work, and how they're used. Also, these chapters present some key terminology that you will see repeatedly throughout the text. Chapter 3 describes how the fast-paced world of computers has evolved.

Chapter 1

Introduction to the World of Computers

Chapter Outline

Objectives

After completing this chapter you should be able to:

1. Understand why it's important to learn about computers.
2. Identify some of the major components in a computing environment and their relationship to each other.
3. Describe several applications in business and other areas of society where computers play an important role.
4. Define several terms that are useful to know when reading about or discussing computers.
5. Appreciate the social impact of computers.

OVERVIEW

Unless you plan to spend your life raising a small team of sled dogs in the upper reaches of the Yukon, computers will probably have an impact on your life. Whether that makes you glad, sad, or mad really doesn't matter. Computers are here to stay, and it's becoming more difficult to get along, much less get ahead, without some knowledge of what they are and what they do.

Computer systems keep track of our bank accounts and credit card purchases. They control the massive reservations systems of the airlines. They perform the millions upon millions of computations needed to send astronauts into outer space and bring them back safely. They also direct production at our factories and provide executives with the up-to-date information they need to make decisions. They are embedded in watches, microwave ovens, television sets, telephones, automobiles, and probably even the stationary workout bike at your local spa. The applications seem almost endless. Fifty years ago these machines were part of an obscure technology of interest to only a handful of scientists. Today they are part of daily life for millions of people.

Many people are intimidated by computers and think they need an advanced degree to understand them. In fact computers are very much like cars—you don't need to know everything about them to use them effectively. You can learn to drive a car without understanding internal combustion engines, and you can learn to use a computer without knowing about technical details such as logic circuits.

Still, with both cars and computers, a little knowledge can give you a big advantage. Knowing something about cars can help you make wise purchases and save money on repairs. Likewise, knowing something about computers can help you use these machines to better advantage.

This book is about computers—what they are, how they work, and what they do. Its purpose is to give you the knowledge you need to use them effectively today, and through the special Tomorrow boxes, to give you a look into the future. Other boxed features throughout the text provide added insights into the dynamic world of computers.

This book is not designed to make you a computer expert. It's a beginner's guide. If you're considering a career in computers, it will give you a comprehensive introduction to the field. If you're not, it will furnish the basic knowledge you need to understand and use computers in school and on the job. Who knows? Even if you do plan to breed sled dogs in the upper reaches of the Yukon, you may find yourself using a computer.

In the rest of this chapter, we'll first take a look at what computers are and how they work. Then we'll examine an example of a computer system in action. Finally, we'll look at the various sizes in which computers come. The Window that begins on page 25 gives you a glimpse of the myriad applications of computers in today's world.

Keep in mind as you read this text that learning to use computers effectively is going to require some plain, old-fashioned hard work.

Although a few useful things can be picked up rather easily, the biggest advantages of computers come at the expense of spending substantial amounts of time learning how to use them.

WHAT'S A COMPUTER AND WHAT DOES IT DO?

Four words sum up the operation of a computer system: **input, processing, output,** and **storage** (or *memory*). To see what these words mean, let's look at something you probably have in your own home—a stereo system.

A simple stereo system consists of a turntable, an amplifier, and a pair of speakers. To use the system you put a record on the turntable, turn the system on, and place the tone arm on the record. The needle in the tone arm converts the patterns in the grooves of the record into vibrations and transmits them to the amplifier as electronic signals. The amplifier takes the signals, makes them stronger, and transmits them to the speakers, thus producing music. In computer terms the turntable sends signals as *input* to the amplifier. The amplifier *processes* them and sends them to the speakers, which produce a musical *output*. The turntable is an **input device,** the amplifier is a *processing unit,* and the speakers are **output devices.** The amplifier is the heart of the system, and the turntable and speakers are examples of **support equipment.**

Most stereo systems have a variety of other support equipment. A stereo FM tuner and compact disk player, for example, are other kinds of input devices. Headphones are another kind of output device. A tape recorder is both an input and output device—you can use it to play music into the system or to record music from it. The tapes and records in your collection are, in computer terms, **input/output (I/O) media.** They *store* music in a **machine-readable** form—a form that the associated input device (a tape recorder or turntable) can recognize (that is, "read") and convert into signals for the amplifier to process.

Computer Systems

All the elements in a stereo system have their counterparts in a computer system. A **computer system** consists of the computer itself, all the support equipment, and the machine-readable instructions and facts it processes, as well as operating manuals, procedures, and the people who use the system. In other words, all the components that contribute to making the computer a useful tool can be said to be part of a computer system.

At the heart of any computer system—equivalent to the stereo amplifier—is the main **computer** itself, or **central processing unit (CPU).** Like a stereo amplifier, the CPU can't do anything useful without support equipment for input and output and I/O media for storage. Computer input and output devices include, to name just a few, display devices, disk units, tape units, and printers. I/O media include disks, tapes, and paper. We will discuss these and many other items in Chapters 2, 5, and 6.

A computer system, of course, is not a stereo system, and a computer is much more sophisticated than a stereo amplifier. For example:

✖ A computer can perform an enormous variety of processing tasks; a stereo amplifier performs only a few.

✖ A computer can support a much greater variety of input and output devices than can a stereo amplifier.

✖ A computer operates at fantastically higher speeds than that at which a stereo amplifier would ever need to operate.

What gives a computer its flexibility? The answer, in a word, is *memory*. A computer has access to a memory, or "workspace," that allows it to store whatever input it receives and whatever results it produces from

Getting Fit by Computer

A GROWING ASSORTMENT OF COMPUTER PRODUCTS IS AVAILABLE TO SEE TO IT THAT YOU KEEP FIT

It's raining—and just when you wanted to go to the local track to run your daily mile. If it's any consolation, rest assured that the computer revolution has addressed this problem, and has provided some solutions that may make you want to give up that unreliable lap track for a more exciting indoor version. If you had a product such as a Tredex electronic running track, for example, you could run in your garage or basement while rain or snow fell outside. The Tredex has a belt on which you run, while electronic sensors and a computer system monitor the distance you've traveled, your time, and your speed. These statistics are constantly available to you on an LED (for *L*ight-*E*mitting *D*iode) display.

If biking is your thing, you could hop up on a product such as Universal's computerized Aerobicycle, which features five preprogrammed exercise modes. The "steady climb" mode, for example, sets up the bike to deliver a constant resistance to your pedaling action,

while the "rolling hills" option varies the resistance by simulating slopes randomly. Moreover, with electronic bikes such as the Aerobicycle, you can have your pulse monitored and see a display of the calories you're burning up. As with the electronic track, an LCD screen apprises you of your progress, keeping your mind occupied as you pump away.

Even the venerable running shoe has gone digital.

And if you'd rather walk than pedal, consider an electronic staircase such as Tri-Tech's StairMaster (see photo). The StairMaster lets you key in the number of flights you want to walk and then keeps you apprised of these inputs. An ordinary stereo amplifier has no such memory; what's playing on a record, compact disk, or tape passes directly through the amplifier to the speakers. Because computers can store materials in such a workspace, they can be directed by *programs* (discussed shortly) to rearrange or recombine that material in an amazing variety of ways before sending it along as output. Thus if you could hook up a fully fledged computer and a good chunk of electronic workspace to your home stereo, you'd be able to do such things as play the selections on a record in any order you wished, create your own music, or combine and manipulate music from many different sources.

Most stereo equipment sold today is in fact built with inexpensive computer and memory chips. These chips have made possible such conveniences as quartz tuning and assigning favorite radio frequencies to push buttons. Also, other technological breakthroughs such as the compact disk are pushing conventional consumer products more and more into the computer age.

your progress. It has a "famous landmarks" feature that enables you to choose, say, a Statue of Liberty option (for 34 flights of walking) or Toronto's CN tower (for 159 flights). Like many of the computerized exercise bikes, there are several settings to vary the resistance, and your pulse is monitored as you walk. The StairMaster is also available with a 13-inch display screen that shows you how you're doing.

Even the venerable running shoe has gone digital. For example, Adidas has a shoe with an on-board microprocessor chip, so joggers can keep track of their speed, stride, and calorie consumption. Moreover, there are microprocessor-driven rowing and golfing aids if those are your sports of choice.

Once you've finished with the exercise hardware, there is a collection of software products to help you along further. For example, nutrition counseling software such as *The Original Boston Computer Diet* will tailor a diet for you based on your responses to a series of questions. These questions cover such things as your medical history, eating habits, and weight-loss objectives. Each day you enter a description of the meals or snacks you've eaten into your computer system and the nutri-

Stepping it up in a high-tech spa.

tion counselor reacts accordingly. For example, if you were to snack too much, you might get a display-screen lecture on how to overcome it. If you tend to eat the wrong foods, the nutrition counselor will have something specific and unpleasant to say about that, too.

And if you want a running coach to help you set a goal and stay on course, consider an electronic one. As you exercise on a daily basis, you report your results to the software package, which makes suggestions on your next workout. Many coaching programs also have routines that help you monitor your diet as well, since exercise and nutrition go hand in hand.

Data and Programs

The material that a computer receives as input is of two kinds: data and programs. **Data** are, essentially, facts. **Programs** are instructions that tell the computer how to process those facts to produce the results that the person using the computer system wants. To return to our example of a computer-driven stereo system, we could say that the tunes input to the system by the turntable or tape deck are data (facts), and the instructions that tell the computer system the order in which to play those tunes are a program. Let's discuss these important terms in a little more detail.

DATA.   Almost any kind of fact can become computer data—facts about a company's employees, facts about airline flight schedules, or facts about the orbit of a satellite. When we input data into a computer system, we usually aren't interested in getting them back just as we entered them. We want the system to process the data and give us useful, new **information.** (*Information,* in the language of computers, usually means data that have been processed.) We might want to know, for example, how many employees make over $15,000, how many seats are available on flight 495 from Los Angeles to San Francisco, or when a damaged satellite might plunge back into the earth's atmosphere.

Of course you don't need a computer system to get this kind of information from a set of facts. For example, anyone can go through an employee file and make a list of people earning a certain salary. But to do so would take a lot of time, especially for a company with thousands of employees. Computers, because they work at electronically fast speeds, can do such jobs almost instantly. The processing of data on computers is called *electronic data processing* (*EDP*), which, as the title of this book attests, is commonly shortened to **data processing.**

PROGRAMS.   The amplifier in a home stereo system, like most machines, is a special-purpose device. It is designed to do only a few specific jobs—play a record, make a recording on tape, play music into speakers or headphones. These jobs are built into its circuitry. To put it another way, it is "hardwired" to perform a very limited number of specific tasks.

Most computers, in contrast, are *general-purpose* devices. They must perform an enormous variety of tasks, any one of which might involve extremely complex processing. In a small company, for example, one person might want the computer system to scan a list of customer accounts and print a report of all customers who owe more than $300. Another person might want a report, in a different format, of all customers with good credit references. And an assistant might need the computer to help prepare a series of letters to clients.

Because most computers must be flexible, they can't be hardwired to do all the jobs they need to do. Instead they rely on programs to tell them what to do. As we said before, a program is a list of *instructions*. Often a program is read into the computer system followed by the data it is supposed to process. The program then directs the circuits in the computer to open and close in the manner needed to do whatever job needs doing with these data.

Programs cannot be written in ordinary English. They must be written in a **programming language**—a language the computer system can read and translate into the electronic pulses that make it work. Programming languages come in many varieties. In the early days of computers, they consisted of strings of numbers that only experts could understand. Over the years they have become easier for ordinary mortals to use. Programming languages are not universal; any given computer system will understand some languages but not others. Most computer systems, however, enable people to use several different languages. We will discuss programs and programming languages in detail in Module C.

A Look at Computer Memory

So far we've seen that if you want to get something done on a computer system, you must supply it both with facts (data) and with instructions (a program) specifying how to process those facts. For example, if you want the system to write payroll checks, you need to supply such data as employees' names, social security numbers, and salaries. The program instructions must "tell" the system how taxes are computed, how deductions are taken, where and how the checks are to be printed, and so forth. Also, the computer relies on a memory (storage) to remember all these details as it is doing the work.

Actually computer systems contain two types of memory. A **primary memory** (sometimes called **main memory** or **internal memory**), which is often built into the unit that houses the computer, is used to hold the data and programs the computer is currently processing. When data are "captured" in the computer's primary memory or workspace, they can be rearranged or recombined by the instructions in the program.

Data and programs the computer doesn't need for the job at hand are stored in **secondary (external) memory.** In most large computer systems, secondary memory is located in a separate device, apart from the computer itself. This piece of equipment is called a *secondary storage device.* Some secondary storage devices are capable of storing thousands of programs and millions of pieces of data. This enables us to save large quantities of data and programs conveniently in machine-readable form, so we don't have to rekey them into the system every time we want to use them.

When the CPU needs a certain program and set of data, it requests them from the secondary memory device (much as you might request a particular song from a jukebox) and reads them into its primary memory for processing. In other words, secondary memory is a large library of program and data resources on full-time call to the CPU.

Figure 1-1 illustrates the relationships among input, processing, output, primary memory, and secondary memory. We will discuss secondary memory devices and their associated media in Chapter 5.

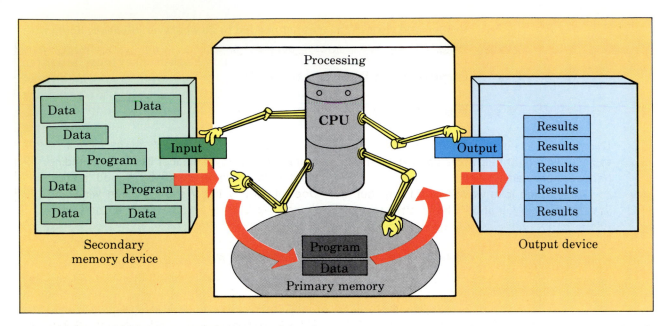

Figure 1-1. *Doing work in a computer system.* The computer system above is obtaining the programs and data it needs from secondary storage, putting them in its primary memory, and processing them according to the instructions in the program. The results are then delivered to an output device.

Hardware and Software

In the world of computers, it is common to distinguish between hardware and software. The word **hardware** refers to the actual machinery that makes up a computer system, for example, the CPU, I/O devices, and storage devices. The word **software** refers to computer programs. It can also refer to the manuals that help people work with the computer system, such as programming language guides and technical manuals for computer operators.

Users and the Experts

In the early days of computers and computing, there was a clear distinction between the people who made the machines work and the people who used the results the machines produced. This distinction still exists, but as computers become more available and easier to use, it is breaking down.

Users are the people who need the output that computer systems produce. They include the accountant who needs a report on a client's taxes, the engineer who needs to know whether a bridge will be structurally sound, the shop-floor supervisor who needs to know whether the day's quotas were met, and the company president who needs a report on the company's profitability over the past ten years. **Programmers** are the people who write the programs to produce this information. There are also *systems analysts* to help users determine their processing needs, as well as other specialists to run, repair, and maintain the machines themselves.

Computer Literacy: What Is It?

CONTROVERSY ABOUNDS ON A KEY ISSUE OF THE 80's

Question: How many programmers does it take to unscrew a light bulb? *Answer:* None—it's a hardware problem.

Maybe the joke wasn't very funny, but if you got it (and you should have after reading this chapter), you may well be on your way to becoming computer literate—at least according to some definitions of the term.

Just what is computer literacy? People disagree. Traditionally the word "literacy" has referred to the ability to read and write, two extremely useful skills for surviving in a modern world. Consequently the term *computer literacy* must refer to learning something useful about computers. It's specifically what that "something" should include that's the matter of heated debate. With regard to the various notions of computer literacy, the following have passed for acceptable definitions:

- Being able to write useful computer programs in one or more programming languages.
- Being able to operate one or more *productivity software* packages; for example, a word processor or spreadsheet package.
- Knowing how and when to take advantage of computer technology to perform your job better.
- Having a sense of where computers are potentially useful in today's world and the possible dangers they pose.
- Having a solid understanding of computer fundamentals (as would, say, a person who has taken a few computer courses and has used a variety of software packages and computers).

And, of course, some people look at computer literacy as involving some combination of these skills, or perhaps as something altogether different from the skills mentioned here. As you can see from the variety of viewpoints, getting a handle on what a person means by computer literacy is almost like understanding what some people mean by "good taste." Does it strictly imply sipping white wine and listening to Vivaldi, or does it also include liking beer and Bob Wills' music?

Despite the fact that there is no universally accepted definition of computer literacy, the issue of how much each of us should know about computers is something we all must face. As you read through this text, you should constantly ask yourself what it is you need to know about computers. And just because you have no desire to be a computer professional, don't think that writing programs and learning how computers work won't help you achieve the type of literacy you seek. Learning these skills might help you overcome fears you have about computers, and make other things—such as working with a word processor or spreadsheet package—seem easier.

The world is becoming frighteningly dependent upon computers and it's likely you'll need to know something about them to do your job better and to live more comfortably, even though there's no pat answer as to what that something is or what the best way is to educate yourself.

Becoming computer literate.

Most large companies have a library of thousands of programs to carry out well-defined tasks—do the payroll, write checks, prepare accounting reports, and so forth. Such companies usually employ a staff of programmers and other experts to write new programs as they are needed, make changes in existing programs, and keep the systems running. Often, however, a user—say, a manager or an executive—will have a desk-top computer and the knowledge to run certain kinds of programs independently. With computer systems becoming cheaper, as well as easier to learn and use, many users are acquiring their own small systems to meet personal information needs that are not being satisfied by other systems within the company.

USING COMPUTERS: A SIMPLE EXAMPLE

Now that we've covered in a very basic way how a computer system works, let's "walk through" an application to put many of the concepts you've just read about into better focus.

Lydia Maxwell is the catering manager at a large hotel. Her job responsibilities are many. She promotes the hotel to convention groups, arranges for groups to reserve hotel facilites, helps groups plan meals, and bills each group when it leaves. There's a lot of paperwork involved—letters back and forth, bills to tally up, reports to file, and so on. Also, Lydia finds that being successful at her job involves a lot of little things that aren't really in her job description, such as preparing an immediate thank-you letter to an important client when the secretary is swamped with other work.

To help her in her work, Lydia has a *microcomputer system* on her desk (see Figure 1-2). You'll be reading more about these computer systems later in the chapter. The hardware in Lydia's microcomputer system consists of five pieces of equipment: a keyboard, a display device, a printer, a system unit, and a floppy disk unit.

The *keyboard,* which resembles that of an ordinary typewriter, enables Lydia to direct the entire computer system to do what she wants. Everything she inputs at the keyboard—and the subsequent responses of the computer system to these inputs—is shown on the *display device,* which resembles a television screen. When she wants something printed out, she directs the computer system to send the output to the *printer.* The *system unit* contains the CPU itself, the CPU's primary and secondary storage, and a lot of other circuitry that we'll talk about later in the book.

Not all microcomputer systems, incidentally, look like Lydia's. For example, in her computer system, the secondary storage device—a *floppy disk unit* (which consists of two *disk drives*)—is housed in the system unit. Many computers, such as the IBM Personal Computer, Apple Macintosh, and Apple IIc, have floppy disk drives built right into their system units (see Figure 1-6 on page 19). Others, such as the Apple IIe, don't. Moreover, the Apple Macintosh's display device and the Apple IIc's keyboard are built into their respective system units.

Figure 1-2. **Example application.** A catering manager at a large hotel interacts with a computer system. She and many other executives in today's world find it necessary to tap into the processing power provided by computers to better perform their jobs.

A *floppy disk* (or *diskette*) is the common input/output medium used to store programs and data on microcomputer systems. People often keep their programs and data on separate disks. Floppy disks must be properly inserted into the computer system's disk drives (see Figure 1-3) if the system is to access the programs and data on them.

Once a program and its data are loaded into the appropriate disk drives, Lydia has turned the computer into a powerful calculating tool. For example, say that she wants a list of her clients, ranked from high to low on the basis of the total amount of money they've spent at the hotel over the past two years. She might load into drive 2 (in Figure 1-3), sometimes called the B drive, *data* on individual client bookings over the past two years. Each client record of data on the disk would likely reflect the name of a client, the beginning and ending dates of a particular booking, and the amount spent during that booking. In drive 1 (sometimes called the A drive) she then loads a *program* that, when run, will total up the dollars spent by each client and, later on, rank the clients from high to low. When she issues a command at the keyboard to run the program with its data, she will see which clients account for her greatest sales volume. Also from her keyboard, she can direct the output to either the display screen or the printer.

Another application for which Lydia finds her computer system useful is meal planning; that is, for searching through descriptions of food dishes to find ones that fit a particular client's needs. On one floppy disk she has hundreds of filled-in "forms" stored, one form for each dish she can offer to guests (see Figure 1-4). Each form contains three separate fields of data: the

Figure 1-3. Inserting a floppy disk into a two-drive system. Users often select the left drive for the program disk and the right drive for the disk containing the program's data.

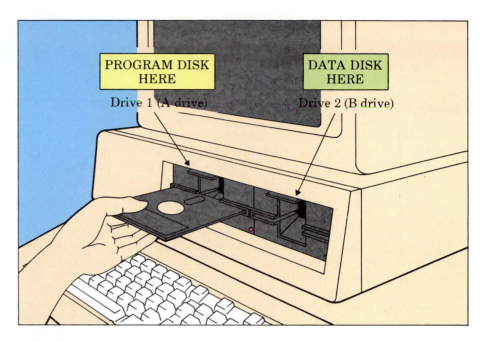

Figure 1-4. Meal-planning data stored on floppy disk. Each set of data consists of a "filled-in form." Several hundred to a thousand or more such forms can often be stored on a single floppy disk.

name of a dish, its ingredients, and a few remarks. She places this data disk in the B drive. In the A drive she places a program called a *file manager,* which can be used to search through the data.

Thus, if she's helping a client plan a Saturday night banquet over the phone, and the client wants a beef dish with mushrooms, Lydia can have her file manager search for all forms on her data disk where "ingredients" contains "beef" and "mushrooms," and "remarks" contains "dinner" and "entrée." She can then have the names of these dishes directed to her display screen. She could, of course, rely on her memory, but having the computer make the search often turns up good alternatives that might not otherwise come to mind. Also, she can save a lot of time on the phone by having her computer system do the searching in the background while she attends to other matters with the client. Lydia's file manager lets her add new forms to the file, delete forms, and modify forms. This is done with a *menu* of processing alternatives (not to be confused with a food menu) that the file manager sends to her display screen, asking her what she wants to do (see Figure 1-5).

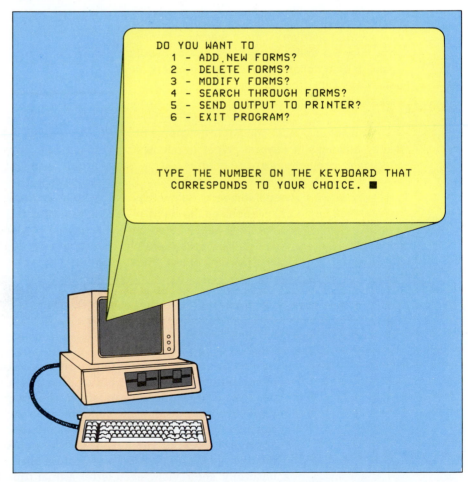

```
DO YOU WANT TO
    1 - ADD NEW FORMS?
    2 - DELETE FORMS?
    3 - MODIFY FORMS?
    4 - SEARCH THROUGH FORMS?
    5 - SEND OUTPUT TO PRINTER?
    6 - EXIT PROGRAM?



TYPE THE NUMBER ON THE KEYBOARD THAT
    CORRESPONDS TO YOUR CHOICE. ■
```

Figure 1-5. A computer menu. Menus beckon a user to choose a specific course of action. Using them effectively requires neither typing skills nor an extensive knowledge of computers.

tomorrow

WHY EVERY BUSINESS STUDENT SHOULD STUDY COMPUTERS TODAY

You'll Need One on Tomorrow's Job

For the past few decades, one of the largest users of computing resources around many college campuses has been the business school or department. Why do business students need to know something about computers? There are a number of reasons.

First, business decisions are often based on money. For example, when a company is considering launching a new product line, a schedule of estimates of probable income and costs has to be made. These estimates can be complicated and very time consuming to prepare. Since a dollar tomorrow won't be worth as much as a dollar today, on long projects all dollar amounts from different years must be deflated to reflect the time value of money (a relatively sophisticated computation).

And not only must one set of estimates be made, but usually several. What happens if 1989 sales projections are 10 percent too low? *What if* bank borrowing rates increase by 2 percent? Or *what if* development is delayed by a year? Refiguring calculations on the basis of all these "what ifs" can take weeks to do by hand. Fortunately, easy-to-use *spreadsheet* packages (discussed in Chapter 12) exist that

will enable almost any businessperson to make such computations quickly and painlessly. A business student without the necessary skills to make convincing quantitative arguments will have a tough time surviving in today's world—and an impossible time getting hired in tomorrow's.

Refiguring calculations can take weeks to do by hand.

Second, many businesspeople make decisions on the basis of information that's stored in computer systems. A businessperson without the wherewithal to access a computer system and navigate through it effectively to locate information will find it difficult to get work done. Can you imagine a stockbroker without easy access to computer-stored stock prices trying to deal effectively with busy

Still another important application Lydia has added to her storehouse of computer skills is client billing. She uses a program that integrates data on client charges into a form letter. The program computes the charges for each client and inserts the amounts into specific places in the letter. Lydia can also insert personalized passages into each final letter by typing in the appropriate text at the keyboard. She quickly reviews each letter on the display screen for correctness before directing it to the printer. And, naturally, she reviews each letter a final time before it is mailed. After all, nothing's perfect—including computer systems.

clients? In Chapter 13 you'll read about *file managers* and *database management systems* that are designed to get to such people, quickly, the information they need on their jobs.

Third, studying business without studying computers is like learning about cars without ever looking at the engine. Computers are, in fact, the engines that power business. They're present in accounting systems, manufacturing systems, systems that help managers make decisions, and other types of important activities. Pull the plugs on their computers, and virtually every large business today would be brought to a standstill.

Fourth, the success of every businessperson often depends on being perceived as organized or on making effective presentations to colleagues and superiors. High-quality, easy-to-use *presentation graphics* software (discussed in Chapter 12) is now readily available on computers to make both of these possible.

Fifth, many businesspeople will someday need to decide what type of computer system to buy for a business. Someone running a small business, for example, will probably need a computer to help run it. And someone working for a large company may be asked to help buy, install, or create a working environment for one or more computers.

The trend to make business students more knowledgeable about computers is on the upswing. Many business students are taking more than the minimum number of computer courses required for their degrees *today* because they sense that computer-related skills will be an asset when looking for *tomorrow's* job.

Business students: Picking up computer skills now a matter of survivability.

COMPUTERS AND SOCIETY

The example we just presented gives you some idea of why computer systems have become such an important part of modern life. Their ability to sort through massive amounts of data and quickly produce useful information for almost any kind of user, from payroll clerk to president, makes them indispensable in a society like ours. Without computers, for instance, the catering manager in our example couldn't provide the services she now extends to clients. The government couldn't tabulate all the data it collects for the census every ten years. Banks would be overwhelmed by the job of keeping track of all the transactions they must process. The efficient telephone service we are used to would be impossible. Moon exploration and the space shuttle would still be science fiction fantasies. The list is virtually endless.

But along with the benefits computers bring to society have come some troubling problems, ranging from health to personal security and privacy. The catering manager in our example, for instance, spends many hours in front of a display screen. Do the radiation and glare emanating from this screen have any effect on her health? Banks keep data about customers' accounts on external storage devices. Can they prevent clever "computer criminals" from using the computer system to steal from those accounts? The government has confidential information about every taxpayer. Can that information be protected from unauthorized use?

These are serious issues, but we can only mention them in this chapter. In Chapter 18, "Computers in Our Lives: The Costs and the Benefits," we discuss them at length.

COMPUTER SYSTEMS TO FIT EVERY NEED AND POCKETBOOK

A great variety of computer systems are available commercially to serve the needs of computer users. In Module D you will learn how computers fit into settings that range from the living room to the offices of giant corporations. Here we'll consider one important way in which computers differ from each other—size.

Computers are generally classified in one of three categories: small, or microcomputers; medium size, or minicomputers; and large, or mainframe computers. In practice the distinction among these different sizes is not always clear. Large minicomputers, for example, are often bigger than small mainframes.

In general, the larger the computer, the greater is its processing power. For example, big computers can process data at faster speeds than can small computers. They also can accommodate larger, more powerful support devices. Naturally, the larger the computer and its support equipment are, the greater is the price. A computer system can cost anywhere from a couple of hundred dollars to many millions.

Microcomputers

A technological breakthrough in the early 1970s made it possible to produce an entire CPU on a single silicon chip smaller than a dime. These "computers-on-a-chip," or microprocessors, can be mass produced at very low cost. They were quickly integrated into all types of products, thus making possible powerful hand-held calculators, digital watches, a variety of electronic toys, and sophisticated controls for household appliances such

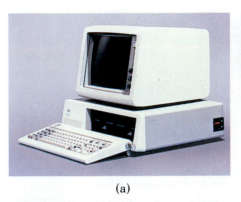 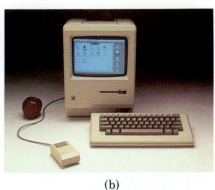 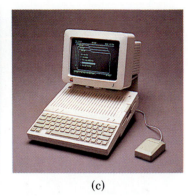

(a)   (b)   (c)

Figure 1-6.   *Three popular microcomputer systems: (a) the IBM PC, (b) the Apple Macintosh, and (c) the Apple IIc.*

as microwave ovens and automatic coffee makers. Microprocessors also made it possible to build inexpensive computer systems that are small enough to fit on a desk top, such as our catering manager's system in Figure 1-2 and the computer systems in Figure 1-6.

These small computer systems are informally called **microcomputers.** Because they are inexpensive and small enough to use at home or work for personal needs, they are also commonly called **personal computers.**

Microcomputers (or micros) appear in homes, offices, and classrooms. At home they help families keep track of their finances, help students write term papers, regulate heating systems to lower fuel bills, and challenge all comers at PAC-MAN®, DONKEY KONG®, and chess. They help businesses keep track of merchandise, prepare correspondence, bill customers, and do routine accounting. Universities, high schools, and elementary schools—attracted by the low cost of these machines and the fact that they are "friendlier" than larger computers—are purchasing micros for courses in computing. In fact, several universities now require entering students to buy or rent their own microcomputers.

Minicomputers

Minicomputers (or minis) are generally regarded as medium-sized computers (see Figure 1-7). Most of them fall between microcomputers and mainframes in their processing power. The very smallest minicomputers, however, are virtually indistinguishable from some microcomputers, and the largest (sometimes called *superminis*) closely resemble mainframes. Minicomputers are generally much more expensive than microcomputers and are not affordable for most individuals.

Any of several factors might lead an organization to choose a minicomputer over a micro or mainframe. A small or medium-sized company, for example, may find microcomputer systems too slow to handle its current volume of paperwork. Or the company may need a computer system that can do several jobs at once and interact with several users at the same time. Most microcomputer systems do not have enough power for such applications. Mainframes, of course, have these capabilities, but they are far larger and more expensive than minis.

Figure 1-7.   A minicomputer system. Digital Equipment Corporation's VAX 11/780 is one of today's most widely used minicomputers.

Mainframes

The **mainframe** (see Figure 1-8) is the mainstay of almost all large organizations. It often operates twenty-four hours a day, serving hundreds of users on display devices during regular business hours, and processing large jobs such as payroll and billing late at night. Many large organizations need several mainframes to complete their computing workloads. Typically these organizations own or lease a variety of computers—mainframes, minis, and micros—to meet all their processing needs.

Figure 1-8.   A mainframe system. IBM's 3090 computer sets the standard for today's mainframes.

Figure 1-9. A supercomputer. The Cray X-MP/48 is one of the world's fastest computers. Whereas most powerful mainframes process at speeds of less than thirty million operations per second, supercomputers churn out anywhere from a few hundred million to a billion or more operations per second.

Some organizations, such as large scientific and research laboratories, have extraordinary demands for processing data. Applications such as sending an astronaut into outer space and weather forecasting, for example, require extreme degrees of accuracy and a wealth of computations. High-quality animation, which produces the images in computer-generated videos and commercials, also demands enormous amounts of high-speed computation. To meet such needs, a few vendors offer very large, sophisticated machines called **supercomputers** (see Figure 1-9). These machines are very expensive, often costing several million dollars.

COMPUTERS IN ACTION

Where would you expect to find computers? In our discussion so far, we've given some indication of the amazing variety of ways in which computers have become part of our lives. As you read through this book, you should get a good idea of what computer systems can and cannot do, and where they do and do not belong. Window 1, page 25, presents an extensive picture essay of computers in action in just a few of the many settings in which you are likely to encounter them.

Summary and Key Terms

Computers are seen almost everywhere in the world today. They're embedded in consumer products, used to run businesses, and employed to direct production in our factories, to name just a few applications.

Four words summarize the operation of a **computer system: input, processing, output,** and **storage.** The processing function is performed by the **computer** itself, which is sometimes called the **central processing unit,** or **CPU.**

The *input* and *output* functions are performed by **support equipment,** such as **input devices** and **output devices.** Just as your stereo amplifier would be useless if it didn't have speakers, headphones, and a turntable to supplement it, the computer would be helpless without this support equipment.

On most of the support equiment are mounted **input/output media (I/O media).** Many of these media *store* materials in **machine-readable** form, a form the computer system can recognize and process.

The materials that a computer receives as input are of two kinds: data and programs. **Data** are facts the computer has at its disposal, and **programs** are instructions that explain to the computer what to do with these facts. Programs must be written in a **programming language** that the computer can understand.

The processing of data on a computer system is commonly referred to as **data processing.** The results produced through data processing are called **information.**

Computer systems have two types of memory, or storage. **Primary memory** (sometimes called **main memory,** or **internal memory,** which is often built into the unit housing the computer itself, holds programs and data the system is currently processing. **Secondary (external) memory** stores other programs and data. In many systems secondary memory is located in a separate hardware device.

In the world of computers, it is common to distinguish between hardware and software. **Hardware** refers to the actual machinery that makes up the computer system, such as the CPU, input and output devices, and secondary memory devices. **Software** refers to computer programs. It can also refer to the manuals that help people work with computer systems.

Users are people who need the output computer systems produce. There are many types of experts in a computing environment who help users meet their computing needs—for example, **programmers,** whose job it is to write programs.

Although computer systems have become an indispensable part of modern life, their growing use often creates troubling problems, ranging from health to personal security and privacy.

Small-sized computers are often called **microcomputers** (or **personal computers**); medium-sized computers, **minicomputers;** and large-sized computers, **mainframes.** The largest of the mainframes are called **supercomputers.** Although classifying computers by size can be helpful in practice, it is sometimes difficult to classify computers that fall on the borderline of these categories.

Review Exercises

Fill-in Questions

1. The computer is sometimes called the _____ (CPU).
2. When programs and data are being processed, they are stored in _____ memory.
3. Processed _____ are called information.
4. Another name for computer programs is _____.
5. When programs and data are not being processed, but need to be "at the fingertips" of the computer, they are stored in _____ memory.
6. A term used for the machinery in a computing environment is _____.
7. A series of instructions that direct a computer system is known as a(n) _____.
8. The hardware, software, data, procedures, and personnel needed to process data successfully are called a(n) _____.

Matching Questions

Match each term with its description.

a. minicomputer   d. supercomputer
b. input device   e. hardware
c. mainframe   f. microcomputer

_____ 1. The actual machinery that makes up a computer system.
_____ 2. Another name for personal computer.
_____ 3. A medium-sized computer.
_____ 4. A large-sized computer.
_____ 5. Any piece of equipment that supplies programs and data to the computer.
_____ 6. The most powerful type of computer.

Discussion Questions

1. What do you believe will be the greatest impact computers will have on your life? On society at large?
2. What is the difference between a computer and a computer system?
3. Name as many computer support devices as you can. What is the purpose of each?
4. What are the major differences between primary and secondary memory?
5. What is the difference between programs and data?
6. Define and give some examples of a computer user.
7. Identify some social problems created by the existence of computer systems.
8. Why is it important that students study computers in school today? Provide several reasons.

Computer Applications

A visual portfolio of the widespread use of computers

Computers have rapidly become an important force in almost every segment of our society. This first "window to the world of computers" presents a small sample of the many tasks to which these machines may be applied. Included are examples from the fields of art, advertising, business and finance, publishing, design and manufacturing, consumer products, and television.

Art

One of the most fascinating and rapidly evolving uses of computers today is in art. The speed and versatility of today's computer systems have added new dimensions to the artist's paintbrush.

1. A digitized rendering of an orange, created on a Genigraphics imaging system.

2

Advertising

Advertisers are increasingly relying on computer graphics to create images that have an impact on buyers. Computers not only provide a high-tech look to advertisements, but also can save several thousands of dollars in development costs and generate ideas that would not be possible to obtain through traditional techniques.

3

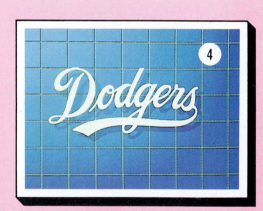

4

5

2–5. Computers are frequently used to create or enhance organizational logos. Logos and many other forms of computer art are created or enhanced on electronic painting systems (or "paintboxes") that provide the computer artist anywhere from 8 to 16,000,000 or more colors to work with.

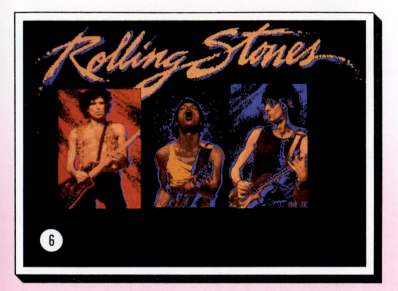

6, 7. Two computer-created images for Rolling Stones promotional shirts.

8. High technology is increasingly being used to develop packaging designs, such as this one for Lipton Tea. The image on the package was created on a computer system that combines traditional graphic and photographic techniques with high-speed computing.

9. A computer-generated image for the fast-foods industry.

Business and Finance

Businesses and financial institutions first used computer systems to tackle their mounting paperwork problems. Today they also use them extensively to provide better customer service and to aid in decision making.

11. Small businesses often meet their processing needs with microcomputer systems such as this Apple IIe. Unlike large computing systems, microcomputer systems often are placed in highly exposed areas, such as on desk tops or table tops, as seen here. One shouldn't get the idea that microcomputer systems are indestructible, however. An errant spray of grease or a spilled cup of coffee on the keyboard—or through an air vent—will disable such a system faster than you can shriek.

12. Automatic teller machines (ATMs) have brought computer technology face-to-face with virtually everyone who has a bank account. For more information about ATMs and how they work, see the related box in Chapter 2.

10. Many large organizations maintain "data centers" to handle the brunt of the massive amounts of processing they must perform daily. The computers and their secondary storage devices at these centers are often housed in secure, dustless, temperature-controlled rooms.

13. "Office automation" is a term frequently used to describe the spread of computer technology into the ordinary office (see Chapter 15). Many office workers—from secretaries to company presidents—have microcomputer-based systems on their desks to aid them in their jobs.

Publishing

Using the computer as a tool to compose text started with magnetic-tape-driven Selectric typewriters only about twenty years ago. Today, getting words into a document is far more spectacular.

14. A digitized photograph, a title logo, and typeset-quality text are computer-combined to produce these attractive face-to-face pages for a cooking magazine.

15. Increasingly, writers, editors, and compositors working for newspapers and journals are using automated pagination systems to develop copy. Text, digitized images of photographs and art, and column headings (in a variety of fonts) can all be stored in the computer and quickly combined into pages—on a display device—before being sent on to the print room.

16. A book cover designed on a computer graphics system.

Design, Manufacturing, and Control

Outside the office, computers are used by organizations to design and manufacture products, as well as to control a variety of industrial processes.

17. A designer models a sailplane in three dimensions on a display terminal. A variety of other products—from jeans to automobiles—are designed on computer terminals prior to manufacturing.

18. Computer-driven robots are used on automobile assembly lines to perform dangerous or monotonous jobs.

19. Computers are used for a variety of control purposes, including monitoring industrial plants and air traffic control.

Consumer Goods

Microprocessors and electronic memories are increasingly being integrated into consumer products, both to enhance product performance and to provide functions that were heretofore not possible. In addition to the products below, microprocessors and memories can be found in goods such as digital watches, scales, washers and dryers, microwave ovens, cameras, and audio and video equipment.

20. A touch screen on the dash panel of a 1986 Buick.

22. Axlon's A.G. (for "Almost Grown") Bear is a cuddly electronic "smart toy" with a microchip for a heart. The microchip "reads" speech pulses in its vicinity by sound recognition and converts them to childlike mumbles of its own. A.G. Bear was created by Nolan Bushnell, who at one time founded Atari with only $250 and later sold it to Warner Communications for $28 million.

21. The Roland G-707 guitar uses computer technology to "memorize" sounds, which can then be played back or blended with other sound by a musician.

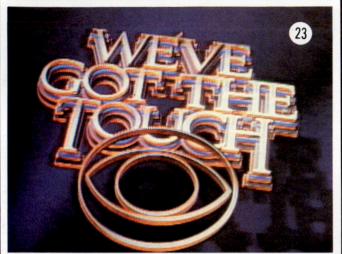

Television Graphics

If you've watched television recently, you've probably noticed a number of flashy graphics that are used for advertising, sports, news, and weather segments. Many of these graphics, such as those below, are created using sophisticated computer hardware and software.

23, 24. Two stills from animated TV segments, created by Teitzell Film of Los Angeles for CBS and NBC, respectively.

25. A computer graphic showing temperatures in Illinois on a fall day. Computers are especially helpful in news and sports broadcasting because deadlines are usually tight.

26. An informative computer graphic showing the current status on hole 3 for golfer Charles Beck. Computers are used both to create a wide variety of attractive sports graphics and to uncover masses of interesting statistical information that satisfy even the most demanding TV sports junkies.

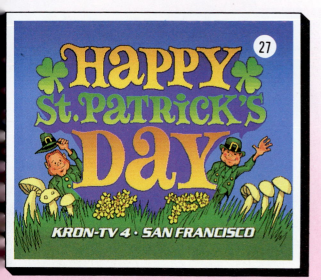

27–29.   These attractive holiday graphics were created on an Aurora/125 paintbox system for KRON-TV in San Francisco.

Chapter 2

How Computer Systems Process Data

Chapter Outline

OVERVIEW
COMPUTER HARDWARE
    Support Equipment
    Is It for Input, Output, or Storage?
    Input/Output Media
    Peripheral and Auxiliary; Online and Offline
    Getting It Together: Combining Hardware Into a System
ORGANIZING DATA FOR COMPUTER SYSTEMS
A BRIEF INTRODUCTION TO SOFTWARE
PROCESSING DATA

Objectives

After completing this chapter you should be able to:

1. Identify several major classes of input, output, processing, and storage hardware.
2. Explain how data are organized in a computing environment.
3. Distinguish between applications and systems software.
4. Describe a few of the ways in which computer systems process data.
5. Define several more key terms that are useful to know when reading about or discussing computers.

OVERVIEW

As you learned in Chapter 1, input, processing, and output, together with storage, are the major aspects of any computer system. In this chapter you will learn in more detail how they work together.

First we'll take a look at computer system hardware. We'll cover some basic hardware concepts and discuss some of the most important kinds of input, output, and storage equipment. Then we'll see how these might be linked together—first in a small computer system and then in a large one. This section will give you an introduction to the detailed discussion of hardware in Module B.

Next we'll take up the subject of data, specifically how data must be organized for processing on a computer system. Study the terms introduced in this section carefully, because you will encounter them frequently throughout the book.

From data we'll go on to a discussion of program software, to give you an introduction to a subject we cover extensively in Module C.

The chapter ends with a discussion of data processing on computer systems. We'll discuss representative examples of some of the most common types of processing to see how hardware, data, software, and users interact to do useful work.

COMPUTER HARDWARE

All computer systems consist of some combination of computers and support equipment. The main **computer** (which is often called the central processing unit, or CPU) is the heart of the system—it's the machine that controls the actual processing of data and programs. Closely tied to the CPU is its *primary memory,* which is almost always housed in the same hardware device, called the **system unit.** Many people refer to the system unit as the computer, but, strictly speaking, it is merely the "box" that contains the computer.

Support equipment consists of all the machines that make it possible to get data and programs into the CPU, get processed information out, and store data and programs for ready access to the CPU. Figure 2-1 summarizes the relationship of these hardware elements and lists some of the most important examples of each.

Support Equipment

There are a number of ways in which to classify support equipment for computer systems. One of the most basic is by function: Is the device predominantly for input, output, or storage? Another is by medium: Does it use tapes or disks? A third is by relation to the CPU: Is it peripheral or auxiliary? Online or offline? Let's consider each of these in turn.

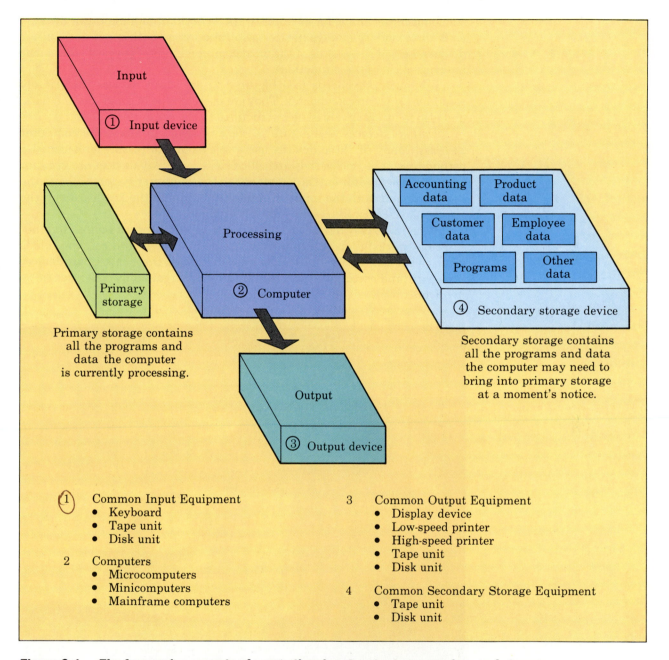

Figure 2-1. *The four major aspects of computing: input, output, processing, and storage.*

Is It for Input, Output, or Storage?

Input devices are machines that convert data and programs into a form that the CPU can understand and process. **Output devices** convert processed data into a form that users can understand. **Secondary storage devices** are machines that can make frequently used data and programs readily available to the CPU. These functions often overlap in a single machine. Some, for example, work as both input and output devices. And all secondary storage devices also function as both input and output devices. Let's discuss some of the most common kinds of support equipment in terms of these three functions.

Computer *keyboards* (see Figure 2-2) are input devices that closely resemble typewriter keyboards. They are used to type in programs and data, and also to interactively issue instructions to the computer system.

Display devices (see Figure 2-3) are involved in almost all computer systems. Many of these devices use a televisionlike picture unit called a cathode-ray tube; hence they are called CRTs. Display devices are used for output. The operator enters commands to the computer system through the keyboard, and both the input the operator enters at the keyboard and the output the CPU produces appear on the screen.

When a display device and a keyboard together form a remote communications workstation to a computer, the display–keyboard combination is often called a *display terminal.* On the other hand, the local display devices that you find with most microcomputers are generally referred to as *monitors.*

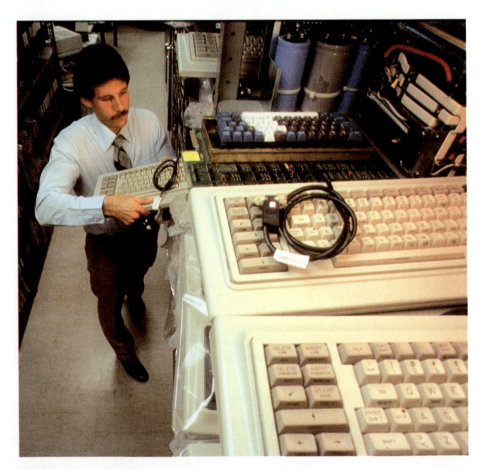

Figure 2-2. Computer keyboards. Although there are many different ways to enter data into today's computer systems, the keyboard remains the most widely used.

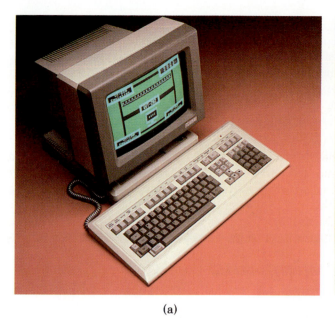

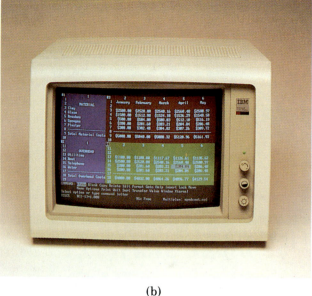

(a)   (b)

Figure 2-3. **Display devices.** (a) A display terminal consists of a screen and a keyboard. (b) A monitor consists of only a screen.

Printers are used to produce output. *Low-speed printers* (Figure 2-4) are designed to output small amounts of printed information. Because of their low cost, they are very popular devices for microcomputer systems. Many low-speed printers that are configured to larger computer systems also contain keyboards, which enable operators to use them to send data to the computer. These devices are called *teleprinters.*

High-speed printers (Figure 2-5) are used to produce extensive printed reports. They may operate at speeds ten to thirty times faster than low-speed devices.

Secondary storage devices hold frequently used data and programs for

Figure 2-4. **Low-speed printer.** The Epson LX-80 is a popular printer for microcomputer systems.

Figure 2-5. **High-speed printer.** "Line printers" are commonly used with mainframes and minicomputers.

ready access to the CPU. They also function as both input and output devices; that is, they contain stored data and programs that are sent to the CPU as input, and the CPU can transmit new data and programs to them as output. The most common types of secondary storage devices are *magnetic tape units* and *magnetic disk units.*

Large tape units (Figure 2-6), which use detachable tape reels as input/output media, are usually associated with large computer systems. *Cartridge* (and *cassette*) *tape units,* which use small tapes enclosed in plastic cases, are usually associated with small computer systems.

Input, Storage, Processing, and Output - ATM Style

STARTED BY THE BANKS, TELLER MACHINES ARE NOW POPPING UP VIRTUALLY EVERYWHERE

A little over two decades ago, the only way you could get your money out of a savings account was to show up at your bank on a weekday during regular banking hours. Then came the *automatic teller machines (ATMs),* which enable a depositor to withdraw money twenty-four hours a day, seven days a week. ATMs were an immediate "hit" with the banking community, because they cut personnel expenditures and provided better service to depositors. They have proved so popular, in fact, that it would be difficult to find a major bank today that has not installed them.

In the past several years, as the accompanying panel of photographs show, ATMs have caught on elsewhere. You now find them in convenience and grocery stores, train and subway stations, gas stations, and even on the ski slopes. Wherever routine transactions occur, ATMs are often busy at work.

Each organization that has automatic tellers uses its own ATM system. Nonetheless, because ATMs are computer systems, they conform to the same basic principles of input–storage–processing–output as do other computer systems. For example, consider the following transaction taking place at a bank:

Input. When you make a withdrawal from a bank ATM, you often begin with two forms of input. First you insert your bank card into the machine. The magnetic stripe on the back of the card contains your name, account number, and other types of important data that identify you to the ATM. Next you must input your *Personal Identification Code* (PIC), which only you and the computer system know.

Storage. Both the data you've entered into the system through your card and the PIC you've typed in are stored in the main memory of your ATM system. In a secondary storage area—waiting to be processed—is a large electronic file containing actual PICs, current bank balances, and other account data for all depositors.

Processing. One form of processing that takes place in a routine withdrawal transaction is that the computer makes a comparison to see that the PIC you've typed in

Disk units store data and programs on magnetized platters called disks. *Hard disk units* (Figure 2-7), which work with rigid disks, are faster than tape units, and can make larger volumes of material immediately available to the CPU. *Floppy disk (diskette) units* (Figure 2-8), which work with flexible disks, are slower than hard disk units and have much less data-carrying capacity. However, they are far less expensive than hard disk units. Hard disk units play an important role in both large and small computer systems, whereas diskette units are generally associated with smaller systems.

is the same as the one it has on file in secondary storage. If it isn't, you may be permitted one or two more attempts to enter your PIC correctly. The computer must process here, too, counting how many times your PIC has been typed in incorrectly and making additional comparisons. If you eventually succeed by typing in the right PIC, the computer system will enable you to make another input—the amount of your withdrawal. If all goes well, the computer will later perform more processing when it checks and updates your account balance.

Output. There are many types of output, or actions, the ATM system could produce during the course of a transaction. For example, if you had failed on the last attempt to input your PIC correctly, the response of the system may be to swallow your card and sound a silent alarm. Or, if the amount you had wanted to withdraw was in excess of your balance, the system might output some sort of "insufficient funds" voice message to you. But if everything had gone smoothly you would have received the best output of them all—cash.

Naturally not all ATM systems are the same as those at the bank. If you are paying for ski-lift tickets, you may have to *input* money or a credit card. The *output* is, of course, your tickets and change. And, at a gas station, the *output* is often the gas you receive at the pump.

The ATM revolution in evidence at a bank, convenience store, and ski slope.

Figure 2-6. **Large tape unit.** The tape reels that are mounted onto this unit can store data at a very low cost.

Figure 2-7. **Hard disk units dot the landscape of a data center.** Hard disk is the most common secondary storage medium used in business because it enables rapid access to data at a reasonable cost.

Figure 2-8.   Floppy disk unit. Floppy disks come in a variety of sizes, as do floppy disk units (drives).

Input/Output Media

Input and output devices are machines for, respectively, getting data and programs into a computer and getting the results out in a usable form. Data and programs, however, are often not permanently stored *in* a particular device. Usually they are recorded *on* **input/output (I/O) media,** in a form the associated device can read and transmit to the CPU. In other words, just as the record player on a stereo system works with vinyl records, input/output devices work with specific input/output media. Four of the most common input/output media in use today are *magnetic tape* (both on *detachable reels* and in *cartridges*), *hard magnetic disks,* and *floppy disks.* These are shown in Figure 2-9 and will be discussed in detail in Chapter 5.

Peripheral and Auxiliary; Online and Offline

Support equipment is either peripheral or auxiliary, online or offline. **Peripheral equipment** consists of machines that can be plugged into the

(a)   (b)

(c)   (d)

Figure 2-9.   Common types of input/output media. (a) Magnetic tape on reels. (b) Cartridge tape. (c) Hard magnetic disks. (d) Floppy disks.

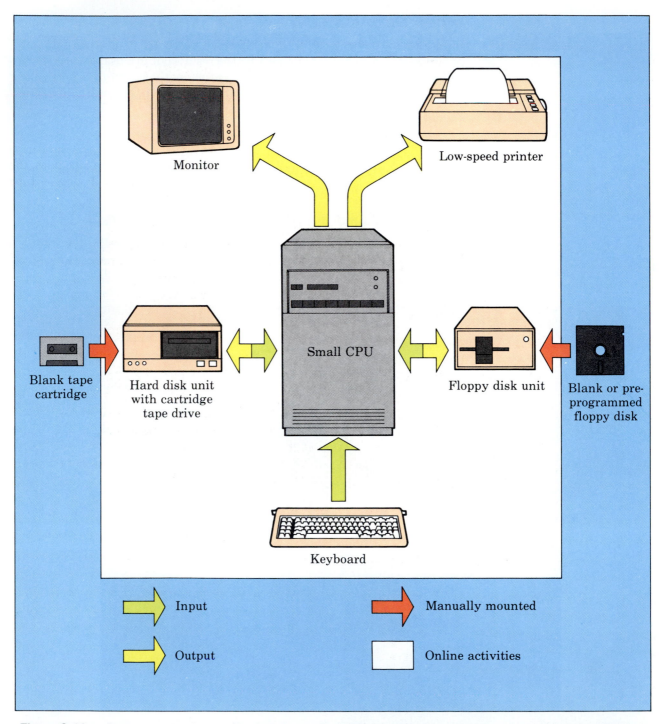

Figure 2-10. *Components of a small computer system run by a microcomputer or a small minicomputer.* In some microcomputer systems, the monitor, keyboard, CPU, floppy disk device, and even the printer all may be housed in the same physical unit.

CPU so that they can communicate with it directly. All the machines we have discussed so far—keyboards, display devices, printers, and secondary storage devices—fall into the peripheral category.

Auxiliary equipment consists of machines that always work independently of the CPU, in what is called the *standalone mode*. Examples are *key-to-tape units* and *key-to-disk units*. These two machines are also examples of **data preparation devices,** because their purpose is to get input material onto a particular input/output medium—tape for a key-to-tape machine and disk for a key-to-disk machine. After the data have been entered onto an input/output medium with one of these machines, the medium must be loaded onto the appropriate peripheral device—a tape unit or disk unit—for the data to be processed by the CPU.

Any device that is ready for or in communication with the computer at a given time is said to be **online** at that time. If a device isn't online, it's **offline.** When peripheral equipment is plugged into the computer, it's considered online. Some peripherals also have standalone capability. Thus when we "pull the plug," taking them away from the computer, they're offline. Auxiliary equipment, since it functions independently of the CPU, is always offline.

Getting It Together: Combining Hardware Into a System

Now that we've covered some basic hardware concepts and discussed some particular machines in terms of these concepts, let's see how hardware is linked together in a computer system. We'll consider two examples: a small computer system and a large computer system.

Figure 2-10 illustrates a system run by a small computer—a microcomputer or a small minicomputer. The system includes a:

- CPU/system unit
- Keyboard
- Monitor
- Floppy disk unit
- Low-speed printer
- Hard disk unit
- Cartridge tape unit

In some computer systems (typically those associated with minicomputers), all these hardware devices will exist as separate units. In microcomputer systems some devices will be combined. For example, the system unit of the Apple Macintosh shown in Figure 1-6 has a built-in monitor.

Figure 2-11 illustrates a large computer system. Such a system might be run by a mainframe computer or a large minicomputer capable of running the most powerful types of support equipment. The simple system shown here includes a:

- CPU/system unit
- Display terminal
- Teleprinter
- High-speed printer
- Key-to-tape unit
- Tape unit
- Key-to-disk unit
- Disk unit

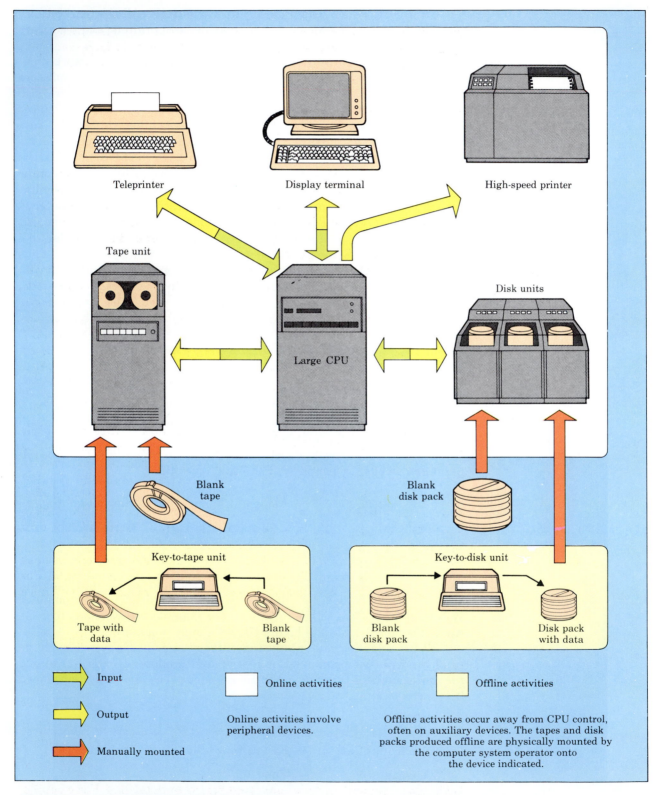

Figure 2-11. *Components of a large computer system run by a mainframe or large minicomputer.* Note the relationship of input / output media to online and offline activities and peripheral and auxiliary devices.

It is not unusual for a system run by a large computer to contain hundreds of display terminals, several tape and disk units, numerous printers, and many other types of equipment. Also, a number of large computer systems contain several computers that are hooked up to each other.

ORGANIZING DATA FOR COMPUTER SYSTEMS

Data, as we said before, are essentially facts. But you can't just randomly input a collection of facts into a computer system and expect to get results. Data to be processed in a computer system must be organized in a systematic way. A common procedure is to organize data into fields, records, files, and databases. These words have precise meanings in a computing environment and you should use them with care.

A **field** is a collection of characters (a character is a single digit, letter of the alphabet, or special symbol such as the decimal point) that represents a single type of data. A **record** is a collection of related fields, and a **file** is a collection of related records. Files, records, and fields are normally stored on input/output media such as tapes or disks. A school, for example, probably would have a *file,* perhaps stored on tape, of all students currently enrolled (see Figure 2-12). The file would contain a *record* for each student. Each record would have a *field* for various types of data about each student: the student's ID number, name, street, city, state, major subject area, and the like.

The concept of a **database** is a bit more complicated to explain at this point, but you can safely look at it as a collection of data that often contains the contents of several files. A *student database,* for example, may contain the contents of a student address file (such as the one in Figure 2-12), a student history file (showing courses completed and grades earned by each student), and perhaps other data. In other words, most of the information regarding students would be found in the student database. We'll return more formally to the concept of a database in Chapter 13.

In most large computer systems, many data files are kept in disk storage for rapid access. These files often contain operational data. For example, most businesses (such as your local department store) will have data files such as the following:

✕ Daily customer transactions (called a customer *transaction* file)

✕ Key customer data, such as names, addresses, and credit standings (called a customer *master* file)

✕ Amounts owed by customers buying on credit (called a *receivables* file)

✕ Outstanding debts the organization itself must pay (called a *payables* file)

Again, data from related files are often stored in databases. For example, data that would normally appear in the customer transaction file, the

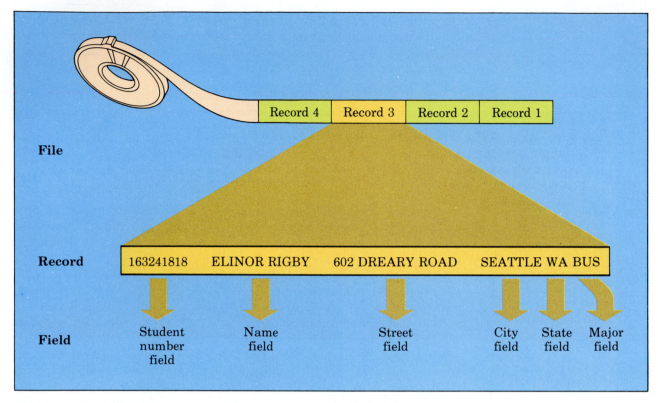

Figure 2-12. *Differences among a file, record, and field.* The file shown contains name and address data on students enrolled at a college. If there were 2000 active students at the college, this file would contain 2000 records. Each record in the file has six data fields—student's number, name, street, city, state, and major.

master file, and the receivables file described above might collectively be stored in a customer database.

Whatever the medium on which they are stored, entities such as files and databases always have a name. The computer system uses this name to identify the file or database when it needs to access it. For example, AR-D200 may be the name of a receivables data file and AR-P201 may be the name of a program that produces from this file a list of customers with overdue balances. Each organization will have its own naming convention. In the preceding example, AR stands for accounts receivable, P for program file, and D for data file. All 100-numbered program files may be related to billing, 200-level files to overdue balances, and so forth.

A BRIEF INTRODUCTION TO SOFTWARE

As mentioned earlier, the word "software" refers to programs. Programs direct the computer system to do specific tasks, just as your thoughts direct your body to speak or move in certain ways. There are two classes of software: applications software and systems software.

Using Computers Down on the Farm

HIGH TECH BEYOND THE CITY

Lawyers, doctors, and well-attired businesspeople are not the only workers who use computers these days. Consider farmers. Although farmers' incomes have been better, microcomputing sales in farming communities have been brisk. Why all this fussing over high tech?

Farming, like other forms of work, constitutes a business. Records must be kept. Income and expenses must be periodically calculated and analyzed. Thousands of dollars depend on things such as which crops are grown, the prices crops will command in the future marketplace, or which bull is chosen to sire. And what better tool is there than a computer to help with these record-keeping and decision-making tasks? Besides, when you're facing tough times and can't afford to make a bad decision, that's when you can't afford not to have a computer around.

Many farmers today have grown up in our high-tech era, so computers don't faze them any more than they do anyone else. And a $3000 price tag for a computer system may not even warrant the batting of an eyelash to someone accustomed to spending $60,000 or more for a tractor, combine, or new building. Farmers also know that you don't save in the long run by buying bargain-basement equip-

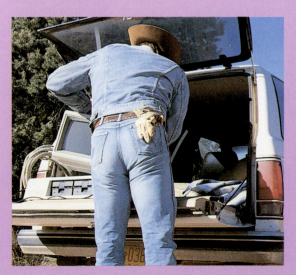

ment in the short run, so they seem to know instinctively how to go about buying a computer system that meets both current and future needs. You don't have to be a computer expert to figure out how to buy and use a computer system sensibly. Necessity often proves to be the mother of invention.

Farming uses of computers are varied, but many fall into the following applications areas:

Bookkeeping and Accounting. A number of programs are available to help farmers record and manage their business transactions. Bookkeeping entries can later be used to prepare taxes and produce summaries of income and expenses.

Least-Cost Feeding Programs. These software packages often use sophisticated mathematical techniques to develop low-cost livestock diets. Generally these packages determine the least-cost mix of feeds that will satisfy the desired nutritional intake of the animals. Software that helps determine optimum planting strategies is also available.

Financial Analysis. Farmers, like other businesspeople, have a need for "what if" types of calculations. Thus software such as spreadsheet packages can be particularly useful to them.

Animal Health, Breeding, and Pedigree Records. Software meeting these needs helps farmers maintain records on each animal, search through records to find animals that have certain characteristics, and analyze records. Such packages are generically called file managers, and some are customized to meet the unique needs of farmers or breeders.

Commodities. The prices crops bring in the marketplace are of particular interest to farmers. By configuring a modem to their computer systems and connecting to an online data service at a remote location, farmers can keep track of the ups and downs of the commodities market.

Applications software is written by users or programmers to perform such tasks as computing the interest or balance in bank accounts, preparing bills, playing games, scheduling passengers on airlines, diagnosing the illnesses of hospital patients, and so forth. In other words, applications software is what enables computers to accomplish the tasks for which people acquire them.

You can buy applications software prepackaged (word processing programs, spreadsheet programs, video games, and the farm programs mentioned in the box on page 49 are examples) or write it yourself. If you write it yourself, you must know a specific programming language. The trade-offs involved with buying or creating software are covered in Chapter 9. Some of the more popular programming languages are discussed in Chapter 11, and prepackaged software is covered in Chapters 12 and 13.

Systems software consists of "background" programs that allow applications software to run smoothly. One of the most important pieces of systems software is the *operating system,* a set of control programs that supervises the work of the computer system. Viewed another way, the operating system enables applications software to interface with a specific set of hardware. Many recent motion pictures have portrayed the role of the operating system, but have shown it in some overly exaggerated way—for example, a demon master control program trying to take over the world. Fortunately operating systems don't control people; rather, people control operating systems. These and other types of systems software are addressed in more depth in Chapter 8.

PROCESSING DATA

Computer systems process data. When we talk about data processing, however, what kinds of processing do we have in mind? The number of things that a fully fledged computer system can do with data is staggering enough to defy a simple, systematic enumeration at this early stage in the book. Rather than trying to look at all of them, let's focus on just a few commonly encountered tasks. This will give you an appreciation for the types of work that you are likely to need a computer system to do.

Some common ways computer systems process data are

- Selection
- Summarizing
- Sorting
- Routine record accounting
- Updating
- Query processing

We will discuss each of these in turn and illustrate each with an example.

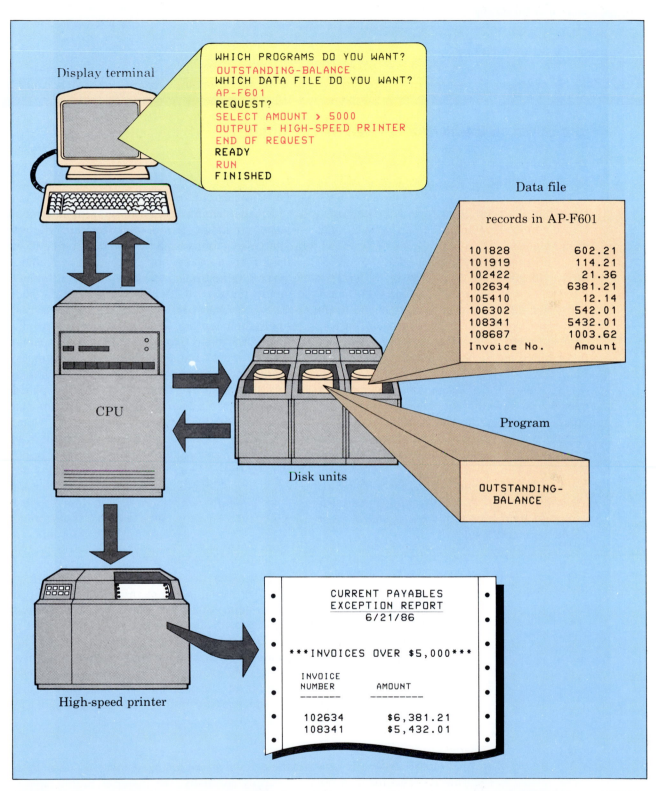

Figure 2-13. **_Selecting records from a file._** A company treasurer has asked for a list of unpaid bills over $5000. Data on all unpaid bills (current payables) are stored on disk in a file named AP-F601. A program called OUTSTANDING-BALANCE, created to process the payables file, is also stored on disk. Using the terminal, the treasurer runs the program with the data file, specifying the records needed and requesting that a printed report be sent to the high-speed printer.

THE QUIET COACH IN THE CORNER OF THE DUGOUT

This One Doesn't Take a Big Byte
Out of Salaries

Bottom of the ninth. Runner on first. Two outs. Score zero–zero. Pitcher due up. Who to send to the plate?

The year is 2000 and it's time to call on MICK. Not Mick the Stick, but the *M*innesota *I*ndians *C*omputerized *K*now-it-all—the computer system that sits on a table at the south side of the dugout. MICK always has an answer (indeed several answers) to everything that takes place on the field. And MICK's advice is often right on the money.

To use MICK at a ballgame, you plug in a memory module that contains an extensive, completely up-to-date history on player performances and games. MICK keeps track of each pitch in the current game, each error and stolen base, and who's been used on each bench. There's even a sensor subsystem attached to MICK to determine for each pitch its speed, its motion to the plate, and whether it was high, low, inside, or outside.

After each pitch MICK suggests the next strategic move for the manager to make and displays it on a small screen. In fact MICK might suggest several strategies, weighing each one according to some sort of a "desirability index." If the club manager doesn't know how MICK arrived at a particular strategy, a "help feature" can be invoked. For example, MICK might explain that the pitcher, Gonzales, should bat now because Gonzales is particularly sharp tonight, the relief pitchers are potentially ineffective, and all the pinch hitters on the bench have done poorly against tonight's opposing pitcher.

Each time the manager wants MICK's opinion on a possible strategic move, a code sequence representing the move can be keyed in on a special pad. For example, the manager may want to send a particular right-handed pinch hitter into the game to bat for the pitcher. These data are keyed in. MICK then quickly

SELECTION.   **Selection** involves going through a set of data and picking out only those items that meet certain criteria. Figure 2-13 illustrates a selection problem and how it could be processed on a computer system. The problem is to select from a data file—in this case one that contains data on a company's unpaid invoices—a specific group of records (unpaid invoices over $5000), and to print a report of the results. The user works at a display terminal, the data file and program are stored on disk, and the report is printed on a high-speed printer.

SUMMARIZING.   **Summarizing** involves reducing a mass of data to a manageable form. A building supply company, for example, might have a file of weekly sales on disk whose records contain fields for product sold, sales region, and number of units sold. If a sales manager wanted to know the total sales of each item in each region, the data would have to be

analyzes the likely consequences of the strategy and reports them on the screen. No, a turkey graphic doesn't appear on the screen if MICK totally disagrees with the manager's train of thinking.

MICK was created in 1995, the brainchild of a crack programmer (who is also a baseball fanatic) and a former major-league manager (who has four World Series rings and a superb won-lost record). More specifically, MICK represents what is known as an *expert system.* These sophisticated systems process data by combining the knowledge and decision-making expertise of people who are considered leaders in their professions with the power of computers.

Although the level of programming required to set up an expert system can be complicated, you can probably appreciate what computers are capable of doing when pushed to the extremes of their potential. And although this story is not true, in tomorrow's world it will probably become real. A few baseball managers today—for example, Davey Johnson of the New York Mets—are integrating computer outputs into their decision making. So it seems only a matter of time before a sophisticated computing device occupies one of those seats on the dugout bench.

Baseball coach, circa 2000.

summarized by product and region. Figure 2-14 shows how such a summarization problem might be processed on a computer system.

SORTING.   **Sorting** involves arranging data in a specific order—a list of names in alphabetic order, for example, or a list of numbers in ascending or descending order. Figure 2-15 shows how a typical sorting problem might be handled on a computer system. A manager wants a report of the company's products listed in order of the amount of sales revenue each generates. Data on the sales revenue for each product are in a file called PRODUCT-SALES. The sorting program is called SORT-CUM. The keyboard operator directs the system to produce the report on a high-speed printer. In addition to showing the rank order of each product by sales, this program also generates information on the percentage of total sales. Reports like these help managers decide which products are making the most money and which need special attention.

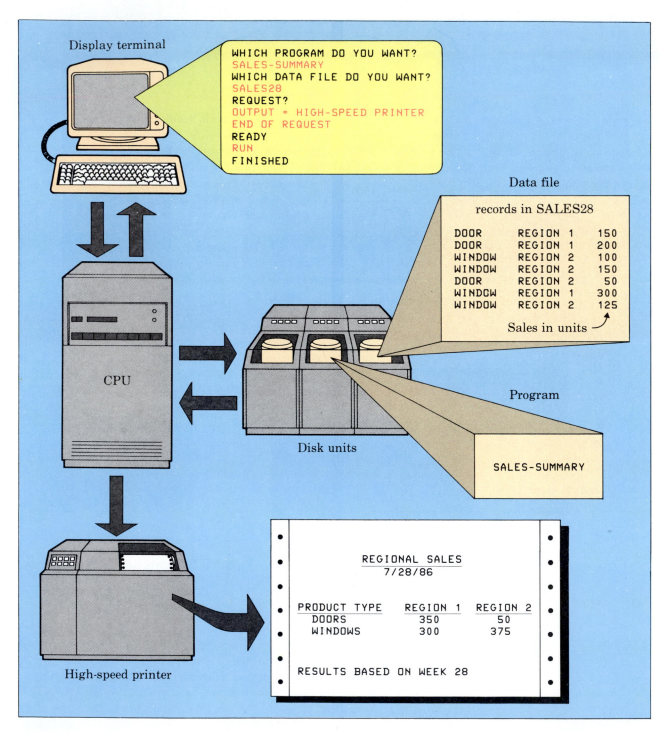

Figure 2-14. *Summarizing information.* A sales manager at a terminal uses a program, SALES-SUMMARY, which contains instructions to total sales data by geographical region and product type. One of the data files that can be used with this program, SALES28, contains data recorded during the twenty-eighth week of the year. SALES-SUMMARY instructs the computer system to total data from this file by region and product type. The manager directs the system to print the results on the high-speed printer.

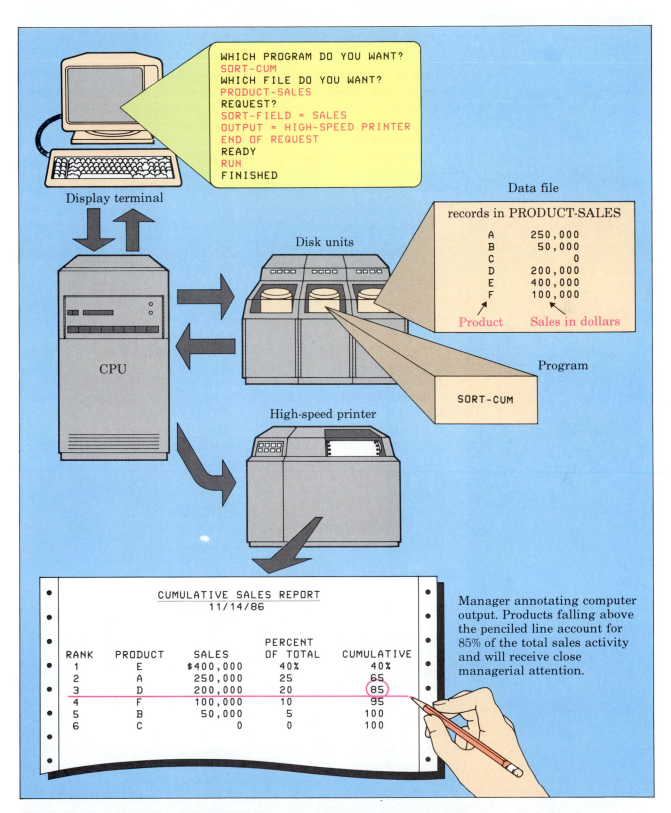

Figure 2-15. *Sorting.* A manager wants to know which of the company's products are producing the most sales revenue. The SORT-CUM program instructs the computer system to sort the data in the PRODUCT-SALES file in rank order by sales. The program also contains instructions directing the computer to calculate useful information on the percent of sales each product generates.

ROUTINE RECORD ACCOUNTING.   Besides producing reports that involve selecting or summarizing data from secondary storage, computer systems are also widely used to input records, perform a series of calculations on each one, and prepare a document for each record on the basis of these computations. This is sometimes called **routine record accounting.** In billing operations, for example, the computer system reads a record of payments and purchases for each customer, computes the amount due, and prepares a bill for each customer. Payroll processing, illustrated in Figure 2-16, is another example.

As the figure shows, computer systems can process data from several sources at once. In this example data come from three sources. The keyboard operator enters each employee's social security number and hours worked that pay period. The EMPLOYEE-MASTER file contains a record for each employee with the employee's social security number, name, and other data. The RATE file contains records with each employee's social security number and pay rate. The PAYROLL program processes these three sources of data, and, following the operator's commands, directs the computer system to print checks on a low-speed printer and a payroll report on a high-speed printer.

Normally payroll processing is much more complicated than Figure 2-16 suggests. Payroll programs must also compute and deduct federal and local taxes and save this information in storage for reporting to the federal and state taxing agencies.

Summarizing, sorting, and routine record accounting are often combined in order to do *control-break reporting,* as illustrated in Figure 2-17. As shown, the computer system "breaks" after processing each department, to print a subtotal. Also, a break is taken to print a final total.

UPDATING.   **Updating** involves changing the data in a file to reflect new information. Credit card companies, for example, update their customer files monthly to reflect payments and purchases their customers have made. Updating is done on either a batch or realtime basis.

Batch processing involves accumulating (batching) transactions over time in a separate file and processing them all at once against a master file. For example, if you update your checkbook at the end of a month, using data from the checking transactions made throughout that month, you are updating on a batch basis.

Many routine record accounting tasks, such as payroll, are done by processing work in a batch. For example, many companies pay employees at the end of the month. Billing is another operation that is often done in the batch mode. Companies maintain a file of customer transactions, which include purchases and payments. At a certain time of the month, this transaction file is processed against a master file of all customer balances. The computer system updates the balance in each account and writes bills that are sent to the customers.

The airline industry updates flight reservations on a realtime basis. Every time a seat is sold by an agent, everyone else using the system needs to know so as to have the most up-to-date information on seat availability.

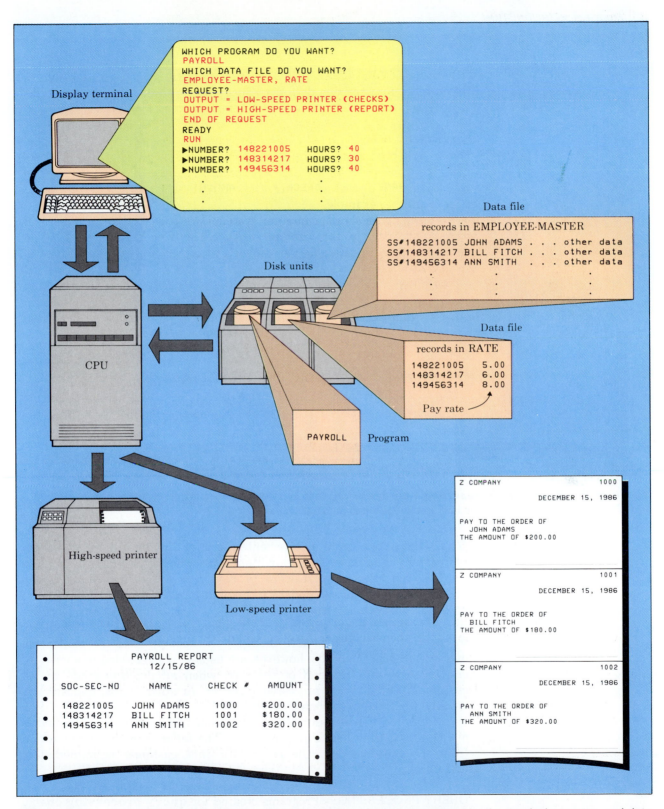

Figure 2-16. **Processing a payroll.** The PAYROLL program uses data entered by the terminal operator, and data stored on disk in the EMPLOYEE-MASTER and RATE files, to calculate each employee's pay. The operator commands the program to print checks on the low-speed printer and to output a payroll report on the high-speed printer.

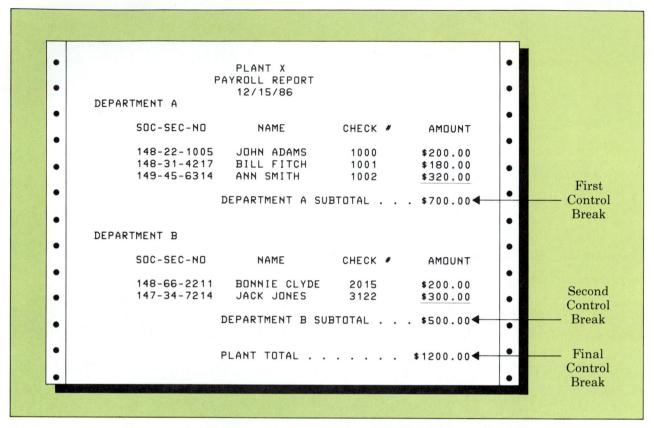

Figure 2-17. ***Control-break reporting.*** After processing each department, the computer system "breaks" to print a subtotal. Often (as shown here), the last break is taken to print the final total.

Realtime processing involves entering data directly into the computer system and updating as each individual transaction takes place.

Another example of realtime processing is found in banking, where tellers with terminals can update an account immediately when a customer makes a withdrawal. If the customer makes the withdrawal at an automatic teller machine, the machine updates the account immediately. The ability to check accounts and update them on the spot protects the bank from overwithdrawals. Deposits, however, are usually not recorded in a customer's balance until the end of the day, when all deposits made by all customers that day are processed together. In other words, deposits are usually processed in the batch mode.

Figure 2-18 illustrates realtime processing in a bank. A customer makes a withdrawal from her savings account. The teller enters the transaction from the terminal, and the record for that customer is immediately updated.

QUERY PROCESSING. Programs created for **query processing** enable users to extract information from a database or many different data files with a series of questions entered at the keyboard. A bank manager, for

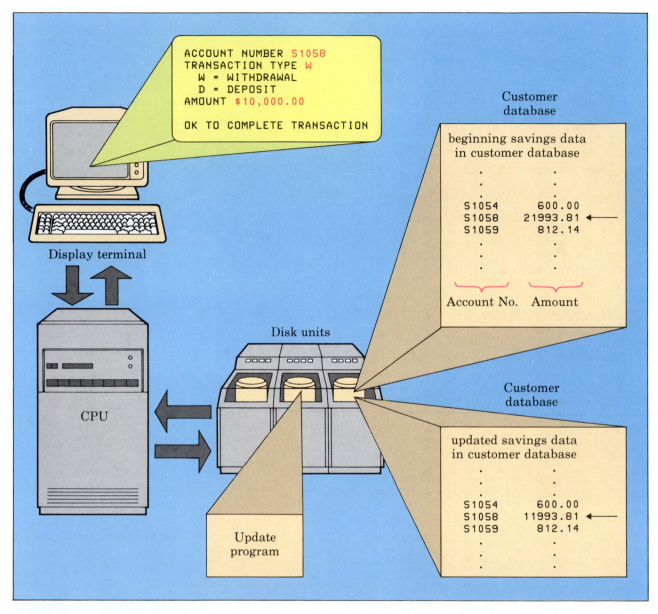

Figure 2-18. *Realtime update at a bank.* When a customer makes a deposit or withdrawal, the teller enters the transaction at a terminal. If the transaction is valid, the computer system immediately updates the customer's account.

example, may want to check a customer's credit rating. The checking, savings, trust, and loan data needed to determine credit ratings are contained in a customer database. A query program responding to the manager's request for a credit check could extract all the needed information from the database and calculate the customer's credit rating automatically. Figure 2-19 illustrates this kind of processing in an inventory environment.

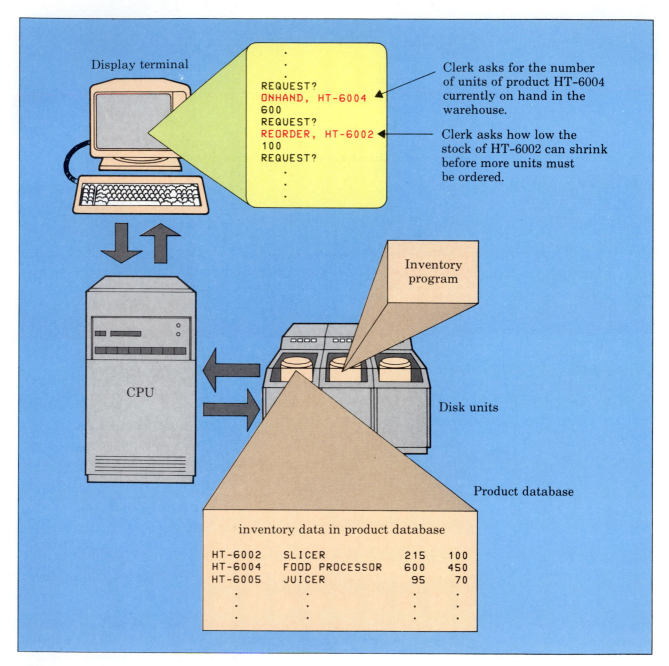

Figure 2-19. *Query in an inventory environment.* A stock clerk retrieves up-to-date information on a company's products at a terminal. If the computer program driving this application is well designed, the user need only learn a few simple commands, like those shown, to query the computer system about the current status of any stored fact.

Summary and Key Terms

All computer systems consist of some combination of **computers,** their primary memories, and **support equipment.** The computer and its primary memory are often housed in the same hardware device, called the **system unit.** The most common types of support equipment are **input devices, output devices,** and **secondary storage devices.**

Input and output devices include *keyboards, display devices* (such as *display terminals* and *monitors*), *low-speed printers,* and *high-speed printers.*

Secondary storage devices include *hard disk units, diskette units, large tape units, cartridge tape units,* and *cassette tape units.* These devices use, respectively, *hard disks, floppy disks* (*diskettes*), *detachable tape reels, cartridge tapes,* and *cassette tapes* as their **input/output media (I/O media).**

If support equipment is capable of being plugged into the computer, it is considered **peripheral equipment.** Otherwise, it's **auxiliary equipment.** Peripheral devices may be either **online** or **offline** to the CPU at any particular point in time. Auxiliary equipment, such as **data preparation devices,** is always offline.

Data are commonly organized into fields, records, files, and databases. A **field** is a collection of individual characters (such as digits and letters of the alphabet). A **record** is a collection of related fields; a **file** is a collection of related records. A **database** often contains the contents of several files.

Software falls into one of two categories: applications software and systems software. **Applications software** enables the computer to accomplish the tasks most people have in mind when they buy a computer system. **Systems software** consists of support programs that keep the applications software running smoothly.

Six common types of data processing are selection, summarizing, sorting, routine record accounting, updating, and query processing. **Selection** involves extracting from files only those fields or records that meet certain criteria. **Summarizing** involves reducing a mass of data to a manageable form. **Sorting** involves arranging data in some specified sequence, such as aphabetical order. **Routine record accounting** involves inputting records, performing a series of calculations on each one, and preparing a document for each record on the basis of the computations. Summarizing, sorting, and routine record accounting are often combined to do *control-break reporting.* **Updating,** which involves changing data in a file to reflect new information, can be done on a periodic or immediate basis. These types of updating are respectively called **batch processing** and **realtime processing**. **Query processing** enables users to extract information from data files.

Review Exercises

Fill-in Questions

1. To be read by a computer system, data must be recorded in machine-readable form on some type of _____.
2. Machines that always work in a standalone mode are referred to as _____ equipment.
3. Another name for a floppy disk is _____.
4. Any device that is ready for or in communication with the CPU at any given time is said to be _____ at that time.
5. _____ software is written by users or programmers to perform such tasks as computing the interest or balance in bank accounts.
6. _____ software consists of "background" programs that enable other programs to run smoothly on a computer system.
7. A(n) _____ is a collection of characters that represents a single type of data.
8. A(n) _____ is a collection of related records.

Matching Questions

Match each term with the example.

a. Query processing   d. Realtime processing
b. Selection   e. Control-break reporting
c. Batch processing   f. Sorting

_____ 1. The registrar at a California state college needs a report listing all students from Sacramento.
_____ 2. A student phone book is produced, with names in alphabetical order.
_____ 3. At the end of each day, a bank records all deposits made to customer accounts.
_____ 4. A terminal's display screen shows information on the sales of a single product, with three subtotals and a grand total.
_____ 5. On a display terminal, a librarian keys in the title of a book to see whether it has been checked out.
_____ 6. Jane Williams withdraws $100 from her checking account and the amount is immediately subtracted from her account balance.

Discussion Questions

1. Name some common types of computer support equipment and state whether each is used for input, output, storage, or some combination of these functions.
2. Name some common types of secondary storage devices and the I/O media each uses.
3. Create a small file of data. Can you identify the records and fields?
4. What is the difference between applications software and systems software?
5. Identify and define the types of data processing discussed in this chapter. Can you think of any other examples of data processing?

Chapter 3

Computers Past and Present

Chapter Outline

Objectives

After completing this chapter you should be able to:

1. Describe some of the key pioneers and events that have influenced today's computers.
2. Understand how hardware and software have evolved over the past half century.
3. Explain the difference between the first, second, third, and fourth generations of computers.
4. Appreciate just how fast the so-called computer revolution is moving along . . . and speculate intelligently about what might evolve in your lifetime.

OVERVIEW

It's natural for many of us to want to dismiss learning about our technological heritage. But the history of a subject gives us insight into the way things are now, and it sharpens our ability to predict events in the future.

Electronic computers as we know them were invented about fifty years ago. Since then, because the need for rapid processing of large volumes of data has been so great, their rise to prominence has been spectacular. But the history of computers goes back much further than fifty years. Since the beginning of civilization, merchants and government officials have used computing devices to help them with calculations and record keeping. The abacus, invented thousands of years ago, is an example of such a device. We will begin, however, in the 1600s, with the invention of the first mechanical calculating machines.

In the first part of this chapter, we will discuss the early advances that made possible today's electronic computer. In the rest of the chapter, we will cover the development of commercial computer systems from the 1950s to the present.

FROM GEARS AND LEVERS TO WIRES AND TUBES

Pascal and Leibniz

Figure 3-1.   Pascal's adding machine. Among its shortcomings was expense— it cost enough to keep an average citizen of seventeenth-century France in reasonable comfort for a year.

Blaise Pascal, the French mathematician, is credited with the invention of the first **mechanical calculating machine,** around 1642. Pascal got the inspiration for his invention when he was nineteen, after spending many hours poring over columns of figures and tediously adding them up. Pascal realized that this thankless chore could be accomplished faster and more accurately by a machine. After much effort he built one. This device—called the **pascaline,** for its inventor—was run by levers and gears and could add and subtract automatically (see Figure 3-1).

Curiously, the pascaline never caught on. Clerks and bookkeepers, fearing for their jobs, refused to use it.

Later in the 1600s, Gottfried von Leibniz, the German philosopher and mathematician, went one step beyond Pascal and devised a machine that could multiply and divide as well as add and subtract. This device, like Pascal's, was also run by levers and gears.

Jacquard's Loom

One important event in the development of the computer might at first glance seem unrelated. In the early 1800s, a weaver named Joseph Jacquard invented a loom that produced patterned cloth automatically. The remarkable thing about this loom was that it used punched cardboard cards to control the pattern in the cloth. The holes in the cards determined which rods in the loom were engaged at any given time.

Jacquard's loom introduced two concepts important to the future development of the computer. One was that information could be coded on punched cards. Punched cards, as we'll see, were to become the main input/output medium for the first "modern" computers. The second important concept was that the information stored in the cards could act as a series of instructions—in effect, a program—when the cards were activated.

Babbage and His Engines

One of the most remarkable figures in the history of computers was the nineteenth-century English mathematician Charles Babbage. About 150 years ago, he designed a machine that was amazing in its similarity to the first modern computers.

Babbage first became interested in mechanical computing devices while studying mathematical tables, which had many errors because they were set into print by hand. Babbage realized that a machine that could

Figure 3-2. The Babbage difference engine. Babbage was constantly at odds with the British government in getting funding for his projects. In 1833, frustrated, he wrote: "... of all countries England is that in which ... the governing powers are most incompetent to understand the merit either of the mechanical or mathematical."

automatically calculate the numbers *and* print the results would produce much more reliable tables.

Babbage was able to get funds from the British government to build such a machine, which he called the **difference engine.** He succeeded in making a small prototype (see Figure 3-2), but his attempts to build a larger version ended in failure, because the technology did not then exist to create the parts he needed.

While working on the difference engine, Babbage conceived of another, much more powerful machine, which he called the **analytical engine.** Like the difference engine, it was to consist of gears and shafts run by a steam engine. It is this machine that is so similar in concept to the modern computer. It was to be a general-purpose machine, capable of many kinds of computing work. It was to be directed by instructions on punched cards. It was to have an internal memory to store instructions and the intermediate results of calculations. And it would automatically print results.

Babbage became obsessed with the analytical engine and devoted all his energy and resources to creating it. But he was never able to complete a working model, and he died without knowing how his vision was to shape the future.

Much of what we know about Charles Babbage's analytical engine comes not from Babbage himself, but from the work of his close friend and associate Ada Augusta, Countess of Lovelace, the daughter of the poet Byron. She has been called "the first programmer" because of her work on the kinds of instructions that would have been fed into the analytical engine to make it work.

Hollerith, the Census, and Punched Cards

Another milestone on the way to the modern computer was passed during the tabulation of the U.S. census of 1890. Until 1890 census figures had been tabulated manually. The census of 1880 took seven years to complete, and officials worried that if something weren't done, the results of the 1890 census would not be completed before it was time to begin the census of 1900.

The government commissioned Herman Hollerith to build a machine to aid in the tabulation of the 1890 census. The machine Hollerith built (Figure 3-3) used punched cards and was powered by electricity. With its help the results of the census were finished in three years.

Hollerith did not rest on his laurels. He founded the Tabulating Machine Company to develop punched-card equipment to sell to business and government. Hollerith's company merged with several others in 1911 to become the Computer-Tabulating-Recording Company. In 1924 this company changed its name to International Business Machines (IBM) Corporation.

IBM rapidly became the leader in the manufacture of punched-card equipment, with an 80 percent market share by the mid-1930s. By this time the mechanical machines of the nineteenth century had been replaced by electromechanical devices such as the one pioneered by Hollerith. **Electromechanical machines** are, simply, mechanical machines driven by electricity. Although these devices were a vast improvement over their

Figure 3-3. *Hollerith and his census tabulator.* Trained as an engineer, Hollerith began work with the U.S. Census Office in 1879. Shortly thereafter, Hollerith later recalled, the head of the division of vital statistics remarked to him ''. . . there ought to be a machine for doing the purely mechanical work of tabulating population and similar statistics.'' The rest is history.

hand-cranked ancestors, they did have some serious drawbacks. Their moving parts took time to align themselves, for example, limiting their speed. Also, the repeated movement of those parts caused wear, making the machines prone to failure.

Aiken, IBM, and the Mark I

The age of electromechanical computing devices reached its zenith in the early 1940s with the work of Howard Aiken of Harvard University. Aiken had long been interested in developing ways to use these machines for scientific calculations. IBM and other manufacturers designed machines with business users in mind, but during the late 1920s and early 1930s, many scientists began to use them also. Aiken had the important insight that the technology of these machines could be adapted to create a *general-purpose computer,* one that could be programmed to do many computing tasks.

Figure 3-4. *The Mark I computer.* Despite its sleek, futuristic look, the electromechanical Mark I was technologically obsolete almost upon completion. The age of electronics was about to dawn, pointing the future of computing in another direction.

With the support of a $500,000 grant from IBM and the help of four of IBM's top engineers, Aiken started work on his machine in 1939. Its official name was "The Automatic Controlled Sequence Calculator," but it came to be called simply the **Mark I.** It was completed in 1944 and was gargantuan, as Figure 3-4 shows. It contained 500 miles of wire and 3 million electrical connections. It could do a multiplication in about six seconds and a division in about twelve seconds.

The ABC

While Aiken and IBM were still at work on the Mark I, others were exploring the use of a new technology in computer design—*electronics*—that was to make the Mark I obsolete almost as soon as it was turned on. Computers with electronic components, unlike electromechanical machines, have no moving parts. In **electronic machines** the main elements change from one state to another, depending on, for example, the presence or absence of current flowing through them. Because they have no moving parts, electronic machines are much faster and more reliable than electromechanical devices.

The first person to design and build an electronic computing machine was John Atanasoff at Iowa State University. Atanasoff, in the late 1930s, wanted a machine that could help his graduate students with the tedious job of solving simultaneous linear equations. None of the machines available at the time met his needs, so he began to design his own.

In early 1939 Atanasoff received a $650 grant from Iowa State University. This sum was enough to buy the part-time services of a graduate student, Clifford Berry, and some materials. He and Berry built a machine they called the **ABC,** for **Atanasoff-Berry computer** (Figure 3-5). The main electronic components in the ABC were 300 vacuum tubes. It could solve a set of twenty-nine simultaneous equations with twenty-nine variables.

Although small and limited in what it could do, the ABC was the first electronic digital computer.

Figure 3-5.   Atanasoff and the ABC. In 1973 a federal judge finally ruled that Atanasoff should be credited as the principle inventor of the electronic computer.

ENIAC

World War II created a sudden demand for computing power. The army, for example, had a pressing need for accurate tables that would tell gunners how to aim their weapons. These tables required vast numbers of arduous calculations. As a result, when J. Presper Eckert, an electrical engineer, and John Mauchly, a physicist, presented a proposal to the army for an electronic computer that could do these calculations in seconds, they received enthusiastic backing.

Eckert and Mauchly's computer, called **ENIAC** (*E*lectronic *N*umerical *I*ntegrator *a*nd *C*alculator), was unveiled in 1946. It was the world's first *large-scale, general-purpose* electronic computer. As you can see in Figure 3-6, compared with today's computers it was enormous. It was 100 feet long, 10 feet high, and 3 feet deep. It contained 18,000 vacuum tubes and consumed 140 kilowatts of electricity when in operation.

Figure 3-6.   ENIAC. Programming ENIAC was often a two-day undertaking. Each time a new program was run, operators had to manually reset thousands of electrical switches and replug hundreds of cables.

Von Neumann and the Stored-Program Concept

A major problem with ENIAC was that every time its operators wanted to do a new series of computations, they had to rewire it and reset switches. This process could take several hours or days. John von Neumann, a mathematician, conceived of a way around this shortcoming. He pointed out that a computer could be designed in which processing instructions could be fed in with the data to be processed. Both the program and the data could be stored in the computer's memory. In such a *stored-program* computer, operators would only have to feed in a new set of instructions when they wanted the computer to execute a new program. They would not have to rewire the machine. With this stored-program concept, the idea of software was born.

The first stored-program computer, called **EDSAC** (*Electronic Delay Storage Automatic Calculator*), was completed in England in 1949. **EDVAC** (*Electronic Discrete Variable Automatic Computer*)—Von Neumann's machine (started in 1946)—was completed in the United States in 1950. With these devices the stage was set for the computer revolution and the explosive growth of the commercial computer industry.

THE COMPUTER AGE

Up until the early 1950s, electronic computers were exclusively the tool of scientists, engineers, and the military. The early machines had been built in military and academic settings with the help of massive support from the government. No electronic computer had yet served a role in commerce. With the success of machines such as ENIAC, EDSAC, and EDVAC, however, big business was ready to enter the field, as both a producer and a user of computers.

The history of commercial computing is often divided into four distinct *generations*. What distinguishes each generation is the main electronic logic element in use at the time. The term *logic elements* refers to the electronic components used to facilitate the circuit functions in the computer. The four generations and their logic elements are as follows:

- First generation (1951–1958): vacuum tube
- Second generation (1959–1964): transistor
- Third generation (1965–1970): integrated circuit
- Fourth generation (1971–?): microminiaturized integrated circuit

Each new logic element led to improvements that made computers significantly faster, smaller, cheaper, more flexible, and capable of more storage than those of past generations.

UNIVAC I: THE FIRST GENERATION BEGINS

The **first generation** and the era of commercial computing began in earnest in June 1951, when the U.S. Census Bureau purchased a computer called **UNIVAC I.** This machine was the brainchild of the pioneers of ENIAC, J. Presper Eckert and John Mauchly. Recognizing the great commercial potential of computers, they had formed their own company. To secure operating capital, they became a subsidiary of Remington-Rand (now known as the Sperry Corporation), which successfully marketed the computer under its own name.

The UNIVAC I differed from its predecessors in a very important respect. It was the first electronic computer manufactured by a business-machine company specifically for commercial data processing applications. A general-purpose machine was now available for payroll processing and other routine, labor-intensive accounting work. Figure 3-7 shows an early UNIVAC I.

Attributes of the First Generation

VACUUM TUBES. The most important attribute of first-generation computers was the use of **vacuum tubes,** like those in old radios and television sets, as the main logic element. Though tubes were a vast improvement over electromechanical parts, like those in the Mark I, they had many problems. They generated excessive heat; they were large; and they were prone to

Figure 3-7.   UNIVAC I. This was the first machine used to tabulate returns in a U.S. presidential election. In 1952 it declared Dwight Eisenhower to be the victor over Adlai Stevenson only for-ty-five minutes after the polls closed.

Figure 3-8. *Punched cards.* Punched cards were the dominant input / output medium of the first generation and were still widely used as late as the 1970s. Today they are primarily found in specialized applications.

frequent failure. Because of the heat the tubes generated, first-generation computers had to be cooled by extensive air-conditioning units. And because the tubes were large, first-generation computers were colossal.

PUNCHED-CARD ORIENTATION.   The punched card (see Figure 3-8), used to process data since the 1800s, continued as the primary input/output medium for computer systems. Processing speeds for punched cards are atrociously slow compared with those of disk and tape, but these latter technologies did not mature until subsequent generations.

MAGNETIC DRUM INTERNAL STORAGE.   Many computers of the first generation used rotating magnetic drums for internal storage. Programs and data could be read from punched cards and stored on the drum, along with intermediate computations and final results. Because drums contain moving parts, they are relatively slow by today's standards.

LIMITED APPLICATIONS.   The typical commercial applications of the first generation were for payroll, billing, and accounting. These applications were very easy to "cost justify." For example, if a computer system could do the work of twenty clerks, who each earned $5000 annually, a cost of $100,000 was a bargain. The system could repay its purchase price in one year.

PROGRAMMING IN MACHINE AND ASSEMBLY LANGUAGES. The first programmers had to work in something called machine language. **Machine-language** instructions consist entirely of strings of 0s and 1s (called *bits*). Each 0 or 1 in an instruction activates or deactivates a circuit in the computer. A machine-language statement might look like this:

01011000011100000000000010000010

Since a program might consist of hundreds of lines such as this, you can imagine that programming in machine language was difficult and that errors were frequent.

Fortunately other languages have since become available to spare people the awesome task of machine-language programming. Dr. Grace Hopper at the University of Pennsylvania made the first breakthrough in 1952 when she produced an assembly language. **Assembly languages** made it possible to write instructions in a shorthand way. The assembly-language equivalent of the machine-language instruction you just read might be

L REG7,A

"L," meaning "load," replaces "01011000" (the first 8 bits); "REG7," meaning "storage register 7," replaces "0111" (the next 4 bits); and so forth. Assembly languages, by replacing numbers with understandable symbols, made it much easier for experienced programmers to code instructions. Assembly-language programming, however, is still tedious and is usually only done by programming experts.

THE SECOND GENERATION (1959–1964): THE TRANSISTOR

In **second-generation** computers, **transistors** replaced vacuum tubes as the main logic element. Transistors perform the same function as tubes, but they are faster, smaller (see Figure 3-9), and more reliable. They also generate less heat and require less power than tubes.

Attributes of the Second Generation

The transistor was only one of several improvements in the second generation. Other noteworthy developments included the rise of magnetic tape and disk, magnetic-core internal storage, modular hardware design, and high-level programming languages.

TAPE AND DISK SECONDARY STORAGE. Although the potential of magnetic tape as a storage medium had been known in the first generation, it was not until the second generation that tape technology developed enough

Figure 3-9. A second-generation transistor compared in size to the first-generation vacuum tube it replaced.

to make it competitive with punched cards. Not only is magnetic tape a faster input/output medium than cards, but it also packs a lot of data into comparatively little space. Today tape is still going strong but punched cards have virtually disappeared.

Disk storage was first introduced during the second generation, although its full potential was not realized until a generation later. The advantage of disk over tape is that it often allows faster access to data. Some commercial applications couldn't exist today, in the form we've grown used to, if fast disk processing weren't available. Making airline reservations, which involves millions of transactions daily, is one of them.

MAGNETIC-CORE INTERNAL STORAGE.   Small, doughnut-shaped **magnetic cores** (see Figure 3-10), which were strung on racks within the computer, began to replace magnetic drums as internal memory devices on many second-generation machines. Core planes offer much faster storage access speeds than first-generation drums. They have no moving parts, so they are not subject to the time-consuming rotation required of mechanically driven drums.

The Computer Museum

A PLACE FOR OLD AND YOUNG ALIKE

Think of Boston and you think of baked beans, New England clam chowder, Cape Cod, the Kennedys, and perhaps that famous tea party. Or, if you're a sports buff, maybe your reference is the Celtics, Bruins, Red Sox, or Patriots. But if you're into computers, a renovated warehouse at 300 Congress Street may come to mind. *The Computer Museum* (see photo), the world's first and only museum devoted solely to computers and computing, is here.

Over half an acre of exhibits chronicles the past half century.

The Computer Museum is an independent, nonprofit institution dedicated to telling the evolving story of the impact of computers on our lives. This story involves the past, present, and future. Over half an acre of exhibits chronicles the enormous changes in the size, capability, applications, and cost of computers over the past half century. Some exhibits are strictly historical, whereas others are "hands-on" and allow you to experiment with the latest technologies. Films, lectures, and an illustrated quarterly magazine complement the exhibits, providing a comprehensive picture of the computer age.

Some of the attractions that you can find at the museum are:

- An original Univac I, the first commercially successful computer.

- A second-generation IBM 1401 computer and old keypunch machines (on which visitors can punch their own cards).
- An original PDP-8, the first minicomputer.
- A computer built entirely of toys, fishing line, and brass pins by students from the Massachusetts Institute of Technology to show that elaborate machines can be built with simple materials.
- The Apollo Guidance Computer that helped astronauts navigate both the spacecraft and lunar lander. (Visitors can perform the same tasks on a working simulator.)
- A large assortment of microcomputer systems that illustrate the changes taking place in this fast-paced area of computing.
- A gallery devoted to computer graphics, showcasing a number of state-of-the-art technologies.

Boston's Computer Museum.

Figure 3-10. Magnetic-core internal memory.
These donut-shaped cores were strung onto racks, which were tiered. Every core in this three-dimensional mass had a coordinate, or address. Data was stored by magnetizing blocks of these cores in a certain way.

MODULAR HARDWARE ELEMENTS.   A big headache with early computers was maintenance. When components failed they had to be replaced individually, which was very time consuming. Manufacturers countered this problem in the second generation by introducing modular design. In *modular* design related components are grouped together onto portable boards. If a component on a board fails, the entire board is replaced. Although this may seem wasteful, modular design makes it easier to diagnose and correct malfunctions.

HIGH-LEVEL LANGUAGES FOR PROGRAMMING.   Software and programming took an important step forward during the second generation with the emergence of **high-level programming languages.** In machine and assembly languages, the programmer has to spell out every step the computer must take in an operation. Getting the computer to add two numbers, for example, might take three separate instructions. In high-level languages, a single simple statement such as

$$A = B + C$$

might accomplish the same result.

Another important feature of high-level languages is that they use simple words and mathematical expressions. As a result they are less intimidating and much easier to learn than are machine and assembly languages.

Among the first high-level languages were *FORTRAN* (*FOR*mula *TRAN*slator) and *COBOL* (*CO*mmon *B*usiness *O*riented *L*anguage). FORTRAN, developed at IBM, was designed for scientific applications. COBOL, developed with support from the government, was designed for business use. Both of these languages are still widely used today.

As high-level languages gained in popularity, users often found that programs they had written for one computer system wouldn't work on equipment made by another manufacturer. This was so because manufacturers often developed radically different versions of the same language. Usually, when a company changed from one kind of equipment to another, it had to rewrite all its programs completely. As a result the American National Standards Institute (ANSI) began to formulate rules—called *standards*—to establish a common approach to the more popular languages. This started to make it possible to write programs on one machine, that, with some minor alterations, could run on another.

THE THIRD GENERATION (1965–1970): THE FAMILY CONCEPT AND THE INTEGRATED CIRCUIT

In mid-1964 IBM made one of the most important product announcements in the history of computers. It had designed a *family* of six upward-compatible computers, the System/360 line. A machine at the "high end" of the line (such as the 360/Model 195) would be bigger and more powerful than one at the "low end" of the line (such as the 360/Model 44). *Upward compatibility* meant that programs written for a low-end machine would work on a larger machine in the series. A company that found itself with growing processing needs and a low-end machine could buy a larger machine in the series without having to redo its applications software. Up until the time of the System/360, conversion from one computer to another normally was quite a headache, requiring massive amounts of reprogramming and staff retraining. A member of the 360 family is shown in Figure 3-11.

Figure 3-11.   An IBM System/360 Model 44. Interestingly enough, many of today's computers are designed much like the popular 360 line.

The System/360 featured, as its main logic element, a device called an **integrated circuit (IC).** The IC, which replaced the second-generation transistor, consists of thousands of small circuits etched onto a small silicon chip. These chips are so tiny that several of them can fit into a thimble.

Since IBM introduced the System/360, the family concept has become widespread in the computer industry. Other major manufacturers quickly followed suit with their own families of machines. With the family concept, users began to feel that they had a solution to the massive conversion problems they had encountered in the transition from the first to the second generation, and later from the second to the third.

Attributes of the Third Generation

Besides the integrated circuit and the family concept, several other noteworthy developments characterized the **third generation.** Perhaps the most important of these are the operating system, continued improvements in software, and the minicomputer.

OPERATING SYSTEMS. An **operating system,** which Chapter 8 covers in detail, is a set of control programs that supervises the work of the computer system. First- and second-generation computers did not use operating systems. Programs were entered one by one and monitored individually by the computer operator. Also, automatic communication between the CPU and devices such as the printer was not then possible. They had to be coordinated manually. With operating systems these tasks are accomplished automatically under program control.

Moreover, computers in the first and second generations were serial processors. That is, a computer would do all its work in a one-program-at-a-time fashion. For example, job 1 would be started and completed, then job 2 would be processed, and so forth. Many modern operating systems enable computer systems to speed up processing by working on several programs at the same time.

IMPROVEMENTS IN SOFTWARE. The development of new high-level languages flourished in the third generation. Each new language was created in response to the needs of an important market of users. *BASIC* (*Beginners All-purpose Symbolic Instruction Code*), for example, was developed in response to the need for a language that was easy to learn and use. It is still one of the most popular languages. Not only is it used extensively to introduce people to computer programming, but it has also evolved as the most popular language for microcomputers.

The development of *RPG* (*Report Program Generator*) in the mid-1960s signaled a new trend in programming languages. With RPG a user or programmer merely describes to the computer system *what* a report is to look like, not *how* to produce it. Once given the input/output formats and formulas for calculations, the computer system automatically generates its own computer program to produce the report. These report generator languages have proved incredibly time-saving, and companies have made extensive use of them.

Figure 3-12. **DEC PDP-8**
minicomputer. At $20,000,
this machine represented a
small fraction of the cost of
mainframes of its day. And it
could be installed almost anywhere—in an engineer's
office, on the factory floor,
and even in a submarine.

An additional boost to the quality of software came in 1969, when IBM decided to "unbundle" pricing on software and hardware. Roughly translated this meant that an organization would be billed separately for hardware and software. Purchasers of IBM equipment were no longer locked into buying their programs from IBM. Almost immediately dozens of companies went into the business of designing better and cheaper software for IBM machines, which dominated the marketplace. Many succeeded, and the software industry soon became a big business. Over the years this industry has expanded so that it now provides software for many other computer products, not just IBM equipment.

TIME-SHARING AND MINICOMPUTERS.   In the mid-1960s, many industry experts, looking at the growing demand for computing services from organizations that could not afford a mainframe, predicted that *time-sharing* would be the wave of the future. In time-sharing several users simultaneously share the resources of a single, large, centralized computer. The users have their own display terminals and low-speed printers that are connected to the central computer. The experts expected that soon there would be many large time-shared computers in every major city, and that small businesses and individuals in droves would hook up to them. A company that owned a time-shared computer would be a utility, just like the phone company.

Companies providing time-sharing services did, in fact, flourish in the late 1960s, and many are still in existence, but by the early 1970s they were on the wane. The cause of the reversal was a relatively new computer maker named Digital Equipment Corporation (DEC). In the late 1960s, DEC had introduced a machine called a *minicomputer,* a scaled-down version of the larger computers of the day (see Figure 3-12). Miniaturization in logic and storage technology had made this innovation possible. Minicomputers are less powerful than mainframes, but they are also much less expensive. After DEC's success, other companies soon started to manufacture minis.

By the early 1970s many small businesses, attracted by the thought of having their own computers, started buying minicomputers and turning away from time-sharing services. Even big companies were snapping up these new machines. Today the minicomputer itself is threatened by another newcomer—the microcomputer.

THE FOURTH GENERATION (1971–?): COMPUTERS EVERYWHERE

The transition from the third to the **fourth generation** is either subtle or great, depending on your frame of reference. It's subtle in that the main logic element of the third generation, the integrated circuit, is still the main logic element of the fourth. But integrated circuits are much smaller, faster, and cheaper now. The availability of compact, low-cost computing has led to an unprecedented growth in computer use. During the fourth generation, computers started showing up virtually everywhere.

The Greening of the Computer Industry

A COMPACT HISTORY OF THE MICROCOMPUTER REVOLUTION

The earliest electronic computers reached fruition largely through the creative efforts of established scholars and the sponsorship of blue-chip corporations, prestigious academic institutions, and the federal government. In contrast the beginnings of the microcomputer industry are absolutely grass roots. The early history of microcomputers is a collage of interesting stories about bright teenagers, high-school dropouts, after-hours hobbyists tinkering in their garages or basements, shoestring budgets, speculative venture capital, and rags-to-riches enterprises.

Let's start our story in the mid-1960s, with the arrival of the first integrated circuits. The shrinkage of electronic circuitry onto small chips made it possible to reduce the size of many electrical products. But these earliest chips were not full-fledged computers, and they were initially employed to build the first electronic calculators, the ancestors of today's pocket calculators. These devices were a major advancement over the clunky, electromechanical desk-top calculators of the time, but they were still limited and expensive by today's standards.

In 1969 an ambitious, although now defunct, Japanese company contracted with a small California firm, Intel, to build logic into a calculator that would give it a variety of new capabilities. The project was assigned to Marcian E. ("Ted") Hoff, called by many an "engineer's engineer." Hoff developed a general-purpose logic chip (the Intel 4004) that would be known as the first *microprocessor,* or computer on a chip. Intel later became the world's leading producer of microprocessor chips.

Once a computer on a chip had become available, the next logical step was for someone to develop it into a complete microcomputer system that the average person could use. One of the first noteworthy efforts in this direction was that of a small group of Air Force personnel working on their own time in an Albuquerque garage. Their firm, *M*icro *I*nstrumentation and *T*elemetry *S*ystems (MITS), initially made electronic calculators. Unfortunately, so did many other firms, enticed by the low costs made possible by chip technology. In the early 1970s, when the bottom fell out of the calculator market, MITS turned its attention to making a kit computer to keep the company afloat. Their machine was called the Altair 8800, and it was the world's first actual microcomputer system.

Most firsts in the history of computing were crude devices, and the 8800 was no exception. You had to be knowledgeable enough to build it yourself from a kit, and it required you to code your own programs in machine language. MITS subsequently hired a Harvard freshman, William Gates, to install the BASIC programming language on the 8800. Although this attempt was successful, MITS went bankrupt a few years later. Gates subsequently dropped out of Harvard and formed

Attributes of the Fourth Generation

Many developments characterize the fourth generation, which is still in progress. These include microminiaturization, semiconductor internal memory, database management systems, and "friendly" productivity software.

Microsoft Corporation, today one of the largest producers of software in the world.

Enter Stephen G. Wozniak, or Woz, as he was known to his friends. A California computer enthusiast, he had dropped out of college. Fortunately for the history of microcomputing, he liked to build computers. Now enter Steven Jobs, another brilliant college dropout and one capable of seeing the potential of Wozniak's work. Under Jobs' direction, thousands of dollars of venture capital was raised, and Apple Computer (see photo)—one of the biggest success stories in modern corporate history—was born. But Apple needed to wait for another verse to be written into computer history before it could savor some of its biggest moments.

On the East Coast a Harvard Business School student, Dan Bricklin, carefully watched his accounting professor erase large chunks of blackboard data every time a single

number changed in an interdependent series of calculations. (Think, for example, of all the recalculations you need to make when you change the amount of wages on your federal income tax return.) Awed by the labor involved, Bricklin and Bob Frankston, a programming friend from the Massachusetts Institute of Technology, went to work on developing Visi-Calc® (the *Visi*ble *Calc*ulator). VisiCalc was the first easy-to-use spreadsheet package. It could do repetitive, accounting-type calculations in a snap.

Suddenly, with spreadsheets, businesspeople (who routinely prepare time-consuming budgets and statements of profit and loss) had a very compelling reason for buying a microcomputer. The first microcomputer manufacturer to adopt VisiCalc was Apple, and Apple computers started selling like tickets to a Michael Jackson concert. Meanwhile, in Armonk, N.Y., giant IBM was taking all of these grass-roots happenings very seriously. And now it was ready for action.

In 1983 IBM entered the microcomputing market with the IBM Personal Computer (IBM PC). This highly successful product immediately cut into sales of Apple's premier product, the Apple II. Another new firm, Lotus Development Corporation (which is today one of the world's biggest software producers), created a spreadsheet product, 1-2-3,® which challenged VisiCalc. Other new companies were entering the hardware and software side of the multibillion-dollar microcomputing industry every day. The grass roots era suddenly vanished, and an age of aggressive marketing began. But that's another story.

The original Apple computer.

MICROMINIATURIZATION.   The technological hallmark of the fourth generation is **microminiaturization.** Over the years more and more circuits have been packed into less and less space, and integrated circuits have become ever smaller. The terms *large-scale integration* (*LSI*) and *very large-scale integration* (*VLSI*) refer to this process. A single silicon chip the size of a fingernail can now contain hundreds of thousands of circuits.

Future systems, experts predict, will contain millions of circuits in the same space, perhaps leading to ultra-large-scale integration (ULSI). The end result is computer systems that are both smaller and more powerful than their predecessors.

Microminiaturization has made possible one of the most important innovations of the fourth generation, the microprocessor. A *microprocessor* is a single silicon chip upon whose surface is etched the circuitry of an entire CPU. These computers on a chip have put processing power into calculators, watches, toys, delicatessen scales, automobiles, TVs, and VCRs. Microprocessors have also made possible a new breed of computer systems—microcomputer systems—that are now placing computing power at the fingertips of almost everyone. Today you can walk into a store and buy a hand-held computer system for less than a hundred dollars or a more sophisticated system for a couple of thousand. Some of the things you probably take for granted today—pocket calculators, Apple computers, electronic games, among others—were virtually nonexistent before 1970 (see box on pages 82–83). Some of the marvels of the age of microminiaturization are observable in Window 2, page 107.

SEMICONDUCTOR INTERNAL MEMORY.   Core memory gave way to MOS (metal oxide semiconductor) memory slowly over the course of the third generation This newer memory proved to be faster, smaller, and cheaper.

Semiconductor memories are similar to microprocessors in that the memory is etched onto a small silicon chip. Also like microprocessors, these chips are commonly mounted onto metal carriers, which plug into a board that resides in the computer's system unit.

PRODUCTIVITY SOFTWARE.   Many people are intimidated by computers, and especially by programming languages. Yet microcomputer systems have a tremendous potential for helping ordinary people do their jobs better, and people who never expected to use a computer are now coming face to face with them. To cushion the shock, software producers are constantly attempting to make software easier to learn and use. (See Figure 3-13.)

A number of software vendors, over the past several years, have developed *productivity software* products that are particularly targeted to the on-the-job needs of noncomputer professionals. These packages—such as *database management systems, spreadsheets,* and *word processors*—are much easier to work with than BASIC, FORTRAN, COBOL, and other high-level languages. However, they are generally tied into specific applications and are not very flexible. For example, you'd be hard pressed to calculate the rate of return on a bank account with a word processing program (which is targeted to typing chores).

Despite its inherent specificity, productivity software is expected to increase the base of computer users substantially by the turn of the next century. Perhaps, after that, we will have created computer systems to understand even the most garbled human voice, thereby laying all existing software to rest with the vacuum tube, electromechanical relay, and Babbage's difference engine.

Figure 3-13.   Productivity software packages. During the fourth generation, user-oriented software became readily available. The two packages pictured above allow users to easily create charts and graphs from computer-stored data.

THE COMPUTER INDUSTRY TODAY

During the first generation, the computer industry consisted of a handful of vendors. Each company produced its own line of hardware and software, and also provided services to its clientele. Multiply the number of computer product vendors that existed thirty years ago by several thousand, and you have an idea of how large the computer industry is today.

HARDWARE. Well over 100 firms today manufacture computer system units. Some are particularly strong in mainframes, others in minis, and still others in microcomputers. Only a few large firms, such as IBM, offer products on all three levels. Many companies that produce their own system units also produce some supporting hardware. Most firms that make peripheral devices, however, do not make system units. Because the computer market is so big, virtually every company specializes in certain areas—for example, Apple and Radio Shack in microcomputing products, Wang in word processing systems, Qume in monitors and low-speed printers, and NCR in retailing and banking applications.

And with so many products made today by companies other than the ones that sell them, it's sometimes hard to tell who does what. In fact some products bear the logo of one company although they are manufactured by another. Companies that buy equipment made by other firms and "manufacture" their own systems out of it (or just merely affix their logos) are sometimes referred to as *original equipment manufacturers* (*OEMs*).

SOFTWARE. In recent years there has been a virtual stampede into the software business. Entrepreneurs have been attracted to the field because the amount of capital required to start a software firm is low. All you really need is time, access to a computer system, and some good ideas.

Most software is produced by independent software firms rather than by companies that also produce hardware. There are few hard and fast rules, however, and companies often expand into new areas on the basis of the talent they have available and the opportunities that lie ahead. Like firms in the hardware sector of the computer industry, software firms usually specialize in a particular area, such as database systems, word processing packages, or accounting packages.

SERVICES. Although advances in microcircuitry have made it easier than ever for a firm to buy its own computer, this is not always the best course of action. In some cases it's still better to do work by hand, or perhaps to share time on someone else's computer system, or even to use someone else's expertise. A small company may not have any equipment or computer knowledge at hand, or a large company may run out of capacity on its own computer system and need to use a piece of someone else's system temporarily. Firms that are in business to sell expertise or computing-related services are called *computer-services companies*.

tomorrow

THE WORLDWIDE COMPUTING PICTURE

Will IBM Still Be on Top Tomorrow?

International Business Machines (IBM) Corporation is enormous. In 1984 IBM's revenues were 50 percent greater than the entire U.S. steel industry's. For about a quarter of a century, it has owned over half of the worldwide computing market. Considering how competitive that market is, that's quite a feat.

At one time IBM and other U.S. computer firms owned virtually the entire worldwide market for computer hardware. Those days are now long gone. Although the United States still supplies most of the computing hardware to the world and is still the world's largest consumer of computers, the situation is rapidly changing. One of the biggest challenges has come from Japan.

In a 1985 survey taken by *Datamation* magazine, companies throughout the world were ranked with respect to their data processing revenues. The United States accounted for eight of the top twelve firms, including the top five (IBM Corporation, Digital Equipment Corporation, Burroughs Corporation, Control Data Corporation, and NCR Corporation). Japan accounted for three out of the twelve, and western Europe for one.

Japan's strength has traditionally been printers and robots. Most of the printers sold at computer stores are made by Japanese companies—NEC, Epson, Toshiba, Brother, Mitsubishi, and others. And Japan both makes and uses over half of the robots worldwide. Recently Japan has also become a major force in the semiconductor chip market and it has announced an intention of becoming the worldwide leader in fifth-generation technologies—those that use artificial intelligence techniques (see Chapter 15, pages 460–467).

We have Toyotas and Datsuns, Panasonic and JVC video cassette recorders, Sony and Sanyo televisions, and Canon copiers to show how successful Japan has been in areas other than computers. But complete computer systems are not the same as cars, copiers, or other consumer products. Computers involve software, and software involves languages.

These companies work in a variety of ways. Some offer a mainframe or minicomputer system, a few software products, and a staff of experts. Their customers generally buy a display terminal and printer from the services company or their own sources and connect them to the services company's system over ordinary phone lines. The services company's staff advises the customer on how to set up applications.

Other computer-services companies may sell only educational services, such as training accounting staff to use productivity software or programmers to learn a new programming language. Still others may offer an online service— such as providing information about securities prices, news items, horoscopes, and so forth. The variations are almost endless.

Summary and Key Terms

The world's oldest computing device, the abacus, dates back thousands of years. The first **mechanical calculating machine,** the **pascaline,** was

Language has traditionally been a barrier to the Japanese, who use a different writing system altogether. Nonetheless, seeing how successful the Japanese have been in almost every market in which they've concentrated, one must certainly wonder if IBM will be at the top twenty years from now.

One of the biggest challenges has come from Japan.

After the United States and Japan in the worldwide computing picture come the western European countries. Among the leading firms here are Siemens (West Germany), Olivetti (Italy), Groupe Bull (France), ICL (England), Nixdorf (West Germany), Ericsson (Sweden), and N. V. Phillips (Netherlands). Another continent away, the Soviets have yet to become a worldwide factor in computing. According to Daniel Seligman in the July 8, 1985, issue of *Fortune:* ''Its hardware isn't modern . . . The telecommunications are terrible. And Soviet managers have lots of sneaky reasons for not wanting effective information systems.''

Despite the fact that there are cultural and language barriers between countries, computer firms internationally are cooperating to pursue mutual goals. For example, Amdahl Corporation, a California mainframe manufacturer, sells Fujitsu supercomputers. IBM once endorsed a product made by Epson as the printer of choice for its IBM PC. And N. V. Phillips of the Netherlands has joined forces with Minneapolis' Control Data to build optical storage devices.

Where the world computing picture will be twenty years from now is anyone's guess. If the history of computing (and business in general) is any barometer of the future, expect IBM to be around and going strong; Japan, western Europe, and other countries to be a much greater force; and a handful of companies to be in control of each major market segment of the computer industry.

developed by Blaise Pascal in the early 1600s. This device could only add and subtract. Later in the 1600s, Gottfried von Leibniz devised a calculator that could also multiply and divide.

The weaver Joseph Jacquard invented an automated loom in the early 1800s that introduced two concepts important to the development of the computer: *data* could be recorded on punched cards, and a sequence of cards could act as a *program.*

The first computing device bearing a resemblance to today's computers was proposed by Charles Babbage in the 1800s. He initially conceived a machine called the **difference engine,** which would both compute and print results. Later he developed a more ambitious machine called the **analytical engine,** which embodied the principles of input, processing, output, and storage found in today's modern computers. Unfortunately Babbage died without seeing either machine completed.

The first **electromechanical machine** to perform computing was built by Herman Hollerith to aid in the tabulation of the 1890 census. Hollerith went on to become a pioneer in the development of business-oriented electromechanical tabulating machines.

Howard Aiken, with the help of IBM, designed and built the first large-scale, general-purpose electromechanical computer. It was completed in 1944 and called the **Mark I.**

While Aiken was constructing his machine, John Atanasoff was at work in the Midwest with a technology that would make the Mark I obsolete almost as soon as it was completed. With the assistance of Clifford Berry, Atanasoff created the **ABC** (for **Atanasoff–Berry computer**), the first **electronic machine** to do computing. A few years later, in 1946, J. Presper Eckert and John Mauchly created the world's first large-scale, general-purpose electronic computer, the **ENIAC.** Later in the 1940s, mathematician John von Neumann developed the concept of *stored programs*. This concept was originally implemented on two computers, the **EDSAC** and **EDVAC.**

The era of commercial computing, which began when the **UNIVAC I** computer was completed and delivered to the U.S. Census Bureau in 1951, is commonly divided into four distinct generations.

First-generation (1951–1958) computers used **vacuum tubes** as the main logic element. They also relied heavily on the use of punched cards and magnetic drum internal storage. Programs were written in either **machine language** or (later) **assembly language.** Most first-generation commercial computers were limited to accounting-type applications, because these were relatively easy to justify in terms of labor savings.

In **second-generation** (1959–1964) computers, **transistors** replaced vacuum tubes as the main logic element. Other noteworthy developments included the rise of magnetic tapes and disks for secondary storage, **magnetic-core** internal storage, modular hardware design, and **high-level programming languages** (such as FORTRAN and COBOL).

In **third-generation** (1965–1970) computers, **integrated circuits** **(ICs)** replaced transistors as the main logic element. Other major developments were the family concept of computers, **operating systems,** improvements in application language software (such as BASIC and RPG), and minicomputers.

Three terms sum up the **fourth generation** (1971 to present): small, smaller, and even smaller. It is a period of **microminiaturization,** characterized by microprocessors (computers on a chip) and **semiconductor memories** (memories on a chip). Microminiaturization has lowered the cost of computing to a level that has made computers widely available. To make computer systems even more accessible, *productivity software*— such as database management systems, spreadsheets, and word processors—has been developed to meet the needs of the growing body of users who are not programmers.

The computer industry consists of firms that sell hardware, software, and services. Most firms in the industry specialize in specific product areas.

Review Exercises

Fill-in Questions

1. The world's first large-scale, general-purpose electronic computer was called the _____.
2. The device developed by Pascal in the 1600s that could add and subtract was called the _____.
3. The first calculating machine to be developed by Charles Babbage was called the _____.
4. The electromechanical computer that was developed jointly in the 1940s by Harvard and IBM was called the _____.
5. The first electronic computer was called by the initials _____.
6. The name of the first electronic computer to be used in business was _____ I.
7. The name of the company that produced the first minicomputer was (is) _____ Corporation.
8. Herman Hollerith's company eventually merged with several others to form _____ Corporation.

Matching Questions

Match each name with its description.

a. Herman Hollerith   e. Blaise Pascal
b. Howard Aiken   f. Charles Babbage
c. John Atanasoff   g. Joseph Jacquard
d. John von Neumann   h. Grace Hopper

_____ 1. A pioneer in the development of assembly language.
_____ 2. Invented the first device that could automatically add numbers.
_____ 3. Nineteenth-century British mathematician who anticipated many of the principles of modern computers.
_____ 4. Invented the automatic weaving machine.
_____ 5. Used punched cards to record census data.
_____ 6. Starting with $650, developed an electronic computer with 300 vacuum tubes in 1939.
_____ 7. The mathematician who pioneered the stored program concept.
_____ 8. Developed the Mark I.

Discussion Questions

1. Identify the major technological developments associated with each of the four generations of commercial computing.
2. Every important technological development in computers has occurred in response to some critical problem. Identify what problem each of the following developments attempted to solve: assembly languages, operating systems, high-level programming languages, and tape and disk secondary storage.
3. What was the significance of the "family concept" of computers?
4. Why did minicomputers become so popular in the early 1970s? Why are microcomputers so popular today?
5. Name three major trends that have existed throughout the evolution of computers.

Module B

HARDWARE

When most people think of computers or computer systems today it is the *hardware* that readily comes to mind. These are the exciting pieces of equipment that are delivered in crates or boxes when you buy a computer system. As you'll find out in this module, there's a rich variety of computer hardware available in today's marketplace. But as you'll learn later in this book, the hardware needs a guiding force—software—to be of any use. Hardware without software is like a human being without the ability to reason and manipulate thoughts.

The hardware in this module is divided into four areas. Chapter 4 describes the role of the CPU—the computer itself. Chapter 5 discusses the hardware that provides an indispensable library of resources for the CPU—secondary storage devices. Chapter 6 delves into input and output devices. Module B closes, in Chapter 7, with a discussion of telecommunications hardware, which makes it possible to transmit data and programs between the hardware devices covered in Chapters 4 to 6.

Chapter 4

The Central Processing Unit (CPU)

Chapter Outline

Objectives

After completing this chapter you should be able to:

1. Describe the differences that exist among computers.
2. Describe how the CPU and its main memory work together to process instructions and data.
3. Identify several binary-based codes that are used in a computing environment.
4. Explain the function of various pieces of hardware commonly found under the cover of the system unit.

OVERVIEW

So far we've considered the system unit—which houses the CPU and its internal memory—to be a mysterious "black box." In this chapter we'll demystify that notion by flipping the lid off the box and examining closely the functions of the parts inside. In doing so we'll try to get a feel for how the CPU, internal memory, and other devices commonly found in the system unit work together.

To start we'll consider the types of computers available today and the features that differentiate the general-purpose CPU from other computing devices. We'll then look at how the CPU is organized and how it interacts with primary memory to carry out processing tasks. Next we'll discuss the way data and programs must be presented to the computer system. Here we'll talk about the codes that have been developed for translating back and forth from symbols the CPU understands to symbols people understand.

These topics will finally lead us into a discussion of how the CPU and its primary memory are packaged with other computing and memory devices inside the system unit (illustrated in Window 2).

TYPES OF COMPUTERS

There are many ways to classify computers. In Chapter 3 we touched upon one such classification—electronic versus nonelectronic computers. Virtually all modern computers are electronic.

A second way to classify computers is by whether they are digital or analog. A **digital computer** is one that *counts*, while an **analog computer** is one that *measures*. Counting and measuring, which are the most basic types of computation, were with us long before computers existed. When we observe that there are fifteen people in a room, for example, we are counting. Entities such as people, books, and dollars are capable of being counted. When we estimate that there are 10 gallons of fuel in a gas tank, on the other hand, we are measuring. There may actually be 10.0001, 9.872, or some other quantity of fuel. Entities such as speed, height, and length are capable only of being measured, because they don't exist naturally as indivisible units.

When we talk about computers today, most of us are referring to digital computers. Digital computers are the ones that help run businesses, sit on desk tops in homes, and perform most of the tasks we generally think of as computer work. In fact digital computers are really what this chapter—and this book—are about. As you'll later see, digital computers convert all programs and their data to strings of 0s and 1s that can be manipulated at electronically fast speeds.

Nonetheless you'll probably encounter several analog computers, devices that measure physical phenomena and convert them to numbers.

For example, a gasoline pump contains an analog computer to measure the amount of gas pumped and convert it into gallon and price amounts that appear on the pump's register. A car has an analog computer to measure drive shaft rotation and to convert it into a speedometer reading. And a thermometer is an analog computer that measures heat and converts it into a temperature reading.

A third way to classify computers is by whether they are the *central* processors (that is, the CPUs) of their computer systems or *specialized* processors relegated to a narrow range of tasks. Since the circuitry for a computer can fit on a tiny silicon chip that costs only a few dollars, you now find specialized computers of all sorts liberally embedded into peripheral devices such as keyboards and printers. In fact you are likely to find several specialized computers under the cover of your computer's system unit (and under the hood of your car, as well). But it is the central processing unit that this chapter is mainly about.

HOW THE CPU WORKS

Every CPU is, basically, a collection of electronic circuits. Electronic impulses come into the CPU from an input device. Within the CPU these impulses are sent under program control through circuits to create a series of new impulses. Eventually a set of impulses leaves the CPU, headed for an output device. What happens in those circuits? To begin to understand this process, we need to know first how the CPU is organized—what its parts are—and then how electronic impulses move from one part to another to process data.

The CPU and Its Primary Memory

The CPU has two major sections: an *arithmetic/logic unit* (ALU) and a *control unit*. Both of these units work closely with *primary memory* to carry out processing tasks inside the system unit.

Primary memory (also called **main memory** and **internal storage**) holds

 The programs and data that have been passed to the computer for processing

 Intermediate processing results

 Output that is ready to be transmitted to secondary storage or to an output device

Once programs, data, intermediate results, and output are stored in primary memory, the CPU has to be able to find them again. Thus each location in primary memory has an address. In many computer systems, a single address will store a single character of data. The size of primary memory varies from computer to computer. The smallest computers have a memory capacity of only a few thousand characters. The largest have a capacity of many million. Whenever an item of data, an instruction, or the result of a calculation is stored in memory, it is assigned an *address* so the CPU can locate it again when it is needed.

Primary memory is relatively expensive and limited in size. For this reason it is only used temporarily. Once the computer has finished processing one program and set of data, another program and set of data are written over them in the storage space they occupy. Thus the contents of each storage location are constantly changing. The address of each location, however, never changes. This process can be compared to what happens to the mailboxes in a post office. The number on each box remains the same, but the contents change as patrons remove their mail and as new mail arrives.

The **arithmetic/logic unit (ALU)** is the section of the CPU that does arithmetic and logical operations on data. *Arithmetic* operations include such tasks as addition, subtraction, multiplication, and division. *Logical* operations involve the comparison of two items of data to determine if they are equal, and if not, which is larger. As we shall see, all data coming into the CPU, including nonnumeric data such as letters of the alphabet, are coded in digital (numeric) form. As a result the ALU can perform logical operations on letters and words as well as on numbers.

Such basic arithmetic and logical operations are the *only* ones the computer can perform. That might not seem very impressive, but when combined in various ways at great speeds, these operations enable computers to perform immensely complex tasks.

The **control unit** is the section of the CPU that directs the flow of electronic traffic between primary memory and the ALU and between the CPU and input and output devices. In other words, it is the mechanism that coordinates the operation of the computer. Figure 4-1 shows the CPU and its primary memory.

Registers

To enhance the effectiveness of the computer, the control unit and ALU contain special storage locations that act as high-speed staging areas. These areas are called **registers.** Since registers are actually a part of the CPU, their contents can be handled much more rapidly than can the contents of primary memory. So to speed up processing, for example, program instructions and data are normally loaded (that is, staged) into the registers from primary memory just before processing. These devices play a crucial role in making computer speeds extremely fast.

There are several types of registers, including those listed here:

Instruction register and address register Before each instruction in a program is processed, the control unit breaks it into two parts. The part that indicates what the ALU is to do next (for example, add, multiply, compare) is placed in the **instruction register.** The part

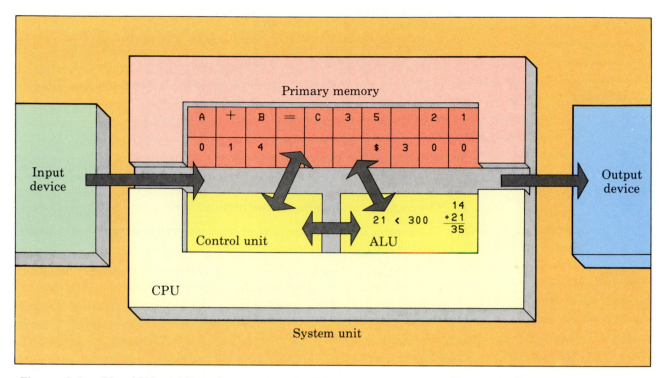

Figure 4-1. ***The CPU and its primary memory.*** Primary memory temporarily stores any program on which the computer is currently working, as well as its input data, intermediate computations, and output. Each location in the memory has an address, and often a single address can store a single character. Although only twenty locations are shown, primary memories typically contain from a few thousand addresses to several million. All "figuring" done by the computer is accomplished in the arithmetic/logic unit (ALU). Data are transferred between primary memory and the ALU under supervision of the control unit.

that gives the address of the data to be used in the operation is placed in the **address register.**

×   *Storage register*   The **storage register** temporarily stores data that have been retrieved from primary memory prior to processing.

×   *Accumulator*   The **accumulator** temporarily stores the results of ongoing arithmetic and logic operations.

The instruction and address registers are often located in the control unit, whereas the storage register and accumulator are often in the ALU.

Machine Cycles

Now that we've discussed the CPU, main memory, and registers, let's see how these elements work together to process an instruction. The processing of a single instruction is called a **machine cycle.** We touched upon machine-language instructions in Chapter 3 and will discuss them further in this chapter.

A machine cycle has two parts: an instruction cycle (I-cycle) and an execution cycle (E-cycle). During the **I-cycle,** the control unit fetches a program instruction from main memory and prepares for subsequent processing. During the **E-cycle,** the data are located and the instruction is executed. Let's see how this works in a little more detail, using a simple addition as an example.

I-cycle

1.   The control unit fetches from main memory the next instruction to be executed.

2.   The control unit decodes the instruction.

3.   The control unit puts the part of the instruction showing what to do into the instruction register.

4.   The control unit puts the part of the instruction showing where the associated data are located into the address register.

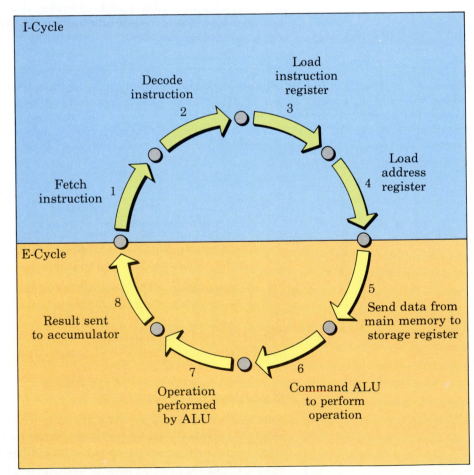

Figure 4-2.   *The machine cycle.* Each statement that you code in languages such as BASIC or Pascal actually requires several machine instructions, or cycles.

E-cycle

5. The control unit, using the information in the address register, retrieves data from main memory and places them into the storage register.

6. The control unit, using the information in the instruction register, commands the ALU to perform the required operation.

7. The ALU performs the required operation, taking the values found in the storage register and the accumulator and adding them together.

8. The result of the operation is placed back into the accumulator, destroying the value that was there previously.

Figure 4-2 summarizes pictorially how the machine cycle works.

All this may seem like an extremely tedious process, especially when you consider that a computer may need to go through thousands, millions, or perhaps billions of machine cycles to process a single program fully. But of course computers are fast—very fast. In the slowest of them, cycle times are measured in **milliseconds** (thousandths of a second). In others they are measured in **microseconds** (millionths of a second). In the fastest they are measured in **nanoseconds** (billionths of a second) or in **picoseconds** (trillionths of a second).

The IBM PC operates at almost five million cycles per second. At the other end of the processing spectrum are supercomputers that are capable of a billion or more operations per second.

BINARY-BASED DATA AND PROGRAM REPRESENTATION

The electronic components of digital computer systems work in two states. A circuit, for example, is either open or closed. A magnetic core is polarized either clockwise or counterclockwise. A magnetic spot is either present or absent, and so forth. This two-state, or **binary,** nature of electronics is illustrated in Figure 4-3. It is convenient to think of these binary states as the *0-state* and the *1-state*. Computer people refer to such zeros and ones as **bits,** which is a contraction from the two words "*bi*nary dig*its*." Computers, being primarily electronic, do all their processing and communicating by representing programs and data in bit form. Binary, or the base-2 numbering system, is the "native tongue" of the computer.

People, of course, don't talk binary. You're not likely to go up to a friend and say

1100100011001001

which, in one binary-based coding system, translates as "Hi." People communicate with each other in *natural languages* such as English, Chinese, and Spanish. In our part of the world, we speak mostly English. Also, we write with a twenty-six-character alphabet, and we use a number system with 10 digits, not just 2.

Figure 4-3.   The binary nature of electronics.
Circuits are either open or closed, a current runs one way or the opposite way, a charge is either present or absent, and so forth. Whatever, the two possible states of an electronic component are referred to as "bits" and represented by computer systems as 0s and 1s.

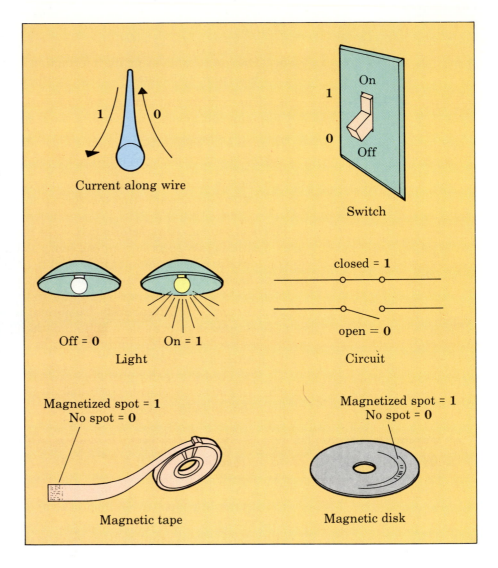

Computers, however, only understand 0 and 1. So for us to interact with a computer, our messages to it must be translated into binary form, and its messages to us must be translated from binary into a natural language.

The programming languages most people use to interact with computer systems consist of a wide variety of natural-language symbols. When we type a message such as

RUN FA-287

at a keyboard, the computer system must translate all the natural-language symbols in the message into 0s and 1s. After processing is finished, the computer system must translate the 0s and 1s it has used to represent the program's results into natural language. This conversion process is illustrated in Figure 4-4.

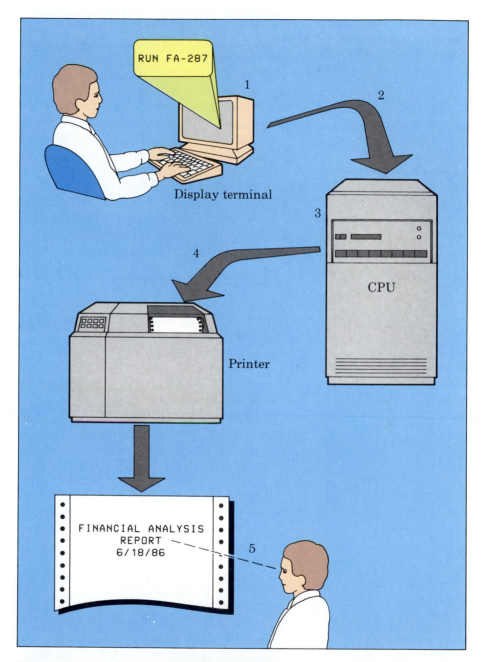

RUN FA-287

Display terminal

CPU

Printer

FINANCIAL ANALYSIS
REPORT
6/18/86

Figure 4-4. *Conversion to and from binary-based form.* (1) The user types in a message in natural-language symbols. (2) The computer system translates the message into binary-based form (this conversion often takes place in the input device). (3) The CPU does all the required processing in binary-based form. (4) The computer system translates the output back into natural-language symbols (this conversion usually takes place in the output device). (5) The user is able to read the output.

Computer systems use a variety of binary-based codes to represent programs and data. For example, when data and programs are being sent to or from the CPU (steps ② and ④ in Figure 4-4), a fixed-length binary-based code such as EBCDIC or ASCII is often used to represent each character transmitted. We shall cover these two codes shortly.

Once data and programs are inside the CPU (step ③ of Figure 4-4), other types of binary-based codes are normally used to handle them. For example, when a program is about to be executed by the computer, it is represented by a binary code known as machine language. Data, on the other hand, may be represented by several different binary-based codes when they are being manipulated by the computer. One such code, which everyone learning how computers store numbers should know, is *true binary representation*. This code, as well as some fundamentals of number systems, is covered in Appendix A.

EBCDIC and ASCII

As mentioned earlier, when data or programs are being sent between the computer and its support equipment, a *fixed-length* binary-based code is commonly used. With a fixed-length code, the transmitting machines can easily tell where one character ends and another begins. Such codes can be used to represent digits, alphabetic characters, and other symbols.

Among the two most popular of these fixed-length codes are **EBCDIC** (*Extended Binary-Coded Decimal Interchange Code*) and **ASCII** (*American Standard Code for Information Interchange*). IBM developed EBCDIC and it is used heavily on IBM mainframes. ASCII, jointly developed by the American National Standards Institute and a number of non-IBM computer vendors, is used on many other CPUs. Even the IBM PC uses ASCII.

Both EBCDIC and ASCII represent each printable character as a unique combination of a fixed number of bits (see Figure 4-5). EBCDIC uses 8 bits to represent a character. A group of 8 bits has 256 (2^8) different combinations, so EBCDIC can represent up to 256 characters. This is more than enough to account for the twenty-six uppercase and twenty-six lowercase characters, the 10 decimal digits, and several special characters.

ASCII was originally designed as a 7-bit code that could represent 128 (2^7) characters. Several 8-bit versions of ASCII (called *ASCII-8*) have also been developed because computers are designed to handle data in chunks of 8 bits. Many computer systems can accept data in either coding system and perform the conversion to its native code. The 8 (or 7) bits used to represent a character in EBCDIC (or ASCII) are referred to as a **byte.**

In many computer systems 1 byte represents a single addressable storage location. For this reason computer manufacturers use the byte measure to define the storage capacity of their machines. As you may have noticed, computer advertisements are filled with references to kilobytes, megabytes, and gigabytes. One **kilobyte (K-byte** or **KB)** is equal to a little more than 1000 bytes (1024 to be precise), 1 **megabyte (M-byte** or **MB)** equals about 1 million bytes, and 1 **gigabyte (G-byte** or **GB)** equals about 1 billion bytes. So, for example, when you read of a system with a 512 KB system unit and a 40 MB hard disk storage unit, it means the primary

Character	EBCDIC Bit Representation	ASCII Bit Representation	Character	EBCDIC Bit Representation	ASCII Bit Representation
0	11110000	0110000	I	11001001	1001001
1	11110001	0110001	J	11010001	1001010
2	11110010	0110010	K	11010010	1001011
3	11110011	0110011	L	11010011	1001100
4	11110100	0110100	M	11010100	1001101
5	11110101	0110101	N	11010101	1001110
6	11110110	0110110	O	11010110	1001111
7	11110111	0110111	P	11010111	1010000
8	11111000	0111000	Q	11011000	1010001
9	11111001	0111001	R	11011001	1010010
A	11000001	1000001	S	11100010	1010011
B	11000010	1000010	T	11100011	1010100
C	11000011	1000011	U	11100100	1010101
D	11000100	1000100	V	11100101	1010110
E	11000101	1000101	W	11100110	1010111
F	11000110	1000110	X	11100111	1011000
G	11000111	1000111	Y	11101000	1011001
H	11001000	1001000	Z	11101001	1011010

Figure 4-5. *EBCDIC and ASCII.* These two common fixed-length codes represent characters in byte form. In EBCDIC, a byte consists of 8 bits; in ASCII, 7 bits.

memory of the computer can store about 512,000 characters of data and the disk unit can store an additional 40 million.

The conversion from natural-language words and numbers to their EBCDIC or ASCII equivalents and back again usually takes place on an input/output device. For example, when a user types in a message such as

RUN

at a keyboard, a specialized processor inside the keyboard usually translates it into EBCDIC (or ASCII) and sends it as a series of bytes to the CPU. The output the CPU sends back to the display screen or to some other output device is also in EBCDIC (or ASCII), which the output device—usually with the aid of another imbedded specialized processor—translates into understandable words and numbers. Thus, if the CPU sent the EBCDIC message

1100100011001001

to your display device, the word "HI" would appear on your screen.

THE PARITY BIT. Suppose you are at a keyboard and press the *B* key. If the keyboard processor supports EBCDIC coding, it will transmit the byte

"11000010" to the CPU. Sometimes, however, something happens during transmission, and the CPU receives a garbled message. Interference on the line, for example, might cause the third bit to change from 0 to 1, and the CPU would receive the message "11100010." Unless it had some way of knowing that a mistake had been made, it would wrongly interpret this byte as the letter *S*.

To enable the CPU to detect such errors, EBCDIC and ASCII have an additional bit position. This bit, called the **parity bit,** is automatically set to either 0 or 1 in order to make all the bits in a byte add up to either an even or an odd number. Computer systems support either an even or an odd parity. In odd-parity systems, the parity bit makes all the 1-bits in a byte add up to an odd number. In even-parity systems, it makes them add up to an even number. Figure 4-6 shows how the parity bit works for the EBCDIC representation of the word "HELLO" on an even-parity system.

The parity bit is automatically generated by the keyboard's processor, so if you typed the *B* character on an even-parity system, "110000101" would be sent up the line to the CPU. If the message were garbled, so that the even-parity computer received "111000101" (an odd number of 1-bits), it would sense the error immediately.

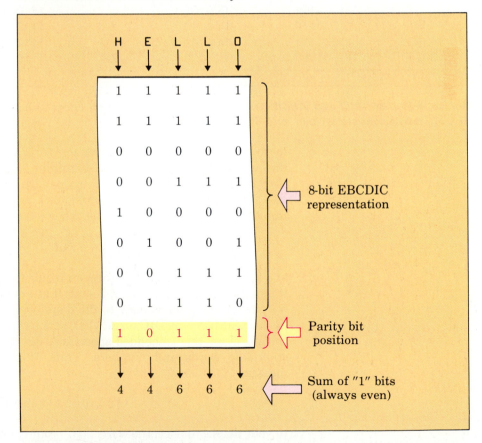

Figure 4-6. **The parity bit.** If the system used supports even parity, as shown here, the 1-bits in every byte must always add up to an even number. The parity bit is set to either 0 or 1 in each byte to force an even number of 1-bits in the byte.

A Closer Look at ASCII

AND THOSE ASCII FILES ON YOUR COMPUTER

Virtually everyone who works with computers at some point will need to create a data file. These files may consist of such items as data for a BASIC program, a word-processed document, or an accounting worksheet. On many microcomputer systems, data files fall into two categories: program-dependent files and ASCII files.

Both types of files consist of sequences of 0s and 1s. The difference is that the strings of 0s and 1s in a standard *ASCII file* represent text that anyone or anything familiar with ASCII can understand, while the strings of 0s and 1s in a *program-dependent file* represent text that only a particular computer program can understand. Most program packages cannot read and translate program-dependent files created by another package. If, say, a word processing package stores documents in its own binary-based form, it's probably impossible to have those documents read by a spreadsheet package that recognizes another form. On the other hand, many software packages can read and understand standard ASCII files, and so if you can find a way to get your document into a standard ASCII file, you can probably get your spreadsheet to read it.

The 7-bit ASCII code runs from 0 to 127. Codes 0 through 32 are control codes, and represent such functions as carriage return, line feed, and form feed. One control code is even assigned to generate a beep or ring a bell. Then begins a string of printable characters; for example, code 33 is the exclamation mark and 76 is the uppercase "L." If all manufacturers of software and hardware used only these 128 standard codes, we would have a lot fewer communications problems.

But since most computers can handle 8 bits, it is possible to generate 128 *additional* ASCII codes. It's these 8-bit forms of ASCII (that is, *ASCII-8*) that cause the interfacing problems, as each software manufacturer uses the additional codes in its own way. For example, some programs use these extra codes to store data more compactly, while others use them to generate special graphics characters and printer sequences. Thus these "extended" ASCII files are completely program dependent. Fortunately many software packages that create program-dependent files provide users with an option for translating these files into standard ASCII.

But getting a file translated into ASCII may be only half the battle in getting one program to handle the data file of another. The

---

Getting a file translated into ASCII may be only half the battle.

---

other half of the battle deals with *formatting differences* between packages. Files consist of records, and each program has its own method of formatting records. One program, for example, might mark the end of each data record with a carriage return character (ASCII 13) whereas another might use a line feed (ASCII 10) instead.

Some software packages offer routines that will automatically translate its files into forms compatible with certain other packages. That is, they will both convert files to another program-dependent form and reformat files for you. For example, Lotus' 1-2-3® has a "transport option" to translate a 1-2-3 file into a dBase® file. Another approach used by software manufacturers to make data files compatible is to generate data files that conform to a particular standard, such as the *Data Interchange Format* (*DIF*). Any program that supports the DIF format can accept files from other programs that use this format.

The parity check is not foolproof. For example, if 2 bits are mistransmitted in a byte, they are self-canceling. A 2-bit error, however, has an extremely small chance of occurring.

Machine Language

Before a program can be executed by a computer, it must be converted into a binary-based code known as **machine language.** An example of a typical machine-language instruction is shown in Figure 4-7. As you can see, what looks like a meaningless string of 0s and 1s actually consists of groups of bits that represent specific locations, operations, and characters. Each computer has its own machine language. A code that is used on an IBM computer will be totally foreign to a Honeywell computer.

Machine-language instructions are what the CPU works on during the machine cycles we discussed earlier in the chapter. Because it is patterned closest to the actual behavior of the computer, machine language is often called a *low-level language. Assembly languages,* developed in the 1950s, are symbolic counterparts of machine languages; they replace binary code with understandable symbols composed of numbers and letters. But because they so closely resemble machine language, and are tedious for the average programmer to work with, assembly languages are also considered low-level languages.

With the first computers, all programs were written in machine language. Today, although it is still possible to write in machine language, hardly anybody does. As mentioned in Chapter 3, programmers can now work in *high-level languages* that are much easier to read. Programs written in high-level languages (such as BASIC or Pascal) or in an assembly language must be translated into machine language, however, before they can be executed. This takes place automatically under the control of a special program called a *language translator* (discussed in Chapter 8).

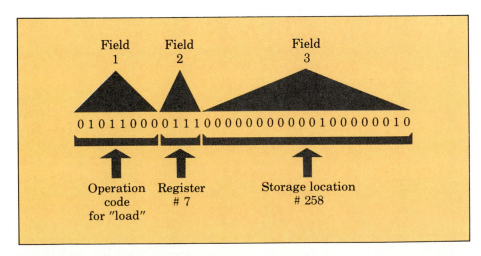

Figure 4-7.   A 32-bit machine-language instruction. The instruction commands the computer to load the contents of main memory location 258 into register 7. In the example, the numbers 7 and 258 are represented in the instruction by their true binary counterparts.

How Computer Chips Are Made

From design to final product assembly

The microprocessor, or computer-on-a-chip, is found in a multitude of products, including toys, phones, digital watches, scales, audio and video equipment, washers and dryers, microwave ovens, and personal computers. The story of how microprocessor chips are produced is a fascinating one. A drawing of the circuits on the chip is first digitized into computer memory. Then it is tested by a series of computer programs and modified appropriately. The final circuit design is later converted back into physical form and, hard as it is to believe, hundreds of thousands—and maybe millions—of circuits are fitted into an area smaller than a fingerprint. The chip design is then replicated many times on a circular silicon wafer. Finally, the individual chips are cut off the wafer, mounted in carrier packages, and sold for a few dollars. Look through this Window to see more clearly how this process takes place.

1. A microchip in its carrier package compared to keys on a computer keyboard.

2. A closeup of a microchip. The twenty-four leads at the center of the carrier package are connected by small wires to edges of the chip to carry out input and output functions.

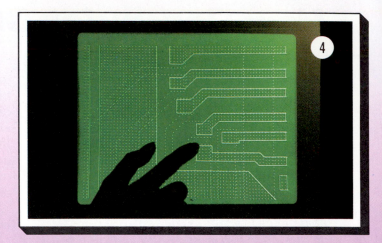

4. Prior to manufacturing, a chip design can be inspected closely for correctness. Later the image will be scaled down photographically to the actual physical size of the chip and replicated several hundred times like a large sheet of postage stamps, on a circular silicon wafer (see photograph 7).

3. A microchip being designed at a display terminal. Often, the circuitry for the chip is started manually on huge sheets of paper by drafters. The drawings are photodigitized and stored in computer memory, where they are corrected and combined with other circuit assemblies.

5. Wafers start as "blank" cylindrical silicon ingots. Silicon is used as a backing for the circuits because it is inert, pure, and abundant. The ingots are then sliced into uniform wafers like rolls of sausage.

6. The wafers are then etched with microscopically visible circuit patterns and baked in a diffusion furnace. The baking operation makes the circuits "permanent" by producing an insulating glass layer over them. Often, the wafer will go through several such etching-baking cycles, with a different set of circuits produced on each layer.

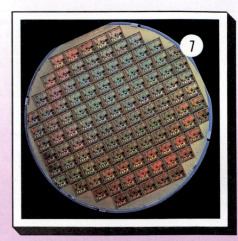

7. A finished wafer of identical micro-chips. At this point, each of the chips is cut from the wafer and separately bonded onto carrier packages such as those shown in photographs 1 and 2.

8. Before each chip is integrated onto a board, it is carefully inspected for flaws.

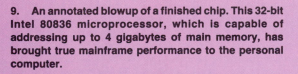

9. An annotated blowup of a finished chip. This 32-bit Intel 80836 microprocessor, which is capable of addressing up to 4 gigabytes of main memory, has brought true mainframe performance to the personal computer.

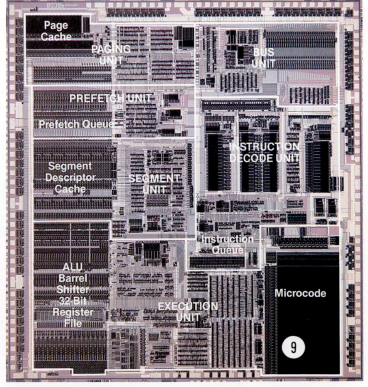

Page Cache

PAGING UNIT

BUS UNIT

PREFETCH UNIT

Prefetch Queue

INSTRUCTION DECODE UNIT

Segment Descriptor Cache

SEGMENT UNIT

Instruction Queue

ALU Barrel Shifter 32-Bit Register File

EXECUTION UNIT

Microcode

10. Once the chip/carrier-package assembly is satisfactory, it is welded onto a board.

11. Each board normally contains a wide assortment of processor and memory chips, as well as related circuitry. As Chaper 4 mentions, each board is generally configured to perform some well-defined function within the computer's system unit.

12. A finished system unit. The computer's system unit may contain anywhere from one to a dozen or more boards. The boards are often fitted into slots inside the unit (see Figure 4-8 in text). Incidently, the system unit is not the only piece of hardware that contains microchips mounted onto boards. You'll also find such assemblies in keyboards, printers, display devices, and a variety of other equipment.

THE SYSTEM UNIT

Now that we've talked conceptually about how the CPU and main memory work, let us consider how they're realized in hardware and how they relate to other devices inside a system unit of, say, a typical microcomputer. Almost all computer systems sold today use a modular hardware approach; for example, related circuitry is etched onto memory or processor chips, the chips are mounted onto carrier packages that are later plugged into boards, and the boards are fitted into slots inside the **system unit.** Let's now look in more detail at the individual hardware components that are involved in this process.

Memory Chips: RAM and ROM

There are basically only two types of chips: memory chips and processor chips. The most popular types of memory chips are RAM and ROM.

RAM.   Primary storage is commonly referred to by the acronym **RAM,** which stands for **random-access memory.** *Random access* means that, since the memory has addresses, the computer can go to the programs and data it wants directly, as opposed to *sequential access,* where the computer must check each memory location in turn. Thus when you see a system unit advertised with 256 KB of RAM, it usually means that the unit has 256 kilobytes of primary memory built into it. The term RAM can be slightly misleading in studying computers. As we'll see in the next chapter, some kinds of secondary storage devices also have random-access capabilities.

One of the most important traits of primary memory is that it is temporary. When the CPU is finished with one set of data and programs in primary memory, it writes another set in its place. To be used again, programs and data must be kept in secondary storage, which is relatively slow.

ROM.   Because of advances in small semiconductor memories, there has been a trend in recent years to build some software functions directly into computer chips. Like RAM, these all-electronic chips are mounted on boards inside the system unit. Once placed on these chips, programs can be accessed very rapidly. On many microcomputers, for example, the operating system is built onto a chip rather than being stored on a floppy disk.

This kind of "software in hardware" is called **firmware.** Several kinds of firmware are available.

Read-only memory (ROM) is by far the most common form of firmware. A ROM module contains a program supplied by the manufacturer. The program can be read from the module, but it is impossible for a user to destroy the contents of the module by accidentally writing over them (hence "read-only").

✖ **Programmable read-only memory (PROM)** is identical to ROM, except that the buyer writes the program. In other words, a PROM module is like a blank ROM module. Special equipment is needed to write a program onto a PROM module, and once the program is on, it can't be erased.

✖ **Erasable programmable read-only memory (EPROM)** is like PROM, except that its contents can be erased by exposure to ultraviolet light and a new program written in. The newest type of EPROM, which is *electrically erasable,* is called EEPROM. EEPROM modules are commonly used in supermarket cash registers to store product prices.

Firmware is often automatically supplied with the computer system you purchase, and it can also be bought separately.

Know Thy Central Processor

A GUIDE TO THE MICROPROCESSOR CHIPS MOST COMMONLY FOUND ON MICROCOMPUTERS

They carry ominous names, such as Z80, WE 32000, 65C02, 68000FN, and 80286. What are they? Microprocessor chips. Although the letters and digits in their names sometimes seem to make no sense at all, having the right microprocessor in your system unit can make all the difference in terms of speed, memory, and the applications software you can run.

Dozens of microprocessor chips are commercially available, but four distinct families of chips have captured the lion's share of today's market: the 6502 family, the Z80, the Intel family of chips, and Motorola 68000-based chips. Let's look more closely at these chip families and where they are used.

6502 Family. MOS Technology's 6502 chip is known primarily for its use on the Apple II and IIe computers. The 6502 is inexpensive and reasonably fast but, being an 8-bit chip, it has a limited instruction set and address space. A newer version of this chip, the 65C02, powers the newer Apple IIc computer. Because a large body of Apple software has been written for 6502-based chips, this family is likely to be around in the years to come.

Z80. Developed by Zilog, the 8-bit Z-80 chip is known for its support of the CP/M operating system. CP/M was once one of the

Four chip families have the lion's share of today's market.

most popular operating systems for microcomputers, but with the arrival of 16-bit processor chips and their more powerful operating systems, its popularity has waned—and with it, the Z80.

The Intel Family of Chips. One chip in this family, the 16-bit Intel 8088, was selected

Computer Chips: The CPU and Specialized Processors

Virtually every microcomputer system sold today runs under the control of a single CPU; that is, a chip that acts as the central processor for the entire system. Some of the more widely used chips, and a few of the computer systems that use them, are discussed in the box on pages 112–113. These chips differ in many respects, one of the most important of which is the word size used.

WORD SIZE.   A computer **word** is a group of bits or bytes that may be manipulated and stored as a unit. It is a critical concept because the internal circuitry of virtually every computer system is designed around a certain word size. Take the IBM Personal Computer, for example, which uses the Intel 8088 chip. The Intel 8088 contains a 16-bit-word internal architecture

by IBM for its Personal Computer. Many computers that look and run like the IBM PC also use this chip (or the faster Intel 8086). The MS-DOS and PC-DOS operating systems were designed specifically to take advantage of the 8088.

When IBM developed the PC AT computer, a more powerful version of the PC, it selected the Intel 80826 chip as the central processor. This newer chip is much faster than both the 8088 and 8086, and can support a multiuser environment as well. Many other computers that look and run like the AT also use the 80286 chip.

Because of IBM's strong support for the 8088 and 80286, and the large body of software available for these chips, the 8088 and 80286 are likely to remain popular for years to come. Intel's latest chip, the 80386—a processor capable of bringing the mainframe power to the desktop—is shown in photograph 9 of Window 2.

The Motorola 68000 Family.   The 32-bit Motorola 68000 family is a powerful line of chips that can address up to 16 megabytes of primary memory. The 68000 (see photo) became a prominent chip when Apple selected

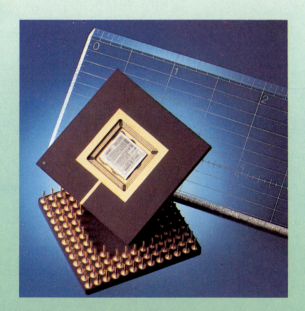

Motorola's popular 68000 computer.

it as the processor to run its Macintosh computer. Several other graphics-oriented computers, such as the Commodore Amiga, also use 68000-based processors. Of the chip families mentioned thus far, many hardware experts consider the 68000 line to be the most advanced.

and an 8-bit-word I/O path. Roughly translated, this means that data are transferred within the CPU chip itself in 16-bit chunks, but there is only an 8-bit-wide data path from the CPU to external devices. The newer and faster Intel 8086 chip, used by the Wang PC (and several other systems), has both a 16-bit *internal architecture* and 16-bit data path. Although the Wang has a faster processor than the IBM Personal Computer, both systems are considered "16-bit computers."

Besides speed, there are many other important reasons to consider word size when buying a computer. A second reason is that the greater the size of the word used, the greater is the number of bits available to represent machine-language instructions. For example, most 32-bit machines are designed so that the first 8 bits are reserved for the instruction type. This permits a total of 2^8, or 256, different instructions. Sixteen-bit machines, on the other hand, have a smaller number of bits available for this purpose. Typically these computers reserve 6 bits for instructions, which permits only 2^6, or 64, different instructions. Thus, the bigger the word size, the larger is the set of instructions available to the computer.

Third, the longer the word size, the greater is the RAM capacity. A 32-bit machine may have over a billion bytes of memory. A 16-bit machine, in contrast, is often limited to several hundred thousand.

Fourth, longer word sizes generally make for greater precision. A big number that occupies one word in a large computer may occupy two words in a smaller machine, which results in some loss of accuracy. On very large scientific computers, where speed and accuracy are extremely important, word sizes as great as 60 or more bits are not unusual.

SPECIALIZED PROCESSORS.   A distinct trend in computing over the past several years has been to download some of the workload of the CPU onto *specialized processor chips*. For example, a companion chip to the Intel 8088 and 8086 CPUs is the Intel 8087 math *coprocessor*. Computer systems using either of these CPU chips are capable of very-high-speed mathematical operations when the 8087 chip is plugged into a board alongside the CPU.

Another specialized processor, the Intel 8048, is used on the keyboard that comes with the IBM PC. The 8048 determines which keys are being depressed, and also checks to see if the keyboard is communicating properly with the CPU. In fact many other peripheral devices that are bought for personal computer systems have one or more specialized processors imbedded in them.

Putting It All Together

Each processor or memory chip, once manufactured, is mounted onto a carrier package, as shown in Window 2. These carrier packages plug into specific socket locations on boards, which are placed inside the system unit.

BOARDS.   A **board** (see Figure 4-8) is a card that contains the circuitry to perform one or more specific functions. The most important board in the microcomputer's system unit is the **system board** (sometimes called the

Figure 4-8.   A board.
Processor chips, as well as RAM and ROM modules, are placed into carrier packages that fit into specific sockets on the board.

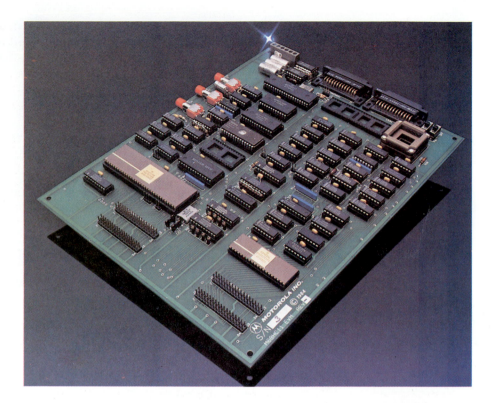

motherboard). This board often contains the CPU and a limited amount of primary memory. On many larger computers, the CPU and its primary memory may require several such boards.

Some microcomputer-system vendors enable you to customize your system by allowing you to choose your own **plug-in boards.** With these boards you can interface with specific types of peripheral devices. For example, if you want a certain model of display unit attached to your computer, you'll need a special *display adapter board* that contains the proper interfacing routine to establish the connection. Hooking up a floppy disk to your system often requires a *floppy disk controller card.* Similarly, you can sometimes increment the RAM on your system board by getting a *memory expansion card* with enough memory chips to bring your total RAM up to the required level.

Because system units that allow plug-in boards have a finite number of slots to accommodate such boards, a popular practice with board manufacturers has been to squeeze as many functions onto a board as practicable. Such products are commonly called *multifunction boards.* A single multifunction board might contain, say, enough memory chips to give your system an additional 384 kilobytes of RAM, as well as a display interface.

System units that allow you to customize with boards are said to possess an *open architecture* (see Figure 4-9). Most microcomputer systems targeted to business users are open-architecture machines. *Closed architecture* machines are generally faster and easier to maintain, but they lack the flexibility you get from being able to configure a wide variety of devices to your computer.

Figure 4-9. Plug-in boards. Open architecture system units enable plug-in boards to fit into slots within the unit.

PORTS.   Most system units, independently of their closed or open architectures, contain sockets that enable you to plug in other devices. These sockets are known as **ports** (see Figure 4-10). *Serial ports* are generally designed to let you connect to remote devices over the phone lines, whereas *parallel ports* facilitate communication with close-by peripherals such as printers. We'll look more closely at serial and parallel interfaces in Chapter 7.

Figure 4-10.   Ports. These external sockets enable you to plug peripheral devices directly into the system unit.

THE COMING CHIP TECHNOLOGIES

Gallium Arsenide — the Next Major Challenger to Silicon

Since the beginning of modern computing, researchers have constantly searched for new types of circuit technologies to hold data and to manipulate them faster. The earliest computers used such hardware as vacuum tubes, magnetic drums, and core planes as their principal circuit components. In the 1970s, when it was possible to pack circuitry onto the head of a pin, another major medium evolved: silicon-based chips. Today, although more than a million microminiaturized components can be placed on a silicon chip, that, too, may not be enough. Researchers are still pressing forward with other approaches.

GaAs. Probably the most promising new technology of today involves chips made from *gallium arsenide* (*GaAs*). Gallium arsenide chips (see photo) are superior to those made of silicon because

- They move electronic impulses around up to ten times faster.
- They enable *optical* transmission, something silicon can't do.
- They can operate at much higher temperatures and emit less power, thus enabling circuits to be packed more densely.

Gallium arsenide products are already moving into the marketplace. For example, some of the more critical components of large computers consist of GaAs chips, and GaAs is rapidly taking hold in areas such as high-speed communications.

But GaAs has some drawbacks. Such chips are still often ten to twenty times more expensive than those made of silicon. And because the newer technology is still in its infancy, GaAs designers can currently squeeze only tens of thousands of circuits onto a single chip. The chances are that GaAs will coexist with silicon for a long time and not replace it entirely.

Nonetheless many knowledgeable people predict that GaAs will launch a quantum leap into a new age of electronics, making possible "supercomputers on a desk top," sophisticated communications-related products, and small direct-broadcast rooftop antennas for satellite TV.

Other Approaches. Despite the enormous potential of GaAs, researchers have not looked at it as the end-all of circuit technologies. Two less-developed approaches, optical processing and biotechnology, may lead to the development of even faster components.

Optical processing uses light waves to do the work of silicon's electrons. As with GaAs chips, the optical components currently available in the marketplace can move data around about ten times faster than can silicon chips. Theoretically an optical processor is capable of speeds hundreds of times faster than that— if one could get data into and out of it fast enough.

Biotechnology offers yet another compelling alternative to today's silicon chip. Scientists have shown that tiny molecules can be grown and shaped to act as circuits. With such a technology, electrons are passed from molecule to molecule. Some scientists believe that, if such a technology were ever perfected, it could result in circuits that are possibly 500 times smaller than today's silicon devices.

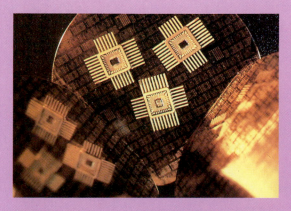

GaAs chips: Faster and denser than silicon.

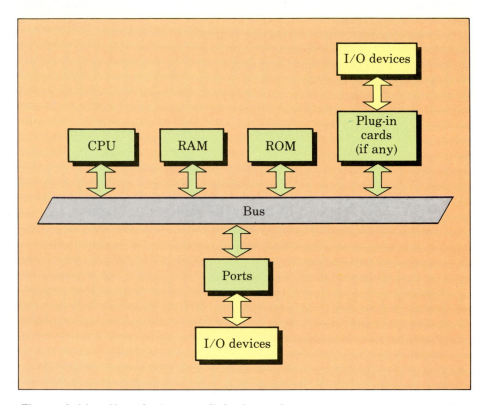

Figure 4-11. *How devices are linked together.* A set of wires or circuits called a bus allows the CPU to communicate with RAM, ROM, and peripheral devices that use internal or external interfaces.

SYSTEM UNIT.   Figure 4-11 shows an example of how many of the devices we've talked about in this chapter may be connected inside the system unit. Coded information travels through the system unit on a **bus,** a set of wires that acts as a data highway between the CPU and other devices. Which devices hook directly into the bus and which into the plug-in boards or I/O ports varies from system to system. Mainframes and minicomputers also contain buses, often several of them.

Under the cover of the system unit you'll sometimes also find a cooling fan (especially if plug-in boards are allowed) and a power source. Additionally, as mentioned in Chapter 1, some system units have peripheral devices that are built in. For example, the Apple Macintosh has a built-in monitor and floppy disk drive.

Summary and Key Terms

There are many ways to classify computers. **Digital computers,** for example, are devices that *count,* whereas **analog computers** are devices that *measure.* Also, some computers are *central* processors whereas others are *specialized* processors.

The CPU has two major sections: an arithmetic/logic unit (ALU) and a control unit. Both of these units work closely with primary memory to carry out processing tasks inside the system unit.

Primary memory (also called **main memory** and **internal storage**) holds the programs and data that have been entered into the computer, the results of intermediate processing, and output that is ready to be transmitted to secondary storage or an output device.

The **arithmetic/logic unit (ALU)** is the section of the CPU that does arithmetic and logical operations on data.

The **control unit** is the section of the CPU that directs the flow of electronic traffic between primary memory and the ALU, and between the CPU and input and output devices.

Registers are high-speed staging areas within the CPU that hold program instructions and data immediately before they're processed. The part of a program instruction that indicates what the ALU is to do next is placed in the **instruction register,** and the part showing the address of the data to be used in the operation is placed in the **address register.** Before data are processed, they are taken from primary memory and placed in the **storage register.** The **accumulator** is a register that temporarily stores the results of ongoing operations.

The processing of a single instruction is called a **machine cycle.** A machine cycle has two parts: an **I-cycle** (instruction cycle), in which the control unit fetches and examines an instruction, and an **E-cycle** (execution cycle), in which the instruction is actually executed by the ALU under control unit supervision. A computer may need to go through thousands, millions, or perhaps billions of machine cycles to process a single program fully. Computer cycle times are generally measured in **milliseconds** (thousandths of a second), **microseconds** (millionths of a second), **nanoseconds** (billionths of a second), or **picoseconds** (trillionths of a second).

The electronic components of digital computers work in a two-state, or **binary,** fashion. It is convenient to think of these binary states as the 0-state and the 1-state. Computer people refer to such 0s and 1s as **bits.**

The computer uses several binary-based codes to process data. Some of these are covered in Appendix A. Two other popular codes are **EBCDIC** and **ASCII.** These fixed-length codes can represent any single character of data—a digit, alphabetic character, or special symbol—as a string of 7 or 8 bits. This string of bits is called a **byte.** EDBDIC and ASCII allow for an additonal bit position, called a **parity bit,** to enable computer systems to check for transmission errors.

The storage capacity of computers is often expressed in **kilobytes (K-bytes, KB),** or thousands of bytes; **megabytes (M-bytes, MB),** or millions of bytes; and **gigabytes (G-bytes, GB),** or billions of bytes.

Machine language is the binary-based code used to represent programs. A program must be translated into machine language before it can be executed on the computer.

Almost all computer systems sold today use a modular hardware approach; that is, related circuitry is etched onto *processor chips* or *memory chips,* the chips are mounted on carrier packages that are later plugged into *boards,* and the boards are fitted into slots inside the **system unit.**

The most popular types of memory chips are RAM and ROM. Primary storage is commonly referred to by the acronym **RAM,** which stands for **random-access memory.** This memory is used to store *temporarily* programs and data with which the computer is currently working. *Permanent* storage of important programs is commonly provided through **firmware,** which is software-in-hardware modules. There are several types of firmware, including **ROM (read-only memory), PROM (programmmable read-only memory),** and **EPROM (erasable programmable read-only memory).**

Processor chips differ in many respects, for example, in word size. A computer **word** is a group of bits or bytes that can be manipulated as a unit. Often the larger the word size, the more powerful is the processor.

Boards contain the circuitry to perform one or more specific functions. The **system board,** for example, contains the CPU and a limited amount of primary memory. Many microcomputer-system vendors enable you to customize your system by allowing you to choose your own **plug-in boards.**

In addition to chips and boards, many system units have external **ports** to enable you to plug in support devices. Also, there must be circuitry to connect everything together within the system unit. A set of wires called a **bus,** for example, connects the CPU to other devices.

Review Exercises

Fill-in Questions

1. A thousandth of a second is called a(n) _____.
2. A millionth of a second is called a(n) _____.
3. A billionth of a second is called a(n) _____.
4. A trillionth of a second is called a(n) _____.
5. A(n) _____ is approximately 1,000 bytes.
6. A(n) _____ is approximately 1,000,000 bytes.
7. A(n) _____ is approximately 1,000,000,000 bytes.

Matching Questions   *Match each term with its description.*

a. ALU   e. ASCII
b. Binary   f. Word
c. Bit   g. EPROM
d. EBCDIC   h. Parity bit

_____ **1.** The base-2 numbering system.
_____ **2.** The fixed-length code most associated with IBM mainframes.
_____ **3.** A type of firmware that is erasable.
_____ **4.** A fixed-length code developed by the American National Standards Institute.
_____ **5.** Used to check for transmission errors.
_____ **6.** The section of the CPU where computations are performed.
_____ **7.** A group of bits or bytes that may be manipulated and stored as a unit.
_____ **8.** A binary digit.

Discussion Questions

1. Distinguish an analog computer from a digital computer.
2. Describe the sections of the CPU and their roles.
3. Explain how a program instruction is executed.
4. Why is the binary system used to represent data and programs?
5. What is the purpose of the parity bit and how does it work?
6. What is the difference between a bit, a byte, a kilobyte, a megabyte, and a word?
7. How does RAM differ from ROM?
8. What devices are contained under the cover of the system unit? What functions do these devices perform?

Chapter 5

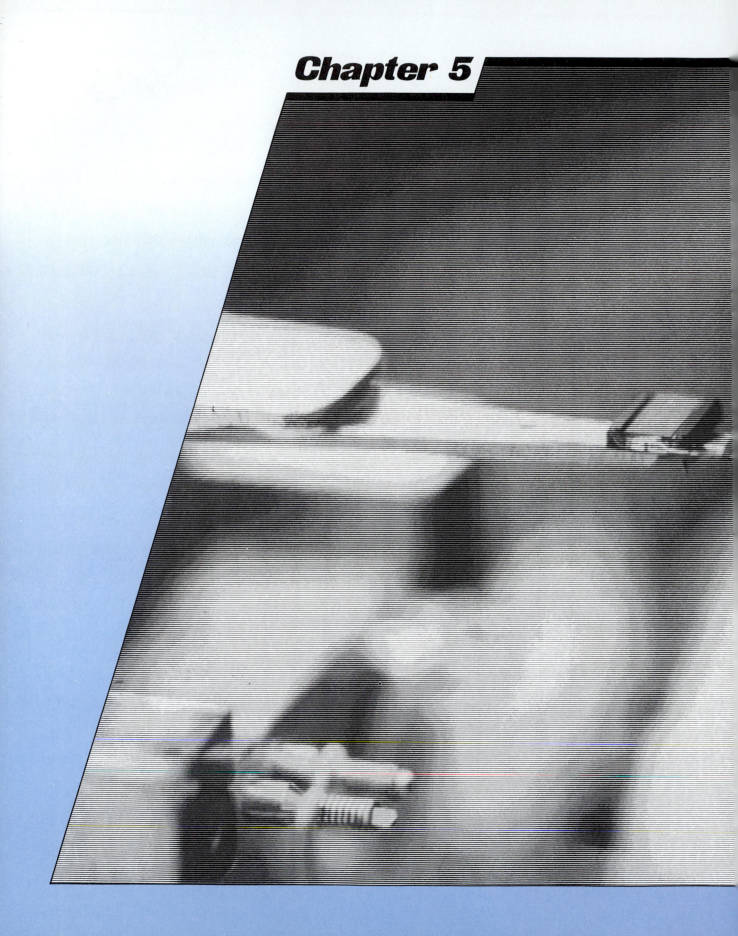

Secondary Storage

Chapter Outline

Objectives

After completing this chapter you should be able to:

1. Identify a number of magnetic tape and disk storage systems, as well as describe how they work and where they are particularly useful.
2. Describe the roles of other secondary storage media and equipment.
3. Explain several types of data access and organization strategies, and identify situations in which each is appropriate.

OVERVIEW

In Chapter 4 we discussed the role of primary (internal) memory. Primary memory is designed to provide immediate access to stored items. It is here that programs, data, intermediate results, and output are temporarily saved. As soon as a program has been executed, however, new data and programs are written over the existing ones. Thus if data, programs, and the results of processing are to be preserved for repeated use, additional storage capacity must be made available. Secondary (external) storage serves this purpose. Although it is slower than primary memory, secondary storage is less expensive and has more storage capacity.

Any secondary storage system involves two physical parts: a peripheral *device* and a *medium*. For example, a tape recorder is a peripheral device and magnetic tape is a medium. Data and programs are written onto and read from the medium. The peripheral device is online to the computer, but the medium, in many cases, must be loaded onto the device before the computer can read data and programs from it or write new data and programs on it. When not in use, these storage media are often kept offline.

We begin this chapter with a discussion of the two most important kinds of secondary storage systems today—those using magnetic tape and those using magnetic disk. We will then look at some less common secondary storage systems, such as those that use optical disks and magnetic bubbles. Finally we'll cover two related subjects—data access and data organization. *Data access* refers to the ways in which computer systems retrieve data from a storage medium. *Data organization* refers to ways of storing data on a medium for efficient access.

MAGNETIC TAPE

For years **magnetic tape** has been one of the most prominent secondary storage alternatives. Although not as popular as disk, it is still very widely used on computer systems of all sizes.

The tapes used with mainframes and minicomputers are often stored on *detachable reels*. The tapes are commonly ½ inch wide, made of plastic Mylar, and coated with a magnetizable substance. A standard diameter for the reels is 10½ inches, although smaller "minireels" are also quite common. A typical 2400-foot reel can pack data at densities as high as 6250 bytes per inch. When such a tape is read, it can transfer more data in one second than many secretaries could type in a month—and without any errors.

For microcomputers magnetic tape is available in cartridge or cassette form, where the tape is housed in a small plastic casing. **Cassette tapes** used for storing data look similar to those used at home for recording music but are of higher quality. However, because cassette tapes are extremely slow for most types of processing, their value is limited.

Figure 5-1. Magnetic tapes: (a) Reels. (b) Cartridge tape.

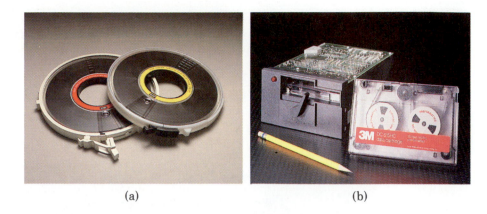

(a)   (b)

Cartridge tapes look a lot like cassettes but are often slightly larger. On microcomputer systems cartridges are commonly used to back up the contents of a hard disk. These tapes can have huge capacities and work very fast. A 600-foot, ¼-inch tape may hold up to 60 megabytes and copy the contents of a disk in a matter of a couple of minutes. Cartridge tapes used for disk backup are sometimes referred to as *streaming tapes*.

The discussion that follows in this section applies principally to the detachable tapes used with mainframes and minicomputers, as they are by far the most important tape media employed in commercial data processing applications. Many of the principles described, however, apply to the smaller tapes as well. An assortment of magnetic tapes is shown in Figure 5-1.

Processing Tapes

A tape must be mounted on an online **tape unit** (see Figure 5-2) if it is to be processed by the computer. For tapes on detachable reels, these units are about the size of a common household refrigerator. The *supply reel* on the

Figure 5-2. Magnetic tape units.

unit contains the tape that is to be read from or written on by the computer system. The *take-up reel* collects the tape as it is unwound from the supply reel. As it is processed, the tape passes a mechanism called a **read/write head,** which reads data from the tape or records data on it. On many devices the tape is allowed to droop in a vacuum chamber so that it will not break if the two reels should move at different speeds. When processing is finished, the tape is rewound onto the supply reel and removed from the unit. The take-up reel never leaves the unit.

Storing Data on Tape

Figure 5-3 shows how data are stored on nine-track magnetic tape. Data may be coded using the 8-bit byte of either EBCDIC or ASCII-8, depending on the equipment used. Magnetized spots of iron oxide represent 1s; nonmagnetized spots represent 0s. The tape contains a **track** for each bit of information in a character, plus an additional parity track so that the computer system can check for transmission errors.

The tape unit reads across the nine tracks to identify the character

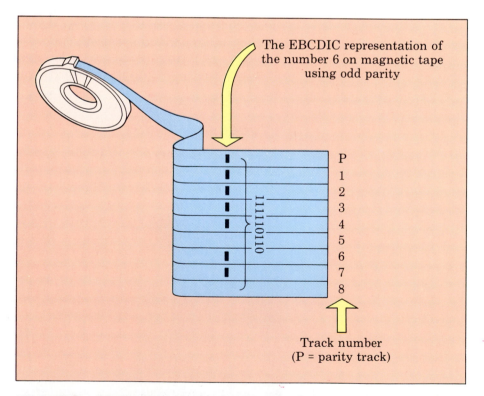

Figure 5-3.   *Storing data on nine-track magnetic tape.* Shown is the number 6 represented in EBCDIC (11110110, or 111110110 with the odd-parity track). In the shaded cross section of the tape, the magnetized spot representing the 1-bit is shown by a vertical mark in the appropriate track. The 0-bit is characterized by the absence of a mark.

represented in each column. You'll recall from reading Chapter 4 that in odd-parity machines, all 1-bits add up to an odd number, and in even-parity machines, to an even number. An incorrect sum indicates an error. The parity bit is included with the byte representation of each character when it is placed on tape.

A magnetic tape is, basically, a long narrow strip, so when the records in a data file are stored on tape, they must be placed one after another in sequence. The sequence is often determined by a **key field**—customer ID number, for example, which can be ordered numerically. The key field generally has a different value for every record.

If you want to read a particular record from a tape, you can't go directly to it. Instead you have to pass through all the records that come before it. In a sense this is similar to the "fast forwarding" you need to do on a music tape when the tune you want to hear is in its middle. Retrieving records in this way—in the order in which they are stored—is called *sequential access,* and organizing data in sequence by a key field is called *sequential organization.* We will talk more about data access and organization later in the chapter.

Blocking Records

Tape units are not purely electronic, as is the CPU. They have moving parts that have to stop and start. Because all records read from tape must pass the read/write heads at the same speed, some "dead space" must exist before and after each record, to allow the tape to speed up and slow down between starts and stops. These spaces are called **interblock gaps** (or **interrecord gaps**). Unfortunately each interblock gap occupies about ½ inch of tape, whereas a single record may use only $\frac{1}{20}$ inch. This means that a tape could conceivably consist of about 10 percent data and 90 percent dead space.

To correct this problem, a solution called **blocking** is often employed. Individual records, called **logical records,** are grouped into larger units of fixed size, called **physical records.** The number of logical records in each physical record is the **blocking factor.** If each physical record contains ten logical records, the blocking factor is ten. An interblock gap is then placed between each of the physical records. This technique is illustrated in Figure 5-4.

Besides the great saving of space, a second reason for blocking is faster processing. Computer systems that permit blocking contain special high-speed memory areas within the computer unit called **buffers.** Buffers used for blocking data function much like the registers in the CPU: they stage data in a fast-access (or "waiting") area just before they are processed by the computer system.

As the tape is being processed, physical records are placed in the buffers, as shown in Figure 5-5. Often there are two of these buffers. Whenever a program issues a READ instruction, the logical record can be retrieved directly from the buffer rather than from the remote tape unit, which must spin and read the tape in response to each request.

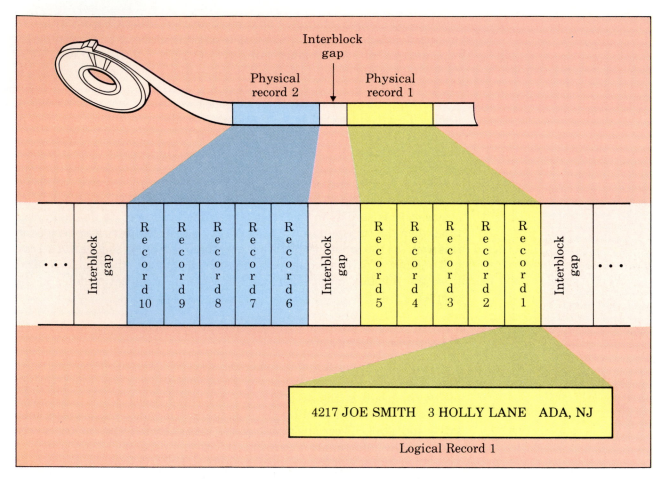

Figure 5-4. **Blocking records on magnetic tape.** Logical records are blocked into physical records. The diagram illustrates a blocking factor of 5. In other words, five logical records form a single physical record. Usually, to save space, much larger blocking factors are employed.

Because the buffers are entirely electronic, like the rest of the computer unit, data can be retrieved much more rapidly than from the mechanical tape unit. When all the logical records in one of the buffers have been processed, reading continues in the other buffer. In the meantime the next physical record on the tape is loaded into the first buffer, writing over the physical record that was stored there before. This process of alternating between the buffers continues until the file is exhausted.

Protecting Tapes

Tape reels are equipped with safety features that prevent operators from destroying the contents of the tape accidentally. One such device is the **file-protection ring** (see Figure 5-6). When tapes are stored offline, these

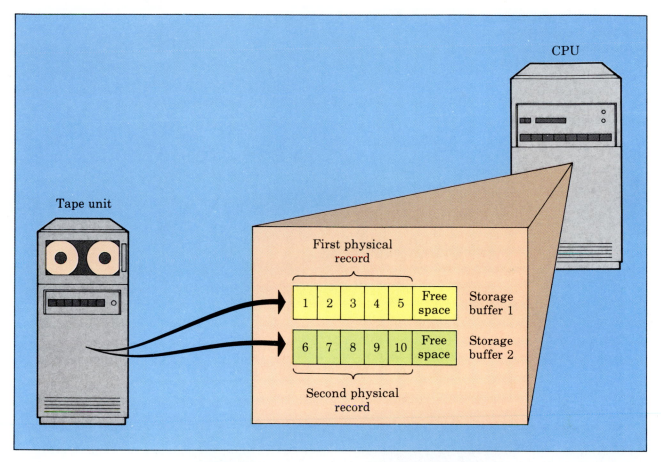

Figure 5-5. **Buffering of physical records in storage.** Suppose records are blocked in the manner suggested by Figure 5-4. The computer's systems software will initially place the first physical record in buffer 1 and the second in buffer 2. All READ instructions in an applications program retrieve data from these buffers, where the computer can retrieve logical records at faster speeds than if they were in secondary storage. When the first buffer has been exhausted, reading shifts to the physical record in the second buffer. Meanwhile the third physical record is loaded into the first buffer.

rings are not mounted on the reel. To write on any part of the tape, thereby destroying any data that may already be stored there, the operator must insert this ring into the center of the reel. The tapes can be read, however, whether or not the ring is present.

Another device designed to protect tapes is the **internal header label.** This label appears at the beginning of the tape and identifies it. The identifying information in the label is usually generated automatically by the computer system or data-entry device. Thus if you were to command the computer system to process tape AP-601, and the operator accidentally

Figure 5-6.   A magnetic tape with a rubber file-protection ring. When the ring is off the reel, you can read from the tape but you can't write onto it. When the ring is on, you can both read from and write onto the tape.

mounted tape AR-601 instead, no processing would take place. Also, a warning message would be sent to the operator.

MAGNETIC DISKS

Magnetic disks are without doubt the most important secondary storage medium in data processing today. Disks permit much faster retrieval of information than do tapes because disks allow *direct access* to data—that is, the computer system can go directly to the location of specific data on the disk. It does not have to read through a series of records before reaching the desired one, as is the case with tapes.

Without disk storage many of the computer applications that we see around us would not be possible. Banking with automatic tellers and airline passenger-reservation systems are just two of the many activities that depend on the rapid access to data that magnetic disks make possible. Also, virtually every business that uses a computer relies on disk for the bulk of its secondary storage needs.

Two popular types of magnetic disk are floppy disks and hard disks. **Hard disks** are round, rigid platters. Because of their large storage capacities and fast-data-retrieval capabilities, these disks are by far the preferred medium on minicomputer and mainframe systems. A growing number of microcomputer users are also finding hard disks helpful in their work. There are many types of hard disk systems in use today. Two that will be discussed here are *removable-pack disk systems,* which often accompany larger computers, and *Winchester disk systems,* which are found with both large and small computers.

The advantages of hard disk notwithstanding, inexpensive **floppy disks**—which are round, flexible platters—are still the medium of choice on most microcomputer systems today. Floppy disks also see occasional (and sometimes heavy) use with minicomputers and mainframes.

In this section we discuss removable-pack systems and floppy systems first, because of their relative presence in the marketplace.

Removable-Pack Disks

Of all the magnetic disk technologies discussed in this chapter, **removable-pack disk** systems are by far the oldest. These systems consist of several hard disks stacked into an indivisible unit, or "pack." It is this unit that can be mounted or *removed* from the associated storage device. Although each pack is capable of storing enormous amounts of data, the secondary storage needs of many organizations are so large that the number of packs required to store these data cannot all fit on the storage device at one time. Hence we have the need for pack removability.

PHYSICAL PROPERTIES.   The disks in removable-pack disk systems are commmonly 14 inches in diameter and coated on both sides with a magnetizable substance such as ferrous oxide. Records are stored in concentric rings, or tracks. Characters are represented by binary bits, which appear as magnetic spots in the tracks (see Figure 5-7). Each track may consist of several logical records, which are often blocked into physical records in a manner similar to blocking on tape.

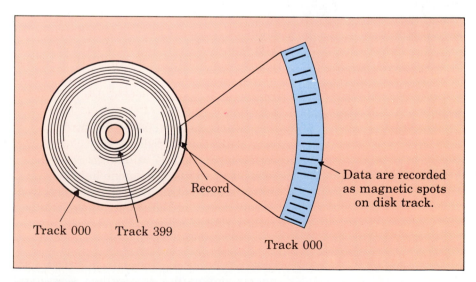

Figure 5-7.   *Surface of a disk.* Unlike a phonograph record, which bears a single spiral groove, a disk is composed of concentric tracks. The number of tracks per surface varies from manufacturer to manufacturer. The hard disk shown here has 400 tracks. Floppy disks commonly have only 40 or 80 tracks.

Figure 5-8.   A disk pack.

On most removable-pack disk systems, each track is designed to carry the same total amount of data, even though the tracks near the outer edge are much longer than those nearer the center and move past the read/write heads faster. This design constraint keeps the data-transfer rate constant throughout the system, independently of the location of the track being accessed. The number of tracks per disk varies with the manufacturer, but it is often several hundred. Data are read or written by a read/write head, which moves above or below the spinning disk to gain access to the disk tracks.

Disk platters on removable-pack systems are often assembled into groups of six, eight, ten, twelve, or some other number, depending on the manufacturer, and mounted on a shaft that spins all the disks at the same rate of speed. The disks are spaced far enough apart to permit the read/write heads to move in and out between the disks. Such an assembly is called a **disk pack** (see Figure 5-8). The disk pack is encased in a plastic shell, similar to a cake cover, to protect the recording surfaces from foreign objects. Usually the top and bottom surfaces of the pack are not used, because they are the ones most exposed to dust.

Disk packs are mounted on a device called a **disk storage unit,** or **disk unit** (see Figure 5-9). These units are plugged into the computer, thus enabling it to access any of the data recorded on the disks. A disk pack stands in the same relation to a disk unit as a row of phonograph records does to a jukebox. The relationship among a disk, disk pack, and disk unit is illustrated in Figure 5-10.

Figure 5-9.   A disk storage unit.

READING AND WRITING DATA.   Data on disk, as on tape, are read or written by a read/write head. In virtually all disk systems, there is at least one read/write head for each recording surface. These heads are mounted on a device called an **access mechanism.** Figure 5-11 shows how access is accomplished with a *movable access mechanism.* The rotating shaft spins at high speeds (3600 revolutions per minute is common), and the mechanism moves the heads in and out *together,* between the disk surfaces, to access the required data. Movable devices are by far the most common type of access mechanism.

A head never touches the surface of a disk, even during reading and writing. Head and disk are very close, however. The IBM 3350 disk heads, for example, glide 17 millionths of an inch above the recording surfaces. If present on a surface, a human hair, or even a smoke particle (about 2500 and 100 millionths of an inch, respectively) would damage the disks and heads. As you can see in Figure 5-12, the results would be like placing a pebble on a record while playing it.

DISK CYLINDERS.   In removable-pack systems, an important principle for understanding disk storage and access strategies is the concept of **disk cylinders.** Again consider the disk system of Figure 5-10. In the disk pack shown, there are eight possible recording surfaces, with 400 tracks per surface. One might envision the disk pack as composed of 400 imaginary, concentric cylinders, each consisting of eight tracks, as illustrated in Figure 5-13. Outer cylinders fit over the inner ones like sleeves. Each cylinder is

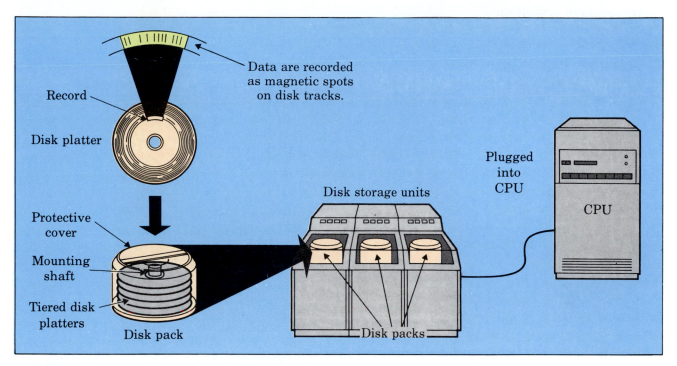

Figure 5-10. **A removable-pack disk system.** Disks are assembled into disk packs, which are mounted in the disk storage unit.

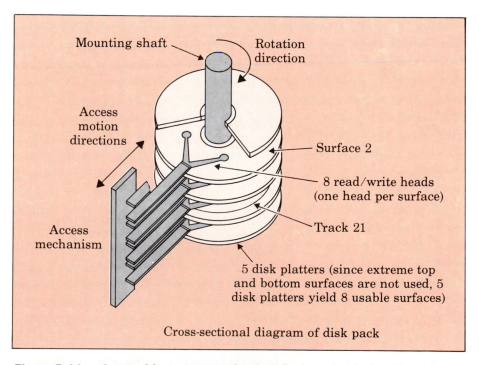

Cross-sectional diagram of disk pack

Figure 5-11. **A movable access mechanism.** Each read/write head is assigned to a particular disk surface. As the mounting shaft spins the disks, the comblike access mechanism moves the heads in or out between the disks to read or write data on the tracks. On most systems all the heads move together. So if you need to retrieve data from track 21 on surface 2, all the read/write heads must move together to track 21. At that point the head assigned to surface 2 will read the data. Only one head may be actively reading or writing at any one time.

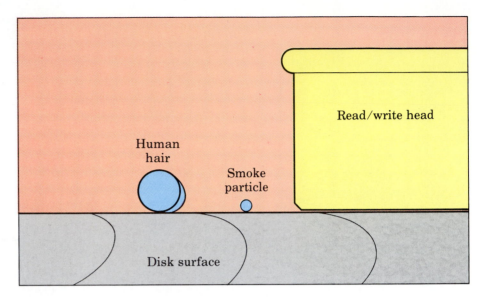

Figure 5-12. *The space between a disk and a read/write head compared with a smoke particle and a human hair.* A human hair, or even a smoke particle, if present on a disk surface, can damage both the surface and the read/write head.

equivalent to a track position to which the heads on the access mechanism can move. With a movable access mechanism, all the read/write heads are positioned on the same cylinder when data are read from or written to one of the tracks on that cylinder.

DISK ACCESS TIME.   In a removable-pack disk system with a movable access mechanism, there are three tasks that must be accomplished in order to access data. First, the read/write head must move to the cylinder on which the data are stored. Suppose, for example, the read/write head is on cylinder 5, and we wish to retrieve data from cylinder 36. To do this the mechanism must move inward to cylinder 36. The time required to do this is referred to as **access motion time.**

Second, when a read or write order is issued, the heads are not usually aligned over the position on the track where the required data are stored. So there is some delay involved while the mounting shaft rotates the disks into the proper position. (The disks are always spinning, whether or not reading or writing is taking place.) The time needed to complete this alignment is called **rotational delay.**

Third, once the read/write head is positioned over the correct data, the data must be read from disk and transferred *to* the computer (or transferred *from* the computer and written onto disk). This last step is known as **data movement time.** The sum of these three components is known as **disk access time.**

In reading from and writing to disk storage, two strategies can be used to reduce disk access time. An inexpensive strategy, which is almost

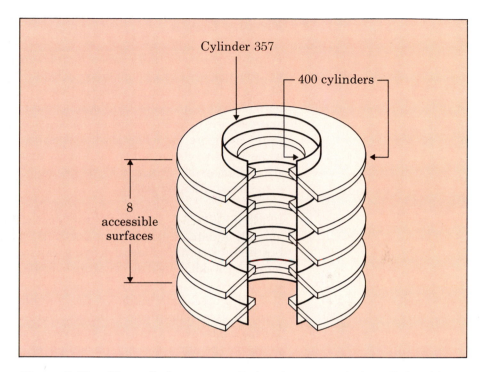

Figure 5-13. **The cylinder concept.** To imagine any particular cylinder, think of pushing an actual cylinder such as a tin can downward through the same track in each disk in the pack. In this example, cylinder 357 is made up of track 357 on surfaces 1–8.

universal in data processing shops, is to store related data on the same cylinder. This sharply reduces access motion time. For example, if we need to store 500 records, and it is possible to place 100 records on a track (requiring five tracks), it is better to select five tracks on the same cylinder rather than on different ones. Thus if we store the 500 records on cylinder 235, we need only one movement of the access mechanism to reach all 500 records.

A second solution is to acquire a disk system with a *fixed access mechanism.* Such a mechanism has a read/write head for each track on every surface, thus eliminating access motion time entirely. For example, eight accessible surfaces and 400 tracks per surface would require a total of 3200 read/write heads mounted onto the eight access-mechanism arms. Fixed access mechanisms are much faster than movable ones, but because they are much more expensive, they are not as widely used.

ADDRESSING.   Every disk system is addressable. This means that each data record or program may be stored and later accessed at a unique **disk address,** which can be automatically determined by the computer system. Procedures to locate records on disk are discussed later, in the section entitled "Data Access and Data Organization."

Floppy Disks

Floppy disks (sometimes called *floppies* or *diskettes*) are round, flexible platters that are encased in plastic jackets. The platters are made of a tough plastic and coated with a substance that can be magnetized. As in the case of hard disks, each side of the floppy contains concentric tracks, which are encoded with 0- and 1-bits when you are writing data and programs to them (refer to Figure 5-7). The plastic jacket is lined with a soft material that wipes the disk clean as it spins. Floppy disks are widely available in three sizes (diameters)—8 inches, 5¼ inches, and 3½ inches. Figure 5-14 shows an assortment of floppy disks.

USING FLOPPIES.   Despite their small size, floppies can store a respectable amount of data. A common capacity for 5¼-inch floppies is 360 kilobytes, but disks with higher data-carrying capacities can store 3 megabytes or more. A 360-kilobyte disk can store over 100 typewritten pages of information.

To protect data diskettes also contain a write-protect notch (Figure 5-15) or insert. This prevents the user from accidentally writing on the disk. With 5¼-inch diameter diskettes, covering the notch makes it impossible to write on the surface. The convention on 3½-inch- and 8-inch-diameter diskettes is completely opposite: exposing the notch or insert makes writing impossible.

Figure 5-14.   Floppy disks. These secondary storage media are highly popular for microcomputer systems.

RAM Disk

THIS INEXPENSIVE APPROACH CAN SPEED CERTAIN SOFTWARE PACKAGES

"RAM disk" (sometimes referred to as electronic disk, E-disk, or disk emulation software) represents an inexpensive approach to overcoming the slow speed involved in fetching program instructions from floppy disk.

Here's how it works: If your system has enough RAM to store one or more files from a floppy disk, the emulation package will load those files into RAM and point the system to this RAM every time it wants to go to the disk to fetch data from the files. Thus, in a way, the emulation software is tricking the system into thinking it's dealing with the disk drive. Such a technique can boost the speed of applications software 50 percent or more.

RAM disk is implemented in a number of ways. For example, many of the vendors who sell such a product might offer it as a function on a multifunction board (see photo). The board may contain, say, a graphics and display interface, a clock/calendar feature so that you don't have to input the date and time every time you turn on your system, and RAM disk circuitry. The board hardware will generally be accompanied by software (on an accompanying disk) that enables you to "tell" the board how many bytes of primary memory you want to set aside for the RAM disk feature.

Another vendor might offer a hardware unit with a built-in static memory, which you can establish as RAM disk. This unit may fit into one of the cavities ordinarily used for a floppy disk drive. Although this second approach may be more expensive, it affords the luxury of not using up the primary memory on your system.

RAM disk works particularly well with software packages that access commands from disk, such as Micropro International's highly successful WordStar® word processing package. For example, when you want to issue commands such as "center" or "delete a line" in WordStar, your system must go out to disk to figure out how to do these things. This can result in an annoying delay as the disk light turns on, the disk whirs around, and mechanical heads read the required instructions—all before anything happens on the screen. However, if WordStar is stored on RAM disk, the response is virtually instantaneous.

RAM disk is not successful in all types of situations. Some software packages require so much primary memory to run that you may not have adequate amounts left to make RAM disk worthwhile. Also, if the software package is designed to eliminate disk fetches, in effect doing what the RAM disk would do, the advantage in having your own RAM disk is lost.

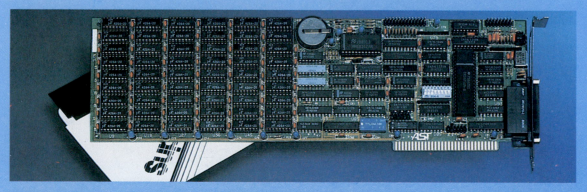

RAM disk on a multifunction board: AST's popular SixPack Plus.

Figure 5-15. **A closeup of a floppy.** On this 5¼ inch floppy, covering the notch prevents one from writing onto the disk.

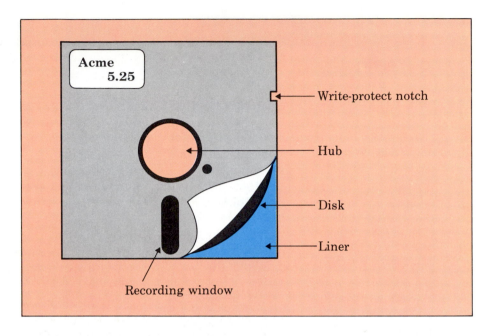

To be used the floppy is inserted into a device called a *floppy disk drive,* as shown in Figure 5-16. Note that the disk can go into the drive correctly in only one way. Once the disk is inserted, the user locks it into place by closing the drive door, by turning a knob, or by some other such means. This "locking-in" step is necessary, or you won't be able to access the disk in the drive.

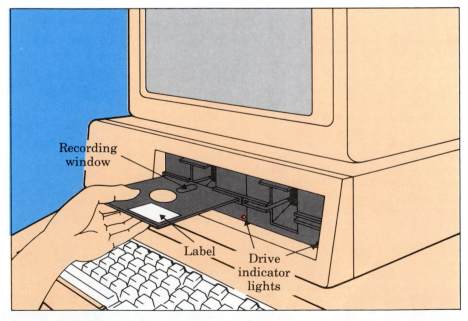

Figure 5-16. **Inserting a floppy into a drive.** Disks correctly fit into the drive one way—usually with the label up and the recording window toward the drive door, as shown.

What the locking-in step accomplishes is to lock the drive—the mechanism that rotates the disk—into the disk's hub. This is similar to fastening a tire to an axle. The disk spins inside its jacket at a rate of about 300 revolutions per minute while the jacket stays fixed in place. While the disk is rotating, the read/write head (or heads) accesses tracks through the recording window. A disk should not be removed while the indicator light for a drive is on (meaning the read/write head is accessing the disk in the drive). To do so is like removing a phonograph record from a record player while the tone arm is still touching it.

TYPES OF FLOPPIES.   In addition to the fact that floppies are available in several diameters, many other physical characteristics differentiate these disks.

First, a floppy can be *soft sectored* or *hard sectored.* As you will later see, **sectors** divide a floppy into manageable pie-shaped pieces. If you buy a soft-sectored disk, you can use your computer system to sector (that is, format) the disk for you. A hard-sectored disk is already presectored for a specific computer system. Hard-sectored disks are faster, but more expensive. Most diskettes sold today offer the flexibility of soft sectoring, because computers and their operating systems differ widely with respect to sectoring requirements.

Second, diskettes are recorded at one of several bit densities. *Single-density* diskettes are written to pack data at 3200 bits per inch, as measured along the innermost track of the disk. *Double-density* diskettes employ a density of 6400 bits per inch, while *quad-density* diskettes are recorded at 12,800 bits per inch.

Third, floppies and their drives are either *single sided* or *double sided.* A double-sided drive can read both a single-sided and a double-sided floppy, but a single-sided drive can only read a single-sided floppy.

Fourth, diskettes differ in the number of tracks per side. For example, diskettes that are used by computers such as the IBM PC, TI Professional, and Zenith Z-150 have forty tracks per side. Newer machines, such as the IBM PC AT and Apple Macintosh, use diskettes that contain 80 tracks per side. The newer IBM PC AT drives can read the older forty-track diskettes, but the older IBM PC drives cannot read the newer 80-track diskettes.

SECTORING ON FLOPPIES.   As mentioned earlier, floppy disks are divided into pie-shaped sectors to store data and programs. Computer systems differ in the number of sectors into which they divide a disk. For example, some use eight sectors, some use nine, and so forth. The Apple Macintosh, which defies conventional disk-storage technology in that it packs more data into outer disk tracks than inner ones, actually varies the number of sectors on a single disk. Thus these newer 3½-inch disks have approximately twice the data-carrying capacity of the older 5¼-inch variety.

Sectoring a disk organizes it into addressable storage locations, as illustrated in Figure 5-17. A directory on the disk, which is automatically maintained by the computer system, is used to keep track of the contents of each location. On most microcomputer systems, the FORMAT command is used to sector the disk, and a disk is not usable for storage unless it has been sectored.

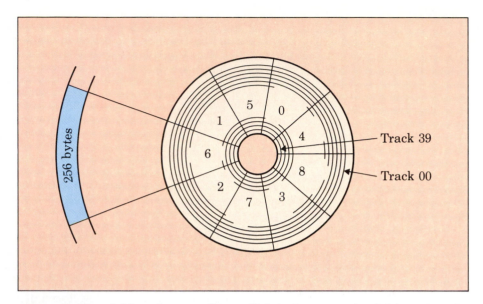

Figure 5-17. **Addressing on a floppy disk.** Let's assume the disk has 40 tracks and the computer system divides the disk into 9 sectors. Formatting the disk causes it to be divided into the 9 pie-shaped sectors 0–8 above. Because the disk has 40 tracks, this results in 9 × 40 = 360 addressable storage locations.

CARING FOR FLOPPY DISKS.   Despite the fact that floppy disks look like inert slabs of plastic, they are extremely sensitive items and must be cared for accordingly. A few fundamentals of caring for floppies are provided in Figure 5-18. Many of these basics are also listed on the disk storage envelopes that accompany the floppies you buy.

Winchester Disks

Although most microcomputer systems use floppy disks, small sealed units called **Winchester disk** systems are also quite popular. These hard disk devices are especially appropriate for users who need greater amounts of online storage than floppies can provide, and for those who require faster access to programs and data.

Winchester disk units consist of rigid metal platters that are tiered in the same way as disks in the removable-pack systems discussed earlier. However, the disks are not removable, but are hermetically sealed in the storage unit along with the access mechanism that contains the read/write heads. Because the storage unit is completely sealed and free from the air contamination that plagues other disk systems, Winchester disks can be rotated at very high rates of speed—typically, 3600 revolutions per minute.

Winchester units for microcomputers are commonly found in capacities of 10, 20, 30, and 40 megabytes. Higher storage capacities are also available. Like other magnetic disks, Winchesters are nonvolatile and hold

Figure 5-18.   The DOs and DON'Ts of floppy disk care.

data even when the computer's power is turned off. Thus, if you have a 10-megabyte Winchester unit, that means you have the storage equivalent of about twenty-five double-sided/double-density floppies immediately online as soon as you turn on the power. And you're not constantly burdened with shuffling floppies in and out of disk drives.

Winchester disk units can be internal or external. An *internal* Winchester system is fitted into your computer's system unit, in the space normally occupied by one of the floppy drives (see Figure 5-19). An *external* system is a detached hardware unit that has its own power supply. Many external systems also have a built-in slot for a tape cartridge, which can be used to back up important programs and data.

The earliest Winchester disks, used with large-computer systems, were 14 inches in diameter, or the same as the standard removable-pack disks. In fact, Winchester disks are still very popular on these computer systems. For smaller computers, Winchesters are now available in 8-inch, 5¼-inch, and 3½-inch diameters.

OTHER SECONDARY STORAGE MEDIA AND EQUIPMENT

Although magnetic tape and disk systems are by far the most common form of secondary storage, a number of other systems are also in use. Among these are the mass storage unit, optical disk storage, and magnetic bubble storage.

Mass Storage Unit

Disk storage units can make large amounts of data available online, but they have limitations. In many systems disk packs must be manually loaded onto the disk unit, which takes time. Disk systems with nonremovable packs avoid this problem but are limited in the amount of data they can store. For most applications these are not serious drawbacks. But because the capacity of the largest disk units is only a few billion characters, organizations that must keep massive amounts of data online to the computer have found **mass storage units** extremely useful. A device such as the IBM 3850 mass storage unit can store 472 billion bytes of data, the equivalent of almost 50,000 reels of magnetic tape.

The IBM 3850 consists of 9440 cylindrical data cells, each capable of storing 50 million bytes of data. Each cell contains a spool of 3-inch magnetic tape, 770 feet long. The cells reside in a honeycomb-shaped rack, as Figure 5-20 shows. When the data in a cell must be retrieved, a mechanical arm pulls the correct cell from its container. Next the tape is unwound, the data are transferred to disk, and processing is performed. All this takes place automatically, without the aid of human operators.

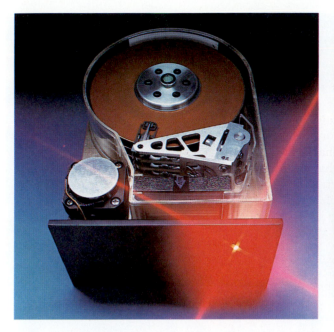

Figure 5-19 An "internal" Winchester disk unit.
Winchester disks are very common on business-related
microcomputer systems. Winchesters are available in
several capacities, the most common being 10, 20, 30,
and 40 megabytes.

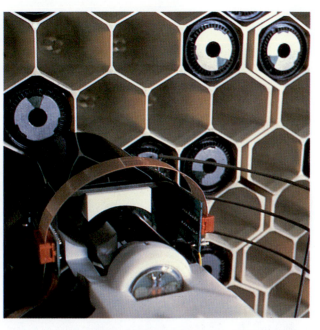

Figure 5-20. Mass storage unit. The device pictured
has enough memory capacity to store a 100-character
record for every person in the world, or, alternatively, the
capacity to hold as many words as there are in 27 million
pages of a typical daily newspaper.

With mass storage the user sacrifices speed to gain storage capacity.
Retrieval of the data cell and transfer of the data to disk may take as long as
fifteen seconds. Compared with the fraction of a second that elapses during
access to disk, this is a long time. Therefore, mass storage is only feasible for
applications with enormous online storage requirements.

Optical Disks

An emerging technology that many expect to have a profound impact on
secondary storage strategies is the **optical disk** (see Figure 5-21). With this
technology laser beams write and read data at incredible densities, several
times finer than the density of a typical magnetic disk. Data are placed onto
optical disks with high-intensity laser beams that burn tiny holes into the
surface of the disk. A laser beam of lower intensity then reads the data that
have been inscribed.

Optical disk systems that are widely available today are still in the
fledgling stage. Most units seen today are of the CD-ROM (*C*ompact
*D*isk/*R*ead-*O*nly *M*emory) type. That is, you buy a prerecorded disk and
"play it" (read it) on the optical disk unit attached to your computer. You
cannot write new data to the disk in any way. There are also systems
available that will let you write once to the disk—that is, once written, data
cannot be erased. These are called WORM disk (for *W*rite *O*nce, *R*ead

Figure 5-21. *An assortment of optical disks.* A single optical disk can store the entire contents of the Encyclopedia Britannica—and more.

*M*ostly) systems. Since optical disks have very large storage capacities, most users can write to the disk for a year or more before using it up. Optical disk systems that allow you to erase unwanted data are also available, but such systems are still far too expensive for most users.

A 5¼-inch optical disk is often capable of storing 250,000 or more pages of text. Roughly speaking that is the capacity of twenty-five 10-megabyte Winchester disks. Nonetheless, hard disks still have a few things going for them: they're faster and there's a lot of software around that must be altered to work on optical disk.

Optical disks used with computers are similar to, but not the same as, the video disks marketed for home use by companies in the entertainment industry (see box on page 145). For one thing video disks are designed to work with a television set. By contrast the optical disk is evolving as a read/write technology available for a wider number of applications. Future optical disk products are expected to provide data, still graphics, motion video, and music, all on one disk.

Magnetic Bubble Storage

Magnetic bubble storage is a secondary memory technology in which thousands of magnetized bubbles, each a fraction of the diameter of a human hair, are arranged on a thin film of magnetic material. The presence of a bubble in a location represents a 1-bit, and its absence, a 0-bit. Bubble storage is often packaged in chip form.

TOMORROW'S OUTLOOK ON INTERACTIVE VIDEO DISK SYSTEMS

Joining Graphics, Video, and Storage Technologies

Interactive video disk systems are already here, although they've barely hit stride yet.

A *video disk* is a shiny round platter that can store text, video images, and audio signals. These data are stored on 54,000 microscopic tracks etched on the disk surface. Video disks are special types of optical disks, so they are read by lasers. A track on the surface of a video disk can be accessed in about three seconds. Virtually all video disks currently marketed are of the CD-ROM type: You can read them but can't output to them.

Video disk systems are used today in a variety of settings. At the Dayton Hudson Corporation department-store chain, for example, customers can use an interactive video disk system— called a *kiosk*—to buy furniture. By utilizing a touch screen, the customers can select furniture and see it in a variety of room settings. All of the appropriate frames are stored on the video disk and the computer searches for specific frames to display based on the customer input.

A video disk system has also been developed in Michigan to help realtors conduct faster searches for homes and properties (see photo). The client describes the type of home wanted—say, three bedrooms, a fireplace, acreage, and under $80,000. The realtor types these data into the system and photo-quality images of homes and facts about them appear on a display screen.

And the applications don't stop there. Video disk has also been used by automobile manufacturers to show their lines, by travel agents to interest clients in resorts, and by various makers of consumer goods to display their wares. In the future, industry observers believe, many automatic teller machines (see box on pages 40–41) will be equipped with video disk components so that consumers don't have to depend so much on clerks and showrooms. When a desired item flashes on the display screen, the customer can insert a credit card and order that item immediately.

As you may have guessed, there has also been a lot of research conducted on bringing these types of consumer services into the home. Many people just don't have the time or interest to do their shopping in person at various stores; it's much easier to pick up a catalog and call an 800 number. But catalogs are becoming increasingly expensive to print and mail. With a remote video disk database, a user can activate frames by keying in commands on a pad attached to a standard TV set. These home-based services are commonly referred to as *videotex*. In Europe home-based videotex has been far more successful than it has in North America.

Interactive videodisk: A high-tech sales tool for real estate and retailing.

Shopping and banking from home notwithstanding, one of the most promising uses of video disk technology lies with faster computers and bigger memories. Together these two trends will make possible realtime animation for the entertainment market. We'll be able to play games and to watch realistic animation sequences resulting from decisions we make on an input device. We'll be able to read interactive novels and create movies, in which we can play our own roles. Some of this is being done today, but that is only the tip of the iceberg.

During the late 1970s, many experts thought that magnetic bubble devices would replace disks as the major secondary storage medium in computer systems. This optimism was grounded in the fact that magnetic bubble units are static; that is, they require no moving parts. By contrast disk units generally employ spinning platters and movable access heads. Besides being faster, static assemblies are generally much more reliable than nonstatic ones, thus resulting in fewer errors and maintenance problems. So far bubble devices have failed to live up to expectations, largely because their cost is still relatively high compared with that of disks.

Despite their apparent failure to capture the market for storage devices, magnetic bubbles are popular components in many electronic machines. They are often used as memory units in terminals, desk-top computers, robots, and communications devices.

DATA ACCESS AND DATA ORGANIZATION

When the computer system is instructed to use data or programs residing in secondary storage, it must be able to find the materials first. The process of retrieving data and programs in storage is called **data access.** Arranging data so they can be retrieved efficiently is called **data organization.**

Of course, the way in which information is organized affects how we gain access to it, as well as how quickly we can do so. Because encyclopedias have an index and are alphabetically arranged, we can find a description of, say, the Oracle at Delphi much more quickly than if we simply thumbed through one volume after another, looking for the appropriate passages. Conversely, the kind of access we want strongly influences the way in which we organize our data. The encyclopedia has been set up deliberately to promote rapid access to information. In the following pages we will see how access and organization are related to each other in the context of secondary storage.

Access Methods

As we have seen, a major difference between, say, tape and disk is that data on tape can only be retrieved sequentially, whereas data on disk can be retrieved both sequentially and in a direct (random) fashion. With **sequential access** the records in a file can only be retrieved in the same sequence in which they are physically stored. With **direct access** (also known as **random access**), a record can be retrieved immediately.

The distinction between sequential and direct access can be observed on a typical home stereo system. Suppose you have both a cassette tape and a phonograph record of the same album of music. Say, for example, you want to hear the fifth song on side one of the record. Suppose also that this song is the fifth selection on the tape. On the tape you must pass sequentially through the first four songs to hear the fifth one. With the phonograph record, however, you can place the needle directly on the fifth song and listen to it immediately.

The phonograph record is also effective as a sequential-access device. If you want to listen to the entire first side of the album, you simply place the needle at the beginning of the record and play the tunes in sequence. Thus the phonograph record is really both a sequential- and direct-access medium, in that we can play a series of songs sequentially or choose individual ones in random order.

Let's apply this distinction to computer systems. Machine-readable magnetic tape has the sequential properties of music tape, and magnetic disk has both the sequential and direct properties of the phonograph record. Moreover, magnetic disk is erasable and can store far more data than you could ever hope to fit on a phonograph record.

Some data processing applications are essentially sequential in nature, and others are direct. For example, the preparation of mailing labels is often a sequential operation. If we want to send Christmas cards to all employees in a company, we can process the computerized employee file sequentially, from the beginning of the list to the end. As names and addresses are extracted from the file, they are printed on the mailing labels. Obtaining the latest inventory information about products, on the other hand, often involves direct processing, because requests are made to the inventory file in random order. For example, a salesperson may want to find out how many units of item 6402 are on hand. A minute later a customer may call to find out the price of item 36. Then a question comes up regarding deliveries of item 988. We move randomly back and forth through the records to obtain information from this file.

We can categorize all secondary storage media and their devices in terms of whether they permit sequential or direct access. Those that are classified as direct, such as disk, generally allow both sequential and direct access.

Organization Methods

Our need for certain access methods necessarily dictates our choice of ways to organize data files. Only if data are organized in certain ways can they be retrieved in others. Let's consider a practical example. Most book libraries are organized with card indexes ordered by title, author, and subject, so you can retrieve books directly. If you want James Martin's *Computer Networks and Distributed Processing,* you simply look up the title of the book in the index, find its call number (QA 76.9 D5), and go directly to the QA shelves to find the book. This type of organization is referred to as an *indexed organization.* Indexed organization schemes facilitate direct access.

Suppose, however, there are no card indexes and books are organized alphabetically by title on a single continuous shelf. With such a *sequential organization* of books, it would take much longer to retrieve the title you want. You might go to the middle of the shelf and find the titles starting with the letter *F.* Then you would backtrack several yards until you saw titles beginning with *C*. Finally you would find *Computer Networks and Distributed Processing*. As you can see, sequential organization does not permit straightforward access to a specific book.

Data organization on computers works in a similar fashion. *First* we decide the type of access we need—direct, sequential, or both. *Then* we organize the data in a way that minimizes the time needed to retrieve data with these types of access.

There are many ways to organize data. Here we will describe three—sequential, indexed sequential, and direct organization.

SEQUENTIAL ORGANIZATION.   In a file characterized by **sequential organization,** records follow one another in a fixed sequence. Sequentially organized files are generally ordered by a *key field* or fields, such as an ID number. Thus if a 4-digit ID number were the key field being used to order the file, the record belonging to ID number 0612, say, would be stored after number 0611 but before number 0613, as shown in Figure 5-22.

Let's see how sequential organization is used in data processing. Many companies update customer balances and prepare bills at the end of the month. Such an operation is known as a *sequential update*. Two data files are used. The *master file* normally contains the ID number of the customer, the amount owed at the beginning of the month, and additional information about the customer. This file is sorted by the key field—customer ID number—and records are arranged in ascending sequence, or from low ID numbers to high. The *transaction file* contains all the transactions carried out during the month by the old customers, who appear in the master file, and by new customers, who do not. Transactions might include purchases and payments. Like the master file, the transaction file is ordered in ascending sequence by customer ID number.

In a sequential update, the two files are processed together, in the manner shown in Figure 5-23. The sequential-update program reads a record from each file. If the key fields match, the operation specified in the

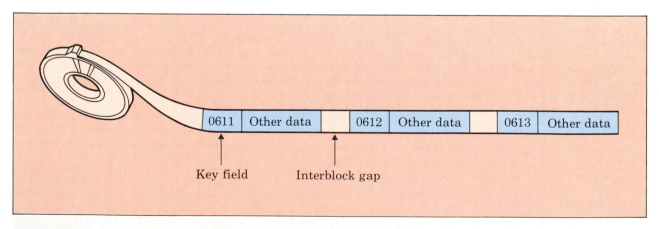

Figure 5-22.   *Sequential organization of records on tape.*

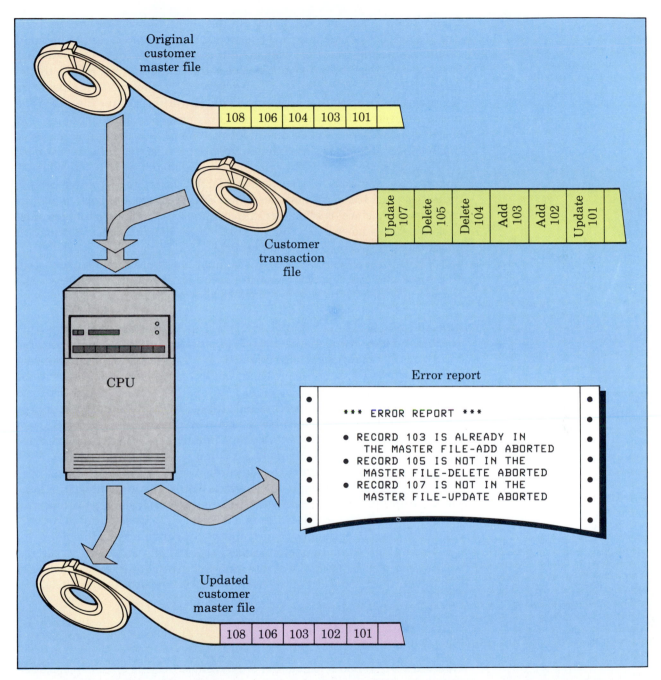

Figure 5-23. *A sequential update of a master file.* Each customer record in the original master file might contain the customer's ID number (the key field), name, address, amount owed, and credit limit. For simplicity, only the key field is shown in the illustration. The transaction file contains a record of each customer transaction. Each record in this file might contain the customer's ID number (the key field), the amount of the purchase or payment, and the type of transaction involved (update, add, or delete). Only the key field and type of transaction are shown in the illustration, again for simplicity. As both files are processed together, an updated master file is produced, as well as a printed listing of records that, for one reason or another, couldn't be processed because of some discrepancy.

transaction file is made. You'll note, in the figure, that the key fields of the first records in each file match. Thus record 101 is updated for the updated customer master file. For example, if the transaction file shows that customer 101 bought a toaster, data on this purchase are added to the master file. Next both files are "rolled forward" to the next records. Here the program observes that customer 102 is not in the master file, since the master file record following 101 is 103. This must be a new customer, and the program will create a new record for customer 102 in the updated master file. At this point only the transaction file will be rolled forward, to customer 103. The program now observes that this record matches the one to which it is currently pointing in the master file. However, the transaction file indicates that 103 is a new customer. Hence there appears to be an inconsistency, since the master file contains only old customers. The program makes no entry in the updated master file but sends information about this transaction to the error report.

The processing continues in this manner until both files are exhausted. The processing is sequential in nature because the computer processes the records in both files in the order in which they physically appear.

INDEXED-SEQUENTIAL ORGANIZATION.   **Indexed-sequential organization** is a way of organizing data for both sequential and direct access. This type of organization requires disk, since tapes can't provide direct access. Records are stored sequentially on the disk by key field. Also, several indexes—which are similar in nature to the page index in a telephone book—are created to find records once they are organized onto disk. For example, if the top of a phone book page reads "Alexander—Ashton," you know that you should look for the phone number of Amazon Sewer Service on that page. When implemented on a computer, as shown in Figure 5-24, such indexes permit rapid access to records.

Many computer systems have systems programs that help programmers set up indexes and indexed-sequential-organized files painlessly. As records are added to or deleted from a file, the systems software automatically adds them to or deletes them from the disk and updates the index.

Since the records remain organized sequentially on the disk, the file can be processed sequentially at any time. Sequential processing may begin either with the first record of the file or with some record further along.

Figure 5-24.   Indexed-sequential organization. Records are ordered sequentially by key on disk, and all disk addresses are entered in an index. To access any record, say number 200, a computer system using cylinders normally proceeds as follows. After the request has been relayed from the terminal to the CPU, the computer system first searches a cylinder index and then a track index for the address of the record. In the cylinder index, it learns that the record is on cylinder 009. The computer system then consults the track index for cylinder 009, where it observes that the record is on track 2 of that cylinder. The access mechanism then proceeds to this track to locate the record.

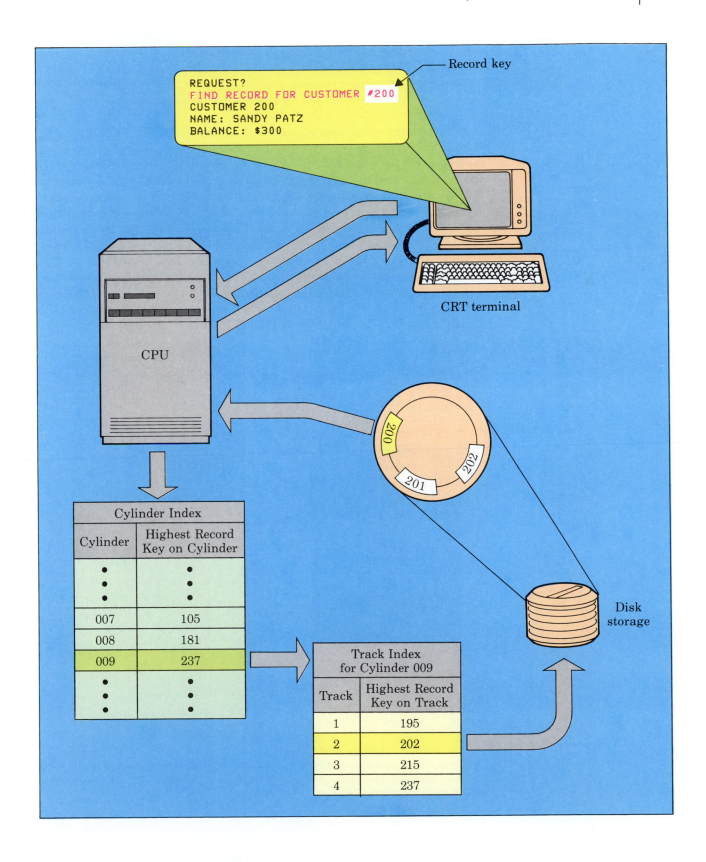

Record key

REQUEST?
FIND RECORD FOR CUSTOMER #200
CUSTOMER 200
NAME: SANDY PATZ
BALANCE: $300

CRT terminal

CPU

Disk storage

Cylinder Index	
Cylinder	Highest Record Key on Cylinder
• • •	• • •
007	105
008	181
009	237
• • •	• • •

Track Index for Cylinder 009	
Track	Highest Record Key on Track
1	195
2	202
3	215
4	237

DIRECT ORGANIZATION. Although indexed files are suitable for many applications, the process of finding disk addresses through index searches can be time consuming. Schemes of direct organization have been developed to overcome this disadvantage by permitting direct access in the shortest possible time.

Direct organization eliminates the need for an index by translating the key field of the record directly into a disk address. This is done by using mathematical formulas called *hashing algorithms.* Several hashing procedures have been developed. One of the simplest involves dividing the key field by the prime number closest to, but not greater than, the number of records to be stored. A prime number can be divided evenly by itself and 1, but not by any other number. The remainder of the division by the prime number (not the quotient) is used to determine the address of the location at which the record will be stored.

Let's consider an example. Suppose a company has 1000 employees, and thus, 1000 active employee numbers. Also suppose that all employee identification numbers (the key field) are 4 digits long. Therefore, the possible range of ID numbers is from 0000 to 9999.

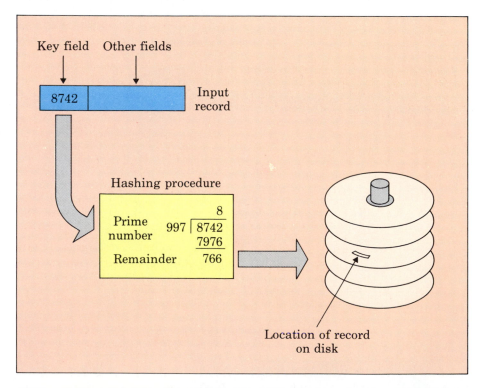

Figure 5-25. Hashing illustrated. The CPU follows a hashing procedure to assign a record to a disk address. In this case the hashing procedure involves dividing the key field by the prime number closest to 1000—or 997. The remainder corresponds to an actual disk address.

Assume that the company wants to place the record of employee number 8742 onto disk. The hashing procedure would take place as follows. The prime number closest to 1000, the number of records to be stored, is 997. Figure 5-25 shows that the hashed address computes to 766. The number 766 is then translated into a cylinder number, surface number, and so forth, that corresponds to an actual disk address. (Note that records organized according to a direct scheme are not stored sequentially by key field, as they are in indexed-sequential organization.) After the record has been placed at the designated address, the computer can retrieve it as needed by applying the hashing procedure to the key field of the record again. Hashing usually cuts storage requirements and consumes much less time than would a search through one or more indexes.

Procedures for hashing are difficult to develop and are certainly not without problems. For example, it is possible for two or more records to be hashed to the same relative disk location. This, of course, means they will "collide" at the same disk address. When this happens, one record is placed in the computed location and assigned a "pointer" that chains it to the other, which is often placed in the available location closest to the hashed address. Good hashing procedures result in few collisions. A detailed discussion is beyond the scope of this book.

Summary and Key Terms

Secondary storage technologies make it economically feasible to keep large quantities of programs and data online to the CPU. The most common types of secondary storage media are magnetic tape and magnetic disk.

Magnetic tape normally consists of ½-inch-wide plastic Mylar, coated with a magnetizable substance, and wound on a 10½-inch-diameter reel. Each character of data is represented in byte form across **tracks** in the tape. Many tapes contain nine tracks—eight corresponding to the 8 bits in a byte, and an additional parity track to check for transmission errors. Magnetic tape is also available for small computers in the form of **cassette tapes** and **cartridge tapes.**

For a tape to be processed by the CPU it must be mounted on a hardware device called a **tape unit.** The drives on the tape unit spin the tape past a **read/write head,** which either reads from or writes to the tape. Records are often systematically organized on a tape with respect to a **key field,** such as a customer ID number.

Because the tape unit requires records to pass the read/write head at a constant speed, **interblock (interrecord) gaps** must be provided on the tape for acceleration and deceleration between records. To minimize the number of these gaps on the tape, a technique called **blocking** is frequently used. With this technique conventional data records (called **logical records**) are grouped, or *blocked,* into **physical records.** The number of logical records blocked into a physical record is called the **blocking factor.**

The size of a physical record depends, to a large extent, on the size of input-record **buffers** within the computer unit. Often there are two of these buffers. Each buffer can contain a complete physical record. Because the buffers are within the all-electronic computer unit, records in them can be fetched quickly by active programs.

Tapes have many features designed to prevent careless processing errors. A **file-protection ring,** for example, must be inserted at the center of a tape reel in order to write on the tape. Also, an **internal header label** is used to carry identifying information about the tape, so this information can be carefully verified by the computer system before any processing takes place.

Magnetic disk is commonly available in the form of hard disks and floppy disks. **Hard disks,** such as removable-pack disks and Winchester disks, consist of round, rigid platters. **Floppy disks,** on the other hand, consist of *flexible* platters.

The disks in **removable-pack disk systems** are frequently 14-inch-diameter platters. Data are represented in byte form on concentric tracks of each disk surface. Often the same amount of data is stored on each track of a disk to keep the data-transfer rate constant throughout the disk system.

In removable-pack systems, several platters are usually assembled into a **disk pack.** The disk pack, in turn, is mounted on a **disk storage unit (disk unit),** which enables the data on the disks to be online to the computer. In most systems a read/write head is assigned to each recordable disk surface. The heads are mounted on an **access mechanism,** which can move them in and out among the concentric tracks to fetch data.

All tracks in the same position on the tiered platters of a disk pack form what is known as a **disk cylinder.**

Three primary factors determine the time needed to read from or write to most disks. **Access motion time** is the time required for the access mechanism to reach a particular track. The time needed for the disk to spin to a specific area of a track is known as **rotational delay.** Once located, data must be transferred to or from the disk, a process known as **data movement time.** The sum of these three time components is called **disk access time.** If related data are placed on tracks that belong to the same disk cylinder, access motion time can be reduced considerably. Disk units that have a read/write head for every track eliminate access motion time entirely.

Each location on disk has a unique **disk address,** so that the computer system can easily keep track of programs and data on the disk unit.

Floppy disks (sometimes called *floppies* or *diskettes*) are commonly used with microcomputers and small minicomputers. Floppies are available in a number of different sizes (diameters) and data densities. They are also available in *soft-sectored* and *hard-sectored* form. **Sectors** divide a floppy into addressable, pie-shaped pieces. Floppy disk drives will work only when the correct type of floppy is inserted into it in the right way.

Small, sealed hard disk units called **Winchester disks** are also becoming very popular for microcomputer systems. Winchesters are faster and have greater data-carrying capacity than floppies.

Besides tape and disk, several other devices may be used for secondary storage. The **mass storage unit** is particularly suitable for storing enormous quantities of data online. Although slower than magnetic disk, it is more cost effective when the CPU must have large quantities of data readily accessible. **Optical disks,** which work with laser read/write devices, are a relatively recent secondary storage technology. Most optical disk systems available today are *CD-ROM* systems, which work with prerecorded disks. The potential of optical disks is yet to be realized. **Magnetic bubble storage** is frequently used for small amounts of local memory in such devices as terminals, desk-top computers, robots, and communications equipment.

The process of retrieving data and programs in storage is called **data access.** Systematically arranging data so they can be retrieved efficiently is called **data organization.**

There are two general classes of access: sequential and direct. In **sequential access** the records in a file are retrieved in the same relative sequence in which they are stored. In **direct (random) access,** the records in a file can be retrieved in any order. Tape is strictly a sequential-access medium. Disk is capable of both sequential and direct access to data.

There are three major methods of storing files in secondary memory: sequential organization, indexed-sequential organization, and direct organization. In **sequential organization** records are generally arranged with respect to a key field. With **indexed-sequential organization,** records are arranged sequentially by key field on the disk to facilitate sequential access. In addition, one or several indexes are available to permit direct access to the records. **Direct organization** facilitates even faster access to data. It uses a process called *hashing* to transform the key field of each record into a disk address.

Review Exercises

Fill-in Questions

1. The number of _____ records per _____ record is known as the blocking factor.
2. A tiered assembly of disk platters enclosed in a protective cover is known as a(n) _____.
3. Each character of data on magnetic tape is represented in byte form across parallel _____ of the tape.
4. In order for data to be written onto a tape, a(n) _____ must be mounted in the center of the tape.
5. For rapid access related data are often stored on the same _____, a collection of disk tracks that are in the same relative position on different disk surfaces of a pack.
6. The time taken for a disk read/write head to be aligned over the proper position on a track once the access mechanism has reached the track is known as _____.
7. A type of hard disk that is becoming very popular for small business systems is the _____ disk.
8. A(n) _____ is a secondary storage device capable of storing almost 500 billion bytes of data online, in honeycombed data cells.

Matching Questions

Match the most appropriate storage technology with its description.

a. Floppy disk
b. Cartridge tape
c. Removable-pack disk unit
d. Winchester disk
e. Mass storage unit
f. Cassette tape

_____ 1. A user needs a lot of fast, random access to run a business on a home microcomputer system.
_____ 2. A storage alternative, often under 1 megabyte in capacity, that is available in a soft-sectored, double-sided, double-density format.
_____ 3. A common storage alternative for minicomputers and mainframes.
_____ 4. An extremely slow secondary storage alternative.
_____ 5. Used by organizations that need extremely large amounts of data online.
_____ 6. A microcomputer user needs daily backup of the full contents of a hard disk.

Discussion Questions

1. How does secondary storage differ from primary storage?
2. Explain how data are stored on magnetic tape.
3. How and why are records blocked on tape?

4. How does buffering work in sequential processing?
5. Identify three types of magnetic disk, and for each type describe a possible situation in which it might be useful.
6. Explain the difference between data access and data organization.
7. Provide examples of sequential access and direct access to data.
8. What are the physical differences among floppy disks?
9. What precautions should one take in caring for floppies?
10. What potential is seen for optical disks?

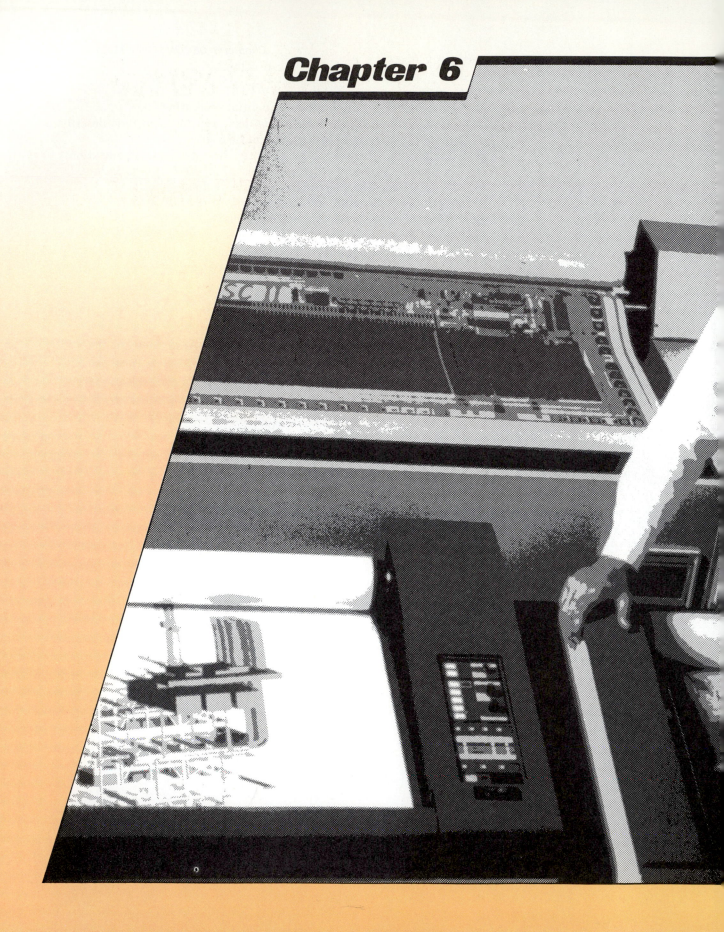

Chapter 6

Input and Output Equipment

Chapter Outline

OVERVIEW
INPUT AND OUTPUT
DISPLAY DEVICES
    Text Versus Graphics
    Monochrome and Color Display Devices
    CRT and Flat-Panel Display Devices
    Terminal Intelligence
    The Operator Interface
PRINTERS
    Impact Printing
    Nonimpact Printing
    Printers for Microcomputers
    Printers for Large Computers
PUNCHED CARDS AND EQUIPMENT
SOURCE DATA AUTOMATION
    Optical Character Recognition (OCR)
    Magnetic Ink Character Recognition (MICR)
    Digitizers
    Voice-Input Devices
SPECIAL-PURPOSE OUTPUT EQUIPMENT
    Computer Output Microfilm (COM)
    Plotters
    Voice-Output Devices

Objectives

After completing this chapter you should be able to:

1. Identify several types of input and output devices, as well as explain the roles of these devices.
2. Describe the differences that exist among display devices.
3. Describe the differences that exist among printers.
4. Explain what source data automation means and discuss several ways in which it may be accomplished.
5. Appreciate the large variety of input and output equipment available in the marketplace.

OVERVIEW

In Chapter 5 we covered secondary storage devices. Although most of those devices perform both input and output operations for the computer, storage is their main role. In this chapter we turn to equipment that is designed primarily for input of programs and data into the computer, for output, or for both. Many of these devices possess a limited amount of storage capacity as well.

We begin the chapter with a look at display devices. These units are ideally suited for applications that require considerable interaction between the operator and the computer. We'll also highlight some of the qualities that distinguish one display device from another.

The second major chapter topic is printers. Printers place the results of computer processing on paper, sometimes at incredible speeds. We'll then turn to punched-card equipment, which represents one of the oldest technologies for translating data into a form the computer system can understand.

Next we'll cover hardware designed for source data automation. This equipment provides fast and efficient input for certain kinds of applications.

Finally, we'll describe some special-purpose output equipment. Included among these devices are machines that can record output onto microfilm, machines that can speak, and plotters.

Keep in mind that the hardware we describe in this chapter is only a small sample of the kinds of input/output equipment available today. There are, in fact, thousands of products in the marketplace, and these can be put together in so many ways that it is possible to create a computer system to fit almost any conceivable need.

INPUT AND OUTPUT

Input and output equipment makes it possible for people and computers to communicate. **Input devices** convert data and programs that humans can understand into a form that is comprehensible to the computer. These devices translate the letters, numbers, and other natural-language symbols that humans conventionally use in reading and writing into the configurations of 0- and 1-bits that the computer uses to process data. **Output devices,** on the other hand, convert the strings of bits used by the computer back into natural-language form to make them understandable to humans. These devices produce output for screen display, output on paper or film, and so forth.

The equipment that we are about to discuss can be classified in a number of ways. Some of it is *peripheral equipment.* This refers to input or output devices that can be plugged into the computer. Display devices, printers, and card readers are examples. Other input or output equipment, such as many optical character recognition (OCR) and computer output microfilm (COM) devices, are *auxiliary equipment.* These devices normally work independently of the CPU. Some auxiliary devices prepare input data so that these data can later be mounted on a peripheral device. Others take output that has been produced on a peripheral device and make it more useful to humans.

The equipment, of course, can also be discussed in terms of its input or output functions. Teleprinters, for example, are capable of both input and output. Keyboards and optical character devices are designed primarily for input. Printers, display devices, and most computer microfilm devices, on the other hand, specialize in output.

DISPLAY DEVICES

Display devices are peripheral devices that contain a televisionlike viewing screen. Most display devices fall into one of two categories: monitors and display terminals. A **monitor** is an *output* device that consists of only the viewing screen, while a **display terminal** is an *input/output* communications workstation that usually consists of the screen (for output) and a keyboard (for input). The difference between a monitor and display terminal can be seen in Figures 6-1*a* and 6-1*b*.

In practice one commonly finds monitors plugged into and sitting on top of the system units of microcomputers. The keyboard is usually a separate input device that also connects to the system unit. Despite the fact that a monitor is strictly an output device, keyboard input can also be seen on the display because the computer routes it to the monitor as computer output. Display terminals, on the other hand, are often hooked up to remote mainframes and minicomputers in a communications network. Here the keyboard unit is cabled directly to the display unit, which in turn is connected to the computer.

Display devices are handy when only small amounts of output are required and it is necessary to see what is being sent as input to the computer system. A student writing a program for a class, an airline clerk making inquiries to a flight information file, a stockbroker analyzing a security, or a bank teller checking the status of a customer account would each employ a display device. The display is useful, however, only up to a point. If, for example, the student writing the program wanted to take a copy of it home, it would be necessary to direct output to a printer.

There are many features that differentiate the hundreds of display devices currently on the market (Figure 6-1). A discussion of some of the more noteworthy features follows.

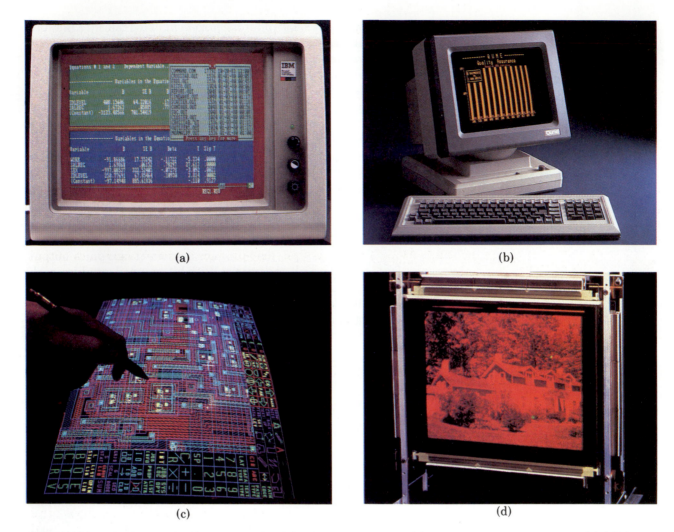

(a)

(b)

(c)

(d)

Figure 6-1. **A variety of display devices.** (a) A CRT-type monitor. (b) A CRT-type display terminal. (c) A light pen terminal. (d) A flat-panel display.

Text Versus Graphics

Many of the display devices sold today are capable of providing both text and graphics output. *Text* output consists of only letters, digits, and special characters. Two examples are program listings and letters to friends. *Graphics* output includes complex picture images, such as charts, maps, and drawings. The terminal shown in Figure 6-1*b* is displaying both text and graphics output on its screen.

RESOLUTION.   A key characteristic of any display device is its resolution, or the sharpness of the screen image. On many displays images are formed by lighting up tiny dots on the screen. On such a device, resolution is measured by the number of these dots, or **pixels** (a contraction of the

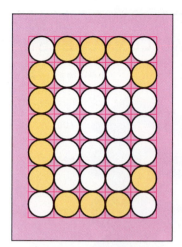

Figure 6-2. A "C" character, as formed by a 5-by-7 dot matrix of pixels. Generally, the more dots available in the matrix to form characters, the better the character resolution.

phrase "picture elements"). The more pixels on the screen, the higher is the resolution (the clearer the picture). A display resolution of, say, 720 by 350 means that the screen consists of 720 columns by 350 rows of dots—that is, $720 \times 350 = 252,000$ pixels.

Text characters are formed on the screen in a dot-matrix configuration, as shown in Figure 6-2. Generally display device manufacturers will select a specific matrix size—say, 5 by 7 (= 35 pixels), or perhaps 7 by 12 (= 84 pixels) to display its standard text. The more pixels used to form characters and the more pixels packed per square inch of screen, the higher is the resolution of the text. Many display devices will use 25 rows of 80-character lines for standard text display. With some devices you may be able to enter a *compressed mode* that will let you display, say, 50 rows of 132-character lines.

BIT MAPPING.   Display devices that produce reasonable graphics output often use a technique called **bit mapping.** With bit-mapped graphics, each pixel on the screen can be individually controlled by the operator. This enables virtually any type of image to be created on the screen.

One of the largest markets for graphics devices is in the engineering and scientific fields. Displays are used for such tasks as contour mapping, circuit design, mechanical design, and drafting. Such applications collectively fall under the heading of *computer-aided design (CAD)*. Many graphics devices that are operated in a CAD environment use a light pen to facilitate drawing directly on the display screen (as in Figure 6-1c). CAD will be discussed in greater detail in Chapter 15.

Another large market for computer graphics is in the business sector. Managers can easily become overwhelmed as they try to make decisions on the basis of piles of raw data. A possible solution is suggested by the old adage, "One picture is worth a thousand words." From a graphics image, a decision maker can more easily spot problems, opportunities, and trends. Many applications of computer graphics in business fall under the general category of *presentation graphics,* which is covered in Chapter 12 and Window 4. With presentation graphics, computer images are used to increase the effectiveness of managerial and sales presentations (Figure 6-3).

Monochrome and Color Display Devices

Just as there are television sets that provide black-and-white or color images, so too are there display devices that are classifiable as monochrome or color.

Monochrome displays (Figures 6-1b and 6-1d) output images using a single foreground color. Like television sets, many of the earliest monochrome devices were of the black-and-white variety—providing white text on a black background. Through a technique known as *reverse video* (i.e., reversing the color of the pixels), black text on a white background is also possible. Over the years a number of studies have shown that people become

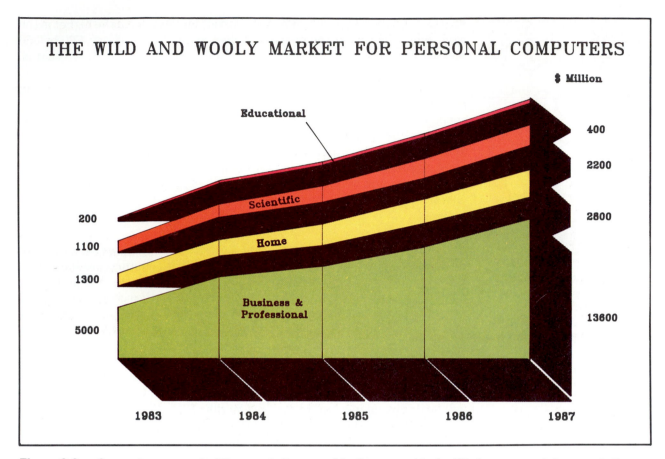

THE WILD AND WOOLY MARKET FOR PERSONAL COMPUTERS

Figure 6-3. *Computer-generated "presentation graphics" are used to facilitate managerial presentations.*

less fatigued when working with amber on a black background, or perhaps green on a black background. Although the studies have produced conflicting results, many of the monochrome display devices available in the marketplace are of the amber or green type.

Most *color displays* (Figures 6-1a and 6-1c) are of the *red-green-blue* (*RGB*) type. Depending on such things as the sophistication of the display unit itself and the amount of RAM available with the computer, users may be able to display from eight to 16,000,000 colors. Business users who require presentation graphics output often need only a few colors, but people such as artists and product designers may need many, many more. Display devices that meet this latter set of needs often cost several thousands of dollars. Nonetheless users who have as few as eight colors available to them can create the illusion of many more colors by painting alternate pixels different colors. For example, painting alternate pixels yellow and green produces a lime color.

Monochrome display devices have advantages over color devices in that they are cheaper, generally provide better resolution for text display (an important consideration if the display will be used extensively for word processing), and emit less radiation. These advantages notwithstanding, if you need more than a single color, only a color display will suffice.

CRT and Flat-Panel Display Devices

Traditionally most display devices have used a large picture-tube element, similar to that in a standard TV set. This type of display device is commonly called a **CRT (cathode-ray tube).** The monitor in Figure 6-1*a* and the terminals in Figure 6-1*b* and 6-1*c* are CRTs. The box on pages 166–167 describes how CRTs work.

Recently monitors and terminals that use charged chemicals sandwiched between panes of glass have become very popular. These slim-profile devices are called **flat-panel displays.** Although they are still relatively expensive when compared with CRTs, and are not yet commercially viable for color output, flat-panel displays are compact and lightweight, require little power, and can provide a resolution sharpness that rivals a photograph's. Because of these advantages over the CRT, they are commonly found on portable computers. Figure 6-1*d* features a flat-panel display that uses a *plasma technology.* Another flat-panel technology, *liquid crystal display* (*LCD*), has been used for years in pocket calculators.

Terminal Intelligence

The *intelligence* of a display terminal is the degree of ability it has to perform certain types of work in a communications network. With respect to intelligence, terminals can be classified into two groups: dumb and intelligent.

DUMB TERMINALS.   **Dumb terminals** can handle only the most unsophisticated types of input and output. Such devices often contain no computing or storage facilities. As a result, when the operator types in characters at the keyboard, they are sent directly "up the line" to the computer. If the operator makes a mistake, it is often necessary to backspace to the error and retype the rest of the line. Although dumb terminals may be purchased cheaply, they contain very few features that make the work of the operator easy.

INTELLIGENT TERMINALS.   **Intelligent terminals,** in contrast, enable operators to edit, manipulate, store, and process data locally. A major attraction of intelligent terminals is cursor flexibility. The **cursor** is a highlighted position on the screen that indicates where the next character to be typed in by the operator will be placed. Whereas the cursor in dumb terminals can move only to the right or left, in intelligent terminals it can move in many directions. This feature, together with local storage capacity, enables operators to transmit a block of several lines to the host computer system at one time, capture blocks of text on the screen and move them around, and the like.

How CRTs Work

A FEW OF THE PRINCIPLES BEHIND THE MOST POPULAR DISPLAY TECHNOLOGY

Cathode Ray Tubes—commonly called *CRTs*—have for many years been the most prominent type of display device. With their large flat ends and long necks, they closely resemble television tubes. Here we'll look at how CRTs work. First, we'll explore the inside of a monochrome CRT, and then we'll turn to color devices.

Most CRTs use raster graphics.

Monochrome CRTs. Most CRTs work according to a principle called *raster graphics.* All of the air inside the tube is removed, thus creating a vacuum. Electrons are shot out in a narrow beam, toward the flat-face end of the tube. The interior of the flat face is coated with phosphorous materials that emit light when struck by electrons at high velocity. As each pixel area is struck by a beam, it glows for a fraction of a second.

Because too many electrons striking the same spot can burn the phosphors, the beam moves in a Z-like pattern (sometimes called a "raster pattern") from pixel to pixel across the entire tube surface. A magnetic field at the neck of the tube deflects the beam precisely to each pixel. Since a pixel glows only for a moment, it constantly has to be "refreshed"— and so the raster pattern is repeated again and again. The number of times per second the electron gun scans the entire surface of the tube is called the CRT's *refresh rate.* Refreshing the screen pixels thirty or more times per second is common. If the refresh rate isn't high enough, the tube will flicker as a result of phosphors momentarily losing their glow.

The luminescence of each pixel on the screen also depends upon the intensity of the electron beam striking it, which in turn depends on the voltage applied to the electron gun. This voltage can be controlled precisely, to turn pixels on and off. The more sophisticated monitors can also control the brightness of the individual pixels by varying the beam intensity.

Color CRTs. In color CRTs several other elements are added to those already described. For example, instead of one gun, there are three—one each for red, green, and blue. Also, the phosphor coating contains triplets of phosphor dots for each pixel, which glow in each of the three colors when struck by

The Operator Interface

Operators interfacing with display devices can do their jobs more effectively if the proper input hardware and display software are available.

HARDWARE INTERFACES. Whether they are using monitors or terminals, most operators will also be working concurrently with some type of input device. Traditionally this input device has been a **keyboard** (Figure 6-4).

Side View

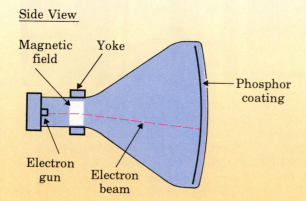

Magnetic field

Yoke

Phosphor coating

Electron gun

Electron beam

Front View

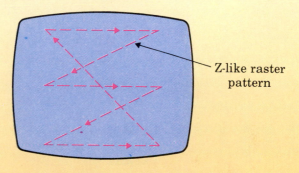

Z-like raster pattern

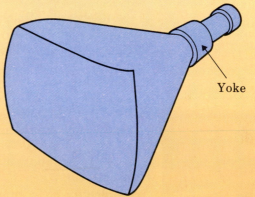

Yoke

a beam. Shades and colors other than red, green, and blue are created by varying the intensity of each of the three beams. The number of colors available on a given CRT depends on how the intensities of the three electron beams are controlled.

The major difference among color monitors has to do with whether one composite signal controls all three guns or each gun is controlled by a separate signal. Those using a single signal are known as *composite* display devices. They employ basically the same technology found in color television sets. Sharper images are possible on CRTs that control the guns with separate signals. These units are called *RGB* (for red–green–blue) display devices.

Not all CRTs use raster graphics. Some of the most sophisticated graphics terminals employ a technique called *stroke* (or *vector*) *graphics*. And flat-panel displays work entirely differently, using image-producing technologies such as gases and chemicals between charged plates.

Keyboards can vary dramatically with respect to touch, number and arrangement of keys, and built-in functions. Many keyboards today are *detachable*, enabling them to be moved around independently of the display, to suit the comfort of the operator.

Typing on computer keyboards is often facilitated by *function keys* (Figure 6-5). When depressed by the operator, these keys initiate a command, or even an entire computer program. Generally speaking each software package will define these function keys differently.

Figure 6-4. *A computer keyboard.* Keyboards can vary dramatically with respect to touch, number and arrangement of keys, and built-in functions. Most include three distinct areas: function keys, a typewriter area, and a numeric keypad.

Figure 6-5. *Function keys.* Each software package defines these keys differently. For example, depressing the F2 key may enable you to block-indent text with your word processor whereas, with your spreadsheet package, it may allow the editing of cells.

Figure 6-6. *A touch screen display device.* This operator interface requires neither typing skills nor a knowledge of programming-language commands. All one does is point to an option and the computer system takes the appropriate action.

Keyboards, although extremely popular, are not the only type of input equipment used to interface with display devices. For example, some displays are designed to respond when the operator touches a finger or light pen to a position on the screen. These interfacing devices are especially appropriate for graphics-oriented work, for applications where the operator is not a typist, and for applications where the operator may be wearing gloves (such as in a factory). Display devices that are designed to allow a finger to activate the screen are commonly called **touch screen devices** (see Figure 6-6).

A **light pen,** such as the one in Figure 6-1c, contains a light-sensitive cell at its tip. When the tip of the pen is placed near the screen, the terminal can identify its position. Some pens are even equipped with a remote-control press-button feature, which enables access to any page-length image on the display screen. This is shown in Figure 6-7.

Besides the input hardware discussed, there are many interfacing devices that, when moved independently of the screen, cause the screen cursor to move. Four such devices are shown in Figure 6-8 (on page 170).

A **joystick,** which looks like a car's stick shift, is often used for computer games and for CAD. With many joysticks, the speed at which they move and the distance they travel determine the speed and distance traveled by the screen cursor.

A **trackball** consists of a sphere resting on rollers, with only its top exposed outside its case. The screen cursor travels in whatever direction the trackball is spun by the operator. A **mouse,** which has become very popular in recent years, is merely a trackball turned upside down and rolled along a desk top or other flat surface.

A **crosshair cursor** is moved over hard-copy images of maps, survey photos, and even large drawings of microchips. The image is digitized into the computer system's memory as the cursor passes over it. Using the keyboard or a keypad on the cursor, the operator can enter supplementary information into the memory. With maps, for example, features such as

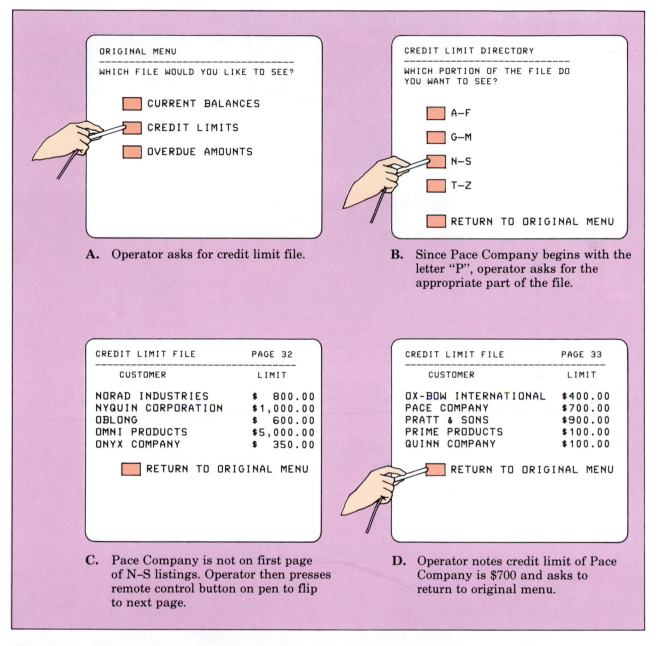

A. Operator asks for credit limit file.

B. Since Pace Company begins with the letter "P", operator asks for the appropriate part of the file.

C. Pace Company is not on first page of N–S listings. Operator then presses remote control button on pen to flip to next page.

D. Operator notes credit limit of Pace Company is $700 and asks to return to original menu.

Figure 6-7. *Simple series of screens presented to an operator of a light pen.* As the light pen is touched to the desired option, the display device automatically takes the appropriate action. In the panel of screens shown, the operator is attempting to locate the credit limit of Pace Company.

rivers, roads, and buildings may be scanned with the crosshair and any identifying labels can be keyed in from the pad. Once the maps are in digital form, the operator can call them up for display on the screen and modify them at will.

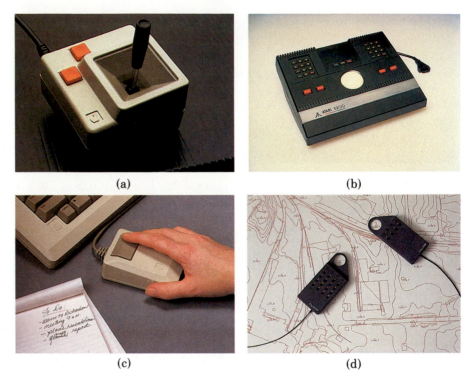

Figure 6-8.   Cursor-movement devices. (a) Joystick. (b) Trackball. (c) Mouse. (d) Crosshair cursor.

SOFTWARE INTERFACES.   There are many types of software products commercially available that make display devices easier to use. For example, *windowing software* subdivides a screen into independent "boxes" of information called *windows.* A screen with, say, three windows may contain a computer program listing in one window, the data for that program in another, and the results from executing the program with its data in a third. Figure 6-1*a* illustrates how a screen looks with windows.

Menus, on the other hand, make display device interaction feasible for people who find it difficult to compose computer commands or to type. What a menu is and how it works are demonstrated in Figure 6-7*a* and 6-7*b.*

Since this is a hardware chapter, these software interfaces will be discussed more fully in the software module.

PRINTERS

Display devices have two major limitations as output devices: (1) only a small amount of data can be shown on the screen at one time, and (2) output is not portable. Also, you must be present at a display device to get any results at all. To preserve output in portable form, you virtually have to take notes.

Printers overcome these limitations by producing *hard copy,* a permanent record of output. Hard copy is created when digital electronic signals from the computer are converted into printed material in a natural language that can be easily read and understood. A great deal of output can be placed onto such computer printouts, although as hard copy accumulates, it can become difficult to handle and store. In fact many executives complain that they are drowning in a sea of computer-generated paperwork.

Printers differ in a number of important respects. One involves the printing technology used—whether it is *impact* or *nonimpact.* Another involves speed of operation. **Low-speed printers** are capable of outputting only a character at a time, whereas **high-speed printers** can output either a full line or a full page at a time.

Impact Printing

Impact printing is the method used by conventional typewriters. A metal "hammer" embossed with a character strikes a print ribbon, which presses the image of the character onto paper. In other cases of impact printing, the hammer strikes the paper instead and presses it into the ribbon. Characters created through impact printing can be formed by either a solid-font or dot-matrix printing mechanism.

SOLID-FONT MECHANISMS. A **solid-font mechanism** produces fully formed characters similar to those from conventional typewriters. One of the most popular devices for producing fully formed characters on low-speed printers is the daisywheel print element, shown in Figure 6-9. *Daisywheel printers* operate at very slow speeds—often in the neighborhood of 30 to 60 characters per second—but the output quality is very high. Thus daisywheel printers are sometimes called *letter-quality printers* because they are often used to produce attractive correspondence that is sent outside the user's organization. Other letter-quality printers in the equipment marketplace include those using *print-thimble* and *golf-ball* print elements in place of the daisywheel.

Many high-speed printers also employ a solid-font mechanism to produce fully formed characters. In chain printers, for example, all characters are mounted on a *print chain* that revolves rapidly past the print positions, as you can see from Figure 6-10. Hammers are lined up opposite each of as many as 132 print positions. These hammers press the paper against a ribbon that, in turn, presses against the appropriate embossed characters on the chain.

DOT-MATRIX MECHANISMS. Most low-speed printers in use today employ a print head that's an **impact dot-matrix mechanism.** Typically such a device constructs printed characters by repeatedly activating a vertical row

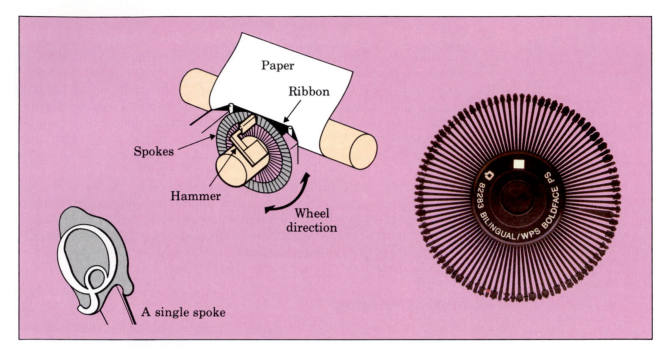

Figure 6-9. **The daisywheel.** Each spoke has an embossed character that strikes the ribbon when struck by a hammer.

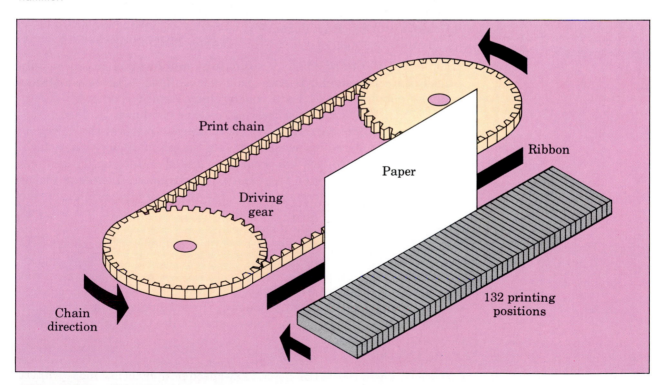

Figure 6-10. **The print chain.** Hammers press the paper against a ribbon that, in turn, presses against the appropriate embossed characters in the chain.

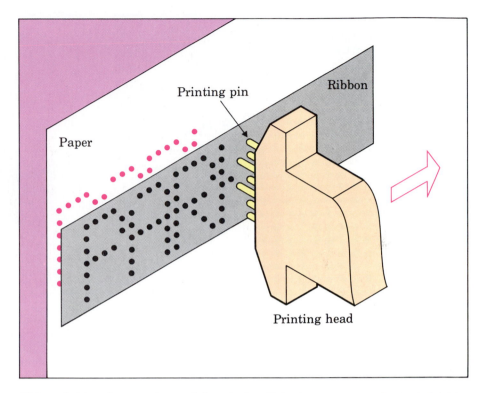

Figure 6-11. *Impact dot-matrix printing.* This character-formation technique is similar to the one used to light up electronic scoreboards at sports stadiums. The printing mechanism contains a vertical line of pins that form the characters on the paper. Depending on the character to be represented, different pins in the mechanism are activated. The characters shown are formed from a 5-by-7 dot matrix. The more dots in the matrix, naturally, the higher the quality of the printed character.

of pins, as illustrated in Figure 6-11. Impact dot-matrix printers are much faster than solid-font printers. For example, a speed of 100 to 200 characters per second is not unusual for a low-speed, impact dot-matrix printer.

Unfortunately the quality of output on dot-matrix devices is low as compared with that from solid-font devices. Nonetheless many relatively inexpensive impact dot-matrix printers are capable of printing very respectable looking output. These printers use strategies such as packing as many pins as possible on the print head, overstriking by making multiple passes on a line, and blending overstrike dots into earlier dots by shifting the paper ever so slightly (see Figure 6-12). In the world of computers, single-pass impact dot-matrix printing is often called *draft-quality* printing and multiple-pass dot-matrix printing is called *near-letter-quality (NLQ)* printing. Today, many dot-matrix printers can create characters that are virtually indistinguishable from those produced by solid-font printers. Some dot-matrix printers have heads with *two* rows of pins, enabling them to produce NLQ output in a single pass.

Figure 6-12. ***Overstrik-***
ing on a dot-matrix printer.
(a) Single striking. (b) Overstriking by multiple passes
produces denser characters.

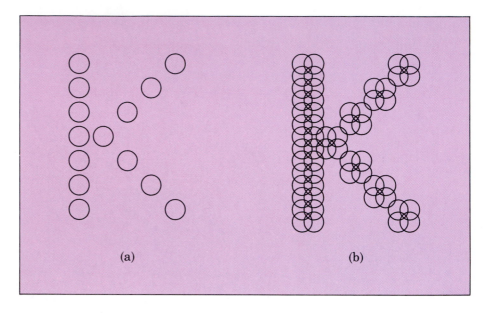

(a)   (b)

Many impact dot-matrix printers can also be used to produce graphical or color output. Graphical output is possible if the printer supports *bit mapping.* In the case of printers, this means that each individual pin on the printing head may be independently software controlled. Color output is often possible through a process called *dithering.* Here a three-color ribbon may be used and—possibly through multiple passes, overstrikes, and ever-so-slight paper shifts—the printer "mixes" new colors and blends colors right on the paper. Dithering isn't elegant, but it can meet the need for inexpensive color output.

Figure 6-13 shows some output samples produced by an impact dot-matrix printer.

Nonimpact Printing

Nonimpact printing, which most often employs dot-matrix characters, does not depend on the impact of metal on paper. In fact no physical contact at all is made between the printing mechanism and the paper. The most popular nonimpact methods today utilize electrothermal, thermal-transfer, ink-jet, laser, and array technologies.

In *electrothermal* printing characters are burned onto a special paper by heated rods on a print head. Electrothermal printers are available at very low cost, but their chief disadvantages are the special paper they require (which some people find unpleasant to touch) and an inability to produce color output.

Thermal-transfer printers, which represent a relatively new technology, thermally transfer ink from a wax-based ribbon onto plain paper. These printers can produce output that rivals a daisywheel's and, because they use a dot-matrix print head, they can support high-quality graphics as well.

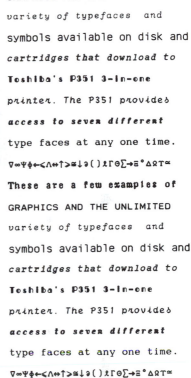

These are a few examples of GRAPHICS AND THE UNLIMITED variety of typefaces and symbols available on disk and cartridges that download to Toshiba's P351 3-in-one printer. The P351 provides access to seven different type faces at any one time. ∇∞Ψφ←≤∧↔↑>≅↓∂()≵ΓΘ∑→Ξ°ΔΩΤ∝

These are a few examples of GRAPHICS AND THE UNLIMITED variety of typefaces and symbols available on disk and cartridges that download to Toshiba's P351 3-in-one printer. The P351 provides access to seven different type faces at any one time. ∇∞Ψφ←≤∧↔↑>≅↓∂()≵ΓΘ∑→Ξ°ΔΩΤ∝

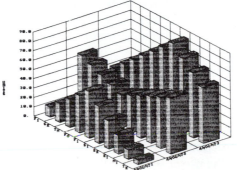

Figure 6-13. Samples of characters produced on an impact dot-matrix printer—the Toshiba P351. The high clarity of some of the characters is made possible by double striking and moving the paper in small increments. The house and three-dimensional graph are achievable because the printer is bit mapped.

Ink-jet printers spray small dots of electrically charged ink onto a page to form images. Many of them will hold several color cartridges simultaneously, so they are excellent for color output.

Laser printers form images by charging thousands of dots on a platen with a very-high-intensity laser beam. Then, as with photocopiers, toner is affixed to the charged positions and, when paper is pressed against the platen, an image is formed. Laser printers produce fast, high-quality work, but they are often more expensive than other types of printers.

Array printers, which first became available in 1985, have many of the same properties as laser printers. They contain fewer moving parts, however, so they are more reliable. They are also more expensive.

There are many important practical differences between impact and nonimpact printers. For example, because nonimpact printers contain fewer moving parts, they are generally much faster and subject to fewer breakdowns. Additionally, because hammers aren't busily striking ribbons, nonimpact printers are quiet. But unless you require very fast speeds or high-quality color, these printers are often an expensive alternative. And, because most nonimpact printers are dot-matrix devices, they generally can't match the letter-quality output produced by impact, solid-font printers. Some other differences between the most common types of impact and nonimpact printers are highlighted in Figure 6-14.

Printers for Microcomputers

Most printers available for microcomputer systems are of the low-speed variety, and output a character at a time. The most common of these low-speed devices are letter-quality, impact dot-matrix, electrothermal, thermal-transfer, and ink-jet printers. The differences among these devices are shown in Figure 6-14.

Low-speed printers typically operate in the range of 10 to 300 characters per second. The slower units print in a single direction, like a conventional typewriter. The faster ones print in two directions (i.e., *bidirectionally*), to save a time-consuming carrige return. Usually these fast devices are also *logic seeking,* in that they are always "peeking" at the next line to decide how to print it the fastest way. Many low-speed printers can output subscripts, superscripts, colors, graphic material, or multilingual and scientific text. Four of the approximately 500 now commercially available are shown in Figure 6-15.

On many low-speed printers, character widths are adjustable, so that the operator can change the number of characters per line or lines per inch. With dot-matrix units, these adjustments can be made by setting a switch or by the use of software. With solid-font devices, however, the operator must change the printing element by hand.

	Device					
Criterion	**Impact Dot Matrix**	**Daisywheel and Print Thimble**	**Ink Jet**	**Electrothermal**	**Thermal Transfer**	**Laser and Array**
Speed	Fast	Slow	Medium to very fast	Medium to fast	Medium to fast	Very fast
Print quality	Fair to very good	Excellent	Good to excellent	Fair to very good	Excellent	Excellent
Cost	Low	Medium	Medium to high	Low	Medium to high	High
Graphics capabilities	Fair	Very limited	Fair to excellent	Good	Good to excellent	Excellent
Color	Fair	Very limited	Excellent (if available)	Not available	Excellent (if available)	Very limited

Figure 6-14. *Comparison of printing technologies.*

Figure 6-15. A variety of low-speed printers. (a) A daisywheel printer. (b) An impact dot-matrix printer. (c) An ink-jet printer. (d) A thermal-transfer printer.

(a)

(b)

(c)

(d)

Low-speed printers utilize either a friction feed or an adjustable tractor feed—and often both. *Friction feeding* holds the paper as a conventional typewriter does. It is the cheapest type of paper-feed mechanism, but continuous-form paper often gets out of alignment after a few pages have been printed and must be readjusted. *Tractor feeding* works with a pair of sprocket mechanisms, which pass through holes on the left and right sides of the paper to keep it in alignment. The sprocket mechanisms can be adjusted by the operator to fit a wide range of paper widths. On many printers the sprocket mechanisms can be slid aside, to enable the operator to friction-feed single sheets of precut letterhead paper.

Perhaps the greatest potential for high-speed printing on microcomputer systems is with laser printing, and recently relatively inexpensive laser devices (available for under $3000) have become available for this use. Laser printing is a special case of page printing, which we shall cover shortly.

Printers for Large Computers

Most of the printing on large computer systems is accomplished by high-speed printers. Whereas low-speed printers top out at speeds of around 300 *characters per second,* the slowest high-speed printers operate

Figure 6-16.   A line printer. Line printers are targeted to larger computers—minicomputers and mainframes—and produce output at speeds ranging from 300 to 3000 lines per minute.

Figure 6-17.   A laser printer. Operating at peak capacity over a weekend, some page printers can produce well over a million pages of output.

Figure 6-18.   A teleprinter terminal. These low-speed devices are handy on large computer systems when a modest amount of hard-copy output is required.

at about 300 *lines per minute* (roughly twice the speed of the fastest low-speed printer). In many commercial settings with both kinds of printers, you will often find the high-speed printers operating at speeds from ten to thirty times faster than the low-speed printers.

High-speed printers fall into two major categories: line printers and page printers. Teleprinter terminals, which are low-speed printing devices, are also commonly configured to large computers.

LINE PRINTERS.   **Line printers** (Figure 6-16) are so named because they print a whole line at a time rather than just a character. One type of line printer uses the solid-font, impact *chain* mechanism (refer to Figure 6-10), which was introduced by IBM in 1959 on its 1403 printer. This device has proved to be the most popular printer of all time, and is still used today. Many other types of line printers use mechanical devices such as print trains, drums, wheels, bands, and belts. Impact line printing is typically done at speeds ranging from 300 to 3000 lines per minute. Although most line printers are of the solid-font impact type, impact dot-matrix and nonimpact devices are also available.

Because line printers typically produce high volumes of output on perforated, continuous-form paper, a piece of special auxiliary equipment called a *burster* is often needed to separate the printed pages. Also, if forms with carbon-paper interleaves are used on an impact printer (nonimpact line printers can't produce multiple copies), another auxiliary machine called a *decollator* removes the carbons. This operation can also be done by hand. If both operations must be performed on the same output, decollating is done before bursting.

PAGE PRINTERS.   As its name suggests, the **page printer** (illustrated in Figure 6-17) can produce a page of output at a time. These devices, which can print up to 20,000 lines per minute, all employ nonimpact technology. Many of them utilize an electrophotographic process, similar to that used in the copying machines found in many offices. Many use lasers or light-emitting-diode arrays to form the printed images.

The printing commonly takes place on standard 8½ by 11-inch paper, which is cheaper than the larger, sprocket-fed paper usually used by line printers. The smaller paper is cheaper to file and mail as well. Also, since page printers do not use carbon paper, the decollating operation that accompanies impact printing is eliminated. Some page printers can print in color or on both sides of the page.

An interesting feature of page printers is their ability to store digital images of forms. In fact users of such systems can even design their own forms. Thus a considerable savings can be realized over the line printer, in which paper and printing elements need to be changed when output requires a new form or format.

Page printers generally cost considerably more than line printers, whose cost ranges from $3000 to $100,000. Page printers for large computers may cost between $150,000 and $300,000. In general an organization that produces over a million lines of output per month should investigate the feasiblity of acquiring one of these machines.

TELEPRINTERS. **Teleprinter terminals** are low-speed printers that have a keyboard for input by an operator. They are handy devices for obtaining small amounts of hard-copy output from a large computer because a short request can be entered from the keyboard and the output is immediately directed back to the teleprinter terminal. A teleprinter terminal is shown in Figure 6-18.

tomorrow

PERIPHERALS OF THE FUTURE

A Marriage of User Needs, Market Potential, and Technology

Input and output used to be relatively straightforward. You keypunched a program and its data onto cards and gave the cards to a computer operator. Perhaps a few hours or a day later, you dropped by the computer center to pick up the printed results, on standard computer paper. This process might not have been very impressive, but at least it was relatively uncomplicated: just punched-card input and printed output.

Today's user of peripheral equipment has a much wider (or should we say "staggering") array of input and output choices. There are now display terminals, complete personal computer systems, OCR devices, plotters, film recorders, digitizers of all types, and a seemingly endless list of other machines. We can input data as text, as sounds, or as images, and get them back in the same or a different form.

And when it comes to choosing one type of device, you may have dozens of options. Take printers, for example. Hundreds of models of printers are available—typeset quality, letter quality, near letter quality, draft quality, print thimble, daisywheel, thermal transfer, dot matrix, logic seeking, color, graphics, and proportional spacing, as well as ribbons of all sorts to choose from, papers and forms of every size and description, and so forth ad nauseum.

Input and output equipment has evolved, and continues to evolve, on the basis of user needs, market potential, and technology. For example, when microcomputers became a force, the market for small printers and inexpensive monitors suddenly exploded with new products. Many "experts" had predicted that improvements in printers would be slow, because printers were mechanical devices that had developed at a relative snail's pace compared with other computing products. But the need for better devices and the market potential caught the attention of aggressive companies that were willing to seek solutions. And printing technology improved dramatically.

Technolgies sometimes develop in a straight direction, but more often than not in the course of computer history, they merge to create opportunities in several areas. For example, lasers, which started as a communications technology, have also made possible new types of storage and printing devices. Thus the growing need for fast, inexpensive printers has pushed even more development money and researchers into the laser field, which will undoubtedly make communications peripherals much better.

It's apparent that the future will bring a variety of new and exciting peripheral devices into the marketplace. It seems as though any time there's a need for processing power in an area where existing input and output devices are insufficient, new peripherals result.

PUNCHED CARDS AND EQUIPMENT

One of the earliest media employed for entering data into computers was the *punched card.* Developed in the 1880s for use with tabulating machines, punched cards have persisted as a data input medium. Even today they are still viable for certain applications—such as warranty cards packed with stereos and microwaves—although they are fading in importance because of their bulkiness and slow speed.

A punched card is a rectangular piece of thin cardboard, cut to a standard size. Characters are represented by columns of holes punched into fixed positons on the card in varying configurations. A *keypunch machine* is used to punch these holes. When enough cards have been generated to form a complete computer program or data file, they are manually inserted into the hopper of a *card reader,* which communicates their contents to the computer.

THE STANDARD PUNCHED CARD.   A standard general-purpose **punched card** appears in Figure 6-19. The 3¼ by 7⅜ inch card contains 80 columns and 12 rows. An advantage of using standard punched cards is that they can be processed by standard punched-card equipment, which is still available.

THE KEYPUNCH MACHINE.   The **keypunch machine** is used to punch holes on cards to represent data. To enter the data, a stack of blank cards is first placed in the input hopper of the machine. The cards are then fed one by one into a punching station, where the operator fills each one with data.

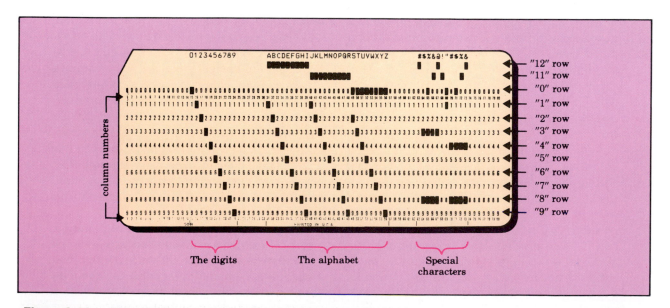

Figure 6-19.   *The standard punched card.* Each column on the card can contain a single number, letter, or special character of data. As the card is punched, each character is represented by its own unique pattern of holes. For example, the letter "A" is always represented by a hole in the "12" row and a hole in the "1" row.

Figure 3-8 on page 74 shows an old keypunch machine, which works in a manner very similar to many later models. Newer keypunches can also be programmed to handle certain functions automatically, such as skipping over unused columns at the end of a field and punching repetitive data.

OTHER PUNCHED-CARD EQUIPMENT.   Another hardware device, known as a **card reader,** is used to communicate the data on punched cards to the computer. The operator places the cards in an input hopper, where they are read sequentially. The contents of each card are scanned as it passes through a reading station. Stations designed to read standard cards often contain twelve photoelectric sensors, corresponding to the twelve rows on the card. As each column passes through the station, the sensors make electrical contact where the holes appear, thus identifying the character coded in the column.

Numerous other types of equipment exist to process punched cards. Probably the most widely used of these today is the *verifier,* which checks to see if data punched onto a card are correct. The verification operation takes place after the cards have been keypunched but before they are sent to the card reader for processing. Even though punched cards are fading from the scene, data verification continues to be an extremely vital operation—and it will remain so until we develop computer systems that can spot all human and machine errors (don't hold your breath waiting for this to happen).

SOURCE DATA AUTOMATION

Before data can be processed, they must often be translated from handwritten form into machine-readable form, a procedure that can involve thousands of hours of duplicated effort. When data input involves keying from coded forms, the process can become time consuming indeed. Data must be collected, entered on the coding forms, keyed into machine-readable form on a data preparation device, verified, and read into the computer.

Source data automation eliminates much of this duplicated effort by making data available in machine-readable form at the time they are collected. Because data about transactions are collected in machine-readable form, source data automation is both fast and accurate.

Source data automation has been applied to a number of tasks. Students record the answers to exams on mark-readable forms, which can be processed by a document reader. A microchip designer draws some circuits on a special pad, and the drawings are immediately digitized and displayed on a terminal screen. Source data automation has also been used to speed checkout lines and inventory-taking at supermarkets, quality-control operations in factories, and the processing of checks by banks.

In the next few pages, we will discuss several technologies that can be used to accomplish source data automation: optical character recognition (OCR), magnetic ink character recognition (MICR), digitizing, and voice input.

Optical Character Recognition (OCR)

Optical character recognition (OCR) refers to a wide range of optical-scanning procedures and equipment designed for machine recognition of *marks, characters,* and *codes.* These symbols are transformed into digital form for storage in the computer. Most symbols designed for OCR can be read by humans as well as by machines. Optical recognition of hand-printed characters is also technically possible but is still in its infancy. OCR equipment is some of the most varied and highly specialized in the data processing industry. A scanner that can read one type of document may be unable to read another.

OPTICAL MARKS.   One of the oldest applications of OCR is the processing of tests and questionnaires completed on special forms (see Figure 6-20).

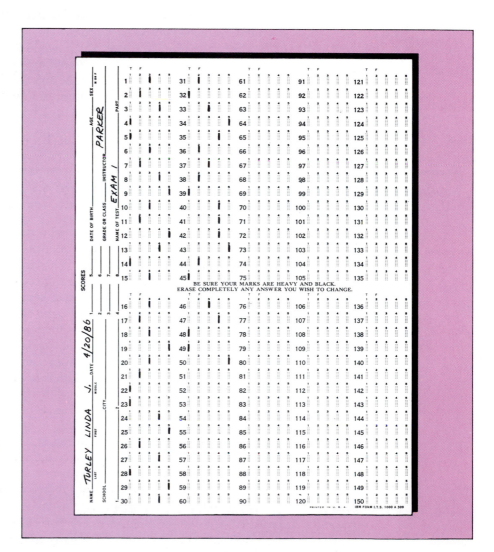

Figure 6-20.   Exam taken on an OCR form. When this completed exam is optically scanned, the scanner can recognize penciled-in areas because light doesn't penetrate those areas.

Figure 6-21. *A selection of characters from an optical character set.*

ABCDEFGHIJKLMN
OPQRSTUVWXYZ
1234567890

Take the case of grading a test. Once respondents have darkened the bubbles on the answer sheet to indicate the answers to multiple-choice questions, an optical document reader scans the answer sheets offline. This machine passes a light beam across the spaces corresponding to the set of possible responses to each question. The light does not penetrate where a response is penciled in, and that choice is tallied by the machine. Some document readers can automatically score the test from a key of correct responses. Others produce a magnetic tape of all the data gathered from the test forms for subsequent grading and analysis by a computer system.

OPTICAL CHARACTERS.   Optical characters are characters that are specially designed to be identifiable by humans as well as some type of OCR reader. They conform to a certain *font,* such as that shown in Figure 6-21. The optical reader reflects light off the characters and converts them into digital patterns for recognition. Only if the reader is familiar with the font used, can it identify the character.

In the early days of optical character reading, fonts differed widely from one OCR manufacturer to another. As years passed, however, a few fonts became industry standards. Today many machines are designed to read a number of fonts, even when these fonts are mixed on a single document. An unusual machine in this regard is the Kurzweil OCR reader, which uses *artificial intelligence* techniques to recognize fonts with which it isn't familiar.

Probably the best known use of optical characters is in **point-of-sale (POS) systems,** employed widely in retail stores. POS systems allow a store to record a purchase automatically, at the time and place it occurs, from machine-readable information attached to the product. Figure 6-22 illustrates an OCR-character-coded price tag being read with a wand reader. The information on the tag is input to a special cash register. Many registers are equipped with direct-access memories that contain descriptions of stocked items, so they can print what each item is along with its price on the customer receipt (see Figure 6-23).

Another common application of optical characters is in billing operations, such as the processing of insurance and utility bills (see Figure 6-24).

Figure 6-22.   A wand reader. The wand scans the information on a price tag printed with OCR characters and sends it to a cash register.

```
YURI'S FOODMART

04/02/86  11:09  2 201  48
KETCHUP                    .89*
RAISIN BRAN               1.09*
     2.34 LB @ 39/LB
PEACHES                   1.59*
QT NONFAT MILK             .79*
DOZ LARGE EGGS             .98*
     SUBTOTAL             5.34
     TAX                   .27
     TOTAL                5.61
     CASH TEND            6.00
     CHANGE DUE            .39
```

Figure 6-23. An informative cash register receipt made possible by a local memory.

OPTICAL CODES.   Probably the most familiar optical code is a *bar code* called the **universal product code (UPC),** commonly found on packaged goods in supermarkets (see Figure 6-25). Because they enable purchases to be recorded immediately, universal product codes are another example of POS systems. The UPC consists of several vertical bars of varying widths, which describe the product and identify the manufacturer. This code has been in use since 1973, and is currently found on over 80 percent of the products sold in supermarkets. Other bar codes are used for applications such as credit card verification and warehouse freight identification.

The UPC can be read either by passing a wand containing a scanning device over the coded label, or by sending the item past a fixed scanning station (see Figure 6-26). By using the data from the code, the terminal/cash register can identify the item, look up its latest price, and print the information on a receipt such as that shown in Figure 6-23.

Another example of source data automation in a UPC environment is shown in Figure 6-27. Here a Red Cross worker in Australia uses a wand reader to verify blood-type labels. The label information is sent to a microcomputer system, which displays the blood type.

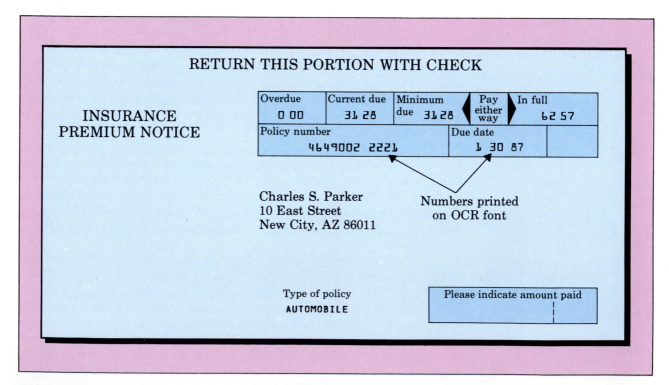

Figure 6-24.   An OCR-readable insurance bill. When this invoice is sent back to the insurance company with the payment, the address and policy number are optically scanned—saving time and minimizing data-entry errors—and the customer's record is updated.

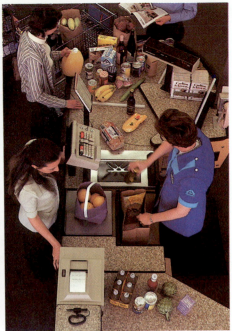

Figure 6-25.   A UPC code used on supermarket goods. Because items bearing a UPC label can be identified by optical means, the supermarket industry has saved millions of dollars in localities where it is permitted to post a single price on the shelf for a product instead of marking the price on each individual item.

Figure 6-26.   A UPC scanning station. If you buy peas selling at two cans for 49 cents, the system will charge you 25 cents for the first can and "remember" to charge you 24 cents on the next can that passes by. Some systems also use a speech synthesizer that names each item and states its price as the item passes over the scanner.

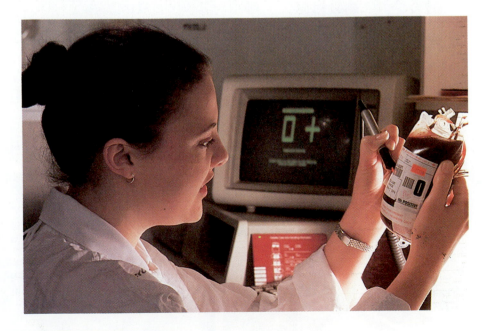

Figure 6-27.   Red Cross worker in Brisbane, Australia, uses a wand reader to verify blood-type labels. Using the keypad on the device, the clerk types in supplementary data such as the number of units in stock.

Creative Computer Output

A peek at the leading edge in computer output

There is probably nothing that better exemplifies the rapid advances made in computer output over the last few years than the field of computer art. As you examine the images on the next few pages, keep in mind that it has only been since about 1980 that the computer has emerged as a viable tool for artistic expression. All of the earliest computer artists were scientists with a keen knowledge of both computers and mathematical modeling, working on large general-purpose computers. As the potential and demand for computer-generated art in business-related fields such as advertising, publishing, and movie production evolved, specialized hardware and software started becoming available for noncomputer professionals to use. The field of computer art is truly in the pioneering stage and one can only guess what the leading edge of computer output will look like ten years from now.

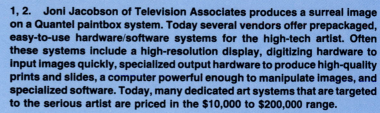

1, 2. Joni Jacobson of Television Associates produces a surreal image on a Quantel paintbox system. Today several vendors offer prepackaged, easy-to-use hardware/software systems for the high-tech artist. Often these systems include a high-resolution display, digitizing hardware to input images quickly, specialized output hardware to produce high-quality prints and slides, a computer powerful enough to manipulate images, and specialized software. Today, many dedicated art systems that are targeted to the serious artist are priced in the $10,000 to $200,000 range.

Abstract Art

3–5. Three abstract images produced on Lightspeed's Quolor™ system. This imaging system, like many others, contains a paintbox feature that enables the artist to "paint" areas of the screen from a large palette of colors. Art systems have an assortment of other features to facilitate inputting, outputting, storing, and manipulating images.

Semi-Realistic Art

6–8. The first two pieces of art (6 and 7) were produced by Bonnie Pelnar on a Genigraphics SG1 imaging system. The picture of the car (6) was inspired by a photograph of her Dad's 1937 Nash, which she digitized, painted, and placed in an exotic backdrop—all in six hours. The picture with the oranges was created by combining several stored images. The train picture was created by Scott Lewczak on an Artronics graphics system.

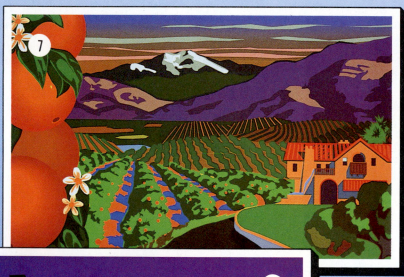

9–11. Image 9 was produced at Cornell University's Program of Computer Graphics on a (general-purpose) VAX 11/750 minicomputer. Image 10 is the work of Olga Antinova of Lightspeed. Image 11, intermixing the subtle beauty of the outside world with high-technology, was created at Cranston-Csuri Productions of Columbus, Ohio.

Assorted Artistic Images

12. "Mt. Fuji," courtesy of Aurora Systems, shows in delicate light blue tones the reflection of a snow-covered mountain.

13. A meadow tree evocative of the French Impressionists, courtesy Robert Bosch Corporation.

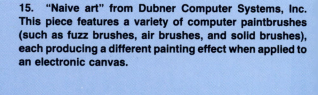

15. "Naive art" from Dubner Computer Systems, Inc. This piece features a variety of computer paintbrushes (such as fuzz brushes, air brushes, and solid brushes), each producing a different painting effect when applied to an electronic canvas.

14. A butterfly image produced on a Robert Bosch FGS-4000 videographic system.

Images from the Land of Make Believe

16, 17. Computer-generated images are often used to create a "storyboard"—a sequence of sketches that depict the significant changes in action or scene in a movie or television program.

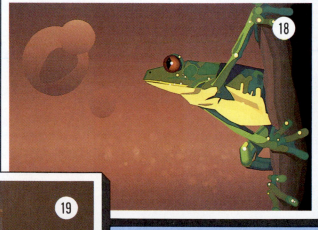

18, 19. Two animal images created by Scott Lewczak of Artronics, Inc. on a vector-based slide-presentation system. Vector graphics systems are more expensive than those using raster graphics (see related box in Chapter 6), but many artists prefer them because they produce stunningly high resolution and clear, crisp edges on surfaces.

20–22.   These three images, courtesy of James Dowlen of Time Arts, Inc., were produced on an ordinary micro-computer system. The software used to create these images can also accept data from commercial spreadsheet packages in order to combine picture images with statistical information (see Window 4, photograph 3).

23.   In "Space," created on an AVL Starburst system, all major components were created as separate files, which were combined to create the final picture. The sky contains 80 different colors.

Figure 6-28. The four-
teen-character E-13B font.
This font has been adopted
as the standard for magnetic
ink character recognition
(MICR) by the banking industry.

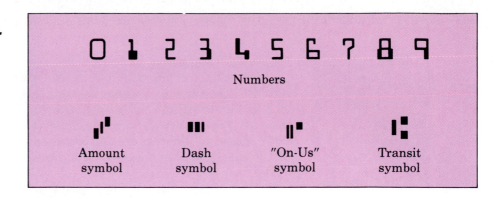

Numbers

Amount
symbol

Dash
symbol

"On-Us"
symbol

Transit
symbol

Magnetic Ink Character Recognition (MICR)

Magnetic ink character recognition (MICR) is a technology that is confined almost exclusively to the banking industry, where it is used for processing checks in high volume. Figure 6-28 shows the fourteen-character font adopted by the industry, and Figure 6-29 illustrates a check that has been encoded with MICR characters.

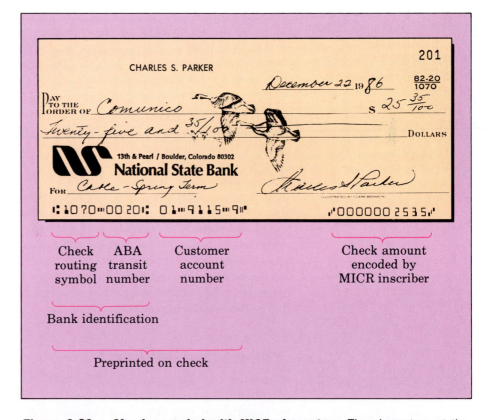

Check
routing
symbol

ABA
transit
number

Customer
account
number

Check amount
encoded by
MICR inscriber

Bank identification

Preprinted on check

Figure 6-29. Check encoded with MICR characters. The characters at the bottom left of the check are preprinted and contain identifying information, including the customer's account number. The characters at the bottom right show the amount of the check and are imprinted by an operator after the check has been cashed. If there is a discrepancy in your account, you should note whether the amount recorded by the operator is the same as the one you wrote on the check.

The characters are written on the check with a special magnetic ink. As with OCR readers, a machine called a MICR reader/sorter senses the identity of an MICR-encoded character on the check by recognizing its shape. But in contrast to OCR, the characters must be magnetized in order to be sensed by the reading device; no optical recognition is used. With MICR checks can be quickly sorted, processed, and routed to the proper banks.

Digitizers

A **digitizer** is a device that converts a measurement into a digital value. When we covered alternatives to keyboards, we saw a few examples of digitizers—for example, light pens, joysticks, and mice. Many digitizing applications are also prime examples of source data automation because source data can easily be collected by a digitizer in machine-readable form.

A type of digitizing device that's especially useful for quickly collecting source data as it's generated is a *digitizing tablet* (see Figure 6-30). A penlike stylus is used by the operator to "draw" on the flat tablet. You can think of the tablet as a matrix of thousands of tiny dots. Each dot has a machine address. When you draw a line on the tablet, the stylus passes over dots, causing the status of these dots in machine memory to change from a 0-state to a 1-state. When the drawing is complete, it is stored in digital form as a large matrix of 0s and 1s and may be recalled at any time.

There have recently been some ambitious, and very successful, efforts at pushing digitizing to even new heights. Some penlike devices will trace over a three-dimensional object so that it can be electronically reconstructed in computer memory, "digitizing copiers" can reproduce photographs and images from a standard TV or video cassette recorder (VCR) into computer memory, and "digitizing cameras" can take a picture of a physical event happening right now and generate a digital image of it based upon the intensity of light incident upon the subjects. Some of the images in Window 3, for example, started from photographs or shapes that were entered into the computer system with such digitizing devices. In Chapter 15 we cover robots, some of which can "see" (that is, "recognize") objects by digitizing their shapes and other physical properties and comparing them with those stored in computer memory.

Voice-Input Devices

Machines that can convert spoken words into digital form for storage and processing by the computer are known as **voice-input devices.** If you stop to think about how complicated the interpretation of spoken words can be for humans, you can begin to realize how tricky it is to design a voice-input device to do much the same thing. Two people may pronounce the same word differently because of accents, personal styles of speech, or the unique sound of each person's voice. Moreover, in listening to others, we not only ignore irrelevant background noises, but also decode complex grammatical constructions as well as sentence fragments.

Equipment designers have tried to overcome these obstacles in a

Figure 6-30. A digitizing tablet and stylus. As the operator traces a drawing on the tablet, the drawing is digitized to 0s and 1s and is stored in computer memory.

number of ways. Voice-input devices are designed to be "trained" by users, who repeat words until the machine knows their voices. These devices can also screen out background noise. Unfortunately voice-input devices can recognize only a limited number of isolated words, generally not whole sentences. Thus the complexity of the messages to which they can respond is quite limited.

Still the possible applications of this technology are quite exciting. In fact its potential is probably far greater than that of voice output (to be discussed later in this chapter), a more mature technology at this time. Imagine speaking into a microphone and having your words typed automatically by a printer. Such a system is commercially available; however, the number of words the computer can "understand" is extremely limited, typically under 1000.

One commercial application of voice input is a system installed by a chemical company to sort the thousands of pieces of mail that it receives each day. An operator speaks the recipient's first initial and the first four letters of the last name into a microphone headset. The corporate mail zone of the employee then appears on a display device and the package can be routed to the right place. The company maintains that this procedure has doubled the operator's productivity.

SPECIAL-PURPOSE OUTPUT EQUIPMENT

In this section we consider output devices that are appropriate for specialized uses. The technologies we describe are computer output microfilm, plotters, and voice-output devices.

Computer Output Microfilm (COM)

Computer output microfilm (COM) is a way of placing computer output on microfilm media, typically either a *microfilm reel* or *microfiche card,* both of which are shown in Figure 6-31. Microfilming can result in tremendous savings in paper cost, storage space, and handling. For example, a 4- by 6-inch microfiche card can contain the equivalent of 270 printed pages. COM is particularly useful to organizations that must keep massive files of information that do not need to be updated. It's also useful to those organizations that need to manipulate large amounts of data but find fast methods of online access too costly.

The process of producing microfilm or microfiche output generally takes place offline on a special COM unit. If a report is to be generated and placed on microfilm, the computer system first dumps it onto magnetic tape. Then the tape is mounted offline on the COM unit, which typically can produce both microfilm and microfiche. This device displays an image of each page on a screen and produces microfilmed photographs from these images. In online processes output passes directly from the computer to the COM unit. Most COM units can work both online and offline, depending on the needs of the organization.

(a)

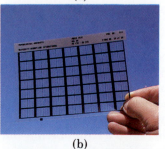

(b)

Figure 6-31. Microfilm and microfiche. (a) Microfilm. (b) Microfiche.

Figure 6-32. A micro-image retrieval station. The Kodak IMT-350 can locate a single image from a roll of thousands of stored frames in a few seconds.

To read the microfilm or microfiche that COM produces, one either selects the reels or cards by hand and mounts them onto the appropriate hand-driven reading device, or one uses an auxiliary retrieval system driven by a microcomputer or minicomputer that automatically locates and displays the desired frames. Such a system is shown in Figure 6-32. Reading usually takes place offline.

Plotters

A **plotter** is an output device that is specifically designed to produce charts, drawings, maps, three-dimensional illustrations, and other forms of graphical hard copy. *Pen plotters* are the most widely used type of plotter. A pen plotter is very similar to a printer, with the primary difference between the two the fact that the plotter uses pens that create images by moving across the paper surface. Pen plotters are of two types: flatbed plotters and drum plotters.

A *flatbed plotter,* which looks like a drafting board with pens mounted on it, is shown in Figure 6-33. Watching this machine draw is a remarkable experience and it always attracts a crowd at a product demonstration. The plotter looks like a mechanical artist working in fast motion. As the plotter switches colors and begins new patterns, it is difficult to guess what it will do next. *Drum plotters,* which draw on paper rolled onto a drumlike mechanism, are also available. A drum plotter is shown in Figure 6-34.

In addition to pen plotters, *electrostatic plotters* are also frequently seen. These plotters are relatively fast but, generally, the output quality is not as high as that of a pen plotter.

Figure 6-33. A flatbed plotter. These devices can be as small as a typewriter or larger than a king-size bed.

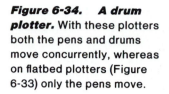

Figure 6-34.   A drum plotter. With these plotters both the pens and drums move concurrently, whereas on flatbed plotters (Figure 6-33) only the pens move.

Voice-Output Devices

For a number of years, computers have been able to communicate with users, after a fashion, by speaking to them. Upon dialing a phone number, one may hear, "We're sorry, the number you are trying to reach is no longer in service," or "The time is 6:15 . . . the downtown temperature is 75 degrees." The machines responsible for such messages, **voice-output devices,** convert digital data in storage into spoken messages. These messages are constructed, as needed, from a file of words that have been prerecorded.

Computerized voice output is also used at airline terminals to broadcast information about flight departures and arrivals, and in the securities business to quote the prices of stocks and bonds. Voice output has great potential in any service company where some employees do little else all day but provide balances and status reports.

One of the main limitations of this technology as it stands now is that the number of potential messages is quite small if the system must create them extemporaneously. Most voice-output devices have a vocabulary of the order of a few hundred words and a limited ability to combine words dynamically to form grammatical sentences. As a result these devices are most useful when their messages are short—a telephone number, a bank balance, a stock price, and so on.

Summary and Key Terms

Input and output devices make it possible for people and computers to communicate. **Input devices** convert data and programs into a form that is comprehensible to the CPU. **Output devices** convert computer-processed information into a form that is comprehensible to people.

Display devices are peripheral devices that contain a televisionlike viewing screen. Most display devices fall into one of two categories: monitors and display terminals. A **monitor** is an output device that consists only of the viewing screen, while a **display terminal** is an input/output communications workstation that usually consists of the screen (for output) and a keyboard (for input).

A key characteristic of any display device is *resolution,* or sharpness of the screen image. On many display devices, resolution is measured by the number of dots, or **pixels,** on the screen. A **bit-mapped** device is one where each individual pixel on the screen is capable of being controlled by the operator.

One common way to classify display devices is by whether they are monochrome or color. *Monochrome displays* output images using a single foreground color, whereas *color displays* often are capable of outputting images in eight or more colors.

Most display devices on the market today use a large picture-tube element, similar to those in standard TV sets. These devices are called **CRTs (cathode-ray tubes).** Recently slim-profile devices called **flat-panel displays** have also become available.

Another major way in which display terminals differ from one another is in degree of intelligence. *Intelligence* refers to the level of ability the machine has to do certain types of work. **Dumb terminals** have few operator conveniences to make work easy. **Intelligent terminals,** in contrast, enable operators to edit, manipulate, store, and process data locally. A major attraction of intelligent terminals is that they enable flexible movement of the **cursor** (a highlighted position on the screen indicating where the next character to be typed in by the operator will be placed).

Operators who are interacting with display devices may use, for input, a hardware device such as a **keyboard, light pen, joystick, trackball, mouse,** or **crosshair cursor.** Display devices that enable a finger to activate the screen are commonly called **touch screen devices.**

Printers, unlike display terminals, produce *hard-copy* output—output printed on paper.

Low-speed printers output a character at a time. Because of their relatively low cost, they are popular units for small computer systems. **High-speed printers,** which can output either a line or a page at a time, are more popular with larger computer systems.

All printers use either an impact or a nonimpact technology. In **impact printing** the paper or ribbon is struck by a hammer or pins to form characters. A **solid-font mechanism** is an impact device that produces a fully formed character such as those made by a typewriter. Most low-speed printers in use today employ a print head that's an **impact dot-matrix mechanism,** which constructs printed characters out of closely packed dots. In **nonimpact printing,** which typically uses dot-matrix characters, a variety of techniques are used to form printed images. The most popular nonimpact methods use *electrothermal, thermal-transfer, ink-jet, laser,* and *array* technologies.

The most common printers available for microcomputer systems are low-speed devices that use either letter-quality, impact dot-matrix, electrothermal, thermal-transfer, or ink-jet technologies. Only recently have relatively inexpensive laser devices become available for microcomputers.

Most of the printing on large computer systems is accomplished by high-speed printers. The most notable exception to this rule is the **teleprinter terminal,** which is a low-speed printer with a keyboard for small amounts of operator input. High-speed printers fall into two major categories: **line printers,** which produce a line of output at a time, and **page printers,** which produce a page of output at a time. Line printers must often be used with auxiliary devices such as *decollators* and *bursters.*

Punched-card equipment is still used in data processing work, although it is losing significance. Two important punched-card devices are the **keypunch machine** and the **card reader.**

Source data automation refers to technologies for collecting data in machine-readable form at the point at which the data originate. Among these technologies are optical character recognition (OCR), magnetic ink character recognition (MICR), digitizing, and voice input.

Optical character recognition (OCR) refers to a wide range of optical scanning procedures and equipment designed for machine recognition of marks, characters, and codes. *Optical marks* are frequently seen in test-taking situations, where students pencil in responses on special forms. Probably the best known use of *optical characters* is the **point-of-sale (POS)** systems used at checkout stations in stores. In many of these systems, the characters on the price tag are coded in a special font that is readable by both machines and humans. Some POS systems use *optical codes,* such as **bar codes.** A famous example of a bar code is the **universal product code (UPC),** which is used on the labels of most packaged supermarket goods.

Magnetic ink character recognition (MICR) is a technology confined almost exclusively to the banking industry. Such characters, preprinted on bank checks, enable the checks to be rapidly sorted, processed, and routed to the proper banks.

A **digitizer** is a device that converts a measurement into a digital value.

Voice-input devices permit computer systems to understand the spoken word. Voice-input technologies have tremendous work-saving potential, but have been slow to mature because of their relative complexity.

A number of special-purpose output devices exist for a variety of data processing applications. Among these are computer output microfilm (COM) equipment, plotters, and voice-output devices.

Computer output microfilm (COM) is a way of placing computer output on microfilm media such as *microfilm* reels or *microfiche* cards. COM can result in tremendous savings in paper cost, storage space, and handling.

A **plotter** is an output device that is specifically designed to produce graphic output such as charts, maps, and engineering drawings. A *flatbed plotter* uses a drawing surface that resembles a drafting table. A *drum plotter* draws on a cylindrically backed surface. In addition to these two types of *pen plotters,* there are also *electrostatic plotters,* which generally produce fast but lower-quality output.

Voice-output devices enable computer systems to compose intelligible spoken messages from digitally stored words and phrases.

Review Exercises

Fill-in Questions

1. Display devices may be classified into _____ and _____.

2. Resolution on a display screen is measured by the number of dots, or _____.

3. A highlighted position on a display screen that indicates where the next character to be typed in by the operator will be placed is called a(n) _____.

4. A display device that outputs images in a single foreground color is known as a(n) _____ display.

5. Multiple-strike dot-matrix printing is sometimes called _____ (NLQ) printing.

6. A(n) _____ print element consists of embossed spokes arranged in a circle.

7. A(n) _____ is a low-speed printer that includes a keyboard for operator input.

8. Two types of pen plotters are _____ and _____ plotters.

Matching Questions

Match each term with its description.

a. Decollator   d. UPC   g. Plotter
b. OCR   e. MICR   h. Digitizer
c. POS   f. COM

_____ **1.** Used almost exclusively by the banking industry.
_____ **2.** Refers to microfilmed output.
_____ **3.** A type of output device used to produce graphical images on paper, with pens.
_____ **4.** A collection of different technologies used for the optical recognition of marks, characters, and codes.
_____ **5.** A code that is prominent on the packaging of most supermarket goods.
_____ **6.** A machine that removes carbon interleaves from impact-printed paper.
_____ **7.** A device that converts a measurement into a digital value.
_____ **8.** Refers to the use of electronic cash registers, optical scanning devices, and so forth, in the retail industry.

Discussion Questions

1. List several types of input and output devices. State whether each device is used for input, output, or both.
2. Identify several ways in which display devices differ.
3. Name some hardware devices that are used in conjuction with display devices for entering data into the computer system.
4. In which major respects do printers differ?
5. What is source-data automation and why is it significant?
6. How does MICR differ from OCR?
7. What are the limitations of voice-input and voice-output devices?
8. What are the major advantages afforded by COM?

Chapter 7

Teleprocessing

Chapter Outline

Objectives

After completing this chapter you should be able to:

1. Identify the hardware and software components of a teleprocessing system.
2. Describe various types of teleprocessing media and explain how messages can be sent over them.
3. Identify some types of communications services and facilities that organizations may acquire.
4. Describe several types of teleprocessing networks.
5. Explain the conventions used by devices to communicate with each other.
6. Describe some of the strategies used to manage networks.

203

OVERVIEW

Teleprocessing is a marriage of two terms, *telecommunications* (communication over a distance) and *data processing.* When two or more machines in a computer system are transmitting data over a distance of more than a few feet, and the data are being processed somewhere in the system, teleprocessing is taking place.

Teleprocessing technologies have long been formally integrated into the routine operations of many organizations. Through teleprocessing, for example, a manager at company headquarters can instantly receive information on inventories from a warehouse in another part of town, and then transmit that information to a division office across the country or on the other side of the world.

The increasing availability of low-cost microcomputers and communications devices has made teleprocessing feasible today for both the home and office. Virtually any microcomputer user can now tie into remote information services for anything from stock prices to airline schedules. And businesspeople of all types are using their microcomputer systems to tie into larger, remote computers for the data they vitally need to perform their jobs.

In this chapter we'll talk about how data are sent over distances. We begin by describing the media, such as telephone wires or microwaves, that carry the data, as well as the nature of the signals in which the data are encoded. Next we'll discuss the various ways in which people or organizations can get the resources they need to teleprocess data. Finally, we'll look at several issues relating to the management of teleprocessing systems. These issues include determining the way communications networks are set up, and dealing with the problems that arise with interfacing numerous pieces of incompatible equipment in a network.

TELEPROCESSING IN ACTION

In the early days of computing, the computer and its support equipment were located, more or less, in the same room. As long as this arrangement was necessary, use of a computer was not very flexible, since people had to come to the computer to take advantage of it. Certain applications, such as computerized passenger-reservation systems for air and train travel, were impossible. However, as computer teleprocessing matured, convenient access to the computer through remote terminals became possible.

Take the case of a mail-order catalog firm. Figure 7-1 shows a teleprocessing network that links the firm's North Chicago headquarters and its South Chicago warehouse to a large computer. Such a configuration can be called a teleprocessing system because data processing is taking place and all the terminals, both at headquarters and at the warehouse, are in a

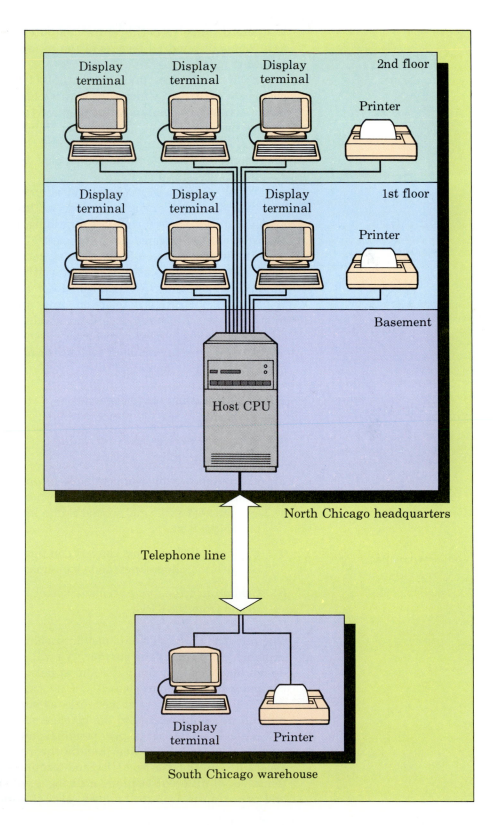

Figure 7-1. Teleprocessing system for a mail-order catalog firm.

location "distant" from the central computer. This distance may be as small as a couple of hundred feet, as in the headquarters, or as great as several thousand miles.

Each day the firm processes nearly 1000 phone and mail orders from its customers. At North Chicago headquarters, eight I/O devices (six display terminals and two printers) are configured to the computer. The computer's storage device contains, among other things, data on up-to-date product prices, the quantity of items in stock, and the firm's customers. Authorized salespeople and warehouse personnel may draw on any of these data in the course of processing an order.

When an order is received at headquarters, it is keyed on a display terminal by a salesperson and routed to the warehouse. Two printers are available at the headquarters site for billing, preparing out-of-stock notices to customers, and various other purposes.

At the warehouse a single display terminal is used by personnel to update stock counts as soon as products either are received from vendors or shipped to customers. All data sent to or received from this terminal are transmitted over ordinary telephone lines and processed by the headquarters computer. A printer is also available at the warehouse to capture customers' orders in hard-copy form.

A *teleprocessing network* such as the one shown in Figure 7-1 consists of the following elements:

1. A central computer, called the *host computer* (or *host*), handles the processing.

2. Peripheral devices, called *terminals,* send data to or receive data from the host computer.

3. The data are sent over *communications media.* In this case, ordinary phone lines carry the data between the remote warehouse peripherals and the host CPU, and special cables link the peripherals at headquarters to the host.

4. Devices called *modems* convert computer signals into a form compatible with the phone lines, and vice versa.

5. *Communications management devices* optimize the flow of messages to and from the CPU.

The role that these elements play in such a teleprocessing network will be explained throughout the chapter. We will also look both at networks that do not involve a host computer and at networks where the "terminals" are computer systems themselves.

Even in teleprocessing networks as simple as the one in Figure 7-1, difficult problems related to the management of remote devices can arise. For example, if several display terminals on the system are competing for service, how will the system handle the requests? This problem can be especially knotty if the host CPU and terminals have been manufactured by a number of different vendors, utilizing a variety of communication codes and data-transmission techniques. Also, if some of the terminals are used very sparingly, how can the teleprocessing system be set up to minimize line costs? These are a few of the problems that this chapter will address. Solutions to such teleprocessing problems are particularly important because communications costs often constitute a major data processing expense. For example, management analysis at General Motors has shown that in recent years 50 percent of that company's total data processing costs have been related to communications.

TELEPROCESSING MEDIA: PROVIDING THE CONNECTION

A simple teleprocessing system is shown in Figure 7-2. Two hardware units, distant from each other, transfer messages over some type of **communications medium.** The hardware units may be a terminal and a computer, two computers, or some other combination of two devices. The medium might be privately operated or public telephone lines, microwave, or some other alternative. When a message is transmitted, one of the hardware units is designated the *sender* and the other the *receiver*. There are several ways in which the message can be sent over the medium, as this section will demonstrate.

Types of Media

Communications media fall into one of two classes: physical lines and microwave signals.

PHYSICAL LINES.   Three types of physical lines are used in teleprocessing systems today: twisted-wire pairs, coaxial cable, and fiber optic cable. **Twisted-wire pairs,** in which strands of wire are twisted in pairs, is the technology that has been in use the longest. The telephone system, which carries most of the data transmitted in this country and abroad, still heavily consists of twisted-wire pairs. In some cases several thousand pairs may be placed in single cables, which might connect switching stations in a city. By contrast only a few pairs are needed to connect a home phone to the closest telephone pole. Generally each twisted-wire pair in a cable can accommodate a single phone call between two people or two machines. Since most of

Figure 7-2. A simple teleprocessing system. As complicated as teleprocessing systems may seem to the casual observer, they reduce simply to one device being able to communicate effectively with another.

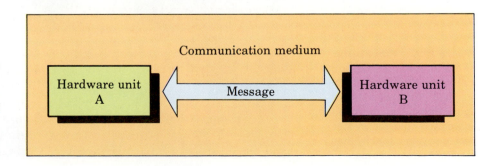

the phone system was set up many years ago to accommodate voice transmission, it is not the ideal medium for computer teleprocessing. Nonetheless the phone system is fast enough for many types of computer applications. And since twisted-wire pairs can be manufactured and installed at a very low cost, they are still a very common means of linking two points in a communications system.

Coaxial cable, the medium employed by cable television, was developed primarily because a phenomenon called crosstalk exists in twisted-wire pairs when transmission occurs at high speeds. Crosstalk results when a conversation taking place in one twisted-wire pair interferes with a conversation taking place in another pair. For example, on many phone lines you sometimes hear background conversations. With voice communication this problem isn't serious. However, crosstalk can inhibit the high-speed transmission required for television reception and some other types of sophisticated communication. Thus coaxial cable was developed to fill the need for a fast, relatively interference-free transmission medium. Coaxial cable is also used extensively by the phone companies, typically as a replacement for twisted-wire pairs in important links of the network.

One of the most promising developments in cable technology is fiber optics. An innovation whose potential is just beginning to be realized, **fiber optic cable,** shown in Figure 7-3, consists of thousands of clear glass fiber strands, each approximately the thickness of a human hair. Transmission is made possible by the transformation of data into light beams, which are sent through the cable by a laser device at incredibly fast speeds—of the order of billions of bits per second. Every hairlike fiber has the capacity to carry a few television stations, or, alternatively, a few thousand two-way voice conversations.

The principal advantages of fiber optics over wire media include speed, size, weight, resistance to tapping, and longevity. For example, it is not unusual for a fiber optic cable to have ten times the data-carrying capacity and one-twentieth the weight of a standard coaxial cable.

Figure 7-3. **Fiber optic cable strand.** Each approximately the thickness of a human hair, these strands are bound into cables that are far lighter and have far greater data-carrying capacity than standard coaxial cable.

MICROWAVE.   **Microwaves** are high-frequency radio signals. Sounds, letters, numbers, and video all can be converted to microwave impulses. Microwave transmission works by what is known as a *line-of-sight* principle. The transmission stations do not have to be within actual sight of each other, but they should have a relatively obstruction-free path. When one microwave station receives a message from another, it amplifies it and passes it on. Because of mountains and the curvature of the earth, microwave stations are often placed on tall buildings and mountaintops to ensure an obstacle-free transmission path.

Microwave signals can be sent in two ways: via terrestrial stations or by way of satellite. Both of these technologies can transmit data in large quantities at much higher rates of speed than twisted-wire pairs.

Terrestrial microwave stations, illustrated in Figure 7-4, must be no greater than 25 to 30 miles apart if they are to communicate with each other directly. This limitation arises because the moisture at the surface of

Figure 7-4.   Terrestrial microwave. (a) Terrestrial microwave transmission. (b) A microwave station.

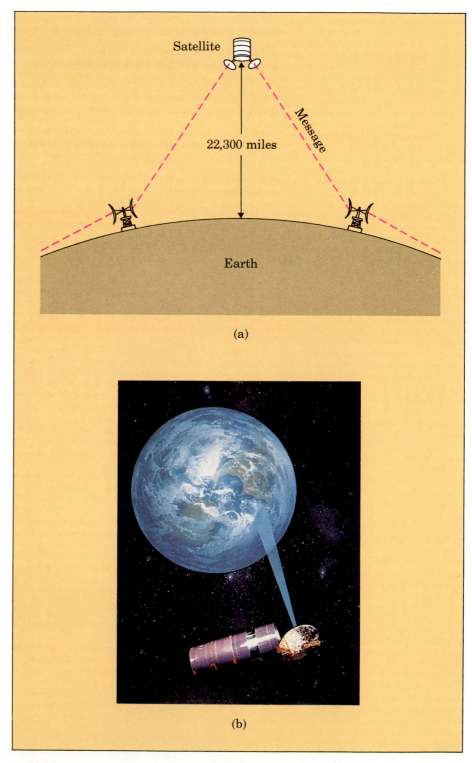

Figure 7-5. *Communications satellites.* (a) Satellite transmission. (b) A commercial satellite.

the earth causes interference, which impedes communication between stations. As you can imagine, it is quite impractical to build all the repeater stations needed to connect distant locations.

Communications satellites were developed to reduce the cost of long-distance transmission via terrestrial repeater stations, as well as to provide a cheaper and better overseas communications medium than undersea cable. Communications satellites, such as the ones shown in Figure 7-5, are usually placed into an orbit about 22,300 miles above the earth. Because they travel at the same speed as the earth rotates, they appear to remain stationary over a particular spot.

Media Speed

The speed of a communications medium, generally measured in terms of the number of bits that can be transmitted per second (**bits per second,** or **bps**), partly determines the uses to which it can be put. Media can be grouped by speed into three grades, or bandwidths. The speed of transmission is proportional to the width of the frequency band.

Narrowband transmission refers to a medium with a data-carrying capacity in the range of 45 to 150 bps. These rates are suitable only for very-low-speed operations such as telegraph and teletype communication.

Voice-grade transmission (300 to 9600 bps) represents a medium level of speed. This kind of transmission derives its name from the fact that spoken messages can be transmitted in this speed range. On regular telephone lines, the most common voice-grade line, speeds of 300, 1200, and 2400 bps are often used to transmit data. To realize higher speeds (up to 9600 bps), a "private" line must usually be obtained and *conditioned*. To condition a line, technicians place amplifiers at given intervals along the line to clean up the interference that accompanies the higher speeds.

Wideband transmission rates (19,200 to 500,000 or more bps) are possible only with coaxial and fiber optic cable, and microwave media.

Media Mode

Communications media can also be classified in terms of whether or not messages can be sent in two directions. In the vernacular of communications, transmission mode is said to be simplex, half duplex, or full duplex.

In **simplex transmission** data can be transmitted in a single, prespecified direction only. An example from everyday life is a doorbell—the signal can go only from the button to the chime. Although simplex lines are cheap, they are not very common for business teleprocessing. Teleprocessing with most peripheral equipment involves two-way communication. Even receive-only (RO) devices, such as printers, communicate an acknowledgment back to the sender device.

In **half-duplex transmission,** messages can be carried in either direction, but only one way at a time. The press-to-talk radio phones in police cars employ this mode of transmission. Only one person can talk at a time. Often the line between a terminal and its host CPU is half duplex. If the computer is transmitting to the terminal, or if it's working on a program, the operator cannot send new messages until the computer is finished.

Full-duplex transmission is like traffic on a busy two-way street. The flow moves in two directions at the same time. Full duplexing is ideal for hardware units that need to pass large amounts of data between themselves, as in computer-to-computer communication. Full-duplex channels are generally not needed for terminal-to-host links, because the response of the terminal operator is often dependent on the results sent back from the computer.

Media Signal

There are two possible ways to classify the signal sent along a medium: analog and digital.

The phone system, established many years ago to handle voice traffic, carries signals in an **analog** fashion—that is, by a *continuous* sine wave over a certain frequency range. The continuous wave reflects the myriad variations in the pitch of the human voice. Unfortunately data processing machines are **digital** devices. They are built to handle data coded into two *discrete* states; that is, as 0- and 1-bits. This difference between analog and digital states is illustrated in Figure 7-6.

THE USE OF MODEMS.   Because digital impulses can't be sent over analog phone lines, some means of translating each kind of signal into the other had to be developed. Conversion of signals from digital to continuous-wave form is called *modulation,* and translation from continuous waves back into digital impulses is termed *demodulation.* A single device called a **modem**

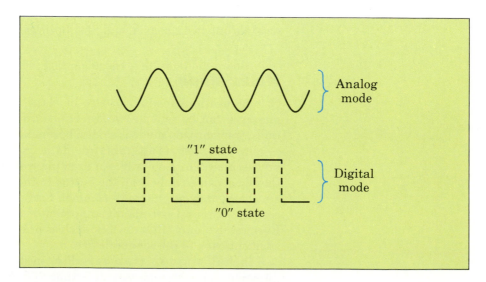

Figure 7-6.   Analog and digital transmission.

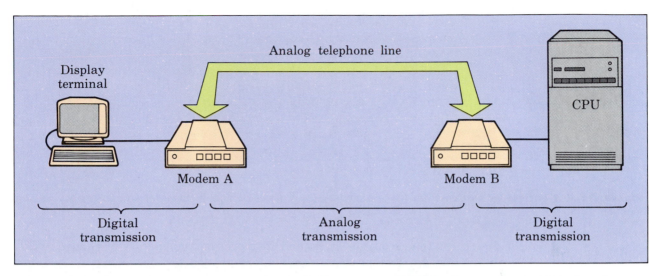

Figure 7-7. How modems work. An operator at a display terminal types in data that are encoded digitally and sent to modem A. Modem A converts the data to analog form and sends them over the phone lines to modem B. Modem B reconverts the data back to digital form and delivers them to the CPU. When the CPU transmits back to the terminal, these steps are reversed.

(coined from the words "*mod*ulation" and "*dem*odulation") takes care of both operations. As Figure 7-7 shows, when a terminal sends a remote CPU a message that must be carried over an analog line, a modem is needed at both the sending end (to convert from digital to analog) and the receiving end (to convert from analog to digital).

TYPES OF MODEMS.   Modems can be classified in a variety of ways. One way is by whether they are standalone or board units. *Standalone (external) modems* are hardware devices that are detached from the CPUs or terminals they serve. *Board (internal) modems,* which have recently become possible with advances in microcircuitry, are built onto plug-in boards that are inserted into an expansion slot inside the computer's system unit. Board modems have the advantage of requiring no desk space, but the disadvantage of using up one of the limited number of slots in the system unit.

Standalone modems are further classifiable into acoustic and direct-connect devices. *Acoustically coupled modems* have a cradle that holds the phone's headset. Users dial the telephone number of the computer system, and when they hear a high-pitched sound, they place the headset into the cradle to establish a connection between their terminals and the CPU. The coupler converts the digital signals of the terminal into audible tones, which the receiver of the phone picks up and sends in analog form to a modem at the other end of the line. There the analog signals are reconverted to digital form for processing by the computer.

Direct-connect modems, on the other hand, completely bypass the telephone headset, plugging directly into a wall phone outlet on one end and the computer on the other. Direct-connect modems offer faster transmis-

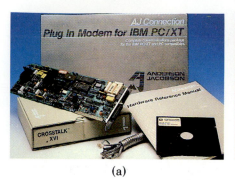
(a)

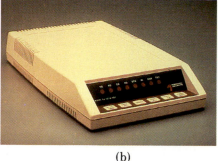
(b)

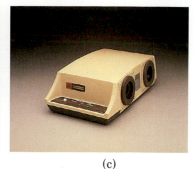
(c)

Figure 7-8. *A variety of modems.* (a) A board modem. (b) A direct-connect modem. (c) An acoustically coupled modem.

sion than acoustic devices and are now priced competitively enough so that they are dominating current standalone modem sales. Nonetheless, if you are a traveling salesperson making a call from a phone booth, where there is no wall outlet, only an acoustic device will put you in contact with the outside world.

MODEMS AND BPS RATES.   Common bps rates found on modems targeted to microcomputer users are 300, 1200, and 2400 bps. Often modems capable of higher speeds have independent circuitry to function at the lower rates as well. Acoustically coupled modems are especially vulnerable to outside interference and are usually limited to speeds of 300 bps or less. Figure 7-8 shows a variety of modems. The box on page 216 describes communications software that is often packaged with modems.

DIGITAL LINES.   Although physical lines have traditionally been analog, *digital lines* are also available. These lines can transmit data (including voice and video) faster and more accurately than their analog counterparts. And, of course, no modem is necessary. The public telephone network is still far from being all digital, but urban areas are rapidly moving in that direction

A summary of communications media and their properties is given in Figure 7-9.

ACQUIRING SERVICES AND FACILITIES

An organization that needs to teleprocess data generally has three choices for services and facilities: the common carriers, which maintain the public-access facilities; the communications media vendors, who provide facilities that may be leased or purchased for one's own use; and the communications services companies, which provide services beyond those offered by the common carrier. Some organizations may be able to build their own

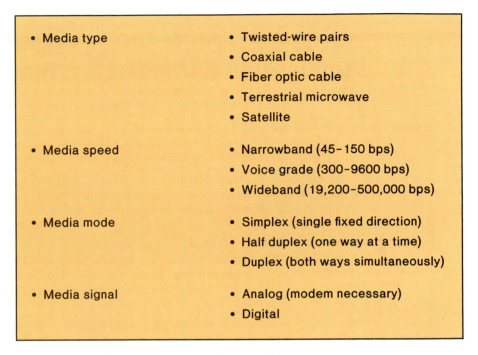

• Media type	• Twisted-wire pairs
	• Coaxial cable
	• Fiber optic cable
	• Terrestrial microwave
	• Satellite
• Media speed	• Narrowband (45–150 bps)
	• Voice grade (300–9600 bps)
	• Wideband (19,200–500,000 bps)
• Media mode	• Simplex (single fixed direction)
	• Half duplex (one way at a time)
	• Duplex (both ways simultaneously)
• Media signal	• Analog (modem necessary)
	• Digital

Figure 7-9. *Communications media at a glance.*

communications networks; however, this option is prohibitively expensive, except in rare instances.

Common Carriers

Common carriers are companies licensed by the government to provide communications services to the general public. The most prominent of these, of course, are the phone companies. Among the less-known common carriers are the *specialized carrier companies,* such as those that provide satellite transmission facilities.

SWITCHED LINES.   Because points in the public telephone system receive calls from different locations, the phone system is designed to route calls into a huge switching network. Remember the telephone operators in those old-time movies who switched plugs in and out of a big board, to connect people? Today's **switched lines** work in much the same way, except that most of the switching is automated rather than manual. Users of these lines can "dial up" computers from their terminals, and the calls are routed, or switched, through paths in the public phone network to the proper destinations.

Switched lines are attractive because a person can dial any computer that has a phone number and gain access to it. Also, using the public phone network is often inexpensive because, like the home phone, charges are

Communications Software for Your Microcomputer's Modem

SOME MODEMS ARE SMARTER THAN OTHERS

Modems, like computers, are hardware devices that use software to work. The programs used with modems are commonly referred to in the microcomputing world as *communications software.*

Communications software for a microcomputer can be acquired in a number of ways. For example, you often buy it when you buy a modem. Sometimes it's included in the price of the modem, and sometimes it's not. There is also some very good communications software—notably PC TALK III and MODEM7—that is available free (or for a voluntary donation) from computer bulletin boards.

Although products in the communications-software marketplace differ in terms of features, most of them enable you to do the following:

- Access information utilities such as CompuServe, The Source, and Dow Jones News/Retrieval Service
- Connect to electronic mail services
- Connect to computer bulletin boards (and possibly build your own)
- Exchange disk files with other microcomputers
- Turn your microcomputer into a terminal that can access a mainframe or minicomputer
- Establish remote access to your microcomputer

In addition, some packages will place and answer calls for you, interface with voice machines, provide security for your online files, and simplify a number of routine, phone-related tasks (such as accessing phone directories and keying in passwords to an information utility). And, naturally, packages differ in that some are much easier to use than others.

But even though you think it's great to have powerful communications features, you may not always want to use them. At 300 bps, for example, it may take a couple of hours to transmit the contents of a disk over the phone lines. If the phone connection is long distance, then, depending on the distance involved and the time of day, you may be paying as much as $30 or more. Alternatively, although it's not as elegant or fast, you can mail a diskette for less than a dollar.

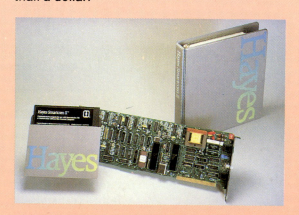

The popular Hayes 1200B (board modem) and its accompanying software.

Some of the communications software packages available are designed for particular modems. If you feel that you need communications capabilities, it's best to shop for the modem and software at the same time. If you already have a modem, then make sure that the features of the software package you like are supported by that modem. As with any other computer-related purchase, assess your needs carefully before buying.

based directly on the number and length of calls. Unfortunately switched lines can transmit data only at slow rates. As a result, they often are not practical for devices such as graphics display terminals, which require fast transmission speeds to communicate pictures. It is also possible to encounter annoying busy signals on switched lines, just as it is on a home phone.

Communications Media Vendors

A *communications media vendor* is a company that sells or leases media for private (as opposed to public) use. These media may consist of dedicated point-to-point lines, switched lines that are not available for public use, or perhaps networks composed of either or both types of these lines.

DEDICATED LINES. **Dedicated lines** (or *nonswitched lines*), which can be leased or purchased from a number of communications media vendors, are used to circumvent many of the problems inherent in public-access switching. Dedicated lines are used to provide an always available point-to-point connection between two devices. Thus you are placed in immediate contact with a given remote computer system every time you activate the "on" switch on the terminal. Additionally, because only the owner or lessee has access to the line, dedicated lines can be especially conditioned to transmit data at higher rates of speed. And you generally are not charged for every call you make on the line, but pay a flat rate.

Thus users of dedicated lines can transmit data quickly and in volume, at a fixed cost, with no threat of busy signals. However, they don't have the flexibility to dial up other computer systems. Figure 7-10 compares the advantages and disadvantages of switched and dedicated lines.

Type of Line	Advantages	Disadvantages
Switched	• Operator can choose calling destination • Inexpensive for low volume of work	• Slower speed • Possible to get busy signal • Expensive for high volume of work
Dedicated	• No busy signals • Higher speed supports more applications • Inexpensive for high volume of work	• No choice of calling destination • Expensive for low volume of work

Figure 7-10. Comparison of switched and dedicated lines.

PRIVATE BRANCH EXCHANGES (PBXs). The phone system consists of several switching stations that are, essentially, *public* branch exchanges. When a company leases or purchases a switching station for its own use, such a facility is known as a **private branch exchange (PBX).** Most PBXs are popularly referred to as "company switchboards"—you call a company's number and a private (company) operator routes you to the proper extension. But in the world of computers, many PBXs need to deal with machines calling other machines. Thus such PBXs are controlled by host computers that route machine-to-machine calls automatically and let the human operator deal with many of the interpersonal communications.

LOCAL NETWORKS. **Local networks** (sometimes called **local area networks,** or **LANs**) consist of privately owned or leased lines that connect terminals and computers in close proximity to each other—for example, in the same building or on the same college campus. An example of a local network is given in Figure 7-11. Note that the local network does not utilize a "visible" host computer (or switching station), as such. Instead "transparent" processors within the network itself manage the devices as they contend for network facilities. Local networks are expected to play a major role in office automation, which is discussed in Chapter 15.

Communications Services Companies

Communications services companies are firms that use the facilities of a common carrier in order to offer subscribers additional services on those facilities. These services—which might include data processing, information retrieval, electronic mail, and the like—are, in turn, sold to the public. Often, in using these services, you are billed by both the phone company (if long-distance charges are involved) and the communications services company.

One very common type of firm offering communications services is the so-called *time-sharing* company. A subscriber to one of these services can call the company's computer system and use whatever facilities are needed and available. The subscriber is then billed.

Another common type of services firm offers *information retrieval* capabilities to the public. Examples of such firms are CompuServe, Dow Jones News/Retrieval Service, and The Source. As a subscriber you have access to large banks of potentially interesting information, such as stock and security prices, baseball scores, news, airline schedules, hotel information, recipes, horoscopes, and journals over the phone lines. Many of these firms also offer "electronic mailboxes," so you can send confidential messages to friends or business associates who also subscribe to the same *electronic mail* service.

Once you've made phone contact with the services company, its software systems generally provide easy-to-use menus of available options, which let you choose from among their information or electronic mail offerings. After you have made a request from your keyboard, the information is sent over the phone lines to your display screen. Generally these companies bill at an hourly rate for the time you are hooked up to them.

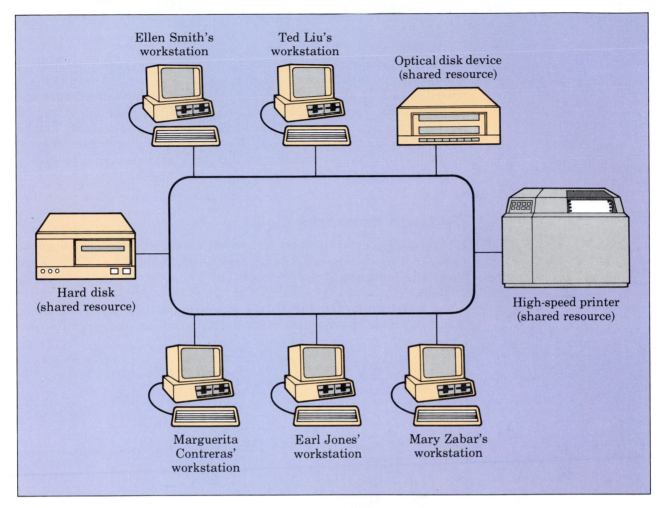

Figure 7-11. **A local network.** The surge in microcomputer usage has made local networking a particularly attractive solution to sharing resources.

There may also be an initial subscription fee and a charge for special services such as electronic mail.

Heavy users of communications services often have a hard disk and a "smart modem" (refer to box on page 216) that operates at a high transmission rate. Such a setup enables line charges to be minimized and information to be transmitted when you're away or asleep. Also, because different services companies may require different transmission rates, a faster modem (which has circuitry to deal with lower transmission rates as well) permits the most flexibility.

NETWORKS AND DISTRIBUTED DATA PROCESSING

So far we've looked at some concepts rather informally. It's now time to consider them more rigorously. Three such concepts are networks, terminals, and host computers. We'll also look at how these concepts tie into distributed data processing systems.

As we have seen, a *teleprocessing network* is composed primarily of computers and I/O devices (including storage devices), all of which are linked in various ways by communications media. A **host computer** is a computer that controls such a network. Any I/O device (or cluster of devices) that is not a host is, technically speaking, a **terminal.** Thus a terminal could conceivably consist of a display device/keyboard workstation (that is, a display terminal), a printer, a hard disk unit, or even a complete microcomputer system.

Types of Networks

Teleprocessing networks can be classified in terms of their topology, or "shape." Three common topologies are the star, bus, and ring. These are illustrated in Figures 7-12, 7-13, and 7-14.

STAR NETWORKS.   A **star network** often consists of a host computer that's directly connected to several display terminals in a point-to-point

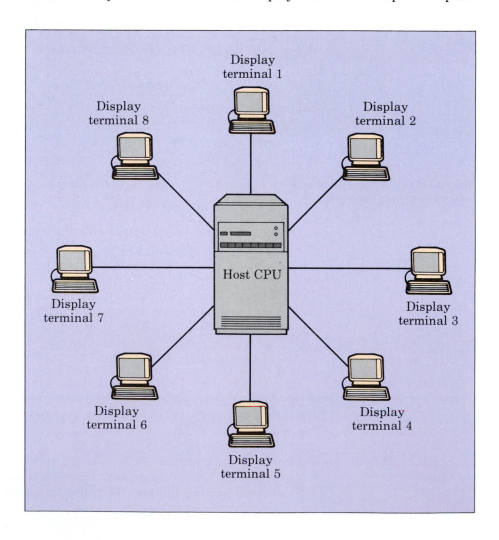

Figure 7-12.   A star network.

Figure 7-13.   A bus network.

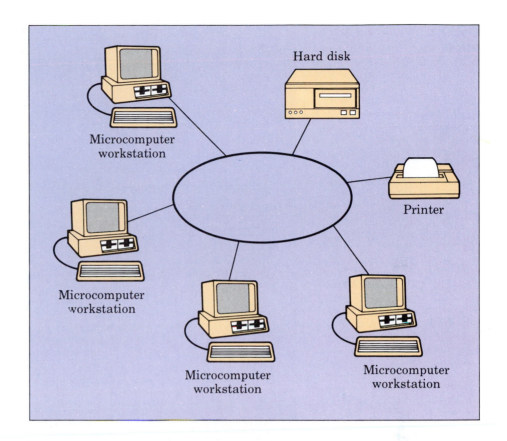

fashion. This configuration is illustrated in Figure 7-12. In a common variant of this pattern, several microcomputer systems (the terminals) are connected to a larger host computer that switches data and programs between them. The private branch exchange (PBX), which we discussed earlier, is also an example of a star network. The star network is especially well suited to an organization with several related plants (or divisions), because each plant may need access to common centralized files, yet also need to do its own local processing.

BUS NETWORKS.   A **bus network** works in much the same way as city buses in ground-based transportation systems. Moreover, the hardware devices are like "bus stops" and the data like "passengers." For example, the network in Figure 7-13 contains six terminal stations (bus stops) at which data (passengers) are "picked up" or "let off." Local networks, which we discussed earlier, typically utilize a bus topology. The loop circuit is commonly made of a high-capacity, high-speed coaxial cable, with inexpensive twisted-wire pairs dropped off at each of the terminal stations. A bus network contains no host computer.

RING NETWORKS.   A less common and more expensive alternative to both the star and bus is the **ring network,** in which a host computer is absent, and a number of computers or other devices are connected serially to one

Figure 7-14.   A ring network.

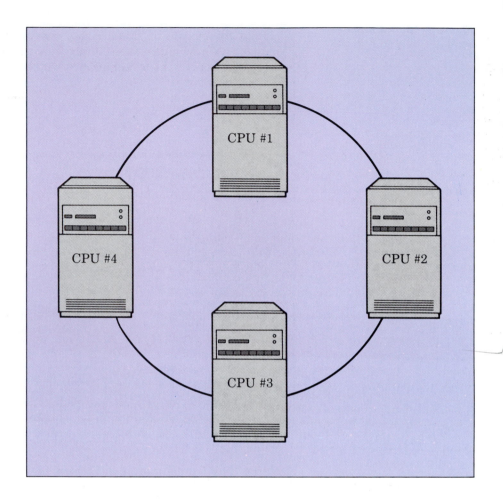

another. A ring network is shown in Figure 7-14. As you can see, a message sent from computer 1 to computer 3 must be routed through computer 2 or 4. A major advantage of this configuration is that terminals in the network are more likely to retain access to each other in case of failure. For example, if the communication path between two of the points breaks down, an alternative path is available.

Distributed Data Processing (DDP)

The term **distributed data processing (DDP)** often is used when referring to networks. Unfortunately DDP is one of those computer terms that can mean different things to different people. Here we'll define it as a system configuration in which work that conceivably could be done on a single computer is divided (that is, "distributed") among two or more computers. These computers may be at different sites. Thus an organization that spreads out (that is, distributes) its processing on two or more computers has a DDP system.

Ring and bus networks, since they generally involve several computers, are almost always DDP systems. Many star networks are also DDP systems as well, unless all of the terminals are "dumb" (in which case the host does all of the processing). Today, with so much of any organization's processing being offloaded to microcomputers and minicomputers, one is hard pressed to find a firm that isn't taking advantage of DDP in some way.

COMMUNICATIONS AMONG DEVICES

In the last few sections, we covered various types of communications media and networks. In this section we will discuss communications standards and special "communications management hardware" that is designed to optimize the flow of communications traffic.

How Do Devices "Talk" to Each Other?

As you learned earlier, hardware devices vary widely in a number of ways, including speed, the binary-based code used (see Chapter 4), and so on. These differences are crucial when devices must communicate with each other, since the sender and receiver need to interface at a common speed and common code to understand each other, just as you would need to interface with a foreigner through a common language. Unfortunately device communications are much more technically complicated than human communications, in that dozens of other factors must also match if the devices are to understand each other at all. In this section we'll consider some of these factors.

PARALLEL AND SERIAL TRANSMISSION.   Devices differ in the number of channels, or tracks, they use to transmit data. The bits used to represent characters may be transmitted in parallel or in serial. If, for example, all the 8 bits needed to convey the letter H are sent out at once in eight separate channels, **parallel transmission** is being used. On the other hand, if the bits representing H are sent out one at a time over a single channel, **serial transmission** is occurring. Figure 7-15 illustrates the difference between the two.

As you might guess from looking at Figure 7-15, parallel transmission is much faster than serial transmission. However, because it requires many more channels, parallel transmission is also more expensive. Thus parallel transmission is usually limited to short distances.

Computers and their remote terminals have traditionally communicated with each other in serial. A common serial interface, the RS-232C, was developed to standardize remote computer-to-terminal connections.

Computers, of course, need to communicate at high speeds with other nearby peripherals such as disk and tape units. Since the distance involved is short, parallel transmission is feasible. In microcomputer systems nearby

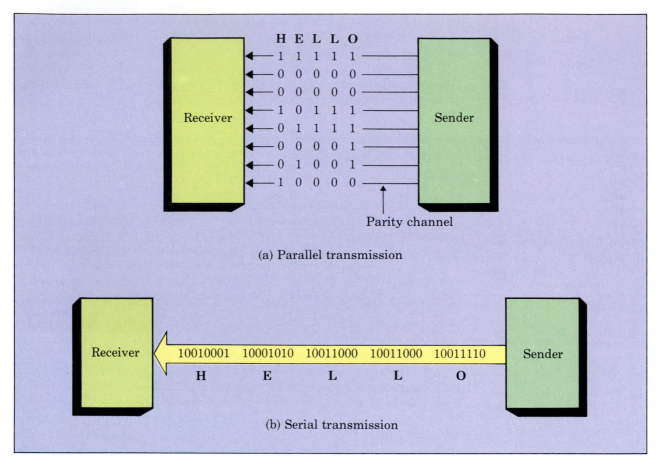

Figure 7-15. *Parallel and serial transmission.* Parallel transmission is faster, but the cabling it uses is more expensive. Consequently, devices in close proximity to each other often communicate in parallel, whereas those far apart communicate serially.

printers are often connected in parallel (see Figure 7-16) to the computer's system unit with a popular standard known as the *Centronics* interface.

ASYNCHRONOUS VERSUS SYNCHRONOUS TRANSMISSION. Serial transmission can be classified further in terms of whether it is asynchronous or synchronous. In **asynchronous transmission** one character at a time is transmitted over a line. When the operator strikes a key on the terminal, the byte representation of the character is sent up the line to the computer. Striking a second key sends a second character, and so forth. Since the amount of data that even the fastest typist can generate is very small compared with the quantity the line can accept, there is a lot of idle time on the line.

Synchronous transmission corrects for this deficiency by dispatching data in blocks of characters rather than one at a time. Each block might consist of thousands of characters. Because there is no idle time between the individual characters in the block, the utilization of the line is much more efficient. Synchronous transmission is made possible by a

Figure 7-16. *One end of a parallel printer cable.* Let the buyer beware that not all parallel printer cables are alike and, because they are expensive, many of them are very short. This limits the distance that printers can be placed from the system unit.

"buffer" in the terminal, a storage area large enough to hold a block of characters. As soon as the buffer is filled, all the characters in the buffer are sent up the line to the computer.

The differences between asynchronous and synchronous transmission are illustrated in Figure 7-17. As the figure indicates, in asynchronous transmission a start bit precedes each byte representation of a character, and a stop bit follows each character. When the sending machine has no character to send, it transmits a steady stream of stop bits. The machine at the receiving end "listens" to the line for the start bit. When it senses this bit, it counts off the regular bits used to represent the character. When it encounters the stop bit, it reverts to a "listen-to-the-line" state, waiting for the next start bit.

In synchronous transmission each block of characters is preceded by one or more "sync" (synchronous) bytes. The machine at the receiving end listens to the line for this byte. When it's sure it has sensed it (some systems use more than one sync byte to ensure this step), the receiving machine starts reading the characters in the block. Since it knows the speed of transmission and number of characters per block, it can interpret the message. After the block is finished, the receiving mechanism continues to "listen" to the line for the next sync byte. Synchronous transmission is commonly used for data speeds of 2400 bps and higher.

Many display terminals are designed for synchronous transmission, especially those that must transfer data at high speeds. Those that aren't so designed, and use asynchronous transmission, are sometimes called *ASCII*

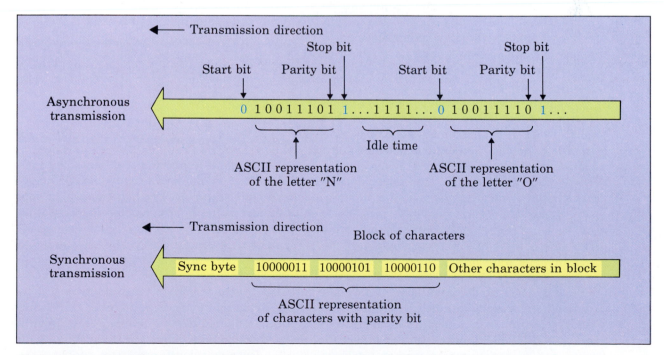

Figure 7-17. *Asynchronous and synchronous transmission.* Each byte is preceded by a start bit and followed by a stop bit in asynchronous transmission, whereas in synchronous transmission, large blocks of bytes are preceded by a sync byte.

terminals. Teleprinters, which are limited by the slow speed of the typing operation on input and by having a slow mechanical printing head for output, almost always use asynchronous transmission.

Synchronous equipment is more expensive and requires a synchronous modem. The greater initial cost, however, may be offset by greater speed and the lower costs resulting from more efficient use of transmission channels.

PROTOCOLS.   Because manufacturers have long produced devices that use a variety of transmission techniques, standards for the industry have

tomorrow

THE MICRO-TO-MAINFRAME CONNECTION

How Fast Will It Improve?

When many businesspeople purchased their first microcomputers they found them particularly useful for simple spreadsheet and file management tasks. As they became more familiar with their micros and software packages, processing needs often increased. In many cases there were a lot of valuable data and processing resources on the company's mainframe computer that could be useful. Was there some way to get the microcomputer to talk to the mainframe?

There is, but the solutions are less than perfect. Why? Most communications that microcomputer people are used to dealing with (that is, computer bulletin boards) are of the *asynchronous* type. They typically buy a standard 300-, 1200-, or 2400-bps asynchronous modem that sends data serially over the telephone lines. Many large mainframe computers, on the other hand, handle data *synchronously* at a rate of 9600 bps. To complicate matters, synchronous transmission uses a nesting of sophisticated *protocols* not found in asynchronous communications. Thus special software is required. And if these things didn't cause enough problems, most microcomputers work in ASCII. IBM mainframes, which account for over half of the business market for large computers, work in EBCDIC.

Because of these communications incompatibilities, the link between the micro and mainframe has been far from perfect. Two alternatives that have evolved for intermachine communication are terminal emulation software and special hardware units that are both a microcomputer system and a terminal.

The link has been far from perfect.

Terminal Emulation Software.   Terminal emulation software enables the microcomputer to function as a dumb (or relatively dumb) terminal to the host computer. Depending on the package used and the data management practices in effect, data may be "uploaded" to the mainframe or "downloaded" from it. Downloading is usually the most common, because both computer people and management personnel are very concerned about "homemade data" entering the mainframe system from a microcomputer station.

Data-download software enables the micro to accept files from the host computer

been a major problem. Everyone recognizes the need for standardizing transmission, but the form that such standards (called **protocols**) should take is still widely debated. Both national and international groups have tried to develop protocols. Among those popular today are SNA, SDLC, OSI, and Ethernet. Nevertheless a number of incompatible guidelines are now in effect. Adding to the problem is the fact that many of the protocols that do exist are still subject to change because major subsections of them have not yet been implemented. Today, and well into the future, you can expect to see many pieces of equipment that simply can't "talk to" one another directly.

and store them locally. In some cases, software is available to structure and format the data for use with a popular microcomputer package, such as Lotus Development Corporation's 1-2-3® or Ashton-Tate's dBaseIII®. Also available is information-extraction software, which provides the microcomputer user with reasonably fast query access to mainframe data. But because the microcomputer only *emulates* a terminal (that is, it uses *slow* software routines to compensate for what *fast* hardware can do), query access is normally not as fast as it would be on a regular terminal.

Microcomputer/Terminal. The other approach, acquiring a combination microcomputer/terminal, involves buying or leasing a piece of hardware such as the IBM 3270 PC (see photo). This machine has the features of both an IBM PC and an IBM 3270-type synchronous terminal, the device most popular on IBM mainframes. Buying such a hybrid device today is a relatively expensive approach to solving the micro-to-mainframe communications problem, however, because you are buying the circuitry to give you the best of both worlds. But tomorrow, as hardware prices continue to fall, cost will be less of a factor.

Combining the power of microcomputers and mainframes has only begun. But the barriers to overcome are intimidating. The future of micro-mainframe communications rests not

The IBM 3270 PC: A microcomputer and communications terminal in one package.

only on technology, but also on transmission standards and data management practices. With regard to technology, although advances in communications networks are taking place rapidly, the lion's share of attention has thus far focused on other areas—specifically, microcomputer-based local networks and conventional mainframe-terminal types of networks. As to transmission standards, vendors still disagree widely on protocols and it seems safe to believe that many machines and software packages still won't be able to talk to each other ten years down the road. And concerning data management, more effort must be expended on protecting mainframe data in a world of noncomputer professionals at microcomputer-based workstations.

Hardware for Managing Communications Traffic

Now that we've covered some of the basic elements of teleprocessing systems, let's explore some of the ways in which these systems have been made more efficient. There are a number of machines available to enhance the efficiency of telecommunications networks. The most notable of these *communications management devices* are controllers, multiplexers, concentrators, and front-end processors.

CONTROLLERS. **Controllers,** which are often specialized minicomputers, are devices that supervise communications traffic in a teleprocessing environment. Hence they relieve the host CPU of a considerable processing burden. In large data processing systems, most peripheral devices communicate directly with controllers, which manage the messages and communicate them to the CPU. When the CPU finishes processing the work, it sends it back to the controller, leaving it to the controller to route the outputs to the proper peripheral devices.

One type of controller, the terminal controller, specializes in coordinating the activities of a number of low-speed terminals. As shown in Figure 7-18, terminals, controllers, and the CPU may be connected in either a point-to-point (star) configuration or a multidrop (buslike) configuration. In a **point-to-point configuration,** each terminal is connected directly to the computer (Figure 7-18*a*) or its controller (Figure 7-18*b*). In a **multidrop configuration,** a number of terminals are attached to the same line, which connects with a controller (Figure 7-18*c*).

Controllers collect messages from the terminals connected to them, and pass them on to the CPU when appropriate. The CPU processes the messages and sends them back to the controllers for delivery to the terminals. Thus controllers free the CPU from the need to deal with, in some cases, as many as several hundred terminals.

Two major protocols used by controllers are polling and contention. Both can be illustrated with the terminal configuration shown in Figure 7-18*c*. There terminals are multidropped off a single line from each controller. When **contention** is used, each terminal "contends" for use of the line. If a terminal is unsuccessful in seizing the line, it gets a busy signal and must try again. The line might have enough capacity for a few terminals, but with contention, there is never enough line capacity to service all the dropped terminals at once.

With **polling** the controller polls the terminals in a round-robin fashion, asking each if there is a message to send. If there is, it's sent; if not, the next terminal on the controller's polling list is queried. In Figure 7-18*c* the terminals attached to the controller at the left may be polled in the order 1, 2, 3, 1, 2, 3, and so on. If one terminal is sending more often than the others, it can be polled more regularly. So if terminal 3 normally accounts for 50 percent of the activity, the polling sequence might be 3, 1, 3, 2, 3, 1, 3, 2, and so on.

MULTIPLEXERS. Communications lines almost always have far greater capacity than a single terminal can use. Many terminals can work

Figure 7-18. Terminal controllers. The computer in A has no controllers and must manage nine different terminals. In B and C controllers coordinate clusters of three terminals. Because messages can be collected before they are sent, the CPU is relieved of the burden of communicating directly with the terminals.

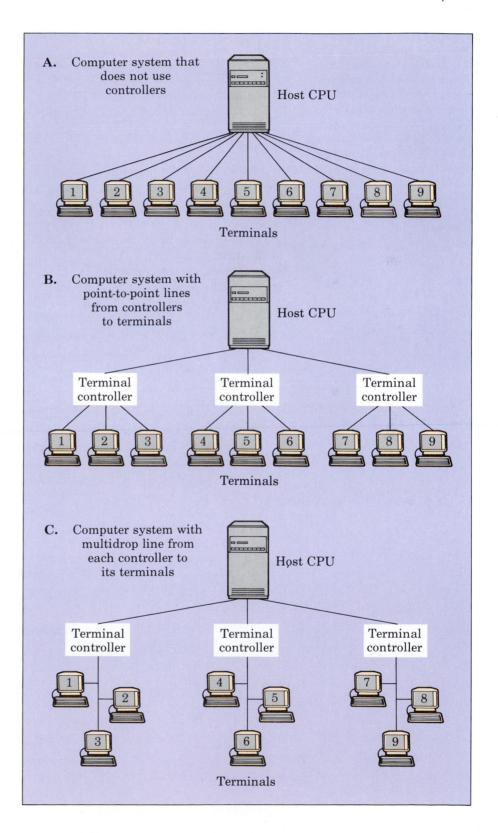

A. Computer system that does not use controllers

Host CPU

Terminals

B. Computer system with point-to-point lines from controllers to terminals

Host CPU

Terminal controller   Terminal controller   Terminal controller

Terminals

C. Computer system with multidrop line from each controller to its terminals

Host CPU

Terminal controller   Terminal controller   Terminal controller

Terminals

Figure 7-19. A system with two multiplexers. Assume that terminals 1, 2, and 4 are sending a continuous stream of characters, whereas terminal 3 is sending nothing. The messages are intertwined (multiplexed) at multiplexer A, sent over the high-speed line, and then separated (demultiplexed) at B. When the CPU transmits to the terminals, these steps are reversed.

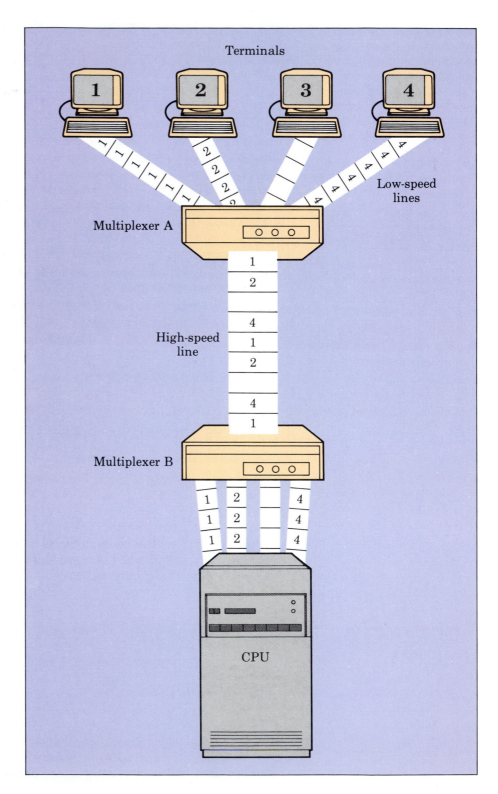

adequately at speeds of 300 bps, and voice-grade lines can transmit up to 9600 bps. Since communications lines are expensive, it is desirable for several low-speed devices to share the same line. A device called a **multiplexer** makes such line sharing possible.

Figure 7-19 illustrates the use of two multiplexers servicing several terminals and a host CPU. The first *multiplexes,* or combines, the data from low-speed lines into a high-speed line. The second unit *demultiplexes* the incoming character stream, so that the CPU appears to get the messages from the terminals individually. The device shown in the figure, known as a *time-division multiplexer,* provides a time slice on the high-speed line for each terminal, whether the terminal is active or not. A more sophisticated class of devices, called *statistical multiplexers,* allocates more time slices to busy terminals than to less active ones.

CONCENTRATORS.   A **concentrator** is a hardware device that combines control and multiplexing functions, as well as other things. Commonly it is a minicomputer that provides a store-and-forward capability. Thus messages from slow devices such as asynchronous terminals can be stored at the concentrator until enough characters are collected to make forwarding to another device worthwhile.

In airline passenger-reservations systems, concentrators placed at key sites, such as Boston, New York, Los Angeles, and other transportation centers, allow many agents to share communications lines economically. Messages initiated by agents are sent to the concentrator, stored, multiplexed with messages from other agents, and transmitted at very high speed over long-distance lines to a central processing site. Use of the long-distance line in such a fashion minimizes communications costs.

FRONT-END PROCESSORS.   A **front-end processor** is the most sophisticated type of communications management device. Generally it is a programmable minicomputer located at the site of the host CPU. It can perform all the communications functions of a concentrator, as well as relieve the host of routine computational burdens. For example, a front-end processor can check for valid user account numbers and validate or change the format of incoming data.

Summary and Key Terms

A **teleprocessing** system is one in which data processing is taking place and the data are being transmitted over a distance of more than a few feet.

Messages sent in a teleprocessing system are communicated over some type of **communications medium.** Physical lines, such as **twisted-wire pairs, coaxial cable,** and **fiber optic cable,** constitute one major class of media. Messages are also commonly sent through the air, in the form of **microwave** signals. **Terrestrial microwave stations** are used to accommodate land-based microwaves. **Communications satellites** are used to reduce the cost of long-distance transmission via terrestrial microwave stations and to provide better overseas communications.

The *speed* of a data-communications medium is measured in **bits per second (bps).** The slowest rates of speed are referred to as **narrowband transmission.** Medium-speed lines, which are the type commonly found in the public phone network, are capable of **voice-grade transmission.** The highest rates of speed, referred to as **wideband transmission,** are possible only with coaxial cable, fiber optic cable, and microwaves.

Communications media can be either in the simplex, half-duplex, or full-duplex *mode.* In **simplex transmission** messages can only be sent in a single direction (for example, a doorbell). In **half-duplex transmission,** messages can be sent both ways but not simultaneously (for example, press-to-talk phones). **Full-duplex transmission** permits transmission in two directions simultaneously (for example, a busy two-way street).

Signals sent along a phone line travel in an **analog** fashion, as continuous waves. Computers and their support equipment, however, are **digital** devices that handle data coded into two discrete states—0s and 1s. For two or more digital devices to communicate with each other over the analog phone lines, a device called a **modem** must be placed between each piece of equipment and the phone lines. Modems perform digital-to-analog and analog-to-digital conversion.

Modems can be classified in a variety of ways. *Standalone (external) modems* are hardware devices that are detached from the CPUs or terminals they serve. *Board (internal) modems* are built into plug-in boards that are inserted into an expansion slot inside the computer's system unit. Standalone modems are further classifiable into *acoustically coupled modems* and *direct-connect modems.* Modems can be bypassed when *digital lines* are used to interconnect transmitting devices.

Common carriers are companies licensed by the government to provide communications services to the public. Carriers generally provide access to the **switched lines** of the public telephone system to subscribers.

A *communications media vendor* is a company that sells or leases media for private (as opposed to public) use. These media may consist of **dedicated lines** or switched lines. A switching station that is not intended for public use is often called a **private branch exchange (PBX).** Privately owned or leased lines that connect terminals and computers that are in close proximity to each other, without a central switching device, are called **local networks** or **local area networks (LANs).**

Communications services companies are firms that use the facilities of a common carrier in order to offer subscribers additional services on those facilities. Examples are firms that provide time-sharing, information retrieval, and electronic mail services to the public.

A *teleprocessing network* is composed primarily of computers and I/O devices, all of which are linked in various ways by communications media. A **host computer** is a computer that controls such a network. An I/O device (or cluster of devices) not considered a host is, technically speaking, a **terminal.** Three common types of teleprocessing networks are **star networks, bus networks,** and **ring networks.** Teleprocessing networks are considered **distributed data processing (DDP)** systems when two or more computers perform work that conceivably could be done on one computer.

Terminals and computers communicate with each other in a variety of ways. To exchange data two machines must use the same communications codes. Transmission between compatible machines is either in **parallel** or in **serial, synchronous** or **asynchronous.** Factors that determine which of these types of transmission are used include the speed at which data must be transferred between the machines and the capabilities of both the machines and communications media. Because there are so many ways to transmit data, many industry groups have tried to develop sets of standards (called **protocols**). Nonetheless a number of incompatible guidelines are in effect.

Communications management devices enhance the efficiency of teleprocessing traffic. Common devices are controllers, multiplexers, concentrators, and front-end processors.

Controllers are machines that supervise communications traffic between the CPU and terminals. Terminals can be hooked up to a controller or CPU in either a **point-to-point configuration** (one line from each terminal to the controller or CPU) or **multidrop configuration** (a single line sent out from the controller to service a cluster of terminals). Terminals must either compete with each other for service, a process called **contention,** or they are polled in an orderly (noncompeting) fashion, a process called **polling.**

Multiplexers are devices that enable several low-speed devices to share a high-speed line. **Concentrators** are machines that perform the functions of both the controller and the multiplexer, among other things. A **front-end processor** is the most sophisticated communications management device—it can perform the concentrator's function as well as some of the tasks normally done by the computer.

Review Exercises

Fill-in Questions

1. The telephone system, which carries most of the data transmitted in teleprocessing systems, consists predominantly of _____.

2. _____, the medium employed by cable television, was developed primarily because a phenomenon called "crosstalk" exists with lower-grade wire at high speeds.

3. In contrast to the continuous waves used to represent analog signals over phone lines, computers generate _____ signals.

4. _____ refers to the medium that involves laser-generated light waves sent over transparent, hair-thin strands.

5. Conversion from analog to digital and digital to analog is performed by a(n) _____.

6. _____ transmission involves sending data along a communications line in blocks of several characters at a time.

7. _____ are companies licensed by the government to provide communications services to the public.

8. _____ transmission is a type of serial transmission in which each character is preceded by a "start" bit and followed by a "stop" bit.

9. A non-switched line is frequently called a _____ line.

10. A PBX is an example of a _____ network topology.

Matching Questions

Match each term with its description.

a. Front-end processor   d. Multiplexer
b. External modem   e. Controller
c. Internal modem   f. Protocol

_____ 1. A device that combines several low-speed lines into a high-speed line.

_____ 2. A hardware device that is often used to help the CPU manage traffic from terminals.

_____ 3. An example is a device that contains a cradle to hold the headset part of a phone.

_____ 4. The most sophisticated type of communications management device.

_____ 5. Built into a plug-in board that fits into an expansion slot in a microcomputer's system unit.

_____ 6. A standard used to make communications devices more compatible.

Discussion Questions

1. What is teleprocessing?

2. Name some types of communications media and explain how they differ.

3. What are the differences among simplex, half-duplex, and full-duplex transmission?
4. Identify some alternatives for acquiring network facilities.
5. What is the difference between a local network and a PBX?
6. What is meant by distributed data processing?
7. How do parallel and serial communications differ?
8. Identify the different strategies used by terminal controllers to manage terminals.

Module C

SOFTWARE

So far you've read a great deal about the hardware parts of a computer system—the CPU, storage devices, input and output equipment, and communications devices. But hardware by itself cannot process data any more than the various instruments of an orchestra can play a symphony without musicians, a conductor, and a musical score. Without *software* a computer system would be interesting to look at, perhaps, but essentially useless.

As mentioned earlier, the term software often includes programs, manuals, and processing procedures. Alternatively, software may be thought of as the collection of all instructions that enable data to be processsed on computer systems. Programs are the kind of software of most interest to us here. Without programs the computer is just a useless hunk of metal. Because programs are so important, the terms *software* and *programs* are often used interchangeably in practice.

Computer programs fall into two general categories—systems programs and applications programs. The former are programs that assist the running of other programs. These include the operating system, language translators, and utility programs. Applications software, in contrast, consists of programs that perform the processing tasks that directly produce the information users need in their jobs. Among these are programs for payroll, transaction processing, billing, inventory control, managment reports, and word processing—as well as thousands of other tasks.

Systems software is discussed in Chapter 8. Applications software development and the programming languages that are used to code these applications are discussed in Chapters 9 to 11. Productivity software packages—such as word processing, spreadsheet, and data management programs—are the subject of Chapters 12 and 13.

Chapter 8

Systems Software

Chapter Outline

OVERVIEW
THE ROLE OF SYSTEMS SOFTWARE
THE OPERATING SYSTEM
    Functions of the Operating System
    Interleaved Processing Techniques
LANGUAGE TRANSLATORS
UTILITY PROGRAMS

Objectives

After completing this chapter you should be able to:

1. Describe the role of systems software.
2. Explain the activities carried out by an operating system.
3. Describe several ways computer systems interleave operations to process data more efficiently.
4. Explain the role of a language translator and describe several types of language translators.
5. Explain the role of a utility program and describe several types of utility programs.

OVERVIEW

Systems software consists of programs that coordinate the various parts of the computer system to make it run rapidly and efficiently. The activities carried on by systems programs are quite diverse.

On most microcomputers these programs format disks so they can be used by your hardware; they copy program or data files from one disk to another; and they systematically store any programs or data you enter into your computer system. On larger computers, systems programs perform most of the tasks their microcomputer counterparts do, and many more as well. Because larger computers will generally serve many people at the same time, their systems software must be sophisticated enough to be able to schedule the many jobs awaiting processing and keep track of all of the people using the computer.

In this chapter we'll first look closely at the role of systems software. Then we'll turn to the *operating system,* the piece of systems software that controls computer system operations by assigning and scheduling resources as well as keeping track of user activities. Here we'll look at some of the features you're likely to find on operating systems that are used on small computers and on large ones. We will conclude the chapter with a discussion of *language translators* and *utility programs,* which perform other vital services for users and programmers.

THE ROLE OF SYSTEMS SOFTWARE

The role of **systems software** is basically to act as a mediator between applications programs and the hardware of the computer system. Systems software interprets the requirements of every incoming program and makes available whatever hardware, software, and data resources are needed to produce the desired results.

Most users aren't aware of what systems software is doing for them. On microcomputer systems, for example, saving a program onto disk requires systems software to look for adequate space on the disk, write the program onto "addresses" of this space, and update a directory indicating the addresses where the program is located. On larger computer systems, when you log on, you may not realize that a system program is put to work checking the validity of your ID number. And although it may seem to you, as you type at your terminal, that the computer system is responding to your commands only, it actually may be dealing with dozens of other users at almost the same time. It is systems software that makes this illusion possible.

THE OPERATING SYSTEM

Before the 1960s, human operators ran computers manually to a large extent. For each incoming data processing job, the operator had to reset by hand a number of circuits on the computer. In fact every role of the computer system—input, output, processing, and storage—required substantial operator supervision and intervention.

On these early computers, jobs could be processed only in a serial fashion, one program at a time. Because they could only handle programs serially, these computers sat idle for long periods of time while the operators took care of manual procedures between jobs.

The development of operating systems greatly improved the efficiency of computers. An **operating system** is a collection of programs that manage the activities of the computer system. Operating systems do away with much of the manual work formerly required to process programs. Many of today's operating systems enable the processing of several jobs concurrently, and also permit the computer to be left completely unattended while programs are running.

The primary chores of the operating system are management and control. It makes sure each valid, incoming program is processed in an orderly fashion and that the computer system's resources are made available to run the programs optimally. To help you understand the role of the operating system, we can compare its activities to those of a receptionist working in the lobby of a large office.

The main duties of the receptionist are to screen visitors and direct them to the right people. After visitors have identified themselves satisfactorily, the receptionist finds out what they want. If, for example, a visitor wished to obtain information for a magazine story, the receptionist might direct that visitor to a public relations person on the fifth floor. If a call revealed that the person were available, the visitor would be routed upstairs. All visitors must sign a logbook at the reception desk before they enter the offices and as they leave.

Operating systems do many of the same kinds of things. For example, on large computer systems, they check to see that people trying to gain access to the system are authorized users. When a user's identification number is found to be valid, he or she is signed in (or "logged on"). Then the operating system determines which resources of the computer system will be needed to do the user's job, and automatically assigns these resources to the work request if and when they become available.

Generally the user will need to tap a number of the system's resources. A typical job might need the number-crunching power of the CPU, a language translator that understands how to interpret the programming language commands that the user types in, primary memory to store intermediate results, secondary memory for storing data and programs, and a printer for output. It is the operating system that makes all these facilities available. Finally, when the user leaves the computer system, he or she is

Operating System	Description
PC-DOS	The operating system most commonly used on the IBM PC
MS-DOS	The operating system most commonly used on computers that function like the IBM PC
Apple DOS, Apple ProDOS	Operating systems used on the Apple II series of computers
UNIX	A multiuser, multitasking operating system used with minicomputers and powerful microcomputers
Xenix, Venix	Two UNIX-like operating systems
CP/M	An operating system popular with 8-bit microcomputers
TRS-DOS	The operating system commonly used with Tandy's TRS-80 series of microcomputers
AmigaDos	The operating system of the Commodore Amiga
p-System	An operating system that is sometimes used with Pascal applications programs
MVS, OS/VS, VM	Operating systems used with IBM mainframes
GCOS	An operating system available for Honeywell mainframes
VAX/VMS	An operating system available for DEC's VAX series of minicomputers
AOS/VS	An operating system available for Data General minicomputers

Figure 8-1. Some popular operating systems.
Each operating system is targeted to one or more specific types of computers. Operating systems can differ substantially with respect to ease of use, speed, number of features available, portability, and cost.

automatically logged off. In effect the operating system is the go-between, meshing the user's application program with the resources of the system.

Because of the central role of the operating system in managing the activities of the entire computer system, it's considered by many to be the most critical piece of software imaginable. Without an operating system, none of the other programs can run.

There is a wide selection of operating systems available in the marketplace (see Figure 8-1). Just as you would expect the executives who manage and control busy corporations to differ in many important respects, so do operating systems differ. For example, some operating systems are designed for only one brand of computer, whereas others are general enough to work on several brands. Other important differences concern ease of use, speed, number of features available, portability, and cost. Often these criteria conflict—for example, an operating system that's designed to be easy to use generally isn't fast. And, as you might expect, a system that's packaged with an assortment of powerful features isn't likely to be cheap.

Functions of the Operating System

Now that you have a general idea of what operating systems do, we can discuss their functions in greater detail. As we examine these functions, keep in mind that not all of them may apply to the operating system that you are using on your computer. For example, consider the difference between operating systems on large computers and those on small systems. Large computers— such as mainframes, minicomputers, and top-of-the-line microcomputers—require powerful, sophisticated operating systems. Because these machines normally have several people logged on at the same time (through terminals), their operating systems must be able to balance the needs of these people and their jobs concurrently. Many microcomputers have operating systems that permit only one user on the computer at a time, working on only one program. Thus features relating to an environment with several users and several concurrent programs don't apply.

ASSIGNMENT OF SYSTEM RESOURCES.   When most computers are first activated, a program called the **supervisor,** a major component of the operating system, is also activated. On some systems this program may be referred to as the *monitor,* the *kernel,* or even something else. The supervisor will always be in primary memory when the computer is on. On many computers other programs in the operating system are brought into primary memory from secondary storage only as they are needed. The supervisor has the ability to mobilize these other programs to perform system tasks for applications programs.

Once the supervisor activates any other program in the operating system, the supervisor cedes control to that program until its role is complete. On completion control returns to the supervisor, which may call up other systems programs required by the job. The supervisor operates somewhat like a master of ceremonies, introducing the next speaker on the program after each previous one has finished his or her talk.

In addition to the supervisor, a number of other programs in the operating system have a hand in determining what parts of the computer system will be mobilized for any given job. One of these is the **command-language translator.** This program reads instructions to the operating system written by the user or programmer. These instructions, coded in a **command language** (sometimes referred to as a *job-control language,* or *JCL*), permit users and programmers to specify instructions for retrieving, saving, deleting, copying, or moving files; what I/O devices are to be used; which language the user or programmer is employing; any customized requests for output format; and any other special processing needs of the applications program. The command language, in effect, gives the user a channel for communicating directly with the operating system.

In the absence of special command language instructions from the user, the operating system makes some standard assumptions about how things are to be done. These assumptions are called **defaults.** Often you can override the defaults by typing in your own commands. Thus, if the default on output is 24-line screen images delivered to the display, and you want hard-copy output from the printer—say, five copies at fifty lines per page—you may be able to override the default by entering a command such as

```
PRINTER, LINES = 50, COPIES = 5
```

Operating systems can differ significantly in how command language instructions are invoked—to delete a file, for instance. With operating systems such as MS-DOS and PC-DOS, which are used on the IBM PC and similar computers, you would type in a command such as

ERASE FRED

to delete a file named FRED. On computers such as the Apple Macintosh, **icons**—which are geometric symbols that represent operations—are used in conjunction with a pointing device called a mouse to carry out such operations. To delete FRED you would use the *mouse* to point to a file-folder-shaped icon labeled FRED, and then to the waste-basket-shaped icon to activate the delete operation.

Figure 8-2 shows some functions that are often performed through a command language. Keep in mind that not every command language is capable of carrying out all of these functions. In general the smaller the computer, the less powerful are the associated operating system and its command language. Figure 8-3 shows some commands that you'll find helpful if you're using PC- or MS-DOS. Figure 8-4 shows an icon-oriented command screen popularized by the Apple Macintosh and used with many other microcomputers.

Besides enabling you to do things through a command language, operating systems often make other types of assignments that are tranpar-

USES OF COMMAND LANGUAGES

- Identifying the names of users and the users' account numbers.

- Retrieving, saving, deleting, moving, copying, or renaming files.

- Declaring any unusual requirements that exceed the standard allowances of the computer center—for example, any extraordinarily large storage, CPU time, or printed output needs.

- Identifying the software package, programming language, or files to be used.

- Identifying the organization or access methods to be used on the files.

- Specifying special instructions for output—for example, the input/output device used, the number of copies of output desired, and any special printing fonts that are needed.

- Stating directions to operate a device in a certain way; for example, should a display device have 40, 80, or 132 characters per line?

- Assigning secret passwords to data files or programs.

Figure 8-2. **Some functions of command languages.**

Command	Implementation
Formatting a disk in the A drive	FORMAT
Formatting a disk in the B drive	FORMAT B:
Copying the contents of a disk in the A drive to a disk in the B drive	DISKCOPY A: B:
Copying the contents of a file named FRED from a disk in the A drive to a disk in the B drive	COPY FRED B:
Deleting a file named FRED from a disk in the A drive	ERASE FRED
Deleting a file named FRED from a disk in the B drive	ERASE B:FRED
Invoking BASIC	BASIC
Checking the contents of a disk in the A drive	DIR
Checking the contents of a disk in the B drive	DIR B:

Figure 8-3. How various commands are implemented in PC-DOS and MS-DOS. The given commands assume a two-disk system and working from the A drive.

Figure 8-4. The icon-oriented command screen of the Apple Macintosh. *Icons* (on the left and bottom borders of this screen), *pull down menus* of choices (which are selected on the top of the screen and "pulled down" over the image on the display), and *mouse* pointing have made the Mac both a pioneer and a pacesetter in easy-to-use operator interfaces.

ent to most people. At any time, for example, large computers are likely to be processing a number of programs concurrently, each with its own needs for tape or disk devices, storage requirements, and so on. It is the operating system that keeps track of which facilities in the system are being used and which are free for assignment to new programs. Also, because space in main memory is at a premium, the operating system must allocate shares of it to the various programs, some of which may be very large.

SCHEDULING OF RESOURCES AND JOBS.   Closely related to the process of assigning system resources to a job is that of scheduling resources and jobs. The operating system helps decide not only *what* resources to use (assignment), but also *when* to use them (scheduling). This task can become extremely complicated when the system must handle many jobs at once.

Scheduling programs in the operating system determine the order in which jobs are processed. A job's place in line is not necessarily on a first-come, first-served basis. Some users may have higher priority than others, the devices needed to process the next job in line may not be free, or other factors may affect the order of processing.

The operating system also schedules the operation of parts of the computer system so that they work on different portions of different jobs at the same time. Because input and output devices work much more slowly than the CPU itself, millions of calculations may be performed for several programs while the contents of a single program are printed or displayed. Using a number of techniques, the operating system juggles the various jobs to be done so as to employ system devices as efficiently as possible. Later in the chapter, we'll discuss some of these methods of processing a number of jobs at, more or less, the same time. These procedures are known collectively as *interleaved processing techniques.*

MONITORING ACTIVITIES.   A third general function of operating systems is monitoring—keeping track of activities in the computer system while processing is under way. The operating system terminates programs that contain errors or exceed either their maximum running time or storage allocations. It also sends an appropriate message to the user or operator. Similarly, if any abnormalities arise in I/O devices or elsewhere in the system, the operating system sends a message to the user's or computer operator's terminal.

Bookkeeping and security are also among the monitoring tasks of the operating system. Records may be kept of log-on and log-off times, the running time of programs, a list of programs that each user has run, as well as other information. In some environments, these records enable the organization to bill users. The operating system also can protect the system against unauthorized access by checking the validity of users' ID numbers and reporting attempts to breach the security of the system.

In the following section, we will examine some of the assignment and scheduling techniques that computers employ to handle a large number of jobs at the same time.

Interleaved Processing Techniques

Sophisticated computers often take advantage of interleaved processing techniques such as multiprogramming, multitasking, time-sharing, virtual storage, and multiprocessing to operate more efficiently. These operating system features enable computers to process many programs at almost the same time and consequently to increase the number of jobs that the system can handle in any period of time.

MULTIPROGRAMMING. **Multiprogramming** is somewhat similar to the operation of a busy dentist's office. The dentist *concurrently* attends to several patients in different rooms within a given period of time. The dentist may pull a tooth in room 1, move to room 2 to prepare a cavity for filling, move back to room 1 to treat the hole created by the pulled tooth, and so forth. Assistants do minor tasks as the dentist moves from patient to patient.

In a computer system with a multiprogrammed operating system, several applications programs may be stored in main memory at the same time. The CPU, like the dentist, works on only one program at a time. When it reaches a point in a program at which peripheral devices or other elements of the computer system must take over some of the work, the CPU moves on to another program, then returns to the first program when it is ready to be processed again. While the computer is waiting for data for one program to be accessed on disk, for example, it can perform calculations for another. The systems software for the disk unit works like the dental assistants—it does background work; in this case, retrieving the data stored on disk.

Multiprogramming is feasible because computers can perform thousands of computations in the time it takes to ask for and receive a single piece of data from disk. Such disk I/O operations are much slower than computation because the computer has to interact with and receive communications from an external device to obtain the data it needs. It must also contend with the slower access speeds of secondary memory.

MULTITASKING. **Multitasking** refers to the ability of an operating system to enable two or more programs from any single user to run concurrently on one computer. Thus multitasking is a special case of multiprogramming. This feature enables a user to do such things as editing one program while another program is running, or having two programs displayed on a screen at the same time and modifying them together. Remember, one computer, like one dentist, can only attend to one task at a time. But the computer works so fast that the user is often under the illusion that it is doing two things at once.

One situation in which multitasking is very helpful is when a program has an exceptionally long processing time and the computer is needed for other work. Let's say you want to search through a large employee file to find all people between the ages of 25 and 35 with six years of service and some experience in computers. On a relatively small computer, a search such as this one may take several minutes. During that time you may want

Why UNIX?

A CLOSER LOOK AT THE OPERATING SYSTEM MANY ARE TALKING ABOUT

For the past decade, four letters have usually seemed to surface when computer professionals talk about operating systems they'd like to have on their microcomputers: U-N-I-X. UNIX was developed over a decade ago at Bell Labs as a highly *portable* operating system for minicomputers—that is, an operating system that would work on many different brands of computers. It has since become a systems software package that computer enthusiasts working on all sizes of computer systems are excited about. What is it that makes UNIX so popular?

First, UNIX is a multiuser, multitasking operating system. Because it is a multiuser system, several people can share the same processor concurrently. Because it facilitates multitasking, a user can work on several programs concurrently at a workstation. Until recently microcomputer systems that could take advantage of these two UNIX properties were unavailable. With the arrival of supermicros such as the IBM PC AT, AT&T UNIX PC, and Compaq 286, however, this situation has changed.

Second, UNIX is easy to move to new computers. Unlike other operating systems such as CP/M and MS-DOS, UNIX is written in a high-level language (called "C") and is not built around a single family of microprocessors. Computers from micros to mainframes can run UNIX. In a world where new computer chips come out every month, UNIX's portability is a real asset to software designers.

Third, UNIX has a variety of design features that make it popular with computer scientists and programmers.

Files, for example, are organized hierarchically in directories, which makes keeping track of large volumes of information easy. Moreover, UNIX has a regularity—virtually everything is a file and all files are handled pretty much the same way. Also, it uses a "tool-kit" approach that enables users to customize the operating system with their own commands or features.

But UNIX isn't for everyone.

But UNIX isn't for everyone. If you don't have a multiuser, multitasking system unit, much of its power will be lost to you. Also, UNIX isn't particularly easy to learn as compared with the current crop of microcomputer-based operating systems. Products such as PC-DOS and MS-DOS have already established a strong foothold in the microcomputer marketplace. And applications software for UNIX is relatively scarce.

Nonetheless UNIX appears to have a bright future. If too many incompatible versions of it don't surface before it has a chance to get off the ground, the portability of this powerful operating system will let people take advantage of the features of new computer generations without making their existing software obsolete.

to use the computer for other work. With multitasking you can use your computer to perform another task, on the same or a different program, while the search is taking place in the background. Without multitasking you'll have to find other (offline) work to do, such as eating lunch, while the computer is tied up.

Because multitasking involves using the computer to interleave the processing of a single user's tasks, it is closely associated with *windowing software,* which is discussed later in the chapter under utility programs.

TIME-SHARING. **Time-sharing** is a very popular technique for computer systems that support numerous terminals. The operating system cycles through all the active programs in the system that need processing, giving each one a small time slice on each cycle.

For example, say there are twenty programs in the system and each program is to be allocated a time slice of one second (the time slice is usually much smaller than this, and not all slices are necessarily equal). The computer will work on program 1 for one second, then on program 2 for one second, and so forth. When it finishes working on program 20 for one second, it will go back to program 1 for another second, program 2 for another second, and so on. Thus if there is an average of twenty programs on the system, each program will get a total of three seconds of processing during each minute of actual clock time, or one second in every twenty-second period. As you can see, in a time-sharing system, it is difficult for a single program to dominate the CPU's attention, thereby holding up the processing of shorter programs.

Both time-sharing and multiprogramming are techniques for working on many programs concurrently, by allotting short periods of uninterrupted time to each. They differ, however, in the way in which they allot time. In time-sharing the computer spends a fixed amount of time on each program and then goes on to another. In multiprogramming the computer works on a program until it encounters a logical stopping point, as when more data must be read in, before going on to another. Many computers today combine time-sharing and multiprogramming techniques to expedite processing.

VIRTUAL STORAGE. In the early days of computing, users who had large programs faced numerous problems in loading them into main memory. Often the programmer had to split such programs into pieces manually, so that only small portions of them resided in the limited main memory space at any one time. In the early 1970s, a virtual storage feature became available on some operating systems. It permitted users the luxury of writing extremely long programs that would automatically be split up and managed by the operating system.

Virtual storage refers to the use of disk to extend main memory. This is the way it usually works: The operating system delivers programs to be processed to the virtual storage area on disk. Here the programs are generally divided into either fixed-length "pages" or variable-length "segments." Whether the programs are subdivided into pages or segments depends on the capabilites of the operating system.

A virtual storage system that uses **paging** breaks a program into pages. If a program is 40 kilobytes long, and the paging system divides programs into 4-kilobyte lengths, the program will be divided into ten pages. As the computer works on the program, it stores only a few pages at a time in main memory. As other pages are required during program execution, they are selected from virtual storage and written over the pages in main memory that are no longer needed. All the original pages, or modified ones, remain intact in virtual storage as the computer processes the program. If a page that has been written over in main memory is needed again, it can readily be fetched. This process, illustrated in Figure 8-5, continues until the program is finished. The buffer areas shown in the figure are sometimes referred to as *spooling* areas. We'll talk more about spooling programs later in the chapter.

The operating system may use a variety of rules to determine which pages to keep in primary memory. One rule might require a new page to be written over the page that has been used least recently. On the other hand, a page with a high overall frequency of use (even though it may be the least recently used at any time) is a logical candidate for remaining in primary memory.

Segmentation works somewhat like paging, except that the segments are variable in length. Each segment normally consists of a contiguous block of logically interrelated material from the program. As in paging, a segment that is needed in main memory is written over one that isn't. Many systems that use segmentation employ a combination of segmentation and paging. A program is first segmented into logically related blocks, which are further divided into pages of fixed length.

Not all operating systems on large computers use virtual storage. Although this technique permits processing of larger programs, it requires extra computer time to swap pages or segments into and out of main memory. Also, many microcomputer software packages (such as Word-Star®) have built-in virtual storage features that enable them to work on computers with small main memories (RAM). If you have a lot of RAM and "RAM disk software" (see box on page 137), you can eliminate the time-consuming disk swapping of virtual storage and speed these programs up considerably.

MULTIPROCESSING.   **Multiprocessing** refers to the use of two or more CPUs, linked together, to perform work in parallel; that is, at the same time. Whereas multiprogramming processes several programs *concurrently* on a *single* machine, multiprocessing may handle several jobs *simultaneously* (at precisely the same instant) on *several* machines.

Because of the availability of low-cost microprocessors, many computer manufacturers are designing systems to do multiprocessing. Since the machines can work as a team and can operate in parallel, jobs can be processed much more rapidly than they could be on a single machine. Some manufacturers have employed parallel processing philosophies to build *fault-tolerant computers*. These machines duplicate important circuitry components, so that if one component fails, an identical backup component is automatically invoked.

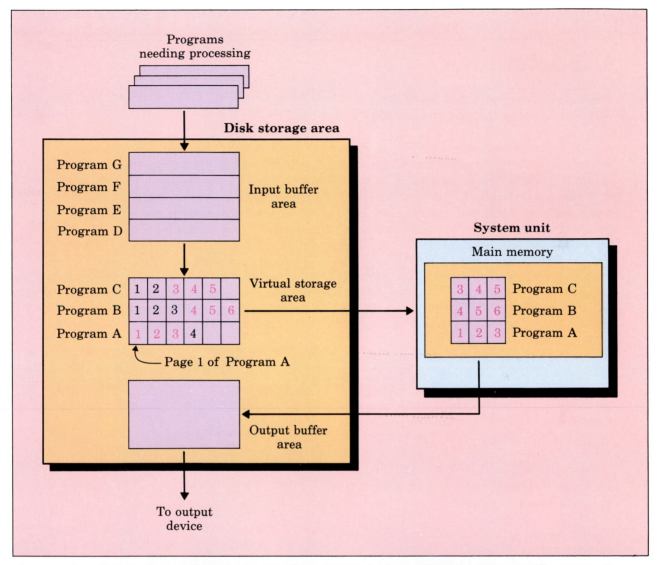

Figure 8-5. *Virtual storage based on a paging system.* In this system, programs awaiting processing are transferred from the input buffer area on disk to the virtual storage area. In the virtual storage area, programs are divided into pages of fixed length, perhaps 4000 bytes each. When the computer is ready to process a program, the operating system transfers a certain number of pages (three, in the example here) into main memory. The computer then processes the program until it needs a new page, whereupon the required page is delivered to main memory, writing over the one that is no longer needed. The computer system continues in this fashion, selecting desired pages of a program from virtual storage, until the program is completed. At that point the program output is delivered to the output buffer area of the disk, to await an output device, and a new program is read into its area of virtual storage.

Multiprocessing is slightly different from *coprocessing,* which was discussed in Chapter 4. In multiprocessing two or more fully fledged, general-purpose CPUs work in parallel. In coprocessing a CPU works in parallel with a *specialized* processor that performs a dedicated chore; for example, high-speed mathematical operations or graphics.

tomorrow

PARALLEL PROCESSING

The Two-Heads-Are-Better-Than-One Approach Applies to Computers As Well

A general principle of work is that two or more workers doing a job together can complete it faster than one of them working alone. Curiously, however, until recently few attempts had been made to apply this principle to computers. Despite the fact that computer systems have evolved at an astounding rate over the past fifty years, most of them are still driven by a single central processor. A single processor can only perform instructions in serial, or one step at a time, whether it is working exclusively on one program or interleaving several.

In the race to develop ever-faster computer systems for tomorrow, scientists are experimenting with ways to have two or more processors and memories perform tasks in parallel. For example, instead of relying on one processor to solve a lengthy calculation, a parallel processing computer assigns portions of the problem to several processors that are operating simultaneously. But just as it is difficult to coordinate two or more workers who are simultaneously dedicated to completing a single job, so too it is difficult to coordinate the parallel efforts of several processors and memories that work together at superhuman speeds. Nonetheless many industry insiders see parallel processing, or multiprocessing, as the wave of the future. Several approaches to such systems are currently in use or under study.

One popular approach to parallel processing is represented by the Cray-2 (see photo), a supercomputer that carries a price tag of several million dollars. The Cray, as do most other supercomputers, employs a common parallel design philosophy—hooking up a small number of expensive, state-of-the-art processors. The Cray-2 uses four such processors, which carry out both parallel and serial processing. Other supercomputers that will be out shortly will have a greater number of parallel processors in operation.

Since not everybody can afford a supercomputer, other parallel processing approaches have evolved. Another common tack is to design parallel machines with a much larger number of relatively inexpensive, off-the-shelf microprocessors. Although devices built this way are less versatile than supercomputers, they can pack together a respectable

The awesome Cray-2.

amount of power at a fraction of the cost. Some computers have been reported in the press that use over 1000 microprocessors hooked up in parallel.

Although computer manufacturers and scientists all over the world are busily at work constructing such machines, it will be several years before parallel processing becomes a widespread reality. Still, because common sense would seem to tell us that 100 heads are better than one, these machines would seem to be a sure bet for tomorrow.

LANGUAGE TRANSLATORS

As mentioned earlier, computers can execute programs only after they've been translated into machine language. There are two reasons why people don't generally write programs in this language. First, machine-language instructions consist of complex-looking strings of 0s and 1s. For example,

0101100001110000000000100000010

Few people enjoy or are successful at writing long programs consisting of statements like this. Second, machine-language instructions have to be written at the most detailed level of exposition. For example, the computer can't directly add A and B, and place the result in C, with a single instruction such as

C = A + B

Even a simple task like this may require three or more machine-language instructions, such as

1. Load the value represented by A from main memory into a register.

2. Add the value represented by B from main memory into the same register.

3. Place the sum obtained into another storage area.

Such detailed statements are sometimes called *machine-level instructions,* since they cannot be subdivided further into smaller commands. An instruction such as C = A + B, on the other hand, is an example of a *macroinstruction.* Macroinstructions must be broken down into machine-level instructions by the computer system before they are processed. All high-level languages (such as BASIC, FORTRAN, and COBOL) use macroinstruction-type statements to spare the programmer the tedious task of explaining in fine detail to the computer how to do work.

A **language translator** is simply a systems program that converts an applications program written in a high-level language or in an assembly language into machine language. In other words, it converts a program with macroinstructions into one with binary-based machine-level instructions. There are three common types of language translators—compilers, interpreters, and assemblers.

COMPILERS. A **compiler** translates a high-level-language program entirely into machine language before the program is executed. Every compiler-oriented language requires its own special compiler. Thus a COBOL program needs a COBOL compiler; it cannot run on a FORTRAN compiler.

The program that you write in a high-level language and enter into the computer is called a **source module** (or **source program**). The machine-level program that the compiler then produces from it is called an **object module** (or **object program**).

Before the object module is actually executed, it is normally bound together with other object modules that the CPU may need in order to process the program. For example, most computers can't compute square roots directly. To do so they rely on small "subprograms," which are stored in secondary memory in object module form. So if your program calls for the calculation of a square root, the operating system will bind the object module version of your program together with this square root routine to form an "executable package" for the computer. The binding process is referred to as *linkage editing* (or the *link-edit stage*), and the executable package that is formed is called a **load module.** A special system program, called a **linkage editor,** is available on computer systems to do the binding automatically.

It is the load module that the computer actually executes, or runs. When your program is ready to run, it has reached the *GO stage.* Figure 8-6 shows the complete process, from compiling to link editing to execution. Both object and load modules can be saved on disk for later use, so that compilation and linkage editing need not be performed every time the program is executed.

INTERPRETERS.   An **interpreter,** unlike a compiler, does not create an object module. Interpreters read, translate, and execute source programs one line at a time. Thus the translation into machine language is performed while the program is being run.

Interpreters have advantages and disadvantages relative to compilers. A major advantage is that the interpreter itself requires relatively little storage space. Also, the interpreter does not generate an object module that has to be stored. Many versions of BASIC use interpreters rather than compilers, and for this reason require less storage than compiler-oriented languages such as COBOL and FORTRAN. This is one reason why BASIC was initially so popular on microcomputers, which had very limited storage capacity in their early days. Another reason is that interpreters are easier for beginners to use.

The major disadvantage of interpreters is that they are slower and less efficient than compilers. The object program produced by a compiler is entirely in machine language, so it can be executed very quickly. Interpreters, in contrast, translate each statement immediately before executing it, which takes more time because a statement must be reinterpreted every time it is executed. In addition the object module of a compiled program can be saved on disk, so the source program doesn't have to be translated again every time the program is run. With an interpreter the program must be translated anew every time it is run.

ASSEMBLERS.   The third type of translator, the **assembler,** is used exclusively with assembly languages. It works like a compiler, producing a stored object module. Each computer system typically has only one assembly language available to it; thus only one assembler need be acquired.

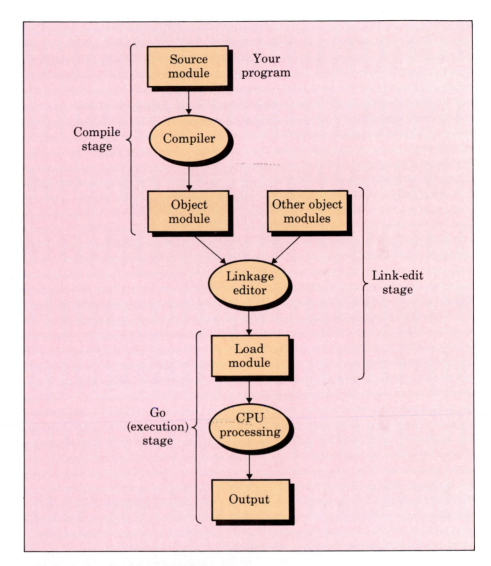

Figure 8-6. *Compile, link edit, GO.* A compiler and a linkage editor convert a source module into a load module, which is processed by the CPU.

UTILITY PROGRAMS

Some tasks are performed so often in the course of processing that it would be extremely inefficient if every user had to code them into programs over and over again. Sorting records and copying programs from tape to disk (or from disk to tape) are examples of such tasks. To eliminate the need for users and programmers to waste time writing such routines, computer systems normally have available several **utility programs** to perform these functions. Typically these programs reside in secondary storage and are summoned by the operating system's supervisor program when needed.

Utility programs are packaged in a variety of ways. Sometimes they are bundled into the operating system. In other cases they can be acquired from independent vendors and made to run with a given operating system. Four popular types of utility routines are sort utilities, spooling software, windowing software, and text editors.

SORT UTILITIES. *Sort utilities* are programs that are used to sort records in a file. To appreciate how a sort utility might work, consider Figure 8-7. This program uses a *primary key,* director, to sort the file initially. A *secondary key,* movie title, is then used to sort movies alphabetically within each director. Although the example shown here uses only two sort keys, some sorting packages will enable you to identify a dozen or more such keys to order a file. Also, you can usually sort records in ascending or descending order on each key you name.

Sort utilities are normally very flexible. You can operate one independently, as illustrated in the figure, even changing the order of the original fields of the file or suppressing some of the fields on output. In addition, some languages permit you to embed a "call" to the sort utility in the computer programs you write. Many productivity software packages, such as Lotus Development Corporation's 1-2-3® and Ashton Tate's dBase III,® have sort utilities embedded in them.

SPOOLING SOFTWARE. Some input and output devices are extremely slow. Tape devices and printers, for example, work at a snail's pace compared with the CPU. If the CPU had to wait for these slower devices to finish their work, the computer system would encounter a horrendous bottleneck. Suppose, for example, that the computer has just completed a five-second job that has generated 100 pages of hard copy for the printer. On a printer that prints 600 lines per minute, this job would take about ten minutes to print. If the CPU had to deal directly with the printer, primary memory would be tied up for ten minutes waiting for the printer to complete the job. As a result other programs could not be processed while this output was being transferred from main memory to paper.

To avoid such a delay, disks on almost all large systems contain *output spooling areas* to store output destined for the printer (Figure 8-8). As the computer processes a program, a **spooling program** rapidly transfers, or "spools," the output from main memory to the disk spooling area. The computer is then free to process another program, leaving it to a spooling program to transfer the output of the first program from disk to printer.

At any one time, the spooling area of a large computer system may contain over 100 completed jobs waiting to be delivered to output devices. As long as space remains in the output spooling area, the CPU can continue to operate without delay. A form of output spooling is popular on microcomputers, too. For example, if your printer is going to be tied up for fifteen minutes or so typing a long document, it's great to have a spooling routine so you can use your computer to edit another document at the same time.

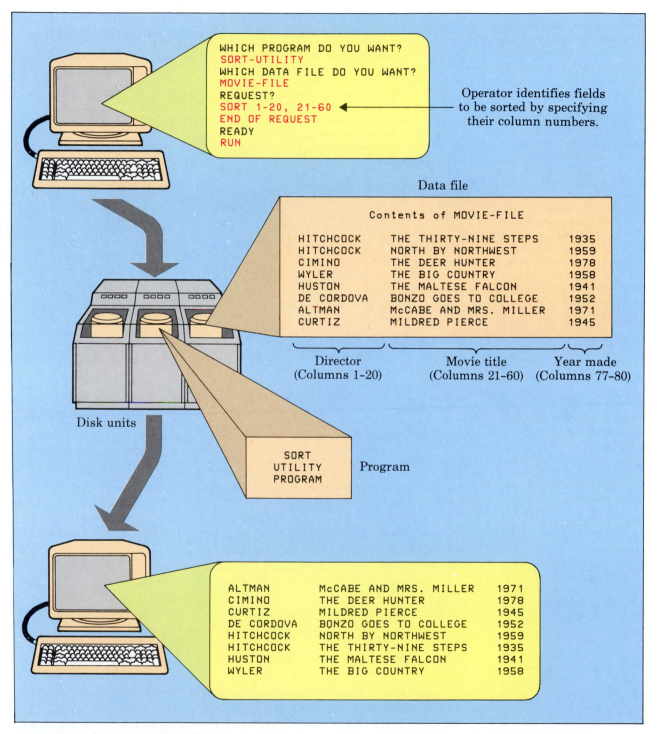

Figure 8-7. *A sort utility program in action.* The terminal operator requests that a movie file be sorted alphabetically, first by director (columns 1–20) and then by movie title (columns 21–60). Note that the second sort reverses the order of the two Alfred Hitchcock movies.

Figure 8-8. **Spooling.** On large computer systems input is spooled while waiting to be processed, and output is spooled before it is sent to the printer.

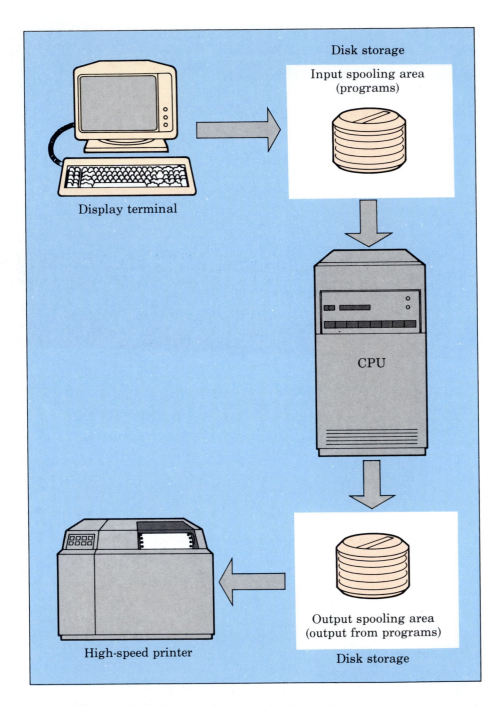

As Figure 8-8 shows, spooling can also be used to hold, or stage, input on its way to the computer. As programs enter the computer system, they are stored in an *input spooling area* (or *queue*). When the operating system is ready to deliver the next program to the CPU, it checks the queue to see which to process next. Often, some users can assign a high priority to their programs. In this case the computer attends to their jobs before those that may have been in the queue longer but have a lower priority.

Figure 8-9. Overlapping windows on a display screen. Windowing software makes it possible for users to see independent blocks of work on the screen at the same time.

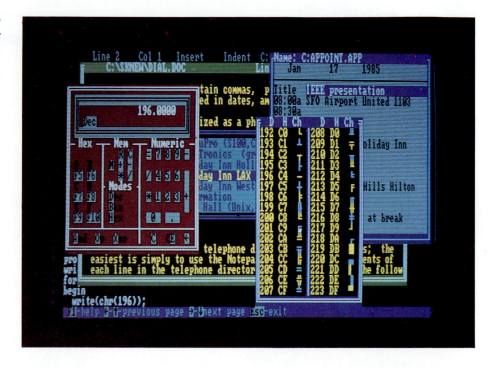

WINDOWING SOFTWARE. In the world of computers, there are two types of **window** environments that you'll encounter. The first, which is discussed in Chapter 12 (in connection with spreadsheets), exists where a document that's too large to fit on a display screen is moved around by the arrow keys on the keyboard so that you can see different portions of it. In other words the screen serves as a single "window" through which you can look to inspect different portions of the document. The second type (see Figure 8-9) is found where several independent "boxes" (i.e., windows) of information are created on the display screen. It is this second window environment to which the term **windowing software** is most commonly applied.

Windowing software may sometimes be bundled into a software package that you buy. Many packages, for example, have built-in windowing routines that let you create windows on your screen to display different aspects of your work. If you're preparing a textual document that will integrate graphs from spreadsheet data, you can display the document in the first window, the spreadsheet in a second, and various possiblities for graphing the spreadsheet data in the third. Windowing packages that you buy separately often allow you to run the software products of a variety of vendors in your windows.

TEXT EDITORS. A **text editor** is a software package that enables you to manipulate text in a file. Whereas words processors are programs that are specifically targeted to preparing such things as memos, letters, and manuscripts (in essence, turning your computer system into a glorified typewriter), text editors offer another dimension to text manipulations.

Desk Accessories

ENHANCE YOUR MICROCOMPUTER'S OPERATING SYSTEM WITH FUNCTIONS AVAILABLE ON MANY DESKTOPS

They come with such names as Sidekick®, My Desk®, and Pop-Up DeskSet Plus®. These window-laden microcomputer-based programs are *desk accessories*. Often they are shells that fit over your operating system, enhancing it with a variety of useful features commonly found on a desk top.

Here's how many of them work. When you boot up the operating system on your microcomputer, you invoke your desk accessory program. This program then essentially creates another operating system, which contains your original operating system and a variety of handy desk-top utilities. You can later call up these utilities when you are working on software such as a word processor or spreadsheet package.

One common utility is a clock program. Let's say you're typing a paper for a class on your word processor and you want to know what time it is. You might press the ALT and F1

keys, and, a small window appears on your screen with the right time. Later, when you press any other key, the window will disappear and you are back into your word processor as if nothing ever happened.

Desk accessory software varies from vendor to vendor, but many of them offer the following features. Often, each feature is implemented by a window, which appears when a specific sequence of keys is activated.

Calculator. Most calculator utilities come with screen graphics that provide an image of the calculator in the display window. Some can export the results of the calculations back to your applications program as well.

Calendar. Calendar programs usually have two levels. At one level they simulate the wall calendars you have at home. Each

With a text editor, you can often carry out such tasks as sorting records in a file, deleting or moving fields in a set of records, or appending fields to a set of records.

Let's look at an example. Say you with to create records that contain names and social security numbers. In each record names are to begin in column 1 and the social security numbers in column 31. But you mistakenly type the social security numbers first, then the names. Many text editors will permit you to correct this mistake quickly, with a single command that changes the positions of the social security number and name data in all the affected records.

Some text editors are *full-screen editors* that let you move the cursor anywhere on the screen, to point as you change text. *Line editors,* on the other hand, keep the cursor constrained to a single line position on the display screen. If you want to move back to an earlier line, you normally must depress a special sequence of keys to tell the line editor that you want to do something out of the normal sequence of operations.

graphical image sent to the window is a grid of the days in a particular month. When you hit specific sequences of keys, you can move forward or backward to other months. At the other level, the graphical image sent to the screen is an appointment-book page for a particular day that enables you to look at, add, or delete entries.

Clock. Besides providing you with the time, some packages have an online alarm-clock feature that causes the audio unit in your computer to beep or chime. Some clocks will even interrupt your application with a preprogrammed message.

Notepad. Many desk accessory programs offer full-screen notepads for writing notes, letters, and other text. In some cases you may be able to export notepad text back to your applications program.

Card File. This feature allows you to store and recall the electronic equivalent of a Rolodex card file on your microcomputer system. Some programs offer a communications interface with the Rolodex feature, so that you can look up the number of an online information service or database and dial it immediately.

A salesperson summons clock and calculator windows while doing some filing.

Desk accessory software is becoming increasingly popular with microcomputer users. Some people claim that, once you use one of these software packages, you'll wonder how you ever did without it.

Text editors are an invaluable aid to programmers in the creation and debugging of programs. Some languages, such as BASIC, have their own built-in editors.

Summary and Key Terms

Systems software consists of programs that coordinate the various parts of the computer system to make it run rapidly and efficiently. The role of systems software is basically to act as a mediator between applications programs and the hardware of the computer system.

An **operating system** is a collection of programs that manage the activities of the computer. The functions of the operating system—which include assignment of system resources, scheduling of resources and jobs, and monitoring activities—can be seen as aspects of a single general mission: to control the operations of the computer system.

Two of the most prominent programs of the operating system are the supervisor and the command-language translator. The **supervisor** is a program that controls all the other parts of the operating system. The **command-language translator** enables both users and programmers to communicate with the operating system with a **command language.** When interfacing with the operating system, one can use the standard system **defaults,** chosen by the operating system, or request customized service through command-language instructions. On some computer systems the operator points on the screen to geometrical images, called **icons,** to carry out such instructions.

Sophisticated computers often take advantage of interleaved processing techniques, such as multiprogramming, multitasking, time-sharing, virtual storage, and mutiprocessing, to operate more efficiently.

In a computer system with **multiprogramming,** the computer can work on several programs concurrently. For example, while the computer is waiting for data from one program to be accessed on disk, it can perform calculations for another.

Multitasking refers to the ability of an operating system to enable two or more programs from any single user to execute concurrently on one computer. Thus multitasking is a special case of multiprogramming.

Time-sharing is a technique in which the operating system cycles through all the active programs in the system that need processing, giving each a small slice of time on each cycle.

Virtual storage refers to using disk to extend main memory. Often, the operating system delivers programs to be processed to the virtual storage area, where they are subdivided into either fixed-length *pages* (a process called **paging**) or variable-length *segments* (a process called **segmentation**).

Multiprocessing refers to the use of two or more computers, linked together, to perform work on programs in parallel; that is, at the *same* time.

A **language translator** is a system program that converts an applications program written in a high-level language or in assembly language into machine language. There are three common types of language translators—compilers, interpreters, and assemblers.

A **compiler** translates a high-level-language program entirely into machine language before the program is executed. The program written by the user or programmer, called a **source module (source program),** is first translated by the compiler into an **object module (object program).** The object module version of the program is then input to a **linkage editor,** which combines it with supplementary object modules needed to run the program, to form a **load module.** It is the load module that is executed by the computer.

Interpreters read, translate, and execute source programs one line at a time. Thus the translation into machine language is performed while the program is being run.

The third type of translator, the **assembler,** is used exclusively with assembly languages.

A **utility program** is a type of system program written to perform repetitive data processing tasks. There are many types of utility programs. *Sort utilities* are programs that are used to sort records in a file. **Spooling programs** are utilities that free the CPU from time-consuming interaction with I/O devices such as printers. **Windowing software** refers to utilities that create several independent "boxes" (i.e., **windows**) of information on a display screen. **Text editors** are utilities that enable users to manipulate text in a file.

Review Exercises

Fill-in Questions

1. _____ software consists of programs that act as a mediator between applications software and the hardware of the computer system.
2. A(n) _____ is a collection of programs that manage the activities of the computer system.
3. In a computer system with _____, the computer works on several programs concurrently, leaving one at some logical stopping point to begin work on another.
4. _____ is a technique in which the operating system cycles through active programs in the system that need processing, giving each one a small slice of time on each cycle.
5. _____ refers to the use of two or more computers linked together to perform work on programs in parallel.
6. A(n) _____ is a systems program that converts an applications program written in a high-level language or an assembly language into machine language.
7. _____ programs are systems programs written to perform repetitive data processing tasks, such as sorting and text editing.

Matching Questions   *Match each term with its description.*

a. Windowing software   e. Interpreter
b. Compiler   f. Text editor
c. Linkage editor   g. Operating system
d. Spooling software

_____   1. A language translator that reads, translates, and executes source programs a line at a time.

_____   2. Enables you to edit a document on your microcomputer system while you are printing out another.

_____   3. Creates several independent boxes of information on the display screen.

_____   4. Binds object modules together.

_____   5. Piece of systems software without which a computer system won't do anything.

_____   6. A language translator that creates an object module.

_____   7. Can do things such as appending fields to records and changing the order of fields in records.

Discussion Questions   1. What is systems software?

2. What is an operating system and what are its major functions?

3. Describe multiprogramming, multitasking, time-sharing, virtual storage, and multiprocessing.

4. What are the differences among a compiler, an interpreter, and an assembler?

5. Describe the differences among a source module, object module, and load module.

6. Identify several types of utility programs and explain what they do.

Chapter 9

Applications Software Development

Chapter Outline

Objectives

After completing this chapter you should be able to:

1. Identify and describe the components of the program development cycle.
2. Recognize when it is more advantageous to develop software in-house than to buy it externally.
3. Describe a number of tools and procedures used by computer professionals to develop software.

OVERVIEW

If you wanted to build a house, you'd probably begin with some research and planning. You might speak to various people about home design, draw up some floor plans, estimate the cost of materials, and so on. In other words, you wouldn't start digging a hole and pouring concrete on the very first day. Producing a successful applications program also requires planning and discipline. The process involved is called *program development*.

Years ago the cost of hardware was the dominant concern in establishing a computer system, and developing good applications program software was often a secondary consideration. The cost of hardware has plunged in recent years, however, whereas the cost of labor has increased dramatically. Writing programs is a labor-intensive task. Thus many organizations are finding that they spend most of their total computing costs on software. What's more, many large organizations have discovered that up to 80 percent of their software costs are just for maintaining existing programs.

In this chapter and the next, we will describe some useful practices for properly developing applications programs. In both these chapters, our focus is on a set of procedures called *structured techniques*. As you read the chapters, keep in mind that it is never enough just to write a program that works. Good programs must be easy to understand and easy to maintain. A well-planned program may take slightly longer to write initially, but the subsequent savings in maintenance costs will generally make the effort well worthwhile.

THE ROLE OF APPLICATIONS SOFTWARE

Applications software consists of programs that direct computer systems to produce outputs for computer users. Every computer application that interfaces with users, from video games to the tracking of a space shuttle, from printing mailing lists to compiling U.S. census returns, requires applications software.

Consider an example. It's a hot Saturday night and you want to cool off at a local movie theater, but you don't have enough cash. You go to the automatic teller machine at your bank, slip in a plastic card, respond to the questions that appear on the screen by pressing the appropriate keys, and presto—movie money. Without an applications program, however, the convenience of automatic tellers would be impossible. It's an applications program that, among other things, tells the system what messages to put on the screen, how to respond to the keys you press, what to do if your balance is too low or if you enter the wrong ID number, and how much cash to deliver.

Creating applications software is closely related to the process of systems development, which we discuss in detail in Chapter 16. Systems

AND NOW THE NEXT MAJOR COMPUTER EXPENDITURE: TRAINING

Will Training Soon Be the Biggest Item on Computing Budgets?

There was a time not too long ago when if a company said it had a computer, people took notice. These machines cost several hundreds of thousands of dollars. But because their software was limited, the software budget of a company might be only several thousands of dollars. Nonetheless these few programs served important applications and the early computer systems paid for themselves.

Training is already a multimillion-dollar industry.

As the price of hardware dropped and computers became flexible enough to do many more things, other software was demanded. Since software is much more labor intensive than hardware, software nudged hardware aside as the major cost in organizational computing. Today, in a typical company, the cost of software can easily be double that of the hardware. Now another major force, more labor intensive than programming software, is waiting in the wings to take a big bite out of every computing dollar—that force is training.

Although the need for quality hardware and software will continue, many of the basic needs in these areas are being satisfied and products are beginning to collide in the marketplace. Hardware and software prices are coming down for products of better quality. With software such as spreadsheets and word processors easily available in the office, more and more people are finding it necessary to be knowledgable about computers.

This is where training comes in. With today's prices a company may figure that it spends $50 per hour on a typical professional employee. As an employee you might see only a small portion of that $50, since it includes health and retirement benefits, employee facilities that need to be maintained, and so forth. If the company sends ten programmers or users to a $10,000 seminar for a week, the total cost of the seminar may be close to $50,000, including expenses. That's a lot of money. Since people often change jobs, training is a continuing large expense. The cost of training can exceed the cost of the software—especially as software prices continue to fall and as more and more people need to interface with computer systems.

Flyers for training programs. If you want a crash course in a specific area, chances are there's a seminar around to meet your needs.

Training is already a multimillion-dollar industry (see photo). In 1982 total spending in the United States on training for personal computers alone was approximately $30 million. And some experts expect that figure to rise to $600 million by 1990. At that rate expect to see training as a strong contender for tomorrow's computing dollar.

development involves the analysis, design, and implementation of complete computer systems, including hardware, systems software, applications software, data, people, and procedures. If a bank without automatic teller machines were to consider installing them, it would probably go through the complete systems development process. Only part of that process would involve designing and creating the applications programs to make the machines do useful work.

Once a system is in place and running, however, there is often still a need for new or modified applications software. The bank may decide, for example, to modify its automatic teller system to permit customers to make withdrawals with their credit cards as well as with their bank cards. Or a bank executive may ask to see a report on machine transactions daily instead of weekly. Thus the development of software for an application is normally a continuing process.

THE PROGRAM DEVELOPMENT CYCLE

There are two ways in which organizations acquire applications programs: writing them internally (sometimes called in-house development) and buying them from an outside source. The method that's chosen generally depends upon such things as the quality of available software in the marketplace, the nature and importance of the application, programmer availability, and cost. Whichever method is chosen, certain steps should be followed to ensure that the software does its job.

The creation of successful programs commonly involves five stages:

Analysis Identifying and defining the problem to be solved; deciding whether the solution involves software; and if it does, defining input, output, and processing requirements.

Design Planning the solution to the problem.

Coding Writing the program.

Debugging Finding and eliminating errors in the program.

Documentation Writing manuals for the people who will use the program and for maintenance programmers.

These five stages are often called the **program development cycle** (or **program life cycle**).

When a program is purchased from an outside source, it will not be necessary to go through all these stages. Some of them, such as designing the program, coding, and documentation, will be done by the vendor. And most of the errors, it is hoped, will have been worked out of the program as well.

In a typical organization, the responsibility for successful program development is that of systems analysts and programmers. **Systems analysts** (or *analysts*) actually specify the requirements the applications

software must meet. They work with the people who will use the software to assess their needs and to translate those needs into a plan (Figure 9-1). They then determine the resources required to implement the plan. For each program, the analysts create a set of technical specifications that outline:

- ✕ What the program must do—that is, the outputs, inputs, and processing requirements
- ✕ The timetable to complete the program
- ✕ What programming language to use
- ✕ How the program will be tested before it is put into use
- ✕ What documentation is required

Figure 9-1.   Users work closely with systems analysts in software development. It is the analyst's role to assess the needs of users for computing resources and to translate those needs into an orderly plan.

Some of these specifications—such as the programming language, testing methods, and documentation requirements—will follow standard organizational practices.

Programmers then use these specifications to design a software solution. Later they translate that design into code— a series of statements in a programming language. **Maintenance programmers** monitor the finished program on an ongoing basis, correcting errors and altering the program as conditions change.

ANALYSIS

A problem for a systems analyst often begins as a request that a computer system produce specific information. The scope of the solution can range from revamping an entire system to simply providing a new piece of information on an existing printed report. **Analysis** of the problem involves two steps: (1) identifying the problem and deciding what kind of solution is called for, and (2) if the solution involves software, developing the requirements the software must meet.

Identifying the Problem

The first thing a systems analyst must do in studying a potential problem is to decide if any problems do, in fact, exist. This may be the most difficult task for the analyst, since it involves a shrewd sense of perspective, a thorough knowledge of the user's job, and excellent communications skills. It requires a sagacity you can't generally learn from books.

Suppose, for example, a sales manager complains that she is getting important information too late and that the reports she is getting are inadequate. The systems analyst must ascertain whether there really are serious problems. Perhaps the information the manager needs is available in reports she already receives, but she doesn't know where to look for it. Also, does she really need the information she is asking for? Does she need it as promptly as she says she does? Getting answers to questions such as these clearly requires sensitivity and tact.

In addition to determining whether or not these problems exist, the analyst must also decide if a computer solution is appropriate. A user has a real need for computing resources if their use will result in benefits to the organization as a whole. These benefits may be realized through reduced costs, better service, and improved information for decision making. Are the benefits of providing the sales manager with the information she needs likely to justify the costs of creating it?

Once the analyst has determined that any of these problems are serious and that the need for computer resources is legitimate, the next question is, "What approaches will best solve the problems?" For the problems posed by the sales manager, some possible approaches are:

✕ Add the manager's name to the circulation list for an existing report that provides the information she needs when she needs it.

✕ Modify existing software and procedures to produce the information she needs.

✕ Develop new software and procedures to produce the information she needs.

✕ Acquire one or more new computer systems to serve both the manager and other users who may have similar problems with the existing system.

And, of course, there may be many other possiblities. Software solutions, as you can see, may be just some of many approaches. For now, however, we will deal only with software development and defer the more general issue of systems development until Chapter 16.

Developing Software Requirements

Once the analyst has settled on a software solution, the next job is to specify the constraints the software must meet. This step involves defining the output the software is to produce, the input needed to produce this output, and the processing tasks the system must perform. Output requirements are always developed first, because you can't know what to put into a system or what to ask it to do without knowing what you need to get out.

DEFINING OUTPUT.   The analyst should define output in terms of content, format, timing, and flexibility.

✕ *Content*   What type of information must the software provide and at what level of detail? For example, a sales manager may want information on year-to-date product sales. Specifically, the manager may require sales figures on each individual product, subtotals taken over each region, and a grand total taken over all products and regions.

✕ **Format**   How should the information be presented? Will it appear as a printed report or on a display screen? If the latter, the analyst should consult the user to see which of a number of screen formats is preferable. Likewise, if the output is to be a printed report, the analyst and the user will have to decide how it is to be organized.

✕ **Timing**   When do users need the information? Daily? Weekly? Monthly? On demand? A sales manager might be content with sales reports on a weekly basis. Other users, such as airline clerks who interact directly with clients, need information constantly, and also need a fast response time. Hence the analyst might require software to provide such users with a response in five seconds or less at least 95 percent of the time.

✕ **Flexibility**   Programs should not be so rigidly designed that they cannot be modified to meet changing conditions. In one well-known case, a bank installed a query system that analysts designed to provide the information users told them they needed. However, the analysts neglected to anticipate that once the system was installed, the users—in this case trust officers—would begin to ask new types of questions and demand new types of information. Since the system wasn't flexible enough to adapt to the new requests, it was regarded as a failure.

DEFINING INPUT.   After specifying the output, analysts must determine what input is needed to produce it. This job involves four issues: data needed, data availability, procedures for new data, and data entry.

✕ **Data needed**   What data does the application require? For example, if the application is to provide a monthly report on the sales of a particular product, the system must have data on each sale of that product and the date of sale.

✕ **Data availability**   Are the data needed currently available? Sales invoices, for example, may contain all the data needed to generate monthly reports on product sales.

✕ **Procedures for new data**   If new data are needed, how are they to be gathered? Suppose a company was trying to decide how to market a product, and it wanted information that showed how many purchases were for home use and how many were for business. The analyst might decide to redesign the sales invoice so that it would provide this information.

✕ **Data entry**   How are the data to be entered into the system? The analyst, for example, may recommend new data-entry procedures or the hiring of new data-entry personnel.

DEFINING PROCESSING.   Processing describes the actual work the system does. The analyst must define the processing tasks involved in the application and the constraints that people and equipment impose on the way those tasks are carried out.

✖ **Processing tasks**   What processing tasks must the software accomplish? Producing a sales report, for example, may require a program that can, among other things, sort a large file of sales data by date and product, classify each sale according to such criteria as product and region, and compute totals and percentages.

✖ **People constraints**   How sophisticated about computers are the users who will interact directly with the system? If they are not very sophisticated, the software will have to be easy to use.

✖ **Facility constraints**   The software must be able to work effectively on the computer, peripheral eqipment, and systems software that are available or feasible to acquire. It's not unusual to hear stories of individuals and organizations that have bought large software packages, which barely fit on their current systems, only to discover later that they have to upgrade their facilities significantly to get acceptable performance from the software.

THE MAKE-OR-BUY DECISION

Once a set of technical requirements has been established for a software solution to a problem, a decision must be made as to whether the programs should be created in-house or acquired from a vendor. This decision, which often takes place after the analysis stage of the program development cycle, is frequently called the *make-or-buy decision*.

In the past several years, packaged applications software has become increasingly available for many common business functions, including payroll, accounting, financial planning, scheduling, and correspondence. These packages normally consist of one or several programs, documentation (usually of fairly high quality), and, possibly, training. Packaged applications software is becoming more and more important to organizations, and we will discuss it at great length in Chapters 12 and 13.

The Pros and Cons of Packaged Software

ADVANTAGES.   Today, for many business applications, a significant amount of the software used in practice is vendor supplied. This makes a great deal of sense from the point of view of timing, uncertainty, and cost.

✖ **Timing**   Vendor-supplied software can be implemented almost immediately. In-house software, in contrast, may take months, or even years, to design, code, and debug.

✖ **Uncertainty**   With packaged software, the shrewd buying organization knows what it's getting—a product of stated quality at a stated price. If the buyer is lucky, the product may also have a track record and an active group of users with whom to "trade notes." When software is developed in-house, it's difficult to predict how the final product will work and what its eventual cost will be. Even estimates of development time are, at best, educated guesses. During the project's duration, a key programmer may resign, technology might change the nature of the application, or potential users may not like the way the system works when it is finally implemented. What's more, since people tend to be overoptimistic when estimating costs, many projects developed in-house are completed over budget.

✖ *Cost*   The economics of purchased software are relatively simple. The cost of the software is distributed over several organizations, so the price per user can be relatively low, even allowing the vendor a substantial profit. Costs for in-house software, on the other hand, are often completely absorbed by a single organization.

Also, when vendor-supplied software already has a large base of users, newly hired programmers may be familiar with it, thus saving the time and cost of training them. And programmers like to work with popular software packages because it increases their marketability.

DISADVANTAGES.   Purchased software, although it has many advantages, is not always appropriate. If a package was originally developed for a business that operates differently from the one to which it is being sold, and the vendor has made only superficial attempts to adapt it to the current buyer's needs, it may prove to be more trouble than it is worth. Also, for some applications little or no appropriate packaged software exists. In such cases in-house development is the only alternative—and it then becomes necessary to proceed to the design stage of the program development cycle.

PROGRAM DESIGN

In the **design** stage of the program development cycle, the software requirements developed in the analysis stage are used to spell out, as precisely as possible, the nature of the programming solution needed. The design, or plan, so formed determines all the tasks each program must do, as well as how they will be organized or sequenced when the program is coded. Only when the design is complete does the next stage begin—the actual coding of the programs.

In the early days of computing, design and coding were not clearly separated. Programmers were relatively free to solve problems in their own way. They would often begin coding with a vague, disorganized notion of the program's requirements. Such a nondisciplined approach involved many problems.

First, a programmer might be making substantial progress on a program only to find that a key function had been omitted. As a result large pieces of the program might have to be reorganized. Second, the logic behind programs written in this freewheeling way was usually obscure. Moreover, each programmer had a personalized coding style. What seemed systematic to one might seem incomprehensible to another.

Why Structured Techniques?

A BRIEF HISTORY OF STRUCTURED METHODOLOGIES

In the early days of computing, there were few rules to govern systems analysis and programming other than the rules of the programming languages themselves. For the most part, people concocted their own methods for developing applications software. With more and more dollars being spent for software, however, it was inevitable that analysis and programming had to graduate from their amateur, seat-of-the-pants status into a more disciplined exercise. *Structured techniques* represent an approach to such discipline.

One of the earliest attempts to elevate programming from an art to a science occurred in the late 1960s when E. W. Dijkstra proposed that GO TO statements be eliminated because they encourage unruly, poorly designed programs. About the same time, two Italian researchers—C. Bohm and G. Jacopini—proved that any program could be written by using only three control structures: sequence, selection, and iteration. These observations collectively led to what is known today as *structured programming.* Although there is considerable debate over how one should define structured programming, it is clear that it represents an attempt to make program development more systematic.

By the mid-1970s, structured philosophies spread to the design phase of programming. The result was a discipline called *structured design.* Structured design focuses primarily on the overall organization of a program rather than the step-by-step procedural logic involved.

Structured techniques are an evolving set of methodologies.

Two relatively common structured design approaches are structure charts and HIPO diagrams.

By the late 1970s, it became apparent that many software problems evolved out of poor specifications established during the analysis phase. Consequently structured techniques spread to this component of the program life cycle and the result was *structured analysis.* A popular structured analysis tool is the data flow diagram, which we will introduce more formally in connection with the systems life cycle in Chapter 16.

There are, of course, structured techniques that cut across analysis, design, and coding. The top-down philosophy, for example, can apply to the development of a system from a lofty goal down to a detailed "game plan," to the design of programs in a modular fashion from the top down, or to an approach to coding programs. Also, walk-through-type techniques can be used in both the coding and design phases of the program's life cycle.

Structured techniques are an evolving set of methodologies. So far they have done much to improve the quality of both programs and larger systems. We are likely to see many changes in these techniques over the coming years that will lead to even more rapid and superior applications development.

Programs written in this way may have "worked"—in the sense that they processed data correctly—but they were very difficult for anyone but the original programmers to understand. They were a nightmare; especially for maintenance programmers, the people who had to keep them up to date whenever some aspect of the application changed. These unfortunates, faced with a tangle of confused code, would usually just patch a program up with their own bit of new code rather than write it over. The result was even more confusion. Organizations found themselves dependent for critical applications on software that no one understood very well. As computer systems came to be used for more and more applications, it became clear that some order was needed to prevent financial calamity.

One solution that evolved was to stress program planning (design) and to separate the planning process from the actual coding. At the same time, a group of methods evolved that made program design more systematic and programs themselves easier to read and maintain (see box on page 276). These methods are usually grouped together under the term *structured techniques*. Techniques that deal specifically with the design and coding of programs are often referred to as structured programming. Actually **structured programming** originally referred only to the use of certain logical structures in programs themselves (we will discuss these structures in Chapter 10), but it has come to apply to a whole body of design and coding practices.

Program Design Tools

Program design tools help either analysts or programmers plan, and later document, programs. Many such tools have been developed, but four of the most important are:

- Structured program flowcharts
- Pseudocode
- Structure charts
- HIPO (Hierarchy plus Input-Process-Output) charts

Structure charts and *HIPO charts* show how the independent parts of a program, called *modules*, relate to each other. As Figure 9-2 shows, each module represents a specific programming task—calculating city tax, for example. The modules are arranged hierarchically in what is called a top-down fashion. *Top-down* implies that the top modules control the ones beneath them, and as the modules are developed, the topmost ones are designed first.

Program flowcharts and *pseudocode* are both tools that outline in detail the steps a program will follow. Flowcharts, as you can see in Figure 9-3, depict the steps and their relation to each other pictorially. Pseudocode, in contrast, outlines the steps of the program in a form that closely resembles actual programming code (hence *pseudocode*).

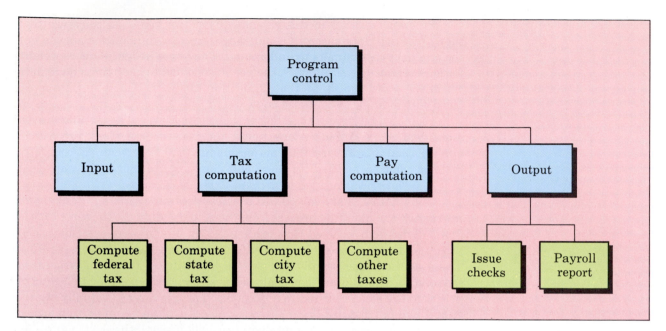

Figure 9-2. **Structure charts.** This technique subdivides a program into individual modules, each of which represents a well-defined processing task. The modules are then arranged hierarchically in a top-down fashion, as illustrated here for a payroll application. HIPO charts use a similar diagram for illustrating the hierarchy of modules in a program.

The use of these design tools varies widely among organizations. In many organizations systems analysts will draw structure charts or HIPO charts to specify the overall design for a program, and the programmers will use flowcharts or pseudocode to design the detailed, step-by-step procedures required to implement the overall design. If the programming project is large, the systems analyst may only provide the programmer with diagrams at the highest level of detail and leave it to the programmer to do most of the "fine tuning."

Choosing a Language

An important decision that must be made during the design phase is the selection of a programming language. Many organizations code the bulk of their applications in a single prespecified language, so this decision is normally very straightforward.

The language choice is closely related to the applications environment. A business-oriented language such as COBOL, for example, is commonly used for business applications, whereas a scientifically oriented language such as FORTRAN is more likely to be used for scientific, mathematical, or engineering applications.

Because it reflects the nature of the application, the choice of a language often also affects the choice of design tools. Some design tools are better suited to certain applications than others. An accounting problem to be coded in a structure-oriented language like COBOL is almost always better suited to structure charts and pseudocode than to flowcharts. On the

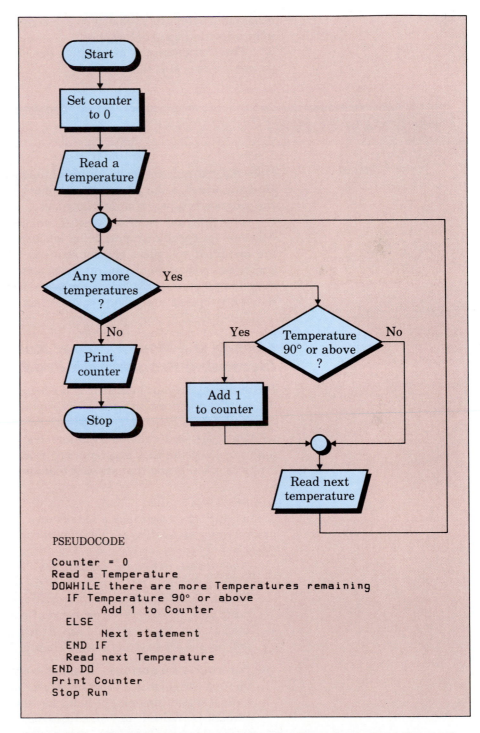

```
PSEUDOCODE

Counter = 0
Read a Temperature
DOWHILE there are more Temperatures remaining
   IF Temperature 90° or above
         Add 1 to Counter
   ELSE
         Next statement
   END IF
   Read next Temperature
END DO
Print Counter
Stop Run
```

Figure 9-3. **The flowchart and pseudocode shown here count the number of temperatures over 90 degrees in a list.** Flowcharts use graphical symbols and arrows to show the operations to be performed and the logical flow of the program. Pseudocode uses English-like statements to achieve the same objectives.

other hand, scientific problems with a high degree of visual content are best planned with the aid of flowcharts.

The characteristics of some of the more popular programming languages are discussed in Chapter 11.

PROGRAM CODING

Once the program design is complete, the next step is to code the program. **Coding,** which is the job of programmers, is the actual process of writing the program in a programming language.

The program is often written on coding forms. These forms are designed for specific programming languages, and the column restrictions are identified to reflect the conventions of each language. Thus coding programs on the forms helps programmers avoid errors. In many organizations the programmer will code the program onto the form and hand it to a data-entry operator, who keys the program exactly as it appears.

Getting the Most for Your Money: Increasing Programmer Productivity

Programming is labor intensive, and when poorly managed, can be a severe drain on an organization's resources. Among the techniques that have been used to increase programmer productivity are coding standards, structured walkthroughs, and chief programmer teams. The purpose of these techniques is to ensure that programmers produce programs that are as free of errors as possible and that are easy to maintain.

CODING STANDARDS.   Many organizations enforce a set of coding standards, which are essentially a list of rules designed to inhibit personalized programming styles. These rules may cover such items as the following:

✖ *Acceptable program structures* Any programming problem has many solutions, but some solutions are more straightforward than others. Many firms require programmers to use only those *programming control structures,* or conventions for grouping program statements, that are acceptable structured programming constructs. (We will discuss these structures in Chapter 10.)

✖ *Naming conventions* Naming conventions are uniform ways of naming variables in a program. For example, a firm might require that variables relating to input fields be labeled with the suffix "-IN," as in "EMPLOYEE-IN" or "ADDRESS-IN."

✖ *Comment conventions* Comments within a program help explain how the program works. They are especially useful in long and logically complex programs. Most firms have conventions that dictate when and how to add comments.

Rules such as these help make programs readable and easy to maintain. If everyone in an organization writes programs according to the same set of conventions, maintenance programmers always know what to expect. Unconstrained creativity is strictly discouraged in commercial programming.

STRUCTURED WALKTHROUGHS. Some organizations employ a technique called a structured walkthrough. A **structured walkthrough,** at the coding stage, is a peer evaluation of a programmer's work. The coding is evaluated by four or five other members of the staff, and a meeting is held to discuss good and bad features of the coding effort. An important topic of discussion is whether the program is being coded consistently and in adherence to the organization's coding standards.

Such a review process is intended to help programmers improve their coding skills and to ensure the success of important programs by subjecting them to close scrutiny. It is not intended as a formal appraisal of performance. In fact, it is recommended that the programmer's boss not participate. Walkthroughs are held early in the coding process, when errors are least costly to fix.

The term **egoless programming** is sometimes used when describing formal reviews such as structured walkthroughs. Some people consider programming an art. Thus they are particularly sensitive to having their programs scrutinized by others who may react negatively to a program's more creative coding aspects. Egoless programming relates to a fundamental philosophy of review methods: One should not take constructive criticism personally.

Some organizations also conduct a walkthrough during the design stage, to ensure that the analyst or programmer has properly planned the application before coding starts. When a walkthrough is conducted at the design stage it is commonly called a *formal design review;* at the coding stage, it is a *formal code inspection.* Some organizations use informal procedures to accomplish walkthrough-type tasks.

CHIEF PROGRAMMER TEAM. When a program (or set of programs) is expected to be very large—with, say, 20,000 or more lines of code—several programmers may be assigned to the coding operation. A **chief programmer team** is simply a team of programmers coordinated by a highly experienced person called a chief programmer. The chief programmer will assign the program modules to the programmers on the team. He or she ordinarily will code the most critical modules and assign less important ones to subordinates. The modules are typically coded in a top-down fashion, in which the higher-level modules are designed and integrated before the ones below them.

The chief programmer is also responsible for fitting all the individual modules into a workable whole by some target date. He or she will normally have the assistance of a *backup programmer,* who helps with the coding and integration of modules, and a *librarian,* who performs many of the clerical tasks associated with the project. An organization chart for a chief programmer team is shown in Figure 9-4.

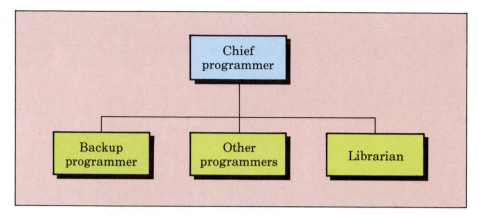

Figure 9-4. *Organization of a chief programmer team.* The chief programmer team is often compared to a surgical team. Each member has a specialized role and there is a careful division of work.

DEBUGGING PROGRAMS

Debugging is the process of making sure that a program is free of errors, or "bugs." Debugging is usually a lengthy process, often accounting for over 50 percent of the total development time for a program.

Preliminary Debugging

The debugging process often begins after the program has been keyed. At this point the programmer will visually inspect the program, before compiling and running it, for typing errors. This is called a *desk check*. When a desk check reveals no apparent errors, the program is submitted to the computer for compiling and subsequent execution.

Rarely are any programs error-free the first time you attempt to compile them. It is not unusual for a very long program to have well over 100 errors at the outset. The systems software of the computer will usually provide a list of informative "error messages" to the programmer that indicates the source of many of the bugs. At this point the programmer again checks the code to see what's wrong and then makes the necessary corrections. This "compile/run/desk check/correct" process may be repeated several times.

Sometimes, after the easy errors have been corrected, the programmer's desk checking may fail to weed out the remaining errors. Diagnostic ("dummy") statements may need to be inserted temporarily to show how the program is executing. Or more drastically, the programmer may need to summon a special diagnostic program to find out what is being stored in computer memory when the program aborts. If all else fails, the programmer can ask someone else for help. Sometimes a few minutes of consultation can save several days of wasted effort. In any case the programmer will normally have to utilize many strategies to get the program in working order.

Testing

At some point in the debugging process, the program will appear to be correct. At this point the original programmer, or preferably someone else, will run the program with extensive *test data*. Good test data will subject the program to all the conditions it might conceivably encounter when finally implemented. The test data should also check for likely sources of coding omissions: For example, will the program issue a check or a bill for a $0.00 amount? Does the program provide for leap years when dating reports? Many more program bugs are often found during the testing phase of the debugging process. Although rigorous testing does significantly decrease the chance of malfunctioning when a program is implemented, there is no foolproof guarantee that the completed program will be free of bugs.

Purchased software should also be tested before implementation. A firm buying a package from an outside vendor must keep in mind that the programs may have been developed for a different type of company or for another type of computer or operating system. If so, modifications may have to be made to enable the programs to work satisfactorily. In any case few packages are completely bug-free to begin with, which is another good reason to test them thoroughly.

Proper debugging is vitally important because an error that may cost a few dollars to fix at this stage in the development process can cost many thousands of dollars to repair after the program is implemented in the real world.

PROGRAM DOCUMENTATION

Program **documentation** includes manuals that enable users, maintenance programmers, and operators to interact successfully with a program.

User documentation normally consists of a user's manual. This manual should provide instructions for running the program, a description of language commands, several examples of situations the user is likely to encounter, and a troubleshooting guide to help with difficulties. The user's manual is an extremely important piece of documentation. If it is poorly written, users may refuse to work with the program altogether.

Programmer documentation usually consists of any tools that simplify maintenance of the program. These might include a program narrative, design tools such as flowcharts and structure charts, a listing of the program, and a description of inputs and outputs. There should also be a set of procedures to help programmers test the program.

Operator documentation includes manuals that assist operators in mounting tapes, printed forms, and the like, which are needed to get programs "up and running." Since operator documentation is machine dependent, a company that purchases a package must often rewrite this part of the vendor-supplied documentation to suit its own equipment.

Although documentation is included here as the last step in the program development cycle, it should be considered an ongoing process. For example, as analysts develop display-screen formats in the analysis stage of development, or HIPO charts in the design stage, they should immediatedly put them in a form suitable for the maintenance programmer's documentation package. If they leave this task until later, they will probably forget many important details.

If you've ever had the frustration of getting something to work from poorly written instructions, you should appreciate how valuable good documentation can be.

Summary and Key Terms

Applications software consists of programs that direct computer systems to produce outputs for computer users. Creating, acquiring, and maintaining good applications software is one of the major data processing expenses in any organization.

In most large organizations, the development of applications software is the job of systems analysts and programmers. **Systems analysts** are the people who work with users to assess needs, translate those needs into a list of technical requirements, and design the necessary software. The design specification is then handed to a **programmer,** who codes the program from it. **Maintenance programmers** monitor the software on an ongoing basis, correcting errors and altering the software as applications change.

Creating successful programs commonly involves five stages: analysis, design, coding, debugging, and documentation. These five stages are often called the **program development cycle** (or **program life cycle**).

Analysis in the program development cycle is the process of identifying and defining the problem to be solved, deciding whether the solution involves software, and if it does, defining input, output, and processing requirements.

Some organizations choose to buy their software rather than create it in-house. This decision, which often takes place after the analysis stage of the program development cycle, is frequently called the *make-or-buy decision.*

In the **design** stage of the program development cycle, analysts work from the software requirements developed in the analysis stage to spell out as precisely as possible the nature of the programming solution that will enable the system to meet those requirements. A group of techniques has evolved that has made program design more systematic and programs themselves easier to read and maintain. These techniques are often grouped together under the term *structured techniques*. Techniques that deal specifically with the design and coding of programs are often referred to as **structured programming.** Many tools are available to help the analyst plan structured programs, including structured program flowcharts, pseudocode, structure charts, and HIPO charts.

Once analysts have finished the program design for an application, the next stage is to code the program. **Coding,** which is the job of programmers, is the process of writing a program from a set of specifications. Programming is labor intensive, and when poorly managed, can be a severe drain on an organization's resources. Among the techniques that have been developed to increase programmer productivity are coding standards, structured walkthroughs, and chief programmer teams.

Many data processing shops employ **structured walkthroughs** during the coding stage. A structured walkthrough is a peer evaluation of a programmer's work. The coding is evaluated by four or five other members of the staff, and a meeting is held to discuss good and bad features of the program. The term **egoless programming** is sometimes used when describing formal reviews such as structured walkthroughs, implying that one shouldn't take constructive criticism personally. Some organizations also conduct a walkthrough during the design stage, to ensure that the systems analyst has properly planned the application.

A **chief programmer team** is simply a team of programmers coordinated by a highly experienced person called a *chief programmer*. The chief programmer will assign the program modules to the programmers on the team and coordinate the fitting of all the indiviual modules into a workable whole by some target date.

Debugging is the process of making sure a program is free of errors, or "bugs." It is usually a lengthy process, and often accounts for over 50 percent of the total development time for an in-house program.

At some point in the debugging process, the program will appear to be correct. Then the programmer, or preferably someone else, will run the original program with extensive *test data*. Good test data will subject the program to all the conditions it might conceivably encounter when finally implemented.

Program **documentation** includes manuals that enable users, maintenance programmers, and operators to interact successfully with a program. Although noted as the final stage of the program development cycle, documentation is an ongoing process that should be addressed from the outset of a project.

Review Exercises

Fill-in Questions

1. _____ are the people who define the requirements that applications software must meet to satisfy the needs of users.

2. _____ are the people involved with keeping an organization's existing programs in proper working order.

3. _____ refers to the writing of computer programs.

4. A formal development process in which the work of a systems analyst or programmer is constructively reviewed by peers is called a(n) _____.

5. The process of detecting or correcting errors in computer programs is called _____.

6. A(n) _____ is a manual inspection process whereby a programmer scans a program for errors prior to submitting it to the computer for execution.

Matching Questions

Match each term with its description.

a. Analysis
b. Design
c. Chief programmer team
d. Documentation
e. Flowchart
f. Pseudocode
g. Module
h. Program design tools

_____ 1. Flowcharts, pseudocode, structure charts, and HIPO charts are examples.

_____ 2. A group of programmers, often assigned to a large programming project, that is coordinated by a highly experienced programmer.

_____ 3. A graphical design tool with boxes and arrows showing, step by step, how a computer program will process data.

_____ 4. The process of planning a program, undertaken after a problem area has been analyzed.

_____ 5. A technique for designing programs that uses English-like statements, resembling actual program statements, to show the step-by-step processing a program will follow.

_____ 6. A well-defined task represented on a structure chart or HIPO chart.

_____ 7. A written description of a program, procedure, or system.

_____ 8. The process of studying a problem area to determine what should be done.

Discussion Questions

1. What is applications software?

2. Name the stages in the program development cycle.

3. What types of decisions must be made in defining software requirements?

4. Name some advantages and disadvantages of buying packaged software.
5. Why have structured techniques evolved as a major strategy in program design?
6. Identify some ways to increase programmer productivity.
7. Why is program documentation important?

Program Design Tools

Chapter Outline

Objectives

After completing this chapter you should be able to:

1. Describe various techniques used to make programs structured and explain why it is desirable to structure programs.
2. Identify the strengths and weaknesses of various program design tools.
3. Draw elementary flowcharts, structure charts, and HIPO charts, as well as construct simple pseudocode.

OVERVIEW

In Chapter 9 you learned how organizations develop applications software. In that chapter we focused on the program development cycle, which begins with problem analysis and ends with a working program. In this chapter we will focus on one stage of that cycle—design.

We will begin with a discussion of one of the earliest and most widely used program design tools, program flowcharts. We then describe some principles of structured programming. Next we will discuss in detail four design tools for structured programming—structured program flowcharts, pseudocode, structure charts, and HIPO charts. Finally we will cover decision tables and other design tools.

WHAT ARE PROGRAM DESIGN TOOLS?

It's extremely difficult just to sit down and write a good program if it is to be long or complex. Before you begin coding, you need a plan for the program. **Program design tools** are, essentially, program planning tools. They consist of various kinds of diagrams, charts, and tables that outline either the organization of program tasks or the steps the program will follow. Once a program is coded and implemented, program design tools also provide excellent documentation for maintenance programmers.

Many of the tools we will discuss in this chapter were developed for structured programming. One of the oldest and still one of the most popular design tools, however, was in use long before structured programming became established. This is the program flowchart.

Because it is difficult to discuss structured programming without resorting to a design tool to help illustrate the concepts involved, we will introduce you to program flowcharts before we move on to structured programming and other design tools.

PROGRAM FLOWCHARTS

Program flowcharts use geometric symbols, such as those in Figure 10-1, and familiar mathematical symbols, such as those in Figure 10-2, to provide a graphic portrayal of the sequence of steps involved in a program. The steps in a flowchart follow each other in the same logical sequence as their corresponding program statements will follow in a program.

For many years flowcharting symbols were nonstandardized, which made it difficult for one programmer to follow the work of another. Today there are a number of standards. Among the most popular are those

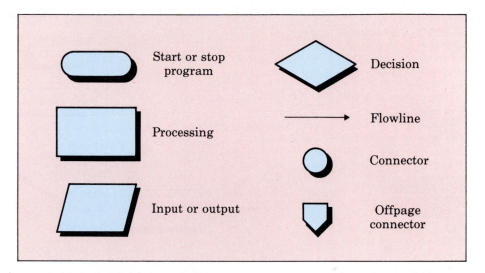

Figure 10-1.   ANSI program flowchart symbols.

Symbol	Meaning
<	Less than
≤	Less than or equal to
>	Greater than
≥	Greater than or equal to
=	Equal to
< >	Not equal to

Figure 10-2.   Mathematical symbols used in flowcharts.

developed by ANSI, the American National Standards Institute (see Figure 10-1). To help you understand what these symbols mean and show you how to use them, let's consider some examples.

SATURDAY PLANS.   The flowchart in Figure 10-3 illustrates the process involved in planning your Saturday activities. This particular flowchart uses four symbols: start/stop, processing, decision, and connector. The lines with arrows that link the symbols are called **flowlines**—they indicate the flow of logic in the flowchart.

Every flowchart begins and ends with an oval-shaped **start/stop symbol.** The first of these symbols in the program contains the word *Start;* the last, the word *Stop.* The diamond-shaped **decision symbol** always indicates a question, which will generally have only two possible answers— yes or no (true or false). Decision symbols should always have one flowline entering and two flowlines (representing the two possible outcomes) exiting.

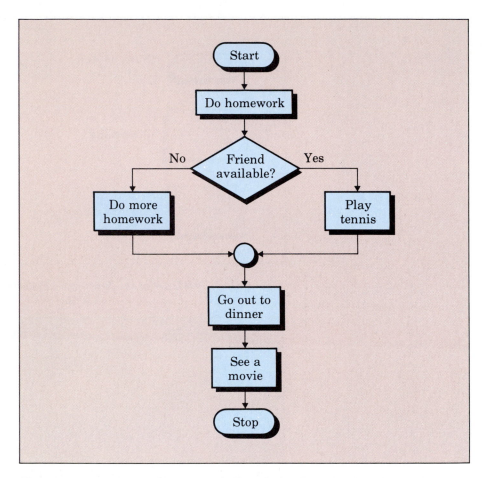

Figure 10-3.   A simple program flowchart. The situation depicted by the flowchart represents your plans for this Saturday. You will start off in the morning by doing homework. If your best friend is free for the afternoon, you will play tennis; otherwise you will do more homework. In any event, during the evening you will go out to dinner and then to a movie.

The rectangular **processing symbol** contains an action that needs to be taken; for example, "Do Homework" or "See a Movie." The **connector symbol** provides a logical point on the flowchart for several flowlines to meet.

SCANNING A FILE FOR EMPLOYEES WITH CERTAIN CHARACTERIS-TICS.   Now let's consider a more complicated example. A common problem in data processing is scanning an employee file for people with certain characteristics. Suppose, for example, the personnel department of a company wanted a printed list of all employees with computer experience and at least five years of company service. A flowchart that shows how to accomplish this task, and also totals the number of employees who meet these conditions, is shown in Figure 10-4.

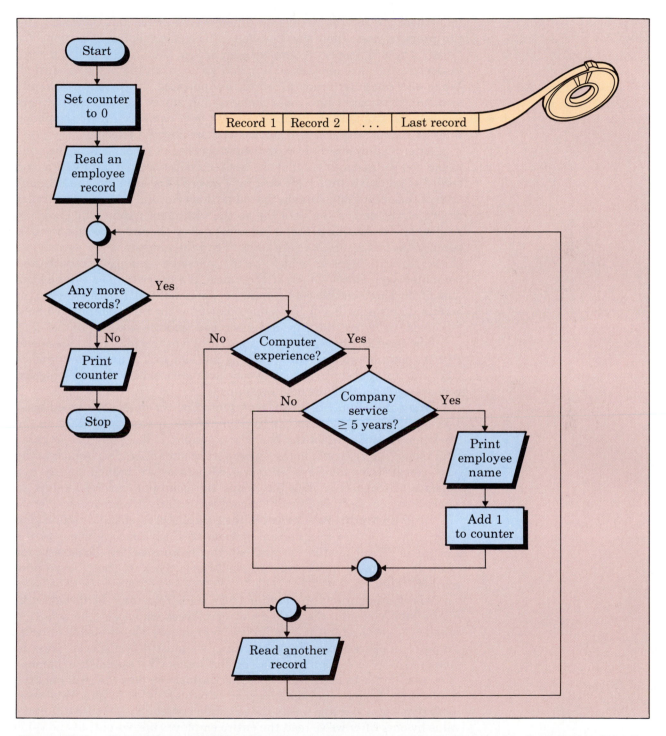

Figure 10-4. Scanning an employee file. The situation represented by the flowchart is the following: Print the names of all people in an employee file with computer experience and at least five years of company service. Also, count the number of such people and print out this count.

There are several interesting differences between this flowchart and the previous one. First, this flowchart involves a *looping* operation. We "read" a record, inspect it, and take an action; then read another record, inspect it, and take another action; and so on, until the file is exhausted. When the computer reads a record, as indicated by the **input/output symbol,** it brings it into main memory and stores its contents (or field values); for example, an employee's ID and name, address, telephone number, department, years of service, and previous experience.

After reading a record, we immediately check to see if it is the last one in the file. We assume here that the last record in the file is not really a true record at all, but a *trailer* (or *sentinel*) record—for example, the "Name" field of this record may contain the value "Last Record." We put this trailer record at the end of the data file so the computer system will know, on reading and inspecting it, that it has encountered the end of the file. If we've reached the last record, we take steps to end the program. If we haven't, we check the two fields in which we're interested—company service and computer experience—to see if they meet the criteria we've established. Only if any employee has *both* computer experience and at least five years of service do we print his or her name (shown by the input/output symbol). Otherwise we bypass the print operation and read the next record.

The flowchart in Figure 10-4 is also different from the previous one in that it contains two types of branching mechanisms. A program *branches* whenever a statement in a block of code is capable of directing the program somewhere other than the next line of code.

In a **conditional branch,** represented by the diamond-shaped decision box, the program proceeds to either of two places, depending on the condition encountered in the box. For example, if the name in the name field is not "Last Record" in the "Any more records?" box, we branch to the box indicated by the "Yes" flowline. Otherwise we branch to the box indicated by the "No" flowline. Thus the condition involved refers to whether or not the "Last Record" record is currently in memory.

In an **unconditional branch,** the program proceeds to a certain step *every time* it comes to a certain statement. Each time we come to the statement "Read another record" at the bottom of the flowchart, for example, we make an unconditional branch back to the "Any more records?" step.

Another important observation to be made regarding the flowchart in Figure 10-4 concerns the totaling of employees who meet the selection criteria. To get this total, we "count" every employee who meets the criteria. To perform operations such as counting, we must define special areas in main memory to hold the values of the totals. We establish a name— "Counter" in the example—to represent the memory area that will hold the total. At the beginning of the program, "Counter" is set to zero. Whenever we find an employee who meets the selection criteria, we increase Counter's value by one. After we've read the entire employee file, we output the value of "Counter" just before the program ends.

It's good practice to set all counts or sums (often referred to as *accumulators*) to zero at the beginning. Otherwise, when the program is coded and executed, you may get incorrect results. Setting a count or sum to a specific value at the beginning of a program or flowchart is called **initializing.**

Figure 10-5. A flowchart showing how to compute the average of a set of examination scores.

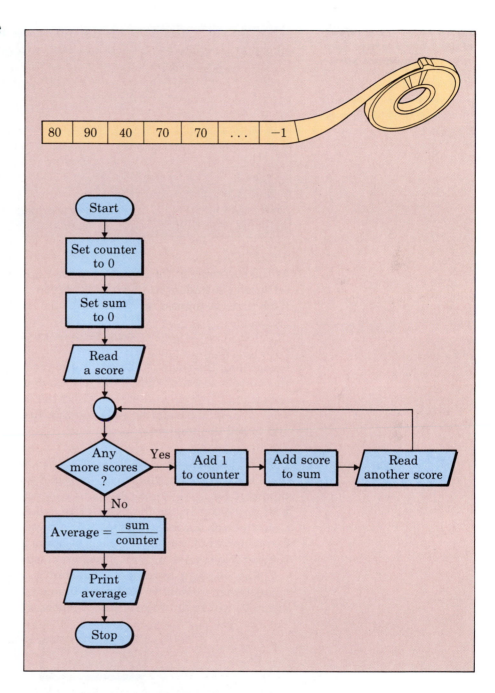

COMPUTING AN AVERAGE. Another common problem encountered in data processing is computing the average of a set of numbers. Figure 10-5 is a flowchart for computing the average of a set of examination scores.

Computing an average involves three basic operations:

✖ *Summing* all scores ("Sum" in the flowchart)

✖ *Counting* the number of scores ("Counter" in the flowchart)

✖ *Dividing* "Sum" by "Counter" (producing "Average" in the flowchart)

When the Value of "Score" Is	The Operation "Add Score to Sum" Does the Following
80	Adds 80 to 0, producing "Sum" = 80
90	Adds 90 to 80, producing "Sum" = 170
40	Adds 40 to 170, producing "Sum" = 210
. . .	. . .
−1	Not performed

At the beginning of the flowchart in Figure 10-5, "Sum" and "Counter" are set to zero. A trailer record with a score of −1 marks the end of the data file. Each time the processing operation

```
Add Score to Sum
```

is executed, the value of "Score" in the record being processed is added to the current value of "Sum." Figure 10-6 summarizes the results of this operation. The trailer value of −1 on the last record alerts the computer system to end the counting and summing, to compute and print the average, and to end the program.

FURTHER USES OF CONNECTOR-TYPE SYMBOLS. As we've already seen, the connector symbol can be used to provide a logical point on the flowchart for flowlines to meet. The connector symbol can also be used to prevent clutter in the flowchart or to avoid the confusion created by the need to cross flowlines. Figure 10-7, a flowchart that computes the wages earned for employees on the basis of hours worked, illustrates the use of a connector symbol to prevent flowchart clutter.

The **offpage connector symbol** is used instead of the connector symbol when we want to continue a flowchart from one page to another. For example, we can draw the offpage connector

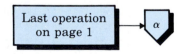

at the bottom of page 1, and at the start of page 2 resume the flowchart with

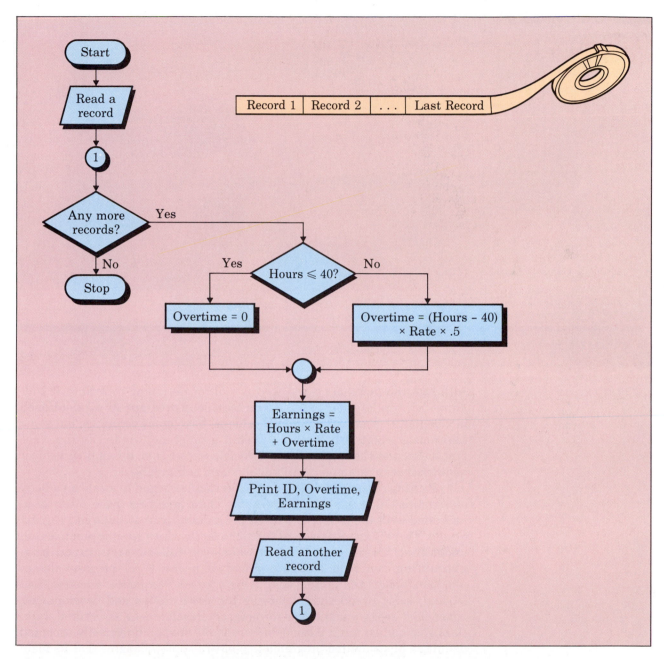

Figure 10-7.   Computing wages. Each record processed contains an employee's ID number, the applicable hourly rate of pay, and the hours worked. The amount earned for each employee is computed as Hourly rate X Hours worked for the first 40 hours worked, and 1.5 X Hourly rate X Hours worked for each hour thereafter.

Flowchart symbols are often drawn with the aid of a plastic *flowcharting template,* such as the one shown in Figure 10-8. These templates are usually available in office supply and college book stores.

Figure 10-8. Flowcharting template.

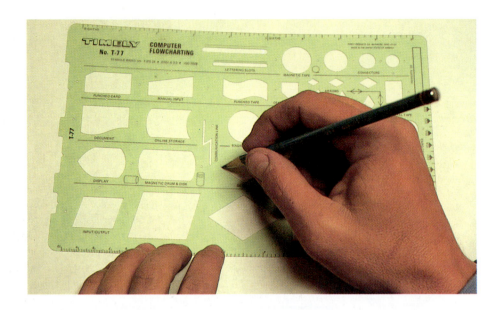

STRUCTURED PROGRAM DESIGN

Although the flowchart is a powerful tool for designing programs, it isn't always appropriate, nor does it guarantee a good program. As we mentioned in Chapter 9, most programming problems have many solutions, but some solutions are better than others. Even if a program "works," in the sense that it executes the application for which it was written, it is of little value if maintenance programmers can't understand and modify it.

Starting in the mid-1960s, a series of studies began to establish a body of practices for good program design. These practices have often been identified with the terms *structured programming* or *structured program design*. There is much debate today over exactly which specific practices fall under these terms. Depending on whom you talk to, **structured programming** can refer to one or more of a variety of program design practices—using the specific control structures of sequence, selection, and looping; using pseudocode; following top-down design and development; using chief programmer teams for program development, structured walk-throughs, and so forth. Although there is no precise, universally accepted definition of structured programming, most people will agree that its main thrust is to:

✕ Increase programmer productivity

✕ Enhance program clarity by minimizing complexity

✕ Reduce program testing time

✕ Decrease program maintenance cost

This section discusses two design practices that are often included under definitions of structured programming: the use of three basic control structures and top-down design.

The Three Basic Control Structures

Advocates of structured programming have shown that any program can be constructed out of three fundamental **control structures:** sequence, selection, and looping. Figure 10-9 illustrates these structures by using flowchart symbols.

A **sequence control structure** is simply a series of procedures that follow one another. The **selection** (or **if-then-else**) **control structure** involves a choice: *if* a certain condition is true, *then* follow one procedure; *else,* if false, follow another. A *loop* is an operation that repeats until a certain condition is met. As the figure shows, a **looping** (or **iteration**) **control structure** can take two forms: DOWHILE and DOUNTIL. With **DOWHILE** a loop is executed as long as a certain condition is true ("do while true"). With **DOUNTIL** a loop continues as long as a certain condition is false ("do until true"). You should also note that a major difference between these two forms of looping control structure is that with DOUNTIL, the loop procedure will be executed at least once, because the procedure appears before any test is made about whether to exit the loop. With DOWHILE the procedure may not be executed at all, because the loop-exit test appears before the procedure.

The three basic control structures are the major building blocks for structured program flowcharts and pseudocode, which are discussed later in the chapter.

THE CASE STRUCTURE. By nesting two or more if-then-else's, you can build a fourth structure, known as the **case control structure.** For example, referring to Figure 10-4, the two individual choices, "Computer Experience?" and "Company Service ≥ 5 Years?," could be joined into the following case structure:

Case I: No Computer Experience, Company Service < 5 Years

Case II: No Computer Experience, Company Service ≥ 5 Years

Case III: Computer Experience, Company Service < 5 Years

Case IV: Computer Experience, Company Service ≥ 5 Years

Many programming languages have statements that enable programmers easily to code case structures.

ONE ENTRY POINT, ONE EXIT POINT. An extremely important fact about the control structures discussed so far is that each of them permits only one entry point into and one exit point out of the structure. This is sometimes called the **one-entry-point/one-exit-point rule.** Observe the marked

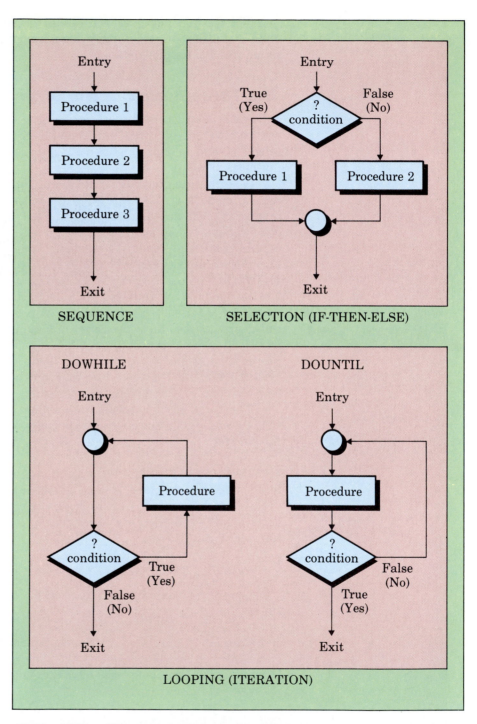

Figure 10-9. *The three fundamental control structures of structured programming.* Note that each structure has one entry point and one exit point.

entry and exit points in Figure 10-9. The one-entry-point/one-exit-point convention encourages a modular programming approach that makes programs more readable.

Top-Down Design

A long book without chapters, sections, or paragraphs would be hard to read. In the same way, programs are easier to read if they are broken down into clearly labeled segments, or **modules,** each of which performs a well-defined task.

Program modules should be arranged hierarchically, in a top-down fashion, so that their relationship to each other is apparent. Such an arrangement is similar to the organization charts many companies use to show the relationships among job titles. **Top-down design** indicates that modules are conceptualized first at the highest levels of the hierarchy, and then at successively lower levels. Lower-level modules should do the actual work in the program, whereas higher-level modules should perform control functions, switching from one lower-level module to another as appropriate.

The use of top-down modular constructions for designing programs is illustrated later in the chapter, in the sections on structure charts and HIPO charts.

TOOLS FOR STRUCTURED PROGRAM DESIGN

An outgrowth of the trend toward structured programming has been the development of a number of tools for structured program design. In this section we will discuss four of these tools—structured program flowcharts, pseudocode, structure charts, and the HIPO method.

Structured Program Flowcharts

Structured program flowcharts are, simply, program flowcharts that have been drawn by using the three control structures of structured programming. All of the flowcharts shown thus far in the chapter are structured. Figures 10-10 and 10-11 demonstrate what these structures look like when imbedded in a complete flowchart (also refer to the box on pages 304–305).

Figure 10-10 is a flowchart for computing payments owed to salespeople. Each record contains the name and number of units sold for each salesperson. The salespeople are paid on commission, which is a percentage of the value of sales. In addition, if they sell over 10,000 units of the company's product, they receive a $100 bonus. As the records are read

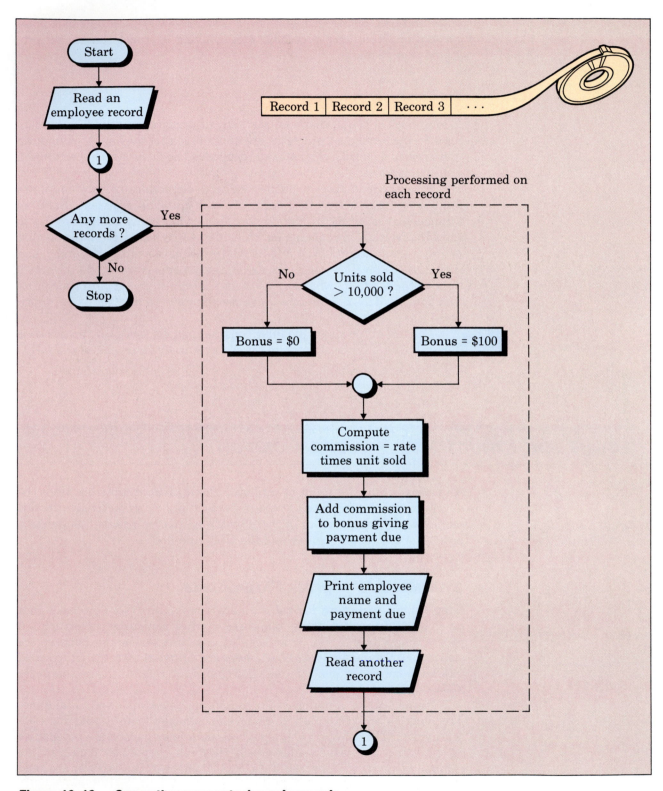

Figure 10-10. *Computing payments due salespeople.*

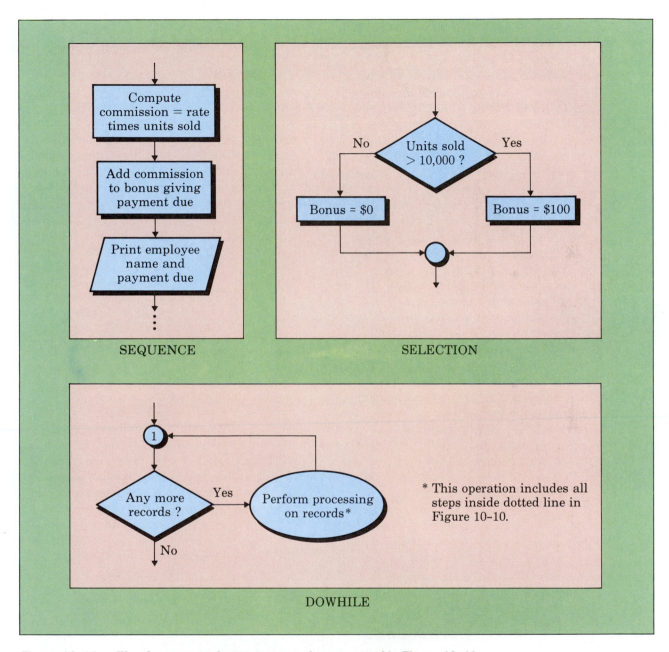

Figure 10-11. **The three control structures as they are used in Figure 10-10.**

sequentially, the payment due is computed and the name of the salesperson is output with the amount due.

The flowchart uses three control structures—SEQUENCE, SELECTION, and DOWHILE—as shown in Figure 10-11. Observe again that the flowchart is constructed entirely from fundamental control structures and that each structure has one entry and one exit point.

Drawing Structured Flowcharts

USING A "PRIMING STATEMENT" TO MAKE FLOWCHARTS MORE STRUCTURED

Program flowcharts were never intended to be tools to support structured programming. It's not that they were originally developed to encourage unruly practices; it's just that people were using them to express program logic well before anyone had even thought of structured programming, or for that matter, program maintenance. Nonetheless they are still extremely useful tools and it will probably be appropriate for programmers to work with them for many years to come.

A major objection to flowcharts raised by structured programming advocates is that it's easy, and often faster, to draw flowcharts that contain structures other than sequence, selection, and iteration. Often these unconventional structures force the programmer to use the GO TO statement when the flowchart is later translated into code. GO TO statements are to be avoided in structured programming because they do not fit within the three control structures and they lead to violation of the one-entry-point/one-exit-point rule.

Let's consider an example. Suppose we wish to design a program that successively reads a number, from a list of positive numbers, and prints it. The last number in the list is −1, a sentinel value that will end the program. A traditional flowchart for solving this problem appears in the accompanying figure. The part of the flowchart in the dashed box is not a conventional iteration structure. Consequently this structure will *always* require a GO TO when we translate the flowchart into code.

If we put another READ statement into the flowchart, however, as shown in the flowchart at the rightmost part of the figure, we have a conventional iteration structure—DOWHILE. In other words, *while* the number in memory is not −1, we *do* the following: print the number and read the next number in the list. If the programming language you are using has a built-in DOWHILE construct, the coded version of the flowchart will *not* require a GO TO. The topmost READ statement in this flowchart is often called a "priming READ," or more generally, a "priming statement."

Priming statements make flowcharts a bit more complicated to draw at first, but they do produce structured programs. Because this text ascribes to a structured philosophy, all of the iteration structures found here conform to this style. If you program in languages such as COBOL and Pascal, it's virtually impossible to

Pseudocode

An alternative to the flowchart that has become extremely popular in recent years is **pseudocode.** This structured technique uses English-like statements in place of the graphic symbols of the flowchart. An example of pseudocode is shown in Figure 10-12 (page 306).

Pseudocode looks more like a program than a flowchart. In fact it's often easier to code a program from pseudocode than from a flowchart because the former provides a codelike outline of the processing to take place. As a result the program designer has more control over the end product—the program itself. Unlike a flowchart, pseudocode is also easy to

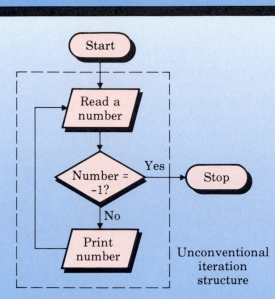

Traditional (unstructured) flowchart

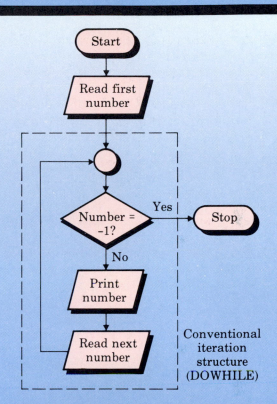

Structured flowchart with priming read

write acceptable programs without following some conventional iteration style, either DOWHILE or DOUNTIL.

The BASIC programming language is a bit more lax with respect to structures, and many versions of it support (and perhaps therefore encourage) unconventional structures. This is not entirely bad, as ignoring rules of structure at the outset often makes it easier for beginners to grasp how programming languages work. Still one should understand that this is *not* the programming style followed by commercial programming shops. If you get into the habit of writing unstructured programs, you may find the habit hard to break.

modify, and it can be embedded in the program as comments. Flowcharts, however, because they are visual, are sometimes better than pseudocode for designing logically complex problems.

There are no standard rules for writing pseudocode, but Figure 10-13 (page 307) describes one set of rules that has a wide following. Note that all words relating to the three control structures of structured programming are capitalized and form a "sandwich" around other processing steps, which are indented. As you can see in Figure 10-14 (page 308), indentation is also used when one control structure is nested within another.

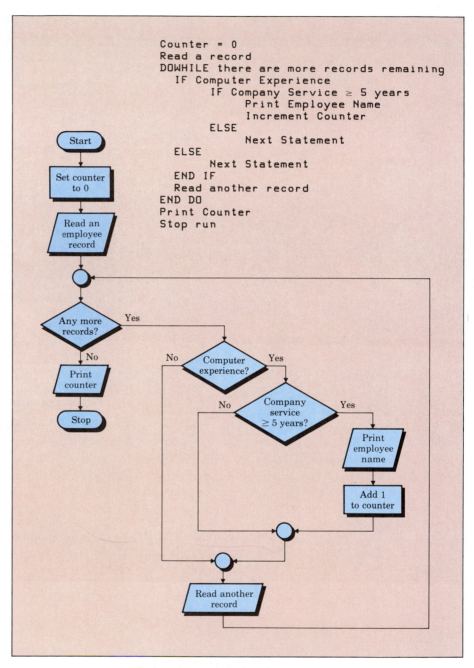

```
Counter = 0
Read a record
DOWHILE there are more records remaining
   IF Computer Experience
         IF Company Service ≥ 5 years
               Print Employee Name
                Increment Counter
            ELSE
                Next Statement
      ELSE
            Next Statement
   END IF
   Read another record
END DO
Print Counter
Stop run
```

Figure 10-12. *Pseudocode to solve the employee file problem of Figure 10-4.* (The flowchart of Fig. 10-4 is at the left.) The problem requires printing the names of all people in an employee file with computer experience and at least five years of company service. A count of the number of such people is also required as output.

SEQUENCE CONTROL STRUCTURE

BEGIN processing task
Processing steps
END processing task

The steps in the sequence structure are normally written in lowercase letters. If the steps make up a well-defined block of code, they should be preceded by the keywords BEGIN and END.

SELECTION CONTROL STRUCTURE

IF condition
Processing steps
ELSE
Processing steps
END IF

The key words IF, ELSE, and END IF are always capitalized and tiered. The condition and processing steps normally are written in lowercase letters. The processing steps are indented from the key words in the manner illustrated.

LOOP (DOWHILE AND DOUNTIL) CONTROL STRUCTURES

DOWHILE condition   DOUNTIL condition
Processing steps   Processing steps
END DO   END DO

The keywords DOWHILE (or DOUNTIL) and END DO are always capitalized and tiered. The condition and processing steps follow the same lowercase convention and indentation rules as the selection control structure.

Figure 10-13.   Some rules for pseudocode.

Structure Charts

Structure charts, unlike flowcharts and pseudocode, depict the overall organization of a program but not the specific processing logic involved in step-by-step execution. They show how the individual segments, or modules, of a program are defined and how they relate to each other. Each module may, of course, consist of one or more fundamental control structures.

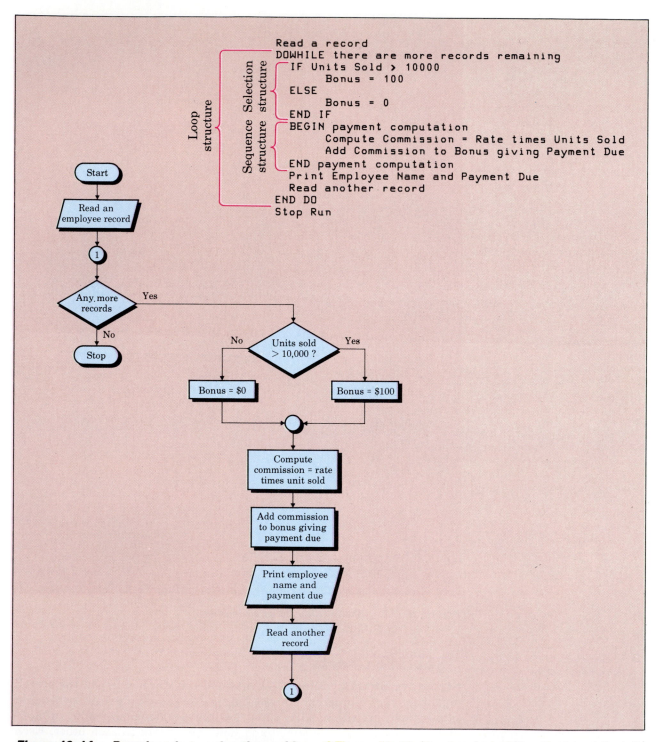

```
                                    Read a record
                                    DOWHILE there are more records remaining
                                      IF Units Sold > 10000
                                            Bonus = 100
                                      ELSE
                                            Bonus = 0
                                      END IF
                                      BEGIN payment computation
                                            Compute Commission = Rate times Units Sold
                                            Add Commission to Bonus giving Payment Due
                                      END payment computation
                                      Print Employee Name and Payment Due
                                      Read another record
                                    END DO
                                    Stop Run
```

Figure 10-14.   *Pseudocode to solve the problem of Figure 10-10.* (The flowchart of Fig. 10-10 is at the left.) Each employee record contains the name and number of units sold for each salesperson. As records are read sequentially, the payment is computed and the name of the salesperson is output with the amount due.

tomorrow

PROGRAM DESIGN TOOLS OF THE FUTURE

**Look at Tomorrow's Needs to Find
Tomorrow's Successful Design Tools**

During the past forty years, computer applications have become more complex. Firms that once used a handful of accounting programs now find themselves with thousands of pieces of applications software (many of them interrelated) that must be managed. The increasing sophistication of the applications development environment has demanded the creation of new tools and management techniques to bring order to what is now a potentially chaotic situation.

All of the development tools that you've studied in this chapter evolved as responses to needs. Program flowcharts, for example, were created decades ago to help people visually organize the steps a program follows as it solves a problem. But the flowchart has limitations, and is not the most appropriate planning tool in many situations. For example, as business applications evolved as a major computing need, and COBOL became dominant, tools such as structure charts and pseudocode were created, and have all but replaced flowcharts for COBOL-based problems. Business programs are characterized by relatively simple logic, an input/output emphasis, structured program modules, and lots of coded statements—all of which make flowcharts less valuable.

Technology has also helped fuel the development of design tools. Word processing and display technologies, for example, have made it easier to use pseudocode as a design and documentation tool. And advancements in graphics software and interactive terminals have made it easier than ever to construct diagrammatic tools such as structure charts and data flow diagrams.

As we head into the 1990s, the new applications environments will give rise to their own set of design tools. For example, as voice input evolves as a technology, we may see tools created that include considerations pertaining to the human voice. Also, future programming languages that involve working with parallel processors are likely to be so different from today's sequential high-level languages that they will also require a new set of tools.

Someone will wrestle with a problem and a new tool may evolve.

Basically this is the way each tool will develop. Someone will be wrestling with a problem and looking for a "systematic handle" to manage it—a checklist, a flowchart, a grid of possibilities, whatever. Somewhere along the line, a new approach (tool) to solving the problem will evolve. If it has merit, the tool will be publicized; for example, someone will present a paper at a conference or submit an article to a professional journal. Other people, including university professors, will evaluate the worth of the tool. If it is still seen as being useful after all of this scrutiny, and has a wide-enough applicability, others will probably try it. Gradually it will be refined and improved. If it's successful, you'll probably be reading about it in a future edition of this textbook.

A typical structure chart looks like a corporate organization chart. It consists of several rows of boxes connected by lines. Each box represents a program module. The modules in the upper rows serve *control* functions, directing the program to process modules under them as appropriate. Those modules in the lowest boxes serve specific processing functions. These are the modules that do all the program "work." The lines connecting the boxes indicate the relationship of higher-level to lower-level modules. Figure 10-15*b* is a structure chart for a program that produces the sales report in Figure 10-15*a*.

HIPO Charts

Another useful tool for structured design is the **HIPO (Hierarchy plus Input-Process-Output) chart.** The HIPO method involves the preparation of a set of three different types of diagrams, which vary in the level of detail they address.

The most general of the diagrams is the *Visual Table of Contents* (*VTOC*), shown in Figure 10-16. The VTOC is identical to a structure chart, except that it contains hierarchically sequenced reference numbers in the lower-right-hand corner of each module.

At the second level of detail in the HIPO method are the *overview diagrams,* which show the input, processing, and output involved in each module. Each overview diagram also has a module reference number that corresponds to a module in the VTOC diagram. Figure 10-17 shows overview diagrams for three of the modules in Figure 10-16.

The third level of detail in the HIPO method, the *detail diagram,* contains complete information about the data required and the processing to be performed in each module. The contents of a detail diagram often depend on the complexity of the module it represents, since its main purpose is to aid the programmer in coding.

DECISION TABLES

All the tools discussed in the preceding section can be used to design an entire program. **Decision tables,** in contrast, are generally used to design only a portion of a program. They are especially useful for clarifying a series of complicated conditions—namely, those you find in nested if-then-else or case structures. Whenever a choice among actions depends on which of many possible combinations of criteria have been met, a decison table ensures that no possible combinations are overlooked.

Figure 10-18 shows the format for decision tables. The heading describes the problem to be solved. Under it, in the rows, are listed the important criteria (*conditions*) to be satisfied, followed by the possible *actions* to be taken. The vertical columns (*rules*) represent all the possible cases that may be encountered in practice.

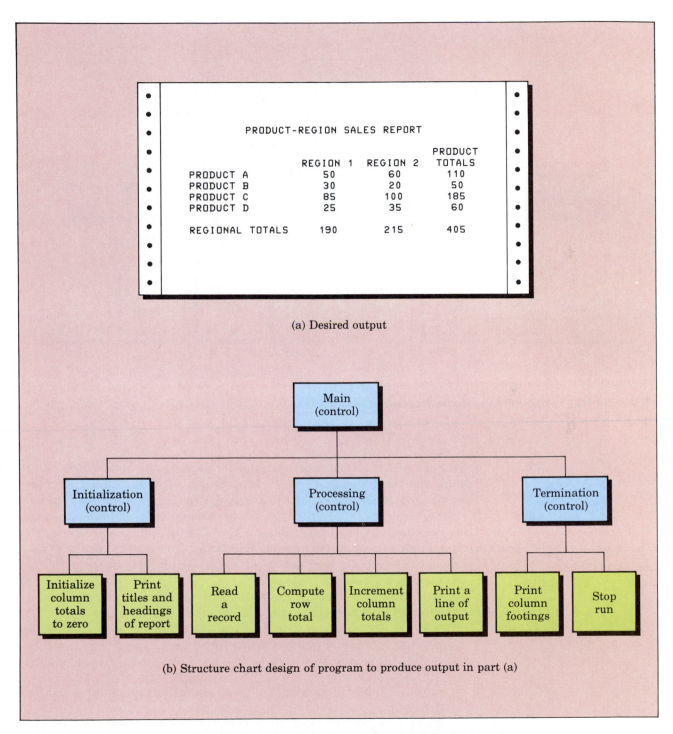

(a) Desired output

(b) Structure chart design of program to produce output in part (a)

Figure 10-15. *Program output and the structure chart of the associated program.*

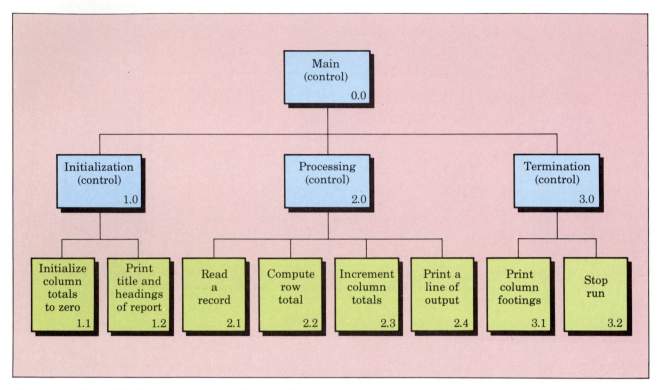

Figure 10-16. **VTOC of the problem depicted in Figure 10-15.**

Figure 10-19 shows a decision table for determining how to respond to people applying for a job. There are two possible responses: send a rejection letter or grant an interview. The response chosen for any applicant depends on three criteria: college education, previous experience, and other qualifications. An applicant who satisfies any two of these criteria will be granted an interview; others will get a rejection letter. In each vertical column of the table, a "Y" signifies a "yes," an "N" a "no." A blank entry indicates that it doesn't matter if the answer is Y or N.

Although the problem in Figure 10-19 is a simple one, decision tables can represent extremely complex situations. They can have:

X Any number of condition and action rows

X Several Y and N values in any single column

X Several X values in any single column (indicating that multiple actions are possible)

In fact the more complicated the situation, the more useful is a decision table. Many people can keep track of the possible outcomes of a simple problem in their heads, but as the number of criteria and actions multiplies, a tool like a decision table becomes imperative.

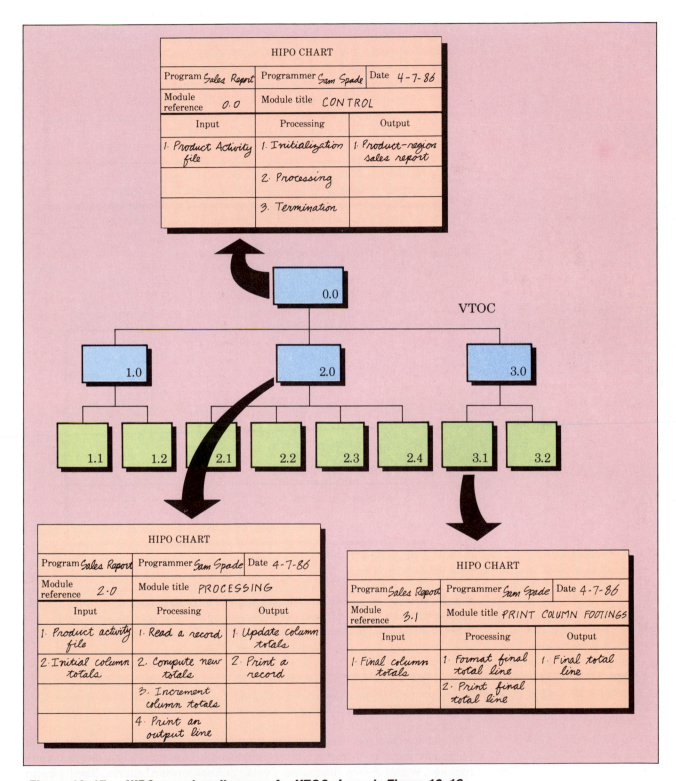

Figure 10-17.   **HIPO overview diagrams for VTOC shown in Figure 10-16.**

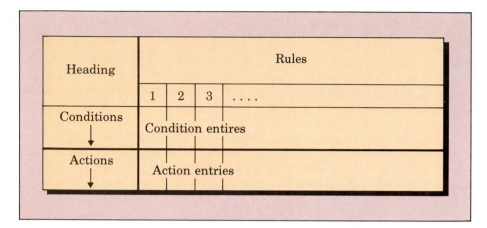

Figure 10-18. *The format of a decision table.*

Hiring Applicants		Rules					
		1	2	3	4	5	6
Conditions	College education?	N	N		Y	Y	
	Experienced?	N		N	Y		Y
	Other qualifications?		N	N		Y	Y
Actions	Rejection letter	X	X	X			
	Interview				X	X	X

Figure 10-19. *A simple decision table.* The table specifies the following: If a job applicant does not meet at least two important criteria (conditions), send a rejection letter (the first action); otherwise grant an interview (the second action).

OTHER DESIGN TOOLS

The design tools covered in this chapter are only a sampling of those currently used by commercial organizations. Other widely used methods include Warnier-Orr diagrams, Nassi-Schneiderman charts (see box on pages 316–317), Meta Stepwise Refinement, and Chapin charts. Some organizations have even created their own design tools for specialized problems. Many schools offer advanced computer courses that place these tools in their proper perspectives.

Summary and Key Terms

Program design tools are program planning tools. They consist of various kinds of diagrams, charts, and tables that outline either the organization of a program or the steps it will follow. Once a program has been coded and implemented, program design tools also provide excellent documentation for maintenance programmers.

Program flowcharts use geometric symbols and familiar mathematical symbols to provide a graphic display of the sequence of steps involved in a program. The steps in a flowchart follow each other in the same logical sequence that their corresponding statements will follow in a program.

The lines with arrows that link the symbols in a flowchart are called **flowlines.** They indicate the flow of logic in the flowchart. Every flowchart begins and ends with a **start/stop symbol.** The diamond-shaped **decision symbol** always indicates a question, which will generally have only two possible answers, such as "yes" or "no." The rectangular **processing symbol** contains an action that needs to be taken. The **input/output symbol** can be used to indicate a read operation or the production of a report. The **connector symbol** provides a logical point on the flowchart for several flowlines to meet. The **offpage connector symbol** is used instead of the connector symbol to continue a flowchart from one page to another.

A program *branches* whenever a statement in a block of code is capable of directing the program somewhere besides the next line of code. In a **conditional branch,** represented by the diamond-shaped decision box, the program proceeds to either of two places, depending on the condition encountered in the box. In an **unconditional branch,** the program proceeds to a certain step every time it comes to a certain statement.

It's good practice in any flowchart to set all counts or sums to zero at the beginning. Otherwise, when the program is coded and executed, you may get incorrect results. Setting a count or sum to a specific value at the beginning of a program or flowchart is called **initializing.**

Beginning in the mid-1960s, a series of studies began to establish a body of practices for good program design. These practices have often been identified by the term *structured programming* (or *structured program design*). There is indeed much debate today over exactly which specific practices fall under these terms.

Nassi-Schneiderman Charts

A STRUCTURED ALTERNATIVE TO TRADITIONAL FLOWCHARTING

Program flowcharts, as noted earlier, were developed well before anyone thought of structured programming. Consequently they are not the ideal tool for designing structured programs. Although we can structure flowcharts by using tools such as ''priming statements'' (see box on pages 304–305), one has to be very careful when drawing the flowchart to make sure that no unconventional structures creep into it.

N-S charts force you to write structured programs.

Nassi-Schneiderman (N-S) charts, in contrast to flowcharts, have built-in, ''idiotproof'' properties to support structured programming. It's impossible to draw an N-S chart with unconventional program structures, and also without exactly one entry point into and one exit point out of each structure. Unconditional branching instructions (which are equivalent to the flowlines interrupting the normal sequence in a flowchart, or a GO TO in a program) are just *not* permitted. Consequently N-S charts force you to write structured, modular programs in spite of yourself. There's just no other alternative.

The three fundamental control structures of structured programming—sequence, selection, and iteration—are shown in the form required by N-S charts in Figure 1. *Sequence* is depicted by a vertical stack of boxes, each containing an operation. *Selection* uses a box divided into five areas: the condition to be tested, ''T,'' ''F,'' the operation to be performed if the condition is true, and the operation to be performed if the condition is false. If more than one operation is to be performed for either condition state, each of these latter two areas may, of course, be subdivided into a sequence of boxes. *Iteration* has two possible forms—one for DOWHILE and another for DOUNTIL—as shown.

How these constructs can be used to draw a complete N-S chart is demonstrated in Figure 2. The problem considered is the salesperson-commission problem described and solved (by flowcharts and pseudocode) in Figure 10-14 (page 308).

In addition to their structured orientation, N-S charts are easy to read and to convert into program code. But they are not always easy to draw, and can often take much longer to develop than equivalent flowcharts and pseudocode. Also, because flowcharts have been around for decades and N-S charts have been available only since 1973, flowcharts are still often the design tool of choice for many programmers.

Although there is no precise, universally accepted definition of **structured programming,** most people will agree that its main thrust is to increase programmer productivity, enhance program clarity by minimizing complexity, reduce program testing time, and decrease program maintenance cost.

Advocates of structured programming have shown that any program can be constructed out of three fundamental **control structures**—sequence, selection, and looping.

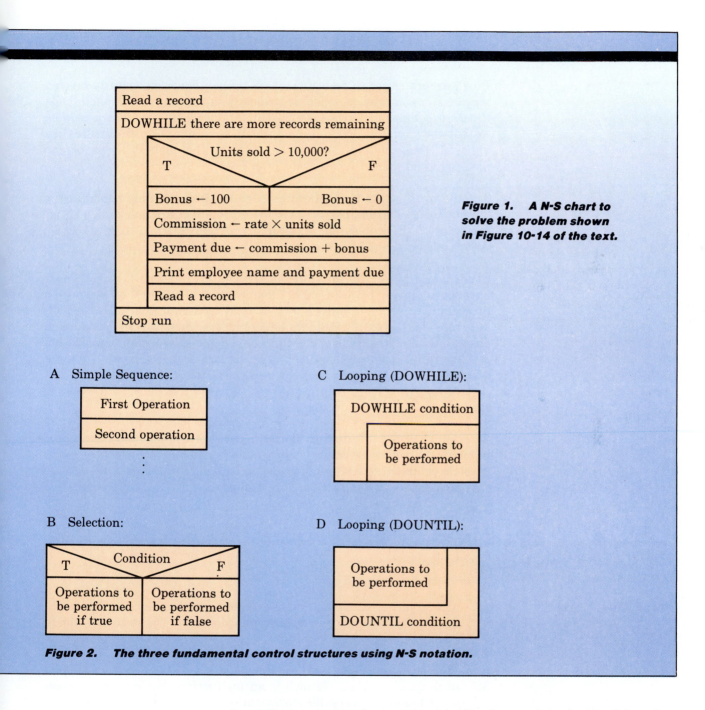

Read a record

DOWHILE there are more records remaining

Units sold > 10,000?

T   F

| Bonus ← 100 | Bonus ← 0 |

Commission ← rate × units sold

Payment due ← commission + bonus

Print employee name and payment due

Read a record

Stop run

Figure 1.   A N-S chart to solve the problem shown in Figure 10-14 of the text.

A   Simple Sequence:

| First Operation |
| Second operation |
.
.
.

B   Selection:

Condition	
T	F
Operations to be performed if true	Operations to be performed if false

C   Looping (DOWHILE):

DOWHILE condition

Operations to be performed

D   Looping (DOUNTIL):

Operations to be performed

DOUNTIL condition

Figure 2.   The three fundamental control structures using N-S notation.

A **sequence control structure** is simply a series of procedures that follow one another. The **selection** (or **if-then-else**) **control structure** involves a choice: *if* a certain condition is true, *then* follow one procedure; *else,* if false, follow another. A **looping** (or **iteration**) **control structure** repeats until a certain condition is met. A loop can take two forms: **DOWHILE** and **DOUNTIL**. By nesting two or more if-then-else's, you can build a fourth control structure, known as a **case control structure**. All of these control structures follow the **one-entry-point/one-exit-**

point rule—that is, a structure can have only one way into it and one way out of it.

Programs are easier to read if they are broken down into clearly labeled segments, or **modules,** each of which performs a well-defined task. Program modules should be organized hierarchically, in a top-down fashion, so that their relationship to each other is apparent. **Top-down design** indicates that modules are defined first at the highest levels of the hierarchy, and then at successively lower levels.

An outgrowth of the trend toward structured programming has been the development of a number of tools for structured program design. Four examples of these tools are structured program flowcharts, pseudocode, structure charts, and HIPO charts.

Structured program flowcharts are, simply, program flowcharts that have been drawn by using the three control structures of structured programming. **Pseudocode** is a structured technique that uses English-like statements in place of the graphic symbols of the flowchart. **Structure charts,** unlike flowcharts and pseudocode, depict the overall organization of a program but not the specific processing logic involved in step- by-step execution. **HIPO (Hierarchy plus Input-Process-Output) charts** involve preparing a set of three different types of diagrams, which vary in the level of detail they address.

Decision tables are used to clarify a series of complicated conditional branches. Whenever a choice among actions depends on which of many possible combinations of criteria have been met, a decision table ensures that no possible combinations are overlooked.

Review Exercises

Fill-in Questions

1. A program _____ uses geometric symbols and familiar mathematical sysmbols to provide a graphic display of the steps involved in a program.
2. A(n) _____ branch is an instruction used to represent a choice in a processing path.
3. A(n) _____ branch is an instruction that causes the computer to execute a specific statement other than the one that immediately follows in the normal sequence.
4. Setting a count or sum to a specific value at the beginning of a program or flowchart is called _____.
5. In _____ design program modules at the highest levels of the hierarchy are defined first, and then those at successively lower levels.
6. _____ is a program design tool that uses English-like statements.

7. _____ and _____ are program design tools that depict the overall organization of a program, rather than the specific processing logic involved in step-by-step execution.

8. _____ are program design tools that use a tabular format and are especially useful for clarifying a series of complicated conditional branches.

Matching Questions

Match each term with its description.

a. Flowlines
b. Start/stop symbol
c. Decision symbol
d. Processing symbol
e. Connector symbol
f. Input/output symbol

_____ 1. A rectangular flowcharting symbol used to represent an operation such as a computation.
_____ 2. The flowcharting symbol used for the READ operation.
_____ 3. The arrows that link the geometric symbols in a flowchart.
_____ 4. A flowcharting symbol used to avoid flowchart clutter.
_____ 5. Used to begin and end every flowchart.
_____ 6. A diamond-shaped flowcharting symbol.

Discussion Questions

1. What is the purpose of each of the flowcharting symbols depicted in Figure 10-1?
2. Provide a flowchart to read a list of positive values and output the number of those values that are greater than 25. Assume the sentinel value -1 appears at the end of the list.
3. What are the objectives of structured programming?
4. Name the three fundamental control structures of structured programming and provide an example of each.
5. What is the difference between the DOWHILE and DOUNTIL control structures?
6. Provide an example that shows the similarity between the case structure and the if-then-else structure.
7. What does the one-entry-point/one-exit-point rule stipulate?
8. What is the difference between a flowchart and a structure chart?
9. Provide a pseudocode solution to the flowchart in Figure 10-5.
10. What is the purpose of a decision table?

Chapter 11

Programming Languages

Chapter Outline

Objectives

After completing this chapter you should be able to:

1. Distinguish between low-level, high-level, and very-high-level programming languages.
2. Identify the uses, key features, and limitations of a number of widely used programming languages.
3. Recognize when one programming language is more suitable than another for a particular application.

OVERVIEW

Programming languages were developed so that people could get the computer to do useful things. Because people vary in their ability to deal with computers and there is an astounding variety of complicated tasks that computers can do, a large number of programming languages have come to the fore. As you will learn in this chapter, each language was created to meet a specific need. There are languages for children and rank beginners, languages for scientists, languages to facilitate typing, languages for projects that require the collective coding efforts of several programmers, languages that take maximum advantage of the computer's speed, languages designed to work on extremely small computers, languages that work best on large computers, and so forth.

A **programming language** can broadly be defined as a set of rules that enable instructions to be written for a computer. The so-called "traditional" programming languages—such as BASIC, Pascal, COBOL,

How to Sharpen Your Thinking:
One Teacher's Opinion

LEARN TO PROGRAM? WHO ME?

When I was a kid, I really hated spinach. As I endlessly rolled it around with a fork from one side of the plate to the other, secretly hoping it would disappear, Mom would always have the same line ready: "If you eat your spinach, you'll be strong like Popeye." So if you ask me why you should learn a programming language, my response is along similar lines: "Learn one and you may someday be able to reason more clearly."

Let's first clear up a few misconceptions you may have about programming. First, although it's true that computers are important and we should all learn more about them, it's not essential that you know how to program expertly in a high-level language to be able to survive in tomorrow's world. Easy-to-use packaged software is available now, and more will be in the future, for you to do most of the things you need to do on a computer. Nonetheless just as learning Latin will enable you to learn

other spoken languages more quickly, learning a high-level programming language will enable you to pick up other things you ought to know about computers more quickly.

A second misconception is that if you can't program well, you might as well not learn to program at all. Using a computer is very much like playing tennis. We don't all have to be able to play at the level of a John McEnroe in order to enjoy it and benefit by it. Anyone who takes the time can learn a lot of valuable computer skills by learning how to program.

Programming is a tool that promotes a logical way to think about problems. For example, you may find that your ability to organize thoughts increases dramatically after you learn to program. Whether you become a doctor, lawyer, or businessperson you'll constantly need to evaluate what strategies are open to you and what possibilities might arise from those strategies. Through the use of

and FORTRAN—are the subject of this chapter. These are the languages that most people think of when they hear the term "programming language." They are the tools of the professional programmer. Later, in Chapters 12 and 13, we'll look at several special-purpose languages that have recently evolved to make noncomputer professionals more productive.

A BRIEF HISTORY OF PROGRAMMING LANGUAGES

The earliest programming languages—machine and assembly languages—are called **low-level languages** because programmers coding in these languages must write instructions at the finest level of detail. This level is closest to that of the computer itself, which is the "base level." Each line of code corresponds to a single action of the computer system.

Machine language, which consists of strings of 0- and 1-bits, is the "speaking tongue" of the computer. Few people actually write programs in

constructs such as if-then-else (selection) structures and decision tables, you'll become more rigorous about taking all conditions into account on any strategical matters. You'll be less likely to let things fall through the cracks.

Learning constructs such as loops often can help you understand concepts in fields such as mathematics. In math you have to deal with such entities as vectors, arrays, and approximations—things that can be expressed readily in program loop structures. Surprisingly, you may even learn how to write better, as programming languages have their own syntax, grammars, and style rules just as the English language does.

And then consider the process of debugging computer programs, which has its real-life counterpart in solving problems. For example, when I was a youngster, my father was always good at fixing things, and I always took my broken gadgets to him. When I grew up and went off to live on my own, I seemed to have my hands full with such problems as car troubles and broken plumbing—the problems that my father usually solved. Fortunately my computer

programming and flowcharting experiences came to bat for me. Every time something went wrong, I would decompose the problem into simple parts and go through a testing process similar to rooting out program bugs to come up with a solution.

Well, I never ate my spinach and perhaps that's why I don't look like Popeye. But learning how to program certainly taught me a lot about how to do a wide range of things in life better.

machine language any more, but all programs written in higher-level languages must eventually be translated into machine language to be executed. We discussed the software that does the translating (assemblers, compilers, and interpreters) in Chapter 8. *Assembly languages,* which represent these detailed machine instructions in a code that is easier to understand than strings of 0s and 1s, is still used frequently by some programmers but is beyond the grasp of most end users.

The next languages to appear were **high-level languages.** Included in this category are what have come to be known as the traditional types of programming languages; for example, BASIC, COBOL, FORTRAN, Pascal, PL/1, APL, and many others. Over 100 such languages are currently in use, and many of these are available in several versions. High-level languages differ from their low-level ancestors in that they require less coding detail. For example, low-level languages require programmers to assign values to specific storage locations and registers in the CPU. The programmer isn't burdened with these tasks when coding in the high-level languages. The translators that convert high-level languages to machine language supply the detail. As a result programs in high-level languages are shorter and easier to write than those in their low-level counterparts.

Some high-level languages, such as BASIC, are relatively easy even for users to learn. However, many dislike programming in any high-level language. Some feel that there are too many rules to remember and that the step-by-step logic involved is too complex. Other users are just too busy to do the volume of programming required to meet their needs with these languages. Yet many of these people could benefit by writing their own programs, if this task were somehow made easier. **Very-high-level languages,** which first began to appear in the 1960s, were developed to meet this need.

We can compare a very-high-level language to a knowledgeable chauffeur. To get where we want to go, we need only give the chauffeur instructions at a general level, such as "Take me to City Hall," instead of a detailed one, such as "From here you make a right; then three blocks later make a left . . ." In the same way, with very-high-level languages, we need only prescribe *what* the computer is to do rather than *how* it is to do it.

For example, we might sum numbers with a very-high-level language by pointing on the screen to the instruction "SUM" and then pointing to the numbers to be summed. This is much easier than creating a mathematical looping procedure to "teach" the computer system how to sum numbers and then typing in and debugging that procedure, as would be required with a low-level or high-level language. Thus low- and high-level languages are sometimes called **procedural languages,** because they require people to define detailed statements that represent sequential steps, or *procedures,* to be performed during program execution. Very-high-level languages, in contrast, are called **nonprocedural languages.**

Very-high-level languages, as well as advances in interactive display technology, are bringing more people into contact with the computer than ever before. These languages do have some serious disadvantages, however. For one thing, they lack flexibility; generally each is designed to do one specific kind of task. You can't, for example, process a payroll with a word processing language. A second major disadvantage is that there are many important applications that are not served by these languages. Nonetheless, for the areas in which they are available, they offer obvious advantages to both programmers and users.

In this chapter RPG is the only very-high-level language discussed. All of the *productivity software packages* covered in Chapters 12 and 13 use very-high-level languages.

ASSEMBLY LANGUAGES

Assembly languages are like machine languages in that each line of code corresponds to a single action of the computer system. But assembly languages replace the 0s and 1s of machine language with symbols (called mnemonics) that are easier to understand and remember, such as "A" for "Add" and "L" for "Load." Because they are closely related to machine languages, which take special advantage of the way the processors on which they run are built, assembly programs often consume less storage and run much faster than their easier-to-use high-level-language counterparts. This efficiency constitutes their primary advantage. Many of the word processing and spreadsheet packages you can buy at your local computer store, for example, are written in assembly language (rather than in BASIC or Pascal).

Unfortunately assembly-language programs take longer to write and maintain than those written in high-level languages such as BASIC, or Pascal. Also, they are very machine dependent. An assembly-language program that works on an IBM Personal Computer, for example, would need substantial modification to run on an Apple Macintosh, which is built around a different microprocessor chip than the IBM. With hardware costs decreasing and software development costs on the rise, assembly languages are gradually losing their competitive edge to higher-level languages in many applications. Yet they are still frequently used because of their speed, efficiency, and ability to meet special-purpose needs.

Some assembly-language commands are provided in Figure 11-1.

BASIC

In the early days of computing, before microcomputers, display devices, and sophisticated communications systems, writing and debugging programs was a painfully slow process. Would-be programmers submitted their punched-card programs to the operator of the computer system and then

Command	Example	Description
LR	LR 7,4	Load the contents of register 4 into register 7.
L	L 8,X	Load the contents of the main-memory location defined by the variable X into register 8.
ST	ST 5,X	Store the contents of register 5 in the main-memory location defined by the variable X.
AR	AR 5,2	Add the contents of register 2 to the contents of register 5, storing the result in register 5.
A	A 5,X	Add the contents of the main-memory location defined by the variable X to the contents of register 5, storing the result in register 5.
SR	SR 5,2	Subtract the contents of register 2 from the contents of register 5, placing the result in register 5.
S	S 5,X	Subtract the contents of the main-memory location defined by the variable X from the contents of register 5, placing the result in register 5.
B	B LOOP	Branch to the statement labeled LOOP.

Figure 11-1. Some examples of assembly-language commands. Note that, as opposed to most high-level languages, there are several commands for each "type" of operation. For example, L, LR, and ST are all "move" operations. The appropriate operation to use depends on whether you want to move values from one register to another, from main memory to a register, or from a register to main memory. Believe it or not, it is not unusual for an assembly language to have *two dozen or more* different commands just to move data.

waited as long as several hours or a day or two for the results. Often the program wouldn't work, and the programmer would receive instead a list of cryptic error messages. These had to be properly diagnosed, the bugs corrected, and the program resubmitted. Getting even a modest program written and debugged could take several days or weeks. It thus took a special kind of persistence to master programming, and many people just weren't interested.

Computer scholars, however, realized that the computer was potentially a tool that could benefit noncomputer professionals in many ways, but only if they could be encouraged to learn programming. Clearly there was a need for an easy-to-learn beginner's language that could work in a "friendly," nonfrustrating programming environment.

BASIC (*B*eginner's *A*ll-purpose *S*ymbolic *I*nstruction *C*ode) was designed to meet these needs. It was developed at Dartmouth College in combination with the world's first time-sharing system. Students communicated with the computer through their own terminals, and turnaround time was usually a matter of seconds. A modest program could easily be conceived, coded, and debugged in a few hours. BASIC also proved to be extremely easy to learn, and many students found it possible to write programs after only a few hours of training.

Over the years BASIC has evolved into one of the most popular and widely available programming languages. Because it is easy to use and the storage requirements for its language translator are small, it works well on almost all general-purpose microcomputers. Many versions of BASIC are available, from stripped-down ones suitable for pocket computers to powerful mainframe versions that rival the processing power of COBOL.

KEY FEATURES. Almost every key feature of BASIC is related to its ease of use for beginners. Among such features are simplified naming of variables, optional formatting, conversational programming mode, and simple diagnostics.

Simplified Naming of Variables. The rules for classifying and naming variables in BASIC are generally simple. Variables are classified as either numeric (for example, A = 6) or alphanumeric (for example, A\$ = "HELLO"). Variable names can begin with any letter of the alphabet. This straightforward naming convention permits beginners to move on quickly to other features of the language.

Optional Formatting. Languages such as COBOL have a detailed set of rules that one must always follow in specifying the format of inputs and outputs. Although such "data declaration" rules are useful for complex programs, they are often a distracting nuisance to the beginner. Mastering them can interfere with learning how computers solve problems. With most versions of BASIC, however, beginners can almost completely ignore formatting data at the outset and learn advanced techniques later.

Conversational Programming Mode. Because BASIC was specifically designed to work on terminals, almost all versions easily enable users and programmers to "converse" interactively with the computer. This makes it possible for beginners to use BASIC to write programs that accept input as the program is running.

Simple Diagnostics. The quality of the error messages generated by a language is extremely important to a beginner. Error messages are supposed to indicate why a program has failed to work. But if a 200-line program

```
10 REM PROGRAM TO COMPUTE SALES
20 REM AUTHOR - C.S. PARKER
30 PRINT "     DESCRIPTION          PRICE          UNITS          TOTAL VALUE"
40 A$="\                    \     $###.##        #,###          $###,###"
50 READ N$,P,U
60 IF N$="LAST RECORD" THEN 150
70 S=P*U
80 PRINT USING A$;N$,P,U,S
90 READ N$,P,U
100 GOTO 60
110 DATA "SMALL WIDGETS",150,100
120 DATA "LARGE SKY HOOKS",200,50
130 DATA "BLIVETS",100,3000
140 DATA "LAST RECORD",0,0
150 END
```

(a) A BASIC program.

DESCRIPTION	PRICE	UNITS	TOTAL VALUE
SMALL WIDGETS	$150.00	100	$ 15,000
LARGE SKY HOOKS	$200.00	50	$ 10,000
BLIVETS	$100.00	3,000	$300,000

(b) Output from the program.

Figure 11-2. **A sample BASIC program and its output.** This program is designed to accept as input the name of a product, its unit selling price, and the number of units sold, and to output this information along with the total dollar value of sales.

doesn't work, and the error messages are confusing or too technical, the result is often frustration. In BASIC the error messages are easier to understand than in most other languages. Also, many versions of BASIC come with a realtime syntax checker that identifies certain kinds of errors in each line of code as it is keyed into the computer system.

LIMITATIONS. Some experts feel that BASIC's chief strength—ease of learning and use—is also its major drawback. Because beginners can get started quickly, they sometimes get started on the wrong foot by sacrificing good programming habits to quick results. Many versions of BASIC support unstructured, trial-and-error coding, so it's easy to write confusing, poorly organized programs. Also, since so many versions of BASIC are available, a program developed on one computer may need substantial modifications to run on another. Finally, because most versions of BASIC use interpreters rather than compilers, BASIC programs often run slowly as compared with programs in other languages.

A sample BASIC program is shown in Figure 11-2.

PASCAL

Pascal, named for the mathematician Blaise Pascal, is a relatively new programming language. It was developed about 1970 by Professor Niklaus Wirth of Zurich, Switzerland.

KEY FEATURES. Pascal was originally created to fill the need for a teaching vehicle that would encourage structured programming. The key features of this language are a structured orientation and memory efficiency.

Structured Orientation. Although BASIC still remains a strong favorite among beginners, many people consider Pascal far superior to most versions of BASIC (and even COBOL) in its structured programming capability.

To say that Pascal is a structured language means that, generally speaking, Pascal programs are made up of smaller subprograms, each of which is itself a structured program. This modular building block approach makes large programs easier to develop. Additionally, Pascal contains a rich variety of control structures—such as DOWHILE and DOUNTIL—that enable programmers to manipulate these modules in a systematic fashion.

Pascal also has an explicit data declaration facility to aid in program development. Because Pascal variables must be declared at the beginning of each program or subprogram with respect to the data type each supports, many errors can be detected before a program ever reaches the testing stage.

Finally, Pascal supports a rich variety of data types, and even lets you create new ones. For example, you could define a data type called FRIENDS, with values of ERNIE, SARAH, DEBORAH, and MIGUEL, and another type called ENEMIES, with values DARTH, BARTH, ZARTH, and GARTH. Later you could manipulate these names in your program by referencing the corresponding data type. If you wanted to, you could even create a third data type called ACQUAINTANCES that consisted of FRIENDS and ENEMIES, the two types you had declared earlier. This is yet another example of Pascal's structured, building-block orientation.

Because its structured emphasis leads to good programming practices, Pascal has been enthusiastically received. Experts generally consider it an important language for anyone studying computer science or learning programming. And the College Entrance Examination Board has chosen Pascal as the required language for advanced-placement courses in computer science for high schools.

Memory Efficiency. Pascal compilers are extremely small, given the processing power of the language. Thus the language can be implemented

```
PROGRAM SALES (INPUT, OUTPUT);
(* PROGRAM TO COMPUTE SALES *)
(* AUTHOR -- C. S. PARKER *)

VAR   UNITS, INDEX          :INTEGER;
      PRICE, TOTAL          :REAL;
      PART                  :ARRAY [1..20] OF CHAR;

BEGIN
WRITELIN ('      DESCRIPTION              PRICE       UNITS      TOTAL VALUE ');
FOR INDEX :=. 1 TO 20 DO
   READ (PART[INDEX]);
   READLN (PRICE, UNITS);
WHILE NOT EOF DO
      BEGIN
      TOTAL := PRICE * UNITS;
      FOR INDEX := 1 TO 20 DO
        WRITE (PART[INDEX]);
        WRITELIN ('        $', PRICE:6:2, UNITS:11,'      $', TOTAL:9:2);
      FOR INDEX := 1 TO 20 DO
        READ (PART [INDEX]);
        READLN (PRICE, UNITS);
      END;
END.
```

(a) A Pascal program.

DESCRIPTION	PRICE	UNITS	TOTAL VALUE
SMALL WIDGETS	$150.00	100	$ 15,000
LARGE SKY HOOKS	$200.00	50	$ 10,000
BLIVETS	$100.00	3,000	$300,000

(b) Output from the program.

Figure 11-3. *A sample Pascal program and its output.* This program solves the same sales problem as does the BASIC program in Figure 11-2.

easily on most microcomputer systems, where main memory capacity may be somewhat limited. This feature also makes the language ideal for educational environments.

LIMITATIONS. Pascal's major weakness is that it has marginal input/output capabilities, and so is not as suitable as COBOL for business data processing applications. As a problem-solving language, however, Pascal can be expected to give both FORTRAN and BASIC a run for their money.

A sample Pascal program appears in Figure 11-3.

COBOL

COBOL (*CO*mmon *B*usiness-*O*riented *L*anguage), which was first introduced in the early 1960s, is the primary business data processing language in use today. Until it appeared there was no language particularly suitable for such business data processing applications as payroll, billing, and payables and receivables. After all, the early language pioneers were engineers and mathematicians, not accountants. But as more and more businesses purchased computer systems, the need for a business-oriented language became apparent. Representatives from the major computer manufacturers met in Washington, D.C., with users from industry and government to discuss such a product. They subsequently formed a committee to draft a language, and the result was COBOL.

KEY FEATURES.   Many features differentiate COBOL from other languages. Almost all of them relate to its business data processing orientation, including machine independence, self-documentation, and input/output orientation.

Machine Independence.   Business data processing programs generally have to last a long time. For example, a company may expect to use many of its payroll or accounts receivable programs for ten or even twenty years. During this span of time, the organization may buy new hardware or change completely from one computer system to another. Thus programs written for one system should be able to run on another with little modification. In other words, the language in which the programs are written should be relatively *machine independent*. COBOL was specifically developed to meet this important requirement.

In 1968 ANSI established a successful COBOL standard, which was revised in 1974. An updated standard, COBOL-85, has recently been developed. Over the years vendors have supplied language translators that meet these standards, so that COBOL programs written in conformation with the standard will generally work on any type of computer system, with little modification.

Self-documentation.   Because business data processing programs must last a long time, they need ongoing maintenance. As business conditions change, the programs often have to be modified. A change in tax policy, for example, could require several modifications in a payroll program. Since programmers tend to switch jobs often, the person doing the maintenance is not likely to be the original author of the program. Thus it's extremely important for program logic to be easy for others to follow. As we saw in Chapters 9 and 10, good design techniques promote logical, easily maintained programs. COBOL lends itself to good program design in three ways: readability, modularity, and heavy reliance on the three control structures of structured programming.

Readability is important because business data processing programs usually consist of thousands of lines of code. To promote readability COBOL permits variable names of up to thirty characters. Thus variable names (for example, TAXES, GROSS-PAY, NET-PAY) can be written out fully and not compressed into obscure abbreviations. COBOL also uses English-like verbs (such as SUBTRACT) and connectives (such as FROM and GIVING) to enhance readability. As a result statements in COBOL often tend to read like regular English sentences; for example,

```
SUBTRACT TAXES FROM GROSS-PAY GIVING NET-PAY.
```

Modularity is important because programs are easier to develop and maintain if they are divided into clearly defined segments, where each segment performs an independent task. COBOL is designed to encourage such modularity. It is easy to represent functional hierarchies in COBOL, and the language lends itself to structured design tools such as structure charts (see Chapter 10). A good COBOL program looks like a well-organized outline. Virtually all COBOL compilers require that every COBOL program be divided into four distinct divisions:

1. An *Identification Division,* which identifies the name of the program, the author, and other details. This division exists mostly for documentation purposes.

2. An *Environment Division,* in which the file names created by the programmer are linked to specific input/output equipment. Here, for example, the programmer would specify that a particular input file, say DISKFILE, is located on disk, and that a particular output file, say PRINTFILE, is to be routed to a printer.

3. A *Data Division,* in which the programmer names and defines all the variables in the program and indicates their relationship to each other.

4. A *Procedure Division,* which specifies the actual procedures the computer system must follow to create the desired output.

The first three divisions ensure that all important specifications are stated explicitly in the program. In other languages, such as BASIC, many of these specifications are implied rather than stated, which makes long programs more difficult to maintain.

Divisions of COBOL programs may be subdivided into sections, and sections further subdivided into paragraphs. Each paragraph may contain one or more statements. For example, a payroll program may have a section named TAX-SECTION in its Procedure Division. Within that section it may have paragraphs such as FEDERAL-TAX-PARA, STATE-TAX-PARA, and CITY-TAX-PARA. The individual statements in these paragraphs would do the work of the program, such as computing taxes.

Finally, because it supports the three major program control structures—sequence, selection, and looping—better than many other languages, COBOL lends itself to well-structured programs.

Input/Output Orientation. Business data processing, in contrast to scientific, mathematical, and engineering applications, involves the manipulation of large files with many business-type records. Much of the work in business data processing applications, therefore, relates to reading and writing records, and COBOL has been designed to be particularly effective in this area. It contains provisions for defining, explicitly and easily, the format of input and output records. For example, it is a very straightforward process to edit dollar amounts on output with dollar signs, decimal points, and commas, and also to round off these amounts.

LIMITATIONS. Because COBOL programs use long, English-like names and specify formats in fine detail, they tend to be lengthy. Also, a large and sophisticated language translator is needed to convert programs into machine language, making COBOL difficult to implement on many smaller computers. And because of its business data processing orientation, it is usually not suitable for scientific, mathematical, or engineering applications, which use a number of complicated formulas.

Despite its limitations, however, COBOL is very good at what it does—business data processing. Currently some 70–80 percent of computerized business applications in large firms are coded in COBOL. With millions of dollars invested in COBOL programs, and thousands of programmers versed in its use, it seems likely that the language will endure for many more years. Despite the many claims that the language is old-fashioned, cumbersome, and inelegant, the fact remains that if you're interested in making money as an applications programmer, COBOL is still clearly your best bet.

A sample COBOL program is shown in Figure 11-4.

FORTRAN

FORTRAN (*FOR*mula *TRAN*slator), which dates to 1954, has the distinction of being the first high-level programming language to become widely used. It has shown remarkable staying power, and is today the oldest surviving commercial high-level language. In a world where everything seems to be changing rapidly, FORTRAN has been altered remarkably little in thirty years. FORTRAN was designed by scientists and is oriented toward scientific, mathematical, and engineering problem solving.

```
          IDENTIFICATION DIVISION.
            PROGRAM-ID. SALES
            AUTHOR. PARKER.

          ENVIRONMENT DIVISION
          CONFIGURATION SECTION.
            SOURCE-COMPUTER. UNIVAC-VS9.
            OBJECT-COMPUTER. UNIVAC-VS9.
          INPUT-OUTPUT SECTION.
            FILE-CONTROL.
              SELECT DISKFILE ASSIGN TO DISK-A1F2-V.
              SELECT PRINTFILE ASSIGN TO SYSLST.

          DATA DIVISION.
          FILE SECTION.
          FD  DISKFILE
              LABEL RECORDS ARE STANDARD.
          01  DISKREC.
              05 PART-DESCRIPTION-IN      PIC X(20).
              05 PRICE-IN                 PIC 999.
              05 UNITS-SOLD-IN            PIC 9(5).
          FD  PRINTFILE
              LABEL RECORDS ARE OMITTED.
          01  PRINTLINE                   PIC X(120).
          WORKING-STORAGE SECTION.
          01  FLAGS.
              05 WS-END-OF-FILE.          PIC X(3) VALUE 'NO'.
          01  HEADING-LINE.
              05 FILLER                   PIC X(9)  VALUE SPACES.
              05 FILLER                   PIC X(11) VALUE 'DESCRIPTION'.
              05 FILLER                   PIC X(10) VALUE SPACES.
              05 FILLER                   PIC X(5)  VALUE 'PRICE'.
              05 FILLER                   PIC X(7)  VALUE SPACES.
              05 FILLER                   PIC X(5)  VALUE 'UNITS'.
              05 FILLER                   PIC X(4)  VALUE SPACES.
              05 FILLER                   PIC X(11) VALUE 'TOTAL VALUE'.
          01  DETAIL-LINE.
              05 FILLER                   PIC X(5)  VALUE SPACES.
              05 PART-DESCRIPTION-OUT     PIC X(20).
              05 FILLER                   PIC X(4)  VALUE SPACES.
              05 PRICE-OUT                PIC $ZZ9.99.
              05 FILLER                   PIC X(5)  VALUE SPACES.
              05 UNITS-SOLD-OUT           PIC ZZ,ZZ9.
              05 FILLER                   PIC X(5)  VALUE SPACES.
              05 SALES-VALUE              PIC $ZZZ,ZZ9.
```

Figure 11-4.   A sample COBOL program and its output. This program solves the same sales problem as does the BASIC program in Figure 11-2.

```
PROCEDURE DIVISION.
010-HOUSEKEEPING.
    OPEN INPUT DISKFILE
        OUTPUT PRINTFILE.
    READ DISKFILE
        AT END MOVE 'YES' TO WS-END-OF-FILE.
    PERFORM 020-HEADINGS.
    PERFORM 030-PROCESSIT
        UNTIL WS-END-OF-FILE = 'YES'.
    CLOSE DISKFILE
        PRINTFILE.
    STOP RUN.
020-HEADINGS.
    WRITE PRINTLINE FROM HEADING-LINE
        AFTER ADVANCING 1 LINE.
030-PROCESSIT.
    MULTIPLY    UNITS-SOLD-IN
        BY      PRICE-IN
        GIVING SALES-VALUE.
    MOVE PART-DESCRIPTION-IN TO PART-DESCRIPTION-OUT.
    MOVE PRICE-IN            TO PRICE-OUT.
    MOVE UNITS-SOLD-IN       TO UNITS-SOLD-OUT.
    WRITE PRINTLINE FROM DETAIL-LINE
        AFTER ADVANCING 1 LINE.
    READ DISKFILE
        AT END MOVE 'YES' TO WS-END-OF-FILE.
```

(a) A COBOL program.

DESCRIPTION	PRICE	UNITS	TOTAL VALUE
SMALL WIDGETS	$150.00	100	$ 15,000
LARGE SKY HOOKS	$200.00	50	$ 10,000
BLIVETS	$100.00	3,000	$300,000

(b) Output from the program.

Figure 11-4. *(Continued)*

Business data processing applications involve sophisticated input/output operations and relatively simple computations. Scientific, mathematical, and engineering applications, in contrast, require complex computations and relatively simple input/output operations. For example, determining the trajectory of a rocket—a classic engineering application—requires intricate and precise computations. In contrast, preparing a payroll—a typical business data processing application—involves reading employee records and writing checks and reports. The computations performed on each record are relatively simple.

tomorrow

COBOL VERSUS THE 4GLs

Will COBOL Be Replaced by Younger, Sleeker Software?

Virtually everyone who has used COBOL complains that the language is verbose and out of date. COBOL programs can take a long time to write, and users often need new types of information immediately. Finding an available COBOL applications programmer and getting a COBOL program written is a process that can take weeks, months, or even years—if it is possible at all. To fill the need for quick retrieval of new types of information, a body of software known as *fourth-generation languages* (*4GLs*) has surfaced.

Since 4GLs are still evolving, they're difficult to define. To get a handle on what they are, let's take a peek at what some of them do and how far they've come.

Some of the early 4GLs were called "data management systems." For the most part, they were *file managers* (see Chapter 13, pages 390–392) that required users to fill out a form stating their processing needs. The form was then keyed into the computer system. The information on the form represented a nonprocedural program. When invoked it activated a program generator that would produce a procedural program to perform the processing requirements.

Later, with the arrival of desk-top terminals, 4GLs provided easy-to-use on-screen forms—or *templates*—that enabled both users and programmers to bypass keypunch operators. Today many 4GLs interface with or are part of *database management systems* (see Chapter 13, pages 392–404). But whatever types of computing technologies they employ, 4GLs have made it possible in many cases to bypass writing lengthy COBOL programs. Programming managers claim that it takes at least ten times longer to write a COBOL program than an equivalent 4GL program.

So COBOL is dead—right? Wrong. Although 4GLs do fill a niche not met by COBOL, they are not all things to all people. Many 4GLs work smoothly, for example, when users choose a number of standard defaults. But if users have specialized needs, the 4GLs become harder to use. Also, because 4GLs involve sophisticated software, they eat up a lot of system resources and can quickly degrade response time to other users.

COBOL has survived for three decades.

Let's not lose sight of the fact that COBOL has survived for three decades as the reigning king of data processing languages. Millions of dollars worth of applications programs are coded in it, and it's been apparent for many years that most employable graduates of computer-related academic programs get jobs as COBOL programmers.

As one noted computer scientist recently remarked, one of the most likely of today's languages still to be on the computing scene in the year 2000 is COBOL. What COBOL does, it does well. There was a term coined in the cold-war era to describe Western–Soviet relations—"peaceful coexistence." Expect that to be the relationship between COBOL and the 4GLs in the year 2000.

Because of FORTRAN's ability to perform sophisticated computations, however, it has proved useful for certain kinds of business applications. These are applications that are of a problem-solving nature rather than routine data processing involving massive files of records. They include sales and econometric forecasting, determining the least expensive way to manufacture a product (linear programming), and simulating complex production processes.

KEY FEATURES. A key feature of FORTRAN is its ability to express sophisticated formulas easily. Complicated algebraic expressions are written in FORTRAN in nearly the same way as in conventional mathematical notation. Although BASIC, a language that was created as a simplified version of FORTRAN, is competitive in this area, FORTRAN is generally superior for two reasons: faster program execution and a large bank of preprogrammed routines.

Fast Program Execution. FORTRAN generally uses a compiler as its language translator. Compilers run programs faster than the interpreters used by most versions of BASIC because they translate each statement only once, rather than several times. Since scientific, mathematical, and engineering programs are characterized by many computations and frequent looping, execution speed is a primary concern. Most FORTRAN compilers are so effective at "number crunching," in fact, that they are superior in this respect to the compilers of most modern languages. The reasons for this are found in history. When FORTRAN was developed in the 1950s, it had to compete with assembly languages for execution efficiency, and that has remained an important force in its design ever since.

Preprogrammed Routines. Programmers working on scientific, engineering, and mathematical applications often find that huge portions of their programs involve solving problems that others have tackled before. An econometric forecast, for example, may involve computing the determinant or inverse of a matrix. Likewise, a statistical test may involve fitting a curve to a set of field observations. Fortunately several published libraries of precoded FORTRAN routines (called *subroutines*) are available for doing tasks of this sort. All the programmer need do is find the subroutine in one of the libraries and incorporate it into his or her program. This can save weeks or months of agonizing coding time and testing.

LIMITATIONS. FORTRAN was developed well before structured programming began to be emphasized, so it is somewhat weak in this area when compared with many of the newer languages. The latest ANSI standard on FORTRAN, however, created in 1977, provided a number of structured facilities for the language to make it competitive with some of the modern structured languages. Nonetheless many existing commercial FORTRAN programs and subroutines were written under the 1966 ANSI standard, in an age predating the arrival of structured programming theory.

```
C THIS PROGRAM COMPUTES SALES
C AUTHOR - C. S. PARKER
          CHARACTER PART*20
          INTEGER UNITS
          WRITE (6, 200)
200       FORMAT (5X,'DESCRIPTION',12X,'PRICE',7X,'UNITS',5X,'TOTAL VALUE')
 10       READ (5, 100, END=99) PART, PRICE, UNITS
100       FORMAT (A20,F6.2,I4)
          TOTAL = PRICE * UNITS
          WRITE (6, 201) PART, PRICE, UNITS, TOTAL
201       FORMAT (1X,A,'        $',F6.2,I11,'        $',F9.2)
          GO TO 10
 99       STOP
          END
```

(a) A FORTRAN program.

```
      DESCRIPTION              PRICE       UNITS       TOTAL VALUE
   SMALL WIDGETS             $150.00         100      $ 15000.00
   LARGE SKY HOOKS           $200.00          50      $ 10000.00
   BLIVETS                   $100.00       3,000      $300000.00
```

(b) Output from the program.

Figure 11-5. *A sample FORTRAN program and its output.* This program solves the same sales problem as does the BASIC program in Figure 11-2.

In addition, the logic of FORTRAN programs is more difficult to follow than the logic of many other languages, and it is very easy to make a typographical error that results in a syntactically correct program that produces erroneous results. Still, FORTRAN will probably remain a popular scientific, mathematical, and engineering language for years to come. It has a large base of loyal, satisfied users and its compilers are widely available.

A sample FORTRAN program is shown in Figure 11-5.

OTHER PROGRAMMING LANGUAGES

PL/1

PL/1 (*Programming Language 1*) was introduced in the mid-1960s by IBM as a general-purpose language. That is, it was designed for both scientific and business data processing applications. It's an extremely powerful language, with strong capabilities for structured programming. Variants of

PL/1, such as PL/C (created at Cornell), have been developed for teaching purposes.

Despite PL/1's credentials, it has not been used as widely as one might expect. There are several reasons for this. First, the language was initially available only on IBM machines, and other computer manufacturers were slow to adopt it on their equipment. Since IBM mainframes are found less commonly in academic settings than in industry, few programmers learned to use PL/1 in school. Second, COBOL had a substantial head start in business data processing. Not only did companies have many thousands of dollars invested in working COBOL programs, but also COBOL programmers have always been more available in the marketplace. Third, BASIC and FORTRAN were already well entrenched for scientific, mathematical, engineering, and business problem-solving applications. They were generally perceived as easier to use than PL/1 and their language translators were more widely available. Nonetheless, PL/1 has a respectable following, and those that use the language swear by it.

APL

APL (*A P*rogramming *L*anguage) began in the early 1960s as a mathematical notation, created by a Harvard professor to teach courses. Somewhere along the way, through the support of IBM, it evolved into a full-blown programming language.

The major objective of APL is to enable programmers to code rapidly. It is a tremendously compact language, and it can only be used with a special keyboard. Like BASIC, it is highly interactive.

APL has two modes of operation: calculator and program. In the *calculator mode,* APL is like a powerful desk calculator. The user types in an APL expression, and the computer system instantly supplies a response. APL uses a special set of symbols to enable users to perform complex mathematical computations in a single step. For example, the single statement below

$$(+ / X) / \rho X$$

computes the average of a predefined list of numbers (called X). The $+/$ part sums the numbers of the list, the ρ (rho) part counts the size of the list, and the $/$ divides the sum by the count to produce the average. Another APL command

$$\nabla X$$

can be used to sort the list, again in a single step. The same special symbols can be used to write complete computer programs in the *program mode.*

Supporters claim that APL programs can be written in a small fraction of the time it takes to write comparable FORTRAN programs. After all, look at all the code you can cram into a single statement. Critics argue that APL is difficult to learn because it uses too many special symbols and employs certain programming conventions that are completely contrary to those of other languages. Most APL programs are extremely difficult for anyone but the original programmer to read. This trait is often acceptable in scientific, mathematical, and engineering environments, however, where programs often have short useful lives.

Ada

For many years much of the software written for the armed services was in machine or assembly language. In the 1970s many branches of the services began to convert applications to high-level languages. There was no single standard for all the branches, however, and systems developed by one branch were not always compatible with those of the others. The U.S. Department of Defense soon declared a moratorium on these divergent efforts and directed the branches to cooperate in creating a single language standard. Existing languages were surveyed and, for one reason or another, rejected. The end result, in 1980, was the development of a new structured language, **Ada,** named for the Countess of Lovelace, a colleague of the nineteenth-century computer pioneer Charles Babbage.

Although the design of Ada is based largely on Pascal, Ada is a much bigger, more complex language. It includes several features that have no counterparts in Pascal, such as realtime control of tasks, concurrent processing, exception handling, and abstract data types.

It is still too early to tell what effect Ada will have both in and beyond the Department of Defense. Supporters predict that the language will be widely embraced by both the academic and business worlds. Critics point to PL/1 and history. "Who," they ask, "needs another programming language?"

C

C, created under the auspices of Bell Labs in the early 1970s, is a high-level language with many of the advantages of an assembly language. It's so named simply because earlier versions of it were called A and B. Today, due largely to its role in packaged software development and its association with the UNIX operating system, it's become one of the hottest languages for programmers to learn.

For the past several years, the packaged software market has been extremely competitive. Once a software product—such as a word processor or spreadsheet—is developed for one microprocessor, it is crucial to develop versions of the product for the other leading microprocessors as soon as possible. The earlier a software product is available in the marketplace, the harder it is for competing products to succeed. Thus packaged software developers need a "mid-range" language—one that has both the portability of a high-level language like Pascal and the execution efficiency of a low-level assembly language. C, which is sometimes referred to as a "portable assembly language," conveniently fills this niche. It is also structured, which makes modifications easy to implement and test, and it is far easier to learn than assembly language.

UNIX, described in the box on page 248 of Chapter 8 as an operating system for smaller computers, is among the many software packages written in C. C and UNIX also both share the same "tool kit" programming approach—that is, if a feature you like isn't available in the language, you can add it yourself.

C is primarily used by computer professionals. Code written in C looks somewhat like Pascal; however, C is not a recommended language for beginners.

Logo

Logo is a programming language that also represents a philosophy to learning. It was developed in the 1970s by Seymour Papert of The Massachusetts Institute of Technology, who incorporated into its specification some of the learning theories of Swiss psychologist Jean Piaget. Logo has been very popular with children, many of whom find it both easy to learn and exciting.

Logo is *easy to learn* because its instructions are relatively straightforward. For example, the following program

```
FORWARD 25 RIGHT 90
FORWARD 25 RIGHT 90
FORWARD 25 RIGHT 90
FORWARD 25 RIGHT 90
```

creates a square with twenty-five units on a side. The first command draws one side, and points the cursorlike device on the screen 90 degrees to the right. The second command draws the second side, and so forth. As the programmer becomes more advanced, a more sophisticated command to do the same thing can be used; for example,

```
REPEAT 4 (FORWARD 25 RIGHT 90)
```

You can probably appreciate how easy Logo is to learn and use when you consider how you would draw a square in another language with which you are familiar.

Logo is *exciting* because it has a lot of psychological hooks that get children involved. For example, one of Logo's strengths is graphics, and how many children prefer writing accounting programs to drawing pictures on a screen? Also, Logo calls its triangular cursorlike device a *turtle*. The turtle can be given commands such as FORWARD (to move), RIGHT or LEFT (to turn), PENUP (to raise the turtle's pen and allow it to move without drawing a line), and PENDOWN (to lower the pen). Inhibitions about using a computer are reduced as children imagine the cursorlike device to be an animal leaving a trail on the screen and not just a boring, insensitive, run-of-the-mill cursor. Logo's *turtle graphics* have found their way into other languages as well, including Pascal.

RPG

Most business reports have a number of characteristics in common. For example, they usually contain a title page, column headings, a main body, column totals and subtotals, and page footings. **RPG** (*Report Program Generator*), developed by IBM in the early 1960s to produce reports quickly on small computers, capitalizes on these similarities of format. Unlike the languages discussed so far in this chapter, RPG is a very specialized nonprocedural language. However, because it is generally considered a "programmer's language," it's included here.

RPG works as follows: Programmers provide facts about how a report should look. These facts are often supplied on special forms, which are subsequently machine coded. The information declared on the form includes answers to such questions as the following:

✖ *What* records in a file will be used to produce the report?

✖ *What* fields should be read from each record?

✖ *What* computations are to be done?

✖ *What* subtotals and totals should be taken?

✖ *How* will the report be formatted?

The RPG language package then determines how the job will be done and creates (generates) a computer program to produce the report. When used for the right kinds of tasks, RPG can save a considerable amount of coding and debugging time as compared with a procedural language such as COBOL. Unfortunately RPG is much more limited in what it can do.

Several improvements have been made on RPG over the years. Updated versions of the language, such as RPGII and RPGIII, are currently very popular. Because RPG compilers are normally small, the language is widely used on small business systems. RPG is not standardized like many of the high-level languages, however, so there are different versions for different computer systems.

Summary and Key Terms

A **programming language** can broadly be defined as a set of rules that enable instructions to be written for a computer.

The earliest programming languages—machine and assembly languages— are called **low-level languages** because programmers coding in these languages must write instructions at the finest level of detail.

The next languages to appear were the **high-level languages.** Included in this class are what have come to be known as the "traditional" types of programming languages—BASIC, COBOL, FORTRAN, Pascal, PL/1,

APL, and many others. High-level languages differ from their low-level ancestors in that they require less coding detail and make programs easier to write.

Very-high-level languages are those in which users prescribe *what* the computer is to do rather than how it is to do it. This type of facility makes programming much easier. Low- and high-level languages are sometimes called **procedural languages,** because they require people to write detailed statements that represent sequential steps to be performed during program execution. Very-high-level languages, in contrast, are called **non-procedural languages.**

Assembly languages are like machine languages in that each line of code corresponds to a single action of the computer system. But assembly languages replace the 0s and 1s of machine language with symbols that are easier to understand and remember. The big advantage of assembly-language programs is executional efficiency—they're fast and consume relatively little storage compared with their high-level counterparts. Unfortunately assembly-language programs take longer to write and maintain than those written in high-level languages. They are also very machine dependent.

BASIC (*B*eginner's *A*ll-purpose *S*ymbolic *I*nstuction *C*ode) was designed to meet the need for an easy-to-learn beginner's language that could work in a "friendly," nonfrustrating programming environment. Over the years BASIC has evolved into one of the most popular and widely available programming languages. Because it is easy to learn and use, and the storage requirements for its language translator are small, it works well on almost all microcomputers. Nearly every advantage of BASIC is related to its ease of use for beginners. Among these advantages are simplified naming of variables, optional formatting, conversational programming mode, and simple diagnostics. A key weakness in many versions of BASIC is that their ease of use leads to sloppy programming practices.

Pascal, named for the mathematician Blaise Pascal, is a relatively new programming language. Pascal was created primarily to fill the need for a teaching vehicle that would encourage structured programming.

COBOL *CO*mmon *B*usiness-*O*riented *L*anguage) is the primary business data processing language in use today. Almost all of its key features relate to its business data processing orientation. These include machine independence, self-documentation, and input/output orientation. The primary disadvantages of COBOL are that programs tend to be lengthy, the language is difficult to implement on many smaller computers, and it is usually not suitable for scientific, mathematical, or engineering applications.

FORTRAN (*FOR*mula *TRAN*slator), which dates back to 1954, is the oldest surviving commercial high-level language. It was designed by scientists and is oriented toward scientific, mathematical, and engineering problem solving. The key strengths of FORTRAN are fast program execution and a large bank of preprogrammed subroutines. The weaknesses include some drawbacks in the area of structured programming.

PL/1 (*Programming Language 1*) was introduced in the mid-1960s by IBM as a general-purpose language. That is, it was designed for both scientific *and* business data processing applications. It's an extremely powerful language with strong capabilities for structured programming.

APL (*A Programming Language*) was developed in the early 1960s to enable programmers to code rapidly. It is a tremendously compact language, and is used with a special keyboard.

Ada is a relatively new structured language initiated by the U.S. Department of Defense. It is still too early to guess what success the language will have in the business and academic worlds.

C combines the best features of a structured, high-level language and an assembler language. It's currently one of the hottest languages for programmers to learn, largely because of its role in packaged software development and its association with the UNIX operating system.

Logo is a programming language that also represents a philosophy of learning. It's been very popular with children, many of whom find it both easy to learn and exciting.

RPG (*Report Program Generator*) was developed by IBM in the early 1960s to produce reports quickly on small computers. Programmers provide facts on special coding forms about how a report should look. After the forms are machine coded, the RPG package determines how the job will be done and creates (generates) a computer program to produce the report.

Review Exercises

Fill-in Questions

1. _____ is a language that was developed at Dartmouth College to meet the need for an easy-to-learn beginner's language that could work in a "friendly," nonfrustrating programming environment.

2. The oldest surviving commercial high-level language is _____.

3. _____ is the primary business data processing language in use today.

4. _____, created about 1970, was developed primarily to fill the need for a teaching vehicle that would encourage structured programming.

5. _____ was introduced in the mid-1960s by IBM as a powerful, general-purpose language.
6. _____ is a relatively new programming language, developed in 1980 by the U.S. Department of Defense.
7. _____ has both the portability of a high-level language and the executional efficiency of an assembly language.
8. _____ is a programming language that popularized the use of "turtle graphics."

Matching Questions

Match each term with its description.

a. Low-level languages
b. High-level languages
c. Very-high-level languages
d. Procedural languages
e. Nonprocedural languages
f. Assembly language
g. Machine language

_____ 1. The language that works with 0s and 1s.
_____ 2. Machine and assembly languages.
_____ 3. Nonprocedural languages.
_____ 4. Languages that work by having the programmer tell the computer system, step by step, how to solve a problem.
_____ 5. Problem-dependent, very-high-level languages.
_____ 6. A low-level language that uses symbols such as "A" for "Add" and "L" for "Load."
_____ 7. Procedural languages such as BASIC, COBOL, and FORTRAN.

Discussion Questions

1. What are the primary differences among low-level, high-level, and very-high-level languages?
2. What are the chief strengths and weaknesses of assembly language?
3. What are the particular strengths and weaknesses of BASIC?
4. What needs are served by the following languages: BASIC, COBOL, FORTRAN, Pascal, C, APL, RPG?
5. What are the features of COBOL that make it attractive for business data processing applications?
6. Many people feel that PL/1 is superior to COBOL and FORTRAN, yet it's not as widely used as these languages. Why?
7. What motivated the development of Ada?
8. What makes RPG different from other languages discussed in this chapter?

Chapter 12

THE RISING SUN

Increase in Industrial Production

Since 1967

'67 '69 '71 '73 '75 '77 '79 '81

Word Processing, Spreadsheets, and Presentation Graphics

Chapter Outline

Objectives

After completing this chapter you should be able to:

1. Identify the operations that are common to most types of productivity software packages.
2. Identify the operations you must master to use word processing software effectively.
3. Identify the operations you must master to use spreadsheet software effectively.
4. Explain the differences among word processing packages and among spreadsheet packages.
5. Understand how presentation graphics packages work and describe the images you can create with them.

Until the last decade, many of the people who used computer output rarely interacted directly with the computer themselves. They depended completely on in-house systems analysts and programmers to design, code, debug, and run the programs that produced the outputs they needed. The hardware that would enable most people to work conveniently and inexpensively with computer systems simply wasn't available—and neither was the software. If you wanted to use a computer system to make you more productive at work, you either had to know how to program in a high-level language or had to have enough clout to hire your own programmer. Then suddenly, things changed. The microprocessor arrived.

The microprocessor made possible desk-top microcomputers. Advances in microcircuitry also paved the way for inexpensive display devices and printers. At first only the hobbyists were interested. Then some easy-to-use microcomputer software was introduced that took the bite out of learning how to program. Word processing programs came to the fore that were much more cost effective than typewriters. Shortly thereafter powerful spreadsheet packages were created that were not much harder to learn and use than pocket calculators. At this point business people became interested. Here were some tools that would clearly make them or their offices more productive.

This chapter and the next cover **productivity software**—the program packages that make businesspeople more productive in their jobs. All of the software functions discussed in the chapters have been implemented on both large and small computers. Chapter 12 covers word processors, spreadsheets, and presentation graphics, while Chapter 13 deals with the data management tools—file managers and database management systems. Productivity packages that integrate some or all of the aforementioned functions are also discussed in Chapter 13.

WORD PROCESSING SOFTWARE

When you use your computer to do the kinds of work that you normally do on a typewriter, you're doing word processing. **Word processing** is using computer technology to create, manipulate, and print text materials such as letters, legal contracts, manuscripts, and other documents. Word processing is such a time saver, in fact, that most people who learn to do it let their typewriters gather dust. As you will discover in this chapter, the two features that give word processors their power are computer-assisted *text editing* and *print formatting* (see Figure 12-1). But before we examine how these tasks are carried out, let's look at some of the types of word processors currently available in the marketplace.

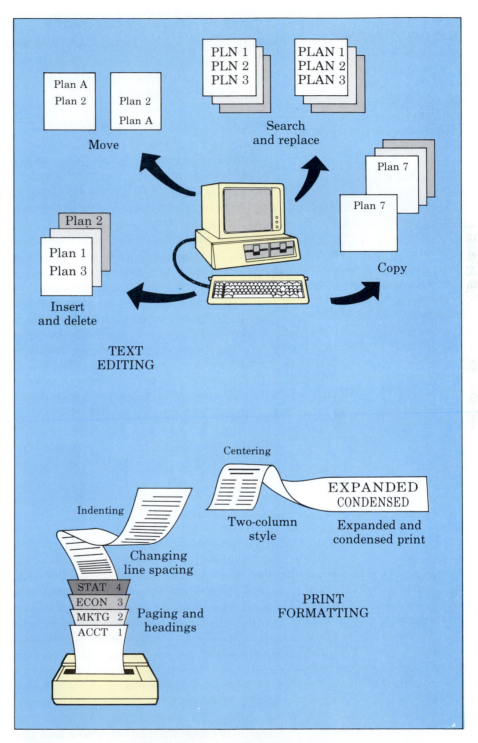

Figure 12-1. *Text editing and print formatting.* Text editing operations allow you to "cut and paste" text materials in electronic memory, whereas print formatting operations make it possible to output those materials in a visually appealing way.

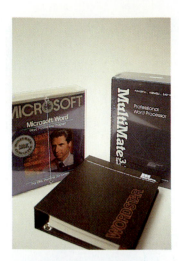

Figure 12-2. *A few of the word processing packages available for general-purpose microcomputers.*

Types of Word Processors

Word processing can be performed in several ways. First, you can do it on either a dedicated word processing system or a general-purpose computer. Second, you can work with either a screen-oriented or an imbedded-command word processor.

DEDICATED VERSUS GENERAL-PURPOSE SYSTEMS. One of the best, and also one of the most expensive, ways to do word processing is to use a *dedicated word processing system.* These systems are generally microcomputers or minicomputers that are rigged with special keys and packaged with special software to make word processing as painless as possible. For people such as secretaries or authors, who need a computer system *exclusively* for high-volume word processing, this is usually the best way to go. Unfortunately the special-purpose nature of these systems often makes them either incapable of or poor at doing things other than word processing. So if you need a single system for a wide variety of purposes—say, word processing, spreadsheets, data management, and writing your own BASIC or Pascal programs—a dedicated word processor is a bad choice. A general-purpose computer system is more appropriate.

General-purpose computer systems are computer systems that are configured to do a variety of tasks. If you want to do word processing, you load a word processing software package onto the system; if you want to run Pascal programs, you load a Pascal compiler; and so on. Word processing software packages are widely available for virtually all sizes of computers (see Figure 12-2 for an assortment of microcomputer-based packages). You might pay as little as $30 to acquire a software package or hundreds of dollars, depending upon the computer you are using and the level of sophistication you require from the software.

SCREEN-ORIENTED VERSUS IMBEDDED-COMMAND SYSTEMS. The majority of commercially available word processors today are screen-oriented. **Screen-oriented word processors** show on the display screen exactly, or almost exactly, how a document will appear before it's printed. Figure 12-3 shows a document being prepared by a screen-oriented package. Shown also is what the document will look like when it's printed out. As you'll observe, what you *see* (on the screen) is very close to what you *get* (in print). Some word processors will not show certain things on the screen; for example, italic or boldface characters. Very inexpensive word processors may not even show page breaks. Nonetheless, in a screen-oriented package, each screen line corresponds to a printed-page line, so you are rarely surprised at how the document looks when it's finally printed.

Imbedded-command word processors, such as the package illustrated in Figure 12-4, produce displays on the screen that consist of text sandwiched between commands. With these word processors, the text is usually not formatted on the screen as it will appear in print, so you may be surprised at the appearance of the final document. As you'll notice in the figure, every line represents either a formatting command (which *isn't* printed on the document) or text (which *is*). In the example, if a line begins

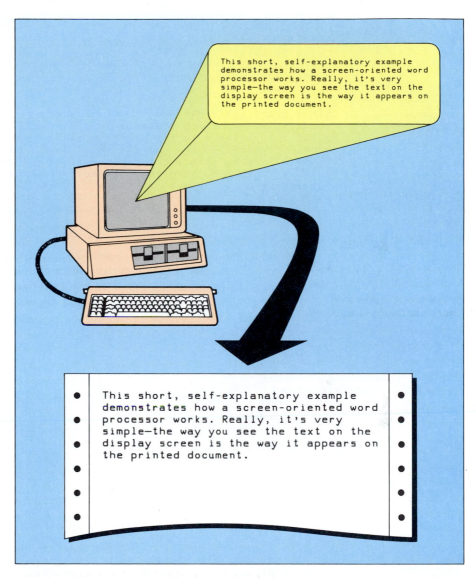

Figure 12-3.   Screen-oriented word processing. The way you see a document formatted on the screen is generally the way you see it in print.

with a period; the package knows that a command follows. If a line begins with any other character, the package treats the entire line as text. You should also observe that the sandwiched text and formatting commands in part *a* of the diagram form a procedural program. However, this program is much easier to follow than programs written in languages such as BASIC and Pascal because there are no looping or transfer-of-control operations.

Many screen-oriented word processors also permit users to work with some imbedded formatting commands, which are displayed on the screen but not printed. WordStar,® for example, has a set of "dot commands" that

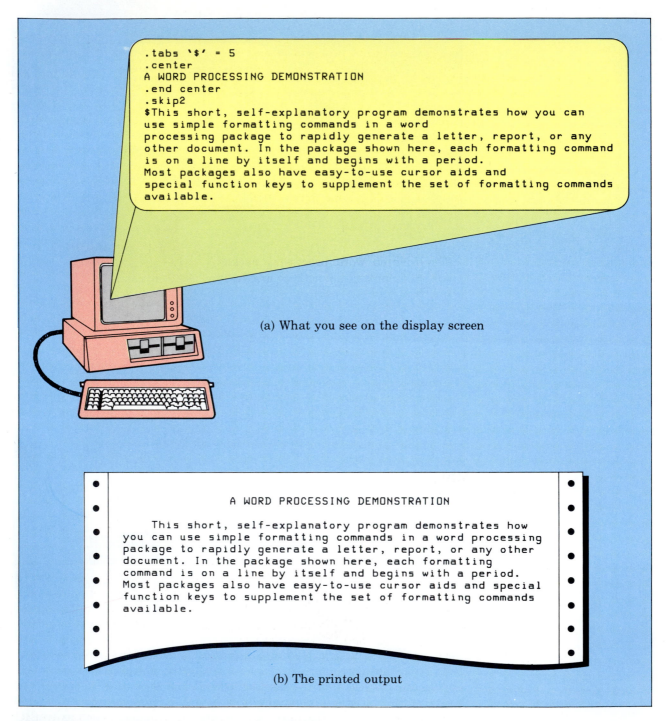

```
.tabs '$' = 5
.center
A WORD PROCESSING DEMONSTRATION
.end center
.skip2
$This short, self-explanatory program demonstrates how you can
use simple formatting commands in a word
processing package to rapidly generate a letter, report, or any
other document. In the package shown here, each formatting command
is on a line by itself and begins with a period.
Most packages also have easy-to-use cursor aids and
special function keys to supplement the set of formatting commands
available.
```

(a) What you see on the display screen

```
              A WORD PROCESSING DEMONSTRATION

     This short, self-explanatory program demonstrates how
you can use simple formatting commands in a word processing
package to rapidly generate a letter, report, or any other
document. In the package shown here, each formatting
command is on a line by itself and begins with a period.
Most packages also have easy-to-use cursor aids and special
function keys to supplement the set of formatting commands
available.
```

(b) The printed output

Figure 12-4. *Imbedded-command word processing.* (a) This part of the figure shows what the user has typed in. After a simple "RUN" or "EXECUTE" command is issued, the document shown in part (b) of the figure is produced.

allow users to do things such as omit page numbers and print headings or footings on the finished document. It is, therefore, largely a matter of degree that makes a word processor either the screen-oriented or the imbedded-command type. There is considerable debate over which approach is easier to learn and use.

SPECIALIZED WORD PROCESSORS.   In addition to the types of packages we've already mentioned, a number of *specialized word processors* are commercially available. For example, there are word processors that have features for printing mathematically oriented documents (with their abundance of special symbols) and others designed for the unique needs of movie scriptwriters. However, the vast majority of software in the marketplace is aimed at people with ordinary needs.

The remainder of this section on word processing will address ordinary, screen-oriented word processing packages that are targeted to general-purpose computers, since these are the types of word processors that most people encounter in practice.

Learning to Use a Word Processor: The Basics

No matter what type of car you drive, there are certain basic operations, common to all cars, that you need to know—for example, how to turn on the ignition, move from a stationary position, stop, and turn off the ignition. Yet each of these operations may be implemented in different ways on different cars. The ignition may be on the steering column in one car and on the main panel in another. Or one car may have standard transmission and another automatic.

Word processing packages are much like cars in this respect. There's a set of basic operations that almost all packages do, but every package implements each of these operations in its own way. For example, almost all packages contain a centering command. After all most people who type have to center text (such as titles and headings) at one time or another. One package may center text when, say, the characters "O" and "C" are typed in (with the control key held down), a second may center text when the "F2" function key is depressed, and a third may center text when a "..C" is typed. Moreover every word processing package needs to be able to *save* or *delete* documents, two other basic operations. If you randomly examined five word processing packages at a computer store, you'd probably find five different ways to save or delete text.

Virtually all word processing packages have some method of implementing these basic operations, because such operations often account for 90 percent or so of the command invocations most people issue during the course of word processing a document. This basic set of word processing commands may be classified as general operations, entering and editing operations, and print-formatting operations.

How to Buy Productivity Software for Your Micro

NOT MUCH DIFFERENT THAN BUYING A CAR

Spending money on costly goods of any type conforms, more or less, to the same five-step buying formula:

1. Analyze what it is you really want by preparing a specifications checklist.
2. Make a list of products and alternatives that appear to meet the specifications.
3. Examine how the products and alternatives meet the criteria on your checklist and get the opinions of knowledgeable friends.
4. Compare the most promising products or alternatives on your list with respect to cost, quality, and other important criteria.
5. Make a choice.

Buying computer products—such as productivity software packages—is no exception.

When you buy a car, for example, you normally list certain features you absolutely require—perhaps automatic transmission, air conditioning, and seating for five people. You would probably also specify certain performance or convenience features that are important to you, such as acceleration potential, comfort, and front-wheel drive. And, naturally, you normally have some price range in mind.

After this analysis step, you'll probably make a list of cars that you should check out more closely. Of course, another alternative you may discover in the analysis step is that you can't afford the car you really want. But if you really think you should get a car, you'll probably want to examine those on your list more closely.

You may then go to dealer showrooms, examine how each of the cars on your list meets the specifications you've set, and take a test drive or two. And if you're like most people, you'll probably talk your observations over with close friends. Perhaps they know something important that you don't about a particular car or feature you're considering.

Finally, all of the facts have to be weighed. There's no pat formula, unfortunately, for determining whether the $12,000 car that's tops on your list is a better buy than a $9000 one you don't like quite as much. It's often something very subjective that influences our final choice.

To show you how similar buying a microcomputer-based productivity software package is to decisions such as buying a car, this text contains three related boxes:

- Tips on Buying a Word Processing Package for Your Micro (pages 358–359)
- Tips on Buying a Spreadsheet Package for Your Micro (page 370)
- Tips on Buying Data Management Software for Your Micro (pages 400–401 in Chapter 13)

Each of these boxes looks at considerations that need to be taken into account during each phase of the five-step buying formula outlined here.

GENERAL OPERATIONS FOR USING PRODUCTIVITY SOFTWARE

- *Accessing* your package from the operating system.

- Informing the package that you either want to *create* a new file or to *retrieve* an old one from disk.

- Commanding the package to *save* a file onto disk.

- Commanding the package to *print* a file.

- Commanding the package to *delete* a file that's on disk.

- Indicating to the package that you want to *quit* working on your current file and do something on another file.

- *Terminating* your work on the package and getting back to the operating system.

Figure 12-5. *The seven general operations you need to master to operate any productivity software package.* Depending on the package you use, the file that you work on may be a word-processed document, a worksheet, a graph, or a collection of database records.

GENERAL OPERATIONS. To use virtually any type of productivity package—word processor, spreadsheet, or whatever—on your computer, you need to know how to carry out the seven general operations outlined in Figure 12-5. These operations are the functional equivalents of starting and stopping a car.

ENTERING AND EDITING OPERATIONS. Nearly every word processor contains entering and editing operations that implement the following tasks. These tasks are associated with keying in and manipulating text on the screen.

✖ *Moving the cursor* Moving the cursor around the screen is a task that many word processors have more than a dozen ways of accomplishing. You can usually move the cursor a character, a line, a screen, or a word at a time, as well as to the front or rear of the screen or document. The cursor can usually be moved either by typing in a command or by depressing one of several *function keys* or *cursor-movement* keys. If you're a beginner in word processing, you'll probably be typing short documents, so be content with moving around with the *arrow keys* for awhile and memorizing the other ways of moving the cursor later (see Figure 12-6).

✖ *Scrolling* Scrolling moves contiguous lines of text up and down on the screen in a way similar to that in which the roll on a player piano is

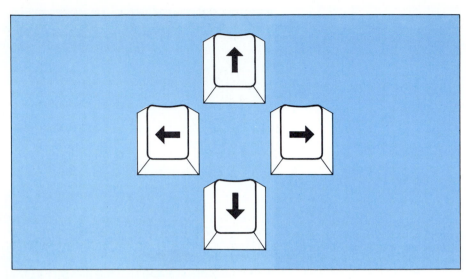

Figure 12-6.   The arrow keys. These are among the handiest cursor-control keys for using any type of productivity software package.

unwound. As lines successively disappear from the top of the screen, for example, new ones appear from the bottom. On many word processing packages, you can use the arrow keys to scroll a document.

Line return   A line return is often accomplished by hitting the "return" (or "enter") key, as you would on a standard typewriter. This is sometimes referred to as a *hard carriage return*. Most word processors also have a *wordwrap* feature so you don't have to hit the return key at the end of each line. Wordwrapping automatically produces a *soft carriage return* when the cursor reaches a certain column position at the right-hand-side of a page.

Inserting and deleting   Inserting and deleting are two of the most basic types of editing. For example, you may have typed in

THE HAVE WON THE CHAMPIONSHIP

and forgot to type in the name of the winning team. If the Hoboken Zephyrs won the championship, you'd have to insert the phrase "HOBOKEN ZEPHYRS" between "THE" and "HAVE."

If you later decided you wanted to delete the word HOBOKEN, the word processor would also enable you to do this. On most packages you can also insert or delete text a phrase (or several phrases) at a time in any portion of the document.

Moving and copying   Moving and copying text allow you to "cut and paste" with a word processor. Moving means identifying a specific block of text and physically relocating it in a new place in the document. In a typical move operation, the block no longer remains in

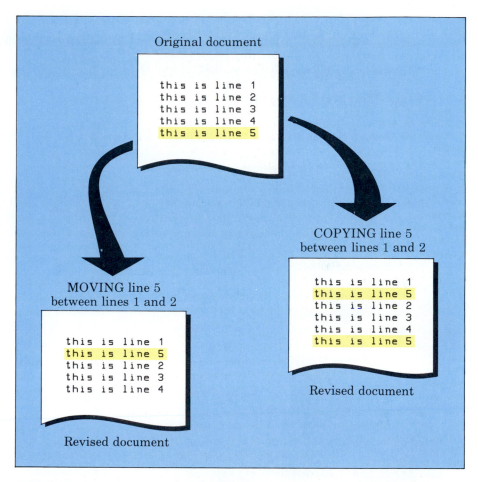

Figure 12-7. *Moving versus copying.* With moving, the highlighted line no longer appears in its original position on the document, whereas with copying, it does.

its original place in the document. Copying is similar to moving, however, a copy of the block remains in its original place, as well. Figure 12-7 illustrates the difference between moving and copying.

✖ ***Searching and replacing*** Searching and replacing are extremely useful features. They enable you to search automatically for all occurrences of a particular word or phrase and to change it to something else. Say, for example, that you've typed out a long document that repeatedly makes reference to a person named Snider. If you've misspelled this name as Schneider, you can usually have a word processor look up all occurrences of Schneider and change them to Snider.

Some people take dangerous short cuts in searching and replacing. For example, we could have asked the package to change all occurrences of "chne" to "n." This would have changed all Schneider occurrences to Snider, but it also would have changed a name such as Schneymann to Snymann, which probably was not intended.

Tips on Buying a Word Processing Package for Your Micro

THE RIGHT PRINTER IS AS IMPORTANT AS THE RIGHT SOFTWARE PACKAGE

As suggested in the box on page 354, buying a software package involves five steps: analyzing needs, listing products and alternatives, examining products, comparing products, and choosing among them. In this box we look at how this five-step buying formula relates to microcomputer-based word processing packages.

Analyzing Needs Most people buy a word processor—such as WordStar®, Word®, Volkswriter®, Multimate®, or Bank Street Writer®, to name a few—that satisfies a wide range of needs. These packages are general purpose and are not targeted to any particular type of user or application. Such software may cost anywhere from $50 to $500.

As a first step to analyzing needs you should carefully list the entering, editing, print formatting, and advanced operations (pages 355–364) that you absolutely require. Here you

must think about the type of word processing you'll be doing—for example, preparing large mailings, writing an occasional letter to friends, or writing a book. If you have highly specialized needs, as would a mathematician or professional typesetter (who respectively require systems that can deal effectively with formulas or special graphics fonts), you may need to look at special-purpose word processors that handle these things.

List Products and Alternatives This is where you make a list of word processors that you'd like to look at further. If you don't know the names or features of any, make a preliminary visit to a computer store to get an idea about what is available. Also, the leading microcomputer journals typically report the results of comparative studies made on the leading word processors, so visit your library and do some digging.

PRINT-FORMATTING OPERATIONS. Print-formatting operations tell the printer how to output the text onto paper. These operations include the following functions.

✗ *Adjusting line spacing* Adjusting line spacing is an important word processing operation. You may want to type letters to potential employers single spaced, but your English 101 instructor may want all the essays you hand in double spaced. If, say, you originally typed in a document single spaced, most word processors would automatically reformat it to double spaced for you upon request.

✗ *Indenting* Indenting (or adjusting margins) on your package is useful when you are typing a paper with a lot of quotations and want to indent these from the main text.

✗ *Reformatting* Reformatting is normally necessary when you insert text, delete text, need to change line spacing, or need to readjust

And consider printers, too, because the quality of the printed document is important to word processing. You'll find that most word processors work best with only certain types of printers. Not all printers, for example, will allow you the luxury of subscripts and superscripts. So even if your word processing package supports these features, if your printer can't handle them, you're in trouble.

Examine the Products At this point you want to look more closely at as many word processors and printers as you have the time and patience to examine. Word processors can vary dramatically in the way they imple-

ment commands, and a package that has the right feel to one person might feel totally unnatural to another. You should go to your local computer store and test some products. Often the salesperson will have a demonstration to show you. You should also try to "test drive" the products yourself. Perhaps something the demonstration didn't cover is of particular importance to you. Or, the quality of the printed documents may look much worse than in the promotional literature you've seen. Also, at this point, you may want to reread those comparative studies you've collected from the library, to make sure that the packages you're considering don't have a "skeleton in the closet."

Comparison Now is the time to cull the choice packages from the "also-rans" and do some hard thinking about the quality you're getting for the cost. Generally, as with anything else, the more you pay the more quality you get. With word processing software and printers, however, you can get surprisingly good quality at a relatively low price.

Choice Make a software (and possibly hardware) selection.

margins in your document. Figure 12-8 illustrates these four occasions for reformatting. After the insertion, deletion, choice of new line spacing, or choice of new margins is accomplished, the operator may need to issue one or more commands to reformat the appropriate sections of the document.

✖ *Centering* Centering text is a very important task for most people. Many packages require the user to have the cursor pointing to the line containing the text to be centered when invoking the centering command.

✖ *Tabbing* Tabbing is a formatting feature that typists have relied on for years. Figure 12-9 shows three useful ways to tab text. The tab at the beginning of the paragraph (Figure 12-9*a*) and tab-stopping numbers into columns (Figure 12-9*b*) can often be done by merely depressing the tab key on the computer's keyboard. The paragraph tab (Figure 12-9*c*) is usually done with a special command issued through the word processing package.

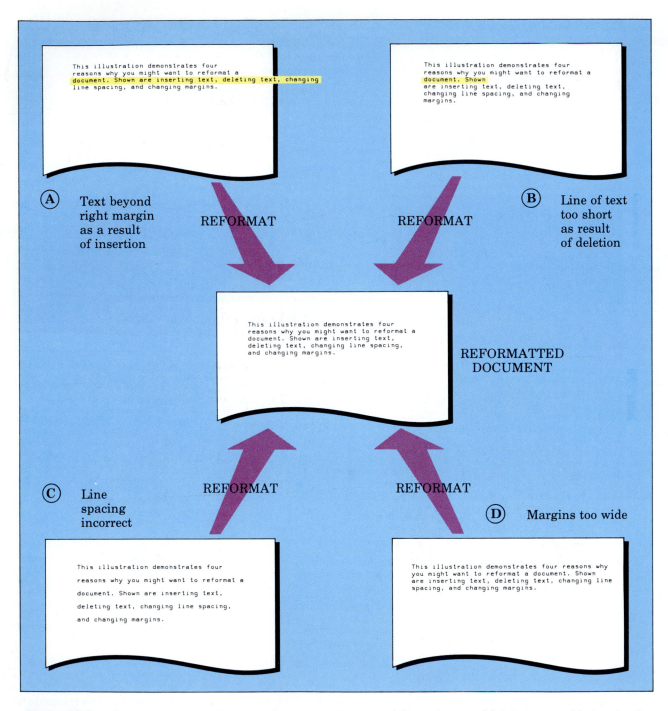

Figure 12-8.   Four reasons to reformat a document. Shown are (a) inserting text, (b) deleting text, (c) changing line spacing, and (d) changing margins.

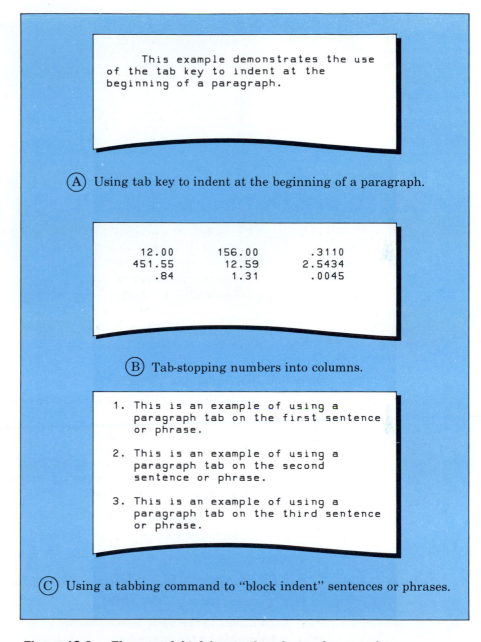

```
        This example demonstrates the use
of the tab key to indent at the
beginning of a paragraph.
```

(A) Using tab key to indent at the beginning of a paragraph.

```
    12.00         156.00           .3110
   451.55          12.59          2.5434
      .84           1.31           .0045
```

(B) Tab-stopping numbers into columns.

```
  1. This is an example of using a
     paragraph tab on the first sentence
     or phrase.

  2. This is an example of using a
     paragraph tab on the second
     sentence or phrase.

  3. This is an example of using a
     paragraph tab on the third sentence
     or phrase.
```

(C) Using a tabbing command to "block indent" sentences or phrases.

Figure 12-9.   Three useful tab invocations in word processing.

✕ *Pagination* Pagination is a feature that provides you with the choice of whether to number pages in a document. For example, you may want page numbers placed on reports you type for a class but not on short letters you prepare. An especially useful pagination feature of some packages is the ability to place the page numbers *where* you specify them. Additionally you may be able to print a standard heading or footing on each page.

Figure 12-10. Some typefaces available for the Apple Macintosh computer. If both your printer and monitor allow bit-mapped graphics (see Chapter 6), you can produce attractive documents using these and many other typefaces.

✕ *Font selection*   Font selection features are those that enable you to use boldface, italicize, underline, produce subscript or superscript characters, or print characters in a variety of typefaces. Both the word processor and the printer on your system must support any of these features in order for you to use them. Figure 12-10 shows some typefaces available for the Apple Macintosh. If you also have a laser printer, you can produce typeset-quality documents such as those in photos 23 and 24 of Window 5.

✕ *Multiple columns*   Multiple-column formatting lets you print text in a columnar format, similar to that used in newspapers and magazines.

Learning to Use a Word Processor: Advanced Operations

In addition to the basic operations we've just covered, the more sophisticated word processors enable you to do a number of other useful tasks. Some of these may be especially valuable if you are a professional typist or an author, or if your business requires a lot of correspondence. Three such tasks are proportional spacing, spelling checks, and mailing list/mail merge operations.

PROPORTIONAL SPACING.   This textbook, like most others, was typeset on a system that spaces characters proportionally. **Proportional spacing** is a feature that allocates more horizontal space on a line to some characters than to others (for example, a capital "M" takes up more space than does a lowercase "i"). A microspacing feature may also be available. With **micro-**

Figure 12-11. Proportionally spaced characters with microspacing.

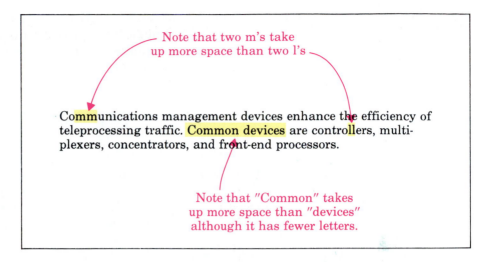

spacing fractions of a full blank space are inserted in each line in places where they aren't likely to be noticed, to fill out the line to full width so that the left- and right-hand margins are flush. Proportional spacing and microspacing are shown in Figure 12-11. Both your word processor and your printer must support proportional spacing and microspacing to produce such typeset-quality documents.

SPELLING CHECKERS.   Some word processing packages include a routine that will read through a document and search for misspelled words. Such a routine is called a **spelling checker.** If a spelling checker feature does not come with your word processor, one may be available as a supplemental package from an independent vendor.

Spelling checkers can vary dramatically in what they do. Some have dictionaries in the neighborhood of 10,000 words, whereas others have 50,000 or more. A particularly important feature is one that allows you to add your own words to the spelling checker's dictionary. A writer of a computer text or a medical article, for example, uses very specialized terms, most of which aren't in the dictionaries of standard spelling checkers.

MAILING LIST / MAIL MERGE PROGRAMS.   Like spelling checkers, mailing list and mail merge programs are often supplements to word processing packages.

A **mailing list program** is used to generate mailing labels. With such a program, you can generally sort records on a specific field (such as Zip code) or extract records with special characteristics (such as all alumni from the class of 1975 who live in San Francisco), prior to processing the labels. Mailing list programs are simplified versions of file managers, which will be discussed in Chapter 13.

A **mail merge program** is specifically designed to produce form letters. This program is so named because such letters are usually printed in volume by merging a file containing a list of names and addresses with a file containing a form letter.

Although many word processors themselves will enable you to do modest amounts of mailing list or form letter preparation, these supplemental packages are much more powerful for these tasks, and are a must if a sizable number of records are to be processed.

SPREADSHEET SOFTWARE

Electronic spreadsheets first came to public notice in the late 1970s when a Harvard Business School student and a programmer friend produced a microcomputer package called VisiCalc® (the *Visible Calculator*). To say it was a huge success is an understatement. It shattered sales

tomorrow

TRENDS IN WORD PROCESSING

Will Tomorrow's Word Processor Be Just Another Word Processor?

The term "word processing" was coined around 1964, to describe a new feature IBM had made available for its Selectric typewriters. The Magnetic Tape Selectric Typewriter (MT/ST) contained a small magnetic tape unit that allowed users to store preprepared portions of popular documents. These materials could later be interwoven with fresh text— such as the name and address of a proposed recipient—thus enabling so-called "canned letters" to be mass produced. Since then word processing has never been the same.

Today, of course, we routinely not only save text, but can manipulate it on a screen prior to printing. Moreover, many people take advantage of enhancement packages such as spelling checkers and mail merge routines to expand their word processing capabilities even further. Other add-on software commonly used with word processors today includes:

Idea Processors. These packages, sometimes referred to as "mindware," enable you to put down thoughts and ideas in a random order, and attach a number or keyword to each. Later you can organize the ideas into an outline, or possibly a complete paper. These processors are ideal for writers, business users, and students. Some writers swear by them, and claim they improve the quality of a written piece and reduce the time it takes to create it.

Macro Processors. These packages let you save files consisting of large blocks of text or multiple program commands, and later invoke these files with one or two keystrokes. You could, for example, store a pre-prepared thank-you letter that pops up on the screen every time you hit the ALT and F keys. Macro processors also generally allow you to redefine the keys on your keyboard, which comes in handy if you don't like certain key positions.

Grammar and Style Checkers. These packages analyze your documents for readability, looking specifically for constructions such as excessively long sentences, passive verbs, wordy phrases, and words longer than two syllables. Single or infrequent occurrences of these things aren't necessarily bad, but too many of them

records for software and, according to many, revolutionized microcomputing. Also, it perhaps once and for all put to rest the question: "Can a businessperson do anything serious with a microcomputer?" VisiCalc is easy to use and clearly has made managers who mastered it more productive.

Today spreadsheet software abounds in the marketplace, for all sizes of computers. A few of the spreadsheet packages available for microcomputers are shown in Figure 12-12.

How Spreadsheets Work: A Quick Overview

The principle behind electronic spreadsheets is to view the display screen as a *window* looking in on a big grid, called a **worksheet.** The worksheet is similar to the large columnar paper on which accountants frequently work.

make a document hard to read. Grammar and style checkers will often provide you with readability measures and specific suggestions for improving the document. *Typesetting and Graphics Packages.* Software that falls into this category enables you to dress up an otherwise drab-looking document with special printing fonts and graphical images. Some packages also let you create and store your own forms, greeting cards, and signs.

In the future we can expect many functions carried out by these add-on packages to be utility routines that are part of the word processor itself, making the word processing package a complete production, writing, and composition system. And, of course, many word processors will also have routines that will enable you to perform spreadsheet, presentation graphics, data management, and communications functions. This is available to some extent today, however, most such "integrated packages" revolve around the spreadsheet function and word processing is relegated to a support activity. We are also likely to see word processing moving closer to *image processing,* as it becomes easier to interweave a variety of drawings and photographs into text (see photo).

And considering the progress that's being made in voice recognition, it seems inevitable that someday we'll regularly be speaking to machines that are not only dictation takers, but authors and writing teachers as well.

Today's business composition systems: How soon will they be regular fare on tomorrow's word processor?

But don't expect that word processor you've become accustomed to using to be obsolete soon. It's probably easy to use and, besides, most people feel that they have modest writing needs. These things will probably make your present word processing software useful for a long time to come in tomorrow's fast-paced world.

Figure 12-12. A few of the spreadsheet packages available for microcomputers. Many spreadsheet-oriented packages, such as Lotus Development Corporation's 1-2-3 (above) also have other software functions integrated into them.

It may consist of, say, 256 rows and 64 columns. Each of the 16,384 (256 × 64) *cells* formed at the intersection of the rows and columns may contain a word, number, or formula. The display screen is only large enough to allow users to see a few rows and columns at any one time. However, they can press keys on the keyboard (usually the arrow keys) that will move the worksheet around so they can see other portions of it through the window.

The use of an electronic spreadsheet is illustrated in Figure 12-13. In this example the user wishes to compute a business income statement, where expenses are 60 percent of sales and profit is the difference between sales and expenses. The *status area* (or *control panel*) is the portion of the screen where users perform such tasks as placing text or numbers into any of the cells of the worksheet. Columns are identified by letters and rows by numbers, and each cell by a letter and number pair. In the world of spreadsheets, a *label* (L) is an entry that cannot be manipulated mathematically. A *value* (V) is an entry that can. In the figure the user has entered the following six commands into the status area:

1.	A1 (L) SALES	**4.**	B1 (V) 200
2.	A2 (L) EXPENSES	**5.**	B2 (V) .6*B1
3.	A3 (L) PROFIT	**6.**	B3 (V) +B1-B2

As each command is issued in the status area, it is processed, and the results are transferred by the software package to the worksheet in the

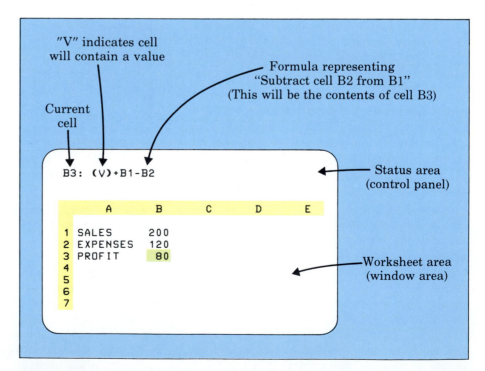

Figure 12-13. An electronic spreadsheet package at work. It's the *recalculation feature* of spreadsheet packages—the ability to quickly rework thousands of tedious calculations—that makes them so valuable to users.

worksheet area (or *window area*). In commands 1 to 4, a direct transfer is made. In commands 5 and 6, the computer first makes the computation indicated by the formulas and then transfers the result to the corresponding cells in the worksheet.

Electronic spreadsheet packages are particularly useful for "what-if" types of queries. For example, suppose the user in Figure 12-13 wanted to know what the profit would be if sales were $5000. The user would simply type in the command

B1 (V) 5000

and the software package automatically would rework all the figures according to the formulas. Thus the computer would respond:

SALES   5000
EXPENSES   3000
PROFIT   2000

Electronic spreadsheets can perform recalculations in seconds that would require several hours to do manually or by writing a program in a high-level language. In fact it's this **recalculation feature** that makes spreadsheets so popular and it is probably the most important thing you should know about them.

A particularly attractive feature of spreadsheet packages is that users can learn to prepare budgets and financial schedules with them after only a few hours of training.

Learning to Use a Spreadsheet

Now that you have an idea of how spreadsheet packages work, let's look more closely at a few important features that are common to most of them.

GENERAL OPERATIONS. As mentioned earlier regarding word processing packages, there are seven general operations with which one needs to become familiar when using virtually any productivity software package. These operations—which include (in the case of spreadsheet packages) such tasks as accessing the spreadsheet program package from the operating system, saving worksheets, and retrieving worksheets—were highlighted, in Figure 12- 5. You should make careful note of how each of these commands is invoked on the spreadsheet package you plan to use.

PHYSICAL MAKEUP. Spreadsheet products are strikingly alike in their physical makeup. For example, there are remarkable similarities in screen layout, pointing mechanisms, and procedures for filling in cells.

Screen layout As Figure 12-13 shows, a spreadsheet window consists of two major sections: a **status area** (or **control panel**) and a **worksheet area** (or **window area**).

Most worksheet areas have columns that are labeled by letters and rows that are labeled by numbers, as shown in the figure. Some

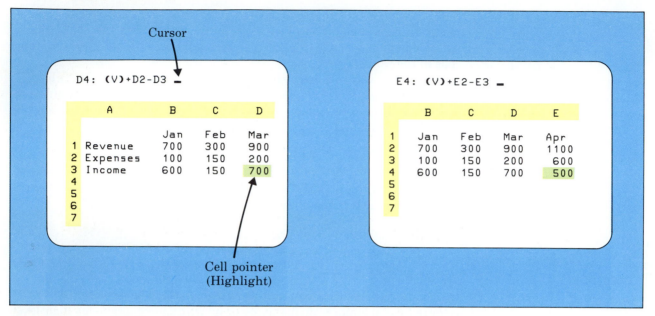

Cursor

D4: (V)+D2-D3 _

	A	B	C	D
		Jan	Feb	Mar
1	Revenue	700	300	900
2	Expenses	100	150	200
3	Income	600	150	700
4				
5				
6				
7				

E4: (V)+E2-E3 _

	B	C	D	E
1	Jan	Feb	Mar	Apr
2	700	300	900	1100
3	100	150	200	600
4	600	150	700	500
5				
6				
7				

Cell pointer
(Highlight)

Figure 12-14. *Scrolling the worksheet to see other parts of it.* In the diagram shown, the right-arrow key has been depressed once.

spreadsheet packages permit thousands of rows and columns. Any **cell** in the worksheet is identified by its column and row—for example, cell K25 is found at the intersection of column K and row 25. The arrow keys on the keyboard enable one to scroll the window around to other parts of the worksheet in order to see them or to enter new data (see Figure 12-14).

The status area is generally used to display the coordinates and the contents of the cell on which the user currently is working, which is called the **current cell** (or **active cell**), as well as a menu of useful worksheet commands. Spreadsheet packages differ in the way in which this is implemented.

Pointing mechanisms In most spreadsheet packages, there are two pointing mechanisms: a cursor and a cell pointer (or highlight). The **cursor** is associated with the status area—it points to the place in that area where the next character typed in by the user will appear. The **cell pointer** (or **highlight**) is associated with the worksheet area, and points to the current cell.

Both the cursor and cell pointer are labeled in Figure 12-14. Depressing any of the arrow keys, which changes the current cell, changes the display in the status area. Note in the figure that when the right-arrow key is depressed, the current cell (in the status area) changes from D4 to E4. And the cell pointer, of course, now highlights cell E4 (instead of D4) in the worksheet area. Many people prefer using a mouse, rather than the keyboard, to move around the worksheet.

Cell-filling procedures In most spreadsheet products, a cell can contain either a "label" or a "value." A **label** is an entry that cannot be manipulated mathematically, whereas a **value** is an entry that can. Some spreadsheets automatically assume that an entry that starts with a letter is a label unless it is preceded by a +, −, or @ character.

A value is generally one of three types: a *numeric constant* (for example, 200); a *formula* (for example, +B1−B2, which tells the package that the value in the current cell is computed as the value in cell B1 minus the value in cell B2); or a *function* (for example, @SUM(B1..B3), which tells the package that the value in the current cell is computed as a function—in this case the sum—of the values in cells B1, B2, and B3).

As you type in a label or value for a cell, the keystrokes are shown in the status area. If you make a mistake, you can always send the cursor back to the point of error and retype over your mistake. When you are satisfied with what you've typed, you depress the return key, which will automatically transfer the appropriate status-area contents into the current cell on the worksheet. Then you move on to the next cell with one of the arrow keys and do the same thing.

ENTERING AND EDITING OPERATIONS.   In addition to enabling users to type in labels and values and have results calculated and displayed immediately, spreadsheet packages also have numerous features to facilitate entering and editing data. The following is a sample of these features.

Inserting and deleting   Virtually all spreadsheet packages allow you to insert new columns or rows into the spreadsheet. Also, you can delete columns or rows that are no longer needed. Generally inserting or deleting involves moving the cell pointer to the appropriate position on the worksheet (relative to the row or column to be added or deleted) and issuing the proper command. Figure 12-15*a* (page 372) illustrates inserting a blank row to make a worksheet more attractive.

Copying   Most spreadsheets have a command that enables you to copy the contents of one cell (or several cells) into another cell (or several others). The command usually prompts you for a source range that contains the data to be copied, and a destination range that will receive the copied data. A valid range is one that, perhaps, consists of contiguous cells from a single row or a single column—for example, F8..Z8, or B9..B28.

If you are copying cells that contain formulas, you will generally be asked to state whether you want the cell references in the formulas to be "relative" or "absolute." For example, say we want the value of each cell in column C to equal the corresponding column A entry minus the corresponding column B entry. In other words, we want

$$C1 = A1 - B1$$
$$C2 = A2 - B2$$
$$C3 = A3 - B3$$
$$C4 = A4 - B4$$

We can generally do this by placing the cell pointer at C1 and typing +A1 − B1. We can then copy this formula into cells C2..C4 in the

Tips on Buying a Spreadsheet Package for Your Micro

A GRAPHICS PACKAGE OFTEN MAKES A GOOD COMPANION

As suggested in the box on page 354, buying a software package involves five steps: analyzing needs, listing products and alternatives, examining products, comparing products, and choosing among them. In this box we look at how this five-step buying formula relates to microcomputer-based spreadsheet packages.

Analyzing Needs　Unlike word processors, spreadsheet packages work alike and look alike in many respects. Still the buyer must beware. Don't neglect listing the entering, editing, and advanced features you require, and make sure the software packages you later consider have them. If you often prepare worksheets that have columns of various widths, for example, you should make absolutely sure the spreadsheet software you eventually buy will allow this. And, incidentally, not all do.

List Products and Alternatives　As with selecting word processors, ask questions and read comparative studies if you're not familiar with any packages. A common spreadsheet need is to graph worksheet data, so you may want to consider jointly acquiring graphics software, a graphics board for your monitor, and a graphics-oriented (i.e., dot-matrix) printer. You may even want color output, but that can increase the cost of your system considerably.

Many spreadsheets are components of integrated software packages (see Chapter 13, pages 404–405), which contain built-in graphics and data management routines that supplement the spreadsheet offerings. Integrated software packages are more expensive than standalone spreadsheets, so if you really

don't need the extra features, don't buy a package that makes you pay for them (unless there are other compelling reasons).

Examine the Products　Among types of productivity software, spreadsheet packages probably have fewer surprises that are likely to surface during a demonstration or test drive. This, of course, is because many of them work the same way. Nonetheless it's always best to become familiar with the features of the products you're considering buying. You may also want to reread the comparative studies you've seen on the spreadsheet packages to make sure you haven't overlooked anything.

Comparison　As many spreadsheet packages have the same "standard" features for manipulating cell values, it's often a certain ineffable "feel" or "bells and whistles" that

distinguishes one product from another. For example, if you sometimes prepare worksheets that consist of rows that require sorting, a spreadsheet package with a sorting feature might sway your decision.

Choice　Make a selection.

manner described by specifying *relative replication.* If we had asked for *absolute replication,* the spreadsheet package would have copied the formula verbatim and all four cells would erroneously contain the value of the expression $+A1 - B1$ (see Figure 12-15*b,c*).

Moving "Cutting and pasting" are often just as important in developing worksheets as in developing word-processed documents. Almost all spreadsheets enable you to move any row or any column into another row or column position on the worksheet. For example, you may decide to move row 5 into the row 2 position, as in Figure 12-15*d*. When moving, formulas are revised automatically by the software so that cell references point to the new worksheet locations. If the spreadsheet package allows you to cut and paste larger areas, you may be able to move, say, a contiguous twenty-by-forty block of cells from one part of the worksheet to another.

Editing dollar amounts Since spreadsheets are particularly useful for preparing financial schedules, it follows that many of the cells in the spreadsheet will contain values that represent monetary amounts. Most packages include facilities that enable you quickly to put dollar signs, commas, and decimal points into these values (for example, to change 90000 to $90,000.00).

Selecting column widths Many spreadsheet packages allow you to change the width of columns on the spreadsheet. In some packages you can assign widths to each column individually; in others you can only select a single, "global width" that must apply to all columns. Many spreadsheet packages also have a "spillover feature," which permits particularly long labels to spill over into adjacent columns without causing problems.

Establishing titles Some spreadsheet packages have a "titles command," which allows you to keep a portion of the worksheet locked in place on the screen regardless of how the rest of the worksheet is scrolled about. For example, if we used the titles command to establish the first four rows of Figure 12-15*e* as titles, we can use the down-arrow key to scroll through data in the worksheet while the titles remain on the screen.

Using templates A **template** is a worksheet that has all of the rows and columns prelabeled for you. Also, many of the cells will already have titles and formulas. The only thing missing are the data. Thus all of the work involved in setting up the worksheet has already been done, leaving you with more time for entering and analyzing data. A template is shown in Figure 12-15*f*.

In addition to containing the features just mentioned, some of the more powerful spreadsheet packages have facilities for sorting data, searching for records with specific characteristics, and doing presentation graphics. We'll discuss such *integrated packages* in Chapter 13.

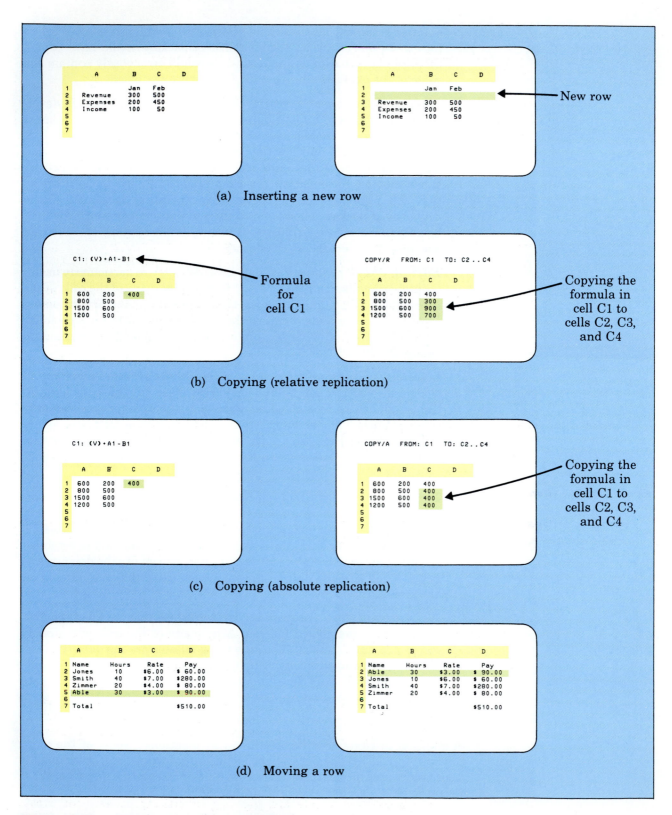

(a) Inserting a new row

(b) Copying (relative replication)

(c) Copying (absolute replication)

(d) Moving a row

Figure 12-15. Entering and editing operations.

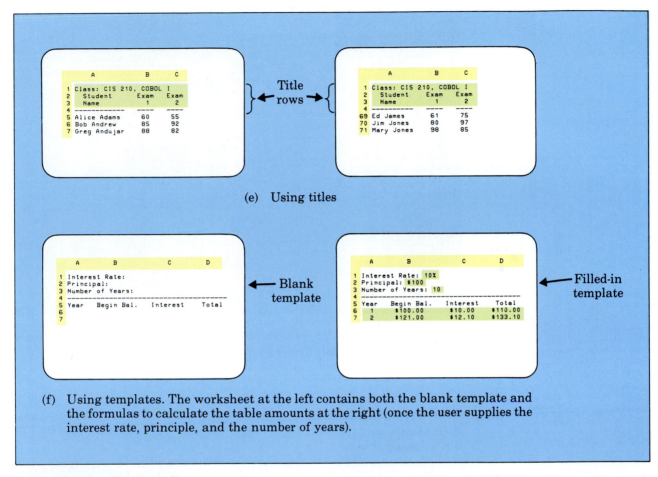

(e) Using titles

(f) Using templates. The worksheet at the left contains both the blank template and the formulas to calculate the table amounts at the right (once the user supplies the interest rate, principle, and the number of years).

Figure 12-15. (Continued)

PRESENTATION GRAPHICS SOFTWARE

The two types of software packages discussed so far (word processors and spreadsheets) typically manipulate text; that is, words and numbers. Graphics packages, on the other hand, manipulate pictures, or graphics. These packages make it possible to generate images relatively painlessly, on either a display device, a printer, or a plotter.

There are two general types of graphics software:

✗ *Presentation graphics software*   **Presentation graphics software** enables you to draw bar charts, pie charts, line charts, and the like, in order to present information in a visual, easily understood way.

✗ *Computer-aided design (CAD) software*   This type of software is used to design houses, clothing, cars, planes, tools, and so forth. It can be employed to create art, produce advertising images, and create props for theatrical productions, as well.

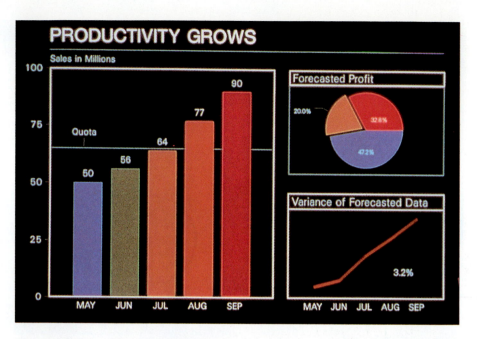

Figure 12-16. *Types of presentation graphics: a bar chart (left), pie chart (top right), and line chart (lower right).*

Because spreadsheet software is often integrated into a graphics package, presentation graphics is treated in this chapter. CAD software is deferred until Chapter 15.

Presentation graphics packages vary in the way they work, but most are capable of producing bar charts, line charts, pie charts, and several other types of information-intensive images (see Figure 12-16 and Window 4). Once the graphics package is invoked, you generally decide on the type of graph to be created, identify the data used to plot the graph, and indicate your preferences on such matters as titles, coloring, and cross-hatching. As with other productivity software, the graphics package usually lets you do such things as save, delete, and print graphs. To get the output in hard-copy form, you normally need either a dot-matrix impact printer that can work in a graphics mode, an ink-jet printer, a laser printer, a plotter, or a camera.

An example of a presentation graphics package in operation is shown in Figure 12-17. The user is first presented with a menu, such as that shown in Figure 12-17a. After the user selects the pie-chart option, a "form" is presented on the screen for the user to fill in (Figure 12-17b). Often the screen is entirely preformatted, and once the user has typed an entry into a field, the package automatically tabs to the next field. When the user is finished, a "Y" (signifying "yes") is typed in the appropriate place. Then the graphic image shown in Figure 12-17c is produced on an output device. Note that the entries in the value column of Figure 12-17b are automatically calculated as percentages of the total when output on the pie chart.

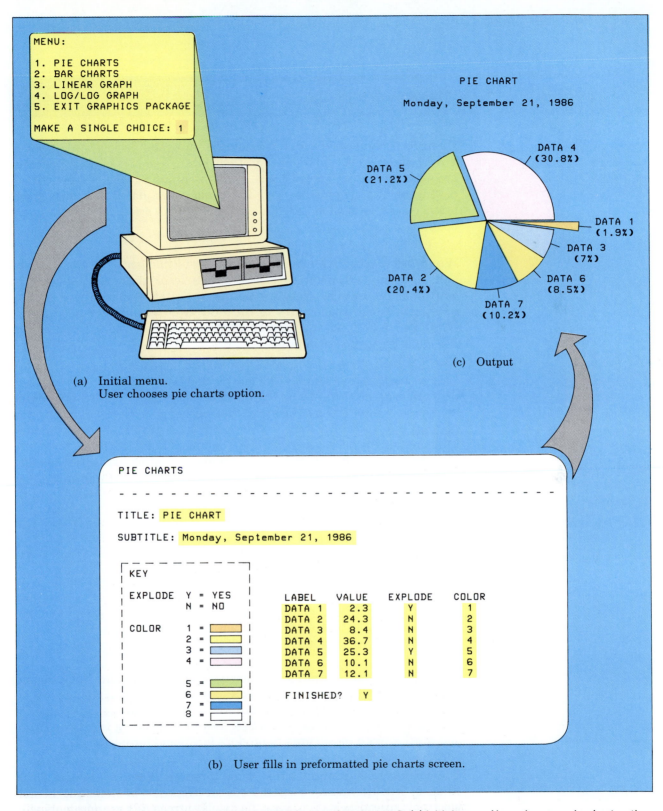

Figure 12-17. *How some presentation graphics packages work.* (a) Initial menu. User chooses pie chart option. (b) Filling out the preformatted pie charts screen. (c) The completed pie chart output.

Summary and Key Terms

Productivity software refers to the program packages that make businesspeople more productive in their jobs. Examples of such packages are word processors, spreadsheets, and presentation graphics software (all covered in this chapter), as well as file managers, database management systems, and integrated software packages (which are covered in the next chapter).

Word processing refers to using computer technology to create, manipulate, and print text materials such as letters, legal contracts, manuscripts, and other documents. Word processors are often classified as **screen-oriented word processors** or **imbedded-command word processors,** depending on how closely what you see on the display screen resembles what you see in print.

Using a word processor, or for that matter, any type of productivity software package requires learning several general operations. These operations include *accessing* the package from the operating system, informing the package that you either want to *create* a new file or to *retrieve* an old one, commanding the package to *save* a file, commanding the package to *print* a file, commanding the package to *delete* a file, indicating to the package that you want to *quit* working on your current file and do something on another file, and *terminating* the package and getting back to the operating system.

Learning to use a word processor at a minimal level involves mastering a number of elementary entering and editing operations as well as several print-formatting commands. Entering and editing operations include moving the cursor, scrolling, line return, inserting and deleting, moving and copying, and searching and replacing. Among the print formatting operations one must learn are adjusting line spacing, indenting, reformatting, centering, tabbing, pagination, font selection, and multiple columns.

Sophisticated users of word processing packages often require software and hardware that provide **proportional spacing** and **microspacing** to enable typeset-quality output. In addition, such users often acquire adjunct packages such as **spelling checkers,** as well as **mailing list programs** and **mail merge programs** to produce labels and form letters.

Electronic spreadsheets first came to public notice in the late 1970s when a product named VisiCalc was developed. The principle behind electronic spreadsheets is to view the display screen as a *window* looking in on a big grid, called a **worksheet.** The worksheet is similar to the large columnar paper on which accountants frequently work.

Presentation Graphics

A picture is worth a thousand words

Presentation graphics involves the use of computer graphics techniques to present information to others in a useful and interesting way. Often data is first assembled into information with a spreadsheet package. Then, a graphics package—which may also contain art software (see Window 3)—is used to put the information into a pictorial format. Output is often accomplished with slide-making hardware or a plotter.

GOVERNMENT SPENDING
Military Pay

20%

2

Where the Dollar Goes

Pie charts, perhaps because they are the same shape as coins, have traditionally been used to show how the dollar is spent.

3.   A spectacular three-dimensional graphic, produced on a microcomputer-based art system, showing that Forest Department spending has increased every year in the first half of this decade.

2.   A simple graphic illustrating that military pay accounts for 20 percent of government spending.

FOREST DEPT. SPENDING

1981
1982
1983
1984
1985

=$1 BILLION

3

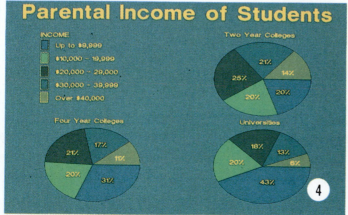

Parental Income of Students

INCOME
Up to $9,999
$10,000 – 19,999
$20,000 – 29,000
$30,000 – 39,999
Over $40,000

Two Year Colleges
21%
14%
25%
20%
20%

Four Year Colleges
17%
21%
11%
20%
31%

Universities
18%
13%
6%
20%
43%

4

4.   A multiple-pie chart showing parental income of students.

Bar Chart Variations

Whereas pie charts are ideal for showing how much each part contributes to some whole, bar charts are useful for comparing items in other ways. This page has several graphics that show how one can use bar charts effectively.

5. A clustered bar chart.

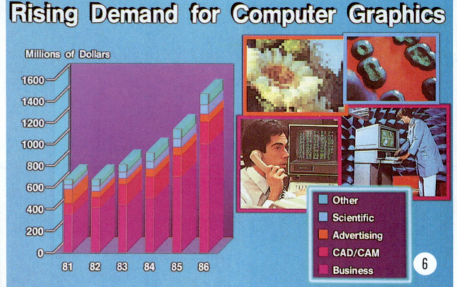

6. A stacked bar chart. This graphic is particularly striking because it uses the computer to incorporate several digitized photographs directly into the presentation material.

7. A three-dimensional stacked bar chart showing millions of instructions per second (mips) at five data centers.

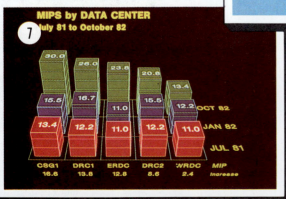

8. A detailed, stacked bar chart graphic from a Versatec color plotter.

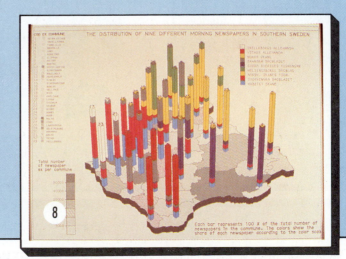

Incorporating the Subject Matter into the Graphic

Researchers have shown that information is more effectively presented when done in an interesting way. The images on these two pages each attempt to do this by presenting numerical or qualitative information along with graphical images that pertain to the subject of the presentation.

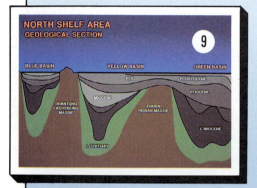

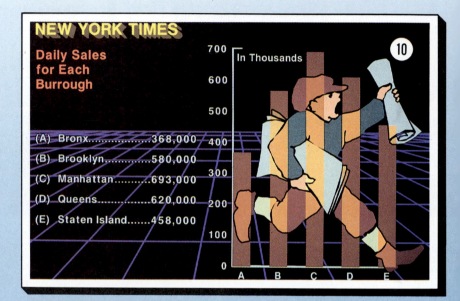

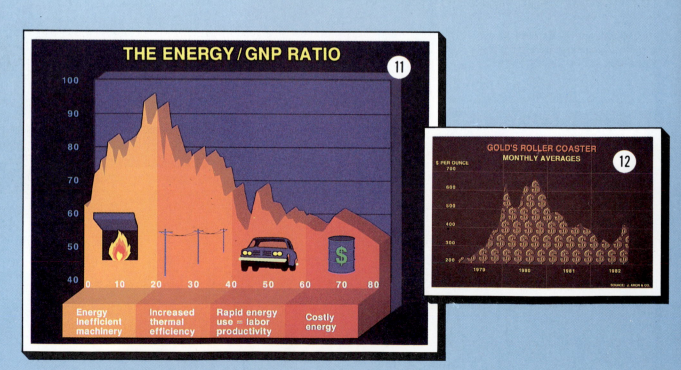

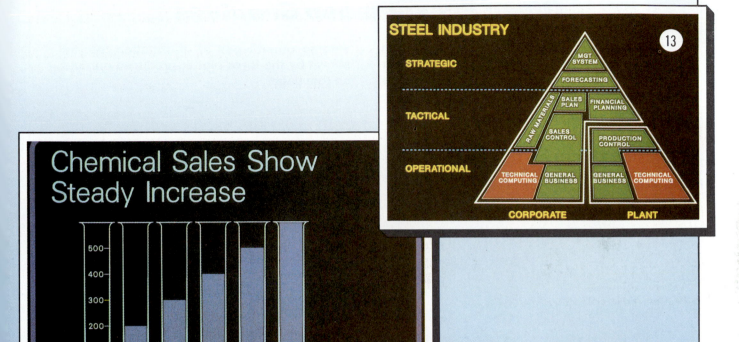

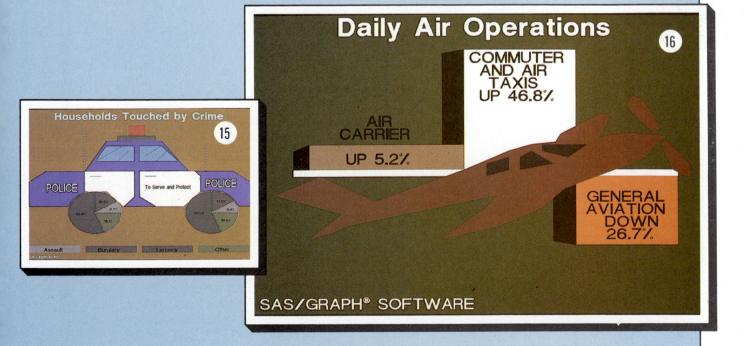

Other Presentation Graphics

Most of the graphics shown so far in this Window are statistical, showing, for example, percentages attributable to different phenomena. But presentation graphics are useful for presenting other types of information too, as shown by the three plotter-produced outputs on this page.

1986 PRICING REVIEW

OCTOBER 17

	30–4	7–10	14–18	21–25
Set Objectives				
Identify Factors				
Establish Strategy		DEPTS. MUST AGREE BY 10th!		
Review Guidlines				
Set Price				
Develop Discounts				

Marketing   Finance

17. A Gantt chart (see Chapter 16) is commonly used to establish schedules, such as this one for developing a pricing strategy.

ONLINE '85
AT A GLANCE ...   TUESDAY, M. 18

9:00	GENERAL SESSION Speaker: Christopher Morgan		
10:00	INTRODUCTION TO MICRO SOFTWARE AND HARDWARE	BEYOND BIBLIOGRAPHIES: THE FUTURE OF THE ONLINE INDUSTRY	INTRODUCTION TO ONLINE SEARCHING AND DATABASES FOR END USERS
10:15	COFFEE BREAK		
10:30	GRAPHIC SOFTWARE O'Connor	NATIONAL TELETEXT Sinter	STRATEGIC PLANNING Marsh
11:15	VISICALC Shaw	FACSIMILE SERVICES Pfaffenberg	DATABASE Botee
12:00	LUNCHEON Speaker: Joseph Becker		

18. A morning itinerary for a conference.

Job Performance and Job Satisfacti 19
What is their bottom–line value to an organization

DESIGN CONCERN	HAS AN EFFECT ON		
	Job satisfaction	Job performance	Ease of communication
Degree of enclosure			✓
Layout			✓
Temperature/air quality	✓		
Lighting	✓	✓	
Windows	✓	✓	
Access control		✓	
Noise	✓		
Speech privecy			✓
Comfort	✓		
Participation	✓	✓	
Flexibilty	✓		

19. A table showing the effects certain attributes have on various aspects of one's job.

Spreadsheet packages are particularly valuable because they provide a **relcalculation feature**—that is, they can perform recalculations in seconds that would require several hours to do manually or by writing a program in a high-level language. Users can learn to prepare budgets and financial schedules with spreadsheet packages after only a few hours of training. In fact it's this recalculation feature that makes spreadsheets so popular and it is probably the most important thing you should know about them.

Worksheets commonly consist of two major sections: a **status area** (or **control panel**) and a **worksheet area** (or **window area**). Most worksheet areas have columns that are labeled by letters and rows that are labeled by numbers. Any **cell** in the worksheet is identified by its column and row. The status area is generally used to display the coordinates and the contents of the cell on which the user is currently working, which is called the **current cell** (or **active cell**), as well as a menu of useful worksheet commands.

In most spreadsheet packages, there are two pointing mechanisms: a cursor and a cell pointer (or highlight). The **cursor** is associated with the status area, and points to the place in that area where the next character typed in by the user will appear. The **cell pointer** (or **highlight**) is associated with the worksheet area; it points to the current cell.

In most spreadsheet products, a cell can contain either a "label" or a "value." A **label** is an entry that cannot be manipulated mathematically, whereas a **value** is an entry that can.

In addition to enabling users to type in labels and values and have results calculated and displayed immediately, spreadsheet packages also have numerous features to facilitate entering and editing of data. These operations include inserting and deleting rows or columns, moving and copying the contents of cells from one part of the worksheet to another, editing dollar amounts, selecting column widths, and establishing titles.

Also, many packages have a **template** feature that enables worksheets to be created and saved that have all of the rows and columns prelabeled, with only the data to be filled in.

Presentation graphics software enables you to draw bar charts, pie charts, and the like, in order to present information to others in a visual, easily understood way. Presentation graphics packages vary in the way they work. Generally, once the graphics package is invoked, you decide on the type of graph to be created, identify the data that's used to plot the graph, and indicate your preferences on such matters as titles, coloring, and cross-hatching. As with other productivity software, the graphics package usually lets you do such things as save, delete, and print graphs.

Review Exercises

Fill-in Questions

1. Most word processors have a _____ feature that automatically produces a soft carriage return.
2. _____ is a word processing feature that allocates more horizontal space on a line to some characters than to others.
3. The principle behind electronic spreadsheets is to view the display screen as a(n) _____ looking in on a big grid, called a(n) _____.
4. In most spreadsheet packages, there are two pointing mechanisms: a(n) _____ and a(n) _____.
5. Two types of copying operations available in many spreadsheet packages are _____ and _____ replication.
6. A worksheet that has all of the rows and columns prelabeled is called a(n) _____.

Matching Questions

Match each term with its description.

a. Copying   d. Inserting
b. Carriage return e. Scrolling
c. Proportional spacing f. Moving

_____ 1. Moving contiguous lines of text up and down on a screen similarly to the way the roll on a player piano is unwound.
_____ 2. Classified as "soft" and "hard" in the world of word processing.
_____ 3. An operation that involves replication.
_____ 4. An operation that involves physically relocating text from one place to another so the text no longer appears in its original location.
_____ 5. A word processing feature that gives text a typeset-quality look.
_____ 6. An operation you would use on a word processor to quickly change the string "MISSIPPI" to "MISSISSIPPI."

Discussion Questions

1. What is productivity software?
2. Explain the difference between a screen-oriented word processor and an imbedded-command word processor.
3. Identify the seven general operations one must master to operate virtually any type of productivity software package.
4. What can one do with an electronic spreadsheet?

5. What is the difference between a "label" and a "value" with regard to spreadsheets?

6. What types of graphical images can be constructed with presentation graphics software?

...icador para seleccionar una ficha .

Sr. Benjamin Rojas
Criollitos de Venezuela.
(043) 21-046

Num Pad   3   1

9:54

File Managers and Database Management Systems

Chapter Outline

Objectives

After completing this chapter you should be able to:

1. Describe what file managers can do and how they work.
2. Explain what database management systems are and how they differ from file managers.
3. Identify the various approaches used for database management on both large and small computer systems.
4. Understand what integrated software does and where it is appropriate.

OVERVIEW

Figure 13-1.   Data management software. These packages specialize in retrieving the information managers need to do their jobs. Data management software is rapidly replacing many of those thick, hard-copy manuals that these same managers once had to thumb through by hand.

People often have a need for rapidly summoning large amounts of data. An airline agent, on the phone to a client, may need to search quickly through mounds of data to find the least-cost available flight path from Tucson to Toronto two weeks hence. The registrar of a university might have to scan student records swiftly to find the grade-point averages of all students slated to graduate in June. And an engineer may need to test several structural-design alternatives against volumes of complicated safety and feasibility criteria before proceeding further with a design strategy.

This chapter covers productivity software that's used specifically for such *data management* tasks. In a sense this is the class of software that's rapidly replacing those thick, hard-copy manuals that people have traditionally needed to thumb through to fetch the information they use on their jobs. Data management software is often categorized into two major types: *file managers* and *database management systems*. As with other types of productivity software, an abundance of these packages is available for both large and small computer systems (see Figure 13-1). File managers are easier to use and understand, so we'll discuss those first. We'll then turn to database systems. Finally we'll look at *integrated software*—packages that often include some data management features with the word processing, spreadsheet, and graphics functions described in Chapter 12.

Before reading this chapter, you should review the section in Chapter 2 entitled "Organizing Data for Computer Systems" (pages 47–48), as well as the "Data Access and Data Organization" section in Chapter 5 (pages 146–153). The terms file, record, and field (introduced in Chapter 2) are used throughout the discussions on data management in this chapter. The Chapter 5 topics—organization and access—are really what data management is all about: organizing data on disk so that you can effectively retrieve them in the ways that you need to.

FILE MANAGEMENT SOFTWARE

A **file manager** (or *record management system*) is a software package that enables you to organize data into files and to process the data a single file at a time. For example, you might first use the package to search for and print out the names of all recipes, in a recipe file, that contain kumquats as an ingredient. Minutes later, you may summon the same package to scan an employee file and total the number of employees in your organization who will be having birthdays in April.

You can use the package to create and store as many files as you want, but since you can only activate one file at a time, the package can't interrelate data appearing in different files for you. Thus you couldn't find, say, the birthday of the employee (in your employee file) who gave you the candied kumquats recipe (in your recipe file) without making two separate file calls and making two separate queries (one for each file).

The one-file-at-a-time drawback aside, file managers are both powerful and extremely useful. Besides enabling you to search for records with specific characteristics, most packages permit you to sort records and to produce both summary information and detailed reports from selected records. They also will let you add, delete, or modify data.

How File Managers Work

Let's look at an example to get a feel for how file managers process data. Suppose an organization has 1000 employees. The organization maintains a "form" on each employee, like the one shown on the display screen in Figure 13-2. Such an *onscreen form,* or **template,** is commonly used for entering data into files. Each file that's created will have its own distinctive template.

As you place data into records of a file, you start with an unfilled template for each record to be keyed in. Then you repeatedly fill the template at the keyboard and save the records onto disk. At any later point, records can be modified or deleted from the file, and new records can be added.

SETTING UP A FILE. Before we look at some of the ways in which we can process the employee file, let's look more closely at the template in Figure 13-2. You'll notice that it contains ten fields: name, social security number, street, and so on.

With most file management packages, users can design their own templates. A chef, for example, in creating a template for a recipe file will probably set up a recipe-name field, an ingredients field, and a directions field. There may even be a field for calories, as well. Generally the file management package will contain a "DESIGN FILE" option that'll enable you to design whatever type of templates you need for your applications. Records in a given file usually must have the same format, conforming to the chosen template.

To enable you to create templates or process file data, many file management packages will provide you with an "opening menu" of choices, such as the one shown in Figure 13-3, as soon as you call the package from the operating system. At this point you must choose one of the given menu options, and also supply the name of the file you wish to process.

For example, if you were setting up a template for the 1000-record employee file previously mentioned, you would select option 1 (DESIGN FILE) and create a name for the file (say, EMPLOYEE-FILE). Then the package would be likely to summon a routine that would ask you a series of questions about how you want to design the template for this file. Here you would name the fields, define the maximum length of data in each of the fields, and make some choices as to how the template will look on the screen. Many packages will let you set up templates that require more than one screen.

Figure 13-2. An onscreen form (template) representing an employee record. Such forms can be filled out while displayed on the screen.

Once the EMPLOYEE-FILE template had been designed, you would go back to the opening menu and select option 2 (ADD) to fill out 1000 "copies" of the form—one for each employee—and to place them onto disk.

FILE MAINTENANCE.   Once records have been stored on disk, you can later add new records (opening menu option 2: ADD) or delete records representing departed employees (option 7: REMOVE). Furthermore, if a record contains outdated data, you can change these data by requesting the update mode (option 4: SEARCH/UPDATE) on the menu.

EXTRACTING INFORMATION.   Besides performing file maintenance operations, you can also extract information for screen display and, if desired, produce printed reports. For example, you might use the search/update feature on the opening menu to scan the file for the names of all employees in department 544, or the names of all employees with salaries exceeding

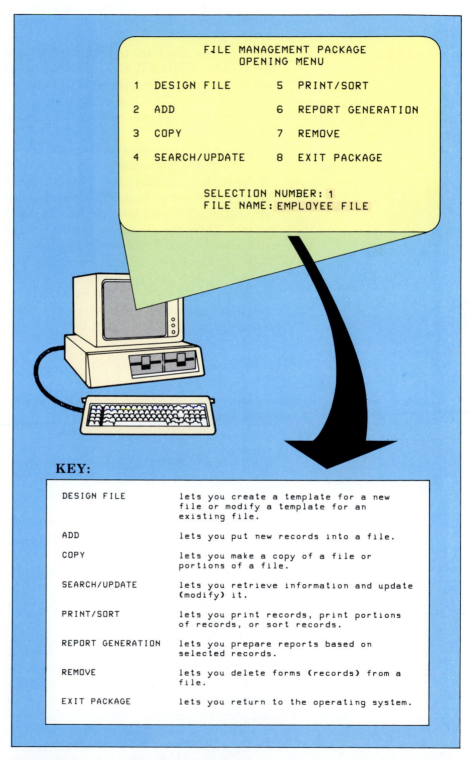

Figure 13-3. *A typical opening menu for a file management package.* In the highlighted areas you key in the processing option you want and the file with which you wish to work.

$40,000. Any of this information can be directed to the screen and, if you wish, printed.

You may also want to produce mailing labels. Thus you could extract the NAME, STREET, CITY, and ZIP fields from selected records by invoking opening menu option 5 (PRINT/SORT). You could then sort these "reduced records" by Zip code before sending them to the printer. The postal service offers reduced rates for large mailings that are presorted by Zip code.

Some packages also have the ability to produce very sophisticated written reports. For example, you might wish to produce a salary report of all employees in departments 212–214, sorted by department and totaled. Again, you would go back to the opening menu, select option 6 (REPORT GENERATION), and identify EMPLOYEE-FILE as the file you wish to process. Then, the file management package would probably present you with a report generation questionnaire, such as the one shown in Figure 13-4a, on which you could describe how to prepare the report. You would merely fill out the questionnaire, hitting the return key after placing responses into each field. The package then would produce the report, as shown in Figure 13-4b. In some cases (such as the one illustrated), the file manager will format the report for you automatically, supply the date, and number pages automatically.

DATABASE MANAGEMENT SYSTEMS

A *database management system* primarily differs from a file manager in that it enables immediate access to data that could conceivably span several files. As a rule, since database management systems are more technically complex than file managers, they are also more expensive and more difficult to master.

Let's look at a case where a database management system might be useful. You are a sales manager, and an order comes in for 10,000 units of product A-211. You first need to find out if the order can be filled from stock in inventory. If it can't, you next need to know how long it will be before enough stock is available. There's an impatient client on the phone and an immediate response is required.

The following scenario would be ideal for you: At the display terminal on your desk, you key in the product number, A-211. The computer system responds with a screen that shows the status of this product, including the current level of uncommitted stock, future delivery dates, and future delivery amounts. Within seconds you are able to satisfy the client's request and place the order.

The type of task we've described is especially suited to a database management system because rapid access to more than one file's worth of data is required. Traditionally an inventory file is used to store current stock levels whereas a vendor order file is used to keep track of future shipments from vendors. The very notion of files is often transparent

Figure 13-4. *Using a file manager to produce a report.* On the display screen, the user fills in blanks on a questionnaire that covers what the report is to look like. The file manager does the rest.

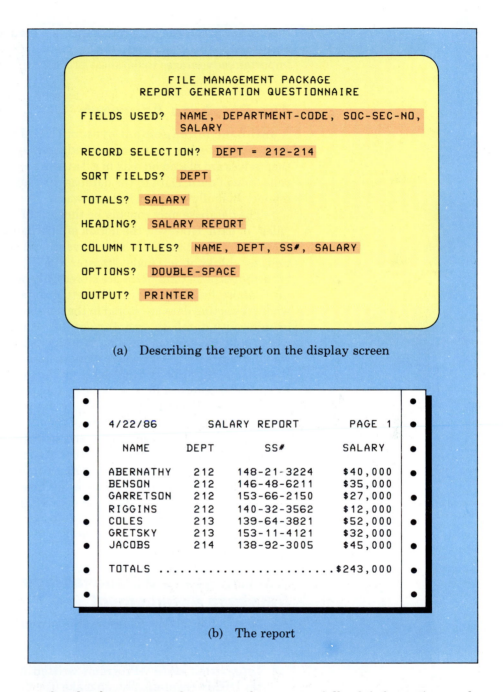

FILE MANAGEMENT PACKAGE
REPORT GENERATION QUESTIONNAIRE

FIELDS USED?   NAME, DEPARTMENT-CODE, SOC-SEC-NO, SALARY

RECORD SELECTION?   DEPT = 212-214

SORT FIELDS?   DEPT

TOTALS?   SALARY

HEADING?   SALARY REPORT

COLUMN TITLES?   NAME, DEPT, SS#, SALARY

OPTIONS?   DOUBLE-SPACE

OUTPUT?   PRINTER

(a)   Describing the report on the display screen

4/22/86	SALARY REPORT		PAGE 1
NAME	DEPT	SS#	SALARY
ABERNATHY	212	148-21-3224	$40,000
BENSON	212	146-48-6211	$35,000
GARRETSON	212	153-66-2150	$27,000
RIGGINS	212	140-32-3562	$12,000
COLES	213	139-64-3821	$52,000
GRETSKY	213	153-11-4121	$32,000
JACOBS	214	138-92-3005	$45,000
TOTALS	. . . .		$243,000

(b)   The report

to the database user, who sees only screens full of information and generally has no idea from where the database system is extracting the information.

You should also observe that a file manager might be unsuitable for the same job we've described. With a file manager, you'd first have to open an inventory file; second, make the stock-level inquiry; third, close the inventory file; fourth (if necessary), open the vendor-order file; and fifth, make the shipment inquiry. Because this serial, "file-conscious" process is slower than having all of the data integrated in a manner transparent to the user, both service to clients and efficiency are sacrificed. There are also other important advantages to database processing, as we'll see later.

The Database Approach

A **database management system (DBMS)** is a sophisticated software system for storing data and providing easy access to them. The data themselves are placed on disk in a **database,** which is simply an integrated collection of data. Data in the database are set up in a common format, in a manner that allows access in many ways.

The database may roughly be thought of as a collection of interrelated "files" of data. However, the notion of files in many database environments is slightly different than it is in conventional circumstances. You might do well to think of a single "master file" (the database), in which all occurrences of all data items are stored only once, and a collection of *logical files,* whose fields consist not of actual data, but of addresses that show where the actual data are stored in the database. A "student file" in a college or university database environment, for example, contains just addresses where student data may be found in the database. Similarly, a "class file" would contain addresses where class rosters might be found. Data such as the ID or social security numbers of students, which would logically appear in both files, physically need appear only once in the database. Although data files per se don't exist physically in many database environments, it often helps to have a logical notion of them.

Users and programmers gain access to the data they need through an easy-to-use *query/update facility* that accompanies the database package, or through an *applications program* written in a programming language (e.g., COBOL). The DBMS serves as an interface between the people and the data. It will locate the data and convert them from the common format into the format required by the user or programmer. A database processing environment is illustrated in Figure 13-5.

Advantages and Disadvantages of Database Management

A sophisticated DBMS offers several advantages over alternative ways to process data. Four such advantages are:

✗ *Integrated data* Programs written in any language supported by the DBMS theoretically can make use of any data in the database. This possiblity enables information that would normally be stored in several independent files to be collected quickly.

✗ *Program-data independence* Because the database data are in their own format and are relatively independent of the programming languages that access them, programs often do not have to be changed when new types of data are added to the database and obsolete types of data are culled.

Figure 13-5. **A college or university database environment.** Database technology makes it possible to combine and efficiently store data that have traditionally existed as separate files.

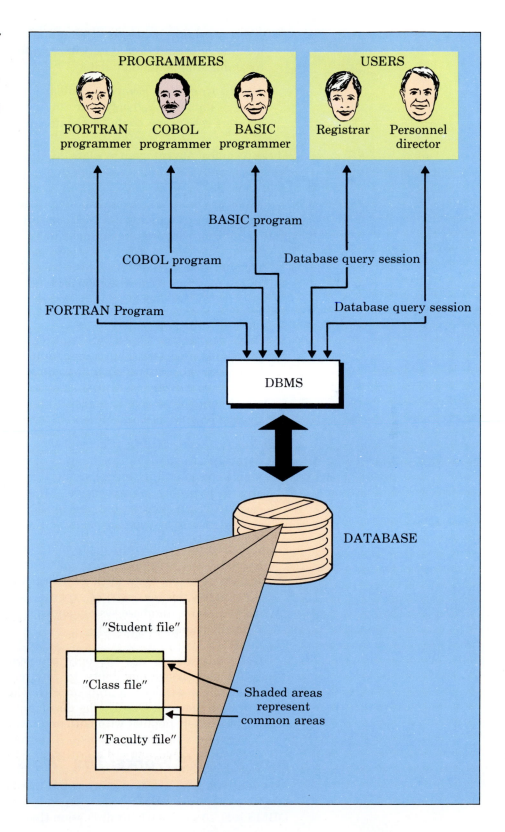

✕ *Nonredundant storage*   Because all occurrences of the same data need be physically stored only once, valuable disk space can be saved by eliminating redundant data.

✕ *Data integrity*   Errors of conflict are avoided because, since each piece of data is stored only once, an update to a piece of data provides all users with access to the same information.

These technical advantages translate into fewer personnel, fast response to problems, and the ability to adapt more rapidly to new and changing environments.

There are, however, several disadvantages to database processing that an organization or individual should consider. The major disadvantage is cost. Significant expenses are normally incurred in the following cost areas:

✕ *Database software*   A sophisticated DBMS is expensive. An organization may spend between $50,000 and $300,000 to obtain one for its mainframe. Microcomputer packages are typically available in the $300–$800 range.

✕ *New hardware*   A DBMS requires a great deal of memory when processing programs. Thus an individual or an organization might find it necessary to upgrade to a bigger, more powerful computer system as a result of a DBMS acquisition. For example, a microcomputer user might suddenly need a hard disk system with a cartridge-tape backup to supplement a newly acquired DBMS.

✕ *Specialized training of personnel*   Both database systems and the databases themselves can be very complex. In large organizations highly specialized personnel are needed to develop and support them, and such people are expensive. Microcomputer-based systems are easier to learn and use, but, are considerably more difficult to master than file managers, spreadsheets, and word processors.

✕ *Conversion effort*   Moving from a traditional file-oriented system to a database system in organizations often entails an expensive, large-scale conversion. Data must be reorganized and programs rewritten. Fortunately this is a one-time expense, as long as the organization stays with the same database system and the vendor of that system doesn't radically change its product.

Cost, however, is not the only problem. Database processing can increase a system's vulnerability to failure. Since the data are highly integrated in the database, a problem with a key element might render the whole system inactive. Despite the disadvantages, however, DBMSs have become immensely popular with both organizations and individuals.

How a DBMS Works: The "Nuts and Bolts"

Now that you have a notion of what DBMSs are, it's time to examine how they work. How a DBMS works depends in large part on what *type* of DBMS it is, so we'll start our discussion there.

TYPES OF DATABASE MANAGEMENT SYSTEMS.   A rather wide variety of database management systems are available for both large and small computers. Each DBMS organizes database data according to some predefined model, called its data structure. A **data structure** specifies relationships among data. As you may remember from Chapter 5, we should *organize* data in accordance with the way in which we want to *access* the data. Thus given the ways we think we might access data, some data structures (and therefore DBMSs) will be more advantageous than others.

Three types of data structures that are very important in database processing are

- Hierarchical (or tree) structures
- Network structures
- Relational structures

Hierarchical and *network* structures have been around the longest, and are still quite useful for many types of applications. But because these database structures are relatively too complicated for the casual user to understand, hierarchical and network databases require professional help to set up and use. Generally this type of work is done by a knowledgeable professional called a **database administrator (DBA).** In large organizations the DBA function may be carried out by several people. Virtually all DBMSs targeted for microcomputers follow the *relational* data model, which is much easier for noncomputer professionals to understand and use.

In hierarchical and network systems, if data are to be accessed in a certain way, a "navigational path" to achieve that access must exist in the database. In other words users aren't free to create new paths on the fly—the DBA must set them up. On the other hand, in relational systems there are no preexisting paths to worry about. As you will shortly see, the data exist in tables and users are free to browse through the data and relate them as they see fit.

Because of their simplicity and flexiblity, relational models are ideal for applications such as *decision support systems* (see Chapter 15), where users require considerable freedom in accessing data authorized to them. Having preexisting paths into the database is generally faster, however, so hierarchical and network databases are useful in environments where people will access the database in predictable ways, such as in routine accounting applications.

SETTING UP THE DATABASE.   The process of setting up, or organizing, the database may involve many steps. Data must be stored as efficiently as possible, indexes and paths may have to be established for rapid access, tight security may have to be established, and so forth. In a large organization, these tasks are carried out by the database administrator. But on most microcomputer systems, such details must be tended to by ordinary users.

One task performed by anyone setting up a database is **data definition,** the process of describing data to the DBMS prior to entering it. For example, say that you've informed your microcomputer's relational database package that you want to create a table called EMPLOYEE-SALARY.

The package may then ask you to describe the data going into the columns of the table. You might then respond as follows:

```
010   SOC-SEC-NUM,C,9
020   EMPLOYEE-NAME,C,30
030   EMPLOYEE-SALARY,N,8,2
```

Roughly translated you've just stated that there will be three table *columns.* SOC-SEC-NUM is the first table column and will consist of text data with a maximum length of nine characters. EMPLOYEE-NAME, the second column, uses thirty characters. EMPLOYEE-SALARY, the third column, will consist of numeric values that are at most eight digits long and have two decimal places. Each table *row* will consist of the social security number, name, and salary of an employee.

PROCESSING DATA.   The process of *using* the database in some hands-on fashion is called **data manipulation.** There are generally two ways to manipulate data in a DBMS—with a query/update facility and with a programming language.

Users such as managers, airline clerks, and university registrars will typically use the **query/update facility** of the DBMS to manipulate data. The query/update facility consists of easy-to-use commands that enable noncomputer professionals to interact with the database without having to learn a programming language.

A programmer, on the other hand, will normally use some sort of *programming language* to write an application-specific program. In the case of microcomputer packages, the programmer often has only one choice—the proprietary "database language" supplied with the DBMS. With DBMS packages targeted to larger computers, programmers normally have several familiar high-level languages to work with, such as COBOL, PL/1, and BASIC. The DBMS vendor will usually extend the power of each of these interfacing languages with a set of database-specific commands.

Database Management on Microcomputers

Microcomputer DBMSs are predominantly relational. As mentioned earlier, they are also relatively simple to learn and use as compared with DBMSs on large computer systems. Many of them come with only a single proprietary language that has commands for data description, query/update, and programming functions. For example, in dBase III®—a popular microcomputer DBMS—the CREATE command is used to set up the database, the BROWSE command enables users to look through the database, and the DO WHILE command enables programmers to set up loops in the programs they create. Although there is no standard relational database language, a number of vendors have chosen to model their languages on IBM's SQL (*Structured Query Language*).

SETTING UP THE DATABASE.   Data in relational databases must be put into *tables,* such as those in Figure 13-6. Each table has a name, such as EMPLOYEE and OFFICE in the example. These tables are similar in

EMPLOYEE		
NAME	**OFFICE-LOCATION**	**DEPARTMENT**
Doney	Phoenix	Acctg.
Black	Denver	Sales
James	Cleveland	Sales
Giles	San Diego	Acctg.
Smith	Miami	Acctg.
Fink	San Diego	Sales
. . .	. . .	. . .

OFFICE	
LOCATION	**MANAGER**
San Diego	Hurt
Cleveland	Holmes
Miami	Jonas
Phoenix	Alexis
. . .	. . .

Figure 13-6. Two database relations. In relational database systems, data exist in tables such as these. Data from two or more files can be combined, or *related*. Through the use of simple database commands, these data can later be extracted and output by the user.

concept to *files*. Moreover, the rows of the tables are like *records* and the columns are like *fields*. Many of the tables have one or more columns in common with other tables. It is through these columns that the data in the tables are *related*. In our example the EMPLOYEE and OFFICE tables are related through the "city" column in each (called OFFICE-LOCATION in one and LOCATION in the other). Defining data in a relational database is often performed in the manner described earlier, on pages 397–398.

PROCESSING DATA.   If, say, we wanted to retrieve the names of all employees in the San Diego office, we could use a query command such as

```
SELECT NAME
     FROM EMPLOYEE
WHERE OFFICE-LOCATION = 'SAN DIEGO'
```

The system would access the EMPLOYEE table to select the names of all employees who worked in San Diego. This query, as you can see, involves only one table.

The power of relational database systems, however, rests in their ability to link the data in more than one table. Suppose, for example, we

Tips on Buying Data Management Software for Your Micro

EASE OF USE AND SPEED ARE THE DIFFERENCE BETWEEN SUCCESS AND DISASTER

As suggested in the box on page 354, buying a software package involves five steps: analyzing needs, listing products and alternatives, examining products, comparing products, and choosing among them. In this box, we look at how this five-step buying formula relates to microcomputer-based data management software packages.

Analyzing Needs. Besides specifying your entering and editing requirements, as you would with word processing and spreadsheet packages, three more things might be added to your data management needs checklist: ease of learning and use, speed, and backup.

With regard to *ease of learning and use,* data management packages can vary remarkably. Generally speaking, file managers are much easier to work with and less expensive than database management systems. If you don't need the power of a database system now or in the future, you probably shouldn't get one. Some database systems are targeted to sophisticated users with a bent for programming and are really not appropriate for the casual user. When evaluating ease of learning, think also of your need for clear, concise documentation—which can also vary dramatically from package to package in the data management area.

Speed is an important consideration because sorting and searching, two common data management tasks, can chew up a lot of time. Since data management packages differ in the ways in which they organize and access data, some are much faster than others for certain types of data management work. Thus you should carefully think about the types of data management tasks you'll be doing, so that later you can evaluate how well the packages rate in this regard.

If you have a transaction-oriented database that is constantly changing, *backup* can

wanted to know which employees worked under the office manager named Jonas. We would enter a query command such as

```
SELECT NAME
    FROM EMPLOYEE
WHERE OFFICE IS IN
    (SELECT LOCATION FROM OFFICE
    WHERE MANAGER = 'JONAS')
```

The system would find Jonas in the OFFICE table, determine that he or she managed the office in Miami, and then use the EMPLOYEE table to find all employees who worked in Miami. In other words, the system would relate these tables to retrieve the needed information.

This principle, applied on a large scale to databases with many tables and many interrelations, provides users with considerable freedom in the retrieval of information. Commands similar to the ones shown here make it

be vital. For example, if a random electrical spike suddenly destroys your database, you want to have a system in effect that provides fast recovery.

List Products and Alternatives. This is where you list the candidate software packages. If you aren't familiar with any packages, visit a computer store or look at comparative product studies in the microcomputer journals at your local library. Because of the acute need for speed, and the fact that data management software might have to access large volumes of data, extra storage hardware such as a hard disk unit may also have to be acquired. If backup is important, you may also need to

consider a tape-streaming device for the hard disk. All of these things can add considerably to the cost of a data management system.

Examine the Products. If you can test candidate products at your local computer store, you'll be able to see which of them works fastest for the type of work you have in mind. And you can assess at the same time how easy they are to use and what the vendor documentation looks like. If the documentation on a product you like is poor or too advanced, check your local bookstore to see if there is a well-written trade book on the product.

Comparison. As with word processors and spreadsheets, this is where you cull the best products from the rest of the lot and scrutinize them closely on the basis of performance and cost.

When data management software is being purchased to run a company, reliability and support may also become major factors to weigh into your final decision. Some people may choose a mature product with a proved track record, or perhaps base the buying decision on the support help available when something goes wrong.

Choice. Make a software (and possibly a hardware) selection.

possible to modify, insert, or delete entries or tables in the database, as well as to retrieve information. In addition, when several such query commands are put together and saved, they form a program. Other commands packaged into microcomputer-based DBMSs allow users to loop, compare, and perform arithmetic on data fields.

Database Management on Large Computers

On large computer systems, DBMSs are necessarily more complex than their microcomputer counterparts. First, they must deal with the problem of several users trying to access the database, perhaps simultaneously. Second, because database technology began evolving at a time when many organizations had thousands of dollars already invested in programs written in popular high-level languages, DBMS vendors had to design their products to interface with these languages.

SETTING UP THE DATABASE. In large DBMS packages, usually a special language is dedicated to the data definition function. This language has generically come to be known as the **data definition language (DDL)**. Besides simply defining data, a major function of the DDL in these large packages is to keep the database protected from unauthorized use.

In setting up a database, for example, the DBA can assign passwords to determine which users may access data. Also, the DBA can allow some users to make modifications to certain data, whereas other users of those data are only permitted query capability. For instance, in an airlines passenger-reservation database, a clerk or agent may not be allowed to rebook a special-rate passenger on an alternate flight, whereas a high-level supervisor (who knows the password) can do so.

The Data Dictionary

A UTILITY TO KEEP TRACK OF DATABASE DATA

Many database management systems, especially those on larger computers, come with a data dictionary facility. The data dictionary and its associated software extend considerably the strength of the data definition function.

A database's *data dictionary* is similar in concept and organization to an ordinary dictionary in that it contains definitions for an alphabetical list of words. The words are those encountered in the company's database environment. Among them would be, for example, names of fields, records, and programs. Thus if we were to look up the field ZIP-CODE in the data dictionary for a typical DBMS, we might find:

• The definition of ZIP-CODE. This definition would probably include a short description of what ZIP-CODE means as well as supplementary information, such as the number of characters in ZIP-CODE and whether or not they are numeric, alphabetic, or something else.

It contains definitions for words in your database.

• The names of all the programs that use ZIP-CODE.
• Any alternate names that ZIP-CODE assumes in programs. For example, ZIP-CODE may be called ZCODE in program T-6742 and ZIPPER in program B-606. These alternate names are known as "aliases."

The data dictionary facility is particularly helpful if, say, a data field changes its properties. For example, if we need to change ZIP-CODE from a 5-digit to a 9-digit field at some point in the future, we can use the dictionary facility to supply the names of all the programs that must be appropriately modified. Also, if a particular type of data is no longer to be kept in the database, and we want the names of all programs that use these data, we can use the dictionary facility for that, too.

PROCESSING DATA. DBMSs targeted for larger computer systems often contain separate language packages to handle query/update and programming tasks. Also, both sets of tasks have their own array of problems that aren't faced by the typical microcomputer DBMS owner.

For example, users on large computer systems (or microcomputer systems linked by a network) often need to access the same data at more or less the same time. This can cause several problems, including:

✖ Suppose a single seat remains available on a flight. Two agents seize it at the same moment and sell it to different customers.

✖ Suppose a program is tallying a series of customer balances in a database. When this program is half finished, another program controlled by someone else transfers $5000 from account 001 (which has already been tallied by the first program) to account 999 (which hasn't). Thus the first program will "double count" the $5000 and obtain erroneous results.

To prevent such **concurrent access** problems, most database systems allow users to place a temporary "lock" on certain blocks of data, to ensure that there will be no other modifications to these data while they are being processed.

Another problem unique to DBMSs on large computer systems relates to the fact that these DBMSs must tie into programs coded in popular high-level programming languages. An interfacing feature known as a **data manipulation language (DML)** solves this problem.

The DML is simply a set of commands that enables the language with which the programmer normally works to function in a database environment. For example, if the programmer writes programs in COBOL, a COBOL DML must be used. The DML may consist of thirty or so commands, which are used by the programmer to interact with data in the database (see Figure 13-7 for a sample of these commands). Thus a COBOL program in a database environment consists of a mixture of standard

DML Command	Purpose
CREATE	Creates a record
STORE	Stores data in the database
FETCH	Retrieves data from the database
INSERT	Inserts a record
MODIFY	Changes data in a record
FIND	Locates a record
DELETE	Deletes a record

Figure 13-7. *Some typical DML commands.* Where available, such commands extend the language with which the programmer normally works, tailoring it to a database environment.

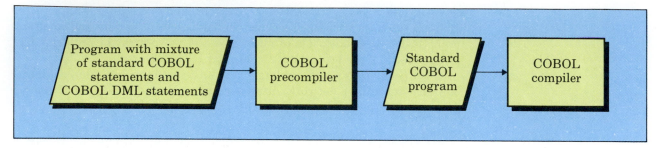

Figure 13-8. *Use of a COBOL precompiler.* The COBOL precompiler translates a COBOL program written with DML commands into a regular COBOL program, which can be run on a standard COBOL compiler.

COBOL statements and COBOL DML statements, such as the small block of code that follows, which deletes an employee's record from a database:

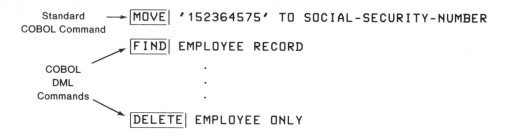

The program containing this mixture of statements is then fed to the DBMS's COBOL precompiler, as shown in Figure 13-8. The **precompiler** translates this program into a standard COBOL program, which can then be executed with the regular COBOL compiler available on the system.

The high-level languages that are supported by their own DMLs are called **host languages.** Several of them may be available on any particular system. Languages that a DBMS commonly employs as hosts are COBOL, FORTRAN, PL/1, and BASIC.

INTEGRATED SOFTWARE PACKAGES

This chapter and the previous one have described various types of productivity software—specifically, word processors, spreadsheets, presentation graphics packages, file managers, and database management systems. An **integrated software package** is one that bundles two or more of these software functions, and perhaps others, into a single "megapackage." Symphony® and Jazz® (see Figure 13-9), which bundle together a spreadsheet, file manager, presentation graphics routine, word processor, and communications software (see box on page 216 of Chapter 7), are examples of integrated software products. So, too, is Framework®—which combines a spreadsheet, database management system, presentation graph-

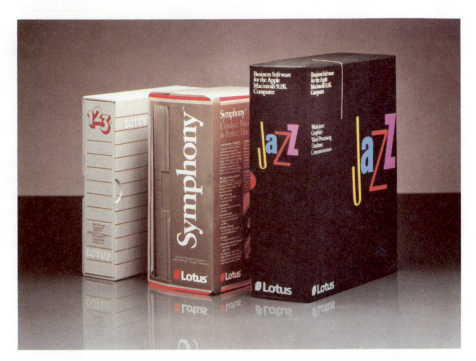

Figure 13-9. ***Three popular integrated software packages.*** These packages bundle into a single product two or more software functions that would normally be sold separately.

ics routine, word processor, and communications software—and Micro Data Base Systems' Knowledge Manager® (Knowledge Man).

Integrated software provides you with the convenience of learning a single command or menu structure, rather than suffering through the software-approach differences of, say, three or four different vendors. Additionally a bundled package normally costs less than if the individual software components were purchased separately. And, perhaps most important, one can integrate data from the various package components—for example, inserting a graph into a word-processed document—because all of the software components are compatible with each other.

On the negative side, integrated packages normally have one or two strong components and several weak ones. Thus an author who requires a top-of-the-line word processor is often better off getting a dedicated word processing package and leaving integrated packages that cater to spreadsheet or database users alone. A second disadvantage of these packages is that the user might not need all of the features that are integrated into them. For example, a user without phone access certainly wouldn't get his or her money's worth out of a communications-software feature.

Integrated packages perform some of the same types of applications integration as *windowing software,* which was covered in Chapter 8. Depending upon one's needs, one might actually be better off buying separate, dedicated packages and tying them together in a windowing environment.

tomorrow

DATABASES, PERSONAL PRIVACY, AND BIG BROTHER

Some Dangers Posed by Database Technology

One of the nice things about database technology is that it enables us to examine data quickly that would otherwise exist in scores of different files.

We can compare the advantage that database management gives us over conventional file management techniques by looking at a real-life counterpart. Consider, for exam-

All those easy-to-get-at data make it easier than ever for people to gather facts about us.

ple, how long it would take to ask twenty people in a room a (nonconfidential) question and get responses, as opposed to asking people the same question individually. That's essentially the convenience difference of database technology versus file management. And, of course, there are advantages to having all the people together in the room, so that you can easily pose new questions and cover ground faster, just as there are advantages to having all the data together in a DBMS.

But there is also a less advantageous side to what database technology brings to us. All those easy-to-get-at data make it easier than ever for people to gather facts about us

and to interrelate them in ways we never thought possible. How would you like a sorry incident that took place when you were fifteen years old to surface thirty years later when you were applying for a bank loan or seeking a promotion? Or how about your buying or spending habits analyzed as a result of machine-readable credit card purchases you've made and checks you've written? Or your reading habits determined from the magazines you subscribe to? If what we hear about a checkless and cashless society comes true, every cent you spend can theoretically be traced and scrutinized—perhaps to your disadvantage.

Fortunately, today there are privacy laws (see Chapter 18) to protect us from such abuses. Nonetheless privacy is a matter of public policy. If someday that Orwellian nightmare of "Big Brother" watching us does to some extent become true, it will be database technology that will have paved a good part of the way.

Summary and Key Terms

A **file manager** (or *record management system*) is a software package that enables one to organize data into files and to process the data a single file at a time.

Many file managers employ an *onscreen form,* or **template,** to assist users in placing data into records of a file. At any later point, records can be modified or deleted from the file, and new records can be added.

A **database management system (DBMS)** primarily differs from a file manager in that it enables immediate access to data that could conceivably span several files. As a rule, since database management systems are technically more complex than file managers, they are also more expensive and more difficult to master.

The data in a DBMS are placed on disk in a database. A **database** is an integrated collection of data. Users and programmers gain access to the data they need through an easy-to-use *query/update facility* that accompanies the DBMS, or through an *applications program* written in a programming language (e.g., COBOL).

The major advantages of a DBMS include integrated data, program/data independence, nonredundant storage, and data integrity. These technical advantages translate into fewer personnel, fast response to problems, and an ability to adapt more rapidly to new and changing environments. The major disadvantage of a DBMS is cost. Significant expenses are normally incurred in purchasing database software, upgrading hardware, acquiring specialized personnel, and converting to a database system.

A rather wide variety of database management systems are available for both large and small computers. Each DBMS organizes database data according to some predefined model, called its **data structure.** A data structure specifies relationships among data.

Three types of data structures that are very important in database processing are *hierarchical (tree) structures, network structures,* and *relational structures.* Hierarchical and network databases are relatively too complicated for casual users to set up and use on their own, and they are generally established with the help of a competent professional known as a **database administrator (DBA).** Virtually all DBMSs targeted for microcomputers follow the relational data model, which is much easier for noncomputer professionals to understand and use.

One task performed by anyone setting up a database is **data definition**— the process of describing data to the DBMS prior to entering them.

The process of using the database in some hands-on fashion is called **data manipulation.** There are generally two ways to manipulate data in a DBMS—with a **query/update facility** or with a *programming language.*

Many microcomputer-oriented DBMSs come with only a single proprietary language that has commands for data description, query/update, and programming functions. On large computer systems that use sophisticated DBMSs, there is usually a special language dedicated to each of these tasks. For example, a **data definition language (DDL)** is used to handle data definition chores, while a **data manipulation language (DML)** is used to extend the language the programmer normally works with into a database environment. Languages that are supported by their own DMLs are called **host languages.** A program called a **precompiler** is used to translate DML commands into host-language commmands, which can then be executed on the regular compilers available at the computer site.

On large computer systems, DBMS packages must also deal with the problem of several users trying to access the database simultaneously. To prevent such **concurrent access** problems, most database systems allow users to place a temporary "lock" on certain blocks of data, to ensure that there will be no other modifications to these data while they are being processed.

An **integrated software package** bundles one or more individual productivity software functions—such as word processing, spreadsheets, presentation graphics, file management, database management, and the like—into a single "metapackage."

Review Exercises

Fill-in Questions

1. The two major types of data management packages are called _____ and _____.
2. The onscreen form used to create records in a data management environment is often called a(n) _____.
3. An integrated collection of data is called a(n) _____.
4. The three most common types of database data structures are the _____, _____, and _____ structures.
5. For complicated data structures, a knowledgeable professional known as a(n) _____ is often called upon to set up the database and assist users.
6. The problem of _____ access often arises when two or more people try to seize and modify data at the same time.

Matching Questions   *Match each term with its description.*

a. Precompiler	d. Query/update facility
b. Data definition language (DDL)	e. Host language
c. Data manipulation	f. Data description

_____ **1.** A language used to describe database data.

_____ **2.** A language supported by a DML (data manipulation language).

_____ **3.** A translator used to translate DML commands into commands that can be input to a regular language translator.

_____ **4.** A database software product that permits both programmers and nonprogrammers to retrieve, add, delete, or modify database data easily with simple, English-like commands.

_____ **5.** Organization of data in the database so that programmers and users have access to them, so that they are stored as efficiently as possible, and so that the security of the database is maintained.

_____ **6.** A task that can be achieved through either a query/update facility or a programming language.

Discussion Questions

1. What is a file manager?
2. What is a database management system and how does it differ from a file manager?
3. Identify the advantages and disadvantages of database management systems.
4. What is the difference between data description and data manipulation?
5. How do database management systems solve the problem of concurrent access?
6. What is an integrated software package?

Module D

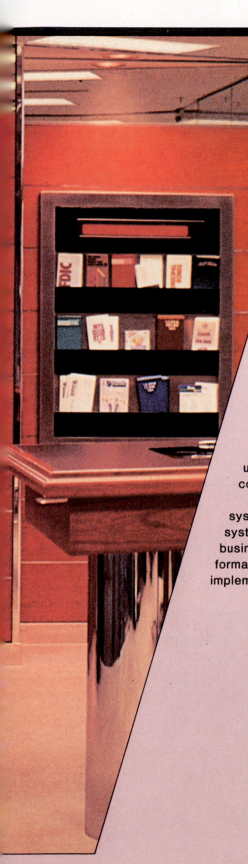

COMPUTER SYSTEMS

This module integrates many of the concepts from earlier chapters, which introduced various parts of computer systems. A computer system consists of the computer itself, as well as any support equipment, programs, data, procedures, and people found in its environment. In other words, all the components that contribute to making the computer a useful tool can be said to be part of a computer system.

Chapters 14 and 15 discuss various types of computer systems. Chapter 14 focuses on personal uses of computer systems and Chapter 15 on more formal uses of computers in businesses and other organizations. Chapter 16 discusses how formal systems are developed, from preliminary investigation to implementation.

Chapter 14

Microcomputer Systems

Chapter Outline

Objectives

After completing this chapter you should be able to:

1. Distinguish among the various types of microcomputer systems currently on the market.
2. Identify the major hardware and software components found in most microcomputer systems.
3. Explain how you would go about selecting a microcomputer system and how you would maintain it.

413

OVERVIEW

Often affordably priced between a few hundred and a few thousand dollars, microcomputer systems have been available since the mid-1970s. The earliest systems were targeted to electronics hobbyists, but rapid improvements on both the software and hardware fronts soon made them practical for both business and home use. Today microcomputer-based processing is one of the fastest growing areas in the computer field. Some industry observers predict that by 1990 there will be as many as 100 million systems in operation.

We begin the chapter by covering the common types of hardware and software found with microcomputer systems. Where appropriate, we'll look at product differences that are particularly important to know about when buying (or leasing) systems. We then cover various topics that are of interest to virtually any microcomputer user, such as where to go to learn more about microcomputer systems and how to maintain a microcomputer system once it's on your desk.

In Window 5 a panel of photographs further illustrates the nature and use of microcomputers.

TYPES OF MICROCOMPUTER SYSTEMS

Microcomputer systems, as we mentioned earlier, are computer systems driven by microprocessors. A **microprocessor** is a computer that is engraved on a silicon chip no larger than a fingernail. The microprocessor, memory chips, and circuitry of various sorts are packaged into a unit called the *system unit*. Besides microcomputer systems, microprocessors are also put into such consumer products as electronic scales, digital watches, children's learning toys, microwave ovens, washers and dryers, and video games.

Personal computer systems are, technically, microcomputer systems used by individuals to meet various *personal* needs, whether at work or at home. The terms *personal computer* and *microcomputer* are often used synonymously in practice.

Microprocessors can be classified in many ways; for example, by the number of bits they can manipulate per operation. The microprocessors that power electronic gadgets such as watches and toys typically manipulate a small number of bits at one time, often 2, 4, or 8. The microprocessors that are used as the CPUs in microcomputer systems, on the other hand, typically can handle 8, 16, or 32 bits at once.

Classifying Microcomputer Systems

Microcomputer system units currently available for business and home use can be classified into the following four categories (also see Figure 14-1).

Figure 14-1. Four types of microcomputer systems. (a) Pocket (hand-held). (b) Portable (lap-top). (c) Desk top. (d) Supermicro.

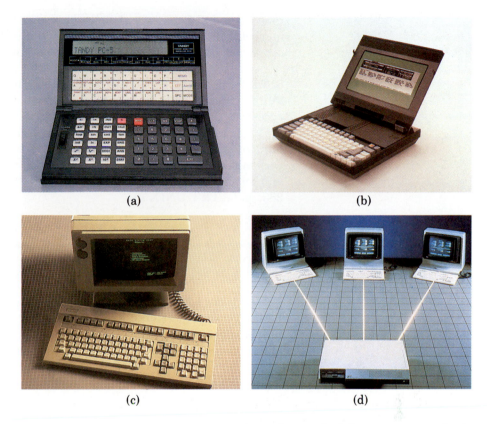

(a)

(b)

(c)

(d)

1. POCKET (HAND-HELD) UNITS. **Pocket (hand-held) computers** look and behave a lot like standard pocket calculators. You can fit one into your pocket and you can hold the entire unit in your hand while operating it. These microcomputer systems often come with built-in printers, multiline displays, slots to accept program cards or cartridges, and even I/O ports for attached peripherals (such as cassette tape).

2. PORTABLE (LAP-TOP) UNITS. **Portable (lap-top) computers** are designed for users who need both hardware portability and more "computing power" than is currently possible in pocket units. They are characterized by being lightweight (8–12 pounds) and compact (the size of a briefcase). Typical users of lap-top units include field engineers, sales representatives, executives who travel a lot, and people who may need to give computer-assisted management presentations in places where it's inconvenient to lug in a larger unit. Although many portables are just as powerful as their larger-sized, desk-top cousins (discussed next), they generally suffer from the disadvantages of being more expensive, having smaller screens (which often bothers spreadsheet users), and having a dense arrangement of keys (which may hamper word processing).

3. DESK-TOP UNITS. **Desk-top computers** are those you see most often—in schools, homes, and businesses. These are the computer systems with the familiar household names: IBM PC; Apple II, IIe, IIc, and Macintosh; TI Professional; TRS-80; Commodore 64 and Amiga; to name a

few. Because of the overwhelming presence of desk-top machines in the marketplace, the discussion of microcomputers in both this chapter and others has been heavily oriented toward them.

SUPERMICRO UNITS.   **Supermicrocomputer** (or **supermicro**) system units—which also fit on a desk top—enable two or more people to have access at, more or less, the same time (note the three terminals in Figure 14-1*d*). Multiuser systems have prevailed in the world of mainframes and minicomputers for a long time, but they are a relatively new development with microcomputers. Some examples of systems that are widely seen in the marketplace are the IBM PC AT, Kaypro 286i, TI Business Pro, Compaq 286, and AT&T UNIX PC.

HARDWARE

Many desk-top microcomputer systems contain at least five pieces of hardware: the system unit itself, a secondary storage device, a video display unit, a keyboard, and a printer. In some systems all or most of these devices are housed in a single hardware unit, whereas with others you can select each device separately. Let's now look at each of these devices in detail. Then we'll discuss how they and other hardware devices fit together into a "typical" system.

The System Unit

The **system unit** often minimally consists of a microprocessor chip, memory (RAM and ROM) chips, internal boards upon which these chips and others are mounted, ports that provide connections for external devices, a power supply, and internal circuitry to hook everything together. Most of these hardware devices were discussed in some detail in Chapter 4.

Figure 14-2.   A micropro-cessor chip in its carrier package. The carrier package is plugged into the system unit's *system board,* which also usually contains a limited amount of memory.

MICROPROCESSOR CHIPS.   When you buy a microcomputer system unit, you'll find that it contains a specific microprocessor chip as its CPU. This chip is put into a carrier package, as shown in Figure 14-2, and the carrier package is plugged into a special board that fits inside the system unit. Figure 14-3 lists some popular system units and the microprocessors that run them.

The microprocessors used to run microcomputer systems typically can handle 8, 16, or 32 bits at once. As you may remember from the discussion of **word** size in Chapter 4, the more bits a computer can manipulate at a time, generally the faster it is and the greater the main memory it can accommodate. You may also recall from Chapter 4 that word size can be deceiving. For example, what one vendor calls a "32-bit computer" may actually be slower and support less memory than what another calls a "16-bit computer." Furthermore, two 16-bit computers may provide drastically different performances.

System Unit	Microprocessor
Apple Macintosh	Motorola 68000
Apple II	MOS Technology 6502
Apple IIc	MOS Technology 65C02
Apple IIe	MOS Technology 6502
Atari 520ST	Motorola 68000
AT&T UNIX PC	Motorola 68010
AT&T 6300	Intel 8086
Commodore Amiga	Motorola 68000
Commodore 64	MOS Technology 6510
Commodore VIC-20	Zilog Z-80A
Compaq DeskPro 286	Intel 80286
Compaq Plus	Intel 8088
Compaq Portable Computer	Intel 8088
Data General One	Intel 80C88
HP 150	Intel 8088
IBM PC (and PC / XT)	Intel 8088
IBM PC AT	Intel 80286
Kaypro II	Zilog Z-80A
Tandy 1000	Intel 8088
Tandy 3000	Intel 80286
TI Professional	Intel 8088
TI Business Pro	Intel 80286
TRS-80, Model 4	Zilog Z-80A
Wang PC	Intel 8086
Zenith Z-150	Intel 8088

Figure 14-3. *System units and their microprocessors.* Four families of chips—the Intel family, Motorola 68000 family, 6502 family, and Z80—dominate the microprocessor scene (see box on page 112 of Chapter 4).

The type of chip in your computer's system unit also greatly affects what you can do with your computer system. Operating systems are written to serve a specific chip, and an applications program that works with one operating system generally does not function on another, unless modified. So if the chip that supports your computer is rare, you will have difficulty finding applications programs that run on it.

RAM.   The primary memory of microcomputer systems (as does the microprocessor) consists of circuits etched onto silicon chips. As mentioned in Chapter 4, this kind of primary memory is commonly called **random-access memory (RAM).** Most desk-top microcomputer systems in use today have between 64 kilobytes and 1 megabyte of RAM. If the RAM you currently have is insufficient, many computer systems allow expansion.

Most RAM is *volatile,* which means that the contents of memory are lost when the computer is shut off. *Nonvolatile* RAM, called "CMOS RAM," is also available, but is more expensive. (CMOS RAM is mounted onto boards containing small batteries, which allow the chips to retain data and programs for several months or more. The batteries are automatically recharged every time the system unit is turned on.)

ROM.   As we discussed in Chapter 4, **ROM** stands for **read-only memory.** It consists of nonerasable hardware modules that contain programs. These modules are plugged into one or more boards inside the system unit. You can neither write over these ROM programs (that's why they're called "read-only") nor destroy their contents when you shut off the computer's power (that is, they're nonvolatile).

Often key systems software such as the operating system are stored in ROM. This arrangement makes the operating system available to perform useful tasks at the moment the computer's power is turned on. Some computer systems even enable you to purchase a few of your favorite software packages, such as BASIC or certain electronic spreadsheets, in ROM form. If you buy packages in this form, you avoid having to load them from disk every time you want to use them.

INTERNAL AND EXTERNAL INTERFACES.   Many system units contain a limited number of internal "slots," into which **plug-in boards** can be mounted by the user (see Figure 14-4). This arrangement offers the user a great deal of flexibility in personalizing a system. For example, if more main memory is needed, a *memory expansion board* may be acquired that contains the appropriate number of additional memory chips and the circuitry needed to get your computer system to access them. Other plug-in

Figure 14-4.   Plug-in boards fit into slots within the system unit. Many of these boards perform an interfacing role, enabling users to "personalize" their computer systems. You select the peripheral equipment that meets your needs and then the boards that will allow this equipment to interface with your system.

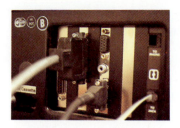

Figure 14-5.   Ports in the back of a system unit. A port is a socket through which a specific type of peripheral device is plugged into the system unit.

boards may be required to enable the user to interface a particular hard disk or display device.

Because there are a limited number of internal slots, many board manufacturers make *multifunction boards* that combine several of these functions. Thus a user might be able to buy a single board that contains both extra memory and a display–device interface.

Not all manufacturers produce system units that allow such *internal* expansion. One compelling argument against internal expansion is that the slots require space that many people would not use. Another is that flexibility is added at the expense of the streamlining that accompanies a highly specialized machine.

Although only some system units provide for internal expansion, virtually all have *external* I/O **ports** that enable peripherals to be plugged into them. As mentioned in Chapter 7, for example, printers "talk to the CPU" through either serial or parallel interfaces. The interfacing is done through ports. As shown in Figure 14-5, these ports are generally found in the back of the system unit.

Often ports for printers and modems are attached to boards in the computer's system unit. These ports, too, are external, as they extend through openings in the back of the unit.

Secondary Storage

As with larger computers, the primary memory of microcomputers can hold only the data and programs the computer is currently processing. As discussed in Chapter 5, if you want to keep data and programs for repeated use, you must have a secondary storage unit. Both tape and disk devices are available for use with microcomputers.

FLOPPY DISKS.   For desk-top systems, **floppy disk** is by far the most popular storage medium. Although disks are available in several sizes (diameters), the 5¼ inch and 3½ inch ones are the most popular. Floppy disks have various other properties— for example, they may be double sided, double density, soft sectored, and the like. These and other properties were discussed in detail in Chapter 5. It's important that the disks you use be compatible with the floppy disk drives on your microcomputer system.

HARD DISKS.   In Chapter 5 we also discussed **Winchester disk** drives for microcomputer systems. In these *hard disk* devices, the disks, access arms, and read/write heads are all sealed in the same container. Winchester systems are much faster and can store much more than floppy disk systems, but they are comparatively expensive. Although many microcomputer users don't need and can't afford Winchesters, they are becoming very popular for business applications.

OTHER DEVICES.   For many low-end desk-top systems, some portable systems, and most pocket systems, *cassette tape* is a useful secondary storage medium. But because cassette tape lacks direct-access capability, it's not often found on high-end products. *Cartridge tapes* (sometimes called *streaming tapes*), which look like oversized cassettes, are often used to back up hard disk systems.

Some high-end microcomputer users are now enjoying the benefits of *optical disk* secondary storage, although this technology is still in its infancy. "CD-ROM" optical disks for microcomputers can store 100 megabytes or more.

The Keyboard

For most people a personal computer system would be useless without a **keyboard,** since it is often the main vehicle for input. Potential buyers should carefully evaluate keyboards, in terms of several factors.

First, not all keyboards have the same key arrangement. For example, the QWERTY keyboard uses the format of the conventional typewriter, whereas the newer and more sensibly designed Dvorak keyboard uses another arrangement (see Figure 14-6).

Second, keyboards differ with respect to touch. Some are sculpted to match the contour of the fingertips; others have either flat (calculator-style) keys or a flat membrane panel with touch-sensitive keys. Additionally, manufacturers space keys differently, so keys that feel just right to one person may feel too far apart to another. Key spacing can be a real problem for word processing users who want a portable computer, as keyboards on these units are designed to be as compact as possible.

Third, the keyboards of most microcomputer systems have several special keys that communicate specific software commands when they are depressed. A "delete" key, for example, deletes characters from the screen, and a "page up" key flips through screen-length units of a file one at a time. The number of such keys, as well as their functions and placement, vary widely among manufacturers.

Finally, many keyboards are separate hardware units that can be placed wherever convenient, even in the user's lap, whereas other are built into the display or system unit.

As discussed in Chapter 6, users may desire other input devices to supplement or replace keyboard operations. One of the most popular of these is the **mouse,** a cursor-movement device that's a standard item on computers such as the Apple Macintosh. Many other computer systems support the mouse as an optional device.

The Monitor

Almost every microcomputer system has a video display unit, or **monitor.** A monitor resembles a television set with only one channel. It allows you to see your input as you enter it and the computer's output as the computer responds.

The differences among monitors are numerous and were highlighted in Chapter 6. Most people interacting with a microcomputer system will be using either a monochrome or full-color monitor. A *monochrome monitor* is

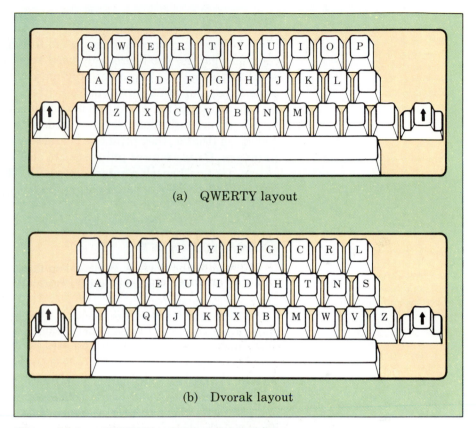

(a)   QWERTY layout

(b)   Dvorak layout

Figure 14-6.   QWERTY and Dvorak keyboards.

one that outputs in a single foreground color—for example, green, amber, or white. *Full-color monitors* generally will output in at least eight different colors. Most monitors made today allow users to produce both text and graphics on the display screen. However, on many microcomputer systems, a display adapter board with a graphics interface must be acquired to provide the graphical output.

Many microcomputer systems permit you to use a television set as a monitor. A small device called an RF-modulator converts the computer's output into a form that can be received over a regular channel on your television set.

Unfortunately the picture provided by the standard television set is not as clear as that of a monitor especially designed for a computer system. Although your home television might be adequate for video games, it is probably not suitable for applications such as word processing, where you must be able to examine small characters of text with care, perhaps for long periods of time.

Monochrome (CRT-type) monitors are currently available for as little as $100, whereas full-color (CRT-type) monitors are more expensive and are often priced somewhere in the $400 to $600 range.

The Printer

If you are using your computer system for any purpose other than playing computer games, you'll probably need some form of printed output. You may want a copy of a computer program you've just debugged, for example, or perhaps a copy of a paper you've written.

As with monitors the differences among printers (discussed in Chapter 6) are numerous. Most devices used with microcomputer systems are low-speed (that is, they print one character at a time) **impact dot-matrix printers. Daisywheel printers** are also very popular for *letter-quality* output. Generally each printer comes with its own special cable that hooks into either a parallel or serial port in the back of the computer unit.

Other Hardware

In addition to the devices discussed so far, many other hardware units are commonly found on microcomputer systems. Two popular ones are modems and power managers.

Modems are used to convert the binary pulses generated by a computer system into other pulses that are compatible with your phone lines. They were discussed in some detail in Chapter 7.

Many microcomputer-system owners also invest in a unit called a **power manager** (see Figure 14-7). Power managers enable you to turn on all of your computer hardware devices (such as the system unit, monitor, and printer) and even a nearby lamp or two with the flick of a single switch. They usually also accommodate *surge suppression,* which prevents random, electrical power spikes from causing damage. The power going into most homes and offices is uneven, and power spikes can "zap" your RAM at unexpected times. This may result in loss of memory when your system is on. Some power managers can also handle brownouts (the reverse of a power spike), and even blackouts (complete loss of power).

There are, of course, other hardware devices that can be interfaced to a microcomputer system, but it would probably take a book the size of this text to describe them all.

Connecting All of the Equipment Together

The types of, number of, and power of peripheral devices that a microcomputer system can support are largely determined by the system unit. In Figure 14-8, which shows a hypothetical configuration that closely resembles the IBM Personal Computer system, you can observe some of the principles involved in connecting peripherals to the system unit.

In the system shown in Figure 14-8, there are built-in ports for a cassette tape unit, a speaker, and a keyboard. By using special cables, the user can plug these peripherals directly into the ports allocated to them. Each port is designed to accommodate a specific peripheral device and its matching cable.

Figure 14-7. *Power manager.* The CPU and its support devices feed into the power manager, and the power manager is plugged into a standard wall outlet. This permits you to turn all your equipment on or off with the flick of a single switch.

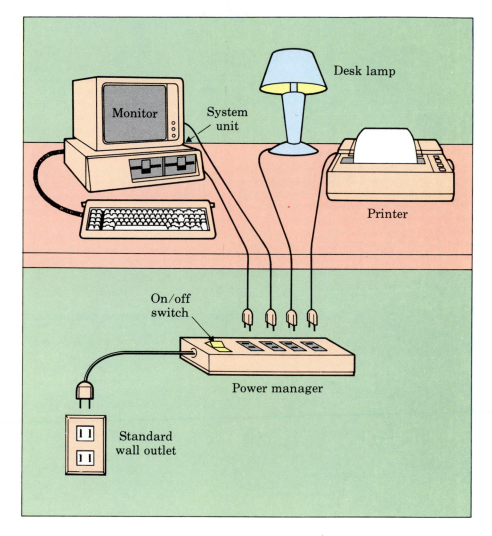

The computer shown also has five expansion slots, which can accept plug-in boards that accommodate any of a variety of specific devices. Among the devices that can be added to the depicted microcomputer system are a game-control adapter, a modem, almost any type of low-speed printer, secondary storage devices, monitors (both monochrome and color), and primary memory. These devices must compete for the available expansion slots. Each slot can accommodate one plug-in board, and each board can support a limited number of specific devices. Ultimately, however, the number of peripherals is restricted by the capacity of the microprocessor and its primary memory.

Microcomputer systems differ widely in the way their individual hardware devices are connected together. When you are selecting components for a system, you must pay careful attention to which devices plug in where, what types of special cables are needed to establish hookups, and what possiblities (if any) you have for expansion as your needs grow.

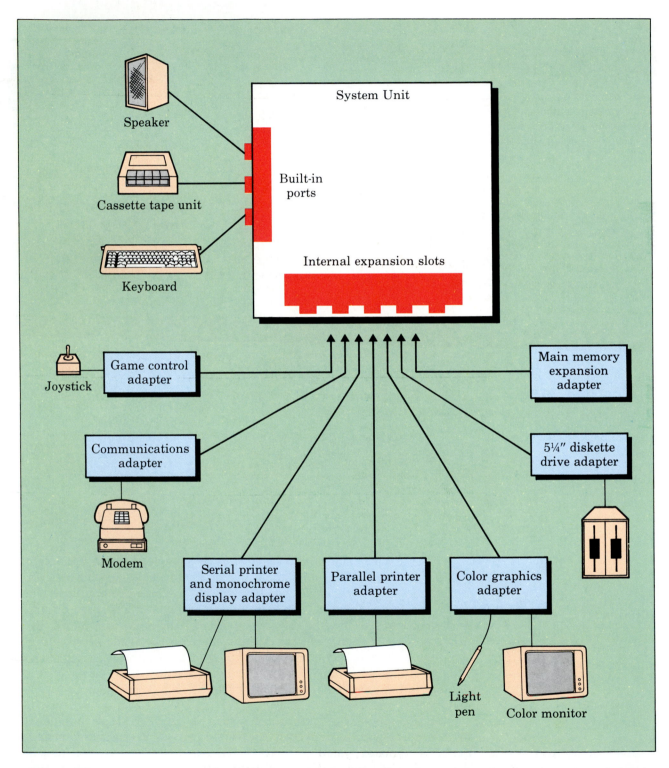

Figure 14-8. **Connecting peripheral devices to a microcomputer.** The system shown has three external ports for a keyboard, cassette tape unit, and a speaker. It also has five expansion slots that can accommodate a variety of other peripheral devices.

APPLICATIONS SOFTWARE

The variety of tasks microcomputer systems can handle is quite extensive. Historically, as the need for microcomputer programs developed, software firms and individual entrepreneurs quickly appeared to satisfy the demand. Some important applications and the software that accommodates them are discussed here.

Productivity Software

Figure 14-9. Productivity software packages. Such products—covered extensively in Chapters 12 and 13—have the goal of making people more productive at their work.

Productivity software constitutes such an important class of programs that two chapters in this book—Chapters 12 and 13—are devoted to it exclusively. These software packages are designed to make virtually any office worker more productive. The four most important types of productivity software packages are:

✗ *Spreadsheets*   These packages, which are used heavily in budget preparation and other financial planning applications, turn the computer system into a sophisticated electronic calculator.

✗ *Word processors*   These packages turn the computer system into a powerful typewriting tool and, in some cases, a typesetting and mailing-list system as well.

✗ *File managers and database managers*   These packages turn the computer into an electronic research assistant, capable of searching through mounds of data to prepare reports or answer queries for information.

✗ *Presentation graphics packages*   These packages take data and painlessly convert them into bar charts, line charts, and the like, for management presentations.

When two or more of these functions (and perhaps others) are combined into a single product, the resulting software is commonly referred to as an **integrated software package.** For example, Lotus Development Corporation's 1-2-3® is an integrated software package that combines spreadsheets, file management, and presentation graphics into a single product.

Figure 14-9 shows how a variety of productivity software products are packaged. Generally the program disks, an easy-to-follow tutorial disk, and a reference manual are fitted into attractive shrink-wrapped boxes, such as those shown in the photo. When buying a package, make sure you get the version intended for both your system unit and your operating system.

Educational Software

Education by computer can take many forms. You can learn arithmetic, spelling, music, foreign languages, chemistry, and even programming languages by interacting at your own pace with instructional programs that you can buy from a number of software firms. These programs vary widely in difficulty. An elementary one might require you to compute the daily profit made at a front-yard lemonade stand, whereas a complex one might ask you to create three-dimensional surfaces with multivariate calculus. The use of educational software to provide paced instruction is sometimes called *computer-assisted instruction* (*CAI*).

Home Software

Although we're still a long way from seeing a computer in every home, it does seem inevitable that the home computer will someday be as prevalent as the home phone. In fact the phone and computer have already been bundled together into a single product to provide powerful access to a wide variety of data resources. Yet, today, many people still feel that they don't need a computer at home. Certainly we're still far from seeing it as indispensable as the phone.

The most popular use of computers in the home is for electronic games. Home computer systems intended for extensive game playing generally can be equipped with a game controller to load prepackaged cartridges; a joystick, which looks like the stick shift in an automobile (and can move spaceships, Pac-people, and the like in different directions on the monitor screen); and an audio output unit, which makes sounds to accompany exciting action on the screen.

Computers are, of course, also used in the home for productivity and educational purposes. For example, computer systems are now inexpensive enough to consider buying as a powerful home typewriter or a sophisticated home calculator. Also, communications software can be acquired to electronically check account balances, make banking or securities transactions, or even interface with a large information network electronically. With respect to education, parents often bring a computer into the home so that their children can learn a programming language or pick up computer-based, problem-solving skills.

You can even use your microcomputer to manage your home environment automatically. Computers can help regulate temperature, manage fuel consumption, open and close drapes, control kitchen appliances, turn lights on and off, supervise security, and monitor the watering of your garden.

SYSTEMS SOFTWARE

The most important piece of software on any microcomputer system is the **operating system.** A variety of operating systems are available for microcomputers, of which some of the more famous are MS-DOS, PC-DOS, CP/M, TRSDOS, Apple ProDos, UNIX, and XENIX. Each of these operating systems has a *syntax,* or set of grammatical and structural rules, like any other programming language. An exception is the icon-oriented operating system for Apple's Macintosh computer, which has neither a syntax nor a name.

Operating systems are developed to conform to the physical limitations of specific microprocessor chips and are often written in the assembly language available with the chip. Chips differ in the number of registers available, amount of RAM, types of ROM, and so forth. As a result their assembly languages, which address specific memory modules and storage locations, are not interchangeable. Since prepackaged application programs are written to interface with a particular operating system, a version of a program that works with one operating system usually does not work with another. Thus the choice of an operating system is critical.

CP/M, developed by Digital Research, Inc., has long been a popular operating system on 8-bit machines because so many applications programs are available to interface with it. It was initially written for the 8-bit Intel 8080 chip and subsequently modified to run on several other chips, most notably the Zilog Z-80. PC-DOS, which uses Intel's newer 16-bit 8088 and 8086 microprocessors, quickly became a major operating system when IBM announced in 1983 that its Personal Computer would support it. MS-DOS, used by many other microcomputer systems that look and behave like the IBM PC, is virtually identical to PC-DOS and is another major operating system. Both PC-DOS and MS-DOS were developed by Microsoft Corporation. UNIX, developed by Bell Labs, and versions of it such as XENIX, developed by Microsoft Corporation, are expected to make the same sort of impact as microcomputers evolve beyond the 16-bit word size. Unlike the other operating systems mentioned here, UNIX and XENIX are multi-user systems.

Other microcomputer-based systems software includes *language translators* and *utility programs*—such as editors, windowing programs, and print spoolers. These types of software were covered in some detail in Chapter 8.

SELECTING AND MAINTAINING A SYSTEM

Now that you know about the typical hardware and software found in microcomputer systems, let's consider how you decide what type of a system to buy, how you might shop for such a system, where you go to pick up knowledge that will make your system more useful, and how to care for your system.

Choosing a System

Selecting a microcomputer-based system for home or business use must begin with the all-important question: "What do I want the system to do?" Once you've decided what types of applications the system must service, you must then decide what applications software to buy, given your budget

Tips on Buying a Microcomputer for a Small Business

A DOZEN SUGGESTIONS FOR WHAT TO DO . . . AND NOT DO

There are virtually hundreds of microcomputer-based systems available commercially in today's marketplace. Although this makes it a safe bet that there's a system out there that will meet the needs of almost any small business, it does raise the very serious issue of how to choose among the staggering array of options available. Here are a few hints to help you make a wise selection.

- Don't be conned into thinking that a computer will solve all of your problems. When misapplied the computer will only make things worse than they already are.
- Before buying anything analyze the applications involved and define your needs. Only after you have a general idea of your software requirements should you make decisons on hardware.
- Some vendors have complete hardware/software systems that are particularly tailored to the needs of certain types of small business. Auto parts wholesale dealerships and health clubs are two such examples.

- The software you consider should be easy to learn, easy to use, and able to handle routine operator errors. If the user interface is bad, you'll be hard pressed to get the system to do anything but confuse people.
- If you are inexperienced, retain the services of an independent consultant to help you examine your needs. It also often helps to acquire a system from a local dealer or computer services company that can provide the required support to bring the system into operation and maintain it adequately. Normally computer manufacturers will not furnish this type of service.
- Before you buy check out the experiences of companies similar to yours as well as the experiences of the customers of the vendor from which you are considering buying your system. Ask the customers if the systems have performed as expected and what problems they have encountered. It also helps to visit a customer site or two, because often questions you didn't anticipate will occur to you there.

constraints. Finally, you need to select the hardware and systems software that best meet the requirements imposed by your earlier choices.

People can often justify the purchase or lease of a microcomputer system on the basis of one or two applications. For example, many managers do so much "what-if" type of financial planning that a spreadsheeting capability alone is enough to justify the entire computer system cost. And, of course, many writers find word processing so indispensable to their livelihoods that it matters little what else the computer system can do. On the other hand, if you're really not sure what you want a system to do for you, you'd better think twice about buying one. Computer systems that are heavily configured to serve certain applications (say, games) are often poor at others (such as word processing), so you can easily make some expensive mistakes if you're tentative.

- Make sure the system you buy can be upgraded as processing needs expand. Sometimes a system that looks like a bargain is only a bargain in the short run, if at all. It can cost you much more than you expected as your processing environment changes.
- It's almost always important to have adequate backup or support available if the system you acquire should suddenly break down. Many businesses have a hard disk unit and streaming tape on hand to back up important programs and data. Also, does the dealership from which you bought your system offer an adequate warranty? Is a maintenance contract available? If the computer were to go down, the consequences could be disastrous. Make sure that both your hardware and software contracts cover everything.
- Carefully investigate possible areas of hardware and software compatibility. Not every piece of hardware you may want can be plugged into the system you are thinking of buying. Likewise, not all applications software can be run on the operating system available to you.
- Make sure you can afford the personnel required to keep the system running if you can't do it youself. A widespread myth is that "user friendliness" means that anyone with two fingers can use the system. If you know little about computers, you probably should seek outside help.
- Manual data-handling procedures can be as important as automated ones. Computers have a way of quickly producing volumes of information that, if not managed properly, can drown an organization in a sea of paperwork. Also, be sure to take steps to ensure the accuracy of the data going into the system and information coming out. Because the computer can produce so much output quickly, it would be a shame (at best) or a disaster (at worst) if it were just a pile of garbage.

Shopping for a System

Where should you shop for hardware and software? One possiblity is the computer store. Many stores, such as Computerland and Micro Age, carry the products of a number of vendors in their showrooms. Generally the salespeople at these stores are relatively knowledgeable about computers and will help you try out the equipment before you buy or lease. As is the case with a stereo system, you can buy a whole computer system at once or the individual components separately. Many complete systems, you'll find, include the offerings of more than one vendor, because few companies manufacture a full line of products for personal computers.

Another possible source of computer products is mail-order firms. These companies regularly publish price lists in microcomputer-oriented journals and will ship products to you upon request. Because these companies don't have to pay for a showroom, their prices are often lower than those of computer stores. A disadvantage of shopping this way, however, is that you need to know exactly what you want. And even then buying something by mail generally is riskier than buying locally.

Learning More About Microcomputers

A wealth of resources is available to those who want to learn more about personal computer systems and their uses. Classes, computer clubs, computer shows, magazines, and books are all sources of such information.

CLASSES.   A good way to learn any subject is to take an appropriate class. Many colleges and universities offer microcomputer-oriented courses for both degree-seeking and continuing-education students. Probably the fastest way to find out about such courses is to call a local college and ask to speak to the registrar or some computer-related academic department.

CLUBS.   Computer clubs are another effective vehicle for getting an informal education in computers. They are also a good place to go to get an unbiased and knowledgeable viewpoint about a particular product or vendor. Clubs are generally organized by region, product line, or common interests. Apple computer enthusiasts join such clubs as Apple-Holics (Alaska), Apple Pie (Illinois), or Apple Core (California). Clubs such as the Boston Computer Society, on the other hand, serve the needs of a more diverse group of microcomputer buffs. Many clubs also function as buying groups, and can obtain software or hardware at reduced rates. Computer clubs range in size from two or three members to several thousand.

SHOWS.   Computer shows provide you with a first-hand look at leading hardware and software products. Such shows typically feature a number of vendor exhibits as well as seminars on various aspects of computing. The annual West Coast Computer Faire, held in the San Francisco area, is one event specifically oriented toward smaller computers. Even the nation's largest show, the National Computer Conference, gears several exhibits and seminars to the interests of the microcomputer user.

PERIODICALS.   Periodicals are another good source for information about microcomputers. Magazines such as *Byte, Personal Computing, PC,* and *Macworld* (see Figure 14-10) focus on microcomputers. Computer magazines vary tremendously as to reading level. You can probably browse through all of these publications and more at your local bookstore or computer store.

BOOKS.   One of the best ways to learn about any aspect of personal computing is to read a book on the subject. A host of soft- and hard-covered books are available, ranging in difficulty from simple to highly sophisti-

Figure 14-10.   A variety of microcomputer-oriented journals. Many of these can be found on the periodicals rack of your local bookstore.

cated. These volumes include a large number of "how-to" books on such subjects as operating popular microcomputers or productivity packages, programming in microcomputer-based languages, and the technical fundamentals of microcomputers. You can find such books in your local library, computer stores, and bookstores.

Caring for a System

Microcomputer systems consist of sensitive electronic devices, so they must be treated with appropriate respect. In Figure 5-18 you observed some of the safeguards that should be taken when handling disks. Let us now turn to some of the other safeguards.

DUST, HEAT, AND STATIC.   Each of those tiny processor and memory chips in your hardware units are packed tightly with hundreds or thousands of circuits. Dust particles circulating in the air can easily settle on a chip and cause a short circuit. Many people buy dust covers for their hardware devices to prevent foreign particles in the air from causing hardware failure.

Plug-in-board-oriented system units like the IBM PC and TI Professional require cooling fans. Those boards generate heat, and too much heat inside the system unit can cause various problems. Upon inserting the boards, users should place them as far apart as possible to avoid heat buildup. Also, most boards draw power from the system's main power unit (as do many *internal* hard disks), so you have to be particularly careful about overtaxing the power unit.

Static electricity is especially dangerous because it can damage chips, destroy programs and data in memory, or disable your keyboard. So that those nasty little electrical discharges from your fingertips don't wreak havoc, you might consider buying an antistatic mat for under your workstation chair or an antistatic spray for your keyboard. Static electricity is more likely in dry areas and in the winter (when there's less humidity in the air).

OTHER CAUSES FOR CONCERN.   CRT-type monitors work by having a phosphorescent surface "lit up" by an electronic gun (see box on pages 166–167 of Chapter 6). If you keep your monitor at a high brightness level and abandon it for an hour or two, the phosphorescent surface will be "torched" rather than merely lit up. What this means is that ghosty character images will be permanently etched on the screen, making it harder to read.

Disk drives and printers are particularly prone to failure because they are electromechanical devices. You should have the heads on your disk drives cleaned periodically and, at the same time, check to see that the heads haven't slipped out of alignment. Misregistered heads can usually be adjusted easily. And, of course, never insert a warped disk into a drive.

If you have an impact dot-matrix printer, the most vulnerable mechanism in the unit is the print head. These print heads, like typewriter keys, will wear down over time. You can take precautions to prevent rapid wear,

THE MICROCOMPUTING FALLOUT

Where Will the Pieces Fall After the First Explosion in Microcomputers?

The grass-roots era of microcomputing is well behind us now. Sales of microcomputer systems are leveling off. New software and hardware announcements are creating more confusion than excitement in the marketplace. And one might even guess that if a supercomputer on a chip were announced tomorrow, it would be accompanied by more yawns than anything else. After all, most people are just barely struggling along on the microcomputer systems they have.

As the microcomputer matures as a product, one wonders what ultimately will be its mark on history. Will it lead to that computer in every home we once talked about as the beginning of a brave new world? Will it turn all of us into efficiency-conscious automatons who need to press buttons or finger touch panels every time we want to get something done? Or will it just be looked upon as a tiny footnote in the long history of machinery?

Although more speed, more memory, and more portability for the dollar will make new microcomputing products better every day, it seems as though it will take another big technological breakthrough to get people interested in buying again. Such products as Visi-Calc®, 1-2-3®, WordStar®, and dBase II® sent businesspeople to their checkbooks to acquire their first microcomputers. But those same people are waiting for another giant step in computing—not just a slight improvement over what they have now—before they spend more time and money.

Perhaps something like a fast voice-input word processor that anyone who can speak can easily use might stir up some vigorous interest. Or how about voice-input/voice-output tax planning or legal software that asks you spoken questions to which you respond by voice, and then figures out either a tax or legal strategy for you? That'll send even the most computer-illiterate businesspeople to the computer stores.

Now that the novelty is gone, what problems have been raised?

Now that the general exhilaration that accompanied falling in love with the novelty of microcomputers has passed, we have to think about managing the problems they've raised. Educational institutions, for example, are faced with the rising demands and expectations of people who suddenly want to become computer literate, but are not sure how. Businesses are wondering how they can coordinate and control the mushrooming growth of corporate microcomputers and the data they churn out. And users are nervous about all the changes taking place in products, when they've barely mastered the hardware and software they bought over a year ago.

however, such as making sure the head is cleaned periodically, not using the printer excessively for graphics (which wears the head more rapidly), and ascertaining that the head is not adjusted for carbon copies (which makes the head strike harder) if you want only single copies.

Naturally, as with other electronic devices, you shouldn't switch hardware units on and off to an excessive degree.

Microcomputer Systems

Like death and taxes, interfacing with a microcomputer is inevitable.

In the decade or so that they've been available, microcomputer systems have taken the world by storm. First they were snapped up by hobbyists. Then, as more and more software was developed, people found them increasingly useful for business purposes. As their range of applications widens, it's now conceivable that they will become even more widespread than pocket calculators.

1. A salesperson using a Hewlett-Packard lap-top computer in China.

Some of Today's Leading Desk-Top Systems

There are now well over a hundred models of microcomputer systems, with desk-tops leading the way in popularity. On this and the next page are a dozen of today's best-selling systems.

2. The 16-bit IBM PC is the best-selling microcomputer of all time.

3. The IBM PC AT was one of the first supermicros to do well in the marketplace.

4. The Apple Macintosh was the first microcomputer system to popularize the use of graphics and an easy-to-learn graphics interface.

5. The Apple IIc is Apple's latest model in the popular Apple II line.

6. The Apple IIe, which immediately preceded the IIc, is still a very popular microcomputer system.

7. Texas Instruments' Professional computer was one of the first successful IBM PC "look alikes."

8. The Commodore Amiga boasts a very-high-resolution graphics screen and an easy-to-learn operator interface.

10. AT&T's 16-bit PC 6300 is another popular computer that behaves a lot like the IBM PC.

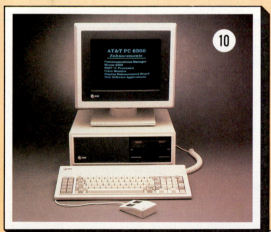

12. Atari's 520 ST has been dubbed the "Jackintosh" because it was introduced by Jack Trameil (Atari president) and it is similar in many ways to Apple's Macintosh.

13. The Kaypro 2 is a desktop computer that folds up into a luggable case for easy transport.

9. The Commodore 128 is an upgraded version of the well-received Commodore 64.

11. Hewlett-Packard's HP 150 PC features a touch screen for easy operation.

Other Hardware

On the previous two pages you saw several examples of system units, monitors, printers, floppy disk units, keyboards, and mice. On this page you'll find other types of hardware that you might want to think about if you purchase a microcomputer system.

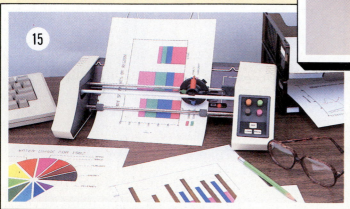

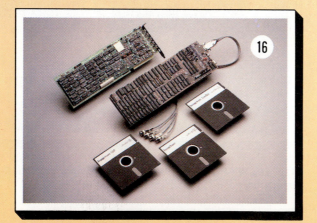

14. A Winchester hard disk is a necessary hardware item for anyone contemplating a microcomputer for business purposes.

15. A plotter is especially useful for presentation graphics (see Window 4—photographs 8, 17, 18, and 19—for plotter-produced outputs.

16. Plug-in boards normally are necessary if you plan to interface other hardware—say a printer or monitor—to your system unit. Boards often are accompanied by disks containing software that enables you to operate the boards in a personalized fashion.

17. Microcomputer users often buy power managers so that they can power up their systems with the flick of a single switch. Many power managers have built-in surge protectors that filter out power spikes.

18. Whenever you are considering a new peripheral for your microcomputer, make sure there's a cable available to hook the peripheral up to your specific brand of system unit. Cables come in different lengths and have different types of plug-in mechanisms.

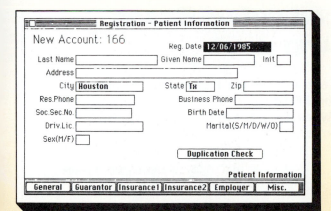

Registration – Patient Information		
New Account: 166	Reg. Date 12/06/1985	

Last Name _____ Given Name _____ Init ___
Address _____
City Houston   State Tx   Zip _____
Res.Phone _____   Business Phone _____
Soc.Sec.No. _____   Birth Date _____
Driv.Lic. _____   Marital(S/M/D/W/O) ___
Sex(M/F) ___

Duplication Check

Patient Information

| General | Guarantor | Insurance1 | Insurance2 | Employer | Misc. |

21

19–21. Productivity software is available to perform a wide variety of tasks. Lotus Development Corporation's 1-2-3® (photo 21)—which integrates spreadsheets, presentation graphics, and data management—is one of the best-selling software packages of all time. Photos 19 and 20 feature Tess System One, a medical office file management system.

Software

Transaction Entry

Anderson, Roy 06-17-01 2501 Bell Ave. Denton Tx 76201

| Account No:1 | Past Due: | 0.00 | current: | 21.20 | BALANCE: | 21.20 |

12-06-85 Office   Anemia

Date	Loc	7800	10.00	Hemoccult X 3	+$	36.00
Diagnosis		7709	15.00	PT	-$	0.00
		7750	15.00	PTT	T$	57.20
Select Patient		3301	120.00	Sigmoidoscopy		
Transaction		9412	50.00	Chemo.Admin.		
		0	10.00	Injection – IM	**Accept**	
		0	10.00	Injection – IV	**Get Info**	
		9163	50.00	ER-Office Hrs.	**Cancel Trans**	
		9073	70.00	ER-After Hrs	**Add To List**	
		9022	95.00	Initial HV	**Review Entries**	
		9019	50.00	Hosp.Visit,Inte	**Appointment**	
Amount		9025	60.00	Hosp.Visit, ICU		
Save trans.		9071	100.00	Detention	**Finished**	
		9029	80.00	CONS-Extensive		

Desk File Edit Tools Font Style   22

LAKEVIEW

NONE

22. With GEM Paint, tools commonly used by artists—such as pencils and paintbrushes—are displayed as icons. Shapes can be enhanced by selecting from twenty-one patterns and up to sixteen colors.

Arch News

23, 24. A promotional mailer and a newsletter produced on an Apple LaserWriter printer.

Microcomputer-Based Publishing

Ever had a desire to produce typeset-quality outputs at home? With the introduction of low-cost copier/printers and powerful typesetting software packages, this is now possible. Observe.

25. A Diconix Dijit 1 printer.

Summary and Key Terms

Microcomputer systems are computer systems driven by microprocessors. **Microprocessors** are the central processors in microcomputer systems, as well as in products such as electronic scales, digital watches, children's learning toys, microwave ovens, washers and dryers, and video games. **Personal computer systems** are, technically, microcomputer systems that are used by individuals to meet various personal needs, whether at work or at home. The terms *personal computer* and *microcomputer* are often used synonymously in practice.

Microcomputer system units currently available for business and home use are often classified into four categories. **Pocket (hand-held) computers** look and behave a lot like standard pocket calculators. **Portable (lap-top) computers** are designed for users who need both hardware portability and more "computing power" than is currently possible in pocket units. **Desktop computers** are those you see most often; these are the systems with the familiar household names—IBM PC, Apple II and Macintosh, TI Professional, and so forth. **Supermicrocomputers** (or **supermicros**) allow two or more people access at, more or less, the same time.

Many microcomputer systems contain five major pieces of hardware: the system unit itself, a secondary storage device, a video display unit, a keyboard, and a printer.

The **system unit** often minimally consists of a microprocessor chip, memory chips, internal boards upon which these chips and others are mounted, ports that provide connections for external devices, a power supply, and internal circuitry to hook everything together.

Microprocessor chips come in various **word** sizes, and, generally, the more bits the chip can manipulate at one time, the faster it is and the greater the main memory it can accommodate. The primary memory chips on microcomputer systems are commonly referred to as **RAM**, for **random-access memory.** Memory chips that contain nonerasable programs are referred to as **ROM**, for **read-only memory.**

Many system units contain a limited number of *internal* "slots," which enable the user to mount **plug-in boards,** Although only some system units provide for internal expansion, virtually all have *external* I/O **ports** that allow peripherals to be plugged into them.

As with larger computers, the primary memory of microcomputers can hold only the data and programs the computer is currently processing. If you want to keep data and programs for repeated use, you must have secondary storage. Two popular secondary storage media are **floppy disk** and **Winchester disk.**

For most people, a microcomputer system would be useless without a **keyboard,** since it is often the main vehicle for input. Potential buyers should carefully evaluate keyboards before deciding on one. There are many other input devices available to supplement keyboard operations—for example, the **mouse.**

Almost every microcomputer system has a video display unit, or **monitor.** Many microcomputer systems allow you to use a television set as a monitor.

If you are using your computer system for any purpose other than for playing games, you'll probably need some form of printed output. Two popular *printers* used in microcomputer systems are the **impact dot-matrix printer** and the **daisywheel printer.**

In addition to the devices discussed so far, many other hardware units are commonly found on microcomputer systems. Two popular ones are **modems** and **power managers.**

The number of peripheral devices that a microcomputer can support is limited by the capacity of the microprocessor and its primary memory.

Applications software for personal computers is numerous and includes **productivity software** (both single-function packages and **integrated software packages**), educational software, and home software. Systems software includes the computer's **operating system,** language translators, and utility programs.

Selecting a microcomputer-based system for home or business use must begin with the all-important question: "What do I want the system to do?" Once you've decided what types of applications the system must service, you must decide what applications software to buy, given your budget constraints. Finally, you need to select the hardware and systems software that best meet the requirements imposed by your earlier choices.

The shopper has numerous options when seeking a microcomputer system, including computer stores and mail-order firms.

A wealth of resources is available to those who want to learn more about microcomputer systems and their uses. Classes, computer clubs, computer shows, magazines, and books are all good sources of information about computers.

Microcomputer systems consist of sensitive electronic devices, so they must be treated with appropriate respect. One should exercise particular care in protecting the system from dust, heat buildup, and static discharges. Disk drives and printers are particularly prone to failure because they are electromechanical devices.

Review Exercises

Fill-in Questions

1. RAM is an acronym for _____.
2. ROM is an acronym for _____.
3. A CPU on a silicon chip is called a(n) _____.
4. Memory whose contents are not destroyed when the power is shut off is _____.
5. As with larger computers, _____ on smaller computers allocate the hardware of a specific computer system to the demands of applications programs.
6. A device that enables microcomputer users to communicate with remote computers over ordinary phone lines is called a(n) _____.
7. A feature on a power manager called _____ prevents random, electrical power spikes from causing damage to a microcomputer system.
8. A board that is capable of performing a variety of diverse tasks is called a(n) _____ board.

Matching Questions

Match each term with its description.

a. Microcomputer   d. ROM   g. Supermicro
b. Monitor   e. Port   h. Mouse
c. RAM   f. Board

_____ 1. Nonerasable hardware modules.
_____ 2. Often found in the back of the system unit.
_____ 3. With microcomputing systems, synonymous with primary memory.
_____ 4. Resembles a television set.
_____ 5. A synonym for personal computer.
_____ 6. A cursor-movement device.
_____ 7. Can be concurrently used by two or more people.
_____ 8. Device into which processor and memory chips plug directly.

Discussion Questions

1. Identify the major types of microcomputing systems and explain how they differ.
2. What are the major pieces of hardware in a microcomputer system?
3. Distinguish among a microprocessor, a microcomputer system, and a personal computer system.
4. What is the significance of the particular microprocessor chip used by a microcomputer system?
5. Name several applications for a microcomputer system.
6. Why is it important to choose a relatively well-known operating system for your microcomputer system?
7. Name some places where you can acquire a microcomputer system.
8. Identify some concerns you should have in caring for a microcomputer system.

Chapter 15

Business Systems

Chapter Outline

Objectives

After completing this chapter you should be able to:

1. Describe several types of computer systems commonly found in business and other environments.
2. Explain how a number of elements you read about in previous chapters fit together into a complete computer system.
3. Appreciate, through Window 6, how designers work with computers to create interesting images.

OVERVIEW

Now that we've covered various types of hardware and software, let's focus on how these combine into the complete computer systems found in businesses and other organizations. Undoubtedly you've already encountered many types of computer systems. When you go into the supermarket, you generally see in use electronic cash registers and various hand-held or laser scanning devices that are obviously a part of some supermarket system. Or when you've registered for classes, perhaps you've observed someone at a display terminal checking to see whether a certain class you want to take is still open or whether you've paid all your bills—apparently as part of a registration system. Also, almost all organizations seem to have some type of accounting system to help handle their business transactions, and many have manufacturing systems that assist in running their factories.

There are perhaps hundreds of types of computer systems in existence today. Many systems in businesses, nonprofit organizations, and government can be described as falling into one or more of six categories:

- *Accounting systems*   Included in this category are record keeping and other accounting tasks that organizations must handle regularly.

- *Management information systems*   These systems generally provide managers with predefined types of information on a periodic basis.

- *Decision support systems*   These systems enable managers to generate their own information from an organization's data.

- *Office systems*   These systems help cut down on the time-consuming paperwork normally generated in the office and make office workers more productive.

- *Design and manufacturing systems*   This category includes computers used to design and make products and guide robots in factories.

- *Artificial intelligence systems*   These programmed decision-making systems use techniques that model human thought processes.

In the following pages, we'll look more closely at each of these common types of systems.

ACCOUNTING SYSTEMS

Virtually every company must support a number of routine operations, most of which involve some form of tedious record keeping. These operations—such as payroll and accounts receivable—were among the earliest commercial applications of computers in organizations, and are still among the most important. As you'll see in the following pages, and as you can learn from a beginning accounting course, many accounting operations are highly interrelated.

PAYROLL. *Payroll systems* compute deductions, subtract them from gross earnings, and write paychecks (Figure 15-1) to employees for the remainder. These systems also contain programs that prepare reports for managerial and taxing agencies of the federal, state, and local governments.

TRANSACTION PROCESSING. Virtually every organizational entity is involved with day-to-day transactions with clients. The accounting systems

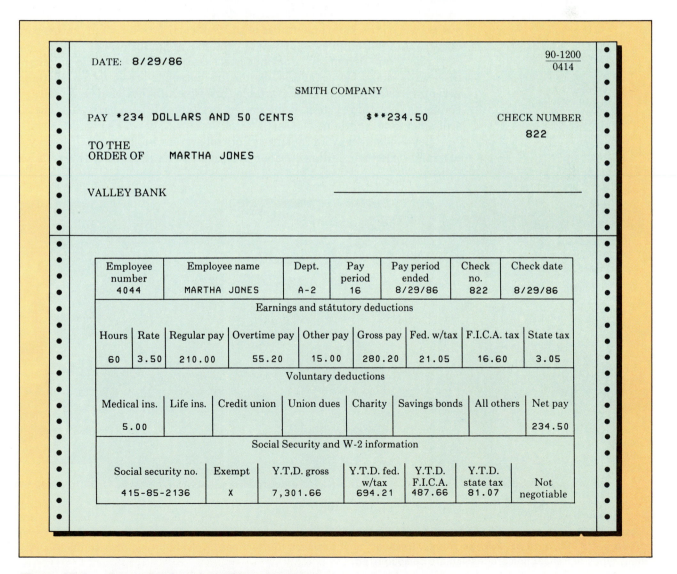

Figure 15-1. A paycheck and earnings statement.

that record and help manage these transactions are called *transaction-processing systems*. For example, banks have automatic teller systems that record certain deposits and withdrawals of depositors and keep track of account balances. The airlines have a reservation system that accounts for all tickets purchased by passengers. Supermarkets and department stores keep track of customer sales with a variety of sophisticated input equipment, some of which you saw in Chapter 6. And colleges and universities record student registration and fees paid by students.

In many cases the transaction-processing system must also interface with an inventory control system, because the stock levels of products are reduced by orders received from customers. A variety of transaction processing environments is depicted in Figure 15-2.

INVENTORY CONTROL.   The units of product that a company has in stock to sell at a given moment is called its *inventory*. An *inventory control system* keeps track of the number of units of each product in inventory and ensures that reasonable quantities of products are maintained.

The term "inventory" does not necessarily refer to tangible merchandise on a shelf. For example, in airline passenger-reservation systems, inventory refers to the seats available for sale on flights, and in a college's course-registration system, it means the available slots in each class that is still open for enrollment.

Let's look at how an inventory control system might work. In the case of a mail-order firm selling outdoor equipment, a clerk at a toll-free number

(a)   (b)   (c)

Figure 15-2.   Computer-based transaction processing at an airlines reservation booth, automatic teller machine (ATM), and brokerage house. Because most business transactions involve a predictable series of steps, many types of transaction processing are computerized.

```
SMITH COMPANY        ***INVENTORY STOCK STATUS***           9/29/86      PAGE 1

ITEM          ITEM          BEG    QTY    QTY     ON     ON    AVAIL    UNIT
            DESCRIPTION      QTY    REC   SOLD    HAND   ORDER          PRICE

1002   RESISTOR-TYPE B        0    600    200    400    100     500     .15
1003   RESISTOR-TYPE D        0      0      0      0    100     100    2.20
1006   RESISTOR-TYPE E        0      0      0      0     50      50    6.85
1008   SEALING TAPE-1 INCH  200    100     50    250      0     250    3.00
1010   SEALING TAPE-1.5 INCH 100     0     30     70      0      70    3.71
1012   LIGHT FIXTURE-TYPE 6   0      0      0      0      0       0    4.31
1014   LIGHT FIXTURE-TYPE 7   0      0      0      0      0       0    4.03
1015   HEX SCREW            300    250     50    500    200     700     .65
1016   BIT NUT               0    600    100    500      0     500     .21
1018   WRENCH                0     30     30      0    100     100    8.55
1020   SOCKET SET          250     40     80    210      0     210   30.35
```

Figure 15-3. *Inventory stock status report.* Often, inventory systems are tied into transaction processing systems. As delivery or sale transactions are processed, the number of units of stock involved is added or subtracted from electronically kept inventory records. These records are used to produce reports such as this one, either periodically or on demand.

might take your order and type it into a terminal that ties into an inventory control system. The system then checks to see if the desired goods are in stock. If they are, the goods are made available for shipment and the number of units ordered is electronically subtracted from inventory balances. The sale is also recorded by the transaction-processing system, which must account for the fact that a business transaction has just taken place. Also, the accounts receivable system must be alerted in order to bill you. If the goods are not in stock, they may be placed on back order.

Besides monitoring stock levels automatically, almost all inventory control systems generate an assortment of reports for management. Among these documents are inventory stock status reports (shown in Figure 15-3) and summaries listing fast-moving and slow-moving items, back orders, and the like.

ACCOUNTS RECEIVABLE. The term *accounts receivable* refers to the amounts owed by customers who have made purchases on credit. Because about 90 percent of the business transacted in the United States is done on a credit basis, the *accounts receivable system* is a critical computer application in most companies. It keeps track of customers' purchases, payments, and account balances. It also calculates and prints customers' bills (a sample of which appears in Figure 15-4) and management reports. Other output includes sales analyses, which describe changing patterns of products and sales, as well as detailed or summary reports of current and past-due accounts.

When interest rates are high, the billing procedures of the accounts receivable system can be especially critical because the sooner the bill is mailed, the sooner it will be paid and the sooner the receipts can begin to

Sold to:	P.J. JOHNSTON 498 CANYON BLVD. BOULDER, CO 80302		Ship to:	E.D. ADAMS 307 EARL PLACE FLAGSTAFF, AZ 86001		SMITH COMPANY Customer no. 807214	

Today's date 09/22/86	Order date 09/22/86	Order no. 61027	Shipping instructions VIA EZ MOVERS	Stated terms 2% 30 DAYS NET 60		Salesperson 4617

Quantity ordered	Quantity shipped	Description	Unit price	Extended amount	Discount amount	Net amount
40	40	RESISTOR-TYPE B	.15	6.00		6.00
100	50	RESISTOR-TYPE E	6.85	342.50	63.25	279.25
100	100	SEALING TAPE-1 INCH	3.00	300.00	50.00	250.00
		FREIGHT CHARGE				37.55
		PACKING CHARGE				75.80

Tax 19.46	Additional charges 53.04	Invoice amount 721.10	Invoice number 12102

Figure 15-4.   A customer's bill (invoice). The billing procedures of the accounts receivable system can be especially critical. The sooner a bill is mailed, the sooner it will be paid and the sooner receipts can begin to earn interest for the company.

earn interest for the company. Also, studies have shown that delays in billing increase the likelihood of nonpayment.

ACCOUNTS PAYABLE.   The term *accounts payable* refers to the money a company owes to other companies for the goods and services it has received. In contrast to receivables, which reflect a portion of the money coming in, payables reflect part of the money being spent.

An *accounts payable system* keeps track of bills and often generates checks to pay those bills. It involves recording who gets paid and when, handling cash disbursements, and advising managers if they should accept discounts offered by vendors in return for early payment. The interest that could be earned by delaying payment might outweigh the value of discounts for early payment.

GENERAL LEDGER.   A *general ledger (G/L) system* keeps track of all financial summaries, including those originating from payroll, accounts receivable, and accounts payable. It also ensures that the books balance

Figure 15-5. *The relationship among accounting systems.*

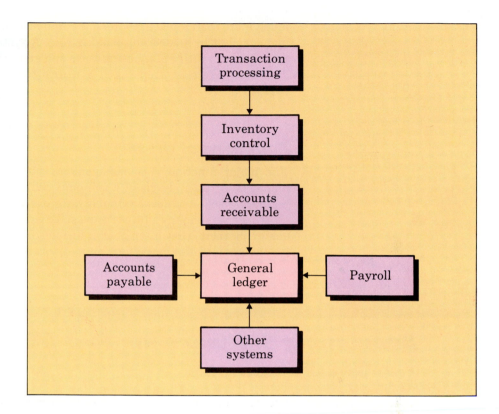

properly. Furthermore, a typical G/L system can produce accounting reports, such as income statements, balance sheets, and general ledger balances.

Once a company has decided to computerize one or more of the routine activities we have just discussed, it must then decide whether to develop the appropriate software itself or buy it from a vendor. Payroll packages are popular to buy from vendors because the payroll operation is similar in many companies, and the cost of keeping up with federal, state, and city tax legislation is almost too much for any one company to bear by itself. Inventory control packages are among the least popular, since inventory practices differ widely among companies.

Figure 15-5 illustrates the relationship among the various systems described in this section. The box on pages 450–451 discusses accounting software currently available for microcomputer-based systems.

MANAGEMENT INFORMATION SYSTEMS

During the early days of commercial computing, businesses purchased computers almost exclusively to perform routine accounting tasks. When used in this way, the computer could cut clerical expenses considerably. However, as time passed, it became apparent that the computer could do much more than replace laborers. It could also provide information to assist management in its decision-making role. A system that performs the dual role of doing routine accounting tasks and generating information for use by decision makers is often called a **management information system (MIS).**

Functions of the MIS

The major function of a management information system is to provide managers at many levels of a company with the kind of information they regularly need. *Top-level managers,* for example, spend much of their time plotting the company's future moves. To establish goals, and objectives for achieving them, they often need information about trends in data, not only for their companies, but about competitors and the economy as well.

Accounting Software for Your Micro and Small Business

QUALITY ACCOUNTING SOFTWARE PRODUCTS ARE FINALLY HERE

In virtually every large business, routine accounting operations are computerized. These operations include such activities as payroll, accounts receivable, accounts payable, and general ledger. *Accounts receivable*

Most packages handle relatively straightforward operations.

represents most of the money coming in; *accounts payable* and *payroll,* most of it going out. The *general ledger* program ties these three important account categories, and several lesser ones, together. The program packages that contain routines to carry out and integrate all of these operations are called *accounting software.*

Large businesses have had accounting software for years, since the days when the only way to get programs was to write them yourself. In these businesses accounting applications have traditionally been, and continue to be, coded by staff programmers in COBOL. There's a good reason for this. Accounting operations form the financial backbone of most companies, and since no two businesses are exactly alike, it pays to have as much control as possible over the software that runs these systems.

But small companies, even though they can't afford a team of programmers, also need to do accounting work. And over 85 percent of the businesses in the United States have fewer than twenty employees. That's about 20 million small businesses and professionals. The microcomputing revolution has made it possible for these health spa owners, plumbers,

The information needs of *middle management* are slightly different. To carry out the strategies devised by their superiors, these managers need to know what is happening in their departments. Therefore, reports summarizing the flow of money and products under their jurisdiction are especially useful. Middle managers also need reports that describe any problems in the performance of production, for example, missed deadlines or quotas.

Lower-level management has yet another set of priorities and information needs. Supervisors are charged with coordinating and controlling the activities of workers so that higher-level goals are met. These managers need reports that help them coordinate workers and materials—reports on inventory, shipping, purchases, payroll, and so on.

Many of the accounting-type clerical tasks mentioned earlier generate data most directly relevant to lower-level management. When these data are summarized and consolidated, they become the information many

interior decorators, and others to have their own computers—as long as someone else writes the software, maintains it, and makes it easy to use. Despite the fact that every business is different, many of their tasks are the same. If a software package were both general and affordable enough, it could be valuable to a large number of companies.

Enter the firms selling generalized accounting packages. The first crop of the microcomputer-oriented versions of such packages were expensive, relatively inflexible,

and full of bugs. Although accounting packages are still more costly than spreadsheets, word processors, and file managers, they have improved substantially in quality. Most of them are designed to handle relatively straightforward accounting operations such as payroll, accounts receivable, accounts payable, and general ledger. Other accounting applications, such as sales order entry, inventory, and job costing, are so different from company to company that packaged software catering to these needs has been far less successful.

In today's market there's no shortage of microcomputer-based accounting packages. Depending on the complexity and versatility of the software, you can find anywhere from a handful to fifty or more integrated accounting functions packaged together. And, since there is less competition in this area than in the spreadsheet and word processing areas, the quality of the documentation can vary considerably among vendors. Some accounting packages are general and simple enough to sell for a few hundred dollars, whereas more complicated ones for a specialized market (such as nonprofit organizations or building contractors) may cost a couple of thousand or more.

An assortment of accounting packages.

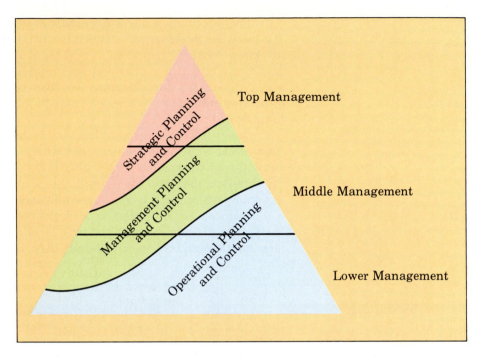

Top Management

Strategic Planning and Control

Management Planning and Control

Middle Management

Operational Planning and Control

Lower Management

Figure 15-6.   The three levels of management and the tasks performed at each level.

middle-level managers need to perform their jobs. Until the recent boom in easy-to-use microcomputing software and online databases, very few top-level managers wanted to interact with computers at all. Although strategic planning and control do involve a lot of information that is impossible to integrate formally into a computer system, it's apparent that computers are becoming increasingly useful tools for many tasks that take place at the highest levels of management.

The roles of these levels of management are illustrated in the pyramid in Figure 15-6.

Limitations of the MIS

When management information systems first became popular, they were plagued by some serious problems. Many company executives, perhaps misled by the exaggerated hype of computer experts (as well as by their own computer illiteracy), expected far more from the systems than the systems could provide. For example, many firms ambitiously undertook the design of some "total system" that would link up every level of the management pyramid and, more or less, "do *everything* a computer system could possibly do, for *everybody*." When executives and users discovered that no MIS could systematically furnish information about all aspects of a business or anticipate all of its needs, many became disillusioned.

Despite the failings of some overambitious systems, however, many MISs survived and have resulted in undeniable benefits to the companies

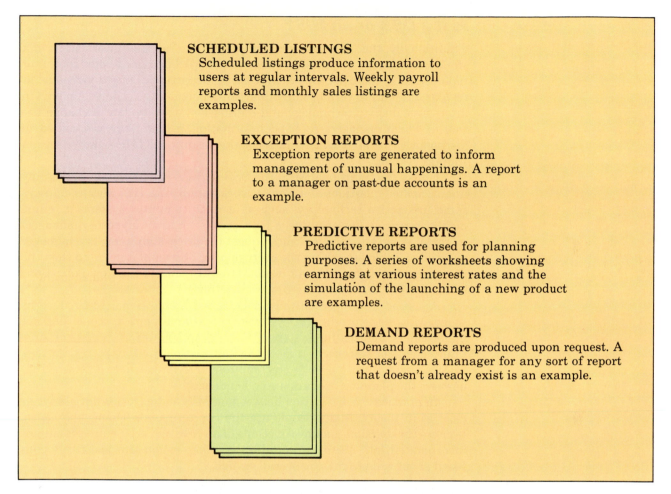

SCHEDULED LISTINGS
Scheduled listings produce information to users at regular intervals. Weekly payroll reports and monthly sales listings are examples.

EXCEPTION REPORTS
Exception reports are generated to inform management of unusual happenings. A report to a manager on past-due accounts is an example.

PREDICTIVE REPORTS
Predictive reports are used for planning purposes. A series of worksheets showing earnings at various interest rates and the simulation of the launching of a new product are examples.

DEMAND REPORTS
Demand reports are produced upon request. A request from a manager for any sort of report that doesn't already exist is an example.

Figure 15-7. *Reports produced by a management information system.*

that developed them. Some of the useful types of reports normally delivered by an MIS are shown in Figure 15-7. With an MIS, management can incorporate much more information into decisions and spend less time gathering it. Managers thus have more time to do the things that they do best—thinking creatively and interacting with people.

DECISION SUPPORT SYSTEMS

During the 1970s, managers began to call for systems that could field questions as they occurred. These systems could prove to be particularly useful to high-level managers, whose requirements for information are somewhat unpredictable. In response the computer industry developed the **decision support system (DSS).** What exactly a DSS does is a matter that's still evolving.

Is It a DSS or an MIS?

Traditionally, the MIS has provided fixed, preformatted information in a standardized way. A typical product of the MIS is a hard-copy computer report that a company's data processing department might circulate at regular intervals to various individuals or departments. As developments in interactive display technology and database systems began to change the way in which managers received information, a new term was coined to distinguish this state of affairs from the traditional MIS—the "decision support system."

Unlike the traditional MIS, the DSS permits one to pose new, possibly unanticipated questions at a display workstation. The DSS always employs some interactive technology, such as a microcomputer system or online display terminal. For example, a DSS user (such as an inventory manager) might sit down at a terminal and request the price of an item. The manager might then decide to ask for the average price of several items, and then the inventory status of a different item. Managers can ask their own questions as the need evolves and receive answers at once.

A second difference between a DSS and a traditional MIS concerns scope. Most decision support systems are less ambitious in scope than are management information systems. Whereas an MIS often consists of large interdependent systems that meet the information needs of scores of users, a DSS might consist of a microcomputer and spreadsheet software that answers the planning needs of a single manager.

In practice the distinction between an MIS and a DSS is not always as clear as in theory. Many people use the two terms interchangeably. Also, because the decision-making functions of an MIS and a DSS are sometimes incorporated into routine accounting systems, people are justifiably confused about what to call the overall system.

DSS Tools

Virtually any interactive software package that gives managers considerable freedom to generate their own information is a decision support system tool. For example, *electronic spreadsheets*, *file managers*, and *relational database management systems*—which were discussed in Chapters 12 and 13—are generally considered DSS tools. Included, too, are the various *financial modeling* and *statistical packages* that are commercially available.

OFFICE SYSTEMS

In recent years computer technology has been applied to the task of increasing productivity in the office. The term **office automation** has been coined to describe this trend. Automating the office can be done through a wide variety of technologies and processing techniques, some of which are discussed here.

Word Processing

Probably the most widespread of the office system technologies is **word processing.** As we've discussed previously in the text, word processing refers to technologies that enable computer systems to automate a variety of typing and document-preparation tasks. Figure 15-8 shows a "dedicated" word processing system. The page-sized screen and specialized keyboard on this system, as well as the software, are especially tailored to the needs of the professional typist or writer.

Decision Support Software

All of the DSS tools that we discussed earlier in the chapter have contributed to automating life at the office. These tools have automated decision processes that were once exclusively carried out with the assistance of ancient (yet still going strong) devices such as pencils, pads of paper, file folders, and filing cabinets.

Electronic Mail

Electronic mail pertains to technologies that make it possible to do such things as send letters, manuscripts, legal documents, and the like from one terminal or computer system to another. The following might be seen as examples of electronic mail.

- A secretary in New York places a document containing both text and pictures into a facsimile (FAX) machine, such as the one in Figure 15-9. The FAX machine digitizes the page image and transmits it over ordinary phone lines to Los Angeles. In Los Angeles another FAX machine receives the page image and reproduces it in hard-copy form. All of this takes place in less than a minute.

- Two people communicate over a *voice mail* system, where the spoken messages of the sender are digitized (by voice tone), and stored in memory on an answering device at the receiver's location. When the receiver presses a "listen" key, the digitized message is reconverted to voice.

- A typist word-processes a manuscript on a microcomputer system and electronically transmits it over the phone lines to a hard disk on an author's system. The author is not home, but communications software on her computer system enables the phone to be answered and the manuscript to be accepted.

- A microcomputer user in Denver types an electronic message and transmits it over the phone lines to the "electronic mailbox" (in Seattle) of a microcomputer user in Spokane. The "post office" that maintains this mailbox, and others, is an online messaging-service company.

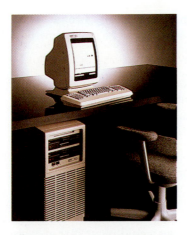

Figure 15-8.   A dedicated word processing system. The page-sized screen, specialized keyboard, and sophisticated software on this system are especially tailored to the needs of the professional typist or writer.

Figure 15-9.   A facsimile machine. Facsimile reproduction has long been a very popular form of electronic mail.

An operator on a large computer system electronically broadcasts a message to online terminal users that the system will be going down for an hour starting at 10:30 A.M.

As with many other evolving concepts in the world of computers, "electronic mail" is a term that's not defined without controversy. For example, some people consider electronic mail to refer exclusively to commercial services that offer an electronic-document delivery alternative that competes with the post office.

Video Teleconferencing

Teleconferencing makes it possible for a group of people to meet electronically, thereby avoiding the time and expense they would incur if they were to get together physically in one spot. **Video teleconferencing** systems permit participants to see each other on video screens, as well as to hear each other (see Figure 15-10).

Although such video systems are gaining in popularity, they do suffer from the disavantage of requiring expensive, specially equipped rooms. Also, they are relatively ineffective in situations where physical confrontation between participants is important. Eventually, however, person-to-person video teleconferencing through "picture phones" may become a widespread reality.

Telecommuting

One of the most interesting ways in which computer technology has automated the office is **telecommuting**—that is, enabling people to work

Figure 15-10. A video teleconference.

at home on a terminal or microcomputer workstation linked to an organization at another location. Many typists and computer programmers, for example, telecommute to their jobs, perhaps because they prefer or need to do so, or because they are more productive at home.

Telecommuting can save workers both the time and expense involved in traveling to work. It can also save businesses the expense of maintaining office and parking space. On the negative side, telecommuting limits the interpersonal contact that often makes working in an office lively and productive. And telecommuting requires a major cultural adjustment for those organizations used to on-site supervision of employees.

DESIGN AND MANUFACTURING SYSTEMS: CAD/CAM

So far we've looked at computers at work crunching out operational documents such as paychecks and bills, supplying information to managers when and where they need it, and streamlining various functions around the office. Now let's look into the design labs and onto the factory floor, to see how computers are used there. Computers are widely used in organizational settings to improve productivity both at the design stage—through computer-aided design (CAD)—and at the manufacturing stage—through computer-aided manufacturing (CAM).

Computer-Aided Design

By using **computer-aided design (CAD),** product designers can dramatically reduce the time they spend at the drawing board. For example, with the use of digitizing devices and specialized graphics workstations (see Figure 15-11), engineers can sketch ideas directly into the computer system, which can then be instructed to analyze the proposed design in terms of how well it meets a number of design criteria. Taking into account the subsequent output of the computer, the designer can modify the drawings until a desirable design is achieved.

Before the arrival of CAD, the designer had to produce hand-drawn preliminary sketches and then advanced designs that represented refinements on the sketches. After models were built and tested, the designer had to prepare production drawings, which are used to build the equipment needed to manufacture the new product, whether a truck or a new toaster. Today computer-aided assistance with all of these tasks is fairly common. CAD is especially helpful in the design of such products as automobiles, aircraft, ships, buildings, electric circuits (including computer chips), and even running shoes.

Besides playing an important role in the design of durable goods, CAD is also very useful in such fields as art, advertising, and movie production (see the Tomorrow box on page 459). Window 6 includes several examples that show how CAD works in these and other environments.

Figure 15-11.   CAD workstations. These units, which are often configured to minicomputers, are targeted to professional designers.

Computer-Aided Manufacturing (CAM)

Computer applications are not limited to the design phases of product development. In fact they were used on the factory floor well before engineers used them interactively for design. With each passing day, more and more of the actual process of production on the factory floor is becoming computerized.

Computer-aided manufacturing (CAM) includes the use of computers to help manage manufacturing operations and to control machinery used in manufacturing processes. One example is a system that observes production in an oil refinery, performs calculations, and opens and shuts appropriate valves when necessary. Another system, commonly used in the steel industry, works from preprogrammed specifications to perform automatically the shaping and assembly of steel parts. CAM is also widely employed to build cars and ships, monitor power plants, manufacture food and chemicals, and perform a number of other functions.

One type of CAM that seems to have caught the attention of people everywhere is **robotics,** the study of the design, building, and use of robots. Robots are machines that, with the help of a computer, can mimic a number of human activities in order to perform jobs that are too monotonous or

tomorrow

COMPUTER-MADE MOVIES

Soon You May Find It Difficult to Distinguish Real Life from Simulated Life

Imagine sitting down with a newspaper twenty or so years from now and reading something like the following:

JACKSON HOLE, WYOMING, January 21, 2008—Cody Wahsach, the popular star of over twenty top-selling music videos, was revealed today to have been a fake, if the word fake can be applied to someone who never existed. Cody, it turns out, was created by sophisticated computer-imaging techniques that can now generate convincingly lifelike pictures. He and his entire band are no more than a collection of refreshed pixels on a video screen.

Although this scenario may seem very sci-fi, we're really not too far away from such a reality. Graphic images can be created by computer that look remarkably real (see photo). Those images can be stored and altered mathematically to produce new images, and all of the images can be used to produce an animated sequence. So far many of the computer-generated images you see on TV and at the movies are such things as whirling logos, bouncing basketballs, and magic-carpet rides over sports stadiums. And the humanlike figures you see seem sticklike and jerky in motion. But quality improvements in the scene simulation area are happening fast.

Historically one of the major problems with computer animation has been raw computational speed. To produce high-quality three-dimensional images, for example, it may take 70 *billion* computations or more per frame. So at 24 frames per second, that means about 50,000 or so billion computations just for 30 seconds of animated film. This is supercomputer-level power. However, advances being made today on products such as gallium arsenide chips and parallel processors (see boxes on pages 117 and 252) will enable the computer to make an even greater number of computations, to produce much more realistic images.

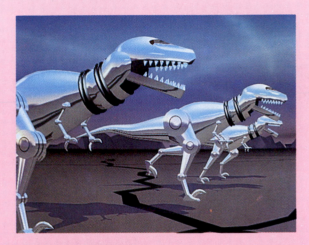

Today's monster from a computer-animated film. Will tomorrow's look as realistic as Godzilla?

In tomorrow's movies it will probably indeed be impossible to tell which is an "actual" object in a scene and which is computer-generated. Already, in movies, it's difficult to tell whether a background is painted or created by computer. But in tomorrow's movies, you'll wonder about everything in the foreground, too.

Figure 15-12.   An industrial robot.

dangerous for their flesh-and-blood counterparts (see Figure 15-12). Some robots can even "see" by means of imbedded cameras and "feel" with sensors that permit them to assess the hardness, temperature, and other qualities of objects. Robots can represent a substantial savings to a corporation, since they don't go on strike, don't need vacations, and don't get sick.

The auto industry uses robots to weld cars and paint them, and electronics firms employ robots to assemble calculators. Elsewhere robots help to mine coal, and even to build other machines. In fact a well-known sushi chef in Japan is not even a human at all, but a robot. So too are a few famous "painters" in the world. There is even a robot in Japan that can read standard sheet music (by optical recognition of notes), and play the music with actual instruments.

Despite this fascination with robots, the acceptance of robot technology has been particularly slow in the United States and Europe, where unions fear that workers will lose their jobs to machines. In Japan, where many companies virtually guarantee workers employment until they reach age 60, robots have been embraced quickly. Japan is now the world's leading robot producer, and represents more than half of the worldwide market.

ARTIFICIAL INTELLIGENCE SYSTEMS

A computer is a device that, given some instructions, can perform work at extremely fast speeds, by drawing upon a large memory. It can also be programmed to draw certain types of conclusions on the basis of the input it receives or the results of computations it performs. A good deal of human mental activity involves these same processes. For this reason the mental acuity attributed to computers is commonly referred to as **artificial intelligence** (*AI*). Consequently the computer systems that embody principles of artificial intelligence are frequently called *artificial intelligence systems.*

The field of AI evolved from attempts to write programs that would enable computers to rival skilled humans at games such as chess and checkers, to prove difficult mathematical theorems, and so forth. Since these tasks normally require a high degree of human intelligence, the feeling has been that the computers that can do them must in some way be mimicking human intelligence.

Early attemps at using computers to do humanlike thinking primarily exploited the awesome speed of these machines. For example, the first chess programs instructed computer systems to make decisions by looking several plays ahead and calculating the effects of all possible moves and countermoves. Unfortunately, planning ten moves ahead is a computationally burdensome chore, even for a computer. It is also not the way skilled chess

The World of CAD

A brief pictorial introduction to computer-aided design

As you've seen in some other Windows in this book, computer systems are capable of producing spectacular images. But how are these images created? Although that would take at least an entire book to adequately describe, this Window provides insight into some of the techniques that are commonly used by computer designers.

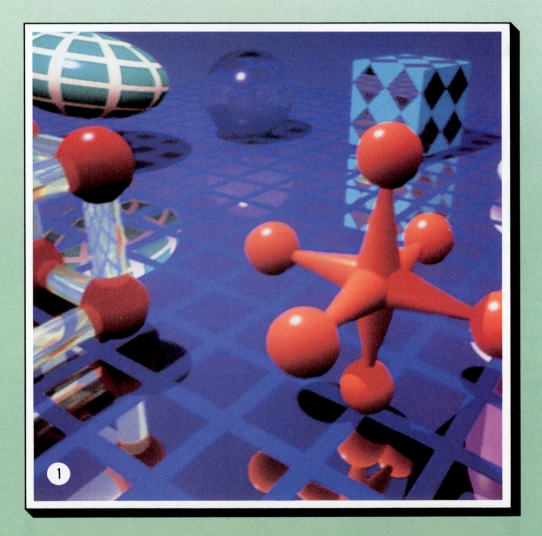

1.   An attractive graphic courtesy of Apollo Computer, Inc. How does one get ultra-smooth shapes, pattern reflections, high-angle views, and shadows? Read on.

Getting Started

Graphical images can be entered into the computer system in a number of ways. One method—using paintbox software to hand-paint the screen—was used in the development of the images in Window 3. Two other methods, mathematical modeling and digitization (which are frequently used in combination with paintbox software), are described below.

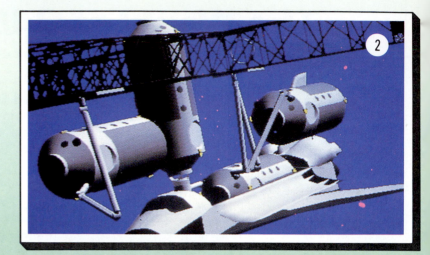

2. Often, three-dimensional objects—such as this space station—are mathematically constructed with solid-modeling software. Solid-modeling software takes advantage of the fact that many objects in nature can be formed from a combination of simple shapes, such as planes, spheres, ellipses, polygons, and so forth—all of which can be described by mathematical formulas.

3. Images can also be directly "digitized" into computer memory from photographs or drawings, as was this wave. A digitizing copier or camera is used to take a picture of the original image and the digitized image is stored as a matrix of colored pixels in computer memory. Although this method is faster than either mathematical modeling or hand-painting for inputting data, it typically provides only a two-dimensional image that can't be rotated in space and examined from other perspectives.

Manipulating the Image

How to electronically alter a picture once it's in memory.

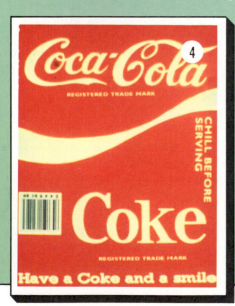

4–6. A common can of Coke Cola, once photodigitized in computer memory, is "wrapped" into a cylinder through mathematical formulas. Moreover, if we wish, we can stretch the can, warp it, or plaster it onto another surface for a wild-looking effect. Paintbox software can later be used by the designer to alter the image on the can.

7, 8. "Zooming" is a technique allowed by many CAD systems. It permits us to get closer or further away from an image, as if we were holding a camera and moving back and forth, constantly refocusing. Also, note that in photograph 8 the soldier has disappeared and both the bear and horse have been rotated. Since the soldier, bear, and horse are saved in memory as separate files, we can make them appear or disappear on the screen just as if we were editing files of ordinary text with a word processor.

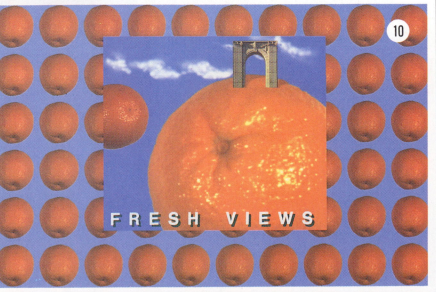

9, 10. "Replication" is a technique whereby we take the file that stores a graphical image and use it to reproduce the image—one or more times—into another image. We can make any "copy" of the original image larger or smaller and, if the image is stored in three dimensions (like the orange), we can rotate it while replicating it.

11. This sea birds image demonstrates how a picture can be "computer enhanced." The image was first digitized from a color photograph. The leftmost third of it was then "block pixellated," the middle section was created using filled polygons to flatten the relief, and the rightmost third was left untouched. Block pixellating is a technique that is getting increasingly popular for creating special effects on television.

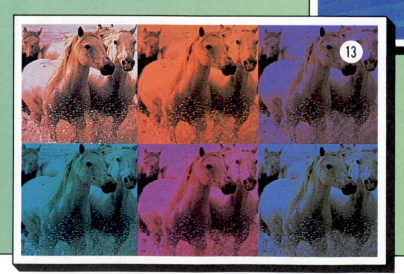

12. "Fractals" refers to a technique that is used to create realistic-looking mountains and other jagged surfaces. The mountains often start as smooth surfaces that are generated from trigonometric formulas. Subsequently, these smooth shapes are bombarded with thousands—or perhaps millions—of randomly sized "pits" to simulate natural erosion.

13. Color filtering is often used to change the mood and quality of an image.

Putting in Shadows and Reflections

When objects are stored in three dimensions, a light source is often simulated into the memory that contains the full image to create realistic shadow effects. For reflections, the image to be reflected is stored separately in its own file and "mapped"—with the use of mathematical formulas—onto the surface that is to carry it.

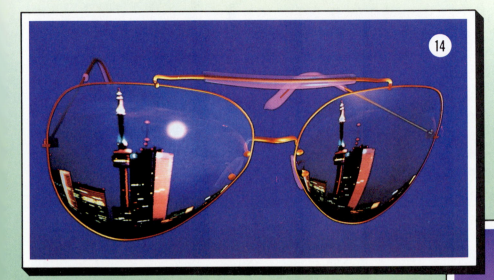

14. A view of Toronto's skyline mapped onto the lenses of a pair of sunglasses.

15. A tree casts a shadow and is also mapped onto a sphere.

16. A plane takes off from a sun-filled runway, casting a shadow.

17. "Kaiser Pass" shows the deep shadows that commonly occur very early or late in the day.

Window 6

Composing a Page Electronically

These three Light-speed images show how a magazine page can be composed electronically.

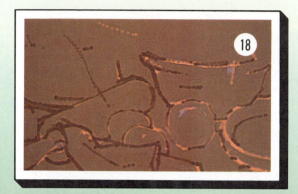

18. Using a paintbox routine, the artist begins creating an image on the screen.

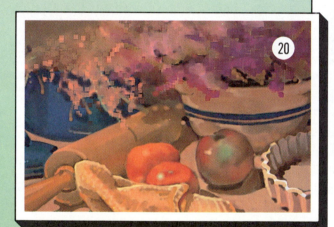

19. The image is refined, and the flowers are block-pixellated for effect.

20. The image is further refined.

21. The preceding three images, which have been saved in computer memory as separate files, are rescaled and combined with both text and typesetting fonts to compose the page.

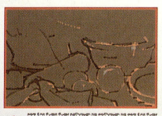

The Electronic Canvas

466

players think. Most chess masters rely on intuitive rules of thumb, called *heuristics*. One highly successful heuristic for playing chess is to control the center of the board. As programmers began supplying computers with the logic for using such heuristics, the quality of chess-playing programs improved dramatically. And as programmers began to supply this same type of "built-in intelligence" to other applications, the field of AI started to attract serious notice. In fact many industry experts now see AI as the key to the fifth generation of computing.

Today the three main areas of AI are expert systems, natural languages, and robotics.

EXPERT SYSTEMS. **Expert systems** (also called *knowledge-based systems*) are an outgrowth of the heuristic-based chess-playing programs of the 1950s and 1960s, when the "expert knowledge" of chess masters was built into programs. Today expert systems are successfully used in such fields as medicine, to incorporate the thinking patterns of some of the world's leading doctors. For example, an expert system might be given a configuration of symptoms exhibited by a patient. If these symptoms could lead to the diagnosis of a disease the program knows something about, the program might ask the attending physician for further information about specific details. Ultimately, through questioning and checking the patient's condition against a large database of successfully diagnosed cases, the program might draw conclusions that the attending physician otherwise may never have reached. And it will do so very quickly.

Expert systems have enormous applications potential. These systems are the key to producing computer systems that can think as people do. Even the IRS is using expert systems to decide whether to audit your income-tax return.

NATURAL LANGUAGES. One of the greatest challenges currently facing scientists in the field of AI is to equip computer systems with the ability to communicate in *natural languages*—English, Spanish, French, Japanese, and so forth. But this challenge is not easily met. People have personalized ways of communicating, and the meaning of words varies with the context in which they are used. Also, the heuristics people employ to reach an understanding of what others are saying are highly complex and still not well understood by language researchers.

Nonetheless researchers have made some large strides in the direction of getting computers to listen to and respond in natural languages. Some of the current high-tech products that incorporate voice input and output were covered in Chapter 6.

ROBOTICS. We've already seen that robots can play an integral role in CAM systems. Although it may seem as though many of these robots are "dumb," they are often aided by AI techniques to identify objects and states in their environments so that they can act accordingly. The ultimate AI product, of course, will be a robot that's virtually indistinguishable from a human being. That, of course, is still far from realization.

Summary and Key Terms

Many computer applications in business, industry, and government fall into one or more of six categories: accounting systems, management information systems, decision support systems, office systems, design and manufacturing systems, and artificial intelligence systems.

Accounting systems generally perform tasks that involve the tedious record keeping that organizations must handle regularly. Among these tasks are payroll, transaction processing, inventory control, accounts receivable, accounts payable, and general ledger.

Management information systems and decision support systems provide decision makers with access to needed information. A system built to perform the dual role of doing routine accounting and generating periodic information for use by decision makers is called a **management information system (MIS)**. Unlike the traditional MIS, a **decision support system (DSS)** permits the definition of new questions at an interactive terminal.

In recent years computer technology has been applied to the task of increasing productivity in the office. The term **office automation** has been coined to describe this trend. Automating the office can be accomplished through a wide variety of technologies and processing techniques, including **word processing** technologies, decision support software, **electronic mail, video teleconferencing,** and **telecommuting.**

Computers are widely used in industry to improve productivity, both at the design stage—through **computer-aided design (CAD)**—and at the manufacturing stage—through **computer-aided manufacturing (CAM).** One type of CAM that has caught the attention of the news media is **robotics,** the study of the design, building, and use of robots.

The mental acuity attributed to computers is commonly referred to as **artificial intelligence (AI).** Consequently the computer systems that embody principles of artificial intelligence are frequently called *artificial intelligence systems.* The three main applications of AI techniques are **expert systems,** natural languages, and robotics.

Review Exercises

Fill-in Questions

1. The term _____ refers to the money a company owes to other companies for the goods and services it has received.
2. The term _____ refers to money owed to a company by customers who have made purchases on credit.

3. A(n) _____ system keeps track of all financial summaries and produces accounting reports such as balance sheets, income statements, and the like.
4. CAD is an acronym for _____.
5. A(n) _____ system makes it possible to send letters, memos, and the like from one computer terminal to another.
6. _____ is an office system technology that makes it possible for a group of people to meet electronically, thus avoiding the time and expense that would be incurred if they were to get together physically in one spot.
7. The study of the design, building, and use of robots comprises the field of _____.

Matching Questions

Match each term with its description.

a. Accounting systems	d. DSS
b. CAM	e. CAD
c. MIS	f. Word processing

_____c_____ 1. A system built to perform the dual role of providing routine data processing and generating information for use by decision makers.

_____a_____ 2. Pertaining to the record-keeping tasks that organizations must handle regularly.

_____f_____ 3. The use of computers to assist in the preparation of letters, memos, documents, and the like.

_____e_____ 4. Pertaining to the use of computers in design.

_____d_____ 5. Pertaining to the use of interactive computer systems for decision support.

_____b_____ 6. Pertaining to the use of computers in manufacturing.

Discussion Questions

1. Name several functions performed by accounting systems.
2. What is the difference between a management information system and a decision support system?
3. Identify some of the computing technologies that comprise the automated office.
4. What is the difference between computer-aided design and computer-aided manufacturing? Provide some examples of each.
5. What is meant by artificial intelligence?
6. Explain what expert systems do.

Chapter 16

Systems Development

Chapter Outline

Objectives

After completing this chapter you should be able to:

1. Explain what a system is.
2. Describe the role of the systems analyst in systems development.
3. Identify and describe the components of the systems development cycle.
4. Explain the difference between prototyping and traditional systems development.

OVERVIEW

As you've seen in Chapter 15, all organizations have systems of various sorts—for example, accounting systems, office systems, and management information systems. Such systems require considerable planning. The process of planning, designing, and implementing systems of any type, whether computerized or not, is called *systems development*.

Unfortunately, since no two organizations are exactly alike and ways of doing things differ among organizations, there is no certain formula for successful systems development. A procedure that works well in one situation may fail miserably in another.

Systems development is often subdivided into five steps, or phases: preliminary investigation, systems analysis, system design, acquisition of resources, and system implementation. These phases are often collectively called the systems development cycle (or systems development life cycle).

In this chapter we'll closely examine an approach to systems development in which phases of the life cycle are performed sequentially. We'll also cover a process called *prototyping,* which raises the issue of conducting systems development in a different way.

ON SYSTEMS

A **system** is a collection of elements and procedures that interact to accomplish a goal. A football game, for example, is played according to a system. It consists of a collection of elements (two teams, a playing field, referees) and procedures (rules) that interact to determine which team is the winner. A transit system is a collection of people, machines, work rules, fares, and schedules that get people from one place to another. And a computer system is a collection of people, hardware, software, data, and procedures that interact to accomplish data processing tasks.

The function of many systems, whether manual or computerized, is to keep an organization well managed and running smoothly. Systems are created and altered in response to changing needs within an organization and shifting conditions in the environment around it. When problems arise in an existing system or a new system is needed, systems development comes into play. **Systems development** is a process that consists of analyzing a system, designing a new system or making modifications to an old one, acquiring needed hardware and software, and getting the new or modified system to work.

Systems development may be required for any of a number of reasons. New laws may call for the collection of data never before assembled. The government may require new data on personnel. Or the introduction of new technology, especially new computer technology, may prompt wholesale revision of a system, as when an organization wishes to switch from a batch-oriented transaction-processing system to an online-oriented system (as many banks and colleges have done) or to convert applications into a database environment. These kinds of pressure can often bring about major changes in the systems by which work is done in an organization.

As you read on in this chapter, there are some facts you should consider about the nature of systems development. First, it is impossible to foresee every possible condition a system will encounter in the future. Because the conditions in which a system must operate are subject to change, some modifications must usually be made in any system at some point. Second, even if perfection were attainable, it is normally economically infeasible to try to solve every conceivable problem. A system that attempts to do everything might be so complicated that it would be impossible to administer efficiently, if at all. Third, there is often considerable uncertainty as to which system will work best in a given situation. Systems development is not an exact science like mathematics, in which a solution can be proved correct. Like most decisions in life, you're never sure that the alternatives you choose are the best ones.

THE ROLE OF THE SYSTEMS ANALYST

In the typical business organization, a number of people share responsibility for the development of systems. The *chief information officer* (*CIO*) holds primary responsibility for systems development. Often this position is at the level of vice president. One of the CIO's duties is to oversee the formulation of a five-year plan that maps out what systems are to be studied and possibly revamped during that period. Because data and information processing affects not only the accounting functions in most firms, but also most other departments (including sales, manufacturing, and personnel), a *steering committee* composed of highest-level executives normally approves the plan. This committee also sets broad guidelines on how computer activities are to be performed. It does not become highly involved with technical details or the administration of particular projects, which are the responsibility of the *data processing department* (see Figure 16-1).

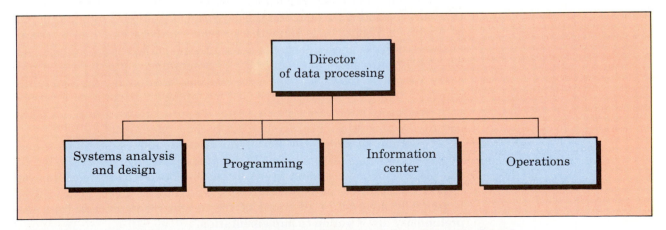

Figure 16-1.   A possible organizational structure for a data processing department.

The Information Center

LIKE A COMPUTER STORE—BUT IT'S IN A PRIVATE COMPANY

The *information center*—sometimes also called the microcomputer support center or corporate computer store—is one of the latest additions to many data processing departments. It was conceived to help individual users in the organization make intelligent choices about the decision support resources (such as microcomputers and fourth-generation languages) that they need to perform their jobs better, and to promote an orderly acquisition of these resources within the organization as a whole. Many information centers are staffed by systems analysts rather than by programmers, and these analysts often have exceptional user-communications skills.

The information center concept is relatively new and still in a highly evolutionary stage. Many are set up in a similar way to a typical computer store. A user talks to a trained analyst about computing needs, and the user and analyst sit down at a system or two and experiment with some software that seems appropriate to the user's job needs. The center may also offer user training, either through formal courses or through self-paced video cassettes.

One of the most serious problems facing organizations today is deciding how far to let users go in creating their own microcomputer systems. Although the information center may exert some control over how these systems are initially developed, it does not eliminate the

The corporate information center: Curbing the uncontrolled proliferation of microcomputer systems.

threat of "homemade data" later wending its way into critical decision-making processes that should be part of a larger, more formal system. If the user's "microcomputer needs" are seen as potentially disruptive to the organization in this regard, the analyst should recommend that the user's problem be handled as part of a formal systems development effort.

The data processing department varies widely in structure from one company to another. In one form the department is divided into four parts, as shown in Figure 16-1. Here the *systems analysis and design group* analyzes, designs, and implements new software and hardware systems. As was discussed in detail in Chapter 9, the *programming group* designs and codes computer programs from specifications created by the **systems analyst.** The *information center* (see box above) assists users primarily with microcomputer-based needs. And the *operations group* manages day-to-day processing once a system has become operational.

Generally speaking, the job of the systems analyst is to plan and implement systems that make use of computers that an organization has or will acquire. When a system needs to be developed, the systems analyst interacts with current and potential users to produce a solution. The analyst is generally involved in all stages of the development process, from the preliminary investigation to implementation.

We can easily understand the varied activities of the analyst if we divide the process of systems development into five steps or phases. These phases are:

✕ Phase 1: Preliminary investigation

✕ Phase 2: Systems analysis

✕ Phase 3: System design

✕ Phase 4: System acquisition

✕ Phase 5: System implementation

These phases are often collectively referred to as the **systems development cycle** (or **systems development life cycle**), since they describe a system from the time it is first studied until the time it is put into use. When a new business pressure necessitates a change in a system, the steps of the cycle begin anew.

The role of the systems analyst in these phases is shown in Figure 16-2.

- *Preliminary investigation* During this phase the analyst studies the problem briefly and suggests a few possible solutions so that management can decide whether the project should be pursued further.

- *Systems analysis* If management decides after the preliminary investigation that further systems development is warranted, the analyst must study the existing system in depth and make specific recommendations for change.

- *System design* During this phase the analyst develops a model of the new system and prepares a detailed list of benefits and costs. Both the model and the list are incorporated into a report to management.

- *System acquisition* Upon management approval of the design model, the analyst must decide what software and hardware to obtain.

- *System implementation* After the components of the system have been acquired, the analyst supervises the lengthy process of adapting old programs and files to the new system, prepares specifications for programmers, and so forth.

Figure 16-2. The role of the systems analyst in the five phases of systems development.

PHASE I: THE PRELIMINARY INVESTIGATION

The first thing the systems analyst does when confronted with a new systems assignment is to conduct a **preliminary investigation.** The purpose of this investigation is to define the problem at hand and to suggest some possible courses of action. Accordingly the investigation should examine the nature of the problem, the scope of the project created by the problem, possible solutions, and the approximate costs and benefits of the alternatives.

The Nature of the Problem

Determining the true nature of a problem is one of the key steps in the preliminary investigation. The analyst must take care at the outset to distinguish *symptoms* from *problems.*

For example, an analyst may be talking to a warehouse manager who complains that product inventories are too high. This may be true, but this fact in itself is not enough to warrant corrective action. It's a symptom, not a problem. There is a problem, however, if these high inventories are causing the company to build an expensive new warehouse or if they are unnecessarily drawing on funds that can be used for other opportunities. Yet even if there is a definable problem, the company may not be able to do anything about it. That is, the problem may not be solvable. For example, the high inventories may be due to a shipping or receiving strike somewhere else.

The analyst must also determine the relative magnitude of a problem. Everyone in an organization has problems they want solved, but the solutions to some problems are more important than others.

The Scope of the Project

In the preliminary investigation, the analyst also has to determine the scope of the project created by the problem. Scope is a function of the nature of the problem and of what management is *willing to spend.* An organization may be ready to spend $100,000 or only $1000. Scope is also a function of what management is *willing to change.* Understandably, people in organizations often hesitate to switch from one procedure to another. If a new system demands too much from people, it will probably fail.

Because most systems in a business organization are interrelated, the analyst must draw some clear boundaries around the systems or subsystems to be studied. Although systems analysts almost always find scores of problems that require attention in any system, they learn to accept some things as given and to find the best solution possible under the constraining circumstances. Completely new systems aren't always the answer. Sometimes a patchwork solution or minor alteration of an old system is all that is necessary.

Possible Solutions

Once the nature and scope of the problem have been defined, a number of solutions may be apparent. The important question at this point is: Does the problem have a simple, inexpensive solution that requires no further study, or is a new system or substantial alteration called for?

A mistake that many people make is to assume that all problems can be satisfactorily solved by computers. Actually the computer often only makes matters worse. An application that is infrequent and involves only a few hours of work is almost always better done the old-fashioned way: manually. Also, to some problems there may not be an absolutely satisfactory solution. For example, no company can completely avoid customers who don't pay their bills, no matter how elegant the billing system is. It is more useful to think of minimizing some problems than eliminating them entirely.

Costs and Benefits

During the preliminary investigation, the analyst should also provide a rough estimate of the costs and benefits of each recommended solution. How much should a company expect to spend on hardware and software? How much time and money would be saved by installing a computer system?

Report to Management

At the end of the preliminary investigation, the analyst writes a report to management with a brief description of the problems and some recommendations. If the problems have a simple solution that requires no further study, the analyst should state this clearly. If the recommendations involve extensive changes that require further study and expense, the analyst must outline the reasons for the proposed changes and summarize their costs and benefits. Once management has a preliminary "ball-park" estimate of the benefits and financial commitment involved, it can decide whether to abandon the project, immediately implement an inexpensive or temporary solution, or press forward to the next phases of development.

PHASE II: SYSTEMS ANALYSIS

Let's assume that, on the basis of the report evolving out of the preliminary investigation, management has decided to pursue systems development further. At this point the **systems analysis** phase begins. During this phase the main objectives are fact collection, analysis, and a report to management.

Fact Collection

The goal of fact collection is to determine what the current system does and what information users need. Later in this phase, these collected facts should enable the analyst to determine what's wrong with the current system and to generate some insights into possible solutions. The decision as to which facts to collect depends largely on the problem being studied. Four sources of information about how the current system works are written documents, questionnaires, interviews, and personal observation.

WRITTEN DOCUMENTS.   Special forms, manuals, diagrams, letters, and other materials can provide helpful information about how the current system functions. For example, an organization chart such as the one in Figure 16-3, which covers the company functions you're studying, is an especially useful document. At the outset of a project, the analyst may not be sure which documents will be most helpful. You can't gather everything in sight, or you'll drown in a sea of paperwork. You should concentrate on collecting documents that tell you the most about how the system works, as well as those that have a bearing on the key problems.

Figure 16-3.   An organization chart. These charts provide an overview of company operations and show the relationships among people and the work they do.

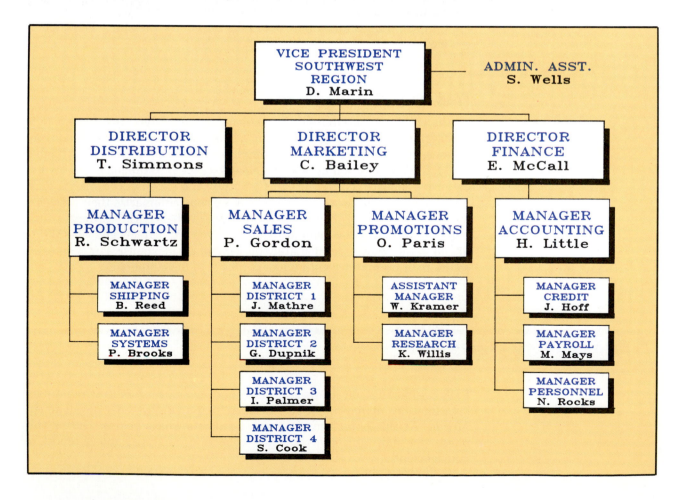

QUESTIONNAIRES.   A list of questions sent to system users is helpful for many reasons. It enables the analyst to obtain information rapidly and inexpensively from a large number of people. Also, it permits anonymous responses. If system users are geographically dispersed, questionnaires may be the only feasible means of getting information from them. Questionnaires do, however, have a number of limitations. If not many users respond, your results may be biased. It is quite easy to create questions that are misleading and confusing, and produce biased, unpredictable answers.

INTERVIEWS.   Both interviews and questionnaires generally serve the same purpose: to gather information from system users. Questionnaires are helpful for amassing a great deal of information rapidly, whereas interviews allow you the flexibility to follow up interesting lines of questioning that you could not have been anticipated in a questionnaire. Also, you can closely tailor an interview to a respondent. Like writing questions, interviewing is a skill.

OBSERVATION.   Observation requires you to go to the workplace to watch the flow of work directly. Sometimes, by watching what people do, you can detect interesting discrepancies between what they've told you in interviews and what they do in fact. Observation can also answer such questions as: Does the system actually work the way the people involved think it does? Is anything happening that I didn't expect?

Analysis

After you've examined the current system, it's time to analyze it to reach some conclusions. These conclusions will serve as the basis for your report to management at the end of the analysis phase. Three useful tools for performing analysis are diagrams, checklists, and synthesis.

DIAGRAMS.   Diagrams of both the existing system and any proposed ones can be particularly helpful. Two commonly used diagram tools are data flow diagrams and system flowcharts. Figure 16-4 shows a **data flow diagram** for the order-entry operation of a mail-order firm. Data flow diagrams provide a visual representation of data movement in an organization. They do not refer to any specific hardware devices. Early commitments to certain types of hardware may limit the way in which you think about the system, and you can easily overlook some promising possibilities.

With **system flowcharts,** on the other hand, the analyst does select specific kinds of hardware devices. Figure 16-5 illustrates how such a flowchart could be created for a portion of the system depicted in Figure 16-5. You should note that the symbol for online storage in Figure 16-4 indicates the need for a disk unit, and the symbol for a document indicates the need for a printer. System flowcharts are not the same as *program flowcharts* (discussed in Chapter 10).

CHECKLISTS.   Checklists can also prove particularly helpful in analysis. You might develop separate checklists for the items listed on page 482.

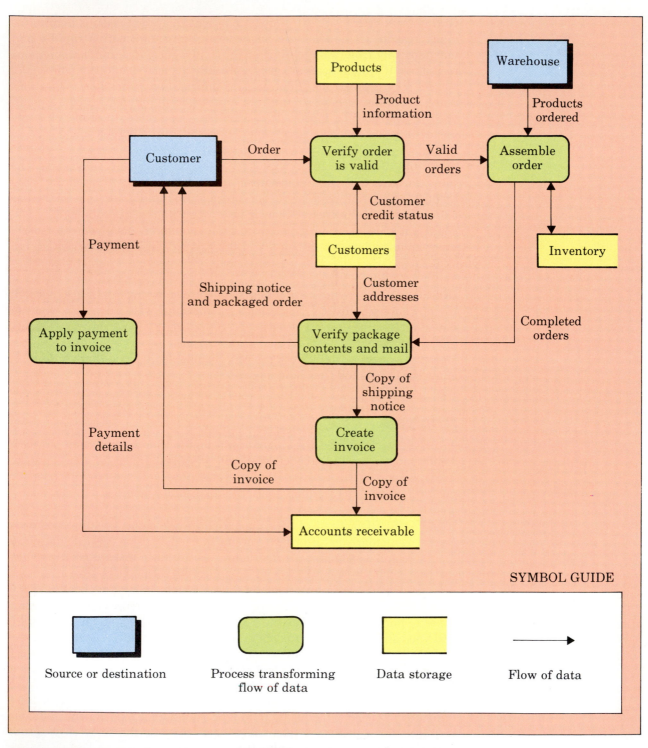

Figure 16-4. A data flow diagram of a mail-order firm. An order triggers the processes of verification and assembly of the goods ordered, and payment is recorded by accounts receivable.

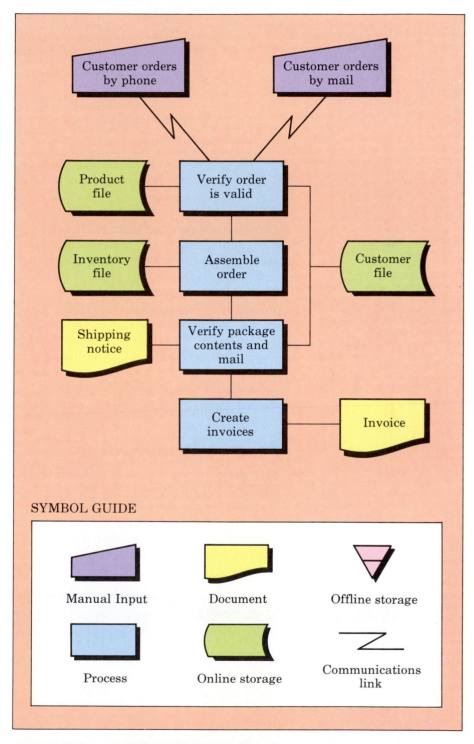

Figure 16-5. **A system flowchart.** This flowchart depicts a portion of the mail-order firm's system shown in Figure 16-4.

✖ *System goals*   For example, an accounts receivable system should get bills out quickly, identify good and bad credit risks for management, and inform customers rapidly about late payments.

✖ *The kinds of information needed to meet these goals*   For example, what information is needed by management to identify good and bad credit risks? How will this information be collected and made available? What timing is required to get information to managers when they need it?

✖ *Strengths and weaknesses of the current system*   For example, how does the present system measure up against these goals and information needs?

There are several other types of checklists you might employ, depending on the requirements of the problem. Common sense must eventually dictate which type of checklist is most appropriate for the situation at hand.

SYNTHESIS.   At some point the moment of truth will arrive: You'll need to provide some recommendations and be able to back them up. This is clearly the part of the analysis that is the most unstructured, and therefore the most difficult. You must be able to *synthesize,* or combine, a number of seemingly unrelated facts into a coherent whole to reach a decision. Because almost every system is different in some respect, you can't depend on a textbook or formula approach to help you here. The ability to synthesize is characterized by a high level of common sense.

Report to Management

After collecting and analyzing the data, the systems analyst must report findings to management. This report covers many of the same subjects as the report at the end of the preliminary investigation, but it is much more thorough. The length and detail of the report should be sufficient to convince management whether it should or should not proceed to the next stage of development, system design.

PHASE III: SYSTEM DESIGN

If the analysis phase indicates that a new system is needed, the system design phase of the development process is begun. The **system design** phase normally consists of four steps:

1.   Review the goals and scope of the project.

2.   Develop a model of the new system.

3.   Perform a detailed analysis of benefits and costs.

4.   Prepare a system design report.

Review the Goals and Scope of the Project

The design of the new system must conform to the goals and scope approved by management in the analysis phase. Thus it is always wise to review these matters carefully before proceeding with the design. They define both the direction and the limits of the development of the project.

Develop a Model of the New System

Once the analyst understands the nature of the design problem, it is usually helpful to draw a number of diagrams of the new system. Both the data flow diagrams and system flowcharts discussed earlier can show how data will logically flow through the new system, as well as how the various physical components of the systems will fit together.

When designing a system, the analyst must take into account output requirements; input requirements; data access, data organization, and storage needs; processing requirements; system controls; and personnel and procedures. Some of the issues that must be covered in the design specification are given in Figure 16-6.

Analysis of Benefits and Costs

As you probably already know, most organizations are acutely sensitive to costs, including computer system costs. Costs include both the initial investment in hardware and software and ongoing costs such as personnel and maintenance. Some benefits can be computed easily by calculating the amount of labor saved, the reduction in paperwork, and so on. These are sometimes called *tangible benefits,* because they are easy to quantify in dollars.

Other benefits, such as better service to customers or improved information for decision makers, are more difficult to convert into dollar amounts. These are often called *intangible benefits.* Clearly the existence of intangible benefits makes it more difficult for management to reach firm decisions. On projects with a high proportion of such benefits, management must ask such questions as, "Are the new services that we can offer to customers worth the $100,000 it will cost us?" In comparing alternative ways to spend its money, management must also take into account taxes and the timing of benefits and costs.

System Design Report

Once the design has been completed, and benefits and costs assessed, the analyst prepares a report for management. This report should provide all the facts that must be weighed before final approval can be given to the system. The analyst might preface such a report with a three- to five-page cover letter summarizing the primary recommendations, the reasoning used to draw conclusions, and other important information. The report itself contains all the details on the system design as well as the associated costs and benefits.

SYSTEM DESIGN ISSUES

OUTPUT CONSIDERATIONS
- What types of information do users need?

- How often is this information needed? Annually? Monthly? Daily? On demand?

- What output devices and media are necessary to provide the required information?

- How should output be formatted or arranged so that it can easily be understood by users?

INPUT CONSIDERATIONS
- What data need to be gathered?

- How often do data need to be gathered?

- What input devices and media are required for data collection?

STORAGE CONSIDERATIONS
- How will data be accessed and, therefore, organized?

- What storage capacity is required?

- How fast must data be accessed?

- What storage devices are appropriate?

PROCESSING CONSIDERATIONS
- What type of "processing power" is required? A mainframe? A minicomputer? A microcomputer?

- What special processing environments must be considered? A communications network? A database processing environment?

SYSTEM CONTROLS
- What measures must be taken to ensure that data are secure from unauthorized use, theft, and natural disasters?

- What measures must be taken to ensure the accuracy and integrity of data going in and information going out?

- What measures must be taken to ensure the privacy of individuals represented by the data?

PERSONNEL AND PROCEDURES
- What personnel are needed to run the system?

- What procedures should be followed on the job?

Figure 16-6.   Issues to cover during the system design specification.

PHASE IV: SYSTEM ACQUISITION

Once a system has been designed and the required types of software and hardware have been specified, the analyst must decide from which vendors to acquire the necessary components. This decision lies at the heart of the **system acquisition** phase.

The Request for Quotation (RFQ)

Many organizations, especially governmental ones, formulate their buying or leasing needs by preparing a document called a **Request for Quotation (RFQ).** This document contains a list of technical specifications for equipment and software, determined during the system design phase. An RFQ may range in length from a few pages to hundreds, depending on the magnitude and complexity of the acquisition. The RFQ is sent to all vendors who might satisfy the organization's needs.

Evaluating Bids

Once vendors have submitted their bids—or quotes—in response to the RFQ, the organization acquiring the resources must decide which bid to accept. Two useful tools to employ in making this choice are a vendor rating system and a benchmark test.

One system for rating vendors is illustrated in Figure 16-7. In many **vendor rating systems,** such as the one in the figure, important criteria for selecting computer system resources are identified and each is given a

Criterion	Weight (Maximum Score)	Vendor 1 Score	Vendor 2 Score
Hardware	60	60	40
Software	80	70	70
Cost	70	50	65
Ease of use	80	70	50
Modularity	50	30	30
Vendor support	50	50	50
Documentation	30	30	20
		360	325

Vendor 1 has
highest total score

Figure 16-7.   A point-scoring approach for evaluating vendors' bids.

weight. For example, in Figure 16-7, the "60" for hardware and "30" for documentation may be loosely interpreted to mean that hardware is twice as important as documentation to this organization. Each vendor who submits an acceptable bid is rated on each criterion, with the associated weight representing the maximum possible score. The buyer then totals the scores and chooses, possibly, the vendor with the highest total. Although such a rating tool does not guarantee that the best vendor will always have the highest point total, it does have the advantage of being simple to apply and objective. If several people are involved in the selection decision, individual biases tend to be averaged out.

Some organizations, after tentatively selecting a vendor, make their choice conditional on the successful completion of a "test drive," or **benchmark test.** Such a test normally consists of running a pilot version of the new system on the hardware and software of the vendor under consideration. To do this the acquiring organization generally visits the

tomorrow

PLANNING FOR TOMORROW BY COMPUTER

A Look at Project Management Software

One of the most important functions of anyone in a planning role, including the systems analyst, is project management. Any project—such as getting a group of programmers to collaborate on a solution to a long programming problem, installing a new computer system and getting it to work, or even bringing a new product to the marketplace—is marked by various milestones that must be reached according to a certain schedule.

For example, If you're planning to create a product and sell it, costs, profits, and risks must be projected so that venture capital may be obtained. Or if you are installing a new computer system, applications have to be converted, people need to be trained, new components must be added and tested, and so forth. When does each activity take place? How much time do you allow for each activity? How vulnerable is the timetable to future delays that inevitably occur? How do you control all of these activities and plan for contingencies?

The answers, of course, lie in using some sensible approach to project management. A number of well-known project management methods currently exist—PERT, CPM, Gantt charts, simulation modeling, decision trees, Bayesian decision models, and a variety of budgeting procedures. When one or more of

Computing power and software have added a new dimension.

these tools are packaged into a software product, the product is known as *project management software.* Although many of these project management techniques were developed independently of the computer revolution, computing power in general, and the surge in microcomputer-based software, have certainly added a new dimension to their usefulness and applicability.

benchmark testing center of the vendor and attempts to determine how well the hardware/software configuration will work if installed. Benchmark tests are expensive and far from foolproof. It's possible that the pilot system will perform admirably at the benchmark site but that the real system, when eventually installed at the site of the acquiring organization, will not.

PHASE V: SYSTEM IMPLEMENTATION

Once arrangements have been made with one or more vendors for delivery of computer resources, the **system implementation** phase begins. This phase includes all the remaining tasks that are necessary to make the system operational and successful.

The computer has improved project management techniques in two major ways. First, because computers can crunch numbers much more quickly than can people working by hand, the projects solved by computer can be very large and complex. Moreover, one can induce uncertainty about the future and randomness into the events, so the project manager can get a good picture of the downside risk of any particular project strategy. It's not only important for mangagement to know what is likely to happen, but also what the consequences will be if something goes wrong.

Second, computer graphics technologies provide us quickly with a good visual sense of what project strategies look like. The project management software enables us to test new strategies quickly and produce sketches of them on the display screen. Project managers available today typically allow us to create entire projects on screen, allow us to schedule tasks over days or years, make it easy for us to generate planning information on each project resource or cost center, and enable us to examine in detail specific portions of the project.

Despite the strides made by computers to enhance the job of project management, more is yet to come. As artificial intelligence techniques creep into software in all areas, we can expect to see more powerful project managers that suggest new ways of organizing activities. In other words we describe the project to the computer system and the system organizes it completely for us. To some extent this is possible today, but only for simple projects. Tomorrow's project managers will have the savvy of both a master scheduler and a super cost accountant.

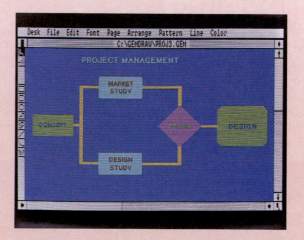

To ensure that the system will be working by a certain date, the analyst must prepare a timetable. One tool for helping with this task is a *Gantt chart*. The chart shows when certain activities related to implementation must start and finish. Packaged programs called *project management software* are widely available to prepare Gantt charts and other such scheduling tools (see box on pages 486–487).

Implementation consists of many activities, including converting programs and data files from the old system to the new one, debugging converted and new applications programs, documentation, training, appraising the performance of the new system, and ongoing maintenance. If the system has been designed well, it should be flexible enough to accommodate changes over a reasonable period of time with minimal disruption. If at some point, however, a major change becomes necessary, another system will be needed to replace the current one. At this point the systems development cycle, from the preliminary investigation to implementation, begins all over again.

PROTOTYPING

Often, in developing systems, it's inappropriate to follow the five phases of systems development in perfect sequence. Some hardware and software may have to be acquired early—perhaps as part of the system design phase—to direct the remainder of the development effort. There are several reasons for this.

First, systems often take too long to analyze, design, and implement. By the time a system is finally put into operation, important new needs surface that were not part of the original plan. Second, the system being developed is often *not* the right one. Managers almost always find it difficult to express their informational needs, and it is not until they begin to use a system that they discover what it is they really need.

To avoid the potentially expensive disaster that could result from having to go through every phase of development before users ever see a system, many analysts have advocated prototyping as part of the design step. The focus in **prototyping** is on developing a small model, or *prototype,* of the overall system. Users work with the prototype and suggest modifications. As soon as the prototype is refined to the point where higher management feels confident that a larger version of the system will be successful, either the prototype can be gradually expanded or the organization can go ahead with the remaining steps of systems development.

Summary and Key Terms

A **system** is a collection of elements and procedures that interact to accomplish a goal. The function of many systems, manual or computerized, is to keep an organization well managed and running smoothly.

Systems development is a process that consists of analyzing a system, designing a new system or making modifications to the old one, acquiring the needed hardware and software, and getting the new or modified system to work. Systems development may be required for any number of reasons; for example, changes in government regulations or some new computer technology.

The chief information officer, or someone with a similar title, holds primary responsibility for the overall direction of systems development. The technical details are the responsibility of the data processing department. The **systems analyst** is the person in the data processing department who is involved most closely with the development of systems from beginning to end.

Systems development is often divided into five phases: preliminary investigation, systems analysis, system design, system acquisition, and system implementation. These phases are often collectively referred to as the **systems development cycle** (or **systems development life cycle**), since they describe a system from the time it is first studied until it is put into use. When a new business pressure necessitates a change in a system, the steps of the cycle begin anew.

The first thing the systems analyst does in a new assignment is to conduct a **preliminary investigation.** This investigation addresses the nature of the problem under study, the potential scope of the systems development project, the possible solutions, and the costs and benefits of these solutions. At the end of the preliminary investigation, the analyst writes a report to management with a brief description of the problem and some recommendations.

If, on the basis of the report evolving out of the preliminary investigation, management decides to pursue systems development further, the **systems analysis** phase begins. During this phase the main objectives are to study the current system in depth to find out how it works and what it does, to compare these findings with some conception of what the system should be doing, and to present a detailed report to management. Stated simply, the three objectives of systems analysis are fact collection, analysis, and a report to management.

The goal of fact collection is to gather evidence about what the current system does and what its users need. Four useful sources are written documents, questionnaires, interviews, and personal observation.

Facts, once gathered, must be analyzed. A number of tools are useful for this task, including **data flow diagrams, system flowcharts,** and checklists. The object of the analysis is to synthesize facts to reach concrete conclusions and recommendations.

After collecting and analyzing the data, the systems analyst must report the findings to management. This report covers many of the same subjects as the report at the end of the preliminary investigation, but it is much more thorough.

The **system design** phase of systems development consists of four steps: (1) reviewing the goals and scope of the project, (2) developing a model of the new system, (3) performing a detailed analysis of benefits and costs, and (4) preparing a system design report.

Once a system has been designed, and the required types of software and hardware have been specified, the analyst must decide from which vendors to acquire the necessary components. This decision lies at the heart of the **system acquisition** phase.

Many organizations formulate their buying or leasing needs by preparing a document called a **Request for Quotation (RFQ).** This document contains a list of technical specifications for equipment and software, determined during the system design phase.

Once vendors have submitted their bids in response to the RFQ, the organization acquiring the resources must decide which bid to accept. Two useful tools for making such a choice are a vendor rating system and a benchmark test. In most **vendor rating systems,** important criteria for selecting computer system resources are identified and weighted. Data processing personnel then rate each vendor on each criterion. A **benchmark test** normally consists of running a pilot version of the new system on the hardware and software of the vendors under consideration.

Once arrangements have been made with one or more vendors for delivery of computer resources, the **system implementation** phase begins. This phase includes all the remaining tasks that are necessary to make the system operational and successful, including programming and file conversion, debugging, documentation, training, performance appraisal, and maintenance.

Prototyping is an approach to systems development in which the five phases of the systems development life cycle are not conducted in perfect sequence. With prototyping users work with a small model (or prototype) of the new system and suggest modifications to direct the remainder of the development effort.

Review Exercises

Fill-in Questions

1. A(n) _____ committee composed of executives in key departments and other members of top management normally approves a plan for systems development.
2. The job of the _____ is to plan and implement systems in an organization.

3. At the end of the preliminary investigation, the analyst writes a report to _____ with a brief description of the problem and some recommendations.
4. Combining a number of seemingly interrelated facts into a coherent whole in order to draw conclusions is known as _____.
5. Developing a model of a new system is part of the _____ phase of systems development.
6. Benefits that are easy to quantify in dollars are called _____ benefits.
7. In many _____ systems, important criteria for selecting computer system resources are identified by the buying organization and each is given a weight. Subsequently each vendor submitting a bid is rated on each criterion, with the associated weight representing the maximum possible score.
8. A(n) _____ consists of running a pilot version of a new system on the hardware and/or software of a vendor under acquisition consideration.

Matching Questions

Match each term with its description.

a. System design
b. System implementation
c. Preliminary investigation
d. Systems analysis
e. System acquisition

_____ 1. The final phase of systems development.
_____ 2. The phase of systems development that involves studying the current system in depth.
_____ 3. The phase of systems development that involves RFQ preparation, vendor rating systems, and benchmark tests.
_____ 4. The first phase of systems development.
_____ 5. The phase of systems development that follows systems analysis.

Discussion Questions

1. Provide some examples of systems, both in business and in society.
2. What is systems development?
3. What are the main duties of the systems analyst?
4. Identify the five phases of systems development.
5. What is the purpose of the preliminary investigation?
6. Why are reports sent to management at the end of both the preliminary investigation and systems analysis phases of development?
7. Why must output requirements be addressed before all other considerations when one is developing a model of a new system?
8. What types of items should be incorporated in the reports sent to management by the systems analyst?
9. What is the purpose of the RFQ?
10. How does prototyping differ from traditional systems development?

Module E

COMPUTERS IN SOCIETY

No study of computers is complete without a look at the impact these machines have had on the very fabric of the society in which we live. In the workplace computers have created many jobs and careers, but have also made others obsolete. Likewise, in society as a whole, they have created both opportunities and problems. Many people praise them as a major source of progress. Others wonder if we are indeed any better off today than we were before ENIAC.

Chapter 17 covers the important subject of computer-related jobs and careers. Chapter 18 discusses many of the opportunities and problems created by the computer revolution.

Chapter 17

Career
Opportunities

Chapter Outline

OVERVIEW
JOBS AND CAREERS
    Computer Jobs
    Career Options
FORMAL EDUCATION FOR ENTRY-LEVEL JOBS
    Computer Curricula
MAINTAINING SKILLS AND DEVELOPING NEW ONES

Objectives

After completing this chapter you should be able to:

1.   Identify the various types of employment available to those seeking a job in the computer field.
2.   Understand the alternatives available to those seeking a career as a computer professional.
3.   Describe the differences among computer curricula offered by colleges and universities.
4.   Describe the resources available to computer professionals as they continue learning about computers.

OVERVIEW

If you're interested in obtaining computer-related employment, welcome to a relatively "hot" job market. The demand for computer professionals in government and industry has been booming over the past decade, a trend expected to continue well into the 1990s. In 1980 some 1.5 million people were involved in the computer industry in the United States. The U.S. Department of Labor predicts that this figure will reach 2 million by 1990, a 33 percent increase. Many of these jobs will not have existed ten years earlier.

The explosive demand for computer professionals has been accompanied by an unusually acute shortage of qualified people, a trend also expected to persist for some time. A major cause of this lack is the short supply of teachers in the field. Because graduates in computer fields can earn almost as much as their professors as soon as they graduate, many would-be instructors are lured away by high-paying jobs in government and industry. Without teachers, colleges and universities find it difficult to expand their academic programs to meet the growing demand. Also, schools find computer curricula expensive to maintain. Not only must top salaries be paid for good teachers, but costly hardware and software must be continually acquired. When academic budgets are being cut, as is often the case today, this need is difficult to fulfill.

Thus a degree in a computer field (if you get into a program) will probably land you several job offers and a good starting salary if your grades are high enough. But beware. Being a computer professional is not suitable for everyone. If you have neither an aptitude for nor an interest in computers, you'd best try your hand at something else as a career. As in other fields, high salaries are generally earned only by people with talent and dedication. Yet even though you may not become a computer professional, computers will probably help you at your job.

This chapter begins by introducing you to some of the jobs and careers possible in the computer field. Next it covers the various educational paths to follow to prepare for entry-level jobs. Finally, it discusses finding a job and ways of maintaining professional skills and developing new ones.

JOBS AND CAREERS

There are so many jobs that classify one as a "computer professional" that it's impossible to cover them all adequately in a single chapter. To set some limit, we'll consider only those that involve supplying users with computer-generated information. These jobs, which require substantial training in a specific computer field, include equipment operators, programmers, systems analysts, and computer managers. Excluded are computer salespeople, personnel engaged in manufacturing computer hardware, and service engineers.

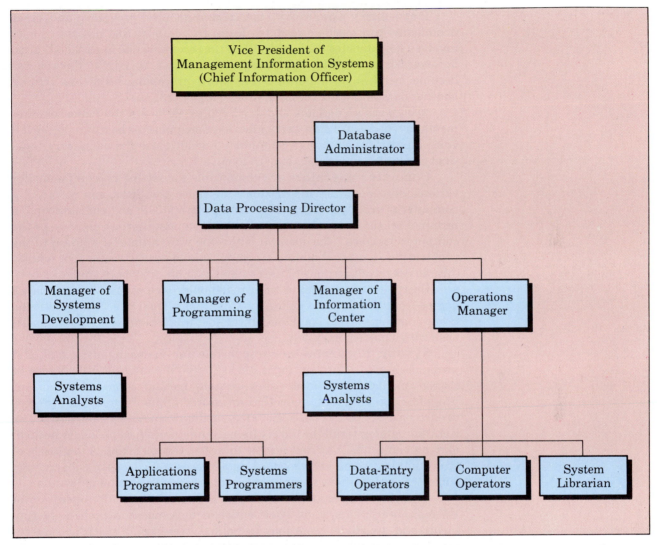

Figure 17-1. *An organization chart showing common computer jobs and their relation to one another.*

In this section we'll look first at some specific jobs that make one a computer professional, and then we'll consider ways to combine jobs into various career paths. Figure 17-1 shows how computer jobs are organized in a typical organization.

Computer Jobs

COMPUTER OPERATIONS PERSONNEL. Such personnel include data-entry operators, computer equipment operators, system librarians, and managers who supervise the day-to-day running of a computing center. All these people perform a service for others who work with large computer systems. Their responsibility lies in making the accounting and information systems operating environment as efficient as possible.

Data-entry operators transcribe data files, programs, and other documents into machine-readable form. In the past this process usually involved keypunching onto cards. With the recent decline in punched cards, however, data entry on key-to-tape, key-to-disk, and OCR devices has become increasingly important. The word processing boom has created another data-entry job: the *word processing operator.*

A high-school diploma and good typing skills are the major requirements for entry-level data-entry jobs. At some point in the future, however, voice input technology may completely revolutionize the data-entry function, and make typing skills superfluous.

Computer operators are responsible for setting up equipment for various jobs, mounting and dismounting tapes and disks, and monitoring computer operations (Figure 17-2). If a program is in an "endless loop," a terminal breaks down, a user is performing an unauthorized activity, or the computer "crashes," the operator is the one who initiates a solution to the problem. Since many commercial computers run nearly twenty-four hours a day, an operator's responsibilities extend over an eight-hour shift.

Entry-level personnel in this area should have at least an associate's degree from a community college or a certificate from a technical institute. Some companies train operators on the job, whereas others require experience with a particular system.

System librarians are responsible for managing data files and programs stored offline on tapes, disks, microfilm, and all other types of storage media. These media may contain backup copies of important programs and data files, items that are stored offline because they are not needed on a day-to-day basis, and archival data kept for legal purposes. The librarian catalogues all the library items, purges materials no longer needed, and prevents unauthorized access to restricted material. A high-school education and some knowledge of data processing concepts are generally sufficient qualifications for an entry-level position as a system librarian.

Computer operations managers oversee the entire operation of the main computer system. Their duties include scheduling jobs to be run, hiring and assigning operations personnel, supervising machine maintenance, and monitoring operations to make sure the system runs efficiently. This is not an entry-level position. Computer operations managers often must have at least three to five years of experience in the operations field.

PROGRAMMERS.   Programmers generally fall into two categories: systems programmers and applications programmers.

Systems programmers write and maintain systems software. Since this class of programs is very technical, systems programmers must have a good technical knowledge of computers. They often have had rigorous training in subjects such as assembly language, compiler design, operating systems, and the architecture of computer systems. An entry-level job usually requires a college degree in a technically oriented field such as computer science.

Applications programmers write and maintain the programs that serve end users. Because there's still a shortage of people in this area in many parts of the country, entry-level requirements vary widely. Many

Figure 17-2. A computer operator at work.

applications programmers have computer-related degrees from four-year or community colleges. Others are certified by technical institutes. In some cases companies hungry for applications programmers have hired people with degrees in other areas virtually "off the street," trained them, and pressed them into service. In general, however, a person seeking an entry-level job as an applications programmer should have a college degree in a computer-related field or in an applied field such as business or science (with a significant number of computer courses supplementing the training in the chosen applied field). A knowledge of accounting and COBOL is also useful.

Some people make programming a career, advancing from trainee to senior-level or chief programmer. In some cases advancement involves specializing in a certain area, such as banking or database applications. It is also possible in many organizations to move from programming to a position in systems analysis. This is not always the best career path, however. Programmers have to spend a lot of time working alone on technical problems, and many have chosen their profession because they enjoy solitude and independence. Systems analysts, in contrast, spend most of their time dealing with other people and must have excellent communications skills.

SYSTEMS ANALYSTS. **Systems analysts** plan and implement computer systems. They form the critical interface between management and users and between users and programmers. Management dictates the priority of the problems to be solved. When given a problem, the analyst must work with users to find the best solutions. The analyst then translates these solutions into a system design and sets the technical specifications for applications programs to be written by programmers. The general duties of the analyst are covered in detail in Chapters 9 and 16. Recently the surge of microcomputers into the office has created new specialized roles for the systems analyst. For example, the *information center consultant* is an analyst who advises current and potential microcomputer users on micro-computing needs.

Good systems analysts literally must be jacks of all trades. They must have a high level of technical knowledge about computers, computer systems, and the computer industry in order to design state-of-the-art systems. They also have to be personable and possess excellent communications skills, since they have to interact with many different kinds of people, including managers, users, and programmers. They must be as comfortable speaking "computerese" with experts as they are speaking plain English with people who have no technical knowledge. Systems analysts should also have some background in business, since most data processing systems are business oriented. Analysts should certainly be familiar with business terms, such as *accounts receivable, pro-forma cash flow, direct costs, gross margin, inventory turnover,* and so on. Some knowledge of accounting is a particularly helpful asset.

Many systems analysts have college degrees in computer-related fields. Some positions, such as the programmer/analyst slot in small companies (which combines the programmer and systems analyst functions), are entry level. Most companies require systems analysts to have a few years of computer-related experience.

DATA PROCESSING AND MIS MANAGEMENT. At the highest level of computer management are positions such as data processing director and vice president of information systems. The exact titles of these jobs vary from company to company.

The **data processing director** oversees all data processing personnel, including programmers, systems analysts, and operations personnel (see Figure 17-1). He or she is given a budget and a long-range plan by the vice president of information systems. In turn the director sets up budgets and plans for the areas under his or her control. Generally this position requires several years of computer-related experience in a variety of jobs.

The **vice president of information systems**—sometimes referred to as the **chief information officer (CIO)**—oversees routine accounting and information systems activities as well as planning in the newer computer-related areas such as teleprocessing, database processing, and decision support systems. He or she also works with key company executives to establish the overall direction of computer activities for the company, such as determining a strategy to coordinate the purchase and development of microcomputer-related resources in the organization. The job usually requires a master's degree in business or computers and extensive computer-related and managerial work experience. A recent survey indicated that the average work experience for a vice president of information systems is almost fifteen years.

Figure 17-3 shows some recent average salaries reported for computer-related jobs. Naturally, overall averages can be misleading, as some industries and firms in some parts of the country pay better than others.

Career Options

There are many ways to build computer-based careers. One possibilty is to begin with an entry-level job and then move up the organizational ladder into positions of greater and greater responsibility. Suppose, for example, you joined a company with an organization like that shown in Figure 17-1. You might start as a programmer trainee; later become a full-fledged applications programmer; and then, after many years' experience, become a manager. A managerial position requires a broad exposure to a number of computer functions as well as an ability to plan and to direct other people. If you supplemented your work experience with additional education or an advanced degree, you might continue up the ladder to a high executive position.

A second possibility is to specialize in a highly marketable area of data processing where the demand for your services is likely to remain strong. There are several ways to do this. Some people specialize by focusing on a certain *industry*. For example, you might choose to become an expert in the analysis and design of computer systems for banks or insurance companies. Or perhaps it's the airline industry that fascinates you. In any case, if you have detailed knowledge of the kinds of computer-related problems faced

Job Title	Annual Salary
Chief information officer	$55,519
Director of data processing	$44,647
Senior systems programmer	$35,416
Senior systems analyst	$34,910
Senior applications programmer	$28,730
Senior systems analyst/programmer	$31,523
Junior systems programmer	$21,687
Junior systems analyst	$25,121
Junior applications programmer	$19,498
Junior systems analyst/programmer	$20,602
Manager of computer operations	$30,364
Computer operator	$15,960
System librarian	$16,611
Data-entry operator	$14,374
Word processing operator	$14,592

Source: *Datamation,* September 15, 1985, page 94. Reprinted with permission of DATAMATION magazine. Copyright by Technical Publishing Company, a Dun and Bradstreet Company, 1985. All rights reserved.

Figure 17-3.   *Recent salaries for computer-related jobs.*

by a specific industry, and if you know how to solve those problems, you will have a competitive advantage when seeking jobs in that industry. Another way to specialize is by choosing a specific *technology*—for example, database processing, teleprocessing, word processing, or small business systems. A database expert, for instance, would be in demand by any company using a database system. Still another option is to specialize in some computer-related *function.* People who can write clear, concise documentation that users can easily understand, for example, are a great asset to any organization.

A third possibility is to mold a career around a certain life-style. Some people, for example, prefer to work part time or during unusual hours. Programming is ideally suited for these people as it allows a great deal of independence. Programmers are pretty much on their own once they understand the technical specifications of a project. Some programmers telecommute—they do their jobs at home on a terminal or microcomputer. This not only saves them gas and commuting time, but also can spare them from unproductive office politics. And if they get their jobs done on schedule, no one cares if they take the afternoon off or work from 1 A.M. to 5 A.M. Other prime candidates for working at home are data-entry clerks and documentation writers. Of course, working at home is not for everyone. Some people need the social stimulus of an office to work well.

FORMAL EDUCATION FOR ENTRY-LEVEL JOBS

Attending school is one of the best ways to train for an entry-level position in computers. Although you can learn a great deal on your own or through on-the-job training, a degree or certificate is often a requirement for obtaining a job. It convinces potential employers that you've had formal training in certain areas and that you've met the standards of a particular institution. In other words, it legitimizes your claim that you know something and can work hard. Besides, most firms would prefer their new employees to arrive on their first day fully equipped to do useful work.

There are many types of schools (beyond high school) that offer education in computers. These include four-year colleges and universities, two-year community colleges, and technical institutes. Course offerings vary widely among such schools. It's wrong to assume that four-year colleges and universities offer better computer education than the community colleges or technical institutes. In many cases the reverse is actually true. And it doesn't necessarily follow that the so-called prestige schools have computer curricula superior to those of lesser known institutions. Computer education is a relatively new phenomenon. Schools that have worked aggressively to make it a top priority are generally the ones that have the best resources and provide the best training.

Computer Curricula

If you're interested in pursuing studies in computers, there are many curricula available to you, the most common of which follow. The specific names given to such programs vary from school to school.

DATA PROCESSING (COMPUTER INFORMATION SYSTEMS).   The **data processing** (or **computer information systems**) **curriculum** is often coordinated by a college or department of business. The primary emphasis is on directly providing services for end users, and many of the computer courses have a "business applications" flavor. These courses often include introductory data processing, microcomputer fundamentals, BASIC or FORTRAN, COBOL, systems analysis and design, database processing, and management information systems. Some schools also offer training in RPG, office systems, and computerized auditing, as well. Because the degree program is coordinated by the business school, students must also take several business courses. These courses can be particularly helpful to anyone aspiring to be a systems analyst or manager. Most of the graduates of these programs go on to entry-level work as applications programmers or programmer/analysts.

COMPUTER SCIENCE.   The **computer science curriculum** is often coordinated by a college or department of computer science, mathematics, or engineering. The training provided is much more technical than that in a data processing/computer information systems program, since the primary emphasis is on the design of software. Graduates of these programs often

tomorrow

UNIVERSITIES PROMOTING MICRO USE FOR MBA STUDENTS

**Learn Computers Today, If Tomorrow
You Want an MBA**

Many students with backgrounds in business, computer science, and other fields go on to get MBA (*M*aster of *B*usiness *A*dministration) degrees. Graduate business programs enrich one's knowledge of business principles, and often sharpen one's ability to make sound decisions. They are often prerequisites to entry into or advancement in some firms. Because most computing is done in businesses, and promotion to the higher levels of the corporate ranks requires some knowledge of business and management principles, MBAs are very popular degrees for computer-oriented people considering careers in business.

Both undergraduate and masters' programs in business schools heavily emphasize computing courses. In fact at some universities, business schools have traditionally accounted for a quarter to a third of the campuswide computing, even though they only represent 10 percent or so of the students. Recently, students seeking MBAs at some schools have been required to have their own microcomputers when they start classes. At Harvard's Graduate School of Business, for example, entering students must own IBM PCs or IBM-PC-compatibles.

Even at schools that don't require entering MBAs to have microcomputers, the use of microcomputers—and computers in general—is heavily stressed. At Dartmouth's Tuck School (see photo), for example, the computer is considered integral to about half of the courses offered—and over half of the courses use the computer for classroom demonstrations. As more and more computer-trained graduate students enter the academic ranks, these percentages are bound to increase, perhaps dramatically.

The surge in microcomputers in business schools mirrors their surge in business.

According to Future Computing Inc., a Texas-based consulting firm, approximately 5–6 percent of office workers in the Fortune 2000 firms used microcomputers. By 1990, the firm predicts, this usage should increase to 50 percent.

By far the most useful and universal tool stressed in MBA programs is the spreadsheet. MBA students must master planning skills that involve scores of profit and cost areas, and be able to make fast, sophisticated judgments.

So if an MBA is in your future, consider getting familiar with microcomputers, and especially spreadsheets, today.

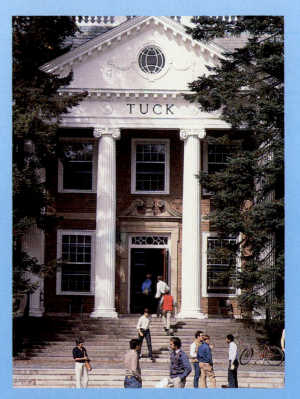

Dartmouth's Tuck School: Making the computer an integral part of MBA education.

find jobs as systems programmers, with responsibility for designing compilers, operating systems, and utility programs. They are also sought for the design of productivity software packages such as database management systems. A surprising number of graduates of these programs, however, take positions as applications programmers. These students have usually prepared themselves by cross-registering for business-oriented courses such as COBOL, database processing, and systems analysis and design. Some even take an accounting course or two, since accounting is generally regarded as the language of business. Of course, cross-registration works both ways. Data processing/computer information systems majors often enroll in computer science courses, such as assembly-language programming and operating systems, which enable them to sharpen their technical skills.

COMPUTER ENGINEERING. Some schools also support a **computer engineering curriculum.** This degree program is designed primarily to prepare students to design computer hardware systems. Graduates of such programs are usually sought by hardware manufacturers.

COMPUTER OPERATIONS. In addition to their other computer offerings, community colleges and technical institutes typically provide practical training in **computer operations.** Students enrolled in these courses often plan to become computer or data-entry operators. Courses involve a great deal of hands-on, practical training, thus enabling students to move on quickly to entry-level positions in government and industry.

MAINTAINING SKILLS AND DEVELOPING NEW ONES

One of the things that people find exciting about the computer field is its rapid rate of change. Someone with "computer fever" trying out new equipment or software is like an excitable five-year-old opening birthday presents. But rapid change also has a less pleasant side—the need for constant retraining. When the computer system you've used for the past five years is unplugged and wheeled away to be replaced by a newer one, you and your co-workers will have to retrain. If the new system involves many recent technologies that you aren't familiar with, the retraining may take a long time.

Retraining is an ongoing fact of life in the computer field. If you want to keep yourself current and marketable, you must have some knowledge of the latest technologies. There are a variety of ways in which you can effectively "retool" yourself or develop new skills. Among them are attending classes, seminars, and exhibitions; reading; and participating in professional associations.

ATTENDING CLASSES. Many universities, community colleges, and computer institutes offer courses on a nondegree or continuing-education basis.

These courses are particularly visible in large cities, where there's a large market for such services. Many of the courses are taught at night to accommodate people who work during the day. Some companies also hold regular classes, and even have schools for training employees in the latest computer technologies.

A more ambitious possibility is to enroll in a graduate school. Many universities have master's and doctoral degree programs in areas such as computer information systems, computer science, and computer engineering.

ATTENDING SEMINARS.   Many individuals and companies offer seminars on a variety of computer topics. An expert on teleprocessing may travel the lecture circuit with an intensive, three-day seminar on the subject, charging, say, $350 per person. The speaker, for example, may present the seminar in Phoenix, then in Los Angeles, then in San Francisco, and so on. Some seminars, especially those conducted by hardware and software vendors, are free. Many computer trade publications publish a list of seminars and details about them.

ATTENDING EXHIBITIONS.   Vendors of computer products frequently participate in joint trade shows to demonstrate new hardware and software to the public. Three of the largest trade shows are the annual U.S. National Computer Conference (NCC); the international, several-times-a-year Computer Dealer Expo (COMDEX) shows; and San Francisco's annual West Coast Computer Faire. Each of these shows attracts hundreds of vendors and thousands of visitors.

READING.   This is one of the most inexpensive ways to learn about new technologies. Fortunately, computer literature is abundant, and several sources carry up-to-date information.

The most current information is found in the so-called computer newspapers. *Computerworld,* which many professionals regard as the *Wall Street Journal* of the computer establishment, contains news items and special features of general interest to a wide audience of professionals. There are several other newspapers targeted to smaller audiences—such as *PC Week,* which specializes in developments of particular interest to owners of IBM PCs or IBM-PC-compatible computers.

A second source of current information is the topical reports that are issued periodically by companies such as *Auerbach* and *Datapro* (see Figure 17-4). These reports, which are usually fewer than thirty pages in length, are assembled into looseleaf binders. Each binder contains current information on related topics that is not easy to find in other places. Even though some of the information may also be available in textbooks, these topical reports are far more current. Also, these reports often contain useful comparisons of specific computer products.

A third source of written information is the computer journals (see Figure 17-5). Many journals are published monthly. Each is generally targeted to a specific audience—small-computer users, the banking industry, and so on. Each journal prints articles of potential interest to its readership.

Figure 17-4.   Some commercially available research reports.

Figure 17-5.   A selection of computer journals and newspapers.

A fourth source is books. If there's a specific topic you want to learn about in some depth, there are generally several books available to meet this need. Some of these are written at very technical levels, whereas others are aimed at audiences who are relatively unsophisticated about computers. One way to learn more about computers is to go to your local library or bookstore and browse through the shelves devoted to computer books, looking for ones that seem interesting and readable.

A fifth source is the information provided by the computer-product vendor. Although such literature is often biased toward the vendor's products, some of it is extremely well presented and informative. And much of it is available without charge.

JOINING PROFESSIONAL ASSOCIATIONS.   Computer people often join professional associations to keep up to date. Members of these associations stay current through meetings, workshops, conferences, and informal contacts with other people with similar interests. Many associations have local chapters in major cities. Organizations such as the ACM (Association for

Professional Computer Organizations

. . . AND A GREAT SOURCE FOR JOB CONTACTS

There are many professional associations serving the computing community. A sample of the more important of these associations is listed here with a brief description of each.

AFIPS.   The American Federation of Information Processing Societies is a national consortium of professional organizations. Its main function is to represent the interests of its member organizations and to distribute information among them. Some of the constituent associations of AFIPS include the American Institute of Certified Public Accountants (AICPA), the Institute of Electrical and Electronics Engineers (IEEE), and the American Statistical Association (ASA), as well as several of the organizations listed below.

ACM.   The Association for Computing Machinery is the largest professional association devoted specifically to computers. The ACM helps to advance the study of an extremely wide range of computer-related areas, including information processing, small systems development, pro-gramming languages, and computer education.

ASM.   The Association for Systems Management is an international organization dedicated to the advancement and continuing education of systems analysts and systems managers in business, industry, and government.

BDPA.   The Black Data Processing Associates, open to people of all races, is dedicated to the professional advancement of minority groups in the data processing community.

DPMA.   The Data Processing Management Association consists of approximately 300 chapters. Its membership includes managers and supervisors of data processing installations, educators and executives with a special interest in data processing, and representatives of vendor organizations. Its activities include many of those supported by ACM, with a particular emphasis on data processing management.

ICCP.   The Institute for Certification of Computer Professionals is a nonprofit orga-nization established to test and certify computer personnel. A major activity is the administration of the Certificate in Data Processing (CDP) examination. The examination consists of five sections— data processing equipment, computer programming and software, principles of management, quantitative methods, and systems analysis and design. All people sitting for the exam must have at least five years of related work experience. Recently the ICCP established the Certificate in Computer Programming (CCP), which gives formal recognition to competence and experience in programming. These certificates, like degrees from colleges and universities, help establish one's claim to knowledge in certain areas of computing. Independent companies have prepared guides and mini-courses to help candidates pass these examinations.

WDP.   Women in Data Processing, open to both males and females, is dedicated to promoting the entry and advancement of women in data processing.

Computing Machinery) and DPMA (Data Processing Management Association) also have student chapters. The box above lists some major associations. Joining a professional association is often a good way to learn about job openings.

Summary and Key Terms

The demand for computer professionals in government and industry has been booming over the past decade, a trend expected to continue into the 1990s. Computer professionals include operations personnel, programmers, systems analysts, and managers.

Computer operations personnel include people such as data-entry operators, computer equipment operators, system librarians, and operations managers.

Data-entry operators transcribe data files, programs, and other documents into machine-readable form. A high-school diploma and good typing skills are needed.

Computer operators are responsible for setting up equipment for various jobs, mounting and dismounting tapes and disks, and monitoring computer operations. Entry-level personnel should have an associate's degree from a community college or a technical institute certificate.

System librarians are responsible for managing data files and programs stored offline on tapes, disks, microfilm, and all other types of storage media. A high-school education and some knowledge of data processing concepts are needed for an entry-level position.

Computer operations managers oversee the entire operation of the main computer system. Their duties include scheduling jobs to be run, hiring and assigning operations personnel, supervising machine maintenance, and monitoring operations to make sure the system runs efficiently.

Programmers generally fall into one of two categories: systems programmers and applications programmers.

Systems programmers write and maintain systems software. An entry-level job usually requires a college degree in a technical field such as computer science.

Applications programmers write and maintain the programs that serve end users. Someone seeking such an entry-level job should have a college degree in a computer-related field or in an applied field such as business or science.

Systems analysts plan and implement computer systems. They form the critical interface between management and users and, subsequently, between users and programmers. Many systems analysts have college degrees in computer-related fields. They also need a few years of experience.

At the highest level of computer management are positions such as data processing director and vice president of information systems.

The **data processing director** oversees all data processing personnel, including programmers, systems analysts, and operations personnel. Generally, this position requires several years of computer-related experience in a variety of jobs.

The **vice president of information systems**—sometimes referred to as the **chief information officer (CIO)**—oversees routine accounting and information systems activities as well as planning in the newer computer-related areas such as teleprocessing, database processing, and decision support systems. This job usually requires a master's degree in business or computers and extensive computer-related and managerial work experience. A recent survey indicated that the average work experience for a vice president of information systems is almost fifteen years.

There are many ways to build computer-based careers. One possibility is to begin with an entry-level job and then move up the organizational ladder into positions of greater and greater responsibility. A second possiblity is to specialize in a highly marketable area of data processing where the demand for your services is likely to remain strong. For example, many people specialize by concentrating on a specific industry, technology, or function. A third possiblity is to mold a career around a certain life-style.

Going to school is one of the best ways to train for an entry-level position in computers. Many types of schools offer some kind of education in computers, including four-year colleges and universities, two-year community colleges, and technical institutes.

If you're interested in pursuing studies in computers, many curricula are available. The **data processing** (or **computer information systems**) **curriculum** is often coordinated by a college or department of business. The primary emphasis is on directly providing services for end users, and many of the computer courses have a "business applications" flavor. The **computer science curriculum** is often coordinated by a college or department of computer science or engineering. The training provided is geared toward the design of software. Some schools also support a **computer engineering curriculum.** This degree program is designed primarily to prepare students to design computer hardware systems. In addition to their other computer offerings, community colleges and technical institutes typically provide practical training in **computer operations.** Students enrolled in these courses often plan to become computer or data-entry operators.

Retraining is a fact of life in the computer field. There are a variety of ways to maintain your skills and develop new ones. Among them are attending classes, seminars, and exhibitions; reading; and participating in professional associations.

Review Exercises

Fill-in Questions

1. _____ transcribe data files, programs, and other documents into machine-readable form.

2. _____ are responsible for setting up equipment for various jobs, mounting and dismounting tapes and disks, and monitoring computer operations.

3. _____ are responsible for managing data files and programs stored offline on tapes, disks, microfilm, and all other types of storage media.

4. _____ oversee the entire operation of the main computer system. Their duties include scheduling jobs to be run, hiring and assigning operations personnel, supervising machine maintenance, and monitoring operations to make sure the system runs efficiently.

5. _____ write and maintain systems software.

6. _____ write and maintain the programs that serve end users.

7. _____ plan and implement computer systems. They form the critical interface between management and users and, subsequently, between users and programmers.

8. The _____ oversees all data processing personnel, including programmers, systems analysts, and operations personnel.

Matching Questions

Match each term with its description.

a. Computer information systems
(or data processing) curriculum
b. Computer science curriculum
c. Computer engineering curriculum
d. Computer operations curriculum

___ⓒ___ 1. The degree program that is tailored primarily to training students to design computer hardware systems.

_____ 2. The degree program, often coordinated by a college or department of business, that trains students as applications programmers and systems analysts.

_____ 3. The degree program, sometimes coordinated by a college of engineering or department of mathematics, that primarily trains students in the design of systems software.

_____ 4. The degree program that trains students as data-entry operators, computer equipment operators, and the like.

Discussion Questions

1. Why is there such a difference between the demand for computer professionals and the supply of qualified ones?
2. Discuss the academic training or experience required to perform the following jobs: data-entry operator, computer operator, system librarian, computer operations manager, systems programmer, applications programmer, systems analyst, data processing director, vice president of information systems.
3. Describe some ways in which to build computer-based careers.
4. Are all academic computer curricula the same? Discuss.
5. Identify several ways in which you can effectively maintain your computer skills or develop new ones.

Chapter 18

Computers in Our Lives: The Costs and the Benefits

Chapter Outline

Objectives

After completing this chapter you should be able to:

1. Describe some of the health-related concerns people have regarding computers.
2. Explain what is meant by computer crime and describe several types of computer crime.
3. Identify several ways that computer technology can be abused to encroach on people's privacy.
4. Describe several applications where computers have an impact on the day-to-day life of the average person.

513

OVERVIEW

Since the early 1950s, when the era of commercial computing began, computers have rapidly woven their way into the very fabric of modern society. In the process they've created both opportunities and problems. Consequently they have been both cursed and applauded—and for good reason.

This book so far has focused on the opportunities. We've especially taken a close look at the impact computers have had in organizations and on the people who work in those organizations. Through the text and Windows, you've seen how these machines have been put to work on routine accounting-type tasks, used to provide managers with better information for decision making, and employed to design and manufacture better products. In this chapter we'll examine some of the effects that computer technology has had, or is likely to have, on our personal lives—that is, our lives outside of the workplace.

But before we look at these social benefits, let's consider some of the problems created by computers. Although the "computer revolution" has brought undeniable benefits to society, it has also brought some troubling side effects. Like any revolution, it has been disruptive in many ways. Some jobs have been created, others lost, and still others threatened. Additionally, an increasing number and variety of health-related concerns have surfaced regarding people who work with computer-related technologies. Computers have also increased access to information immensely, thus creating new possibilities for crime and threatening personal privacy. Clearly some controls will always be needed to limit the dangers these awesome machines pose. This chapter highlights three important problem areas: computers and health in the workplace, computers and crime, and computers and privacy.

COMPUTERS, WORK, AND HEALTH

Computers have been said to pose a threat to both our mental and physical well-being. Although the body of scientific evidence supporting this is far from conclusive, and is likely to be for many more years, we should all be aware of the major concerns that have been raised about the possible effects of computers on our health.

Anxiety-Related Concerns

Emotional problems such as financial worries, feelings of incompetence, and disorientation often produce *anxiety*. These problems, in turn, may have been triggered by layoff and reassignment, fear of falling behind, or job burnout.

LAYOFF OR REASSIGNMENT.   One of the first criticisms leveled at the entry of computers into the workplace was that their very presence resulted in job-related stress. When computers came in, people were often laid off and had to find new jobs, a situation that typically causes anxiety. Clerical workers especially worried about job security. They were often bewildered about the full potential of computers in the office and never knew when a machine might replace them. These fears are still widespread today.

But even a number of people who were not laid off found that their jobs had changed significantly and that they had no choice but to retrain. Airline agents, for example, had to learn how to manipulate a database language and to work with display terminals. And many secretaries were pressured into picking up word processing (and perhaps also electronic spreadsheets and electronic file management) to keep in tune with modern office work. Many of these workers were never able to make the transition successfully, and even many who did succeed find staring at an impersonal tube distasteful.

FEAR OF FALLING BEHIND.   The microcomputing boom is rapidly placing enormous computing power at everyone's fingertips. Some researchers feel that a widespread fear is developing that if you don't learn how to use these machines, you'll "fall behind." An example of this anxiety is parents who fear that their children will fall behind in school without the latest educationally oriented microcomputer system. Another example is the thousands of executives, managers, and even educators who are not computer oriented and see themselves as being upstaged by computer-knowledgeable colleagues. The surge of microcomputers has even made many programmers who work in mainframe environments feel that they somehow are not keeping up.

BURNOUT.   Burnout is caused not by fear of computers (*cyberphobia*), but by overuse of them (*cyberphelia*). Traditionally speaking, perhaps the epitome of burnout by computer has been the "classic" pale, workaholic programmer who seems to live in another world. With the infusion of microcomputers into home and office, new concerns have been raised about what will happen to children who withdraw socially into their computer systems; or to terminal-bound executives who have inadvertently been swept into the computer revolution; or to couples or families whose intimacy is threatened by an overused computer in the home.

Not much research has been done on computer burnout to date. What makes this area so controversial is the compelling flip-side argument—that is, that most people who are victims of computer burnout would burn out on something else even if computers didn't exist.

Ergonomic-Related Concerns

Ergonomics is the field that studies the effects that factors such as computer workspaces have on the productivity and health of employees. Let's consider some of the major fronts of ergonomic research.

DANGERS POSED BY DISPLAY DEVICES. For nearly a decade, large numbers of data-entry operators have reported a variety of physical and mental problems stemming from display device interaction. The complaints have centered primarily on visual, muscular, and emotional disorders that result from long hours of continuous display device use. These include blurred eyesight, eyestrain, acute fatigue, headaches, and backaches. In response to these problems, several states have by passed laws that curb display-device abuse. Consequently vendors of these devices have redesigned their products—with features such as tiltable screens and detachable keyboards—to make them more comfortable to use.

More recent concerns have been voiced about how radiation levels in display devices affect the unborn fetuses of pregnant operators. It will take years of scientific study for the government to draw firm conclusions on this matter, let alone legislate it. In the meantime, groups such as the National Organization for Women (NOW) and 9 to 5 have taken leadership in dealing with this sensitive issue.

WORKSPACE DESIGN. Display devices are not the only things that can torture people at workstations. The furniture might be inappropriate and nonadjustable, forcing the terminal user into awkward postures that produce body kinks. Or the lighting may be so bright as to cause a headache-inducing glare on the display screen. There even may be disconcerting noise levels attributable to poorly designed office equipment or office acoustics. Such problems are being studied by ergonomic researchers and the results of these efforts are becoming obvious in the consumer products offered to the ergonomics-conscious buyer. Some principles of good ergonomic design are illustrated in Figure 18-1.

SOFTWARE ERGONOMICS. The branch of ergonomics that deals with hardware-related issues, such as display-device flicker and radiation levels, is sometimes referred to as *hardware ergonomics*. As you might expect, the branch dealing with software-related issues is called *software ergonomics*. How easy a program is to learn and use, for example, affects both the productivity and well-being of the operator.

Other Areas of Concern

Besides anxiety- and ergonomic-related concerns, there are many other health-related worries regarding computers—for example, we may be coming to rely on them too much. A luminary in the field of artificial intelligence, Dr. Joseph Weizenbaum of the Massachusetts Institute of Technology, has voiced another concern: Will future generations rely on computers so much that they lose sight of the fundamental thought processes that the computer system is intended to model? Teachers already are complaining that many children with pocket calculators can't even do arithmetic by hand.

There is no question, of course, that computers have altered the structure of work and play, just as mechanized farm machinery altered the

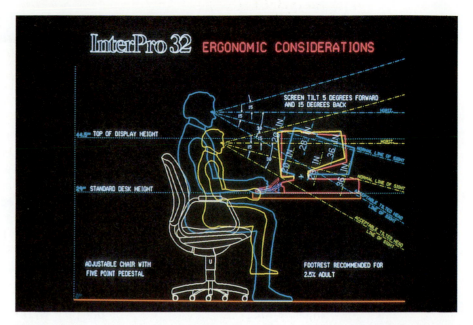

Figure 18-1.   A computer-produced graphic showing principles of good ergonomic design.

nature of agriculture, and airplanes and automobiles altered the nature of travel. Many people have accepted these disruptions as the price of "progress" or "keeping up." Yet almost everyone wonders about what type of world we are creating for ourselves.

COMPUTER CRIME AND ETHICS

Computer crime is loosely defined as the use of computers to commit unauthorized acts. Some states have laws that address computer crime directly; others do not. In practice, however, even in states that do have such laws, computer crime is hard to pin down.

One reason is that it is often difficult to decide when an unauthorized act is really a crime. No one would doubt that a bank employee using a computer system to embezzle funds from customers' accounts is committing a crime. But what about an employee "stealing time" on the company computer to balance a personal checkbook for a home or business? Or even someone using the same computer to word-process a personal letter to a friend? Aren't those acts also unauthorized? Where do you draw the line?

Another problem in pinning down computer crime is that judges and juries are often bewildered by the technical issues involved in such cases. Also, companies that discover computer criminals among their employees are often reluctant to press charges because they fear adverse publicity.

Types of Computer Crime

IT'S NO BALONEY THAT YOU MAY BE SALAMI-SLICED

As in many fields, a specialized jargon has evolved in the area of computer-related crime. Here is a sampling—with definitions—of some of the more colorful terms.

Data Diddling. This is one of the most popular ways to perform a computer crime. It involves altering valid data on the computer system in some unauthorized way. Data diddlers are often found changing grades in university files, falsifying input records on bank transactions, and so forth.

A specialized jargon has evolved.

The Trojan Horse. This is a procedure for adding instructions to a computer program so that it will still work, but will also perform unauthorized duties. For example, a bank worker can subtly alter a large program, containing thousands of lines of code, by adding a small "patch" that instructs the program not to withdraw money from a certain account.

Salami Methods. These involve altering programs so that many small dollar amounts are shaved from a large number of selected transactions or accounts and deposited in another account. The victims of a salami operation generally are unaware that their funds have been tapped, because the amount taken from any individual is trivial. The recipient of the salami slicing, however, benefits from the aggregation of these small shavings. Often these can add up to a substantial amount.

Superzapping. This is a technique made possible by a special program available on most computer systems that bypasses all system controls when the computer "crashes" and cannot be restarted with normal recovery procedures. This program, in effect, is a "master key" that can provide access to any part of the system. The superzap program is a highly privileged "disaster aid," which very few people working with a computer system are authorized to use. In the wrong hands it can be used to do almost any unauthorized task. In one reported case, a computer operator who was allowed to use the superzap program to make certain specific changes fraudulently directed substantial funds to accounts of friends.

Trapdoors. These are diagnostic tools, used in the development of systems programs, that enable programmers to gain access to various

Some Case Studies of Computer Crime

To get some idea of the variety of forms that computer crime can take, and some of the problems involved in dealing with it, let's look at some case studies. All these cases either are true or are closely modeled on actual situations.

CASE 1.   A computer operations employee at a university, who is also a student there, tampers with the student database, changing grades he's

parts of the computer system. Before the programs are marketed, these tools are supposed to be removed. Occasionally, however, some blocks of diagnostic code are overlooked, so that a person using the associated systems program may get unauthorized views of other parts of the computer system. In one publicized case, a trapdoor was discovered by some users of a time-sharing service, and they were able to examine, criminally, a number of supposedly protected passwords. They later used the passwords to gain unauthorized access to confidential programs.

Logic Bombs. These are programs designed to be executed at random or at specific times to perform unauthorized acts. In one celebrated case, a programmer inserted a logic bomb in a system that would cause a company's entire personnel file to be destroyed if his name were removed from it.

Scavenging. As the name implies, this technique involves searching through trash cans, offices, and the like for information that will permit unauthorized access to a computer system. Students, for example, will often look through discarded listings at a computer center for an identification number that will open to them the resources of others' accounts.

Data Leakage. Many pieces of data generated by organizations are highly confidential and not intended for the eyes of outsiders. Generally these organizations will carefully

control any computer outputs leaving their premises. In data leakage, however, confidential data are coded in sophisticated ways so that they can be removed undetected. For example, sensitive data could be transformed through a coding process to make them look like useless nonsense. Then, after they leave the organization virtually unnoticed, they can be decoded and the original output used for unauthorized purposes.

Keeping the scalawags out.

Wiretapping. Remember Watergate? Well, there are many documented cases of people who have wiretapped computer systems to obtain information illegally. Some transmission facilities, such as satellites, are highly susceptible to wiretapping (as evidenced by all those "illegal" rooftop devices that intercept cable TV without pay). Others, such as fiber optic cable, are extremely difficult to penetrate.

received and giving himself credit for courses he hasn't taken. His deceit is discovered by accident and he is pressed to resign. No formal charges are filed against him, however, for two reasons. First, the case would be hard to prosecute because the evidence is circumstantial. It appears as if someone had gained access to the database involved by creating a temporary false user account, but poor systems controls made it impossible to determine who it was. Several people were privileged to authorize such accounts, so the employee could easily argue in court that he had been framed. Second, administrators feared it would cause great embarrassment to the university if the case were made public.

CASE 2.   A programmer working for a bank alters a program so that withdrawals against his own account are never recorded. To keep the books balanced, he taps what appear to be dormant accounts for the funds he withdraws. The employee is discovered when one account he taps turns out not to be dormant. The depositor is persistent enough to persuade the bank to produce an original withdrawal slip for a questionable transaction. It turns out to be missing. Suspicious, the bank investigates further, finally comparing the computer program involved with its backup version. They differ by several lines of code.

The bank has a fairly strong case for embezzlement. The programmer cannot adequately explain why the deposits in his account over a certain period of time are in excess of his income. But fearing that publicity about the case would make depositors think their accounts were in jeopardy, the bank discharges the employee without pressing charges.

CASE 3.   A programmer working for a bank alters a program so that the interest computed in randomly selected, interest-earning accounts is "shaved off" by a few cents and the sums immediately posted to her account. This method of embezzlement is commonly called the *salami technique*. The theory behind it is that since customers have trouble computing interest anyway, and usually quit if they are within a few cents of an expected total, they are not likely to notice the missing funds. A few cents taken from many accounts, however, can amount to a considerable sum over many years when posted to a single account. And since no money is diverted out of the bank's system of accounts, the books of the bank balance.

The programmer's act is discovered during a routine audit, when an accountant with computer expertise tests the program involved with some dummy transactions. Independent tallies differ significantly from the program-generated ones. Again, fearing negative publicity, the bank releases the programmer but does not press charges.

CASE 4.   An accounting manager of a medium-sized company buys a well-known software package for use in the office. Subordinate employees are impressed by what she can do with the package and ask her for copies. She subsequently makes ten copies of the software disk and distributes them to various employees. The vendor of the package hears about the incident and presses charges. The vendor claims that every package it sells is shrink-wrapped with clear plastic and that under the plastic is a highly visible warning stating that copying the program is a crime. The warning also states that, by opening the plastic, one is implicitly agreeing to honor the terms of the vendor. The defense for the manager claims both that someone else opened the package and that simply breaking the plastic doesn't bind one to a contract. The case is eventually settled out of court.

As these cases show, computer crime has many forms. Some cases involve the use of the computer for theft of financial assets, such as money or equipment. Others involve the copying of data processing resources such as programs or data to the disadvantage of the owner. In still other cases, such data as grades are manipulated for personal advantage. Computer crime is estimated to cost individuals and organizations billions of dollars annually. No one knows for sure what the exact figure is, because so many incidents are either undetected or left unreported.

Preventing Computer Crime

There are many ways in which organizations can combat computer crime.

HIRE TRUSTWORTHY PEOPLE. Employers should carefully investigate the background of anyone being considered for sensitive computer work. Some people falsify resumés to get jobs. Others may have criminal records.

SEPARATE EMPLOYEE FUNCTIONS. An employee with many related responsibilities can more easily commit a crime than one with a single responsibility. For example, the person who authorizes adding new vendors to a file should not be the same person who authorizes payments to those vendors.

RESTRICT SYSTEM USE. People using a computer system should have access only to the things they need to use to do their jobs. A computer operator, for example, should be told only how to execute a program and not what the program does.

PROTECT SENSITIVE PROGRAMS AND DATA. On many systems users can protect programs and data with passwords. For example, a user might specify that anyone who wants access to a program named AR-148 must first enter the password "FRED." Users can change passwords frequently, and protect particularly sensitive files with several passwords.

Software vendors often protect their products with small blocks of code that inhibit copying or by enabling buying organizations that want several copies of the product to purchase a *site license*. Site licenses are relatively expensive, but they enable the buying organization to copy the software for site use.

Some users and vendors encrypt data or programs to protect them. *Encryption* is the process of disguising data or programs by using a coding method. The encrypting procedure must provide for both coding and decoding. As with passwords, the encryption method should be changed regularly if it is protecting particularly sensitive materials.

DEVISE STAFF CONTROLS. Overtime work should be carefully scrutinized, because computer crimes often occur at times when the criminal is not likely to be interrupted. Sensitive documents that are no longer needed should be shredded. Access to the computer room or program/data library should be strictly limited to authorized personnel.

RECORD AND MANAGE IMPORTANT SYSTEM TRANSACTIONS. The systems software should include a program for maintaining a log of every person who gains or attempts to gain access to the system. The log should contain information on the terminal used, the data files and programs used, and the times at which the work began and ended. Such a log makes it possible for management to isolate unauthorized use of the system.

CONDUCT REGULAR AUDITS.   Unfortunately many crimes are discovered by accident. Key elements of the system should be inspected and tested on a regular basis to ensure that no foul play is taking place.

Ethical Issues

Ethics is a term that refers to standards of moral conduct. For example, telling the truth is a matter of ethics. Although an unethical act isn't always against the law, sometimes it is. Purposely lying to a friend is unethical, and yet normally is lawful, but perjuring yourself as a courtroom witness is a crime. Whether or not criminal behavior is involved, ethics do play a significant role in shaping the law and in determining how well we get along with other people.

Computer ethics refers to standards of moral conduct shown in computer-related matters. Four important problem areas involving computer ethics are software piracy, hacking, employee loyalty, and gray-market selling.

Figure 18-2.   Software piracy costs vendors millions of dollars a year.

SOFTWARE PIRACY.   **Software piracy**—the unauthorized copying or use of a computer program—is an ethical matter that, like lying, may be a crime (Figure 18-2). If you make an unauthorized copy of a program, you may be found guilty of breaking copyright laws. The law is generally more lenient if you just use an unauthorized copy that was made by someone else, but use may constitute a crime as well. Whether a law is being broken or not, you are probably cheating someone out of deserved royalties.

HACKING.   **Hacking** is a computer term that often relates to the activities of people who use computers or terminals to crack the security of some computer system. Many people engage in hacking purely for the challenge of cracking codes, while others do it to steal computer time or to take a peek at confidential information. Intentions aside, hacking is a breaking-and-entering type of crime just like forced entry into someone else's car or home. Prosecuted hackers (who are often in their teens) have sometimes later claimed they didn't know that merely breaking into someone else's protected database was a crime, although they were sure they were doing something considered wrong in some way.

EMPLOYEE LOYALTY.   Job hopping is prevalent in the computer industry, and so people often have valuable knowledge about their former employer. And if they've taken up employment with a competitor, how much of this knowledge is used to the detriment of the former employer is a matter of ethical concern. Say, for example, that you and a friend you've hired work many hours on a software idea you plan to market. You become sick and are bedridden for a month. During your absence, your friend goes to work for a company that wants to produce a product that will compete with the one you had planned to turn out. When the product is marketed, you notice many similarities between it and the one you designed. Even if you had no legal case, you'd probably feel that your friend (perhaps now a former friend) was unethical.

GRAY-MARKET SELLING.   Many computer hardware manufacturers only sell their goods to so-called authorized dealers. The manufacturers require these dealers to sign a pledge stating that they will not resell the hardware to other dealers or to discount houses, or sell it by mail. Many dealerships sign this pledge and then promptly ignore it, simply because it's more profitable for them to buy huge volumes of hardware at substantial discounts and then resell most of the stock to unauthorized dealers. To make matters worse, many authorized dealers who dabble in this gray market later refuse to service the machines that they sell "out the back door."

COMPUTERS AND PRIVACY

Almost all of us have some aspects of our lives we would rather keep private. These may include a sorry incident from the past, sensitive medical or financial facts, or certain tastes or opinions. Yet we can appreciate that at times selected people or organizations have a legitimate need for some of this information. Doctors need accurate medical histories of patients. Financial information must be disclosed to credit card companies and college scholarship committees. A company or the government may need to probe into the lives of people applying for unusually sensitive jobs.

Once personal information has been made available to others, however, no matter how legitimate the need, there is always the danger that it will be misused. Some of the stored facts may be wrong. Facts may get to the wrong people. Facts may be taken out of context and used to draw distorted conclusions. Facts may be collected without one's knowledge or consent. **Privacy,** with respect to information processing, refers to how information about individuals is used and by whom.

The problem of how to protect privacy and ensure that personal information is not misused was with us long before electronic computers existed. But modern computer systems, with their ability to store and manipulate unprecedented quantities of data, and to make those data available to many locations, have added a new dimension to the privacy issue. The greater the ability to collect, store, and disseminate information, the greater is the potential for abuse of that information.

Some Problem Areas

INVOLUNTARY COLLECTION.   A fear many people have is that sensitive information about them will be gathered without their knowledge and will then fall into the hands of the wrong people. Let's look at a simple example that shows how computer technology has made this type of abuse easier.

Say you enjoy reading and keeping up on a wide variety of topics. You order several books from a mail-order catalog on a controversial subject. Unknowingly you have probably placed yourself on a computerized mailing list. What's more, your order will probably be analyzed by computer to reveal (correctly or incorrectly) your "purchasing tastes." The company that you originally dealt with may also sell its mailing list to other companies interested in people with specific purchasing tastes. Thus a piece of data about you that you may not want widely known has been collected, stored, and distributed. For many months you're flooded with junk mail from various companies with which you'd rather not deal. In fact you have to think twice before asking someone to pick up your mail.

It is, of course, possible to write to the companies and request them to drop your name from their mailing lists. But even if you do, it may be months before the flood begins to ebb. And unfortunately, with so many transactions linked to credit card and banking identification numbers, almost anytime we make a purchase, data can be collected on us and filed in computer data banks without our ever knowing about it.

DISCLOSURE.   Most people would agree that credit card companies should have the right to check the credit history of an applicant, and that employers should be able to check into the backgrounds of people seeking jobs. But when an honest, hardworking person with an impeccable credit history is denied credit, or a qualified applicant is denied a job, a number of questions come to mind. Decisions such as these are often based on data stored in computer files. What types of data are in the files? Where did they come from? Are they accurate? Are the people making the decisions confusing two people with the same name? What procedures are being used to make decisions?

As the many horror stories about people who have suffered because the wrong facts slipped into a data file suggest, these are serious questions. They have led many people to argue for the right of disclosure—the right of a person denied credit or a job to examine the data on which the decison was based and to correct any errors.

UNAUTHORIZED USE.   The federal government, local governments, and private organizations maintain various data banks with enormous amounts of information about millions of people (Figure 18-3). The Internal Revenue Service alone collects detailed information about every taxpayer every year. Many people fear the information in these data banks could easily be abused—to monitor people's lives without their consent, for example, or to harass people who object to government policies. Considering that many data banks maintained by the federal government can be interrelated by social security number, the degree of control that a person or organization with access to just a few of them could exercise is indeed frightening. On the other hand, of course, these data banks do serve legitimate needs.

Figure 18-3. Governments maintain data banks with enormous amounts of information about millions of people.

Legislation

Since the early 1970s, the federal government has sought to protect the rights of citizens by passing legislation to limit the abuse of computer data banks. Some important laws that have been enacted for this purpose are the Fair Credit Reporting Act, the Freedom of Information Act, the Education Privacy Act, and the Privacy Act.

The *Fair Credit Reporting Act (1970)* is designed to prevent private organizations from unfairly denying credit to individuals. It stipulates that people must have the right to inspect their credit records. If a serious objection is raised about the integrity of the data, the credit agency is required by law to investigate the matter.

The *Freedom of Information Act (1970)* gives individuals the right to inspect data concerning them that are stored by the federal government. The law also makes certain data about the operation of federal agencies available for public scrutiny.

The *Education Privacy Act (1974)* protects an individual's right to privacy in both private and public schools that receive any federal funding. It stipulates that an individual has the right to keep such matters as course grades and evaluations of behavior private. Also, individuals must have the opportunity to inspect and challenge their own records.

The *Privacy Act (1974)* primarily protects the public against abuses by the federal government. It stipulates that any data federal agencies collect must have a legitimate purpose. It also states that individuals must be allowed to learn what information is being stored about them and how it's being used, and have the opportunity to correct or remove erroneous or trivial data.

Most privacy legislation, as you can see, relates to the conduct of the federal government and the organizations to which it supplies aid. Similar legislation has been enacted by some state governments to protect individuals from abuses by state agencies. The federal government is currently developing private-sector privacy guidelines that are similar to those of federal and state agencies.

COMPUTERS IN OUR LIVES: TODAY AND TOMORROW

The number of uses to which computers have been put is so large and the uses so heterogeneous that they almost defy classification. As you've already seen, computers are valuable, on-the-job tools whether you are a company executive, a manager, an engineer, a marketing research analyst, an accountant, a financial analyst, a lawyer, a doctor, a dentist, a real estate broker, an architect, or even a farmer or a rancher. And the impact of the computer on those occupations and others is just beginning.

Outside of the workplace, computers have also exerted their presence on our lives. Let's look at how they have, through the text that follows and the photographs in Window 7 (beginning on page 537).

Computers in the Home

People generally spend a good deal of time at home. Home is one's "base"—the place where one eats, sleeps, entertains, "gathers" oneself, and stores most of one's worldly possessions. People have always endeavored to make their homes more comfortable—by arranging it in a certain way or by stocking it with the right sorts of conveniences. Where does the computer fit into all of this?

Actually, it may not. Many people choose to keep their homes as gadgetless as possible, and their home lives will probably continue relatively computer-free in our computer-intensive age. Naturally it's hard to avoid the computer altogether, because most of the products brought into the home are managed, grown, designed, or manufactured through the use of computers. But at home, if you rely heavily on one or more electrical products (such as a phone, TV, VCR, stereo/radio, or any kitchen appliance), then the computer revolution will affect your home life, if it hasn't already. And, of course, if someone in your household wants a computer system, then your home life will probably be greatly affected by the computer revolution.

When inexpensive microcomputer systems first became widely available in the late 1970s, many people predicted that there would shortly be a computer system in every home. After all, computers are useful tools, and look what happened in the case of other great inventions, such as the car, phone, and television. We're still very far from such a reality. Most home computer systems today have been purchased by hobbyists, businesspeople, and parents of children who want a computer on which to play games or learn a computer language. The vast majority of people still feel they really don't need a microcomputer system at home, whether a $200 unit or a $5000 one.

But whether people want computer systems in their homes or not, those brainy little microcomputer and memory chips are rapidly finding their way into electrical household products. Look at all of those "programmable features" on your TV, stereo, or VCR. Once all one had to know to operate a "home viewing system" (i.e., a television) or "home listening system" (i.e., a radio) was how to operate the on–off knob, volume knob, and channel dial. But today it can easily take an entire morning to find out how a new VCR works and how to connect it to the stereo and TV for maximum entertainment value.

As computer and memory chips become cheaper and more powerful, there are many additional ways in which life at home may change. The following are a few possiblities for present and future home computing applications.

COMPUTERIZED HOMES.   We touched upon computerized homes in Chapter 14. Homes today are being built with computer-controlled devices that greet and ascertain the identity of visitors, brew your coffee moments before you awake in the morning, monitor and water your lawn while you're away, and automatically regulate the inside temperature.

PERSONAL ROBOT SERVANTS.   Robots are no longer exclusively in the realm of science fiction. Although most of them today are employed to do dangerous work in factories, personal robot servants are being built and marketed for the home (see Figure 18-4). Even a few "robot stores" have sprouted up to sell robot kits or fully assembled robots to the public. Home robots are still very much in their infancy, but some can now perform acts

tomorrow

CRYSTAL-BALLING TOMORROW

**When Making Predictions,
Consider Human Behavior Before
Technology**

One sage piece of advice that's probably been given to all of us at one point or another is that there are only two things of which one can be certain: death and taxes. Here's a third to add to that list: Humans will always resist change unless motivated strongly by a need to change.

Who can blame us? How would you react if you came in to work one morning, to a job in which you felt really secure, and a salesperson tried to interest you in doing your job with a new machine that you knew nothing about and didn't feel comfortable using? If you weren't forced to use the machine, you'd probably tell the salesperson to take a walk.

New products appear so quickly that they outpace our ability to assimilate them.

New products are being introduced so quickly today that they completely outpace our ability to assimilate them. Even the most computer literate among us don't jump at every new product that comes along. How would you feel if it took you three weeks to learn a spreadsheet package and six months later the spreadsheet vendor wanted you to "move up" to a more sophisticated package that was 10 percent better but would take two additional months to master?

Humans are motivated by needs—surviv-

al, security, power, and love, to name just a few. If a particular need is strong enough, barriers that resist change often come tumbling down. The fact that most typists today learn word processing skills is due mostly to the sad fact that they face an extremely limited future if they confine themselves strictly to conventional typewriters. Survival is one of the stongest needs of all. On the other hand, the "fully equipped microcomputer system in every home" reality that some people have predicted has not come about, because of both resistance to change and the lack of a clear need. Most people, in fact, continue to live quite well without extensive use of even a pocket calculator or conventional typewriter in the home.

People who try to make specific predictions about our computer future are usually more wrong than right. Often these predictions are based more on blind enthusiasm for technology than on human behavior. For example, those who predicted time-sharing to be the wave of the future in the late 1960s overlooked the need for people to have control of their own computers. For similar reasons, bus transportation hasn't caught on in many cities—people prefer driving their own cars. And people who never thought printer technology could improve to the state it is in today overlooked the need for good, cheap printers that would evolve as the microcomputer revolution took shape.

Where there's a will, there seems to be a way. Although we may not be able to predict where technologies will be twenty years from now, we do know—like death and taxes—that humans will probably always be what they are today, and will force the computer technologies of tomorrow in line with their needs.

Figure 18-4.   Heath's HERO JR. personal robot.

once thought impossible, such as greeting specific people by name and bussing snacks around the house.

HOME BANKING AND SHOPPING.   Electronic funds transfer (EFT) systems have long been in existence. The earliest systems enabled funds to be wired between banks. Later came the automatic teller machines. Most recent on the scene are *videotex systems* (see Figure 18-5) which enable people to use their TVs, a special keypad, and membership with an online data service to bank and shop from home. Videotex systems provide online access to information from banks, brokerage houses, travel agents, and stores. Today the promise of videotex remains unfulfilled, although some industry observers see it gaining new strength as concepts such as the "integrated entertainment/education center" and "integrated home work center" evolve.

INTEGRATED ENTERTAINMENT/EDUCATION CENTER.   This concept is developing as people are discovering the advantages of hooking up once separate products into a system. Perhaps you have a stereo system, TV, and VCR connected together so that you can watch movie videotapes in stereo. As new computing and communications breakthroughs take hold, and as these breakthroughs are realized in consumer products, it's not farfetched to believe that people will someday have immediate, in-home access to

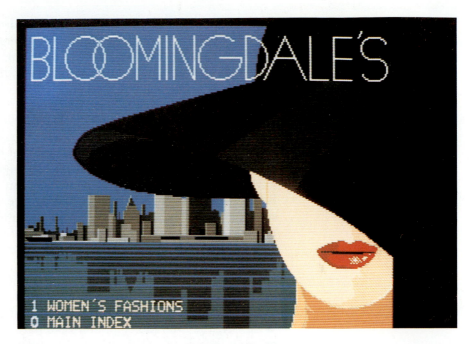

Figure 18-5. A videotex screen for shoppers of Bloomingdale's department store.

almost any movie, game, piece of music, book, or magazine ever produced. Add to this certain authorized forms of local storage and hard-copy reproduction, and the possibilities for media entertainment and education at home seem almost endless.

Figure 18-6. A workstation integrating a computer and a phone.

INTEGRATED HOME WORK CENTER.   In business, many say, the computer and phone will eventually merge into a single product called an "integrated workstation" (see Figure 18-6). This station will be able to carry out many office-type activities that can be automated. Should such a system evolve in business, why not a less expensive version in the home?

There's always the possiblity that the "work center" and "entertainment/education center" could evolve into one system. The preference that individuals seem to possess, though, for having their own systems for their own purposes would seem to indicate otherwise. What we may in fact see is just several "dedicated electronic centers" in the home.

Computers in Education

Some of the earliest electronic computers were installed in academic institutions in the 1940s and 1950s, where they were either studied as a curiosity, or used to perform calculations rapidly. Thus one of the earliest applications of computers in education involved the training of engineers, who had to know how to build computers or use them in their jobs.

Later, as computers found their way into businesses, data processing or information systems courses evolved in business schools. Some academic visionaries, such as John Kemeny at Dartmouth in the 1960s, realized early on that computers would be useful to perform work in a wider variety of disciplines. And so BASIC and the first interactive, time-shared computer system became part of educational life at Dartmouth.

Today computers and education are combined in a wide variety of ways. Let's look at a few of these.

LEARNING ABOUT COMPUTERS. As it is with many other disciplines, the very act of learning about computers can be carried out from several perspectives. Chapter 17 touched on a few of these; for example, *computer science* (a technically oriented perspective), *data processing* or *computer information systems* (a business perspective), and *computer operations* (a hands-on, operational perspective). In a large university, it's not unusual to see fifty or more courses collectively devoted to serving these multiple perspectives. Many large businesses, several independent training houses, and a number of computer camps also provide instruction about computers.

INSTRUCTION. Once just another promising development, *computer-assisted instruction* (*CAI*) has come into its own as an educational tool. With CAI the user and computer take part in an interactive dialogue. For example, a high-school algebra student using a CAI package may be given a problem on the screen to solve. If the answer is correct, the package poses another problem, perhaps one that's more advanced. If the answer is wrong, the package may go into a "remedial mode" by giving hints, or showing how the problem is solved, or providing another problem on the same level. Each student progresses at his or her own pace. At the end of the session, the student is graded. A progress report may also be provided.

In many educational environments, CAI has been very successful. The computer can do a lot of the tedious teaching, while supplemental personalized help is given by a real-life teacher. Also, the teacher becomes less pressured to pace the class according to the efforts of bright, or poor, students. CAI is also used quite heavily by businesses and by the military, which have found it cost effective for certain types of training.

A closely related technology to CAI is *computer-managed instruction* (*CMI*). In a CMI system, the computer merely supervises students, perhaps directing them to read certain books or to see certain library films on their own. On completing one assignment, students return to their computer workstations for testing, and perhaps further assignments. Thus, with CMI, students aren't limited to materials that can be stored and disseminated by a computer system.

Of course, neither CAI nor CMI has ever been recognized as a solution that will meet every teaching need. In many situations the computer may never seriously challenge the purely human, personal approach to education.

RESEARCH. At one time academic and government institutions were the only organizations that paid scholars to do creative research that advanced the technology of computers. As industry giants such as IBM and Xerox evolved, fundamental research involving computers also became a high priority in the private sector. Later, when cheap microcomputer chips became available and were publicized in hobbyist magazines, a grass-roots research movement evolved in such places as Silicon Valley garages and basements. Today virtually everyone with an inclination to do so can develop new computer products on their own.

Computers in Entertainment and Leisure Activities

There are so many types of entertainment and leisure activities where computers are used that these applications are almost impossible to enumerate. Let's consider a few selected applications of general interest—sports, creating movies, creating music, and creating art.

SPORTS.   Among the earliest applications of computers in sports were highly simplified computerized baseball games. You selected opposing lineups and then issued a "RUN" command at your terminal. Subsequently the computer would use random numbers to simulate a ballgame and, within seconds, print out a box score. Not very interesting, perhaps, but better things were to come.

As you listen to and watch televised sports events today, it's not too difficult to guess what did come. Look at all those flashy graphics. There are attractive screens of scores and statistics, possibly a digitized freeze frame of tennis or racing-car action you saw live just seconds ago, and fully animated, cartoonlike sequences of fantasy flights over a basketball court or a football field (Figure 18-7). It's the fast-paced world of computer graphics and animation that's made all of this possible.

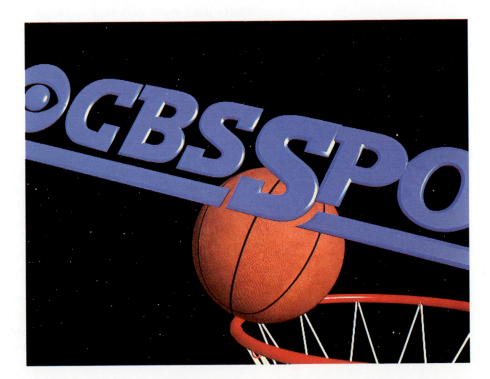

Figure 18-7.   A still from an animated CBS TV sequence. Coming next: Larry Bird versus the Los Angeles Lakers front line.

And, of course, there are all of those impressive player statistics. What else but a computer could quickly determine for you that Gary Carter batted .314 against righthanders and .289 against lefthanders prior to tonight's game? Many clubs now have behind-the-scenes computer people to prepare statistics for the announcers in the broadcast booth.

And how many times have you heard how successful the Dallas Cowboys' computerized recruiting system is? In sports such as baseball, football, tennis, hockey, and basketball, and in Olympic competition, coaches and managers are trusting computers to analyze player performances and game plans.

Combine all of these applications with electronic scoreboards, computer-controlled ticketing, and all of the other conventional accounting- and MIS-related activities performed by profit-making institutions, and you have a very impressive array of computing power in the sports industry today.

MOVIES.   Computers and movies first met when computers became subjects upon which movies were based. Robots were among the earliest of computer technologies to be worthy objects of moviemaking. Then, with the 1950s and UNIVAC I, movies often portrayed the computer as an infallible, big brother type of device that would be used by insensitive power mongers to rule the world. A major emphasis in movies today concerns the notion that computer systems are indeed fallible, and that a human software oversight will cause some global disaster. No wonder a lot of people are afraid of computers.

In the past several years, computers have figured prominently in *creating* the movies themselves. For example, movies such as *Star Wars* would have been absolutely impossible without computers to keep track of and integrate the numerous special effects involved. Many scenes that took place in the spaceships used computers to combine live images, paintings, and dynamic electronic models. Some people feel that the day is not too far distant when the majority of images you see in movies will be computer generated and indistinguishable to most viewers from real-life images (see box on page 459 of Chapter 15).

MUSIC.   While creating music may be an art, the notion of sound is a matter of physics. We can use computers to store sounds, and even recall them from memory in order to have them played. But artistically sequencing sounds of varying length and qualities, and overlapping these sounds to simulate several musicians working together so as to produce a great musical piece, is still unachievable. To a very limited degree, such "generated," or synthesized, music can be created (see Figure 18-8), but it is still much too primitive to cause either Bruce Springsteen, Joan Armitrading, or the members of L'Orchestre de la Suisse Romande any worry about being replaced by a computer.

Important roles of the computer in the creative side of the music industry include the editing and organizing of tasks. Disk jockeys and their staffs, for instance, use computer-controlled equipment to edit and organize music for their radio shows. And performers can store sequences of their

Figure 18-8. *A high-tech music synthesizer.*

music on direct-access devices that enable them later to cut and paste the sequences into a piece. Here the computer isn't really creating sounds, but merely enabling the recording artist to use it as a writer uses a word processor to cut and paste a document.

ART. At one time virtually the only way you could create an artistic image was by being able to paint, draw, weave, sculpt, and the like, completely by your own hand. Then the Guttenberg press arrived and images could be mass produced. Although that event probably caused panic among people contemplating a calligraphy career, the would-be Renoirs and Van Goghs still had little worry of replacement.

The industrial revolution gave further rise to the so-called "industrial arts," and machines such as the Jacquard loom (see Chapter 3), which could weave under program control, appeared. When photography arrived in the mid-1800s, the painters were threatened, but photography later evolved into an art form of its own, with a different set of standards.

Now that the computer has arrived, there are new threats to artists on all levels—but there are also great opportunities. Computers, for example, were used to generate many of the images you see in Windows 1, 3, 4, 6, and 7. By using a computer, images of virtually any shape can be created, colored in any of millions of hues, enlarged, rotated, blended or combined into other images, illuminated by one or more three-dimensional light sources (which can also cast shadows), and so forth. Also, colors, positions, and shapes of objects can be changed at electronically fast speeds to create new images. Thus the artist can see a variety of images and store the most promising of them, all in a short span of time. The artist with only canvas and brush just can't work at that pace, and neither can the traditional film director.

But such artists as painters are still far from being replaced. Like phototgraphy, computer art may become an art form of its own. Handmade art objects seem to have an ineffable quality that's likely to remain desirable.

Computers in Science and Medicine

Science and medicine account for a wide variety of computer applications. In this section we'll look at a few of these applications, specifically, how computers are used for weather forecasting, space exploration, environmental simulations, patient diagnosis, life-support systems, and the treatment of handicapped people.

SCIENCE.   One of the earliest applications of computer power to a scientific field was in weather forecasting. To predict the weather accurately, data on current weather conditions must be input to the computer, which then analyzes mounds of data on past conditions. Because predicting weather is an around-the-clock chore that requires supercomputer-sized computational and storage capacity, it is done at a national level, in such places as the National Center for Atmospheric Research (NCAR) in Boulder, Colorado. The computer, of course, also now comes into play in presenting TV viewers with such interesting weather graphics as satellite maps.

Another ongoing application of computers in science is the exploration of space. There are so many computations that need to be done to send people and spacecraft into the universe that space travel, with any degree of safety, would not be possible without computers. Computers are also used to enhance and study photographs taken in space.

Simulation (see the box on page 535) often involves building a mathematical model of a real-life object or situation, and testing it rigorously with "dummy data" before the object is actually built or the situation encountered. Computer-aided design (CAD), for example, often involves simulation. A car, say, may be modeled on a computer screen. Then the computer simulates real-life events such as accidents and stresses before the car is actually built. Similarly, many airplane pilots are trained today in special "lab cockpits" that simulate encounters with other planes in the air, landings, and the like. Simulation is also useful to both government and business for predicting economic changes in society, the environmental impact of new policies, and consumer reaction to the effects of pricing changes.

MEDICINE.   It is indeed extremely comforting to know that computer systems are hard at work making sure that you remain healthy and that you live longer.

Computer-assisted diagnosis refers to a number of hardware or software technologies that assist physicians in diagnosing the condition of a patient. One example of this is inputting data about a patient's condition to a software program that compares the condition with others (that have

Computer Simulation

A POWERFUL PLANNING TOOL MADE BETTER BY COMPUTERS

One way in which people make decisions is by simulating situations before they actually take place.

Simulation often involves modeling a process as a series of mathematical relationships, and testing the process under a variety of conditions before it is actually implemented. Oil companies, for example, often simulate the loading and unloading of ships at port areas to determine the best possible number of berths to build.

Computer simulations can avoid expensive mistakes or identify new opportunities.

Companies that are actively engaged in research and development or in marketing activities often simulate sales and cost scenarios to assess the riskiness of a new venture before they finally settle on it. In addition, processes such as operating nuclear reactors, using a new highway, or determining the environmental impact of public policy can all be simulated on a computer today to help determine what their individual effects will be tomorrow.

Since the computer can rapidly generate the thousands (or perhaps millions) of different conditions a process might encounter when implemented, as well as record and summarize all of the important events that occur as a result of prevailing conditions, it is a natural tool for conducting simulation studies. In addition, through the use of large databases, graphical display devices, and imaging technologies, the computer can be used to simulate the design and testing of such products as cars and airplanes (see accompanying photo and photos 16 through 21 in Window 7). Because the computer modeling takes place before any actual building or decision making is done, computer simulations can help to avoid expensive mistakes or to identify new opportunities.

Simulation is also a very useful tool for scientists. Researchers—in fields as diverse as medicine, sociology, biology, chemistry, genetics, education, psychology, business, engineering, and physics—have turned to computer simulation as a technique to discover more about how their worlds may look tomorrow on the basis of certain events that are happening today.

A computer-simulated airplane runway.

already been diagnosed) in a large patient database. The program then outputs statistics that will help the attending physicians diagnose the ailment. Many of these programs are considered "expert systems," in that they employ artificial intelligence techniques that enable them actually to draw some conclusions for the doctor.

Computer tomography (sometimes referred to as CAT or PET scanning) is another computer-assisted diagnosis technique. It employs x-ray hardware and computer technology to provide doctors with three-dimensional pictures of the organs in a person's body. Thus the doctors have more information on which to base a diagnosis than they would from the traditional two-dimensional x-ray.

Computerized life-support systems behave a lot like robots, although they usually bear no resemblance to humans. These systems monitor bedridden patients, thus freeing nurses from uninterrupted observation. A system might monitor such factors as heart rate, temperature, and blood pressure—and sound a silent alarm if something is amiss.

Today computers are being used in many ways to help the handicapped. Computer-aided instruction, for example, has been used successfully to help slow learners (see photograph 11 in Window 7). And portable computers have been used to simulate the human voice artificially, thus enabling cerebral palsy victims to "speak." Vision systems—which contain sensors to determine distances of objects and computer systems to determine their identities or properties—are evolving to enable the blind to "see." Figure 18-9 shows an application of computers to help the handicapped.

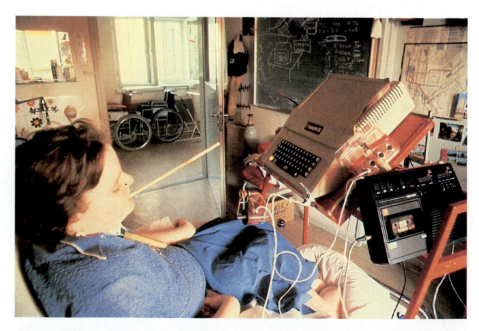

Figure 18-9.   Computers and the handicapped. This woman is using a remote-control pointing device that activates keys on a special keyboard.

Computers in Our World

A sample of the variety of ways computers impact on our lives

Computers affect our daily lives in so many ways that it would require an endless book to catalog all of them. This Window looks at a few of the ways in which we interact socially with computers.

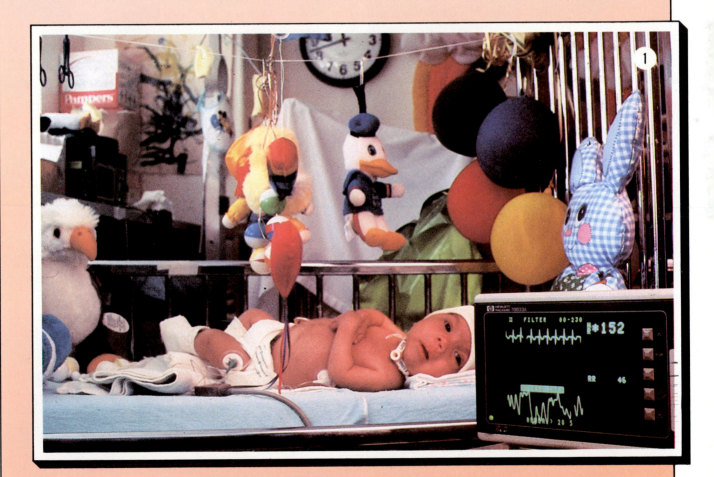

Medicine

1. At Mt. Zion Hospital in San Francisco, patient-monitoring equipment measures a baby's heart and lung functions.

Animation

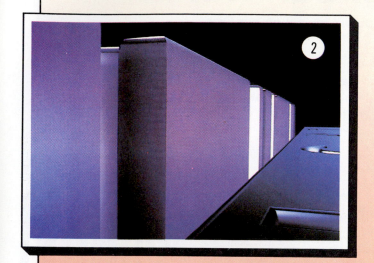

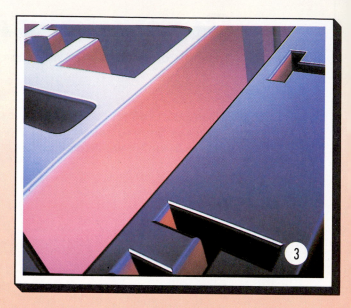

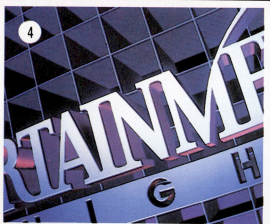

2–5. These Pacific Data Images stills are from the animated sequence that appears at the beginning of CBS's "Entertainment Tonight" TV show. The title logo is stored in a database that models three-dimensional space and the viewer is "navigated" through the letters in the title as if he or she were in a spacecraft.

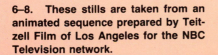

6–8. These stills are taken from an animated sequence prepared by Teitzell Film of Los Angeles for the NBC Television network.

Education

9. Early in grade school students are interacting with computers to do their work and to become literate about the high-tech world around them.

10. A college student using an Apple Macintosh plugs away at the solution to a problem.

11. IBM Personal Computers are used by this student and his classmates in special education classes at a Brooklyn, New York, high school. Computers can be effective equalizers for students who may be at a competitive disadvantage in a conventional classroom environment.

Science and Research

12. Computer-generated animation created by Cranston/Csuri Productions for an educational series entitled, "The Living Body." Scientists and computer modelers are currently experimenting with combining computer animation techniques with x-ray technology to learn more about how organs perform. It may someday be possible to operate the computer like a miniature space ship inside the human body—where the captain is the doctor and the mysterious terrain being explored are the body's organs.

13. At IBM's Rome Scientific Center, experimental image processing techniques have been developed for art restoration. The sixteenth century painting shown here is being restored using computer programs to select colors that will both protect the painting and retain its original integrity.

14. Faculty and graduate students at colleges and universities frequently use computers for research projects.

15. Weather patterns are routinely examined by scientists in labs and displayed to the public on television with computer assistance.

Computer Simulation

16–21. Computers are frequently used to simulate aircraft and automobile operation before the planes and cars are built and put into use. Pilots and drivers can also be trained by simulation techniques.

The Evans & Sutherland systems used to produce these highly complex scenes generate frames in real time at a rate of about fifty frames per second. Realtime simulation means that the frames are not prestored in the computer, but are created—on the fly, so to speak—each time the simulation program is run.

16

20

19

21

Entertainment and Leisure

Five computer-generated outputs from everyday life.

22. An illustration for a greeting card.

23. A news graphic created for KPIX-TV, San Francisco.

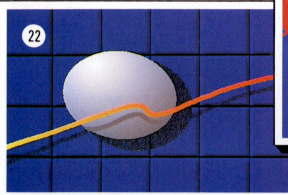

24. A brochure illustration.

25. A design for a surfing poster.

26. A cover for an issue of *Pacific Shipper* magazine.

Summary and Key Terms

Since the early 1950s, when the era of commercial computing began, computers have rapidly woven their way into the very fabric of modern society. In the process they have created both opportunities and problems.

One of the first criticisms leveled at the entry of computers into the workplace was that their very presence resulted in anxiety. Anxiety-related concerns triggered by the so-called computer revolution include fear of layoff or reassignment, fear of falling behind, and job burnout. In addition to these problems, a number of concerns related to **ergonomic** issues—such as display-device usage and workspace design—have surfaced. Moreover many people are worried about society's apparent overreliance on computers.

Computer crime is loosely defined as the use of computers to commit unauthorized acts. Some states have laws that address computer crime directly; others do not. In practice, however, even in states that do have such laws, computer crime is difficult to pin down. It is often hard to decide when an unauthorized act is really a crime, judges and juries are often bewildered by the technical issues involved, and companies are reluctant to press charges.

There are many ways in which organizations can combat computer crimes: hiring trustworthy people, separating employee functions, restricting system use, protecting sensitive programs and data, devising staff controls, recording and managing important system transactions, and conducting regular audits.

Computer ethics refers to standards of moral conduct shown in computer-related matters. Four important problem areas that involve computer ethics are **software piracy, hacking** (breaking a computer code to gain unauthorized entry), employee loyalty, and gray-market selling.

Most of us, understandably, want some control over the kinds of facts that are collected about us, the way they are collected, their accuracy, who uses them, and how they are used. The problem of how to protect **privacy** and ensure that personal information is not misused was with us long before electronic computers existed. But modern computer systems, with their ability to store and manipulate unprecedented quantities of data and make those data available to many locations, have added a new dimension to the privacy issue. The greater the ability to collect, store, and disseminate information, the greater is the potential for abuse of that information.

Since the early 1970s, the federal government has sought to protect the rights of citizens by passing legislation to limit the abuse of computer data banks. Some important laws enacted for this purpose are the Fair Credit Reporting Act, the Freedom of Information Act, the Education Privacy Act, and the Privacy Act.

Today the number of uses to which computers have been put is so large and the uses so heterogeneous that they almost defy classification. The bulk of this text has examined the uses of computers in the ordinary business workplace. Outside of this workplace, computers are found in the home, in educational institutions, in entertainment and leisure activities, and in science and medicine.

Review Exercises

Fill-in Questions

1. Fear of computers is known as _____.
2. _____ is the field that covers the effects that such factors as computer workspaces have on the productivity and health of employees.
3. The criminal act of shaving off small amounts from numerous randomly selected bank accounts is known as the _____ technique.
4. _____ refers to standards of moral conduct in computer-related matters.
5. The unauthorized copying or use of computer programs is known as software _____.
6. _____ is a computer term relating to the activities of people who use computers or terminals to crack the security of computer systems.
7. The _____ Act is designed to prevent private organizations from unfairly denying credit to individuals.
8. The _____ Act protects an individual's right to privacy in both private and public schools that receive federal funding.

Discussion Questions

1. Identify some specific problems caused by the rapid spread of computer use in society.
2. Describe some ways in which computers may affect our health.
3. Why is computer crime so difficult to pin down?

4. Name some of the forms computer crime can take.
5. Name some rights of individuals that computer privacy laws have tried to protect.
6. Name some ways in which computers affect us in our daily lives.

Appendix A

Number Systems

In Chapter 4 you learned that fixed-length codes such as EBCDIC and ASCII are often used to represent numbers, letters of the alphabet, and special characters. Although these codes are handy for storing data and transporting it around a computer system, they are not designed to do arithmetic operations. For this type of use, data must be stored in a "true" binary form that can be manipulated quickly by the computer.

This Appendix covers several fundamentals of numbering systems. The two primary systems discussed are the decimal numbering system (used by people) and the binary numbering system (used by computers). Also discussed are the octal and hexadecimal numbering systems, both of which are shorthand ways of representing long strings of binary numbers so they are more understandable to people.

A *number system* is a way of representing numbers. The system we most commonly use is called the *decimal,* or base 10, system (the word decimal comes from the Latin word for ten). It is called base 10 because it uses ten symbols—the digits 0, 1, 2, 3, 4, 5, 6, 7, 8, 9—to represent all possible numbers. Numbers greater than nine are represented by a combination of these symbols.

Because we are so familiar with the decimal system, it never occurs to most of us that we could represent numbers in any other way. In fact, however, there is nothing that says a number system has to have ten possible symbols. Many other numbers would do as a base.

We saw in Chapter 4 that the *binary,* or base 2, system is used extensively by computers to represent numbers and other characters. Computer systems can perform computations and transmit data thousands of times faster in binary form than they can using decimal representations. Thus it's important for anyone studying computers to know how the binary system works. Students contemplating professional careers in computers should also understand the *octal* (base 8) and *hexadecimal* (base 16) systems. But before we examine many of the number systems used in the computing world—and learn how to convert numbers from one system into another—let's look more closely at the decimal numbering system. Insight into how the decimal system works will help us understand more about these other numbering systems.

THE DECIMAL NUMBERING SYSTEM

All numbering systems, including the decimal system with which we work in our everyday lives, represent numbers as a combination of ordered symbols. As stated earlier, the **decimal*** (or base 10) system has ten acceptable symbols—the digits 0, 1, 2, . . . , 9. The positioning of the symbols in a decimal number is significant. For example, 891 is a different number than 918 (with the same symbols occupying different positions).

The position of each symbol in any decimal number represents the number 10 (the base number) raised to a power, or exponent, that is based on that position. Going from right to left, the first position represents 10^0, or 1; the second position represents 10^1, or 10; the third position represents 10^2, or 100, and so forth. Thus, as the box in Figure A-1 shows, a decimal number like 7216 is understood as $7 \times 10^3 + 2 \times 10^2 + 1 \times 10^1 + 6 \times 10^0$.

THE BINARY NUMBERING SYSTEM

The **binary,** or base 2, system works in a manner similar to the decimal system. One major difference is that the binary system has only two symbols—0 and 1—instead of ten. A second major difference is that the

*Terms used in this appendix can be found in the Glossary at the end of the book.

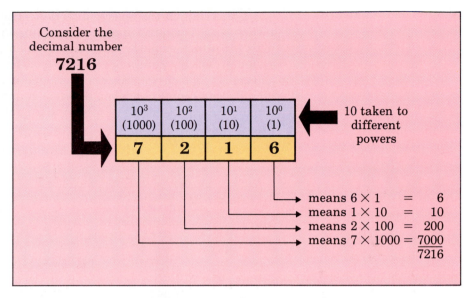

Figure A-1. *How the decimal (base 10) system works.*
Note: $7216 = 7 \times 10^3 + 2 \times 10^2 + 1 \times 10^1 + 6 \times 10^0$.

position of each digit in a binary number represents the number 2 (the base number) raised to an exponent based on that position. Thus the binary number 11100 represents

$$1 \times 2^4 + 1 \times 2^3 + 1 \times 2^2 + 0 \times 2^1 + 0 \times 2^0$$

which, translated into the decimal system, is 28. Another example of a binary-to-decimal conversion is provided in Figure A-2.

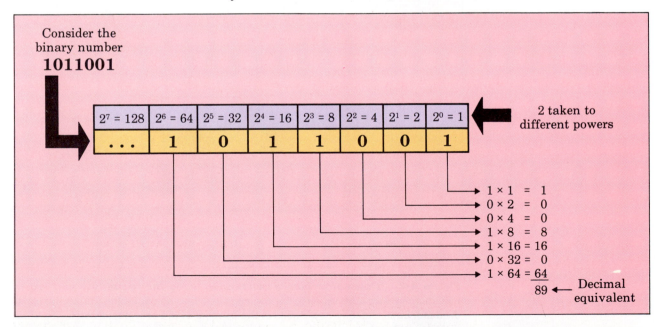

Figure A-2. *Binary-to-decimal conversion.* To convert any binary number to its decimal counterpart, take the rightmost digit and multiply it by 2^0 (or 1), the next to rightmost digit and multiply it by 2^1 (or 2), and so on, as illustrated above. Then add up all the products so formed.

Converting in the reverse direction—from decimal to binary—is also rather easy. A popular approach for doing this is the *remainder method.* This procedure employs successive divisions by the base number of the system to which we are converting. Use of the remainder method to convert a decimal to a binary number is illustrated in Figure A-3.

To avoid confusion when different number bases are being used, it is common to use the base as a subscript. So, referring to Figures A-2 and A-3 for example, we could write

$$89_{10} = 1011001_2$$

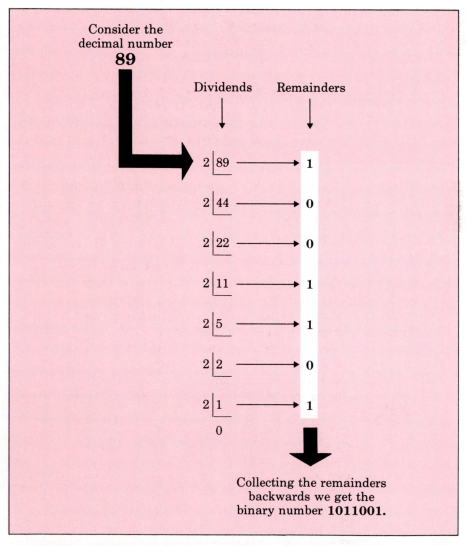

Consider the decimal number **89**

Dividends   Remainders

2	89	→	1
2	44	→	0
2	22	→	0
2	11	→	1
2	5	→	1
2	2	→	0
2	1	→	1
	0		

Collecting the remainders backwards we get the binary number **1011001.**

Figure A-3. *Decimal-to-binary conversion using the remainder method.* In this approach, we start by using the decimal number to be converted (89) as the initial dividend. Each successive dividend is the quotient of the previous division. We keep dividing until we've reached a zero quotient, whereupon the converted number is formed by the remainders taken in reverse order.

Additionally, when we are using number systems other than the decimal system, it is customary to pronounce each symbol individually. For example, 101_2 is pronounced "one-zero-one" rather than "one hundred one." This convention is also used with other nondecimal systems.

The binary system described here is sometimes referred to as *true-binary representation*. True-binary representation does not use a fixed number of bits, as do EBCDIC and ASCII, nor is it used to represent letters or special characters.

THE OCTAL NUMBERING SYSTEM

Because large binary numbers—for example, 11010100010011101_2—can be easily misread by programmers, binary digits are often grouped into units of three or four that, in turn, are represented by other symbols. The octal system uses a grouping of three. Some computer manufacturers use the octal system extensively with their hardware and software documentation, so it is a handy system to know.

As you may already have guessed, the **octal** (or base 8) system uses eight symbols—0, 1, 2, 3, 4, 5, 6, 7. The position of each digit in an octal number represents the number 8 (the base number) raised to an exponent based on that position. Thus a number in base 8 looks like a decimal number, but it has a different meaning than the same pattern of digits in

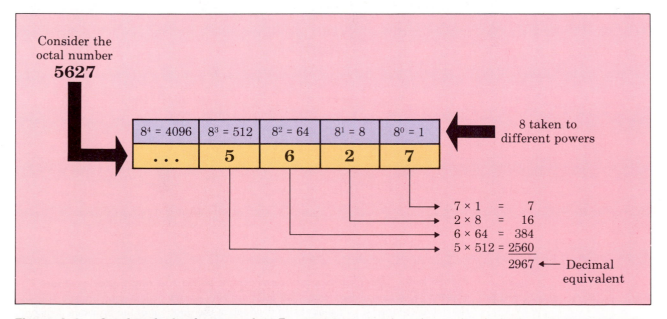

Figure A-4. Octal-to-decimal conversion. To convert any octal number to its decimal counterpart, take the rightmost digit and multiply it by 8^0 (or 1), the next to rightmost digit and multiply it by 8^1 (or 8), and so on as illustrated above. Then add up all the products so formed.

base 10. The base 8 number 725, for example, means

$$7 \times 8^2 + 2 \times 8^1 + 5 \times 8^0$$

which, translated into base 10, is 469. A second example illustrating conversion from octal to decimal is provided in Figure A-4. The procedure employed in this conversion process closely parallels the one used to change binary numbers to decimal numbers.

We can find the octal counterpart of a decimal number by employing the remainder method we used with binary numbers. Instead of successively dividing by 2, however, we divide by 8. Figure A-5 illustrates this process.

To convert from base 8 to base 2, separately convert each octal digit to three binary digits. The table in Figure A-6 will help with this process. So, for example, to convert 7136_8 to base 2, we get

$$\begin{array}{cccc} 7 & 1 & 3 & 6 \\ 111 & 001 & 011 & 110 \end{array}$$

or 111001011110_2. To convert the other way, from base 2 to base 8, we go through the reverse process. If the number of digits in the binary number is

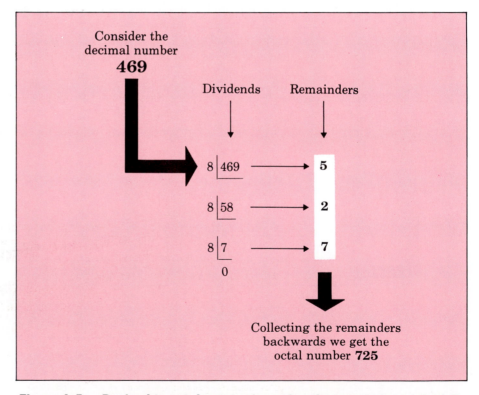

Figure A-5. *Decimal-to-octal conversion using the remainder method.* To convert 469_{10} to an octal number we start our successive divisions by 8 using 469 as the initial dividend. Each successive dividend is the quotient of the previous division. As in Figure A-3, we divide until we've reached a zero quotient, and form the converted number by taking the remainders in reverse order.

Octal Character	Binary Equivalent
0	000
1	001
2	010
3	011
4	100
5	101
6	110
7	111

Figure A-6.   Octal characters and their binary counterparts.

not divisible by 3, add leading zeros to the binary number to force an even division. Thus, for example, to convert 1101100011_2 to base 8 we get

$$001 \quad 101 \quad 100 \quad 011$$
$$1 \qquad 5 \qquad 4 \qquad 3$$

or 1543_8. Note that two leading zeros were added to make this conversion.

THE HEXADECIMAL NUMBERING SYSTEM

Often, diagnostic messages are output to programmers in hexadecimal (or "hex") notation. Hex is a shorthand method for representing the 8-bit bytes that are stored in the computer system.

Hexadecimal means base 16, implying that there are sixteen different symbols in this numbering system. Since we have only ten possible digits to work with, letters are used instead of numbers for the extra six symbols. The sixteen hexadecimal symbols and their decimal and binary counterparts are shown in Figure A-7.

Hexadecimal, like octal, is not itself a code the computer uses to perform computations or to communicate with other machines. It does, however, have a special relationship to the 8-bit bytes of EBCDIC and ASCII-8 that makes it ideal for displaying messages quickly. As you can see in Figure A-7, each hex character has a 4-binary-bit counterpart, so any combination of 8 bits can be represented by exactly two hexadecimal characters. Thus the letter A (represented in EBCDIC by 11000001) has a hex representation of C1.

Let's look at an example to see how to convert from hex to decimal. Suppose you receive the following message on your display screen:

PROGRAM LOADED AT LOCATION 4F6A

Hexadecimal Character	Decimal Equivalent	Binary Equivalent
0	0	0000
1	1	0001
2	2	0010
3	3	0011
4	4	0100
5	5	0101
6	6	0110
7	7	0111
8	8	1000
9	9	1001
A	10	1010
B	11	1011
C	12	1100
D	13	1101
E	14	1110
F	15	1111

Figure A-7. *Hexadecimal characters and their decimal and binary equivalents.*

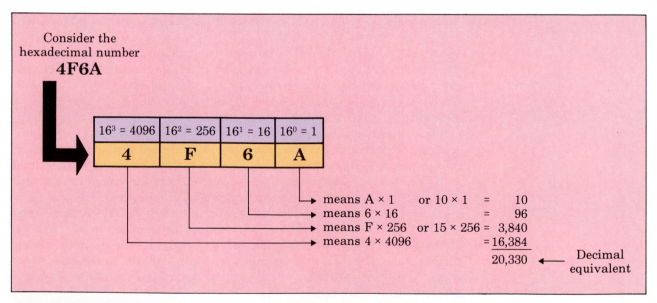

Figure A-8. *Hexadecimal-to-decimal conversion.* To convert any hexadecimal number to its decimal counterpart, take the rightmost digit and multiply it by 16^0 (or 1), the next to rightmost digit and mulitply it by 16^1 (or 16), and so on as illustrated above. Then add up all the products so formed.

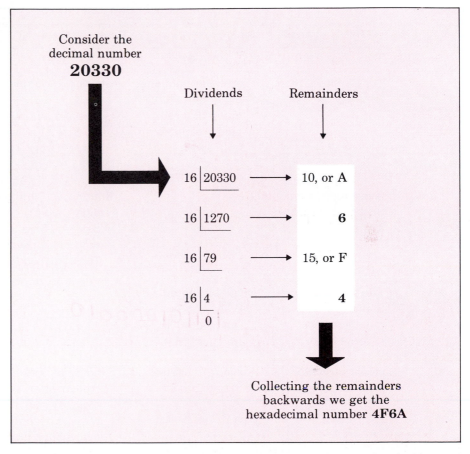

Figure A-9. Decimal-to-hexadecimal conversion using the remainder method. To convert 20330_{10} to a hexadecimal number, we start our successive divisions by 16 using 20330 as the initial dividend. Each successive dividend is the quotient of the previous division. As in Figure A-3, we divide until we've reached a zero quotient, and form the converted number by taking the remainders in reverse order.

This message tells you the location in primary memory of the first byte in your program. To determine the decimal equivalent of a hexadecimal number such as 4F6A, you can use a procedure similar to the binary-to-decimal conversion shown in Figure A-2 (refer to Figure A-8).

To convert the other way—from decimal to hex—we again can use the remainder method, dividing this time by 16. A decimal-to-hex conversion using the remainder method is illustrated in Figure A-9.

To convert from base 16 to base 2, convert each hex digit separately to four binary digits (using the table in Figure A-7). Thus, for example, to convert F6A9 to base 2, we get

$$\begin{array}{cccc} \text{F} & 6 & \text{A} & 9 \\ 1111 & 0110 & 1010 & 1001 \end{array}$$

From Base	To Base			
	2	**8**	**10**	**16**
2		Starting at rightmost digit, convert each group of three binary digits to an octal digit.	Starting at rightmost digit, multiply binary digits by 2^0, 2^1, 2^2, etc., respectively. Then add products.	Starting at rightmost digit, convert each group of four binary digits to a hex digit.
8	Convert each octal digit to three binary digits.		Starting at rightmost digit, multiply octal digits by 8^0, 8^1, 8^2, etc., respectively. Then add products.	Convert to base 2; then to base 16.
10	Divide repeatedly by 2; then collect remainders in reverse order.	Divide repeatedly by 8; then collect remainders in reverse order.		Divide repeatedly by 16; then collect remainders in reverse order.
16	Convert each hex digit to four binary digits.	Convert to base 2; then to base 8.	Starting at rightmost digit, multiply hex digits by 16^0, 16^1, 16^2, etc., respectively. Then add products.	

Figure A-10. *Summary of conversions.*

or 1111011010101001_2. To convert from base 2 to base 16, we go through the reverse process. If the number of digits in the binary number is not divisible by 4, add leading zeros to the binary number to force an even division. So, for example, to convert 1101101010011_2 to base 16 we get

$$0001 \quad 1011 \quad 0101 \quad 0011$$
$$1 \qquad B \qquad 5 \qquad 3$$

or $1B53_{16}$. Note that three leading zeros were added to make this conversion.

A table summarizing all of the conversions covered in this appendix is provided in Figure A-10.

Summary and Key Terms

A *number system* is a way of representing numbers.

The number system we most commonly use is called the **decimal,** or base 10, system. It is called base 10 because it uses ten symbols—the digits 0, 1, 2, 3, 4, 5, 6, 7, 8, 9—to represent all possible numbers. The position of each symbol in any decimal number represents the number 10 (the base number) raised to a power, or exponent, which is based on that position.

The **binary,** or base 2, system works in a manner similar to the decimal system. One major difference is that the binary system has only two symbols—0 and 1—instead of ten. A second major difference is that the position of each digit in a binary number represents the number 2 (the base number) raised to an exponent based on that position.

Because large binary numbers can be easily misread by programmers, binary digits are often grouped into units of three or four that, in turn, are represented by other symbols. The **octal,** or base 8, numbering system corresponds to a grouping of three binary digits. The octal system has eight symbols—0, 1, 2, 3, 4, 5, 6, 7. The position of each digit in an octal number represents the number 8 raised to an exponent based on that position.

The **hexadecimal,** or base 16, system is used to represent a grouping of four binary digits. There are sixteen different symbols in this system. Since we have only ten possible digits to work with, the letters A–F are used instead of numbers for the extra six symbols. The position of each digit in a hexadecimal number represents the number 16 raised to an exponent based on that position.

It is a relatively straightforward process to convert any value in one numbering system into a value in another system.

Exercises

Instructions: Provide an answer to each of the following questions.

1. Convert the following binary numbers to decimal numbers.
   a. 1011_2 _____
   b. 101110_2 _____
   c. 1010011_2 _____

2. Convert the following octal numbers to decimal numbers.
   a. 17_8 _____
   b. 275_8 _____
   c. 3106_8 _____

3. Convert the following decimal numbers to binary numbers.
   a. 51_{10} _____
   b. 260_{10} _____
   c. 500_{10} _____

4. Convert the following decimal numbers to octal numbers.
   a. 92_{10} _____
   b. 153_{10} _____
   c. 6133_{10} _____

5. Convert the following binary numbers to hexadecimal numbers.
   a. 101_2 _____
   b. 11010_2 _____
   c. 111101000010_2 _____

6. Convert the following binary numbers to octal numbers.
   a. 11_2 _____
   b. 1010_2 _____
   c. 10011101000001_2 _____

7. Convert the following hexadecimal numbers to binary numbers.
   a. $F2_{16}$ _____
   b. $1A8_{16}$ _____
   c. $39EB_{16}$ _____

8. Convert the following hexadecimal numbers to decimal numbers.
   a. $B6_{16}$ _____
   b. $5E9_{16}$ _____
   c. $CAFF_{16}$ _____

9. Convert 72_8 to hexadecimal.

10. Drawing upon techniques you've learned in this appendix, how would you convert the base 6 (yes, six) number 451_6 to a decimal number?

```
N 100)
     READ NUMBERS IN
       I=1 TO N
       READ X(I)
     NEXT I
     REM BUBBLE SORT
0    FOR I=1 TO N-1
        FOR J=1 TO
           IF X(J)
              REM
              T=X
80
90              X(
200
210             X(
```

A Beginner's Guide to BASIC

BASIC (Beginner's All-purpose Symbolic Instruction Code) is one of many programming languages widely in use today. A **programming language** is a set of rules used to create a computer program. The **computer program** is what you enter into the computer system to produce results.

A BASIC computer program is very similar to a recipe. It consists of a list of **instructions** the computer must carry out in a specified sequence to produce the desired result. Each of the instructions in a BASIC program must be written in strict accordance with the rules of the BASIC language. These rules are referred to as **syntax.** If you make a seemingly trivial syntax error in writing the program, such as misspelling a word or omitting a comma, the computer system will reject your program or give unexpected, incorrect results.

The purpose of this appendix is to teach you how to write useful, simple BASIC programs. BASIC is one of the easiest to learn of all the major programming languages. You should be able to create programs for business use, game playing, and performing difficult, repetitive computations after reading this appendix and practicing on a computer.

Many versions of the BASIC language are available today. This appendix has been written to conform as closely as possible to the most common BASIC usage, the guidelines for minimal BASIC proposed by the American National Standards Institute (ANSI). Thus the programs that follow will work on most machines. In this appendix program outputs are distinguished from programs and their inputs by a color background.

The need to practice BASIC on a computer can't be emphasized enough. Programming, like driving a car or playing a sport, is a skill that is mastered mostly by practice. Since it is easy for a beginner in any endeavor to make mistakes at the beginning, practicing can initially be very frustrating (can you remember your first day with a musical instrument?). However, if you really want to learn BASIC, and if you start by writing simple programs rather than complicated ones, you will find BASIC relatively easy. So, be patient . . . and start playing with your computer as soon as possible.

Here's what's on the following pages.

Section 1

A BASIC Primer

A SIMPLE EXAMPLE

Let's get into BASIC immediately by looking at a relatively simple problem and developing a BASIC program to solve it. The example given in Figure B1-1 will show you both some of the rules of BASIC and the manner in which computers carry out instructions in a logical, step-by-step fashion.

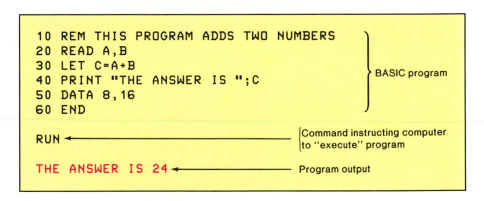

```
10 REM THIS PROGRAM ADDS TWO NUMBERS
20 READ A,B
30 LET C=A+B                            BASIC program
40 PRINT "THE ANSWER IS ";C
50 DATA 8,16
60 END

RUN                                     Command instructing computer
                                        to "execute" program

THE ANSWER IS 24                        Program output
```

Figure B1-1.   A simple BASIC program.

The problem is to write a BASIC program that adds the numbers 8 and 16. We want the computer to print the answer like this:

THE ANSWER IS 24

There are many ways to solve this problem, including the one shown in Figure B1-1.

The six numbered instructions in the figure make up a **BASIC program.** In most cases you will be typing in instructions such as these at a keyboard hooked up to a computer. When you have finished typing the instructions, you normally then type the word RUN, to command the system to execute (that is, to carry out) your program. You should study this program carefully before proceeding further. Sometimes the purpose of an instruction will be obvious. The following comments should clarify the other instructions.

Before we go into detail about precisely how the program works, you should observe the following important points about the program in Figure B1-1:

1. Each of the six numbered instructions is a **BASIC program statement.** The computer completes the operation described in each statement. It then automatically moves on to another statement.

   Each BASIC program statement begins with a key word that tells the computer what type of operation is involved: for example, REM, READ, LET, PRINT, DATA, and END. These key words may be thought of as the vocabulary of the computer system when you are writing BASIC programs. You must always stay strictly within this vocabulary. If, for example, you substitute DATUM or DATTA for DATA in line 50, the computer system will not know what you want to do.

2. Each program statement is identified by a **line number;** for example, 10, 20, 30, and so on. Line numbers are normally written in increments of 10 rather than 1, which allows you easily to insert new statements in the program later. All line numbers must be integers (whole numbers), and all lines must have different line numbers.

   The computer will always execute statements in the sequence specified by the line numbers unless instructed to do otherwise. Ways to do this are discussed later in this section. Because the line numbers specify the order of program statements, you can type in the lines in any order, such as 30, 60, 10, 50, 20, and 40. Before the computer system runs your program, it will automatically put all the statements in proper order (by line number).

3. In this program three **variables** (A, B, and C) are used. When the computer system begins to execute the program, it will set up separate storage locations for A, B, and C. A storage location can be thought of as a "bucket" that can hold only one item (for example, a number) at a time.

   The storage locations represent the memory of the computer with respect to the program being run. For example, when we ask the computer in line 40 to print the value of C, the computer consults its memory to find the value.

   It is possible, as we will see in later programs, to change the values of variables such as A, B, and C several times during the execution of a program. It is because their values are allowed to change that they are known as variables. When A, B, and C are given new values, their old values are lost.

Now let's see, statement by statement, how the program works.

```
10 REM THIS PROGRAM ADDS TWO NUMBERS
```
The REM (remark) statement is actually ignored by the computer. However, even though the computer doesn't use it, the REM statement is very helpful to the programmer. It allows you to place informative comments (such as the program title or description) in the body of the program.

```
20 READ A,B   and   50 DATA 8,16
```
The READ and DATA statements are always used together in BASIC. The

READ statement instructs the computer to assign data to the specified variables. The DATA statement provides these data. Note that the computer assigns values one at a time and in the order they are typed in the READ and DATA statements. Thus when the READ statement is executed, the computer sets A equal to 8 and B equal to 16.

```
30 LET C=A+B
```
The computer system always reacts to a LET statement by computing the value indicated by the expression on the right side of the "=" sign and assigning it to the variable named on the left side. Thus statement 30 will cause the following actions to be taken:

1. The computer system looks up the values of A and B in memory (finding 8 and 16 respectively).

2. The values of A and B are added (producing 24).

3. The value of the right side of the expression (24) is assigned to C.

```
40 PRINT "THE ANSWER IS ";C
```
The PRINT statement is used when we want the computer system to output something, for example, the results of a computation. The PRINT statement above consists of three elements:

1. A phrase appearing inside quotes (THE ANSWER IS). The computer system will print this phrase exactly as it appears. These **literal** phrases are handy in PRINT statements to label output.

2. A formatting character (;). The semicolon instructs the computer system to leave only one space between the literal phrase and the value of C.

3. A variable (C). The computer system will look up the value of C in memory and print its value.

If you are using a display device, PRINT instructs the computer to display the information on the screen. On the IBM Personal Computer and some other machines, you must use the command LPRINT in your program if instead you wish to direct output to your printer.

```
60 END
```
On many computer systems, the END statement physically must be the last statement in the program. It instructs the computer system that the program is finished.

At this point you can start to see how BASIC works. Now is a good time to test your knowledge of some of the fundamental concepts just introduced by practicing on your computer system. You might try some of the following suggestions:

1. Type and run the BASIC program in Figure B1-1. Did you get the same result as in this appendix?

2. Try altering the PRINT statement so it produces nicer output. For example, to get the computer system to output

THE SUM OF 8 AND 16 IS 24

your PRINT statement should look like

```
PRINT "THE SUM OF ";A;" AND ";B;" IS ";C
```

3. Try making the expression in statement 30 more complicated to see what the effects are. For example, A and B could be multiplied by specifying A*B instead of A+B in statement 30. Note that in BASIC an asterisk is used to tell the computer to multiply. Multiplication is explained in more detail later.

   As another example, can you guess what the following program produces?

```
10 READ X,Y,Z
20 LET W=X+Y-Z+100
30 PRINT X;Y;Z;"ANSWER =";W
40 DATA 10,20,30
50 END
```

4. Tinker with the DATA statement by changing the data values (try some negative numbers or numbers with decimal points). Also, experiment to see if it matters where the DATA statement appears. Try placing it as the first, second, or third statement of your program. Finally, try splitting a single DATA statement into several DATA statements. For example, split line 40 of the program in suggestion 3 above into

```
40 DATA 10
41 DATA 20,30
```

Running BASIC programs is a relatively simple task, and is described in some detail later in this section. All you need to concentrate on at this point are the RUN and LIST commands, as well as the instructions relating to correcting or changing lines. The RUN command executes your program and produces output. The LIST command will display the lines of your program in proper order upon your display device. So—get started now! If you can write simple programs today, the complicated ones you encounter later will seem much easier.

A TOUGHER EXAMPLE

The program we just looked at was rather simple. The values of the variables didn't change, and the computer wasn't asked to execute a statement out of numerical order. In most programs, however, the values of the variables do change, and the computer is asked to **branch** to a statement other than the one which immediately follows.

Let's now consider a program that reflects these two added complications. We will write a program to compute and output the squares of 8, 16, and 12.

Before **coding** (that is, writing out) this problem in BASIC, let's consider what tasks are involved in solving this problem. Additionally, let's think about the order in which these tasks must be presented to the computer. The tasks themselves, together with the order in which they are performed, are referred to as an **algorithm.** Designing an algorithm is not that different from building a house. You don't start putting the roof together before you've fully designed the whole structure and decided when the roof will be made relative to other sections. Creating an algorithm is done in the **design phase** of computer program development.

At first glance, it seems that the following algorithm is attractive for solving our problem:

1. Read a number.   **3.** Print out the result of step 2.

2. Square the number.   **4.** Go back to step 1.

The fundamental structure involved here is called a **loop.** Thus the computer system is to read 8, square it (producing 64), output the result (64), loop back to step 1, read 16, square it . . . and so on. There is one major problem with the four-step solution just described—once the computer system fully processes the last number (12) and goes back to step 1, there are no more numbers to read. Thus we need to instruct the loop when to stop. This problem is frequently solved by putting a **trailer** (or **sentinel**) **value** (such as −1) at the end of the data list and directing the computer to leave the loop immediately after this trailer value is read. Thus we could refine our algorithm as follows:

1.   Read a number.

1.5   If the number = −1 go to step 5; otherwise process step 2.

2.   Square the number.

3.   Print out the result of step 2.

4.   Go back to step 1

5.   End the program.

Although this procedure is complete and produces correct results, many professional programmers include an extra "Read" step to make the procedure more *structured*. Many programming languages (such as Pascal and COBOL) make it difficult to code satisfactory programs unless this extra step is taken. (For a full explanation of this extra Read and why it is important for structured programs see the box on page 304 in Chapter 10.)

Inserting the extra Read step (step 3.5) and modifying step 4 so that it points back to step 1.5, we get

1.   Read a number.

1.5   If the number $= -1$ go to step 5; otherwise process step 2.

2.   Square the number.

3.   Print out the result of step 2.

3.5   Read another number.

4.   Go back to step 1.5.

5.   End the program

Once the algorithm is completely designed, coding it in BASIC becomes relatively straightforward, as you will see by observing the program in Figure B1-2.

```
10 REM THIS PROGRAM SQUARES NUMBERS
20 READ A
30 IF A=-1 THEN 90
40 LET B=A^2
50 PRINT "THE SQUARE OF ";A;" IS";B
60 READ A
70 GOTO 30
80 DATA 8,16,12,-1
90 END
RUN
THE SQUARE OF 8 IS 64
THE SQUARE OF 16 IS 256
THE SQUARE OF 12 IS 144
```

Figure B1-2. *Program to compute and output the squares of several numbers.*

It will take the computer 18 steps to execute this program fully, as shown in Figure B1-3.

The design phase of computer programming is extremely critical. Programs used to help run businesses are usually in operation for several years, and they need to be constantly modified to meet changing business conditions. Thus a program that is designed in a hasty fashion will often cause numerous maintenance problems over the years for programmers who have to keep it up to date. Simply stated, poorly designed programs are almost always expensive headaches. A few extra dollars spent on initial design may save hundreds of dollars later.

There are numerous guidelines for good program design. Many of these are covered in Chapters 9 and 10. For example, professional programmers usually write programs that include only certain forms of the three funda-

Step	State- ment Executed	Value of A in Storage	Value of B in Storage	Action Taken
1	20	8		8 taken from data list and assigned to A
2	30	8		8 ≠ −1; therefore, go to next statement
3	40	8	64	B computed
4	50	8	64	Computer system prints THE SQUARE OF 8 IS 64
5	60	16	64	16 taken from data list and assigned to A
6	70	16	64	Computer directed to line 30
7	30	16	64	16 ≠ −1; therefore, go to next statement
8	40	16	256	B computed
9	50	16	256	Computer system prints THE SQUARE OF 16 IS 256
10	60	12	256	12 taken from data list and assigned to A
11	70	12	256	Computer directed to line 30
12	30	12	256	12 ≠ −1; therefore, go to next statement
13	40	12	144	B computed
14	50	12	144	Computer system prints THE SQUARE OF 12 IS 144
15	60	−1	144	−1 taken from data list and assigned to A
16	70	−1	144	Computer directed to line 30
17	30	−1	144	−1 = −1; therefore, go to line 90
18	90	−1	144	The program ends

Figure B1-3. *Steps the computer system must take to fully execute the problem in Figure B1-2.*

mental **control structures: sequence, selection,** and **looping.** Also, good programmers code many comments in their programs as a **documentation** aid, so that other programmers can easily understand how the programs work. Additionally, it is also a good practice to choose variable names carefully and systematically, so that other programmers can quickly grasp the underlying logic involved and you will remember easily what they mean if you have to alter the program months after you wrote it. Most companies will have a set of written guidelines, or *shop rules,* for their programmers to ensure that programs are written in a very consistent and readable fashion. Thus it is very important that from the outset of your programming experience you think very carefully about the design of your programs.

WRITING ACCEPTABLE BASIC EXPRESSIONS

Now that we've covered some broad fundamentals concerning how BASIC works, let's consider more closely rules for writing BASIC instructions. This subsection addresses allowable characters, formation of variables and constants, and the writing of mathematical expressions.

BASIC Character Set

When you are typing in a program you must use only those characters that are understood by the version of BASIC available to your computer system. Such characters are known as the BASIC character set. They fall into three groups:

Alphabetic: ABCDEFGHIJKLMNOPQRSTUVWXYZ

Numeric: 0123456789

Special: . , + & ! < > / @ ( ) - * =   (and so on)

Variables

Variables are of two fundamental types: numeric and string. **Numeric variables** can be assigned only numbers, whereas **string variables** can be assigned any combination of alphabetic, numeric, and special characters. Let's look at numeric variables first.

NUMERIC VARIABLES.   The program below contains six numeric variables:

```
10 LET A=6.5
20 LET B=8.04
30 READ C1,C2,C3
40 LET D=A+B-(C1+C2+C3)
50 PRINT D
60 DATA 3,2,0.04
70 END
RUN
9.5
```

Each of the variables (A, B, C1, C2, C3, and D) is allocated a storage location by the computer at execution time. Each location may store a number while your program is executing.

BASIC varies in the way numeric variable names may be created by the programmer. The most universal convention is to allow the name to be composed of either

1. A single alphabetic character (for example, A, B, and D), or

2. A single alphabetic character followed by a single digit (for example, C1, C2, and C3).

Thus, for example, the following numeric variable names are allowable under this convention:

```
C8, F1, X, I, I8, T
```

whereas those at the top of the next page are not:

C12   Too many characters

8C   First character not alphabetic

F&   Second character must be numeric

If your computer system was purchased within the past few years, it probably allows longer numeric variable names in BASIC—up to 40 characters long in many systems. This allows variable names to be chosen as better reminders of what the variables stand for. The first character must still be alphabetic; other characters can be letters or digits.

In this appendix we will stick with the older convention, since it will work on any computer system using BASIC.

STRING VARIABLES.   A string is a collection of related characters; for example,

```
JOHN Q. DOE
1600 PENNSYLVANIA AVENUE
THX-1138
```

Strings may be assigned to variable names and manipulated by computer systems. For example, the following program contains only string variables

```
10 LET A$="AT THIS EXAMPLE"
20 LET B$="LOOK CAREFULLY "
30 PRINT B$;A$
40 END
RUN
LOOK CAREFULLY AT THIS EXAMPLE
```

There are two string variables in this short program: A$ and B$. The computer allocates storage space to string variables in essentially the same way it allocates storage to numeric variables. In other words the storage location set up for A$ contains the string

AT THIS EXAMPLE

and the location set up for B$ contains the string

LOOK CAREFULLYⱴ   (ⱴ represents a blank space)

Since A$ and B$ are variables, they can contain different strings throughout the course of the program, but only one string at any given time. An important difference between numeric and string variables is that we can perform conventional arithmetic with numeric variables but generally not with string ones.

BASIC varies in the way string variable names may be created by the programmer. The original and most universal rule is to use a single alphabetic character followed by a dollar sign ($). Thus with this convention the following string variable names are allowable:

$$A\$, \quad B\$, \quad C\$, \quad T\$, \quad Z\$$$

but the following are not:

F1   Dollar sign is not second character

P2$ Too many characters

T   Dollar sign missing

$ Leading alphabetic character missing

Again, many newer systems allow longer names.

Some computer systems require that the string assigned to a string variable be enclosed in quotes; for example,

```
10 LET A$="EVERY GOOD "
20 LET C$=" DOES FINE"
30 READ B$
40 PRINT A$;B$;C$
50 READ B$
60 PRINT A$;B$;C$
70 DATA "BOY","GIRL"
80 END
RUN
EVERY GOOD BOY DOES FINE
EVERY GOOD GIRL DOES FINE
```

Constants

Like their variable counterparts, **constants** may be either numeric or string. Unlike variables, however, the value of a constant doesn't change (although constants can be assigned to variables, which can change).

NUMERIC CONSTANTS.   A **numeric constant** is simply a number; for example, 81, -54, .001. When creating arithmetic expressions in BASIC, it is often useful to assign numbers to or to use numbers in combination with numeric variables. Some examples are

```
10 LET A=5.0        5.0 is a numeric constant

10 LET B=A+2        2 is a numeric constant

10 LET C=.01*A+B    .01 is a numeric constant
```

While the numeric constant chosen can be an integer number or a number with a decimal point, the use of commas or dollar signs is not allowed as part of the constant itself. The following are invalid representations of numeric constants in a BASIC program:

```
10 LET A=2,000          Comma invalid. LET A=2000 is valid
100 DATA $6,$3.52       $ invalid. DATA 6,3.52 is valid
```

In many cases we would like to precede a number by a $ sign. This can be done very simply, as the following short example suggests:

```
10 LET A=5.21
20 PRINT "$";A
30 END
RUN
$ 5.21
```

STRING CONSTANTS.   A **string constant** is simply any collection of allowable BASIC characters enclosed in quotes; for example,

```
"HELLO 12?"
"GOODBYE MY LOVELY"
"145-86-7777"
```

String constants can be assigned to string variables, such as

```
10 LET A$="EVERY GOOD "
```

or be declared independently of any variables, as in the PRINT statement below

```
10 PRINT "THE VALUE OF INVENTORY IS $";X
```

A string constant is often referred to as a literal. On many computer systems, string constants appearing in DATA statements need not be enclosed in quotes.

Mathematical Expressions

BASIC allows the programmer to create complex mathematical expressions involving numeric variables and numeric constants. The following operations are permitted:

Operation	BASIC Symbol Used
Addition	+
Subtraction	−
Multiplication	*
Division	/
Exponentiation	$\wedge$ or sometimes **

For example, suppose A = 1, B = 3, and C = 2. The following statements would produce the results indicated:

```
10 LET D=A+B-C
```
(D is assigned a value of 2. The previous value of D is lost.)

```
10 IF B=A+C THEN 70
```
(A+C is computed as 3. Since that is the value of B, the computer branches to statement 70.)

```
10 LET C=B/2
```
(The right-hand side equals 1.5, which is assigned to C. The previous value of C is lost.)

```
10 PRINT A*B
```
(A and B are multiplied, and the product, 3, is printed.)

Now, consider a more complicated expression, such as:

```
10 LET C=C-A+B/(C+4)^2
```

The question arises here as to which operation the computer will perform first. BASIC recognizes the following order of operations (commonly known as the **hierarchy of operations**):

1. All operations within parentheses are performed first, starting with the innermost set of parentheses.

2. Exponentiation is performed next.

3. Multiplication and division are performed next, and the computer executes these from left to right in the expression.

4. Addition and subtraction are performed last, also left to right.

Thus the expression just given would be evaluated as follows under this set of rules:

Step	Operation Performed
1	(C+4) evaluated. Result is 6
2	6^2 evaluated. Result is 36
3	B/36 evaluated. Result is .083333
4	C–A evaluated. Result is 1
5	1 is added to .083333. Result is 1.083333
6	C is assigned the value 1.083333. The previous value of C is lost

To be fully sure that you understand the hierarchy of operations, you should study the examples at the top of the next page. Assume in the examples that W = 1, X = 2, Y = 3, Z = 4.

Example 1   `10 LET A=Y/W*Z`
(A would be assigned a value of 12, since division and multiplication, being on the same level of hierarchy, are performed left to right.)

Example 2   `10 LET B=(X+Y)*(W+1)^2`
(B would be assigned a value of 20. Parenthetical expressions are evaluated first, then exponentiation, and finally multiplication.)

Example 3   `LET C=((Z-W)*X)^2/2`
(C would be assigned a value of 18. The computation in the innermost parentheses is performed first, yielding Z−W=3. Then contents of the outermost parentheses are evaluated, yielding 3*2=6. After all of the parenthetical expressions are evaluated, the 6 is squared. Finally, the result of all the previous operations, 36, is halved to produce 18.)

Most major programming languages have a hierarchy of operations identical to that of BASIC.

MORE ON ELEMENTARY BASIC STATEMENTS

So far, we've informally shown the use of the REM, READ, DATA, IF, LET, PRINT, GOTO, and END statements. Let's consider further the permissible usage of these statements.

READ and DATA Statements

As mentioned earlier, the READ and DATA statements are always used together. When a READ is executed, the computer will assign values appearing in the DATA statements to the respective variables named in the READ. The format of each of these statements is shown below:

> Line # READ list of variables (separated by commas)
> Line # DATA list of data items (separated by commas)

The DATA statements actually are never executed by the computer. Between the time the RUN command is issued and the program is executed, the computer system extracts all of the values from the DATA statements and prepares a "data list." It is this list that is referenced each time a READ is encountered. The DATA statement itself is ignored during program execution.

It is useful to think of a "pointer" attached to the data list. The pointer initially points to the first value in the data list. When this value is assigned, it then points to the second item, and so on. For example, consider the READ and DATA statements for the program in Figure B1-2. The pointer initially points to the 8. When statement 20 is executed, the 8 is assigned to A and the pointer moves to the 16. When the next READ (statement 60) is executed, 16 is assigned to A (the previous value, 8, being erased) and the pointer moves to the 12 . . . and so on. When the -1 is finally assigned to A the data list is exhausted.

Because they are not executed, DATA statements may be placed anywhere in a program. In most implementations they must appear anywhere before the END statement. Also, several DATA statements can be used to hold the data. The program below, which is a rewritten version of the program in Figure B1-2, illustrates these points:

```
 5 DATA 8
 6 DATA 16,12
 7 DATA -1
10 REM THIS PROGRAM SQUARES NUMBERS
20 READ A
30 IF A=-1 THEN 90
40 LET B=A^2
50 PRINT "THE SQUARE OF ";A;" IS";B
60 READ A
70 GOTO 30
90 END
```

You should note, however, that we could *not* have rewritten the data statements as

```
5 DATA -1
6 DATA 8,16
7 DATA 12
```

because the data list formed $(-1, 8, 16, 12)$ would not produce the same results as the original program.

IF Statement

The simplest form of the IF statement follows this format:

Line # IF relational-expression $\begin{Bmatrix} \text{THEN} \\ \text{GOTO} \end{Bmatrix}$ line number

A relational expression is one that contains one of the relational operators in the table at the top of the next page.

Operator	Meaning
<	Less than
<=	Less than or equal to
>	Greater than
>=	Greater than or equal to
=	Equal to
<>	Not equal to

For example, the following are allowable IF statements:

```
10 IF A>B THEN 170
```
  (A>B is the relational expression.)

```
10 IF A-B<=C-D THEN 180
```
  (A−B<=C−D is the relational expression.)

```
10 IF A<>C*(D-E)^F THEN 220
```
  (A<>C*(D−E)^F is the relational expression.)

The computer executes an IF statement as follows:

1. The expression on each side of the relational operator is computed, resulting in a single value on each side.

2. If the statement is true (for example, A>B, where A=3 and B=1), the computer branches to the statement number appearing after the THEN (or GOTO); otherwise the computer goes to the statement that appears immediately after the IF. The IF statement is an example of a **conditional branch.**

An IF statement can contain a relational expression involving string variables; for example,

```
10 IF S$="LAST RECORD" THEN 220
```

Thus, if the string LAST RECORD were stored in S$, this statement would be true.

LET Statement

The LET statement typically follows the format below:

> Line # LET variable-name = expression

An important requirement of this format is that only a single variable name is allowed to appear on the left-hand side of the = sign. Thus

```
10 LET A=6*B-C^(N-1)
10 LET D=0
```

are allowable, whereas

```
LET A+B=C
```

is not. A single variable must appear on the left-hand side because, once the right-hand side expression is computed down to a single value, a storage location (as represented by a single variable) must be declared to store this value. Remember, A, B, C, and so on are acceptable names for storage locations, whereas A+B is not.

The = sign of the LET statement is more properly referred to as an **assignment** (or **replacement**) **symbol** than an "is equal to." To understand the basis of this nomenclature, consider the perfectly acceptable BASIC statement

```
10 LET I=I+1
```

This statement makes absolutely no sense if we interpret the = sign as meaning "is equal to." However, if we interpret this statement as instructing the computer to determine the value of I+1 and to assign the number obtained back to I, it does make sense. Thus if the value 6 were initially stored in I, this statement would add 6 to 1 and assign the result, 7, back to I (erasing the 6 that was there previously).

In most versions of BASIC, the appearance of the word LET is optional in a LET statement. Thus

```
10 I=I+1
```

is equivalent to

```
10 LET I=I+1
```

PRINT Statement

The PRINT statement, being the main vehicle for obtaining BASIC output, is so pivotal that a separate section in this appendix is devoted exclusively to its use (see Section 4). So far we have seen that one acceptable form of the PRINT statement is

$$\text{Line \# PRINT} \begin{Bmatrix} \text{literal,} \\ \text{variable, or} \\ \text{expression} \end{Bmatrix}; \begin{Bmatrix} \text{literal,} \\ \text{variable, or} \\ \text{expression} \end{Bmatrix}; \dots$$

Thus the statements at the top of the next page are allowable:

```
50 PRINT "A=";A
```
If 6 is stored in A, the output is
```
A=6
```

```
50 PRINT A;B;C*Z;M$
```
If 6 is stored in A, 72 in B, 16 in C, 2 in Z, and " ARE THE ANSWERS" in M$, the output is
```
6 72 32 ARE THE ANSWERS
```

```
50 PRINT A$;B$
```
If "HIGH " is stored in A$ and "SCHOOL" in B$, the output is
```
HIGH SCHOOL
```

Other versions of the PRINT statement are covered in Section 4.

GOTO Statement

The simple format of the GOTO statement

> Line # GOTO line-number

makes it one of the easiest BASIC statements to use. For example,

```
200 GOTO 810
```

will direct the computer to statement 810. The GOTO statement is an example of an **unconditional branch.**

Perhaps because of its simplicity, the GOTO statement is frequently overused, leading to programs that are difficult or impossible for a human to follow or "debug" easily. You should never GOTO another GOTO statement. In any case, GOTO should be used as little as possible.

REM Statement

The REM (remark) statement is a very important tool in BASIC—even though it is completely ignored by the computer when the program is executed. Its purpose is to allow you to put useful comments, or blank lines, in the program listing. The format of the REM statement is

> Line # REM any remark

An example of the use of the REM statement is shown in Figure B1-4. The output for the program in Figure B1-4 is exactly the same as the output for the program in Figure B1-2 because the computer system ignores the REM statements. REMs can appear anywhere in a program. In some implementations they must appear before the END statement.

```
10 REM    TITLE:  PROGRAM B1-4
20 REM    DESCRIPTION:  THIS PROGRAM READS
30 REM    NUMBERS, SQUARES THEM, AND OUTPUTS
40 REM    THE RESULTS.
50 REM        AUTHOR - C.S. PARKER
60 REM        DATE - 7/25/85
70 REM *************VARIABLES**************
80 REM      A = THE NUMBER TO BE SQUARED
90 REM      B = THE SQUARE OF THE NUMBER
100 REM ********************************
110 READ A
120 IF A=-1 THEN 180
130 LET B=A^2
140 PRINT "THE SQUARE OF ";A;" IS";B
150 READ A
160 GOTO 120
170 DATA 8,16,12,-1
180 END
```

Figure B1-4.   Program of Figure B1-2 rewritten with REM statements.

END Statement

Generally the END statement is physically the last statement in the program; that is, it is the statement with the highest line number. When the computer encounters this statement, it terminates execution of your program. The format of the END statement is

Line # END

Some versions of BASIC do not require an END statement; however, its use is highly recommended because it leaves no doubt in anyone's mind as to where the program ends. The END statement is frequently used in combination with the STOP statement. The STOP statement is discussed in Section 3.

DEVELOPING AND RUNNING BASIC PROGRAMS ON YOUR COMPUTER SYSTEM

Now that we've covered how to write simple BASIC programs, its time to consider how to develop and run them on your computer system. Systems vary tremendously with regard to the specific *forms* of the system commands used. Fortunately, most of them have the same *types* of commands. These systems often differ only in the specific ways in which the commands must be typed.

System Commands

There are two major types of commands that you will use to write and run BASIC programs on your computer: **BASIC statement commands** (which are the BASIC program statements in the lines of your program), and **BASIC system commands** (which are outside of your program). We have already covered several statement commands (READ, PRINT, GOTO, and so on). These commands instruct the computer system what to do while it is executing your program.

　　System commands, on the other hand, are often used by the programmer to tell the computer to do something before or after it executes the program. Two examples are RUN and LIST. Some examples of common system actions, and how they are implemented on three microcomputer systems, are given in Figure B1-5. The form of these commands on larger computer systems is similar. You should check the system commands for your particular computer.

Interacting with Your System

Let's say that you want to "try out" your computer system by typing in the squares program of Figure B1-4. You would type in all eighteen lines, pressing the RETURN (or ENTER) key after each line, as usual. Many versions of BASIC will check each statement for correct form (or *syntax*) when you press RETURN. Thus suppose you fumble at the keyboard while typing in the eleventh line of your program, producing

```
110 READD A
```

Your keyboard probably has a backspace key that will let you fix the error if you have not hit the return key. If you have already hit the return key to enter the faulty line into the computer system, the following error message might be sent to the output device:

```
INVALID COMMAND
```

At this point you may have to retype the entire line, including the line number.* The computer system will then replace the old line 110 with the corrected version.

---

*Most keyboards sold today have an Insert key, a Delete key, and a set of four "arrow keys" to enable you to rapidly edit your programs. On many computer systems you can correct an error by first displaying the line containing the error, then moving to the point of the error with one of the arrow keys, then using the Insert or Delete key to make the correction and, finally, entering the change by pressing the Return key.

Action Desired	IBM PC (Disk BASIC)	Apple II (Applesoft BASIC)	Apple Macintosh (MS-BASIC)
Turn on System	Power switch is on right side of system unit	Power switch is at left rear of system unit	Power switch is at left rear of system unit
Log into System	Respond to date and time prompts	No response	Insert appropriate disk
Starting BASIC			
User response	Type BASIC or BASICA to A> prompt	System comes up in BASIC, so begin typing program	Insert MS-BASIC disk
Computer response	OK		Display disk directory
User response	Begin typing program		Double click MS-BASIC icon
Computer response			Command box appears
User response			Begin typing program
System commands*			
List program	LIST	LIST	LIST
Run program	RUN	RUN	RUN
Delete a line	DELETE line #	Type line #, then hit RETURN key	Type line #, then hit RETURN key
Save program on disk	SAVE "filename"	SAVE filename	SAVE filename
Save program on tape	Not applicable	SAVE	Not applicable
Retrieve program on disk	LOAD "filename"	LOAD filename	LOAD OPEN filename
Retrieve program on tape	Not applicable	LOAD	Not applicable
Clear memory	NEW	NEW	NEW
Obtain list of files	FILES	CATALOG	Files automatically appear
Log Off System			
User response	No response	No response	Select QUIT from File menu
Computer response	No response	No response	Displays directory
User response	Turn power off	Turn power off	Select CLOSE
			Then, from File menu, select EJECT to leave BASIC
			Turn off power

Figure B1-5. *System commands on three microcomputer systems.*

*System commands on Macintosh can be typed or selected from menu.

When you have finished typing your program, you will probably be anxious for the computer to execute it immediately. Most systems require the user to type in the command

RUN

After you issue this command, one of the following will happen:

1. The program will run successfully, producing the correct answers.

2. The program will run, but produce incorrect answers. This might happen if, for example, you typed in line 130 of the squares program as

130 LET B=A^3

The program would then produce cubes of numbers instead of squares! *Thus it is important that you look at your output carefully before you decide that your program works.*

3. The program stops unexpectedly in the middle of a run. This would happen in the squares program if line 170 were typed in as follows:

170 DATA 8,16,"HELLO",12,-1

The program would compute the squares of 8 and 16 successfully, but would stop (or abort) when it tried to assign the string "HELLO" to the numeric variable A. When BASIC runs into this situation while running the program, it is likely to display a message such as

ATTEMPT TO READ INVALID DATA ON LINE 150

and halt. At this point you must correct the error, or **bug,** in the program and try again. Learning how to correct, or **debug,** faulty programs is one of the most important skills you must develop to program well. As unusual as it may seem, even a good programmer can easily spend 50 percent of the time it takes to develop a program in getting rid of bugs in it. This subject will be addressed in more detail later on.

SOLVED REVIEW PROBLEMS

Example 1

Company X has anywhere from five to twenty students employed on a part-time basis during the summer. This past week five students were on the payroll. The students each worked different hours at different rates of pay, as shown in the table on the next page.

Student Name	Hours Worked	Rate of Pay
John Smith	20	$5.40
Nancy Jones	15	5.60
Bo Weeks	25	5.00
Millicent Smythe	40	4.80
Joe Johnson	20	5.10

The company would like you to write a BASIC program to compute and print the total pay due each student.

Solution

The program must read a number of *records*. Each record contains a name, hours worked, and a rate of pay—that is, a row of data from the table above. The number of records varies from week to week.

To stop the program it is convenient to employ a trailer record. The following steps show how the program might be designed:

1. Read a record (name, hours worked, rate of pay).

2. If Name = "Last Record" (the value on the trailer record), go to step 7; otherwise continue with step 3.

3. Compute pay due.

4. Print student name and pay due.

5. Read another record.

6. Go back to step 2.

7. End program.

This logic leads to the program in Figure B1-6.

Before we leave this example, let's consider some of the problems we might have run into if there were errors in the program. Also, we'll explore how we might correct such errors.

First, suppose we had typed in line 110 as follows:

110 D=H*R

When the computer encounters this statement, it has a value for S$, H, and P. However, it doesn't have the foggiest clue as to what R is, since we never assigned a value to it. In most versions of BASIC, when the computer is requested to use the value of a variable it hasn't yet encountered during execution, it assumes the value is zero. Naturally this can lead to some very

```
10  REM THIS PROGRAM COMPUTES EMPLOYEE PAY
20  REM    AUTHOR: C.S. PARKER
30  REM ***********VARIABLES*************
40  REM    S$ = EMPLOYEE NAME
50  REM    H  = HOURS WORKED
60  REM    P  = HOURLY PAY RATE
70  REM    D  = PAY DUE
80  REM *****************************
90  READ S$,H,P
100 IF S$ = "LAST RECORD" THEN 230
110 D=H*P
120 PRINT S$;" HAS EARNED  $";D
130 READ S$,H,P
140 GOTO 100
150 REM *********DATA STATEMENTS*********
160 DATA "JOHN SMITH",20,5.40
170 DATA "NANCY JONES",15,5.60
180 DATA "BO WEEKS",25,5.00
190 DATA "MILLICENT SMYTHE",40,4.80
200 DATA "JOE JOHNSON",20,5.10
210 DATA "LAST RECORD",0,0
220 REM *****************************
230 END
RUN
JOHN SMITH HAS EARNED  $ 108
NANCY JONES HAS EARNED  $ 84
BO WEEKS HAS EARNED  $ 125
MILLICENT SMYTHE HAS EARNED  $ 192
JOE JOHNSON HAS EARNED  $ 102
```

Figure B1-6. *A program to compute the pay due employees.*

surprising results in your programs. In the current problem, your program would show that everyone has earned $0.

You should quickly be able to find an error like the one just described by making a few simple deductions. For example, since all the values of D are printing as 0 and D is computed by H*R, either H or R (or both of these variables) is equal to zero.

As a second example, suppose we had mistakenly typed in line 190 as follows:

```
190 DATA 40,"MILLICENT SMYTHE",4.80
```

The computer would execute our program successfully until it had printed out

```
BO WEEKS HAS EARNED $125
```

Then we might receive a message such as the following:

ATTEMPT TO READ INVALID DATA ON LINE 130

These two lines of output give us a clue to the error. The computer successfully completed the processing of Bo Weeks's record but subsequently "bombed" on line 130. Thus something must be amiss with the data in the next record. Now we would notice that the number 40 and "MILLICENT SMYTHE" are switched around, and BASIC cannot assign a string constant to a numeric variable.

Debugging programs is a skill that involves a lot of practice. You must learn to make deductions from the information given by the computer system (i.e., partial output, incorrect output, and error messages) to determine the source of the error.

Another technique that's recommended for particularly hard-to-find errors is the so-called dummy (diagnostic) PRINT statement. Suppose again that for line 110 you had typed

110 D=H*R

You have deduced that either H, R, or both of these variables are zero, but you still can't put your finger on the error. However, you could now type the statement

115 PRINT "H =";H;" R =";R

The computer system would then respond with the following outputs after you typed RUN

```
H = 20   R = 0
JOHN SMITH HAS EARNED   $ 0
H = 15   R = 0
NANCY JONES HAS EARNED   $ 0
```

and so on. Now the source of the error is obvious: R is zero for every record in the program.

Once the dummy PRINT statement has served its purpose of uncovering the error, and the error has been corrected, statement 115 should be deleted so that it won't interfere with the normal output of the program. The form for doing this may be

DELETE 115

on your system, or you may be able simply to type

115

and press RETURN (replacing the old statement 115 with a blank statement).

Example 2

ABC Company has a file that keeps the following information on employees:

✖ Name   ✖ Age

✖ Sex (M or F) ✖ Department

The file has approximately 1000 employees, although the exact number is usually unknown. Write a BASIC program that will print out the names of all females over age 40 who work in the accounting department.

Solution

This program involves a series of three IF statements that pose the three conditions we wish to check in each record: in other words, female?, over 40?, and accounting? If a record passes all three checks, we print the associated name; otherwise we read the next record.

Since the data file is not given, we'll make up five "program test records" (including a trailer record) to illustrate how the program works. The program is shown in Figure B1-7.

```
 10 REM THIS PROGRAM SELECTS FROM A FILE ALL
 20 REM FEMALE EMPLOYEES OVER 40 WHO WORK IN
 30 REM THE ACCOUNTING DEPARTMENT
 40 REM    AUTHOR - C.S. PARKER
 50 REM ************VARIABLES***************
 60 REM   N$ = EMPLOYEE NAME
 70 REM   S$ = SEX
 80 REM   A  = AGE
 90 REM   D$ = DEPARTMENT
100 REM *********************************
110 READ N$,S$,A,D$
120 IF N$="LAST RECORD" THEN 260
130 IF S$="M" THEN 170
140 IF A<=40 THEN 170
150 IF D$<>"ACCOUNTING" THEN 170
160 PRINT N$
170 READ N$,S$,A,D$
180 GOTO 120
190 REM *********DATA STATEMENTS***********
200 DATA "JANE CRIBBS","F",25,"ACCOUNTING"
210 DATA "PHIL JONES","M",45,"ACCOUNTING"
220 DATA "ANNE WELLES","F",42,"ACCOUNTING"
230 DATA "MARY SMITH","F",41,"FINANCE"
240 DATA "LAST RECORD","X",99,"NONE"
250 REM *********************************
260 END
RUN
ANNE WELLES
```

Figure B1-7. A selection program.

Problem Decomposition

One of the sad facts of life is that people often give up when trying to solve a complex problem. In many cases the problem is very solvable, but people just stare at it, become intimidated, and quit before even getting started.

An approach that many have used successfully when confronting a tough problem is to *decompose* it into easier-to-solve subproblems. For example, think about writing a textbook such as this one or even a novel. You don't start by writing the first page of Chapter 1, then the second page, and so on. You start by making a broad outline of what each chapter will cover. Then you need to expand each chapter outline to a more detailed list of topics. Once this "skeleton" is erected, you may then want to start writing some of the chapters you find most fascinating—making each of the chapters a project in itself, with its own set of goals and deadlines. And so forth. Most authors think decomposing a book project into manageable pieces is not only the most logical way, but also the *only* way to proceed.

Writing a computer program often involves a similar process of decomposition. It helps, for example, to decompose the program into the *output, input,* and *processing* required—and to take each of these details in turn. For example, say you're required to write a program such as the one in Problem 8, which computes the amount due from students. The *outputs* you must produce are the name of each student and the amount of his or her bill. The *inputs* you're given (i.e., the things that *vary* for each student considered) are the names of the students, credit hours, and scholarship amounts. You're also given a tuition fee formula and an activity fee schedule, but since those *don't vary* on input, they can be built into the *processing* logic of the program.

You can decompose the processing logic further, as follows:

1. Determine *activity fee* from the credit hours taken and activity fee schedule. (This can be done by building the activity

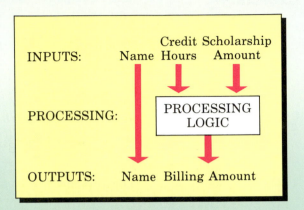

If you thought about it awhile, the decomposed problem might look like this.

fee schedule into one or more IF statements.)
2. Determine *tuition* by multiplying credit hours by $100. (This can be done by a LET statement.)
3. Determine *billing amount* by adding the values found in steps 1 and 2 and subtracting the scholarship amount. (This can be done by a LET statement.)

Thus the solution algorithm is something like the following:

1. Read the record of a student.
2. Go through the series of processing steps.
3. Print results.
4. Loop back to next record.

Of course, you'll also need to build a mechanism into the algorithm to get it to stop when it finishes the last record.

Before you design an algorithm, it's always best to do a few computations by hand to make sure you fully understand the problem and the mental processes you are going through to solve it. Later, when you code the algorithm and get output, it's also important to check the output against hand computations to make sure the program is producing correct results.

Exercises

Instructions: Provide an answer to each of the following questions.

1. Categorize the following variables as numeric, string, or invalid.
   a. A   b. 6F   c. D1   d. B$ e. $R   f. I

2. Write a valid LET statement for each of the following formulas:

   a. $C = \sqrt{A^2 + B^2}$ c. $R = \dfrac{S + T}{U - V} - Y$

   b. $A = \left(\dfrac{B + C}{D}\right) E$ d. $A = \dfrac{3(B - 1)}{T + 2}$

3. Given A = 2, B = 5, and C = 6, determine the value of X in the following BASIC expressions:
   a. `X=(A+B)*C`   c. `X=(A+C/A+1)^2/2`
   b. `X=C/A*B`   d. `X=((3*A)*B)/C-4`

4. Identify the syntax errors, if any, in the following BASIC statements.
   a. `10 GOTO 10 IF X=Y`
   b. `10 LET X+Y=Z`
   c. `98 IF X-Y<=C-D THEN 200`
   d. `20 LET F$=F+5.23`

5. In the expression

   $$X=(Y+Z)^2-2*B$$

   which operation does the computer do
   a. first?   c. third?
   b. second?   d. last?

Programming Problems

Instructions: Write a BASIC program to do each of the following tasks.

1. Find the sum of each of the pairs of numbers below:

   6 and 8
   13 and 25
   14 and 33
   19 and 41

   Use trailer values at the end of your data list so that your program can sense when there are no more data.

2. Below are three sets of data. Each set of data has four variables: A, B, C, and D:

Set	Variables			
	A	B	C	D
1	8	15	10	4
2	6	5	3	2
3	4	0	5	2

Plug the values in each set of data into the formula below, and print out the results:

$$X = A - B * C + A / D$$

3. Team A and Team B, crosstown rivals, played each other in baseball a total of five times over the course of a season. The results were as follows:

Game	Team A Score	Team B Score
1	8	5
2	6	7
3	2	0
4	0	1
5	5	4

Write a program that will output, for each game, the team winning the game.

4. Salespeople at XYZ Company are paid a base salary of $10,000. This salary may be augmented by commissions, which are equal to 10 percent of gross sales, and by a bonus of $500. The bonus is awarded only to salespeople with over $80,000 in gross sales. Compute and output the amounts earned by each of the salespeople below:

Salesperson	Gross Sales
Carlos Ortiz	$90,000
Jill Johnson	$70,000
Don Williams	$20,000
Dee Jones	$95,000
Al Ennis	$40,000

Your output should include the name of each salesperson and his or her earnings. Use trailer values at the end of your data list so that your program can sense when there are no more data.

5. Solve Problem 4 assuming that the commission is computed as follows:

If Gross Sales Are in the Range	The Commission Rate Is
$ 1–$30,000	6%
$30,001–$60,000	8%
$60,001–$80,000	10%
$80,001 and above	12%

Assume that the bonus is still in effect.

6. Grades in a course are awarded as follows: 90 and above = A, 80–89 = B, 70–79 = C, 60–69 = D, below 60 = F. Write a BASIC program that reads the data below and assigns letter grades:

Social Security Number	Score
182-66-1919	63
321-76-4344	81
821-66-0045	90
376-38-3202	54
802-11-1481	79
346-49-8911	75

Your output should include the social security number of each student and that student's letter grade. Use trailer values at the end of your data list so that your program can sense when there are no more items to be read.

7. A company running a copying service charges the following rates:

The first 500 copies are billed at 5 cents per copy
The next 500 copies are billed at 4 cents per copy
Any additional copies are billed at 3 cents per copy

Compute and output the amount each of the following customers is to be billed:

Customer	Copies
XYZ Amalgamated	1200
ABC Industries	200
TR Systems Limited	800

Your output should include the name of each customer as well as the billing amount. Use trailer values at the end of your data list so that your program can sense when there are no more data.

8. Students at a university are billed as follows:

$$\text{Tuition} = \$100 \text{ per credit hour}$$
$$\text{Activity fee} = \begin{array}{l} \$30 \text{ for 6 hours or less} \\ \$60 \text{ for 7–12 hours} \\ \$75 \text{ for more than 12 hours} \end{array}$$

The total amount a student will be billed each semester is computed by the formula below:

$$\text{Tuition fee} + \text{Activity fee} - \text{Scholarship}$$

Compute the amount due from the following students:

Student Name	Credit Hours This Semester	Scholarship Amount
Ed Begay	15	$700
Bill Mendoza	8	0
John Williams	3	0
Nancy Jones	12	500
Dennis Hall	6	0

Your output should include the name of each student as well as the billing amount. Use trailer values at the end of your data list so that your program can sense when there are no more data. [*Hint:* See box on page B-28.]

Section 2
Flowcharting Techniques

INTRODUCTION

A **program flowchart** is a diagram that shows the flow of logic behind a computer program. For example, the flowchart in Figure B2-1 outlines the logic of the program shown in Figure B1-1.

As you can see from the example, a program flowchart consists of geometric symbols and arrows. Each symbol contains an operation the computer must perform, while the arrows show the flow of the program logic (in other words, which operation is to be performed next).

As you have probably already noticed, not all of the symbols have the same shape. The shape of the symbol used depends on the type of operation being performed. The symbols used in this appendix, along with their program statement types, are shown in Figure B2-2.

You should note in Figure B2-1 that not every BASIC program statement will necessarily correspond to a flowchart symbol; conversely, not every flowchart symbol corresponds to a BASIC program statement. For example, there is no BASIC program statement counterpart to the flowcharting "START" symbol. The BASIC program shown actually begins

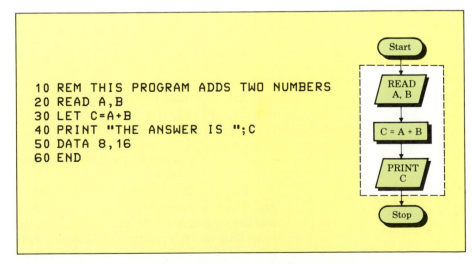

```
10 REM THIS PROGRAM ADDS TWO NUMBERS
20 READ A,B
30 LET C=A+B
40 PRINT "THE ANSWER IS ";C
50 DATA 8,16
60 END
```

Figure B2-1. *A program and flowchart to read two numbers, add them and output the result (previously presented in Figure B1-1).* The highlighted area in the flowchart shows a *sequence* control structure (see the box on page B-35).

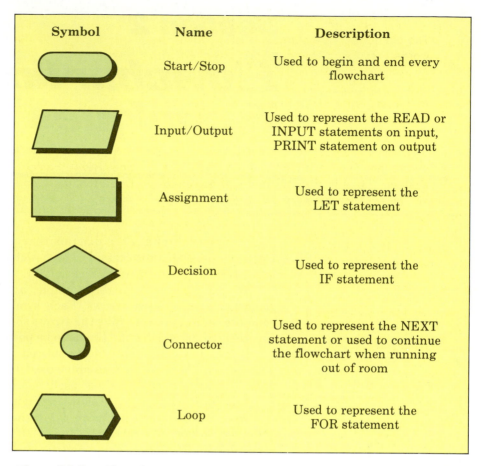

Symbol	Name	Description
	Start/Stop	Used to begin and end every flowchart
	Input/Output	Used to represent the READ or INPUT statements on input, PRINT statement on output
	Assignment	Used to represent the LET statement
	Decision	Used to represent the IF statement
	Connector	Used to represent the NEXT statement or used to continue the flowchart when running out of room
	Loop	Used to represent the FOR statement

Figure B2-2. Flowcharting symbols.

with a REM statement. Also, there is no flowchart symbol for the DATA statement. The flowchart is intended to represent only the flow of program logic. This can be done without specifying actual values for the variables.

You should also note in Figure B2-1 that the flowchart need not contain every detail that will be specified in the program, but only those that are important for understanding the logical flow. Thus the flowchart indicates the output as PRINT C, whereas statement 40 of the corresponding program specifies in more detail:

```
40 PRINT "THE ANSWER IS ";C.
```

Flowcharts are useful both as design tools for developing the program and, later, as a program documentation aid. As a design tool, the flowchart lets the programmer "think through" the logical design of the program prior to writing it. This can be particularly helpful for the same reason a builder of a house consults a floor plan before constructing any individual room. Once the program is written, the flowchart becomes a documentation aid: it generally is easier for others to understand how the program works by studying the flowchart rather than the program itself. Also, because of their simplicity, flowcharts can often be understood by nonprogrammers.

Drawing Structured Flowcharts

The old adage "A picture is worth a thousand words" is the rationale behind flowcharting. Because the processing logic behind the solution to a problem can be complex, it often helps to draw a graphical representation of the steps to be followed to get a feel for how the problem is to be solved. Some computer instructors, in fact, require students to master flowcharting before they even lay their hands on a computer system. These instructors feel that flowcharting gives one valuable planning skills with regard to how computers solve problems— skills that might never be developed if one started coding immediately.

There are many different ways to construct flowcharts. The approach used in this appendix follows the "structured" flowcharting style described in Chapter 10 of this text. This style involves the strict use of three program structures: *sequence, selection,* and *looping* (shown in flowchart form here). Virtually every programming problem that you encounter can be satisfactorily solved by using some combination of these and only these three structures.

Throughout this appendix all of the programs and flowcharts you will see reflect these fundamental structures. For example, the highlighted portion of the flowchart in Figure B2-1 (on page B-33) shows a sequence structure. In this rather straightforward structure, statements are executed in a fixed sequence.

The highlighted portion of the flowchart in Figure B2-4 (on page B-37) shows a selection structure, which reflects a conditional branch. In fact, this flowchart nests several selection structures. A selection structure is highly useful when records with certain characteristics must be "trapped" for processing. In the case of Figure B2-4, records having the characteristics Sex="Female," Age="Over 40," and Department="Accounting" are trapped so they may be output.

The highlighted portion of the flowchart in Figure B2-3 (on page B-36) shows a looping (DOWHILE) structure. That is, while A is not equal to − 1, we continue to do processing. Looping structures are used to repeat any processing steps.

A fourth structure, the "Case" structure (which is a derivative of the selection structure) is described later on (page B-103).

Using these program structures is highly recommended for those who will eventually pursue computer careers. These structures are followed by languages such as COBOL, the language most programmers use in business, and newer languages such as Pascal, C, and Ada. Still, there are other flowcharting styles that are a bit more straightforward for *learning* how to program, and so it's very possible that your computer instructor will follow a style different from the one you see in this appendix.

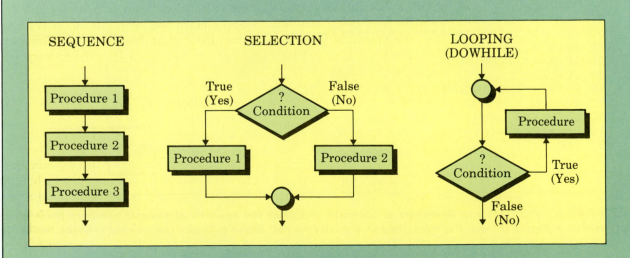

SOME FLOWCHART EXAMPLES

Now that we've covered some of the fundamentals of flowcharting, we'll look at two further examples.

First, let's reconsider the problem of Figure B1-4 (page B-20), which required a procedure to compute and print the squares of several numbers. The flowchart for this problem is given in Figure B2-3.

This flowchart introduces the use of the decision symbol. In BASIC, the diamond-shaped decision symbol always has one arrow leading into it and two arrows leading out. The "Yes" (or "True") branch indicates the THEN condition (in other words, IF A = −1 THEN 180), while the "No" (or "False") branch directs the computer to execute the next statement.

Note that the GOTO statement of BASIC has no associated geometric symbol. It is represented by an arrow leading to the appropriate instruction.

Let's also take another look at the problem solved in Figure B1-7 (page B-27). There we were required to find all employees in a company who are female, over 40, and work in the accounting department. The associated flowchart is shown in Figure B2-4.

Numerous other examples of flowcharts will be presented in later sections of this appendix. Flowcharting is also covered in some detail in Chapter 10.

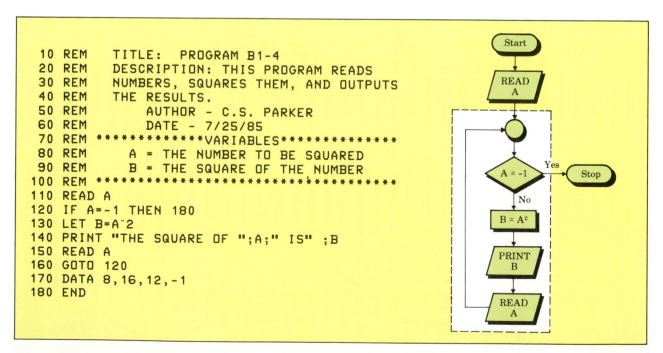

```
 10 REM    TITLE:  PROGRAM B1-4
 20 REM    DESCRIPTION: THIS PROGRAM READS
 30 REM    NUMBERS, SQUARES THEM, AND OUTPUTS
 40 REM    THE RESULTS.
 50 REM        AUTHOR - C.S. PARKER
 60 REM        DATE - 7/25/85
 70 REM ************VARIABLES*************
 80 REM     A = THE NUMBER TO BE SQUARED
 90 REM     B = THE SQUARE OF THE NUMBER
100 REM **********************************
110 READ A
120 IF A=-1 THEN 180
130 LET B=A^2
140 PRINT "THE SQUARE OF ";A;" IS" ;B
150 READ A
160 GOTO 120
170 DATA 8,16,12,-1
180 END
```

Figure B2-3. Program and flowchart to compute and print the squares of several numbers (previously presented in Figure B1-4.). The highlighted area in the flowchart shows a *looping* control structure (see the box on page B-35).

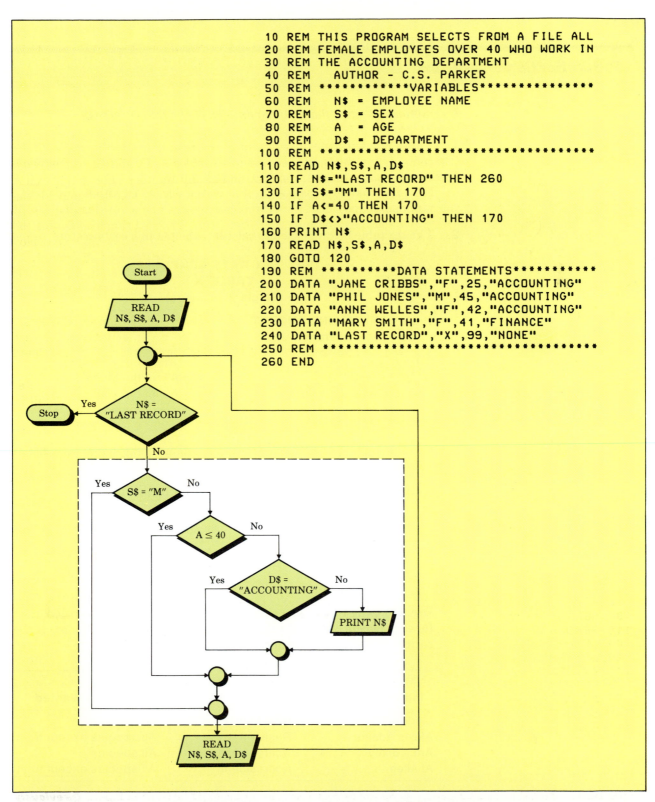

```
 10 REM THIS PROGRAM SELECTS FROM A FILE ALL
 20 REM FEMALE EMPLOYEES OVER 40 WHO WORK IN
 30 REM THE ACCOUNTING DEPARTMENT
 40 REM    AUTHOR - C.S. PARKER
 50 REM ************VARIABLES**************
 60 REM   N$ = EMPLOYEE NAME
 70 REM   S$ = SEX
 80 REM   A  = AGE
 90 REM   D$ = DEPARTMENT
100 REM ********************************
110 READ N$,S$,A,D$
120 IF N$="LAST RECORD" THEN 260
130 IF S$="M" THEN 170
140 IF A<=40 THEN 170
150 IF D$<>"ACCOUNTING" THEN 170
160 PRINT N$
170 READ N$,S$,A,D$
180 GOTO 120
190 REM *********DATA STATEMENTS**********
200 DATA "JANE CRIBBS","F",25,"ACCOUNTING"
210 DATA "PHIL JONES","M",45,"ACCOUNTING"
220 DATA "ANNE WELLES","F",42,"ACCOUNTING"
230 DATA "MARY SMITH","F",41,"FINANCE"
240 DATA "LAST RECORD","X",99,"NONE"
250 REM ********************************
260 END
```

Figure B2-4. *Program and flowchart to solve an employee selection problem (previously presented in Figure B1-7.).* The highlighted area in the flowchart shows a *selection* control structure (see the box on page B-35).

Flowcharting Problems*

Instructions: Write a flowchart to do each of the following tasks.

1. Three numbers (no two of which are equal) are to be read by the computer system and assigned to variables A, B, and C, respectively. Determine the largest, smallest, and middle number. (*For example,* if A is 3, B is 1, and C is 6, then 6 is the largest, 1 is the smallest, and 3 is the middle number.)

2. The tax table below is used to calculate the tax in a certain state.

1987 TAX RATE SCHEDULES
TABLE X
(Single Taxpayers)

If the BOTTOM LINE AMOUNT on your tax return is . . .	Compute your TAX as follows:
$0–1,000	2% of the amount
$1,001–10,000	4% of the amount less $100
$10,001–50,000	6% of the amount less $300
Over $50,000	7% of the amount

Use this table to design a procedure to compute taxes due for a list of taxpayers.

3. A state charges the following annual fees for fishing licenses:

	Resident	Nonresident
All species	$10.00	$22.00
All species except trout	$ 7.00	$15.00

Use this table to design a procedure to compute the fee to be charged for each person buying a license. Below are some sample data to test the correctness of your procedure.

Individual	Residency Status	License Wanted
Merlon Biggs	Resident	All species
Alexis Adams	Resident	All species except trout
Arlen Bixby	Nonresident	All species
Al Allen	Nonresident	All species except trout

*For additional practice with flowcharting, try providing flowchart solutions to the problems described in Programming Problems 3–8 in Section 1 (pages B-30 through B-32). If you want to test your knowledge quickly, try Problems 3, 5, and 8 first.

Section 3

Expanding on the Basics of BASIC

COUNTING AND SUMMING

Now that we've covered a few fundamentals of how BASIC works, let's tackle a slightly more complicated problem. The example in Figure B3-1, a program to compute and print the average of a group of positive numbers, introduces two of the most fundamental operations in data processing: counting and summing. You should observe the "mechanics" of both of these operations very carefully, since they occur in almost every large-scale programming problem.

Three important observations should be made about the program in Figure B3-1:

1. Statements 100 (LET I=0) and 110 (LET S=0) establish *explicitly* the beginning values of I and S. Establishing beginning values for variables is called **initialization.** Most versions of BASIC will *implicitly* initialize all variables to zero before the program is executed; thus statements 100 and 110 are usually unnecessary. It is good practice, however, to explicitly initialize certain variables to zero whether it is necessary or not on your computer system. There are two reasons for this practice:

   a. Many programming languages will not automatically initialize variables to zero. This can lead to surprising results if you didn't explicitly initialize, since numbers from someone else's program may be lurking in the storage locations assigned to your variables. Thus your variables will assume these arbitrary values.

   b. When you initialize explicitly, the intent of your program becomes more evident. In other words, initialization is good documentation.

Only the variables I and S require initialization to zero in this program. These are the variables that the computer needs to "look up" the values for on the right-hand side of the assignment symbol (=) in lines 140 and 150 respectively. The variables X and A don't have to be initialized, since they never appear on the right-hand side of an assignment symbol before the computer has explicitly assigned them a value.

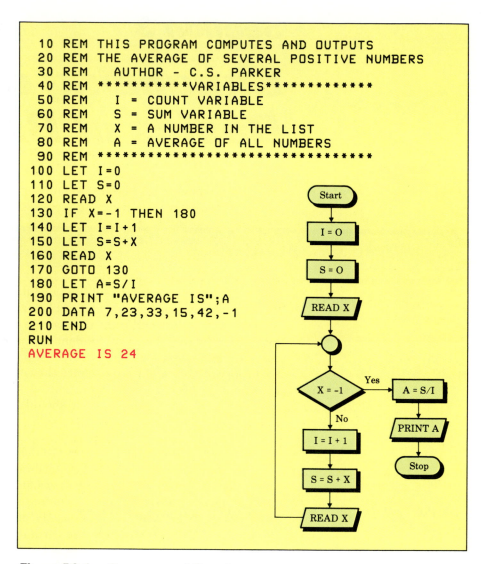

```
 10 REM THIS PROGRAM COMPUTES AND OUTPUTS
 20 REM THE AVERAGE OF SEVERAL POSITIVE NUMBERS
 30 REM    AUTHOR - C.S. PARKER
 40 REM ***********VARIABLES*************
 50 REM    I = COUNT VARIABLE
 60 REM    S = SUM VARIABLE
 70 REM    X = A NUMBER IN THE LIST
 80 REM    A = AVERAGE OF ALL NUMBERS
 90 REM ******************************
100 LET I=0
110 LET S=0
120 READ X
130 IF X=-1 THEN 180
140 LET I=I+1
150 LET S=S+X
160 READ X
170 GOTO 130
180 LET A=S/I
190 PRINT "AVERAGE IS";A
200 DATA 7,23,33,15,42,-1
210 END
RUN
AVERAGE IS 24
```

Figure B3-1.   Program and flowchart to compute the average of several numbers.

2. Statement 140 (LET I = I + 1) *counts* the number of numbers in the list. I is initially assigned a value of zero. Each time a positive number is read into storage for X (so that the "X = −1 test" is failed in line 130 of the program), 1 is added to the current value of I. Since only one number can be assigned to I at any time, the previous value of I is destroyed and lost forever.

3. Statement 150 (LET S = S + X) *sums* the numbers in the list. As with I, S is initially zero. Each time statement 150 is executed, the current value of X is added to the current value of S. Thus S can be seen as a "running total," as indicated in the table that appears at the top of the next page.

When the Value of X Is	Statement 150 Does the Following
7	Adds 7 to the initial sum, 0, producing S = 7
23	Adds 23 to 7, producing S = 30
33	Adds 33 to 30, producing S = 63
15	Adds 15 to 63, producing S = 78
42	Adds 42 to 78, producing S = 120
−1	Statement 150 is not executed when X = −1

You should note that both the counting (I = I + 1) and summing (S = S + X) statements appear after the check for the last record (statement 130, IF X = −1 THEN 180). This is crucial. If these statements appear before the last-record check, the values of I and S will both be in error.

THE INPUT STATEMENT

The INPUT statement is one of the most useful statements in the BASIC language. It permits the program *user* to operate in a **conversational (interactive) mode** with the computer system. In other words, during the course of executing a program, the computer system asks the user for a response, the user answers, and then, based on the response given, the computer system asks the user for a response to another question, and so forth. The format of the INPUT statement is shown below:

> Line # INPUT list of variables (separated by commas)

Figure B3-2 shows the program in Figure B3-1 rewritten with the INPUT statement. You should carefully note the following:

1. The READ statement in Figure B3-1 has been changed to an INPUT statement in Figure B3-2. With the READ statement, all data to be assigned to X are placed in an associated DATA statement; remember, READ and DATA statements are always used together. When we use INPUT X, no corresponding DATA statement is employed. Instead we supply data to the computer system as the program is running.

2. Data are supplied to the computer system as follows: Whenever an INPUT statement is encountered, a "?" is output by the system, and processing temporarily halts. At this point we must enter as many data values as there are variables appearing after the word INPUT in the program. These values must be separated by commas. After we depress the RETURN key, the system will assign the values to their corresponding variables and resume processing. If the same or another INPUT statement is encountered, the system will again respond with a question mark and await more input from the user.

```
 10 REM THIS PROGRAM COMPUTES AND OUTPUTS
 20 REM THE AVERAGE OF SEVERAL POSITIVE NUMBERS
 30 REM    AUTHOR - C.S. PARKER
 40 REM ************VARIABLES***********
 50 REM    I = COUNT VARIABLE
 60 REM    S = SUM VARIABLE
 70 REM    X = A NUMBER IN THE LIST
 80 REM    A = AVERAGE OF ALL NUMBERS
 90 REM ****************************
100 LET I=0
110 LET S=0
120 PRINT "ENTER A POSITIVE NUMBER (OR -1 TO STOP)"
130 INPUT X
140 IF X=-1 THEN 200
150 LET I=I+1
160 LET S=S+X
170 PRINT "ENTER A POSITIVE NUMBER (OR -1 TO STOP)"
180 INPUT X
190 GOTO 140
200 LET A=S/I
210 PRINT "AVERAGE IS";A
220 END
RUN
ENTER A POSITIVE NUMBER (OR -1 TO STOP)
? 7
ENTER A POSITIVE NUMBER (OR -1 TO STOP)
? 23
ENTER A POSITIVE NUMBER (OR -1 TO STOP)
? 33
ENTER A POSITIVE NUMBER (OR -1 TO STOP)
? 15
ENTER A POSITIVE NUMBER (OR -1 TO STOP)
? 42
ENTER A POSITIVE NUMBER (OR -1 TO STOP)
? -1
AVERAGE IS 24
```

Figure B3-2. *Program of Figure B3-1 rewritten with the INPUT statement.*

3. In line 120, just before the INPUT statement, is a PRINT statement that provides instructions for the user of the program. When writing programs that include INPUT statements, it is always a good idea to include such a **prompting** PRINT statement before each INPUT, so that the user will know both how to enter data into the computer and how to stop the program.

The major advantage of the INPUT statement over READ is that the user and computer system are involved in a dynamic dialogue. In many cases the user may not know the inputs in advance, since they depend upon actions taken by the computer. An example of such a dialogue is shown in Figure B3-3.

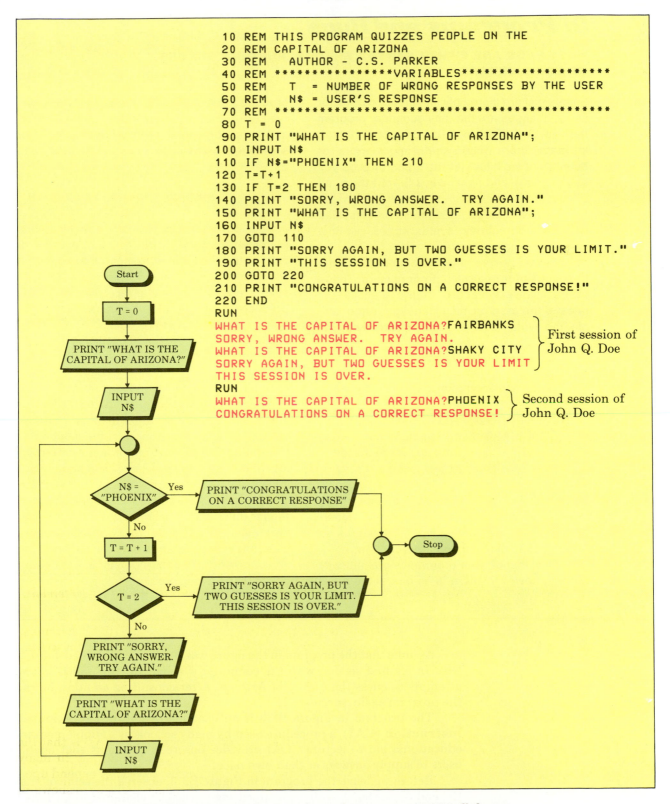

```
 10 REM THIS PROGRAM QUIZZES PEOPLE ON THE
 20 REM CAPITAL OF ARIZONA
 30 REM    AUTHOR - C.S. PARKER
 40 REM *****************VARIABLES*********************
 50 REM    T  = NUMBER OF WRONG RESPONSES BY THE USER
 60 REM    N$ = USER'S RESPONSE
 70 REM ********************************************
 80 T = 0
 90 PRINT "WHAT IS THE CAPITAL OF ARIZONA";
100 INPUT N$
110 IF N$="PHOENIX" THEN 210
120 T=T+1
130 IF T=2 THEN 180
140 PRINT "SORRY, WRONG ANSWER.  TRY AGAIN."
150 PRINT "WHAT IS THE CAPITAL OF ARIZONA";
160 INPUT N$
170 GOTO 110
180 PRINT "SORRY AGAIN, BUT TWO GUESSES IS YOUR LIMIT."
190 PRINT "THIS SESSION IS OVER."
200 GOTO 220
210 PRINT "CONGRATULATIONS ON A CORRECT RESPONSE!"
220 END
RUN
WHAT IS THE CAPITAL OF ARIZONA?FAIRBANKS
SORRY, WRONG ANSWER.  TRY AGAIN.
WHAT IS THE CAPITAL OF ARIZONA?SHAKY CITY
SORRY AGAIN, BUT TWO GUESSES IS YOUR LIMIT
THIS SESSION IS OVER.
RUN
WHAT IS THE CAPITAL OF ARIZONA?PHOENIX
CONGRATULATIONS ON A CORRECT RESPONSE!
```

First session of John Q. Doe

Second session of John Q. Doe

Figure B3-3. *Use of INPUT statement for interdependent user-computer dialogue.*

Of Programs and Bugs

MOST BUGS ARE EITHER SYNTAX ERRORS, RUN-TIME ERRORS, OR LOGIC ERRORS.

Unless you are incredibly intelligent, careful, or lucky, chances are that any computer program that you write will not run correctly at first. Inevitably there will be one or more errors, or bugs. Here we'll look at the types of bugs you can expect—and some ways to root them out of your programs.

Types of Bugs. Bugs can be classified into three categories: syntax errors, run-time errors, and logical errors.

Syntax errors usually cause the most headaches for beginning programmers. These errors involve violations of the grammatical rules of the programming language. For example, the syntax of BASIC's LET statement is

```
10 LET variable-name = expression
```

This syntax implies that statements such as

```
    10 LETT A=B     (LET misspelled)
or  10 LET A+B=A    (A single variable does
                    not appear to the left of
                    the = sign)
```

will result in syntax errors. Although these types of errors can be annoying, BASIC generally provides informative error messages to enable you to pinpoint and correct them.

Even though your program is gramatically correct, however, there is no guarantee it will produce correct results. It may contain a *run-time error;* that is, an error that causes abnormal behavior during program execution. For example, suppose you have a statement such as

```
10 LET A=B/C
```

in your program. Gramatically speaking, this statement is correct. But if C has a value of zero at the time this statement is executed, it will cause your program to terminate. As with syntax errors, run-time errors also generally produce some type of error message, making them relatively easy to pinpoint.

One of the most time-consuming and difficult errors to diagnose is the *logical error.* This is where you have incorrect results, but your program appears to be working properly. Thus, either you've incorrectly translated the problem statement or an algorithm, or perhaps there is an error somewhere in the input data. One reason this type of error is so difficult to locate is that you get no error message—just wrong results. A second reason is that there may be many unanticipated conditions that can trigger this type of error. Thus, except for tiny programs, you can never really be 100 percent sure that your program is entirely correct.

Correcting Bugs. Debugging programs can often be a long process, taking longer than

Assume that the program in the figure was run by a user named John Q. Doe. In his first session with the computer system, Mr. Doe failed in two attempts to guess the capital of Arizona. After consulting an atlas, he ran the program again, successfully.

The program in Figure B3-3 is an example of **computer-assisted instruction (CAI),** a procedure used by many schools as a supplementary educational aid to lectures. CAI provides onscreen questions that enable users to supply answers at their own pace.

Before we leave the program in Figure B3-3, observe the semicolon at the end of line 90. A semicolon appearing as the last character in a PRINT

writing the program itself. Over the years, a number of helpful strategies have evolved to discover and correct bugs. Three of these are diagnostic printing, tracing, and the use of rigorous test data.

Diagnostic printing often involves using PRINT statements to provide you with the current value of certain variables. The use of temporary (or "dummy") PRINT statements was discussed earlier (page B-26). Once the error you are searching for is found, these PRINT statements are removed from your program. Another type of diagnostic printing strategy is *echo printing.* With echo printing, you output the values of variables as soon as they are supplied to a READ or INPUT statement. For example,

```
100 INPUT N$,S
110 PRINT "EMPLOYEE NAME: ";N$
120 PRINT "SALARY :";S
```

The purpose of echo printing is to provide you the opportunity to verify that data are being entered into the computer system correctly. Unlike dummy PRINT statements, echo PRINT statements are generally a permanent part of programs.

Tracing is a technique that allows you to determine the path the computer takes through a program. When tracing is used, the computer prints out the line number of each statement it executes. Thus, you are able to determine the point in the program where the computer has halted processing. On the IBM Personal Computer, the tracing feature is activated by the TRON command and deactivated by the TROFF command. Both of these commands can be used either as BASIC program commands or as BASIC system commands. When the TRON command is activated and the program is run, the line numbers (on the IBM) are printed successively in square brackets, to prevent them from being confused with other program output.

Using rigorous *test data* is one of the most effective ways to root out logical errors in your program. Test data should be chosen so that they subject your program to as many possible situations the program will encounter when it is put into practice. You should test the program with both valid and invalid data, as well as with both ordinary and unusual data. Make sure as well that the test data cover every possible condition that you specify in your IF statements, so you can determine if the program is branching correctly. Also, select some test data that fall on the boundaries of the problems allegedly solvable by your computer program. For example, choose data that set variables to largest- or smallest-allowable values, that cause examination of the first or last item on a list, or that fall on the borderlines of conditions specified in your IF statements. Choosing suitable test data can take time, but it is generally the only way to get a good idea if your program really works.

statement will cause the next item output by the computer system to appear on the same line. In other words, the carriage return is suppressed.

As a third example of the INPUT statement, consider an industrious college student who wishes to send "canned," computerized letters to family and friends. An example of such ingenuity is shown in Figure B3-4.

Such a program is one example of **word processing,** which loosely refers to the computerized organization and generation of documents. You should carefully observe the "blank" PRINT statements in lines 120, 130, 150, 210, 230, and 240. When the word PRINT appears on a line with nothing specified to its right, a line is skipped on the output.

```
10 REM THIS PROGRAM PRODUCES A CANNED LETTER
20 REM    AUTHOR - C.S. PARKER
30 REM ************VARIABLES***************
40 REM    A$=NAME OF RECIPIENT
50 REM    B$=STATE OF RECIPIENT
60 REM *********PROGRAM INPUTS************
70 PRINT "RECIPIENT(S)";
80 INPUT A$
90 PRINT "STATE";
100 INPUT B$
110 REM ********THE LETTER FOLLOWS**********
120 PRINT
130 PRINT
140 PRINT "DEAR ";A$;","
150 PRINT
160 PRINT "     I HAVE BEEN HAVING A GRAND TIME"
170 PRINT "IN COLLEGE, ALTHOUGH SCHOOL IS A"
180 PRINT "LOT OF WORK.  HOPE THINGS ARE GOING"
190 PRINT "WELL FOR YOU BACK IN ";B$;"."
200 PRINT "SEE YOU LATER."
210 PRINT
220 PRINT "                        JOHN"
230 PRINT
240 PRINT
250 REM ************END OF LETTER***********
260 END
RUN
RECIPIENT(S)?MOM AND DAD
STATE?NEBRASKA


DEAR MOM AND DAD,

     I HAVE BEEN HAVING A GRAND TIME
IN COLLEGE, ALTHOUGH SCHOOL IS A
LOT OF WORK.  HOPE THINGS ARE GOING
WELL FOR YOU BACK IN NEBRASKA.
SEE YOU LATER.

                        JOHN


RUN
RECIPIENT(S)?DAISY MAE
STATE?CALIFORNIA


DEAR DAISY MAE,

     I HAVE BEEN HAVING A GRAND TIME
IN COLLEGE, ALTHOUGH SCHOOL IS A
LOT OF WORK.  HOPE THINGS ARE GOING
WELL, FOR YOU BACK IN CALIFORNIA.
SEE YOU LATER.

                        JOHN
```

Figure B3-4. *Use of IN-PUT statement to write a "canned letter."*

THE STOP STATEMENT

Execution of a STOP statement in a program causes the program to halt execution, often by immediate transfer to the END statement. Figure B3-5 illustrates the use of the STOP statement, which has the format below:

Line # STOP

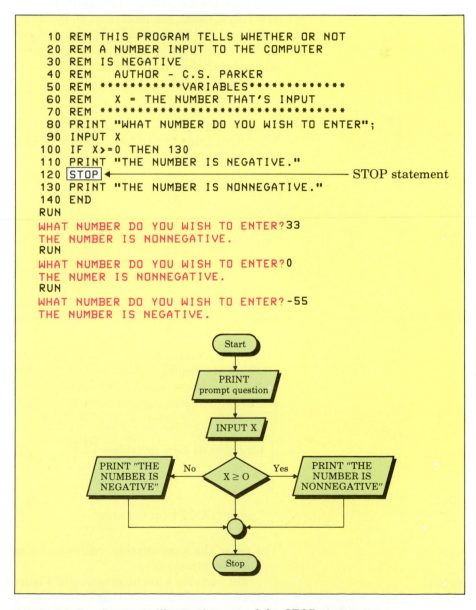

```
 10 REM THIS PROGRAM TELLS WHETHER OR NOT
 20 REM A NUMBER INPUT TO THE COMPUTER
 30 REM IS NEGATIVE
 40 REM    AUTHOR - C.S. PARKER
 50 REM ***********VARIABLES*************
 60 REM    X = THE NUMBER THAT'S INPUT
 70 REM *******************************
 80 PRINT "WHAT NUMBER DO YOU WISH TO ENTER";
 90 INPUT X
100 IF X>=0 THEN 130
110 PRINT "THE NUMBER IS NEGATIVE."
120 STOP                                  ———— STOP statement
130 PRINT "THE NUMBER IS NONNEGATIVE."
140 END
RUN
WHAT NUMBER DO YOU WISH TO ENTER?33
THE NUMBER IS NONNEGATIVE.
RUN
WHAT NUMBER DO YOU WISH TO ENTER?0
THE NUMER IS NONNEGATIVE.
RUN
WHAT NUMBER DO YOU WISH TO ENTER?-55
THE NUMBER IS NEGATIVE.
```

Figure B3-5.   Program illustrating use of the STOP statement.

THE FOR AND NEXT STATEMENTS

The FOR and NEXT statements, which allow the programmer to loop (repeat a program section) automatically, are among the most important statements in BASIC. For example, consider the short program given in Figure B3-6.

The FOR and NEXT statements form a "sandwich," or loop. All statements inside the loop are executed the number of times determined in the FOR statement. (Note that these statements are indented, making the program easier to read.) In Figure B3-6, I is first set equal to 1. Then everything inside the loop (that is, statement 20) is executed; I is then set equal to 2 and statement 20 is executed again, and so forth. After I is set equal to 5, and the loop is executed for the fifth time, control passes to the statement that immediately follows the NEXT statement (in other words, statement 40).

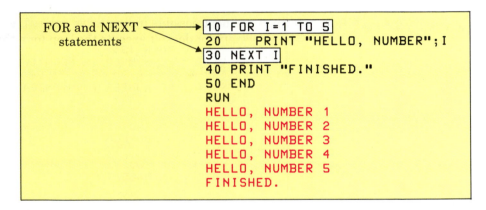

```
FOR and NEXT ──────►  10 FOR I=1 TO 5
statements            20     PRINT "HELLO, NUMBER";I
                      30 NEXT I
                      40 PRINT "FINISHED."
                      50 END
                      RUN
                      HELLO, NUMBER 1
                      HELLO, NUMBER 2
                      HELLO, NUMBER 3
                      HELLO, NUMBER 4
                      HELLO, NUMBER 5
                      FINISHED.
```

Figure B3-6.   *Simple usage of FOR and NEXT statements.*

FOR and NEXT statements are always used together. They physically establish the beginning and end of the loop. Like READ and DATA, one statement makes absolutely no sense unless the other is present. The format of these statements is given below:

$$\text{Line \# FOR loop variable} = \begin{Bmatrix} \text{Beginning} \\ \text{value} \end{Bmatrix} \text{TO} \begin{Bmatrix} \text{Ending} \\ \text{value} \end{Bmatrix} \text{STEP increment}$$
$$\vdots$$
$$\text{Line \# NEXT loop variable}$$

The use of the loop variable, beginning value, ending value, and increment will now be explained.

The variable I in the program of Figure B3-6 is an example of a **loop variable.** Note carefully that the chosen loop variable (which can be any acceptable BASIC numeric variable) must be included in both the FOR statement and its associated NEXT statement, as indicated in the figure.

In Figure B3-6 it was implictly assumed that the loop variable was to be incremented by 1 each time the loop was executed. The increment could also have been explicitly declared in a STEP clause, as shown below:

```
10 FOR I=1 TO 5 STEP 1
```

The results produced would be the same. If, on the other hand, we rewrite line 10 as

```
10 FOR I=1 TO 5 STEP 3
```

and run the program, the computer system would respond

```
HELLO, NUMBER 1
HELLO, NUMBER 4
FINISHED.
```

Since the next possible incremented value, 7, exceeds the terminal value of 5, the computer doesn't execute the loop for a third time, but passes control to statement 40.

It is also possible to let the loop variable work "backwards." For example, if we changed line 10 of Figure B3-6 to read

```
10 FOR I=5 TO 1 STEP -1
```

we would obtain

```
HELLO, NUMBER 5
HELLO, NUMBER 4
HELLO, NUMBER 3
HELLO, NUMBER 2
HELLO, NUMBER 1
FINISHED.
```

BASIC also allows programmers to use variables in FOR and NEXT statements. For example, the following sequence is also acceptable:

```
30 FOR Z=J TO K STEP L
        .
        .
        .
70 NEXT Z
```

If $J = 2$, $K = 10$, and $L = 3$, the loop will be performed 3 times, with Z taking on values of 2, 5, and 8 as the loop is executed.

Let's consider now a more comprehensive example to further explore the concept of looping. Consider again the "averages" problem solved in Figure B3-1 (page B-40). How can we solve this problem using FOR/NEXT loops? The flowchart and program solution appear in Figure B3-7.

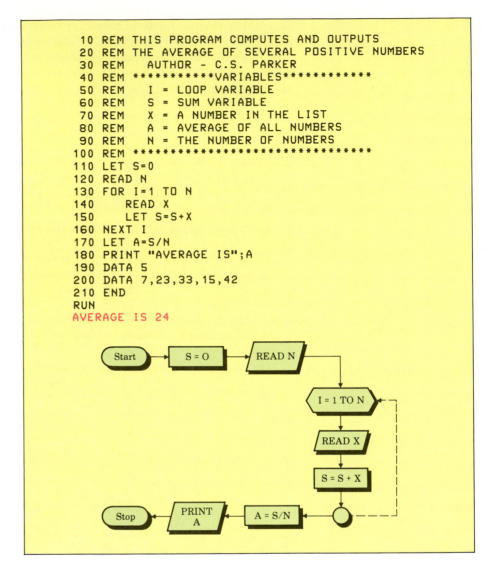

```
10 REM THIS PROGRAM COMPUTES AND OUTPUTS
20 REM THE AVERAGE OF SEVERAL POSITIVE NUMBERS
30 REM    AUTHOR - C.S. PARKER
40 REM ***********VARIABLES************
50 REM    I = LOOP VARIABLE
60 REM    S = SUM VARIABLE
70 REM    X = A NUMBER IN THE LIST
80 REM    A = AVERAGE OF ALL NUMBERS
90 REM    N = THE NUMBER OF NUMBERS
100 REM *****************************
110 LET S=0
120 READ N
130 FOR I=1 TO N
140     READ X
150     LET S=S+X
160 NEXT I
170 LET A=S/N
180 PRINT "AVERAGE IS";A
190 DATA 5
200 DATA 7,23,33,15,42
210 END
RUN
AVERAGE IS 24
```

Figure B3-7. *Flowchart and program solution to the problem of Figure B3-1, using loops.*

You should note the following features in comparing the programs in Figures B3-1 and B3-7:

1. The logic of the program in Figure B3-7 is less complicated than that of Figure B3-1, even though the programs are the same length. A major reason for the gained simplicity is that the automatic initialization, incrementing, and testing done in the loop allow us to eliminate:

    ```
    100 LET I=0
    130 IF X=-1 THEN 180
    140 LET I=I+1
    ```

    Note also that −1 is eliminated in the DATA statement.

2. There are major differences in the flowcharts. Note especially the flowchart symbols used for FOR and NEXT, as well as the dotted line indicating automatic control back to the FOR statement.

You may be wondering at this point why a programming structure like the one shown in Figure B3-1 would ever be used, considering how complicated it is. The major advantage of this structure is that it doesn't require the programmer to know in advance the number of data items processed. In many data processing applications, the number of records processed is unknown. In these situations it is useful to append a trailer record at the end of the data file and use an IF statement to detect it. Thus both of these structures—the FOR/NEXT loop and I=I+1/IF—are frequently used in programs.

Let us now consider branching within a FOR/NEXT loop. For example, suppose that we wanted to read a list of ten numbers, summing only the positive ones. This problem is solved in the short program that appears in Figure B3-8, using the variable-naming convention (lines 40 to 100) of Figure B3-7.

```
10 S=0
20 FOR I=1 TO 10
30    READ X
40    IF X<0 THEN 60
50    S=S+X
60 NEXT I
70 PRINT "THE SUM IS";S
80 DATA 5,-1,3,6,-14,20,4,2,40,10
90 END
RUN
THE SUM IS 90
```

Figure B3-8.   Branching within a FOR/NEXT loop.

Note that if the number is negative ($X < 0$), we wish to bypass the summation operation ($S = X + X$) and read in the next number. However, instead of going directly to the FOR statement, we pass control to the NEXT statement (which will automatically bring us back up to the top of the loop). This raises a key point. If statement 40 were instead

```
40 IF X<0 THEN 20
```

the value of I would be erroneously reset to 1 when the THEN clause is invoked. Note that only through execution of the NEXT statement is the loop variable named in the FOR automatically incremented. If control is passed to a FOR by any statement other than its corresponding NEXT, the loop variable will be set (or reset) to its initial value.

Finally loops within loops (called *nested loops*) are allowed. Observe the program below:

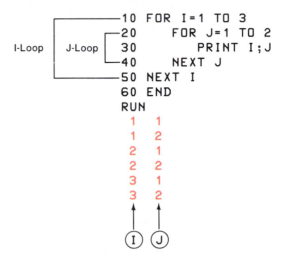

The program executes the PRINT statement a total of 3 * 2 = 6 times. The outer loop variable (I) varies the slowest; the inner loop variable (J), the fastest.

In writing nested-loop programs, it is always important to enclose the inner loop entirely within the outer loop. Thus a program segment such as the one below:

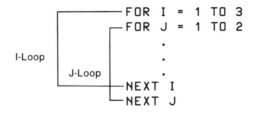

would not work because the loops cross instead of nest.

ELIMINATING GOTOs: THE IF/THEN/ELSE AND WHILE/WEND STATEMENTS

Many recent versions of BASIC enable you to use commands such as IF/THEN/ELSE and WHILE to make program coding more straightforward. IF/THEN/ELSE is a method for coding a *selection* structure, whereas WHILE is a way of coding a *looping* (DOWHILE) structure. Both of these structures are described in the box on page B-35 and are discussed extensively in Chapter 10 of this textbook. Where IF/THEN/ELSE and WHILE are available, they can make developing a program easier—and eliminate many of those GOTO statements (and GOTO clauses) that can make programming logic particularly hard for humans to follow.

IF/THEN/ELSE

As explained earlier, on page B-16, the simplest form of the IF statement involves testing a relational expression and branching to a *line number* if the value of the expression is true. This was the earliest form of the IF statement and is available in virtually all versions of BASIC. The more recent (and increasingly popular) IF/THEN/ELSE statement, as suggested by its format below, allows us to do much more than the simple IF:

$$\text{Line \# IF relational-expression THEN} \begin{Bmatrix} \text{line-number} \\ \text{other statement(s)} \end{Bmatrix}$$
$$\begin{bmatrix} \text{ELSE} \begin{Bmatrix} \text{line-number} \\ \text{other statement(s)} \end{Bmatrix} \end{bmatrix}$$

The square brackets around the ELSE clause means that this clause is optional. Later, we'll look at an instance where we may not want to use an ELSE.

Let's immediately consider an example so you can see how the full form of the IF/THEN/ELSE statement works. Suppose that a list of salespeople is to be processed. If a salesperson sells $5000 or more worth of merchandise in a day, a $50 bonus is to be awarded. A salesperson not achieving that level gets no bonus.

Two short program segments representing this processing task—one using a simple IF and the other using an IF/THEN/ELSE—are provided in Figures B3-9*a* and B3-9*b*, respectively. As you can see, to accomplish the same task (determining whether or not a salesperson gets a bonus), it takes four statements with a simple IF versus a single statement with an IF/THEN/ELSE. Moreover, the IF/THEN/ELSE construct is much easier to follow since it does not involve GOing TO line numbers. Incidentally, many computer systems require you to depress the line feed key when you *continue* a statement from one line to the next (as we've done here in line

```
100  IF S>=5000 THEN 130
110  B=0
120  GOTO 140
130  B=50
140  . . .
```
(a)   Coding a task with a simple IF statement

```
100  IF S>=5000 THEN B=50
                    ELSE B=0
110  . . .
```
(b)   Coding the equivalent task with an IF/THEN/ELSE statement

Note: In the program segments above, S=sales and B=bonus.

Figure B3-9. *Comparison of a simple IF statement and an IF/THEN/ELSE statement.*

100 of Figure B3-9*b*). If your computer does not have a line feed key, depress the Control (Ctrl) key while hitting the "J" key to get a line feed.

In some programs that you write you may want to execute two or more statements if the value of a relational expression is true or, possibly, two or more statements if the value is false. For example, suppose a salesperson selling $5000 or more worth of merchandise is given both a bonus of $50 and a watch (W$="YES"). We might then code the statement in Figure B3-9*b* to inform us of this information as follows:

```
100 IF S>=5000 THEN B=50:W$="YES"
              ELSE B=0:W$="NO"
```

On many computer systems the colon character (:) is used, as shown above, to separate statements appearing on the same line.

Finally, we mentioned earlier that the ELSE clause is optional. So, for example, if we want to increment a counter (C) by one every time a record is read representing a person in the accounting department (D$="AC-COUNTING"), we could use a statement such as

```
200 IF D$="ACCOUNTING" THEN C=C+1
```

As you can see, this form of the IF/THEN/ELSE looks a lot like a simple IF statement. The only difference is that a line number need not follow the THEN clause.

WHILE/WEND

Whereas IF/THEN/ELSE can be used to avoid sloppy branching within a selection structure, many versions of BASIC have a WHILE statement to eliminate the same type of confusion in a looping (DOWHILE) structure. The WHILE statement is similar to the FOR statement in that it uses a companion statement (WEND) to mark the end of the loop. And, also similar to FOR and NEXT, all of the statements appearing between the WHILE and WEND are executed under terms specified by the first statement of the loop: the WHILE statement. The format of the WHILE and WEND statements are provided below:

```
Line # WHILE relational-expression
         .
         .
         .
Line # WEND
```

To see how WHILE and WEND work, let's consider a simple example. Suppose we want to read numbers successively from a list of nonnegative numbers. Each time we read a number, we print it. A negative value (−1) is used as the trailer value on the list to signify its end. Two short program segments representing this processing task are given in Figure B3-10. Figure B3-10*a* shows how we might code the task if no WHILE statement is

```
100 READ X                    100 READ X
110 IF X<0 THEN 150           110 WHILE X>=0
120    PRINT X                120    PRINT X
130    READ X                 130    READ X
140 GOTO 110                  140 WEND
150 . . .                     150 . . .
```

(a) Looping *without* WHILE and WEND   (b) Looping *with* WHILE and WEND

Figure B3-10.   Using the WHILE and WEND statements.

available, whereas the Figure B3-10*b* shows how to proceed with the WHILE. Note that using the WHILE eliminates the confusing line-number transfers in lines 110 and 140 of Figure B3-10*a*. After the loop in Figure B3-10*b* is executed, processing resumes with statement 150.

SOLVED REVIEW PROBLEMS

Example 1
Write a flowchart and BASIC program that will read in the ten values

$$-6, 8, 65, 4, 8, -21, 2, 46, -12, 42$$

and identify the highest number, lowest number, and average.

Solution
The solution shown in Figure B3-11 starts by declaring the first number in the list as both the highest and lowest value in the list.

Then the remaining nine numbers each "get a shot" at competing for highest or lowest value. They are individually read and checked against the current high and low values. As each number is being read and checked, it is accumulated in a sum, so that the average may subsequently be computed. Note in line 190 how the loop variable can be used to "keep tabs" on what the program is doing. Note also in line 330 that a PRINT statement can output a value not calculated until the statement itself is executed.

Example 2
An auto rental company rents three types of cars at the rates below:

Car Type	Fixed Cost per Day	Cost per Mile
Compact	$10	$0.15
Intermediate	$20	$0.18
Large	$30	$0.22

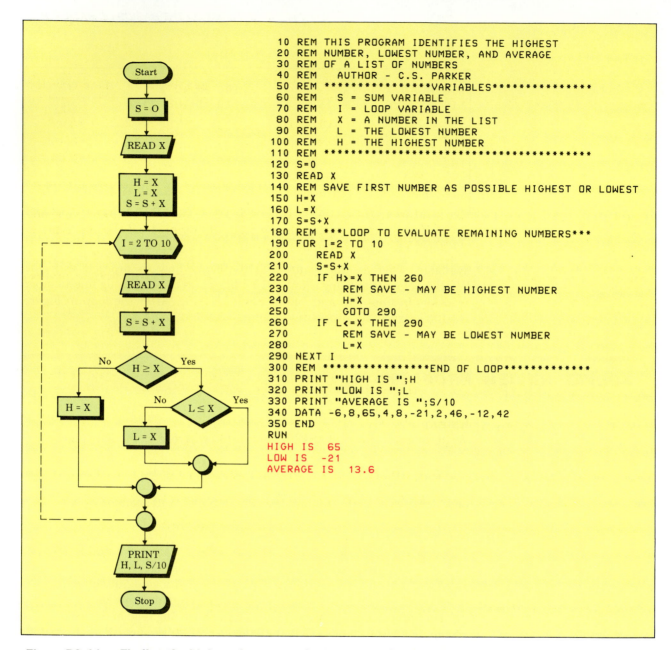

```
10 REM THIS PROGRAM IDENTIFIES THE HIGHEST
20 REM NUMBER, LOWEST NUMBER, AND AVERAGE
30 REM OF A LIST OF NUMBERS
40 REM    AUTHOR - C.S. PARKER
50 REM **************VARIABLES***************
60 REM    S = SUM VARIABLE
70 REM    I = LOOP VARIABLE
80 REM    X = A NUMBER IN THE LIST
90 REM    L = THE LOWEST NUMBER
100 REM   H = THE HIGHEST NUMBER
110 REM ***************************************
120 S=0
130 READ X
140 REM SAVE FIRST NUMBER AS POSSIBLE HIGHEST OR LOWEST
150 H=X
160 L=X
170 S=S+X
180 REM ***LOOP TO EVALUATE REMAINING NUMBERS***
190 FOR I=2 TO 10
200     READ X
210     S=S+X
220     IF H>=X THEN 260
230         REM SAVE - MAY BE HIGHEST NUMBER
240         H=X
250         GOTO 290
260     IF L<=X THEN 290
270         REM SAVE - MAY BE LOWEST NUMBER
280         L=X
290 NEXT I
300 REM ***************END OF LOOP************
310 PRINT "HIGH IS ";H
320 PRINT "LOW IS ";L
330 PRINT "AVERAGE IS ";S/10
340 DATA -6,8,65,4,8,-21,2,46,-12,42
350 END
RUN
HIGH IS  65
LOW IS  -21
AVERAGE IS  13.6
```

Figure B3-11. *Finding the highest, lowest, and average number in a list.*

Thus, for example, a person renting a compact car for 3 days and driving 100 miles would be charged $10 * 3 + .15 * 100 = 45.

Write a flowchart and an interactive BASIC program that will accept

- Customer name
- Number of days car held
- Car type
- Miles traveled

as input. It should output the charge for each customer. Also, have the computer add up the total charges attributable to each type of car. Use the sample data in the table on page B-57 to test your program.

Customer Name	Car Type	Days Held	Miles Traveled
Jones	Large	6	500
Smith	Compact	17	3000
Baker	Intermediate	8	250
Williams	Intermediate	4	1000
Winston	Large	3	500

The solution to this problem is provided in Figure B3-12 (pages B-58 and B-59). You should note that the program will terminate if the user types in "GOODBYE" when asked to supply a customer name.

Exercises

Instructions: Provide an answer to each of the following questions.

1. Identify the syntax errors, if any, in the following basic statements.
   a. `10 FOR I=6 TO 1 STEP 2`
   b. `10 INPUT N$,A,A1`
   c. `10 INPUT T=1, T=2, T=3`
   d. `15 IF N$="PHONY" THEN 25`
   e. `10 FOR I=-5 TO 5`
   f. `10 FOR K=3 TO A STEP 2`

2. Consider the FOR-NEXT loop below:

   ```
   10 FOR I=A TO B STEP C
        .
        .
        .
   20 NEXT I
   ```

   How many times will this loop execute if
   a. A=1, B=7, and C=1?   c. A=5, B=17, and C=3?
   b. A=1, B=7, and C=2?   d. A=5, B=1, and C=−1?

3. Consider the program below:

   ```
   10 FOR I=1 TO 5
   20 FOR J=3 TO 7
   30 A=I*J
   40 NEXT J
   50 NEXT I
   ```

   a. What is the first value assigned to A?
   b. What is the value of A at the end of the program?
   c. What is the value of A the 8th time statement 30 is executed?
   d. What is the value of A the 12th time statement 30 is executed?
   e. How many times will line 30 be executed?

```
 10 REM THIS PROGRAM COMPUTES THE CHARGES DUE ON
 20 REM RENTED AUTOMOBILES
 30 REM      AUTHOR - C.S. PARKER
 40 REM **************VARIABLES*****************
 50 REM     T  = CAR TYPE (1=COMPACT)
 60 REM                   (2=INTERMEDIATE)
 70 REM                   (3=LARGE)
 80 REM     N$ = CUSTOMER NAME
 90 REM     D  = DAYS CAR HELD
100 REM     M  = MILES TRAVELED
110 REM     C  = CHARGE FOR CUSTOMER
120 REM     C1,C2,C3 = TOTAL BILLINGS ON CAR
130 REM          TYPES 1,2 & 3, RESPECTIVELY
140 REM *****************************************
150 LET C1=0
160 LET C2=0
170 LET C3=0
180 PRINT "ENTER CUSTOMER NAME"
190 PRINT "     NOTE: ENTER GOODBYE TO STOP PROGRAM"
200 INPUT N$
210 IF N$="GOODBYE" THEN 470
220 PRINT "ENTER DAYS CAR HELD, MILES TRAVELED, AND CAR TYPE"
230 PRINT "     NOTE: 1=COMPACT  2=INTERMEDIATE  3=LARGE"
240 INPUT D,M,T
250 IF T=1 THEN 310
260 IF T=2 THEN 350
270 IF T=3 THEN 390
280 PRINT "CAR TYPE";T;"DOES NOT EXIST"
290 GOTO 220
300 REM COMPACT CAR CALCULATIONS
310     C=.15*M+10*D
320     C1=C1+C
330     GOTO 410
340 REM INTERMEDIATE CAR CALCULATIONS
350     C=.18*M+20*D
360     C2=C2+C
370     GOTO 410
380 REM LARGE CAR CALCULATIONS
390     C=.22*M+30*D
400     C3=C3+C
410 PRINT N$;"     $";C
420 PRINT
430 PRINT "ENTER CUSTOMER NAME"
440 PRINT "     NOTE: ENTER GOODBYE TO STOP PROGRAM"
450 INPUT N$
460 GOTO 210
470 PRINT "TOTAL CHARGES ON CAR TYPE 1 ARE   $";C1
480 PRINT "TOTAL CHARGES ON CAR TYPE 2 ARE   $";C2
490 PRINT "TOTAL CHARGES ON CAR TYPE 3 ARE   $";C3
500 END
```

Figure B3-12.   *An interactive program to determine auto rental charges.*

```
RUN
ENTER CUSTOMER NAME
      NOTE: ENTER GOODBYE TO STOP PROGRAM
?JONES
ENTER DAYS CAR HELD, MILES TRAVELED, AND CAR TYPE
      NOTE: 1=COMPACT  2=INTERMEDIATE  3=LARGE
?6,500,3
JONES     $ 290

ENTER CUSTOMER NAME
      NOTE: ENTER GOODBYE TO STOP PROGRAM
?SMITH
ENTER DAYS CAR HELD, MILES TRAVELED, AND CAR TYPE
      NOTE: 1=COMPACT  2=INTERMEDIATE  3=LARGE
?17,3000,1
SMITH     $ 620

ENTER CUSTOMER NAME
      NOTE: ENTER GOODBYE TO STOP PROGRAM
?BAKER
ENTER DAYS CAR HELD, MILES TRAVELED, AND CAR TYPE
      NOTE: 1=COMPACT  2=INTERMEDIATE  3=LARGE
?8,250,6
CAR TYPE 6 DOES NOT EXIST
ENTER DAYS CAR HELD, MILES TRAVELED, AND CAR TYPE
      NOTE: 1=COMPACT  2=INTERMEDIATE  3=LARGE
?8,250,2
BAKER     $ 205

ENTER CUSTOMER NAME
      NOTE: ENTER GOODBYE TO STOP PROGRAM
?WILLIAMS
ENTER DAYS CAR HELD, MILES TRAVELED, AND CAR TYPE
      NOTE: 1=COMPACT  2=INTERMEDIATE  3=LARGE
?4,1000,2
WILLIAMS    $ 260

ENTER CUSTOMER NAME
      NOTE: ENTER GOODBYE TO STOP PROGRAM
?WINSTON
ENTER DAYS CAR HELD, MILES TRAVELED, AND CAR TYPE
      NOTE: 1=COMPACT  2=INTERMEDIATE  3=LARGE
?3,500,3
WINSTON    $ 200

ENTER CUSTOMER NAME
      NOTE: ENTER GOODBYE TO STOP PROGRAM
?GOODBYE
TOTAL CHARGES ON CAR TYPE 1 ARE  $ 620
TOTAL CHARGES ON CAR TYPE 2 ARE  $ 465
TOTAL CHARGES ON CAR TYPE 3 ARE  $ 490
```

Figure B3-12.   *(Continued)*

Programming Problems

Instructions: Write a BASIC program to do each of the following tasks.

1. Read a list of positive numbers, sum all of the numbers greater than 10 in the list, and output that sum.

2. Sum all even numbers from 1 to 100 and output the square root of that sum. [*Hint:* The square root of any number X is $X^{1/2}$.]

3. Read a list of positive numbers, find the average of all numbers between 10 and 20 (inclusive) in the list, and output the average.

4. The following data show the weather in a city on ten successive days: Sunny, Cloudy, Rainy, Sunny, Sunny, Cloudy, Sunny, Sunny, Rainy, Cloudy.

   Write a program to read these ten weather observations and then count and output the number of sunny days.

5. Use FOR/NEXT loops to compute the sums S below:

$$S = 1 + 2 + 3 + 4 + \cdots + 10$$
$$S = 3 + 6 + 9 + 12 + \cdots + 30$$
$$S = 1 + 1/2 + 1/3 + 1/4 + \cdots + 1/1000$$

6. Write a program to convert several temperatures from Fahrenheit (F) to centigrade (C). Use the INPUT statement to supply each Fahrenheit temperature to the computer system for conversion. The formula below can be used to make the conversion:

```
C=(5/9)*(F-32)
```

   Use a trailer value, such as 9999 degrees, to stop your program.

7. The cost of sending a telegram is $2.80 for the first 20 (or fewer) words and 10 cents for each additional word. Write a program that will find the cost of a telegram after you have entered the number of words as input at a keyboard.

8. The population growth rate in a city has been projected at 5 percent per year for the next 10 years. The current population in the city is 31,840 residents. Write a program to find the population 10 years from now.

9. Solve Problem 4 in Section 1 (page B-30) using the IF/THEN/ELSE statement in place of the simple IF statement where appropriate.

10. Solve Problem 6 using the WHILE and WEND statements.

Section 4
Formatted Printing

SPACING OUTPUT

Producing neatly formatted output is one of the prized skills of computer programming. A sloppy looking report, even though it contains accurate information, is often not read. Readers of reports are generally favorably inclined toward well-presented output.

So far we have learned two formatting vehicles to use with the PRINT statement:

1. The semicolon. This generally leaves a space or two between printed items.* When it is the last character in the PRINT statement, it forces the next output from the computer system to begin on the same line.

2. The "blank" PRINT statement. This is used to produce blank output lines.

There are three other techniques discussed in this section that will aid in formatting output:

1. The comma (,).

2. The TAB function.

3. The PRINT USING statement.

COMMA PRINT CONTROL

The comma works in a manner somewhat similar to the semicolon, except that

1. It produces more space between the output data items.

2. The items are printed at fixed tab stops.

*The exception is that no spaces are provided between two strings separated by a semicolon (unless, of course, spaces appear within the string).

The fixed tab stops define so-called **print zones.** If you are on an output device that provides 72 characters per line, the zones might be fixed as follows:

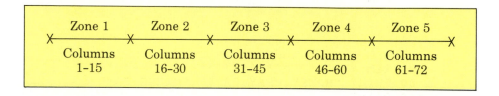

In any case, you should check your output device to find out where the zones begin and end. With the zones given above, the use of commas in a PRINT statement would have the effect shown in Figure B4-1. Positive numbers printed in a zone are preceded by a blank space, negative numbers by a minus sign.

If we wanted to total gross pay in this program and print it neatly on output, we could add the following statements to this program:

```
115 S=0
145 S=S+A
155 PRINT
156 PRINT,,S
```

When the program is run, the output produced will look like this:

```
NAME            PAY RATE        GROSS PAY

JOHN DOE        6.3             200.15
MARY SMITH      7.2             316.4
ANN JONES       5               80

                                596.55
```

There are two other interesting features to note about the use of the comma for spacing in a PRINT statement:

1. If the number of items to be output in a PRINT statement is too large to fit on one line of the output device used, a "wraparound" effect will occur; for example:

```
10 FOR I=1 TO 12
20 PRINT I,
30 NEXT I
40 END
RUN
 1              2               3               4               5
 6              7               8               9               10
 11             12
```

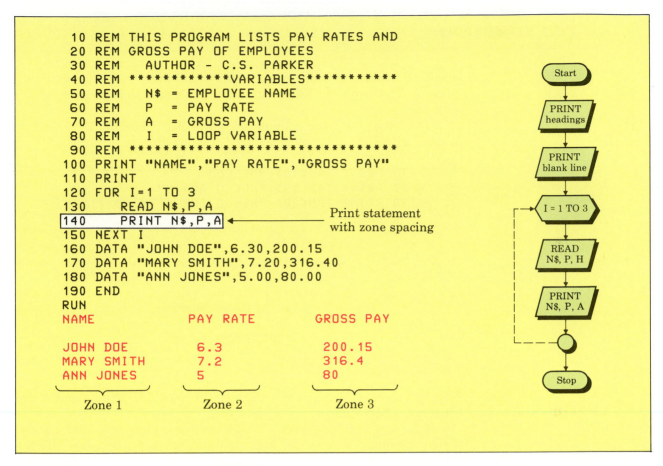

```
 10 REM THIS PROGRAM LISTS PAY RATES AND
 20 REM GROSS PAY OF EMPLOYEES
 30 REM    AUTHOR - C.S. PARKER
 40 REM ***********VARIABLES***********
 50 REM    N$ = EMPLOYEE NAME
 60 REM    P  = PAY RATE
 70 REM    A  = GROSS PAY
 80 REM    I  = LOOP VARIABLE
 90 REM ******************************
100 PRINT "NAME","PAY RATE","GROSS PAY"
110 PRINT
120 FOR I=1 TO 3
130    READ N$,P,A
140    PRINT N$,P,A                    ◄── Print statement
150 NEXT I                                  with zone spacing
160 DATA "JOHN DOE",6.30,200.15
170 DATA "MARY SMITH",7.20,316.40
180 DATA "ANN JONES",5.00,80.00
190 END
RUN
NAME            PAY RATE        GROSS PAY

JOHN DOE        6.3             200.15
MARY SMITH      7.2             316.4
ANN JONES       5               80
```

Zone 1   Zone 2   Zone 3

Flowchart: Start → PRINT headings → PRINT blank line → I = 1 TO 3 → READ N$, P, H → PRINT N$, P, A → Stop

Figure B4-1. *Use of comma in PRINT for spacing.* This simple program reads in names of people, along with associated pay rates and gross pay. This information is then output into print zones.

Only five data items are printed per line because only five print zones are available on the output device used. If we tried running this program on a different output device, say one with six zones, we would get six numbers per line.

2. If a particular data item is too large to occupy a single print zone, it will "overflow" into subsequent zones; for example:

```
10 PRINT "TODAY IS MAY 16, 1987","HELLO"
20 END
RUN
TODAY IS MAY 16, 1987    HELLO
```

└─Begins in zone 1

└─ Begins in zone 3 (because the first literal overflowed into zone 2)

THE TAB FUNCTION

The TAB function of BASIC permits us to "tab" over to any column to start printing. Thus with the TAB function we don't have to begin printing at a zone boundary.

The self-explanatory example below will clarify how the TAB function is used in BASIC.

```
10 PRINT TAB(10);"HELLO"
20 PRINT TAB(15);"HELLO AGAIN"
30 PRINT TAB(20);"HELLO FOR A THIRD TIME"
40 END
RUN
```

```
HELLO
        HELLO AGAIN
             HELLO FOR A THIRD TIME
```

Starts in column 20

Starts in column 15

Starts in column 10

Note that there must be no space between the word TAB in a statement and the opening parenthesis.

It is possible to use several TAB functions on one line. You can also specify tabbing for a single, long output line that spans two PRINT statements. For example:

```
10 PRINT "PART NUMBER";TAB(20);"NAME";TAB(30);
20 PRINT "AMOUNT IN STOCK";TAB(50);"UNIT PRICE"
30 END
RUN
PART NUMBER     NAME     AMOUNT IN STOCK     UNIT PRICE
```

Column 1   Column 20   Column 30   Column 50

Remember, the semicolon at the end of a PRINT statement (see line 10) will keep the output device on the same line.

In many versions of BASIC you can use variable names as tab stops; for example:

```
10 F=25
20 PRINT TAB(F);"GOODBYE"
30 END
RUN
```

```
                    GOODBYE
```

Column 25

THE PRINT USING STATEMENT

The PRINT USING statement is the most powerful instruction in BASIC for formatted printing. The syntax of this statement varies considerably from system to system; however, the one presented below and in the examples to follow is used widely:

> Line # PRINT USING output-image variable;
> list of variables (separated by commas)

A program employing the PRINT USING statement appears in Figure B4-2. This program reads in names (N$), pay rates (P), and hours worked (H). It then computes and sums the amounts earned (A=P∗H). You should examine this example carefully before reading further.

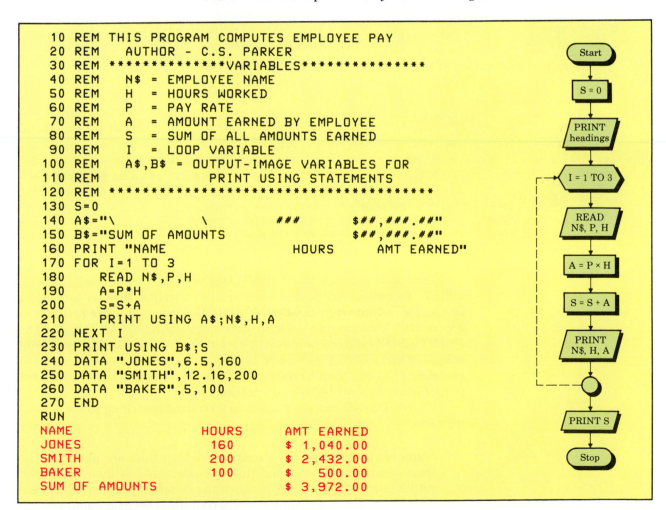

```
 10 REM THIS PROGRAM COMPUTES EMPLOYEE PAY
 20 REM    AUTHOR - C.S. PARKER
 30 REM ***************VARIABLES***************
 40 REM    N$ = EMPLOYEE NAME
 50 REM    H  = HOURS WORKED
 60 REM    P  = PAY RATE
 70 REM    A  = AMOUNT EARNED BY EMPLOYEE
 80 REM    S  = SUM OF ALL AMOUNTS EARNED
 90 REM    I  = LOOP VARIABLE
100 REM    A$,B$ = OUTPUT-IMAGE VARIABLES FOR
110 REM            PRINT USING STATEMENTS
120 REM ******************************************
130 S=0
140 A$="\              \        ###        $##,###.##"
150 B$="SUM OF AMOUNTS              $##,###.##"
160 PRINT "NAME              HOURS      AMT EARNED"
170 FOR I=1 TO 3
180    READ N$,P,H
190    A=P*H
200    S=S+A
210    PRINT USING A$;N$,H,A
220 NEXT I
230 PRINT USING B$;S
240 DATA "JONES",6.5,160
250 DATA "SMITH",12.16,200
260 DATA "BAKER",5,100
270 END
RUN
NAME                HOURS        AMT EARNED
JONES                160         $ 1,040.00
SMITH                200         $ 2,432.00
BAKER                100         $   500.00
SUM OF AMOUNTS                   $ 3,972.00
```

Flowchart: Start → S = 0 → PRINT headings → I = 1 TO 3 → READ N$, P, H → A = P × H → S = S + A → PRINT N$, H, A → (loop) → PRINT S → Stop

Figure B4-2.   *Use of PRINT USING statement.*

How to Dress Up Your Printouts

The appearance of printed documents is important in presenting results to others. As mentioned in this section, one of the best ways to dress up documents is with the PRINT USING statement, which controls the location of each character printed on a page. On many computer systems, you can enhance the appearance of printed documents still further by using a few other simple tricks.

One of the easiest ways to enhance a document is by employing the facilities on your computer system to *expand* or *compress* type. For example,

EXPANDED PRINT

CONDENSED PRINT

SUPERCONDENSED PRINT

To get expanded type on many microcomputer systems, for example, you would issue a command such as:

```
100 LPRINT CHR$(27);"EXPANDED"
```

This command sends an ASCII "escape code" (ASCII character 27) to your printer to tell it to print the string in quotes in an expanded mode. The version of BASIC available to your computer system and the printer you are using both need to "understand" this convention in order for this to happen.

The condensed mode can normally be obtained by another escape sequence or by "DIP switches" on your microcomputer's printer. The DIP switches are generally a collection of eight on–off type of switches that are built into most microcomputer-oriented printers. Leaving certain switches in the on (or off) position will produce condensed print on output. To find out specifically how to do this, you need to consult the manual for your printer to determine which switches to turn on and off. Some printers make this easy for you by having a special button on the panel that, when depressed, will set the DIP switches automatically. In many printers you can also set these switches to produce boldface or correspondence-quality output.

The program uses two PRINT USING statements. Each PRINT USING statement refers to a variable that specifies how to format, or *image,* the output when the PRINT USING is executed. The program in Figure B4-2 contains two such *output-image variables:* A$ and B$. The PRINT USING statement in line 210 references A$, containing the output images of variables N$, H, and A. Similarly, statement 230 references B$, containing the image of variable S. For both A$ and B$ the associated output image appears between quotation marks.

PRINT USING output images are formatted according to the following rules:

✖ *Numeric variables* All numeric variable values are placed in the areas occupied by the pound (number) signs (#) of their associated output images, in the order in which the variable names appear in the PRINT USING. If the variable value contains a decimal point, you can specify where it must appear and the number of digits to the left and right of it. For example, an image such as

#####.##

specifies that 1245.06 be printed as

Ƀ1245.06

In many versions of BASIC, commas can also be automatically placed into numeric values. For example, an image such as

##,###.##

specifies that 1245.06 be printed as

Ƀ1,245.06

If a number to be output with the last image is smaller than 1000, the comma is replaced by a Ƀ. Thus 154.68 is output as

ƁƁƁ154.68

You should note that the # is a special symbol when used to specify an output image.

✕ *String variables*   The symbol pair \ \ is used to specify the maximum number of characters printed out for a string variable. The backslashes plus each space left between them represent the length of output. For example, a declaration such as

\ƁƁƁ\

will accommodate the full contents of any output strings of five characters or less.

✕ *Constants*   Generally any characters other than # (for numeric variables) and the backslashes (for string variables) will be printed as they appear. Thus the dollar sign in lines 140 and 150 and the phrase SUM OF AMOUNTS in line 150 appear exactly on output as they do in the output image.

As you can see by inspecting this program, a major advantage of PRINT USING is that it allows neat decimal-point alignment in columns. This is a "must" for reports used in business. The use of comma spacing or the TAB function does not provide this luxury, since variable values start printing in the zone boundary or tab stop indicated, leaving the decimal point to fall where it may. This can be seen in Figure B4-1; note that the gross pay for Ann Jones is not neatly lined up under the gross pay of the other individuals.

The values of string variables automatically begin at the far left (left-justified) within the \ \ symbol pair. The values of numeric variables are aligned with respect to the decimal point. The following example should make this clear:

```
10 N$="BETSY JONES"
20 A=10
30 B=3.06
40 A$="\              \    ###     ###.##"
50 PRINT USING A$;N$,A,B
60 END
RUN
BETSY JONES            10     3.06
```

First # field (15 characters)   Second # field (3 characters)   Third # field (3 characters to left of decimal point, 2 characters to right)

If the values of any of the variables are too large to fit within the specified \ \ or # sign fields, either truncation, rounding, or output suppression (that is, spaces or nonnumeric symbols) may occur. Referring to the last example, if

```
N$="SHERIDAN P. WHITESIDE"
A=10.6
B=8321.46
```

the following output might be produced:

Truncation   Rounding   Output suppression

SOLVED REVIEW PROBLEMS

Example 1

Compute the square root ($I^{1/2}$), cube root ($I^{1/3}$), and fourth root ($I^{1/4}$) of all integers I in the range 1–10. The output should be neatly labeled and formatted.

Solution

The program and associated output are shown in Figure B4-3. You should note the use of the comma in lines 160 and 200, which keeps the output device printing on the same line. The blank PRINT statement in line 220 is extremely important; it negates the effect of the comma on line 200 when the fourth roots are printed and sends the output device to the next output line.

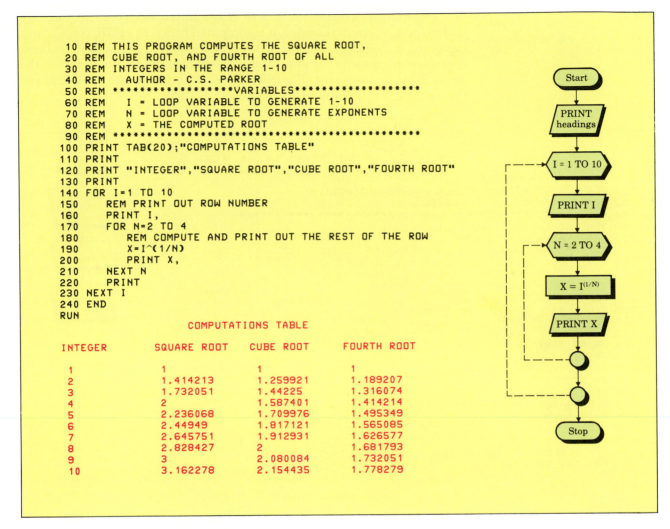

```
 10 REM THIS PROGRAM COMPUTES THE SQUARE ROOT,
 20 REM CUBE ROOT, AND FOURTH ROOT OF ALL
 30 REM INTEGERS IN THE RANGE 1-10
 40 REM    AUTHOR - C.S. PARKER
 50 REM *****************VARIABLES*****************
 60 REM    I = LOOP VARIABLE TO GENERATE 1-10
 70 REM    N = LOOP VARIABLE TO GENERATE EXPONENTS
 80 REM    X = THE COMPUTED ROOT
 90 REM ********************************************
100 PRINT TAB(20);"COMPUTATIONS TABLE"
110 PRINT
120 PRINT "INTEGER","SQUARE ROOT","CUBE ROOT","FOURTH ROOT"
130 PRINT
140 FOR I=1 TO 10
150    REM PRINT OUT ROW NUMBER
160    PRINT I,
170    FOR N=2 TO 4
180       REM COMPUTE AND PRINT OUT THE REST OF THE ROW
190       X=I^(1/N)
200       PRINT X,
210    NEXT N
220    PRINT
230 NEXT I
240 END
RUN
              COMPUTATIONS TABLE

INTEGER        SQUARE ROOT     CUBE ROOT       FOURTH ROOT

1              1               1               1
2              1.414213        1.259921        1.189207
3              1.732051        1.44225         1.316074
4              2               1.587401        1.414214
5              2.236068        1.709976        1.495349
6              2.44949         1.817121        1.565085
7              2.645751        1.912931        1.626577
8              2.828427        2               1.681793
9              3               2.080084        1.732051
10             3.162278        2.154435        1.778279
```

Figure B4-3. *A program to compute roots.*

Example 2

Straight-line depreciation expenses are computed by the formula:

$$\text{Annual depreciation charge} = \frac{\text{Original cost} - \text{Salvage value}}{\text{Useful life}}$$

Provide a depreciation schedule for a car that originally cost $7328 and will be worth approximately $600 at the end of its ten-year useful life. The depreciation schedule should show (for each year) the depreciation charge, total depreciation so far, and the (undepreciated) balance.

Solution
The program and associated output are shown in Figure B4-4.

The annual depreciation charge is computed in line 210. Since the charge for each year is the same, it is computed before the FOR/NEXT loop beginning in line 250. This loop is used to compute the total accumulated depreciation, compute the undepreciated balance, and produce most of the output lines for the report. The PRINT USING statement in line 280 aligns the output neatly in formatted columns.

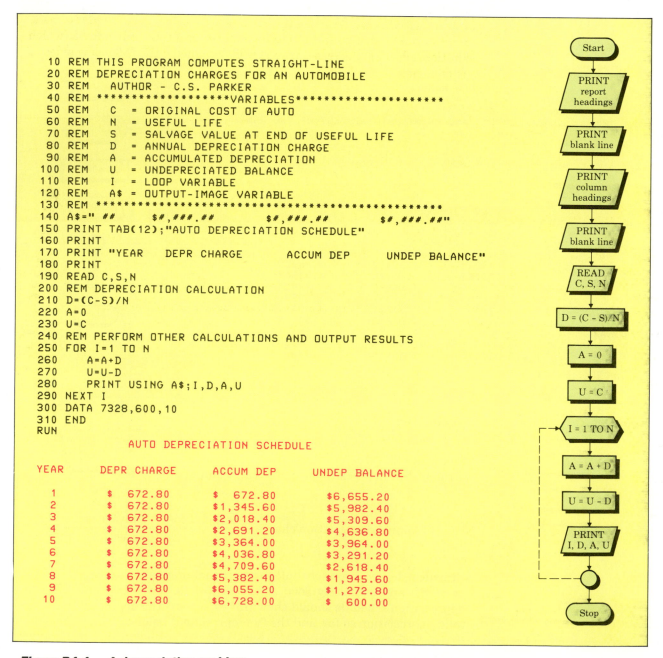

```
10 REM THIS PROGRAM COMPUTES STRAIGHT-LINE
20 REM DEPRECIATION CHARGES FOR AN AUTOMOBILE
30 REM    AUTHOR - C.S. PARKER
40 REM ******************VARIABLES********************
50 REM   C  = ORIGINAL COST OF AUTO
60 REM   N  = USEFUL LIFE
70 REM   S  = SALVAGE VALUE AT END OF USEFUL LIFE
80 REM   D  = ANNUAL DEPRECIATION CHARGE
90 REM   A  = ACCUMULATED DEPRECIATION
100 REM  U  = UNDEPRECIATED BALANCE
110 REM  I  = LOOP VARIABLE
120 REM  A$ = OUTPUT-IMAGE VARIABLE
130 REM ********************************************
140 A$="  ##      $#,###.##      $#,###.##      $#,###.##"
150 PRINT TAB(12);"AUTO DEPRECIATION SCHEDULE"
160 PRINT
170 PRINT "YEAR   DEPR CHARGE      ACCUM DEP      UNDEP BALANCE"
180 PRINT
190 READ C,S,N
200 REM DEPRECIATION CALCULATION
210 D=(C-S)/N
220 A=0
230 U=C
240 REM PERFORM OTHER CALCULATIONS AND OUTPUT RESULTS
250 FOR I=1 TO N
260    A=A+D
270    U=U-D
280    PRINT USING A$;I,D,A,U
290 NEXT I
300 DATA 7328,600,10
310 END
RUN
```

```
              AUTO DEPRECIATION SCHEDULE

YEAR    DEPR CHARGE      ACCUM DEP      UNDEP BALANCE

  1      $   672.80      $   672.80      $6,655.20
  2      $   672.80      $1,345.60      $5,982.40
  3      $   672.80      $2,018.40      $5,309.60
  4      $   672.80      $2,691.20      $4,636.80
  5      $   672.80      $3,364.00      $3,964.00
  6      $   672.80      $4,036.80      $3,291.20
  7      $   672.80      $4,709.60      $2,618.40
  8      $   672.80      $5,382.40      $1,945.60
  9      $   672.80      $6,055.20      $1,272.80
 10      $   672.80      $6,728.00      $   600.00
```

Flowchart:
Start → PRINT report headings → PRINT blank line → PRINT column headings → PRINT blank line → READ C, S, N → D = (C − S)/N → A = 0 → U = C → I = 1 TO N → A = A + D → U = U − D → PRINT I, D, A, U → Stop

Figure B4-4. A depreciation problem.

Example 3

The TAB function is extremely helpful for printing various types of geometrical designs. The program in Figure B4-5 uses the TAB function to print a triangle.

The triangle in the figure consists of eleven lines of output. The top line of twenty-one asterisks and the bottom line of one asterisk are each produced by a single statement—statements 100 and 160 respectively. The middle nine lines of output each consists of two asterisks and are produced in the FOR/NEXT loop, using the variables S1 and S2. As each pass is made in the loop, S1 (which is initialized to 1) increases by one unit, and S2 (which is initialized to 21) decreases by one unit, producing the collapsing sides of the triangle.

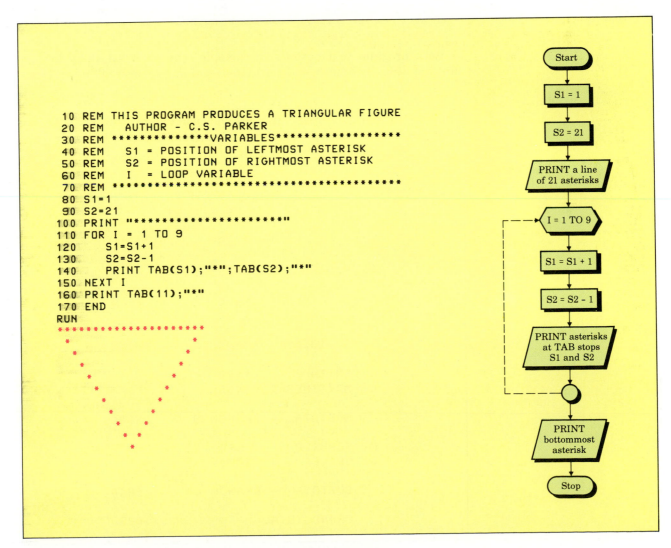

Figure B4-5. *A program and flowchart to produce a triangle.*

Example 4
The table below provides a list of salespeople at XYZ Company, their branch affiliations, and their sales booked last week.

Name	Branch	Sales
M. Vincent	A	$1020
T. Loux	A	$1090
J. Jefferson	A	$1400
A. T. Jones	A	$1700
C. Smith	B	$1100
L. Martinez	B	$1400
M. Schurer	C	$1550
G. Seaver	C	$1090

Write a program that outputs salespeople (and their sales) by branch, subtotals sales by branch, and calculates a grand total over all branches.

Solution
The program and associated output are shown in Figure B4-6. The subtotals that "foot" each branch are examples of **control breaks.** In the program variable B$ (branch) is referred to as the *control-break variable.* B$

```
            XYZ SALES REPORT

      NAME              SALES

      M. VINCENT        1020
      T. LOUX           1090
      J. JEFFERSON      1400
      A.T. JONES        1700

         SUBTOTAL - BRANCH A      5210

      C. SMITH          1100
      L. MARTINEZ       1400

         SUBTOTAL - BRANCH B      2500

      M. SCHURER        1550
      G. SEAVER         1090

         SUBTOTAL - BRANCH C      2640

         GRAND TOTAL             10350
```

Figure B4-6. *(a) Output of control-break program.*

"breaks" two times—when branch changes from A to B and, later, from B to C. At each break a subtotal is printed. Before the program ends, it prints out the final subtotal and the grand total. The program uses a "holding variable" (H$) to hold the value of B$ from the last processed record, and uses a check (in line 200) to signal when a new record represents a change in branch. For this program to work, the data must be presorted by branch.

```
10 REM THIS PROGRAM COMPUTES SUBTOTALS BY BRANCH
20 REM    AUTHOR - C.S. PARKER
30 REM **************VARIABLES*****************
40 REM    T  = BRANCH SUBTOTAL
50 REM    G  = GRAND TOTAL
60 REM    N$ = SALESPERSON NAME
70 REM    S  = SALESPERSON SALES
80 REM    B$ = BRANCH
90 REM    H$ = HOLDING VARIABLE FOR BRANCH
100 REM ****************************************
110 T=0
120 G=0
130 PRINT TAB(10);"XYZ SALES REPORT"
140 PRINT
150 PRINT "NAME","SALES"
160 PRINT
170 READ N$,B$,S
180 H$=B$
190 IF N$="LAST RECORD" THEN 310
200    IF B$=H$ THEN 260
210       PRINT
220       PRINT "    SUBTOTAL - BRANCH ";H$,T
230       PRINT
240       T=0
250       H$=B$
260    G=G+S
270    T=T+S
280    PRINT N$,S
290    READ N$,B$,S
300    GOTO 190
310 PRINT
320 PRINT "    SUBTOTAL - BRANCH ";H$,T
330 PRINT
340 PRINT "    GRAND TOTAL",G
350 DATA "M. VINCENT","A",1020,"T. LOUX","A",1090
360 DATA "J. JEFFERSON","A",1400,"A.T. JONES","A",1700
370 DATA "C. SMITH","B",1100,"L. MARTINEZ","B",1400
380 DATA "M. SCHURER","C",1550,"G. SEAVER","C",1090
390 DATA "LAST RECORD","Z",0
400 END
```

Figure B4-6.   **(b) The control-break program.**

Exercises

Instructions: Provide an answer to each of the following questions.

1. Consider this program.

   ```
   10 FOR I=1 TO 3
   20 PRINT "HELLO NUMBER";I
   30 FOR J=1 TO 4
   40 PRINT X=I*J,
   50 NEXT J
   60 PRINT
   70 NEXT I
   ```

   a. How many lines will be printed by this program?
   b. How many times will line 20 be executed?
   c. What will be the fourth line printed by this program?
   d. How many times will line 40 be executed?
   e. What will be the value of X at the end of the program?

2. How would your answers to Exercise 1 change if the following changes were made to the program?

   ```
    5 LET X=0
   35 LET X=X+I*J
   40 PRINT X,
   ```

3. Consider the program below:

   ```
   10 READ A,B,C,D,E
   20 PRINT...
   30 DATA  (data values)
   ```

   Write a PRINT statement for line 20 that will do the following:
   a. Place the values of A, B, and C in print zones 1, 2, and 3 respectively.
   b. Place the value of A in all five print zones.
   c. Place the values of C, D, and E in print zones 3, 4, and 5 respectively.
   d. Place the values of A, B, and C in print zones 1, 3, and 5 respectively.

4. Assume X has a value of 2590.86. Show how this value would be output when assigned to the output-image fields below. (Use b̸ to represent a blank space.)
   a. `####`
   b. `##,###.##`
   c. `$#,###`
   d. `#.##`

5. Assume N$ has a value of JONES. Show how this value would be output when assigned to the output-image fields below. (Use ƀ to represent a blank space.)

a. \ƀƀƀƀƀƀ\
b. \ƀƀƀ\
c. \ƀ\
d. #####

Programming Problems

Instructions: Write a BASIC program to do each of the following tasks.

1. Students in a class are required to take three exams. The class performed as follows on the exams last semester:

Student Name	Scores		
	Exam 1	Exam 2	Exam 3
Jo Smith	70	80	90
Ed Lynn	40	65	59
Richard Johnson	86	93	72
Linda Harris	95	75	86
Wendy Williams	77	83	78
David Rudolph	55	83	78

Compute the average on each of the 3 exams, the average of each of the 6 students, and the overall average of the 18 scores. Print the table with these computed averages shown in their appropriate row and column positions. Use trailer values at the end of your data list so that your program can sense when there are no more records to be read.

2. Solve Problem 1 by printing letter grades in place of the average score of each of the six students. Use the following formula to assign grades to numbers: 90 and above = A, 80–89 = B, 70–79 = C, 60–69 = D, below 60 = F.

3. Redo the table below so that all of the decimal points line up and each column of data is centered below its column title:

```
NAME           GROSS PAY
----           ---------
ZELDA SMITH    $ 1000
ZEB TSOSIE     $ 83.25
ZENON JONES    $ .50
```

4. If P dollars are invested in an account today at a compounded interest rate of R percent per period, the amount in the account at the end of N periods is given by

$$S = P(1 + R/100)^N$$

For example, \$100 will be worth \$129.15 on 12/31/88 if it was invested on 12/31/83 at an interest rate of 5.25 percent compounded annually; that is,

$$S = 100 (1 + 5.25/100)^5$$
$$= 100 (1.0525)^5 = 129.15$$

Produce a table showing the value of 1 dollar at the end of $1, 2, 3, \ldots, 10$ years at interest rates of 10 percent, 10.5 percent, 11 percent, 11.5 percent, and 12 percent. The years should appear as rows of the table, and the interest rates as columns. Make sure that your decimal points are lined up so that your output looks neat and professional.

5. Figure B4-5 shows how to use the TAB function to produce a triangle. Use the TAB function to produce a square with ten asterisks on each side.

6. The program given in Figure B4-5 shows how to produce a hollow triangle. Revise this program so that the triangle is completely filled with asterisks.

Section 5
Single Subscripting

INTRODUCTION

Subscripting is one of the most useful tools in BASIC, enabling the programmer to build and store lists of numbers or strings. Such lists are commonly called **arrays.** A **subscript** is simply a number that refers to a position in the list or array. For example, suppose that we wanted to place the data in the "averages" program of Figure B3-1 (page B-40) in a list. If we decided to call the list X, it might look as follows:

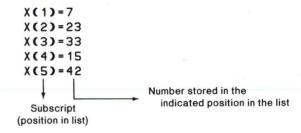

$$X(1)=7$$
$$X(2)=23$$
$$X(3)=33$$
$$X(4)=15$$
$$X(5)=42$$

Subscript
(position in list)

Number stored in the
indicated position in the list

You should make certain you fully grasp the difference between a position in the list and the number stored in that position before reading further. If, for example, you were asked if $X(3) < X(4)$, how would you respond? (*Note:* 33 is not less than 15, so the answer is no.)

A SIMPLE SUBSCRIPTING PROBLEM

Let's again find the average of a set of numbers, expanding the problem to twelve values. Also, let's assume that we wish to output the difference of each of the numbers in the list from the average. A program to solve this problem is shown in Figure B5-1. As usual, study the problem carefully before reading the commentary which follows.

The first thing that you may have noticed is the DIM (dimension) statement in line 120. This statement instructs the computer to reserve 12* storage positions for array X. This is necessary because each number in the

---

*Many versions of BASIC will also reserve a 13th storage location, for X(0). Many skilled programmers, however, choose to ignore this storage position, since other programming languages often prohibit a zero subscript.

```
 10 REM THIS PROGRAM COMPUTES THE DIFFERENCES BETWEEN
 20 REM NUMBERS IN A LIST FROM THE AVERAGE OF THE LIST
 30 REM    AUTHOR - C.S. PARKER
 40 REM ****************VARIABLES*************************
 50 REM    I  = THE LOOP VARIABLE
 60 REM    X  = THE ARRAY OF NUMBERS
 70 REM    N  = THE NUMBER OF NUMBERS IN THE LIST
 80 REM    S  = THE SUM OF THE NUMBERS IN THE LIST
 90 REM    A  = THE AVERAGE OF THE NUMBERS
100 REM    D  = THE DEVIATION OF A NUMBER FROM THE AVERAGE
110 REM ***************************************************
120 REM DIM X(12)
130 LET S=0
140 READ N
150 REM READ AND SUM NUMBERS
160 FOR I=1 TO N
170    READ X(I)
180    LET S=S+X(I)
190 NEXT I
200 LET A=S/N
210 PRINT "NUMBER","AVERAGE","DIFFERENCE"
220 PRINT
230 REM RECALL VALUES, COMPUTE DEVIATIONS, AND OUTPUT RESULTS
240 FOR I=1 TO N
250    LET D=X(I)-A
260    PRINT X(I),A,D
270 NEXT I
280 DATA 12
290 DATA 5,10,11,13,4,6,8,14,2,15,1,7
300 END
RUN
```

NUMBER	AVERAGE	DIFFERENCE
5	8	-3
10	8	2
11	8	3
13	8	5
4	8	-4
6	8	-2
8	8	0
14	8	6
2	8	-6
15	8	7
1	8	-7
7	8	-1

Figure B5.1. *Program to compute differences of numbers in a list from the average of the list.*

array is assigned to a different variable—that is, X(1), X(2), . . . , X(12)—and, as is the usual practice, each variable corresponds to a single storage location. Thus a total of 17 storage positions will be allocated to the variables in this program, as shown below:

```
X(1), X(2), X(3), ..., X(12), S, N, I, A, D
```

Specified by the DIM statement
Nonsubscripted variables in program

Many versions of BASIC will allow you to omit the DIM statement if the length of the array stored is 10 positions or less. In other words, the computer will react as if you had specified

```
120 DIM X(10)
```

in your program, even though this statement is absent. This is called *implicit* dimensioning. Most skilled programmers, however, prefer *explicit* dimensioning, where all arrays are declared in one or more DIM statements. The reasons for this are similar to the ones for explicitly initializing count and sum variables to zero: the intent is made clear, the opportunity for mistakes is minimized, and the practice is a good one to adopt if you program in other languages (BASIC is among a minority of languages permitting implicit dimensioning).

Since the array in our program has 12 positions, X must be dimensioned explicitly. If the DIM statement is absent, the computer will not automatically reserve space for X(11) and X(12). Thus the program will "bomb" when the computer attempts to manipulate one of these variables. It is, however, acceptable to reserve more storage positions in a DIM statement than you actually use.

The DIM statement, like a DATA statement, is not executed by the computer. Although there are several acceptable places to position it, it is good practice to put it at the beginning of the program to avoid potential problems.

If several arrays need to be dimensioned, it is possible to use one DIM statement or several. For example, both

```
10 DIM A(250),X(15),Y(20),Z(200),T(6)
```

and the combination

```
10 DIM A(250),X(15)
20 DIM Y(20),Z(200),T(6)
```

are acceptable to dimension the five arrays shown.

Another interesting feature of the program in Figure B5-1 concerns statements 170 and 180, which are contained in the first loop. Each time I is incremented, a single number is taken from statement 290 and assigned to

Surviving Subscripts

The bane of most beginning programmers' existence is subscripts. Although some people understand subscripts right off the bat, many find them tricky to grasp. Certainly statements such as

$$X = Y(R(I), X(J))$$

or

$$Z(J) = X(J+1)$$

will cause almost anyone who just learned how to program a few weeks ago to look at them in amazement.

Many *business data processing* problems—such as computing a payroll or printing out all people with computer experience in an employee file—can be done with a minimal knowledge of subscripting. However, *scientific, mathematical,* and *engineering* problems—such as computing the time-series trajectory of a rocket or the inverse of a matrix—can be very subscript intensive. For almost anyone contemplating a career in computers, it is

certainly worthwhile to learn some subscripting rather than sweep it under the carpet. One never knows when it might come in handy.

Although subscripting may seem to you an order of magnitude harder than anything you learned in Sections 1 to 4 of this appendix, don't be discouraged. Most people take a while longer to learn it than other concepts. But like anything else, determination and spending the time studying certainly help.

the Ith variable in the X array. Thus when $I = 1$, $X(1)$ is assigned 5; when $I = 2$, $X(2)$ is assigned 10; and so on. When the computer exits the first loop and makes the computation in line 200, storage looks as follows*:

X(1) 5	X(2) 10	X(3) 11	X(4) 13
X(5) 4	X(6) 6	X(7) 8	X(8) 14
X(9) 2	X(10) 15	X(11) 1	X(12) 7
S 96	I 12	N 12	A 8
D 0			

When the second loop is encountered (line 240), the computer has all the information it needs in storage to compute the twelve differences ($D = X(I) - A$). Thus all that needs to be done in this loop is to successively recall from storage $X(1), X(2), \ldots, X(12)$, subtract A from these values, and compute the difference, D.

---

*In some versions of BASIC I would be set to 13, even though the loop was only executed 12 times. This is because the first time NEXT is encountered, I is set to 2; the twelfth and last time NEXT is encountered, I is set to 13. Some computer systems will "roll back" this value to 12 upon leaving the loop.

You should note that it would be extremely inconvenient to solve a problem like the one in Figure B5-1 without the use of subscripts. This is so because we need to consider the values in the array twice—once to compute the average, and again to compute the differences.

The general format of the DIM statement is shown below:

Line # DIM list of dimensional arrays (separated by commas)

A TOUGHER EXAMPLE

A common application is that of generating a frequency distribution from raw data. For example, suppose that all ten automobiles in a used-car lot possess a sales price under $5000. We would like to determine the number (or frequency) of cars for sale in each of the brackets below:

Bracket 1	$0.00–$999.99
Bracket 2	$1,000.00–$1,999.99
Bracket 3	$2,000.00–$2,999.99
Bracket 4	$3,000.00–$3,999.99
Bracket 5	$4,000.00–$4,999.99

Before creating a BASIC program to solve this problem, let's examine a useful "trick" we'll exploit to convert the car prices into the proper brackets. Assume that the brackets are numbered 1 through 5.

If a car is priced at $2350, for example, it should fall into bracket 3. We can convert this price into the number "3" by performing the steps below:

1. Divide the price by 1000. (2350/1000 = 2.35)

2. Truncate the fraction from step 1. (2.35, when truncated, produces 2.)

3. Add 1 to the result of step 2. (2 + 1 = 3)

This "trick" will work for any of the prices encountered in this problem. Also, BASIC has a built-in function (INT) to enable you to rapidly do the truncation required in step 2. Thus if P = 2.35,

$$INT(P)=INT(2.35)=2*$$

---

*You should note further that if A = 3.68, B = 4.30, and C = .01,

$$INT(A+B+C)=INT(3.68+4.30+.01)=INT(7.99)=7$$

suggesting that the argument in the INT function can be any valid BASIC arithmetic expression.

```
 10 REM THIS PROGRAM GENERATES A FREQUENCY DISTRIBUTION
 20 REM     AUTHOR - C.S. PARKER
 30 REM ******************VARIABLES********************
 40 REM     I,J = LOOP VARIABLES
 50 REM     C   = THE ARRAY OF BRACKET COUNTS
 60 REM     P   = THE PRICE OF A CAR
 70 REM     K   = THE CLASS A CAR FALLS IN TO
 80 REM *********************************************
 90 DIM C(5)
100 REM INITIALIZE BRACKET COUNTS TO ZERO
110 FOR I=1 TO 5
120    LET C(I)=0
130 NEXT I
140 REM DETERMINE A CAR'S BRACKET AND INCREMENT BRACKET COUNT
150 FOR I=1 TO 10
160    READ P
170    LET K=INT(P/1000)+1
180    LET C(K)=C(K)+1
190 NEXT I
200 PRINT TAB(15);"***CAR DISTRIBUTION***"
210 PRINT
220 PRINT "AT LEAST","BUT LESS THAN",,"COUNT"
230 PRINT
240 REM OUTPUT RESULTS
250 FOR J=1 TO 5
260    PRINT (J-1)*1000,J*1000,,C(J)
270 NEXT J
280 DATA 1400,2170,682,3340,4100
290 DATA 810,1258,750,3800,2801
300 END
RUN
```

```
            ***CAR DISTRIBUTION***

AT LEAST       BUT LESS THAN                COUNT
   0              1000                         3
 1000             2000                         2
 2000             3000                         2
 3000             4000                         2
 4000             5000                         1
```

Figure B5-2. *Program to generate a car price distribution.*

A program to solve the frequency distribution problem is given in Figure B5-2.

Observe especially the following features in the program:

1. The "three steps" just presented are accomplished in one statement:

```
170 LET K=INT(P/1000)+1
```

Thus when P = 1400, K = INT(1.4) + 1 = 2, identifying this price as belonging in bracket 2. When K = 2, the next statement,

$$180\ \ \text{LET}\ \ C(K)=C(K)+1$$

is processed as C(2) = C(2) + 1. Thus the computer is instructed to increment the count in bracket 2 by 1. At the end of the program, C(1) will represent the number of cars falling into bracket 1, C(2), the number of cars falling into bracket 2, and so on.

2. The C list is referenced by three different subscripts, I, K, and J. Note C(I) in line 120, C(K) in line 180, and C(J) in line 260. Remember, the argument (in other words, the quantity within the parentheses) only represents a position in the list; any acceptable BASIC expression will suffice to identify this position.

STRING LISTS

The examples provided in the previous subsections illustrated lists of *numbers*. BASIC also allows the programmer to form lists of *strings*. For example, suppose we wish to create a list of fruits (say, APPLES, ORANGES, BANANAS, PEACHES, and CHERRIES) and then output the list in reverse order. The program in Figure B5-3 does just this. Note that subscripted string variables are named in the same way as unsubscripted (**scalar**) ones—a single letter followed by the dollar sign.

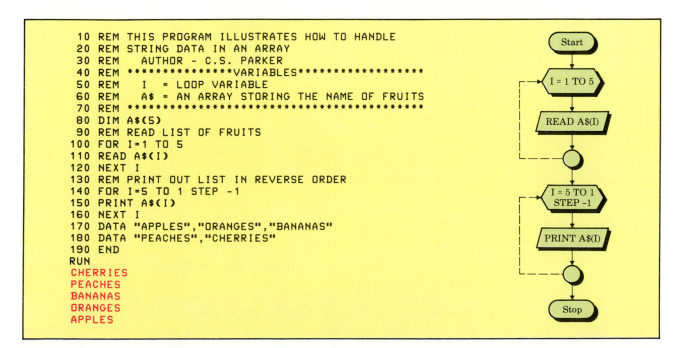

```
 10 REM THIS PROGRAM ILLUSTRATES HOW TO HANDLE
 20 REM STRING DATA IN AN ARRAY
 30 REM   AUTHOR - C.S. PARKER
 40 REM ***************VARIABLES*****************
 50 REM   I = LOOP VARIABLE
 60 REM   A$ = AN ARRAY STORING THE NAME OF FRUITS
 70 REM ****************************************
 80 DIM A$(5)
 90 REM READ LIST OF FRUITS
100 FOR I=1 TO 5
110 READ A$(I)
120 NEXT I
130 REM PRINT OUT LIST IN REVERSE ORDER
140 FOR I=5 TO 1 STEP -1
150 PRINT A$(I)
160 NEXT I
170 DATA "APPLES","ORANGES","BANANAS"
180 DATA "PEACHES","CHERRIES"
190 END
RUN
CHERRIES
PEACHES
BANANAS
ORANGES
APPLES
```

Figure B5.3.   *A program that manipulates a string list.*

SOLVED REVIEW PROBLEMS

Example 1

A company that produces three products currently has eight salespeople. The sales of each product by each salesperson are given in the table that appears below:

	Units Sold		
Salesperson	**Product 1**	**Product 2**	**Product 3**
William Ing	100	50	65
Ed Wilson	500	0	0
Ann Johnson	200	25	600
Edna Farber	150	30	500
Norris Ames	600	80	150
Elma Jace	100	410	800
Vilmos Zisk	300	30	60
Ellen Venn	400	0	0

The latest unit prices on products 1, 2, and 3 are $1, 1.25, and .85 respectively.

Use the data above to produce the table below. Use subscripted variables to represent the totals associated with the three products and eight salespeople.

```
   NAME            PRODUCT1    PRODUCT2    PRODUCT3      TOTAL

WILLIAM ING         100.00       62.50       55.25      217.75
ED WILSON           500.00        0.00        0.00      500.00
ANN JOHNSON         200.00       31.25      510.00      741.25
EDNA FARBER         150.00       37.50      425.00      612.50
NORRIS AMES         600.00      100.00      127.50      827.50
ELMA JACE           100.00      512.50      680.00    1,292.50
VILMOS ZISK         300.00       37.50       51.00      388.50
ELLEN VENN          400.00        0.00        0.00      400.00

TOTALS            2,350.00      781.25    1,848.75    4,980.00
```

Solution

A program solution to this problem is given in Figure B5-4, which appears on page B-85.

The outer loop (lines 300–410) is used to read each salesperson record. The inner loop (lines 330–390)—which executes three times for every iteration of the outer loop—is used to multiply sales of each of the three products by its price, accumulate the row totals, and accumulate the column footings.

```
 10 REM THIS PROGRAM CALCULATES PRODUCT SALES ATTRIBUTABLE
 20 REM TO VARIOUS SALESPEOPLE IN A COMPANY
 30 REM     AUTHOR - C.S. PARKER
 40 REM *********************VARIABLES*********************
 50 REM    N$     = THE SALESPERSON NAME
 60 REM    M      = THE NUMBER OF SALESPEOPLE
 70 REM    P      = THE ARRAY OF PRODUCT PRICES
 80 REM    Q      = THE UNITS OF A PRODUCT SOLD BY A SALESPERSON
 90 REM    S      = THE ARRAY SAVING PRODUCT SALES
100 REM                   IN EACH ROW BEFORE THEY ARE OUTPUT
110 REM    T      = THE ROW TOTALS
120 REM    C      = THE ARRAY SAVING THE COLUMN TOTALS
130 REM    G      = THE GRAND TOTAL OF ALL SALES
140        I,J    = LOOP VARIABLES
150 REM    A$,B$  = OUTPUT-IMAGE VARIABLES FOR PRINT USING
160 REM ******************************************************
170 DIM C(3),P(3),S(3)
180 PRINT "    NAME         PRODUCT1   PRODUCT2   PRODUCT3    TOTAL"
190 PRINT
200 READ M
210 REM INITIALIZATIONS
220 FOR I=1 TO 3
230    C(I)=0
240    READ P(I)
250 NEXT I
260 G=0
270 A$="\            \    #,###.##    #,###.##   #,###.##    #,###.##"
280 B$="TOTALS          #,###.##    #,###.##   #,###.##    #,###.##"
290 REM MAIN COMPUTATIONS
300 FOR I=1 TO M
310    T=0
320    READ N$
330    FOR J=1 TO 3
340       READ Q
350       S(J)=Q*P(J)
360       C(J)=C(J)+S(J)
370       T=T+S(J)
380       G=G+S(J)
390    NEXT J
400    PRINT USING A$;N$,S(1),S(2),S(3),T
410 NEXT I
420 PRINT
430 PRINT USING B$;C(1),C(2),C(3),G
440 DATA 8
450 DATA 1,1.25,.85
460 DATA "WILLIAM ING",100,50,65
470 DATA "ED WILSON",500,0,0
480 DATA "ANN JOHNSON",200,25,600
490 DATA "EDNA FARBER",150,30,500
500 DATA "NORRIS AMES",600,80,150
510 DATA "ELMA JACE",100,410,800
520 DATA "VILMOS ZISK",300,30,60
530 DATA "ELLEN VENN",400,0,0
540 END
```

Figure B5-4.   A program to cross-classify sales data.

Example 2

Produce a flowchart and program to sort the following numbers from low to high: 7, 4, 1, 3, 2.

Solution

Although the task seems relatively simple, the computer must perform several operations to complete it. There are many ways to sort numbers. One of the simplest of these is the **bubble sort,** which is illustrated in Figure B5-5.

The sorting begins by first comparing the first and second numbers in the list (line 190). If they are in the correct order, we leave them alone;

```
 10 REM THIS PROGRAM SORTS A LIST OF NUMBERS
 20 REM     AUTHOR    - C.S. PARKER
 30 REM *****************VARIABLES***************
 40 REM     X    = THE ARRAY OF NUMBERS
 50 REM     I,J = LOOP VARIABLES
 60 REM     N    = THE NUMBER OF NUMBERS IN THE LIST
 70 REM     T    = A VARIABLE TO TEMPORARILY STORE
 80 REM                    A VALUE
 90 REM *****************************************
100 DIM X(100)
110 READ N
120 REM READ NUMBERS INTO ARRAY
130 FOR I=1 TO N
140     READ X(I)
150 NEXT I
160 REM BUBBLE SORT ROUTINE
170 FOR I=1 TO N-1
180     FOR J=1 TO N-I
190         IF X(J)<=X(J+1) THEN 240
200             REM EXCHANGE OPERATION
210             T=X(J)
220             X(J)=X(J+1)
230             X(J+1)=T
240     NEXT J
250 NEXT I
260 REM OUTPUT ROUTINE
270 FOR I=1 TO N
280     PRINT X(I);
290 NEXT I
300 DATA 5
310 DATA 7,4,1,3,2
320 END
RUN
 1   2   3   4   7
```

Figure B5-5. *(a) Program to sort numbers with a bubble sort.*

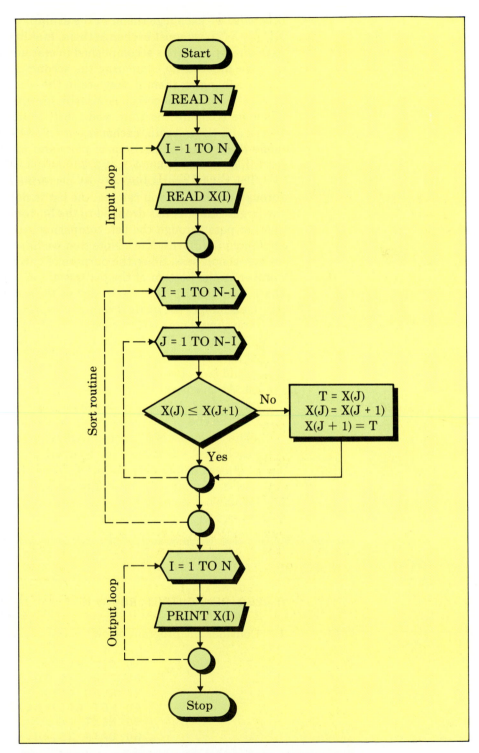

Figure B5-5.   *(b) Flowchart for the bubble sort program.*

otherwise we exchange them. In the example, X(1) = 7 and X(2) = 4. Since X(1) > X(2), we must exchange them, making X(1) = 4 and X(2) = 7. The exchange operation is accomplished in statements 210–230.

We proceed by comparing the second and third numbers in the list, again exchanging them if they are in the wrong order. Since X(2) = 7 and X(3) = 1, an exchange is again made, producing X(2) = 1 and X(3) = 7. Then we compare the third and fourth numbers, and, subsequently, the fourth and fifth. Again, exchanges are made if appropriate. After we have made these four comparisons of pairs and any appropriate exchanges, the list will be in this order: 4, 1, 3, 2, 7.

The set of operations we just performed constitutes our "first pass" through the list. As you can see, the list is not completely sorted; however, the largest number has dropped to the bottom. At this point we must make another pass through the list, comparing X(1) with X(2), X(2) with X(3), and finally X(3) with X(4). Note that we have one less comparison to make on the second pass. Since the purpose of the first pass is to drop the largest number to the bottom of the list, assigning it to X(5), it is unnecessary to check X(4) against X(5). Again, during the second pass (and any subsequent ones), exchanges are made if they are appropriate.

You should note that the list at the end of the second pass will be in the order 1, 3, 2, 4, 7. The list is not completely sorted; however, the second-largest number has fallen to the next-to-bottom position. Thus at the end of the second pass, two values, X(4) and X(5), are in their correct positions in the list. At this point a third pass is made, comparing X(1) with X(2), and X(2) with X(3). A fourth pass will also be necessary, comparing X(1) with X(2). At the end of the fourth pass, the list will be in sorted order.

Note that a list of *N* numbers will require *N* − 1 passes in a bubble sort. Also, each pass will involve the comparison of one fewer pairs of numbers than the pass before it. To make sure you fully understand how a bubble sort works, get out a pencil and paper and jot down what the computer is doing and what it has in storage at each step in the program execution.

Exercises

Instructions: Provide an answer to each of the following questions.

1. Consider the program below.

```
10 DIM A(5)
20 FOR I=1 TO 5
30 READ A(I)
40 LET A(I)=A(I)+1
50 NEXT I
60 DATA 35,18,-6,42,27
```

What is the final value of
a. A(1)? b. A(2)? c. A(3)? d. A(4)? e. A(5)?

2. Consider the program below:

```
10 DIM A(6)
20 A(1)=0
30 FOR I=2 TO 6
40 READ A(I)
50 LET A(I)=A(I-1)
60 NEXT I
70 DATA 35,18,-6,42,27
```

What is the final value of
a. A(1)? b. A(2)? c. A(3)? d. A(4)? e. A(5)?

3. How would you change the program in Exercise 2 so that the final values of A(1) through A(5) would be 0, 35, 18, −6, and 27 respectively?

Programming Problems

Instructions: Write a BASIC program to do each of the following tasks.

1. The following is a list of salaries of the six employees in a certain company:

Name	Salary
T. Jones	$43,000
F. Smith	$31,000
K. Johnston	$22,000
P. Miner	$18,000
C. Altman	$27,000
A. Barth	$19,000

Calculate and output the average salary for the company, as well as the names of all people whose salaries exceed the average.

2. Read the ten numbers in the list shown below and then output the list in reverse order (that is, 12, 43, 6, etc.):

31, 15, 85, 36, 22, 81, 70, 6, 43, 12

3. The following list contains names and sexes of people at XYZ company: Janice Jones (female), Bill Smith (male), Debra Parks (female), Elaine Johnson (female), William Anderson (male), Art James (male), Bill Finley (male), and Ellen Ott (female).

Read the list into the computer in the order given; then prepare and output two separate lists—one composed of all of the males, and the other of all of the females.

4. Twenty-five people took an exam, the scores being distributed as follows:

$$91, 83, 69, 35, 99, 64, 78, 71, 52, 89, 72, 100, 56, 63,$$
$$72, 77, 82, 95, 85, 71, 66, 54, 63, 82, 94$$

Prepare a frequency distribution of scores such as:

RANGE	NUMBER OF SCORES IN RANGE
90–100	?
80–89	?
. . . and so on	

5. An eight-student class in data processing has taken four tests in a semester, with the following results:

	Grade			
Student	Exam 1	Exam 2	Exam 3	Exam 4
Joan Blow	83	64	75	91
Cleon Jones	78	71	60	80
Jane Jackson	65	98	98	69
Bob Smith	81	45	72	55
Leon Russell	68	42	81	76
Sue James	80	70	60	96
John Doe	54	88	92	65
Linda Johnson	88	86	65	74

Write a BASIC program to produce a listing of students in descending order of total points scored on the examinations. List student name and total points scored on your output. (*Hint:* Each time you exchange the total points for two students in the list, you must also exchange their names.)

Section 6
Advanced Topics

DOUBLE SUBSCRIPTING

Data to be processed by the computer system are sometimes better represented in two-dimensional (table) form than in one-dimensional (list) form. For example, consider the data below, which show the vote distribution on a certain issue in different divisions of a university:

	Voted Yes	Voted No	Didn't Vote
Business	205	152	38
Liberal arts	670	381	115
Engineering	306	251	47
Forestry	112	33	14

The above data, which include four rows and three columns of numbers, exist naturally in the form of a table. It would be most convenient if we could give the table a name (V, for example), and store any number in the table with reference to its row and column position. For example, 115, which is in row 2 and column 3, would be referenced by the subscripted variable $V(2, 3)$.

Fortunately BASIC permits us to represent two-dimensional tables in the simple manner just described. Thus we could store the table numbers in the 12 variables below:

$$V(1, 1) = 205 \qquad V(1, 2) = 152 \qquad V(1, 3) = 38$$
$$V(2, 1) = 670 \qquad V(2, 2) = 381 \qquad V(2, 3) = 115$$
$$V(3, 1) = 306 \qquad V(3, 2) = 251 \qquad V(3, 3) = 47$$
$$V(4, 1) = 112 \qquad V(4, 2) = 33 \qquad V(4, 3) = 14$$

It is relatively easy to create such a table in BASIC, and later to access each of the numbers and process it as needed. To see how this might be done, refer to the program in Figure B6-1 (on page B-92) , which totals all of the numbers in the table and subsequently divides each number in the table by this total.

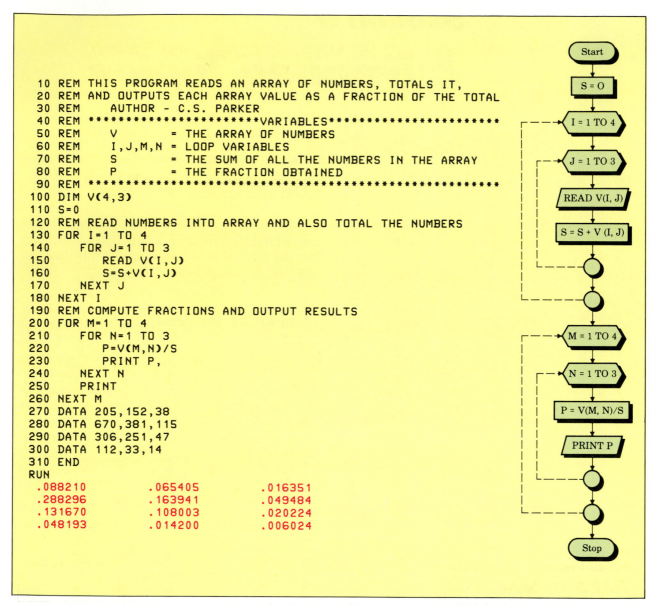

```
 10 REM THIS PROGRAM READS AN ARRAY OF NUMBERS, TOTALS IT,
 20 REM AND OUTPUTS EACH ARRAY VALUE AS A FRACTION OF THE TOTAL
 30 REM      AUTHOR - C.S. PARKER
 40 REM *********************VARIABLES*********************
 50 REM      V       = THE ARRAY OF NUMBERS
 60 REM      I,J,M,N = LOOP VARIABLES
 70 REM      S       = THE SUM OF ALL THE NUMBERS IN THE ARRAY
 80 REM      P       = THE FRACTION OBTAINED
 90 REM ***************************************************
100 DIM V(4,3)
110 S=0
120 REM READ NUMBERS INTO ARRAY AND ALSO TOTAL THE NUMBERS
130 FOR I=1 TO 4
140     FOR J=1 TO 3
150         READ V(I,J)
160         S=S+V(I,J)
170     NEXT J
180 NEXT I
190 REM COMPUTE FRACTIONS AND OUTPUT RESULTS
200 FOR M=1 TO 4
210     FOR N=1 TO 3
220         P=V(M,N)/S
230         PRINT P,
240     NEXT N
250     PRINT
260 NEXT M
270 DATA 205,152,38
280 DATA 670,381,115
290 DATA 306,251,47
300 DATA 112,33,14
310 END
RUN
 .088210        .065405        .016351
 .288296        .163941        .049484
 .131670        .108003        .020224
 .048193        .014200        .006024
```

Figure B6-1. *Program to read a table, total all the numbers in the table, and print the fraction that each number is with regard to the sum.*

You should observe that in this program, as is the usual practice with subscripts, a DIM statement is immediately employed to declare the size of the table. Then nested loops are established in statements 130–180 to generate automatically the row (I = 1, 2, 3, 4) and column (J = 1, 2, 3) subscripts. Thus the first time these nested loops are executed,

I = 1, J = 1, V(1, 1) is assigned 205, and S = 0 + 205 = 205

The second time,

$I = 1, J = 2, V(1, 2)$ is assigned 152, and $S = 205 + 152 = 357$

The third time,

$I = 1, J = 3, V(1, 3)$ is assigned 38, and $S = 357 + 38 = 395$

The fourth time,

$I = 2, J = 1, V(2, 1)$ is assigned 670, and $S = 395 + 670 = 1065$

and so on.

The twelfth time,

$I = 4, J = 3, V(4, 3)$ is assigned 14, and $S = 2310 + 14 = 2324$

In the nested loops in statements 200–260, we simply recall $V(1, 1)$, $V(1, 2), \ldots, V(4, 3)$ successively from storage and, as we do so, divide each by the table sum and print out the fraction obtained. Note that the variables (M, N) used to represent the subscripts in the second set of nested loops are different than those (I, J) used in the first set. Although we could have used I and J again, the example illustrates that any choice of a subscript variable will do as long as the proper numbers are substituted by the computer to represent the row and column involved.

Two final points on the program in Figure B6-1 deserve your close attention. First, note that the PRINT statement in line 230 contains a comma. This keeps output belonging in the same row printing on the same line. Second, note the blank PRINT statement on line 250. This statement forces the output device onto a new line, where a new row of numbers is printed.

RANDOM NUMBERS

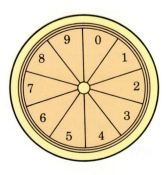

Many computer languages provide a means to generate random numbers automatically, and BASIC is no exception. **Random numbers** introduce the element of chance into a program, enabling the computer system, for example, to pick different cards from an imaginary deck, provide fictional athletic teams with unpredictable successes or failures with selected game strategies, and so forth.

A random number is a number that is formed through laws of probability. One easy way to generate random numbers is to use a ten-position "roulette wheel," such as the one shown at the left.

If we wanted to generate, say, a three-digit random number, we could spin the wheel three times. Perhaps we might obtain "4" on the first try, "0" on the second, and "8" on the third, thereby producing the random number 408. If we tried this repeatedly, we could form a list of several random numbers, such as 408, 616, 832, 009, and so on.

Random numbers are normally generated to **simulate** some real-world physical process. For example, we could use the three-digit numbers just introduced to play a game of baseball. Thus we might arbitrarily choose the following:

Any number generated between 000 and 699 represents an out.

Any number generated between 700 and 849 represents a single.

Any number generated between 850 and 929 represents a double.

Any number generated between 930 and 949 represents a triple.

Any number generated between 950 and 999 represents a home run.

For example, if a batter came to the plate and the number 408 was selected, the batter would be out. The selection of the number 962, on the other hand, would correspond to the batter hitting a home run, and so on. It's not too difficult to write a program to keep track of outs, innings, batters on base, and the score. If different random numbers are generated each time a game is played, we will get different results for each game.

BASIC provides a built-in function, RND, to allow us automatically to generate random numbers on computer systems. For example, the statement

```
10 LET X=RND
```

will request the computer system to generate a random number and place it in the storage location assigned to X. If we want to generate three random numbers and output them, we simply sandwich this statement, with a PRINT, in a FOR/NEXT loop, as in Figure B6-2.

People normally have different requirements for the selection of random numbers: some want three-digit fractions, others want two-digit

```
10 FOR I=1 TO 3
20     X=RND
30     PRINT X,
40 NEXT I
50 END
RUN
  .186255          .413305          .987024
```

Figure B6-2.   A program that generates three random numbers.

integers, and still others want integers only in a certain range (say 1–52, representing the 52 cards in a deck). To accommodate these different needs, BASIC always supplies the random number in the same form—usually as a fraction between .000000 and .999999—and leaves it to each programmer to transform this fraction into a form that meets the particular needs of the application. Observe that the program in Figure B6-2 has generated fractions in the range .000000–.999999.

When we want the random numbers in integer rather than fractional form, we can use the INT function to make the necessary transformation. In the program of Figure B6-2, all we need to do is modify the statement in line 20. For example, consider the following two transformations:

1. Suppose that we want only random integers between 0 and 999 (inclusive). If we change line 20 to read

```
20 X=INT(RND*1000)
```

we will get the desired results. For example, when RND is supplied as .186255, multiplying this number by 1000 yields 186.255. Then, INT(186.255) = 186.

2. Suppose that we want only two-digit random integers in the range 10–30. There are 21 integers in this range: 10, 11, 12, . . . , 30. We must change line 20 to read

```
20 X=INT(21*RND+10)
```

Note that since RND can only be in the range .000000–.999999, it is impossible for X to be any integer outside the range 10–30. At one extreme, when RND = .000000, the formula will yield X = 10; at the other, when RND = .999999, X = INT(20.999979 + 10) = INT(30.999979) = 30.

It is important to realize that most computerized random number generators will produce the same sequence of fractions every time a RUN command is issued. Thus if we ran the program in Figure B6-2 50 times, we would generate the same sequence (.186255, .413305, and .987024) 50 times. To generate a different sequence of random numbers every time the program is run, you should insert the command

```
5 RANDOMIZE
```

in the program. This will place the random number generator at a different "starting point," so that the values of RND produced will be somewhat unpredictable.

Now that we've covered the fundamentals of generating random numbers, let's see how we can use RND in a BASIC program. Consider a bakery that can sell between 15 and 20 wedding cakes per day. Cakes must be baked at the beginning of the day, when it is not known how many cakes will be sold. Cakes cost \$11 to make, and they sell for \$20. A cake baked but not sold can be sold the next day for \$5 at a day-old bake sale. We wish to know:

1. The expected average daily profit if 17 cakes are baked every day.

2. If baking 17 cakes daily is the best strategy for the bakery.

The bakery is faced with a classic supply–demand problem. If few cakes are baked, say 15, and 20 are demanded, the opportunity for \$9 profit on each of the five extra cakes is lost. On the other hand, if several are baked, say 19, and only 16 are demanded, the bakery loses \$6 (\$11 − \$5) on each of the three extra cakes baked. With a strategy of producing 17 cakes daily, the bakery will either underbake, overbake, or bake the right amount on any given day.

We will solve this problem by simulating daily bakery operations over a long period of time (1000 days). To solve part 1 of the problem, we'll assume that each day the baker will bake (supply) 17 cakes. We'll have the computer system select a random integer in the range 15–20 each day. This number will represent the number of cakes demanded that day. Then, knowing supply ($S = 17$) and demand (D = some integer between 15 and 20) for the day, we can compute the profit for the day. If we average the profit for 1000 days, then we'll know how well the strategy "bake 17 cakes" is working. The program to solve part 1 of the problem is given in Figure B6-3. It is annotated to make it easier to follow.

```
 10 REM THIS PROGRAM SIMULATES A BAKERY OPERATION
 20 REM      AUTHOR - C.S. PARKER
 30 REM ***************VARIABLES****************
 40 REM     S  = NUMBER OF CAKES BAKED DAILY
 50 REM     D  = NUMBER OF CAKES DEMANDED DAILY
 60 REM     P1 = AVERAGE DAILY PROFIT
 70 REM     P  = TOTAL PROFIT OVER 1000 DAYS
 80 REM     I  = LOOP VARIABLE
 90 REM ****************************************
100 S=17
110 P=0
120 FOR I=1 TO 1000
130     D=INT(6*RND+15)          This formula generates
                                 random integers in the
                                 range 15-20
140     IF S<=D THEN P=P+(S*9)   S*9 is the profit when
                                 supply ≤ demand
        ELSE P=P+(D*9-6* (S-D))  D*9 − 6*(S − D) is the
                                 profit when supply > demand
150 NEXT I
160 P1=P/1000
170 PRINT "AVERAGE DAILY PROFIT IS $";P1
180 END
RUN
AVERAGE DAILY PROFIT IS $ 145.935
```

Figure B6-3.   *Simulating average daily profit for the strategy "bake 17 cakes."*

```
10 REM THIS PROGRAM SIMULATES A BAKERY OPERATION
20 REM     AUTHOR - C.S. PARKER
30 REM *****************VARIABLES****************
40 REM     S  = NUMBER OF CAKES BAKED DAILY
50 REM     D  = NUMBER OF CAKES DEMANDED DAILY
60 REM     P1 = AVERAGE DAILY PROFIT
70 REM     P  = TOTAL PROFIT OVER 1000 DAYS
80 REM     I  = LOOP VARIABLE
90 REM **************************************
100 FOR S=15 TO 20
110    P=0
120    FOR I=1 TO 1000
130       D=INT(6*RND+15)
140       IF S<=D THEN P=P+(S*9)
                ELSE P=P+(D*9-6*(S-D))
150    NEXT I
160    P1=P/1000
170    PRINT "AVERAGE DAILY PROFIT FOR";S;"CAKES IS $";P1
180 NEXT S
190 END
RUN
PROFIT FOR 15 CAKES IS $ 135
PROFIT FOR 16 CAKES IS $ 141.51
PROFIT FOR 17 CAKES IS $ 145.53
PROFIT FOR 18 CAKES IS $ 146.82
PROFIT FOR 19 CAKES IS $ 145.77
PROFIT FOR 20 CAKES IS $ 142.86
```

These three statements are the only changes made from Figure B6-3

Figure B6-4. *Simulating average daily profit for all baking strategies between 15 and 20 cakes.*

To solve part 2 of the problem, all we need to do is compare the average daily profits for all possible strategies—that is, bake 15, 16, 17, 18, 19, or 20 cakes. The solution is given in Figure B6-4.

Note that the program in Figure B6-4 is created very easily from the one in Figure B6-3. All we needed to do was place an extra loop around the program (to vary S automatically from 15 to 20) and modify the PRINT statement in line 200 slightly.

A computerized simulation, such as the one just shown, enables the management of a company easily to answer "what-if" types of questions that might have a significant impact on operations. For example:

1. What will be the effect if the cost of making a cake rises to $12? Note that the only changes which need to be made in the program of Figure B6-4 are in the profit margins:

```
140 IF S<=D THEN P=P+(S*8)
          ELSE P=P+(D*8-7*(S-D))
```

2. What if the only other bakery in town closes, so that potential demand is now somewhere in the range of 18–25 cakes? Note that the only changes required in Figure B6-4 are the supply–demand statements:

```
100 FOR S=18 TO 25
130 D=INT(8*RND+18)
```

With a computerized simulation, it is relatively easy to answer such "what if" questions within minutes. Often such questions may take days or even weeks for an analyst to solve by hand.

FUNCTIONS AND SUBROUTINES

Functions

A *function* is a precoded formula that is referenced in a computer program. BASIC permits two types of function: **library (built-in) functions** and **user-defined functions.** We have already covered two library functions: INT and RND. Since these functions are built into the BASIC language, the computer system knows exactly what type of action to take when it runs into one of them. Many other library functions are probably available with the version of BASIC used by your computer system. Below is a partial list of some of the more common ones:

Function	Purpose
ABS(X)	Returns the absolute value of X
SQR(X)	Calculates the square root of X (X must be $>=0$)
RND	Returns a random number between .000000 and .999999
SIN(X)	Computes the sine of X (X must be in radians)
COS(X)	Computes the cosine of X (X must be in radians)
TAN(X)	Computes the tangent of X (X must be in radians)
LOG(X)	Calculates the natural logarithm of X (X must be positive)
EXP(X)	Calculates the term e^x, where e is approximately 2.718
INT(X)	Returns the greatest integer $<=X$

Programmers also have the ability to define their own functions. This can be useful when there is a formula you need to use repeatedly which is not a library function. User-defined functions are specified with the DEF statement. For example, suppose we wanted to compute the commission due a salesperson as

15 percent of gross sales of "brand-name" items

10 percent of gross sales of "nonbrand" items

Thus if S1 represents gross sales of brand-name items and S2 is gross sales of nonbrand items, the commission C may be calculated as

$$C=.15*S1+.10*S2$$

A program that computes this commission for three salespeople is given in Figure B6-5. You should inspect this program carefully before proceeding further.

```
 10 REM THIS PROGRAM COMPUTES SALES COMMISSIONS
 20 REM     AUTHOR - C.S. PARKER
 30 REM **************VARIABLES**************
 40 REM     S1,S2 = DUMMY ARGUMENTS
 50 REM     A,B   = REAL ARGUMENTS
 60 REM     N$    = SALESPERSON NAME
 70 REM     I     = LOOP VARIABLE
 80 REM ****************************************
 90 DEF FNC(S1,S2)=.15*S1+.10*S2   ◄── The function is defined here
100 FOR I=1 TO 3
120     READ N$,A,B
120     PRINT N$,FNC(A,B)   ◄── The function is executed here
130 NEXT I
140 DATA "JOE SMITH",700.00,1000.00
150 DATA "ZELDA GREY",600.00,1200.00
160 DATA "SUE JOHNSON",1000.00,500.00
170 END
RUN
JOE SMITH          205
ZELDA GREY         210
SUE JOHNSON        200
```

Figure B6-5.   *Use of user-defined function to compute commissions.*

Note in the program that the formula for computing the commissions is defined in line 90. The formula must be defined (with a DEF statement) before it can be used (as in statement 120).

The format of the DEF statement is

Line # DEF FNx (y) = z

where x is a single alphabetic letter chosen by the programmer, y is a list of arguments (which may be as large as 5 variables, depending on the computer system used), and z is a valid BASIC expression. It is also permissible to use several DEF statements in a single program. Note that the word DEF must be followed by a space and then FN. You must remember, however, to define the functions early in your program, before you reference them.

You should also note that the formula, or function, in the figure also contains two *dummy arguments,* S1 and S2. The only significance of dummy arguments is that they demonstrate how the function will be computed. After reading in the salesperson information in line 110, the computer system prints out in line 120 the salesperson's name and total commission due. Before the computer calculates and prints the commission, it "refers" to line 90 and substitutes A for S1 and B for S2.

A and B are called *real arguments.* Real arguments are always substituted for corresponding dummy arguments, according to their respective positioning within the parentheses, whenever the function is used in the programs.

The program could have also been written by using the same variable names as both dummy and real arguments. All that you would need to change are lines 110 and 120:

```
110 READ N$,S1,S2
120 PRINT N$,FNC(S1,S2)
```

This ability to define a function is one of the most useful and most powerful features of BASIC. It is also the capability most overlooked, even by many skilled programmers.

Subroutines

BASIC **subroutines** are partial programs, or subprograms, that are contained within a BASIC program (called the "main program"). They are particularly effective when a series of statements in a program is to be performed numerous times or, perhaps, at many different places in the overall program.

Subroutines introduce two new statements, GOSUB and RETURN, which have the formats below:

```
Line # GOSUB line number
      .
      .
      .
Line # RETURN
```

The GOSUB statement causes immediate branching to the first statement in the subroutine. The RETURN statement causes branching back to the main program, to the statement that immediately follows the invoking GOSUB (that is, the GOSUB that caused the branching). An example of a program that uses subroutines is given in Figure B6-6. A sample of its output appears in Figure B6-7.

The program processes accounting expenses for the past month. Users of the program have several options—for example, finding the category with the greatest expense, computing total expenses (over all categories), or listing all categories with an expense exceeding $1000. These options are presented to the user in the form of a **menu.** Once the user selects a choice on the menu, either a 1, 2, 3, or 4 is typed in, corresponding to the options in lines 230–260. Given the choice, the computer then branches to the appropriate subroutine to be processed (or ends the program). If, for example, the user selects option 2 (total cost), the computer branches to line 540 and proceeds from that point until line 630 (RETURN) is encountered. It then goes back to the main part of the program and continues with the statement following the invoking GOSUB (in other words, statement 350).

```
10 REM THIS PROGRAM DEMONSTRATES THE USE OF
20 REM SUBROUTINES AND MENUS
30 REM    AUTHOR - C.S. PARKER
40 REM ***************VARIABLES******************
50 REM   C$,A$ = ARRAYS TO HOLD EXPENSE CATEGORIES
60 REM               AND AMOUNTS
60 REM       N = NUMBER OF RECORDS
70 REM       X = MENU-SELECTION VARIABLE
80 REM     H,H$ = HOLDING VARIABLES FOR LARGEST
90 REM              EXPENSE AND CATEGORY
100          T = TOTAL EXPENSES
110 REM ******************************************
120 DIM C$(100),A(100)
130 REM DATA ENTRY
140 READ N
150    FOR I=1 TO N
160       READ C$(I),A(I)
170    NEXT I
180 REM MENU AND SELECTION
190    PRINT
200    PRINT
210    PRINT "PROGRAM OPTIONS"
220    PRINT
230    PRINT "    1 - THE LARGEST CATEGORY"
240    PRINT "    2 - TOTAL COST"
250    PRINT "    3 - ALL CATEGORIES EXCEEDING $1000"
260    PRINT "    4 - END PROGRAM"
270    PRINT
280    PRINT "WHICH OPTION DO YOU WISH TO TAKE (TYPE IN NUMBER)";
290    INPUT X
300 REM CASE STRUCTURE FOR SUBROUTINE TRANSFER
310    ON X GOTO 320,340,360,380
320    GOSUB 400
330    GOTO 310
340      GOSUB 540
350      GOTO 310
360        GOSUB 650
370        GOTO 310
380          STOP
```

Figure B6-6. *A menu-selection program using subroutines.*

```
390 REM *************LARGEST COST SUBROUTINE***************
400    H=A(1)
410    H$=C$(1)
420    FOR I=2 TO N
430    IF A(I)<=H THEN 460
440       H=A(I)
450       H$=C$(I)
460    NEXT I
470    PRINT
480    PRINT "LARGEST EXPENSE:";H$;"  (AMOUNT =";H;")"
490    PRINT
500    PRINT "NEXT MENU SELECTION (TYPE IN NUMBER)";
510    INPUT X
520    RETURN
530 REM **************TOTAL COST SUBROUTINE***************
540    T=0
550    FOR I=1 TO N
560       T=T+A(I)
570    NEXT I
580    PRINT
590    PRINT "TOTAL COST IS...$";T
600    PRINT
610    PRINT "NEXT MENU SELECTION (TYPE IN NUMBER)";
620    INPUT X
630    RETURN
640 REM ************$1000-OR-MORE SUBROUTINE***************
650    PRINT
660    PRINT " CATEGORIES EXCEEDING $1000"
670    PRINT
680    PRINT "CATEGORY", "EXPENSE"
690    FOR I=1 TO N
700       IF A(I)<1000 THEN 720
710          PRINT C$(I),A(I)
720    NEXT I
730    PRINT
740    PRINT "NEXT MENU SELECTION (TYPE IN NUMBER)";
750    INPUT X
760    RETURN
770 REM **************DATA STATEMENTS*****************
780 DATA 8
790 DATA "SALARIES",8500,"RENT",2000,"ADVERTISING",1100
800 DATA "UTILITIES",590,"SUPPLIES",200,"DEPRECIATION",1200
810 DATA "INSURANCE",300,"TAXES",150
820 END
```

Figure B6-6.   *(Continued)*

```
PROGRAM OPTIONS

    1 - THE LARGEST CATEGORY
    2 - TOTAL COST
    3 - ALL CATEGORIES EXCEEDING $1000
    4 - END PROGRAM

WHICH OPTION DO YOU WISH TO TAKE (TYPE IN NUMBER)? 3

CATEGORIES EXCEEDING $1000

CATEGORY         EXPENSE
SALARIES         8500
RENT             2000
ADVERTISING      1100
DEPRECIATION     1200

NEXT MENU SELECTION (TYPE IN NUMBER)?
```

Figure B6-7.   *Output for menu-selection program in Figure B6-6.*

The program in Figure B6-6 also demonstrates the use of the ON GOTO statement (line 310). The format of this statement is

> Line # ON case-variable GOTO line-number, line-number, . . .

A *case variable* (X in our program) is one that has values such as 1, 2, 3, and so forth, that correspond to special situations, or "cases," that must be processed. If X is equal to 1, the computer branches to the first line number after the GOTO, if X is equal to 2, it branches to the second line number, and so on. The *case structure* made possible by BASIC's ON GOTO is ideal for menu-selection programs and is a special form of the selection structure discussed earlier.

Subroutines are useful because the programmer can assign complicated tasks or calculations to several subroutines and avoid cluttering up the main part of the program. Each independent task should be done in a separate subroutine, making the main program logic much easier to follow. Such a *modular programming style* allows new programmers hired by a company to understand more quickly how existing programs work. It also makes debugging easier, since each subroutine can be tested independently with dummy variables. Finally, it is not uncommon for a programmer to have to revise his or her own program months after it was first written. You will be amazed at how hard it is to figure out what a badly organized program is doing—even if you yourself wrote the original program!

Programming Tips

In most programming languages, including BASIC, there are many ways to solve a problem. Moreover, there are good ways and bad ways. Below are some coding tips that may help you write better BASIC programs:

1. If the code you are writing looks overly complicated, stop and think of a better way to solve the problem. Beginning programmers sometimes try to do too much at one time. Often, it's advantageous to retrench and find a way to decompose the solution into easier subproblems. Most programs can be written in a very simple, straightforward manner.

2. If you can't solve an entire problem, consider solving only part of it. Oddly enough, if you've successfully solved part of the problem and you're determined to solve all of it, the solution to the remainder might later hit you when you're brushing your teeth or walking your dog.

Choose meaningful variable names.

3. Choose meaningful variable names. If you are going to represent "gross pay" by a variable, for example, use names such as G or GROSSPAY. Don't choose such names as X or VAR1.

4. Initialize all program variables used as accumulators. For example, if you have counts and sums that start at zero, and

you've coded statements such as

$$I = I + 1 \quad \text{and} \quad S = S + X$$

to represent them, initialize I and S to zero first. Although BASIC is forgiving and will automatically set I and S to zero before it executes these statements, other languages you may learn ordinarily will not do this and may produce unpredictable results in your program.

Prove every result.

5. Prove the correctness of every result you get from the computer. Many beginners are satisfied that their programs work as soon as they get any sort of reasonable looking output. The logic used to write the program unfortunately might be totally incorrect.

6. Use comments in a program (i.e., REM statements) where appropriate. Using *too few* comments will often leave people who read your program bewildered at what it does. Unfortunately using *too many* comments will also produce the same result.

7. Avoid recomputing constants in a loop. For example, the code

```
100 FOR I = 1 TO 10
110     A = 3 * B
120     READ X
130     S = S + X
140 NEXT I
150 S = S + A
```

should be rewritten as

```
100 FOR I = 1 TO 10
110    READ X
120    S=S+X
130 NEXT I
140 S=S+3*B
```

Avoid tricky code.

8. Write clearly and avoid tricky code. For example, many versions of BASIC allow the two operators AND and OR. An all-inclusive IF statement that is coded in the form

```
100 IF X=3 AND Y=2 OR B=5 THEN 210
```

is not as clear as the equivalent block of code:

```
100 IF X=3 AND Y=2 THEN 210
110 IF B=5 THEN 210
```

Some programmers insist on cramming as much code as possible into as few lines as possible, making programs very hard to read or debug.

9. Avoid unnecessary GOTO statements. For example, if the version of BASIC you are using supports the WHILE or IF/THEN/ELSE statements, use them to avoid backward-pointing GOTOs.

10. Order IF statements that will appear together by putting the most frequently occurring conditions first. For example, if

you put statements in the order

```
100 IF T$="TYPEA" THEN 200
110 IF T$="TYPEB" THEN 210
120 IF T$="TYPEC" THEN 220
```

and most of the records you are examining are TYPEC, the computer will be going through many needless comparisons. The program would execute faster if statement 120 came first.

Use subroutines where possible.

11. Use subroutines where possible. Many languages, such as COBOL and Pascal, emphasize breaking a program up into independent modules and using subroutines or subroutine-like statements to access them. If you plan a computer career, it would be well worth your time to consider this approach to coding programs.

12. If your program is computationally intensive, it is useful to know that computers perform addition faster than multiplication. Thus a statement that computes an expression such as

```
100 A=B+B+B
```

will operate faster than one that does the same computation as

```
100 A=3*B
```

Exercises

Instructions: Provide an answer to each of the following questions.

1. Consider the program below:

    ```
    10 DIM A(4,4)
    20 FOR I=1 TO 4
    30 FOR J=1 TO 4
    40 READ A(I,J)
    50 NEXT J
    60 NEXT I
    70 DATA 12,2,0,3,1,4,2,7,6,10,9,0,11,3,8,7
    ```

    What is the value of the following variables?

    a. A(1,3)   b. A(2,2)   c. A(3,4)   d. A(4,3)

2. How would you change your responses to Exercise 1 if statement 40 were changed to:

    ```
    40 READ A(J,I)
    ```

3. Write a single LET statement to generate the following:
    a. Random numbers in the range .000000–.999999 (inclusive).
    b. Random integers in the range 0–99 (inclusive).
    c. Random integers in the range 1–100 (inclusive).
    d. Random integers in the range 37–46 (inclusive).

Programming Problems

Instructions: Write a BASIC program to do each of the following tasks.

1. Write a program that reads the matrix

    $$\begin{bmatrix} 8 & 7 & 3 \\ 2 & 4 & 1 \\ 6 & 5 & 8 \end{bmatrix}$$

    adds the number 5 to each element (number) of the matrix, and prints the resulting matrix.

2. Generate 1000 random integers in the range 1–100 (inclusive) and determine the number that are between 10 and 30 (inclusive).

3. Write a program to simulate the flipping of a coin. For example, generate 1000 random numbers between .000000 and .999999. If a random number is less than .5, it counts as a "head;" otherwise it counts as a "tail." Output the number of heads and tails found in the 1000 "flips."

4. ABC Company has the following "accounts receivables" data:

Customer Name	Previous Balance	Payments	New Purchases
Clara Bronson	$700	$500	$300
Lon Brooks	100	100	0
Louise Chaplin	0	0	100
Jack Davies	50	0	0
Emil Murray	600	600	200
Tom Swanson	300	100	50
Lucy Allen	500	500	80

Write a subroutine that computes the new balance for each customer. Assume that unpaid portions of previous balances are assessed a 2 percent finance charge each month. The main part of your program should perform all the input/output functions necessary to support and supplement the subroutine.

BASIC STATEMENT COMMANDS

Statement	Description	Example
DEF	Sets up a user-defined function (B-99)	`90 DEF FNC(S1,S2)=.15*S1+.10*S2`
DIM	Dimensions an array (B-77)	`120 DIM X(12)`
END	The last statement in a program (B-5, B-20)	`250 END`

FOR/NEXT	The beginning and ending statements in a loop (B-48)	`160 FOR I=1 TO N`
		`   .`
		`   .`
		`   .`
		`190 NEXT I`

GOSUB/RETURN	Branch to a subroutine; Return to main program from subroutine (B-100)	`120 GOSUB 150`
		`   .`
		`   .`
		`   .`
		`190 RETURN`

GOTO	An unconditional branch (B-19)	`140 GOTO 100`
IF	A conditional branch (B-16)	`110 IF A=-1 THEN 160`
IF/THEN/ELSE	A conditional branch (B-53)	`110 IF S>5000 THEN B=500` `             ELSE B=0`
INPUT	Enables data to be entered interactively (B-41)	`80 INPUT X`
LET	An assignment (replacement) statement (B-5, B-17)	`30 LET C=A+B`
ON GOTO	Branches to a specific case (B-103)	`100 ON M GOTO 300,400,500`
PRINT	Displays or prints program output (B-5, B-18)	`160 PRINT N$`

PRINT USING	Enables neatly-formatted output (B-65)	`100 A$=" ###.##"`
		`   .`
		`   .`
		`   .`
		`200 PRINT USING A$;X`

READ/DATA	Assigns values to variables from a list of data (B-4, B-15)	`20 READ A,B`
		`   .`
		`   .`
		`50 DATA 8,16`

REM	A program remark (B-4, B-19)	`100 REM DEPRECIATION CALCULATION`
STOP	Stops a program (B-47)	`80 STOP`

WHILE/WEND	The beginning and ending statements in a loop (B-54)	`150 WHILE X>0`
		`   .`
		`   .`
		`   .`
		`200 WEND`

Numbers in parentheses in the second column are the pages on which the statement is described.

BASIC Glossary/Index

The number in parentheses at the end of each definition is the page of Appendix B on which the term is boldfaced.

Algorithm. A statement of the steps to be followed in solving a problem or performing a process. **(B-7)**

Array. A one- or two-dimensional subscripted variable list. **(B-77)**

Assignment (replacement) symbol. The "=" symbol used in a LET statement, which assigns the value implied on the right-hand side of the symbol to the variable declared on the left-hand side. **(B-18)**

BASIC (Beginner's All-purpose Symbolic Instruction Code). An easy-to-learn programming language developed at Dartmouth College in the 1960s. BASIC is widely used for instructional purposes and is the most popular language implemented on personal computers. **(B-1)**

BASIC program. A set of BASIC program statements that can be executed by the computer to produce useful output. **(B-3)**

BASIC program statement. See BASIC statement command. **(B-4)**

BASIC statement command. An instruction written in the BASIC programming language—for example, READ, LET, PRINT, and so forth. **(B-21)**

BASIC system command. An instruction that performs an action on a BASIC program—for example, RUN, LIST, DELETE, and so forth. **(B-21)**

Branch. The process of transferring control from one statement in a program to any statement out of the normal sequence. **(B-7)**

Bubble sort. A sorting method that works by successive comparisons and exchanges of values in a list, "bubbling" the largest (or smallest) value on each pass up (or down) the list. **(B-86)**

Bug. An error in a program or system. **(B-23)**

Coding. The writing of instructions that will cause the computer system to perform a specific set of actions. **(B-7)**

Computer-assisted instruction (CAI). The use of computers to supplement personalized teaching instruction by providing the student with sequences of questions under program control. The progression through the questions in such a system enables students to learn at their own rate. **(B-44)**

Computer program. A set of instructions that causes the computer system to perform a specific set of actions. **(B-1)**

Conditional branch. An instruction that may cause the computer to execute an instruction, other than the one that immediately follows, depending on the results of an operation, the contents of a storage location, and so forth. **(B-17)**

Constant. A value that doesn't change. **(B-12)**

Control break. The process of a variable (called a control variable) changing its value from one record to the next. **(B-72)**

Control structure. A pattern for controlling the flow of logic in a computer program. **(B-9)**

Conversational (interactive) mode. The use of the INPUT statement to enable a program user to interact with a program as it is running. **(B-41)**

Debug. The process of detecting and correcting errors in computer programs or in the computer system itself. **(B-23)**

Design phase. In program development, the process of planning a program prior to coding it. **(B-7)**

Documentation. Any nonexecutable written description of a program, procedure, or system **(B-9)**

Hierarchy of operations. The order of operations followed by a programming language when evaluating an expression. **(B-14)**

Initializing. Presetting a variable to a prespecified value before using it in a computation. **(B-39)**

Instruction. A program or system command that will cause the computer to take some action. **(B-1)**

Library (built-in) function. A mathematical function that is built into the BASIC language—for example, RND, INT, SIN, and so forth. **(B-98)**

Line number. An integer number that begins and identifies every BASIC program statement. **(B-4)**

Literal. Another name for a string constant. **(B-5)**

Loop. A series of program statements that are executed repeatedly until one or more conditions are satisfied. **(B-7)**

Looping. The control structure used to represent a loop operation. **(B-9)**

Loop variable. A variable used to control the number of times a loop is executed. **(B-48)**

Menu. A schedule of choices presented to a program user. **(B-101)**

Numeric constant. A constant that has a numeric value. **(B-12)**

Numeric variable. A variable that can assume only numeric values. **(B-10)**

Print zone. An output field where the output device may be directed when a comma is encountered in a PRINT statement. **(B-62)**

Program flowchart. A visual program design tool showing, step-by-step, how a computer program processes data. **(B-33)**

Programming language. A language used to write computer programs. **(B-1)**

Prompt. A message output by an interactive program explaining to the program user what input data are to be entered. **(B-42)**

Random number. An unpredictable number produced by chance. **(B-93)**

Scalar variable. A nonsubscripted variable. **(B-83)**

Selection. The control structure used to represent the decision operation. **(B-9)**

Sentinel value. See trailer value. **(B-7)**

Sequence. The control structure used to represent operations that take place one after another. **(B-9)**

Simulation. The representation of a real-world process by a computer program. **(B-94)**

String constant. A constant that may be composed of any mix of characters from the BASIC character set. **(B-12)**

String variable. A variable that may assume any mix of characters from the BASIC character set as its values. **(B-10)**

Subroutine. A partial program, internal or external to a main program, that is invoked by some statement in the main program. **(B-100)**

Subscript. A quantity used to identify a position in an array. **(B-77)**

Syntax. The grammatical and structural rules of a programming language. **(B-1)**

Trailer value. A "dummy" value placed at the end of a data list to denote an end-of-data condition. **(B-7)**

Unconditional branch. An instruction that causes the computer to execute a specific statement other than the one that immediately follows in the normal sequence. **(B-19)**

User-defined function. A function created by a programmer with the DEF statement. **(B-98)**

Variable. A quantity that can assume any of a given set of data values. **(B-4)**

Word processing. The use of computer technology to create, manipulate, and print text material such as letters, documents, and manuscripts. **(B-45)**

Glossary

The terms shown in color were presented in the text as key terms. The boldfaced number in parentheses at the end of the definition of each of these terms indicates the page (or pages) on which it is boldfaced in the text. The terms shown in black are other commonly used and important words one often encounters in computer and data processing discussions. The number in parentheses after the definition of each of these terms indicates the page on which it is discussed.

A

ABC. See Atanasoff–Berry Computer. **(70)**

Access mechanism. A mechanical device in the disk pack or storage unit that positions the read/write heads on the proper tracks. **(132)**

Access motion time. The time taken by the access mechanism on a disk unit to move from one track position, or cylinder, to another when reading or writing data. **(134)**

Accumulator. A register that stores the result of an arithmetic or logical operation. **(97)**

Acoustically coupled modem. A special modem that converts electric signals to or from audible tones that can be transmitted over ordinary telephone wires. The device contains an acoustic cradle to receive a conventional telephone headset. (213)

Active cell. In spreadsheet software the worksheet cell at which the highlight is currently positioned. Also called the current cell. **(368)**

Ada. A structured programming language developed by the Department of Defense and named for Ada Augusta Byron, the world's first programmer. **(340)**

Address. An identifiable location in memory where data may be stored. Primary memory and I/O media such as disk are addressable. (96)

Address register. A register containing the memory location of an instruction to be executed. **(97)**

AI. See Artificial intelligence. **(460)**

ALU. See Arithmetic/logic unit. **(96)**

American National Standards Institute (ANSI). An organization that acts as a national clearinghouse for standards in the United States. (79)

Analog computer. A computer that measures continuous phenomena—such as speed and height—and converts them to numbers. **(94)**

Analog transmission. The transmission of data as continuous wave patterns. **(212)**

Analysis. In program and system development, the process of studying a problem area to determine what should be done. **(271)**

Analytical engine. A device conceived by Charles Babbage in the 1800s to perform computations. This machine is considered the forerunner of today's modern electronic computer. **(68)**

ANSI. See American National Standards Institute. (79)

APL. See A Programming Language. **(339)**

Applications programmer. A programmer who codes programs that do the useful work—such as payroll, inventory control, and accounting tasks—for end users of a computer system. Contrast with systems programmer. **(498)**

Applications software. Programs that do the useful work—such as payroll, inventory control, and accounting tasks—for end users of a computer system. Contrast with systems software. **(50, 268)**

A Programming Language (APL). A highly compact programming language that is popular for problem-solving applications. **(339)**

Arithmetic/logic unit (ALU). The part of the computer that contains the circuitry to perform addition, subtraction, multiplication, division, and comparing operations. **(96)**

Artificial intelligence (AI). The ability of a machine to perform actions that are characteristic of human intelligence, such as reasoning and learning. **(460)**

ASCII. An acronym for *American Standard*

Code for Information Interchange. ASCII is a 7-bit code widely used to represent data for processing and communications. **(102)**

Assembler. A computer program that takes assembly-language instructions and converts them to machine language. **(254)**

Assembly language. A low-level programming language that uses mnemonic codes in place of the 0s and 1s of machine language. **(75, 325)**

Asynchronous transmission. The transmission of data over a line one character at a time. Each character is preceded by a "start bit" and followed by a "stop bit." Contrast with synchronous transmission. **(224)**

Atanasoff-Berry Computer (ABC). The world's first electronic digital computer, built in the early 1940s by Dr. John V. Atanasoff and his assistant, Clifford Berry. **(70)**

Auxiliary equipment. Equipment that works in a "standalone" mode, independent of direct CPU interaction. Examples are bursters, decollators, key-to-disk, and key-to-tape units. **(45)**

B

Bar code. A machine-readable code consisting of sets of bars of varying widths. The codes are prominently displayed on the packaging of many retail goods and are commonly read with wand readers. (184)

BASIC. See Beginner's All-purpose Symbolic Instruction Code. **(327)**

Batch processing. Processing transactions or other data in groups, at periodic times. Contrast with realtime processing. **(56)**

Beginner's All-purpose Symbolic Instruction Code (BASIC). An easy-to-learn high-level programming language developed at Dartmouth College in the 1960s. **(327)**

Benchmark test. A test to measure computer system performance, under typical use conditions, prior to purchase. The test is analogous to the rigorous "test drive" you might take with a car before you buy it. **(486)**

Binary. A number system with two possible states. The binary system is fundamental to computers because electronic devices often

function in two possible states—for example, "on" or "off," "current present" or "current not present," "clockwise" or "counterclockwise." **(99, A-2)**

Bit. A binary digit, such as 0 or 1. The 0 or 1 states are used by computer systems to take advantage of the binary nature of electronics. Bits are often assembled into bytes and words when manipulated or stored. **(99)**

Bit mapping. A term, used with certain display devices and dot-matrix printers, that implies that each of the dots in the image may be individually operator controlled. **(163)**

Bits per second (bps). A frequently used measure of the speed of a communications medium or device. **(211)**

Blocking. The combining of two or more records (into a "block") to conserve storage space and to increase processing efficiency. **(127)**

Blocking factor. The number of logical records per physical record on tape or disk. **(127)**

Board. A hardware device into which processor chips and memory chips are fitted, along with related circuitry. **(114)**

Bps. See Bits per second. **(211)**

Buffer. A temporary storage area used to balance the speed differences between two devices. For example, buffers are used within the computer unit to store physical records so that the logical records that comprise them may be processed faster. Buffers are also used in many terminals and data communications devices to store characters in large blocks before they are sent to another device. **(127)**

Bug. An error in a program or system. (282)

Burster. A device used to separate perforated, fan-fold paper into single sheets. (178)

Bus. A set of wires that acts as a data highway between the CPU and other devices. **(118)**

Bus network. A teleprocessing network that consists of a loop circuit and several devices that tap into the loop to communicate with one another. The network is so named because data are passed around from device to device similar to the way in which passengers are picked up and dropped off at bus stations in towns and cities. **(221)**

Byte. A configuration of 7 or 8 bits used to represent a single character of information. **(102)**

C

C. A programming language that has the portability of a high-level language and the executional efficiency of an assembly language. **(340)**

CAD. See Computer-aided design. **(457)**

CAD/CAM. An acronym for computer-aided design/computer-aided manufacturing. CAD/CAM is a general term applied to the use of computer technology to automate design and manufacturing operations in industry. (457)

CAI. See Computer-assisted instruction. (426)

CAM. See Computer-aided manufacturing. **(458)**

Card reader. An input device that reads punched cards. **(181)**

Cartridge tape. Magnetic tape that is contained in a small plastic cartridge. These tapes look a lot like cassette tapes but are often slightly larger. **(125)**

Case control structure. A control structure that can be formed by nesting two or more selection control structures. **(299)**

Cassette tape. Magnetic tape, approximately ⅛ inch wide, that is housed in a small plastic cartridge. Cassette tape is read on a cassette tape unit. **(124)**

Cathode-ray tube (CRT). A peripheral device containing a televisionlike display screen. A CRT is often used as a synonym for *display device,* although other types of display devices commonly are found in computing environments. **(165)**

Cell. In spreadsheet software an area of the worksheet that can hold a single label or value. **(368)**

Cell pointer. In spreadsheet software a cursorlike mechanism used to point to cells on the display screen. **(368)**

Central processing unit (CPU). The piece of hardware, also known as the "computer," that interprets and executes program instructions and communicates with input, output, and storage devices. **(5)**

Chief information officer (CIO). See Vice president of information systems. **(500)**

Chief programmer team. A team of programmers, generally assigned to a large programming project, that is coordinated by a highly experienced person called the chief programmer. **(281)**

CIO. See Chief information officer. **(500)**

Coaxial cable. A transmission line developed for sending data and video images at high speeds. **(208)**

COBOL. See Common Business-Oriented Language. **(331)**

Coding. The writing of instructions in a programming language that will cause the computer system to perform a specific set of operations. **(280)**

COM. See Computer output microfilm. **(195)**

Command language. A programming language that is used to communicate with the operating system. **(243)**

Command language translator. A language that translates instructions written in a command language into machine language instructions. **(243)**

Common Business-Oriented Language (COBOL). A high-level programming language developed for business data processing applications. **(331)**

Common carrier. A government-regulated private organization that provides communications services to the public. **(215)**

Communications medium. The intervening substance, such as a telephone wire or cable, that connects two physically distant hardware devices. **(207)**

Communications satellite. An earth-orbiting device that relays communications signals over long distances. **(211)**

Communications services company. A company that provides communications-related services to the general public. **(218)**

Compiler. A computer program that translates a source program written by a user or programmer in a high-level programming language into machine language. The translation takes place before the translated program is executed. Contrast with interpreter. **(253)**

Computer. See Central processing unit. **(5)**

Computer-aided design (CAD). A general term applied to the use of computer technology to automate design functions in industry. **(457)**

Computer-aided manufacturing (CAM). A general term applied to the use of computer technology to automate manufacturing functions in industry. **(458)**

Computer-assisted instruction (CAI). The use of computers to supplement personalized teaching instruction by providing the student with sequences of instruction under program control. The progression through the instructional materials in such a system enables students to learn at their own rate. (426)

Computer crime. The use of computers to commit unauthorized acts. **(517)**

Computer engineering. The field of knowledge that includes the design of computer hardware systems. Computer engineering is offered as a degree program in several colleges and universities. **(504)**

Computer ethics. A term that refers to ethical behavior with regard to computer-related issues. **(522)**

Computer information systems curriculum. See Data processing curriculum. **(502)**

Computer operations. (1) The functions related to the physical operation of the computer system. (2) A curriculum offered in many schools that is oriented toward training students to enter the computer operations field. Computer operations curricula often train students to become computer or data-entry operators. **(504)**

Computer operations manager. The person who oversees the computer operations area in an organization. The computer operations manager is responsible for tasks such as hiring operations personnel and scheduling work that the system is to perform. **(498)**

Computer operator. A person skilled in the operation of the computer and its support devices. The operator is responsible for such tasks as mounting and dismounting tapes and disks and removing printouts from the line printer. **(498)**

Computer output microfilm (COM). A term that refers to equipment and media that reduce computer output to microscopic form and put it on photosensitive film. **(195)**

Computer science curriculum. A course of study that includes all technical aspects of the design and use of computers. Computer science is offered as a degree program in many institutions of higher learning. **(502)**

Computer system. When applied to buying a "computer system" in a store, the term generally refers to the equipment and programs one is being sold. When applied to a computer-based operation in an organization, it is commonly defined as all the equipment, programs, data, procedures, and personnel supporting that operation. **(5)**

Concentrator. A communications device that combines the features of controllers and multiplexers. Concentrators also have a store-and-forward capability that enables them to store messages from several low-speed devices before forwarding them—at high speeds—to another device. **(231)**

Concurrent access. A term that refers to two or more users attempting interactively to access the same data at, more or less, the same time. **(403)**

Conditional branch. An instruction that may cause the computer to execute an instruction other than the one that immediately follows in the program sequence. **(294)**

Connector symbol. A flowcharting symbol used to represent a junction to connect broken paths in a line of flow. **(292)**

Contention. A condition in a communications system in which two or more devices compete for use of a line. **(228)**

Control-break reporting. A term that refers to "breaks," in the normal flow of information in a computer report, that periodically take place for subtotals and totals. (56)

Controller. A device that supervises communications traffic in a teleprocessing environment, relieving the computer of a heavy processing burden. **(228)**

Control panel. In spreadsheet software the portion of the screen display that is used for issuing commands and observing what is being typed in to the computer system. **(367)**

Control structure. A pattern for controlling the flow of logic in a computer program. The three basic control structures are sequence, selection (IF/THEN/ELSE), and looping (iteration). **(299)**

Control unit. The part of the CPU that coordinates the execution of program instructions. **(96)**

Coprocessor. A specialized processor chip that is invoked by the CPU to do certain types of processing. (114)

CPU. See Central processing unit. **(5)**

Crosshair cursor. A digitizing device that is often moved over hard-copy images of maps and drawings, to enter these images into the computer system. **(168)**

CRT. See Cathode-ray tube. **(165)**

Current cell. See Active cell. **(368)**

Cursor. A highlighting symbol that appears on a video screen to indicate the position where the next character typed in will appear. **(165, 368)**

D

Daisywheel printer. A low-speed printer with a solid-font printing mechanism consisting of a spoked wheel of embossed characters. Daisywheel printers are capable of producing letter-quality output. **(422)**

Data. A collection of unorganized facts that are not yet processed into information. **(18)**

Data access. Reading data from a device, either sequentially or directly. **(146)**

Database. An integrated collection of data stored on a direct-access storage device. **(47, 394)**

Database adminstrator (DBA). The person or group of people in charge of designing, implementing, and managing the ongoing operation of a database. **(397)**

Database management system (DBMS). A software package designed to store an integrated collection of data and provide easy access to it. **(394)**

Data definition. The process of describing the characteristics of data that are to be handled by a database management system. **(397)**

Data definition language (DDL). A language used by a database administrator to create, store, and manage data in a database environment. **(402)**

Data dictionary. A facility that informs users and programmers about characteristics of data in a database or computer system. (402)

Data-entry operator. A member of a computer operations staff who is responsible for keying data into the computer system. **(498)**

Data flow diagram. A graphic systems analysis and design tool that enables a systems analyst to represent the flow of data through a system. **(479)**

Data manipulation. The process of using language commands to add, delete, modify, or retrieve data in a file or database. **(398)**

Data manipulation language (DML). A language used by programmers to supplement some high-level language supported in a database environment. **(403)**

Data movement time. The time taken to transfer data to or from disk once the read/write head is properly positioned on a disk track. **(134)**

Data organization. The process of establishing a data file so that it may subsequently be accessed in some desired way. Three common methods of organizing data are sequential organization, indexed-sequential organization, and direct organization. **(146)**

Data preparation device. An auxiliary device used to prepare data in machine-readable form. Two examples of data preparation devices are key-to-tape units and key-to-disk units. **(45)**

Data processing. Operations performed on data to provide useful information to users. **(8)**

Data processing curriculum. A course of study, normally offered by a business school, that prepares students for entry-level jobs as applications programmers or systems analysts. Also see Computer information systems curriculum. **(502)**

Data processing director. The person in charge of developing and/or implementing the overall plan for data processing in an organization and for overseeing the activities of programmers, systems analysts, and operations personnel. **(500)**

Data structure. The relationship between data items. **(397)**

DBA. See Database administrator. **(397)**

DBMS. See Database management system. **(394)**

DDL. See Data definition language. **(402)**

DDP. See Distributed data processing. **(222)**

Debugging. The process of detecting and correcting errors in computer programs or in the computer system itself. **(282)**

Decimal. A number system with ten symbols— 0, 1, 2, 3, 4, 5, 6, 7, 8, and 9. **(A-2)**

Decision support system (DSS). A system designed to provide information to managers to enable them to make decisions. Many decision support systems use interactive terminals and enable managers to define their own information needs creatively when using the system. **(453)**

Decision symbol. A diamond-shaped flowcharting symbol that is used to represent a choice in the processing path. **(291)**

Decision table. A table that shows all the circumstances to be considered in a problem as well as the outcomes from any given set of circumstances. **(310)**

Decollator. A device that automatically removes carbon interleaves from continuous, fan-fold paper. (178)

Dedicated lines. Lines used to provide an always available point-to-point connection between two or more devices. **(217)**

Default. The assumption made by a computer program when no specific choice is indicated by the user or programmer. **(243)**

Design. The process of planning a program or system. Design is normally undertaken after a problem has been thoroughly analyzed and a set of specifications for the solution has been established. **(275)**

Desk check. A manual checking process whereby a programmer or user scans a program listing for possible errors before submitting the program to the computer for execution. (282)

Desk-top computer. A microcomputer system that can fit on a desk top. Some familiar examples are the IBM PC, Apple IIc, and Apple Macintosh. **(415)**

Diagnostic. A message sent to the user by the computer system pinpointing errors in syntax or logic. Diagnostics are often referred to as *error messages*. (282)

Difference engine. A mechanical machine devised by Charles Babbage in the 1800s to perform computations automatically and print their results. **(68)**

Digital computer. A computer that counts discrete phenomena, such as people or dollars. Virtually all computers that are used in businesses or in the home for personal computing are digital computers. **(94)**

Digital transmission. The transmission of data as discrete impulses. **(212)**

Digitizer. An input device that converts a measurement into a digital value. **(194)**

Direct access. Reading or writing data in storage in such a way that the access time involved is relatively independent of the location of the data. **(146)**

Direct organization. A method of organizing data on a device so they can be accessed directly (randomly). **(152)**

Disk access time. The time taken to locate and read (or position and write) data on a disk device. **(134)**

Disk address. An identifiable location on disk where data may be stored. **(135)**

Disk cylinder. All tracks on a disk pack that are accessible with a single movement of the access mechanism. **(132)**

Disk drive. A mechanism within the disk storage unit on which disk packs or diskettes are placed to be accessed. (12)

Diskette. See Floppy disk. (131, 419)

Disk pack. A group of tiered hard disks mounted on a shaft and treated as a unit. A disk pack must be placed on a disk storage unit to be accessed. **(132)**

Disk storage unit. A direct-access secondary memory device on which disk packs, sealed disk modules, or floppy disks are mounted. **(132)**

Display device. A peripheral device containing a viewing screen. **(161)**

Display terminal. A communications workstation that consists of a display device and, normally, a keyboard. **(161)**

Disk unit. See Disk storage unit. **(132)**

Distributed data processing (DDP). A system configuration in which work that conceivably could be done on a single computer is distributed to two or more computers. **(222)**

DML. See Data manipulation language. **(403)**

Documentation. A detailed written description of a program, procedure, or system. **(283)**

Dot-matrix character. A character composed from a rectangular matrix of dots. (163)

DOUNTIL control structure. A looping control structure in which the looping continues as long as a certain condition is false (i.e., "do until true"). **(299)**

DOWHILE control structure. A looping control structure in which the looping continues as long as a certain condition is true (i.e., "do while true"). **(299)**

Drum plotter. An output device that draws on paper rolled along a cylindrically shaped drum. (196)

DSS. See Decision support system. **(453)**

Dumb terminal. A terminal that is capable of only the simplest types of input and output operations. Such terminals, although inexpensive, contain few operator conveniences. **(165)**

E

E-cycle. The part of the machine cycle in which data are located, an instruction is executed, and the results stored. **(98)**

EBCDIC. An acronym for *Extended Binary-Coded Decimal Interchange Code.* EBCDIC uses an 8-bit byte and can be used to represent up to 256 characters. **(102)**

EDSAC. An acronym for *Electronic Delay Storage Automatic Calculator.* EDSAC was the world's first stored-program computer and was completed in England in 1949. **(72)**

EDVAC. An acronym for *Electronic Discrete Variable Automatic Calculator.* Completed in 1950, EDVAC was the first stored-program computer built in the United States. **(72)**

EEPROM. See Electrically erasable programmable read-only memory. (112)

EFT. See Electronic funds transfer. (528)

Egoless programming. A term coined to emphasize that programmers having their work criticized in a structured walkthrough

should not let their egos stand in the way of gaining constructive feedback. **(281)**

Electrically erasable programmable read-only memory (EEPROM). An EPROM module capable of having its contents altered when plugged into a peripheral device. (112)

Electromechanical machine. A device that has both electrical and mechanical features. **(68)**

Electronic funds transfer (EFT). Pertaining to systems that transfer funds "by computer" from one account to another, without the use of written checks. (528)

Electronic machine. A device containing electronic components. **(70)**

Electronic mail. A software facility that enables users to send letters, memos, documents, and the like from one computer terminal to another. **(455)**

Electronic spreadsheet. A productivity software package that enables operators to create tables and financial schedules quickly by entering labels and values into cells on a display-screen grid. **(364)**

ENIAC. An acronym for *Electronic Numerical Integrator and Calculator.* Unveiled in 1946, ENIAC was the world's first large-scale, general-purpose computer. **(71)**

EPROM. See Erasable programmable read-only memory. **(112)**

Erasable programmable read-only memory (EPROM). A software-in-hardware module that can be programmed and reprogrammed under certain limited conditions, yet cannot be casually erased by users or programmers. **(112)**

Ergonomics. The field that studies the effects that such things as computer workspaces have on the productivity and health of employees. **(515)**

Expert system. A program or computer system that can reach conclusions on a problem similar to those that can be reached by a human expert who has studied that problem. **(467)**

External disk. A disk unit that is not housed within the computer's system unit. (142)

External memory. See Secondary memory. **(9)**

External modem. A modem that is not housed within the computer's system unit. (213)

F

Facsimile machine. A device that can transmit the images of text, pictures, maps, diagrams, and so forth. (455)

Fiber optic cable. A cable composed of thousands of hair-thin transparent fibers along which data are passed from lasers as light waves. (208)

Field. A collection of related characters. (47)

File. A collection of related records. (47)

File manager. A productivity software package that is used to manage records and files. (388)

File-protection ring. A plastic ring that must be mounted at the center of a tape reel for data to be written onto the tape. (128)

Firmware. Software instructions that are written onto a hardware module. (111)

First generation. The first era of commercial computers, from 1951 to 1958, which was characterized by vacuum tubes as the main logic element. (73)

Flatbed plotter. An output device that draws on paper that is mounted on a flat drawing table. (196)

Flat-panel display. A slim-profile display device. (165)

Floppy disk. A small disk made of a tough, flexible plastic and coated with a substance that can be magnetized. Floppy disks are popular in small computer systems. Floppies are often called *diskettes*. (131, 419)

Flowchart. See Structured program flowchart or System flowchart. (301, 479)

Flowline. A flowcharting symbol used to represent the connecting path between other flowcharting symbols. (291)

FORmula TRANslator (FORTRAN). A high-level programming language used for mathematical, scientific, and engineering applications. (333)

FORTRAN. See FORmula TRANslator. (333)

Fourth generation. The fourth era of commercial computing, from 1971 to the present, which is characterized by microminiaturization and the rise of microcomputing. (81)

Front-end processor. A computer located at the front end of the main computer that relieves the main computer of certain computational chores. Such a device is often found in communications environments, where it receives inputs from remote devices and processes some inputs itself and sends others (possibly partially processed) on to the main computer. (231)

Full-duplex transmission. Any type of transmission in which messages may be sent in two directions, simultaneously, along a communications path. (212)

Function key. A special keyboard key that executes a preprogrammed routine when depressed. (167)

G

Gantt chart. A bar chart used to represent scheduled deadlines, project milestones, and the duration of project activities. (488)

GB. See Gigabyte. (102)

General-purpose computer. A computer capable of being programmed to solve a wide range of problems. (350)

Gigabyte (GB). Approximately one billion bytes. (102)

H

Hacking. A term that, when used with computers, often relates to using a microcomputer system or terminal to break into the security of a large computer system. (522)

Half-duplex transmission. Any type of transmission in which messages may be sent in two directions—but only one way at a time—along a communications path. (211)

Hard copy. A printed copy of machine output— for example, reports and program listings. (171)

Hard disk. A rigid platter that has been coated with a magnetizable substance. Hard disks are popular on both large and small computer systems. (130)

Hardware. Physical equipment in a computing environment, such as the computer and its support devices. (10)

Hashing. A key-to-disk mathematical transformation where the key field on each record determines where the record is stored. (152)

Heuristic. An intuitively appealing "rule of thumb" that is often used as part of a trial-and-error process to find a workable solution to a problem. (467)

Hexadecimal. Pertaining to the number system with sixteen symbols: 0, 1, 2, 3, 4, 5, 6, 7, 8, 9, A, B, C, D, E, and F. **(A-7)**

Hierarchy plus Input-Process-Output (HIPO) charts. A set of diagrams and procedures used to describe program functions from a general to a detailed level. **(310)**

High-level language. See High-level programming language. **(78, 324)**

High-level programming language. The class of programming languages used by most professional programmers to solve a wide range of problems. Some examples are BASIC, COBOL, FORTRAN, and Pascal. **(78, 324)**

Highlight. See Cell pointer. **(368)**

High-speed printer. A line or page printer that produces printed output at a rate of 300 lines or more per minute. **(171)**

HIPO charts. See Hierarchy plus Input-Process-Output charts. **(310)**

Host computer. In teleprocessing, a computer that is used to control a communications network. **(220)**

Host language. A programming language available for use on a specific computer system or subsystem. **(404)**

I

IC. See Integrated circuit. **(80)**

Icon. A graphical image on a display screen that, when selected by the operator, invokes a particular program action. **(244)**

I-cycle. The part of the machine cycle in which the control unit fetches an instruction from main memory and prepares it for subsequent processing. **(98)**

If/then/else (selection) control structure. See Selection control structure. **(299)**

Imbedded-command word processor. A word processor that works predominantly by imbedded formatting and printing commands,

which are sandwiched between blocks of text that are to be output. **(350)**

Impact dot-matrix mechanism. A print head that forms dot-matrix characters through impact printing. **(171)**

Impact dot-matrix printer. A printer whose print head is an impact dot-matrix mechanism. **(422)**

Impact printing. The formation of characters by causing a metal hammer to strike a ribbon onto paper or paper onto a ribbon. Contrast with nonimpact printing. **(171)**

Indexed-sequential organization. A method of organizing data on a direct-access medium in such a way that it can be accessed directly (through an index) or sequentially. **(150)**

Information. Data that have been processed. **(8)**

Information center. A facility in an organization where users can meet their microcomputing needs and acquire other types of decision-support resources. **(474)**

Initialize. To preset a variable to a prespecified value before using it in computations. **(294)**

Input. Anything supplied to a process or involved with the beginning of a process. For example, data must be input to a computer system. Or data must be keyed in to the system on an input device. Contrast with output. **(5)**

Input device. A machine used to supply data to the computer. Contrast with output device. **(5, 37, 160)**

Input/output (I/O) media. Objects used to hold data or information being input or output. Examples include punched cards, magnetic disk and tape, and paper. **(5, 43)**

Input/output symbol. A parallelogram-shaped flowcharting symbol used to represent an input or output operation. **(294)**

Instruction register. The register that holds the part of the instruction indicating what the computer is to do next. **(96)**

Integrated circuit (IC). A series of complex circuits that are etched on a small silicon chip. **(80)**

Integrated software package. A software package that bundles two or more major software functions together, into a single package. **(404, 425)**

Intelligent terminal. A terminal that enables operators easily to edit, manipulate, store, and process data. **(165)**

Interblock gap. The distance on magnetic tape or disk between the end of one physical record and the start of another. **(127)**

Internal disk. A disk unit that is housed inside the computer's system unit. (142)

Internal header label. An identifying label appearing at the beginning of a tape reel. **(129)**

Internal memory. See Primary memory. **(9, 95)**

Internal modem. A modem that is housed inside the computer's system unit. (213)

Internal storage. See Primary memory. **(9, 95)**

Interpreter. A computer program that translates a source program written by a user or programmer in a high-level language into machine language. The translation takes place on a line-by-line basis as each statement is executed. Contrast with compiler. **(254)**

Interrecord gap. See Interblock gap. **(127)**

I/O media. See Input/output media. **(5, 43)**

Iteration control structure. See Looping control structure. **(299)**

J

Joystick. An input device, which resembles a car's stick shift, that is often used for computer games and computer-aided design (CAD) work. **(168)**

K

KB. See Kilobyte. **(102)**

Keyboard. An input device that is composed of several typewriterlike keys, arranged in a configuration similar to that of a typewriter. Computer keyboards also have a number of special keys that, when activated, initiate preprogrammed routines. **(166)**

Key field. A field that is used to identify a record. **(127)**

Keypunch machine. An auxiliary device that uses a keyboard unit to place data directly on punched cards. **(180)**

Key-to-disk unit. An auxiliary device that uses

a keyboard unit to place data directly on magnetic disk. (45)

Key-to-tape unit. An auxiliary device that uses a keyboard unit to place data directly on magnetic tape. (45)

Kilobyte (KB). Approximately 1000 (1024 to be exact) bytes. Primary memory on smaller computer systems is often measured in kilobytes. **(102)**

L

Label. In spreadsheet software a cell entry that cannot be manipulated mathematically. **(368)**

LAN. See Local area network. **(218)**

Language translator. A system program that converts an applications program into machine language. **(253)**

Large-scale integration (LSI). The process of placing a large number of integrated circuits (usually over 100) on a single silicon chip. (83)

Light pen. An electronic device, resembling an ordinary pen, that can be used to enter input on a display screen. **(168)**

Line printer. A high-speed printer that produces output a line at a time. **(178)**

Linkage editor. A system program that binds together related object module program segments so that they may be run as a unit. **(254)**

Load module. A complete machine-language program that is ready to be executed by the computer. **(254)**

Local network. A privately run communications network of several machines located within a mile or so of each other. **(218)**

Local area network (LAN). See Local network. **(218)**

Logical record. A data record from the point of view of a user or programmer. **(127)**

Logic element. The electronic component used to facilitate circuit functions within the computer. (72)

Logo. A programming language that is often used to teach children how to program. **(341)**

Looping (iteration) control structure. The control structure used to represent a looping operation. Also see DOUNTIL control structure and DOWHILE control structure. **(299)**

Low-level language. A highly detailed, machine-dependent programming language. Included in the class of low-level languages are machine language and assembly language. **(323)**

Low-speed printer. A small printer designed to output a character at a time, at speeds from about 10 to 300 characters per second. **(171)**

LSI. See Large-scale integration. (83)

M

Machine cycle. The series of operations involved in the execution of a single machine-language instruction. **(97)**

Machine language. A binary-based programming language that can be executed directly by the computer. **(75, 106)**

Machine-readable. Any form in which data are encoded so that they can be read by a machine. **(5)**

Magnetic bubble storage. A memory that uses magnetic bubbles to indicate the 0- and 1-bit states. **(144)**

Magnetic core. A tiny, ring-shaped piece of magnetizable material capable of storing a single binary digit. Magnetic cores were popular as internal memories in second- and third-generation computers, but they have given way to semiconductor storage devices in the fourth generation. **(76)**

Magnetic disk. A secondary storage medium consisting of platters made of rigid metal (hard disk) or flexible plastic (floppy disk). **(130)**

Magnetic ink character recognition (MICR). A technology confined almost exclusively to the banking industry, MICR involves the processing of checks inscribed with special characters set in a special magnetic ink. **(193)**

Magnetic tape. A plastic tape with a magnetic surface for storing data as a series of magnetic spots. **(124)**

Mailing list program. A program that is used to generate mailing labels. **(363)**

Mail merge program. A program that is specifically designed to produce form letters. **(363)**

Mainframe. A large computer capable of supporting powerful peripheral devices. **(20)**

Main memory. See Primary memory. **(9, 95)**

Maintenance programmer. A programmer involved with keeping an organization's existing programs in proper working order. **(271)**

Management information system (MIS). A system designed to provide information to managers to enable them to make decisions. **(450)**

Mark I. Completed in 1944 by Harold Aiken of Harvard University, the Mark I was the first large-scale electromechanical computer. **(70)**

Mass storage unit. A storage device capable of storing billions of bytes of data online. **(142)**

Master file. A file containing relatively permanent information, such as customer names and addresses. The file is usually updated periodically. (47)

MB. See Megabyte. **(102)**

Mechanical calculating machine A computer that works by means of gears and levers rather than by means of electric power. **(66)**

Megabyte (MB). Approximately one million bytes. **(102)**

Menu. A set of options, provided at a display device, from which the operator is to make a selection. (15)

MICR. See Magnetic ink character recognition. **(193)**

Microcomputer. See Microcomputer system. **(414)**

Microcomputer system. The smallest and least expensive type of computer system. **(414)**

Microfiche. A sheet of film, often 4 by 6 inches, on which the images of computer output are stored. (195)

Microminiaturization. A term that implies a very small size. **(83)**

Microprocessor. A CPU on a silicon chip. **(414)**

Microsecond. One millionth of a second. **(99)**

Microspacing. A technique used by some printers to insert fractional spaces between characters, to give text a typeset look. **(362)**

Microwave. An electromagnetic wave in the high-frequency range. **(209)**

Millisecond. One thousandth of a second. **(99)**

Minicomputer. An intermediate-sized and medium-priced type of computer. **(19)**

MIS. See Management information system. **(450)**

Modem. A contraction of the words *mo*dulation and *dem*odulation. A communications device that enables computers and their support devices to communicate over ordinary telephone lines. **(212, 422)**

Module. A related group of entities that may be treated effectively as a unit. **(301)**

Monitor. (1) A video display. (2) The supervisor program of an operating system. **(161, 420)**

Monochrome. A term used to refer to a display device that operates in a single foreground color. (163)

Mouse. A device used to move a cursor rapidly around a display screen. **(168)**

Multidrop configuration. A communications configuration that uses a single line to service several terminals. **(228)**

Multifunction board. A board that can perform a variety of distinct functions. (115)

Multiplexer. A communications device that interleaves the messages of several low-speed devices and sends them along a single, high-speed transmission path. **(231)**

Multiprocessing. The *simultaneous* execution of two or more program sequences by multiple computers operating under common control. **(250)**

Multiprogramming. The execution of two or more programs *concurrently* on the same computer. **(247)**

Multitasking. The ability of an operating system to enable two or more programs from any single user to execute concurrently on one computer. **(247)**

N

Nanosecond. One billionth of a second. **(99)**

Narrowband transmission. Low-speed transmission, characterized by telegraph transmission. **(211)**

Network. A system of machines that communicate with one another. (206)

Nonimpact printing. The formation of characters on a surface by means of heat, lasers, photography, or ink jets. Contrast with impact printing. **(174)**

Nonprocedural language. A very-high-level, problem-dependent programming language that informs the computer system *what* work is to be done rather than *how* to do the work. Contrast with procedural language. **(324)**

Nonvolvatile storage. Storage that retains its contents when the power is shut off. (418)

O

Object module. The machine-language program that is the output from a language translator. Also called *object program*. **(254)**

OCR. See Optical character recognition. **(182)**

Octal. Pertaining to the number system with eight symbols—0, 1, 2, 3, 4, 5, 6, and 7. **(A-5)**

OEM. See Original equipment manufacturer. (85)

Office automation. Referring to the use of computer-based, office-oriented technologies such as word processing, electronic mail, video teleconferencing, and the like. **(454)**

Offline. Anything not in or prepared for communication with the CPU. **(45)**

Offpage connector symbol. A flowchart symbol used to connect other flowchart symbols logically from page to page. **(296)**

One-entry-point/one-exit-point rule. The rule stating that each program control structure will have only one entry point into it and one exit point out of it. **(299)**

Online. Anything that is ready for or in communication with the CPU. **(45)**

Operating system. A collection of systems software that enables the computer system to manage the resources under its control. **(80, 241, 426)**

Optical character recognition (OCR). An information processing technology that takes machine-readable marks, characters, or codes and converts them into a form suitable for computer processing. **(182)**

Optical disk. A disk that is read by optical rather than magnetic means. **(143)**

Original equipment manufacturer (OEM). A company that buys hardware from manufacturers and integrates it into its own systems. (85)

Output. Anything resulting from a process or involved with the end result of a process. For example, processed data are output as information. Or information may be printed using an output device. Contrast with input. **(5)**

Output device. A machine used to output computer-processed data, or information. Contrast with input device. **(5, 37, 160)**

P

Page printer. A high-speed printer that delivers output one page at a time. **(178)**

Paging. A technique for dividing programs into fixed-length blocks or pages. **(250)**

Parallel transmission. Data transmission in which each bit in a byte has its own path. All bits in a byte are transmitted simultaneously. Contrast with serial transmission. **(223)**

Parity bit. An extra bit added to the byte representation of a character to ensure that there is always either an odd or even number of 1-bits transmitted with every character. **(104)**

Pascal. A structured high-level programming language that is often used to teach programming. **(329)**

Pascaline. A mechanical calculating machine developed by Blaise Pascal in the 1600s. **(66)**

PBX. See Private branch exchange. **(218)**

Peripheral equipment. The input and output devices and secondary storage units in a computer system. **(43)**

Personal computer. See Personal computer system. **(19, 414)**

Personal computer system. A microcomputer system used to meet personal needs. **(19, 414)**

Physical record. A block of logical records. **(127)**

Picosecond. A trillionth of a second. **(99)**

Pixel. On a display screen, a single dot that is used to compose dot-matrix characters and other images. **(162)**

Plotter. An output device used for drawing graphs and diagrams. **(196)**

PL/1. See Programming Language/1. **(338)**

Plug-in board. A board that may be inserted into the computer's system unit to perform one or more functions. **(115, 418)**

Pocket (hand-held) computer. A microcomputer system that is small enough to fit in one's pocket. **(415)**

Point-of-sale (POS) system. A system, commonly found in department store and supermarket environments, that uses electronic cash register terminals to monitor and record sales transactions, and, possibly, to perform other data-handling functions. **(183)**

Point-to-point configuration. A communications configuration in which there is a direct line from each machine to every machine that is served by it. **(228)**

Polling. In data communications a line control method in which a computer or controller asks one terminal after another if it has any data to send. **(228)**

Port. An outlet on the computer's system unit through which a peripheral device may communicate. **(116, 419)**

Portable (lap-top) computer. A microcomputer system that is small enough to fit on one's lap. **(415)**

POS. See Point-of-sale system. **(183)**

Power manager. A device that can be used to control the power going to several other devices in a computer system. **(422)**

Precompiler. A computer program that translates an extended set of commands available with a programming language to standard commands of the language. **(404)**

Preliminary investigation. In systems development a brief study of a problem area to assess whether or not a full-scale investigation should be undertaken. **(476)**

Presentation graphics software. A productivity software package used to prepare line charts, bar charts, pie charts, and other information-intensive images. **(373)**

Primary key. A key in a record that is often used to sequence or access the record. Generally each record will have a different value for its primary key. For example, many records kept on individuals use the social security number as the primary key. (256)

Primary memory. Also known as main memory, internal storage, and primary storage, this part of the system unit temporarily holds data and program instructions awaiting processing, intermediate results, and output produced from processing. **(9, 95)**

Printer. A device that delivers computer output to paper. **(171)**

Privacy. In a data processing context, a term referring to how information about individuals is used and by whom. **(523)**

Private branch exchange (PBX). A switching station that an organization has acquired for its own use. **(218)**

Procedural language. A high-level programming language designed to solve a large class of problems. Procedural languages work by having the programmer code a set of procedures that tell the computer, step by step, how to solve a problem. Contrast with nonprocedural language. **(324)**

Processing. See Data processing. **(8)**

Processing symbol. A rectangular flowcharting symbol used to indicate a processing operation such as a computation. **(292)**

Productivity software. Software—such as word processors, spreadsheets, presentation-graphics packages, file managers, and database management systems—that is designed to make many types of ordinary workers more productive at their jobs. **(348, 425)**

Program. A set of instructions that causes the computer system to perform specific actions. **(8)**

Program design tool. A tool—such as a flowchart, pseudocode, or structure chart—that helps the systems analyst or programmer decide how a program is to work. **(290)**

Program development cycle. All the steps an organization must go through to bring a computer program into operation. The steps of the program development cycle include analysis, design, coding, debugging, and documentation. Also called the program life cycle. **(270)**

Program flowchart. A visual design tool showing, step by step, how a computer program will process data. Contrast with system flowchart. **(290)**

Program life cycle. See Program development cycle. **(270)**

Programmable read-only memory (PROM). A software-in-hardware module that can be programmed under certain restricted conditions and, once programmed, cannot be altered or erased. **(112)**

Programmer. A person whose job it is to write, maintain, and test computer programs. **(10, 271)**

Programming language. A language used to write computer programs. **(9, 322)**

Programming Language/1 (PL/1). A structured, general-purpose, high-level language that can be used for mathematical, scientific, engineering, and business applications. **(338)**

PROM. See Programmable read-only memory. **(112)**

Proportional spacing. A printing feature that allocates more horizontal space on a line to some characters than to others. **(362)**

Protocol. A set of conventions used by machines to establish communication with each other in a teleprocessing environment. **(227)**

Prototyping. A systems development alternative whereby a small model, or prototype, of the system is built before a full-scale systems development effort is undertaken. **(488)**

Pseudocode. A technique for structured program design that uses English-like statements to outline the logic of a program. Pseudocode statements closely resemble actual programming code. **(304)**

Punched card. A cardboard card used with computer systems on which small punched holes are used to represent letters, digits, or special characters. **(180)**

Q

Query processing. Processing that involves requesting information through an online terminal. **(58)**

Query/update facility. An easy-to-learn language that enables users to add, delete, modify, or retrieve data from computer files or databases. **(398)**

Queue. A group of items awaiting computer processing. (258)

R

RAM. See Random-access memory. **(111, 417)**

Random access. See Direct access. **(146)**

Random-access memory (RAM). Any memory capable of being accessed directly. In the world of microcomputers, the acronym RAM generally applies only to primary memory. **(111, 417)**

Read-only memory (ROM). A software-in-hardware module that can be read but not written upon. **(111, 418)**

Read/write head. A magnetic head on a disk access mechanism or tape unit that reads or writes data. **(126)**

Realtime processing. Updating data immediately on a computer system, as the transactions that affect the updates take place. Contrast with batch processing. **(58)**

Recalculation feature. The ability of spreadsheet software to recalculate quickly and automatically the contents of several cells, based on new operator inputs. **(367)**

Record. A collection of related fields. **(47)**

Register. A high-speed staging area within the computer that temporarily stores data during processing. **(96)**

Relational data structure. A data structure in which the relationships among data are represented in interrelated tables. (397)

Removable-pack disk. Refers to hard disks that are placed in disk packs that can be removed from the disk storage unit. **(131)**

Report Program Generator (RPG). A report-generation language popular with small businesses. **(342)**

Request for Quotation (RFQ). A document containing a list of technical specifications for hardware, software, and services that an organization wishes to acquire. The RFQ is submitted to vendors, who subsequently prepare a bid based on the resources they are able to supply. **(485)**

Resolution. A term referring to the sharpness of the images on a display screen. (162)

Response time. The time it takes the computer system to respond to a specific input. (273)

RFQ. See Request for quotation. **(485)**

Ring network. A teleprocessing network in which machines are connected together serially, in a closed loop. **(221)**

Robotics. The field devoted to the study of robot technology. **(458)**

ROM. See Read-only memory. **(111, 418)**

Rotational delay. In disk processing, the time it takes for the read/write heads to be aligned over the proper position on a track once the access mechanism has reached the track. **(134)**

Routine record accounting. A term referring to record keeping and other accounting tasks that organizations must handle regularly. **(56)**

RPG. See Report Program Generator. **(342)**

S

Screen-oriented word processor. A word processor that will, for the most part, give you in print exactly (or almost exactly) what you see on the screen. **(350)**

Secondary key. A key that is often used to search through a file or a database. Unlike with a primary key, two records can often have the same value for a secondary key. For example, a person's name is often a secondary key in records kept on people and, of course, two people can have the same name. (256)

Secondary memory. Memory provided by technologies such as tape, disk, or mass storage, that supplements primary memory. Also called external memory. **(9)**

Secondary storage device. A machine—such as a tape unit, disk unit, or mass storage device—capable of providing storage to supplement primary memory. **(37)**

Second generation. The second era of commercial computers, from 1959 to 1964, which was characterized by transistor circuitry. **(75)**

Sector. A pie-shaped area on a disk. Many disks are addressed through sectors. **(139)**

Segmentation. A technique for dividing programs into logical, variable-length blocks. **(250)**

Selection. The process of going through a set of data and picking out only those data elements that meet certain criteria. **(50)**

Selection (if/then/else) control structure. The control structure used to represent a decision operation. **(299)**

Semiconductor memory. A memory whose components are etched onto small silicon chips. **(84)**

Sentinel record. The final record in a set of records. Also called a trailer record. (294)

Sequence control structure. The control

structure used to represent operations that take place one after another. **(299)**

Sequential access. Reading or writing data in storage in a serial fashion. **(146)**

Sequential organization. A method of organizing data on a medium in such a way that access can only be achieved in a serial fashion. **(148)**

Serial transmission. Data transmission in which every bit in a byte must travel down the same path, one after the other. Contrast with parallel transmission. **(223)**

Simplex transmission. Any type of transmission in which a message can be sent along a path in only a single prespecified direction. **(211)**

Simulation. A technique whereby a model is built of a real-life object or situation, and tested, prior to the object being built or the situation being encountered. (534)

Software. Although generally synonymous with computer programs, the term software also includes the manuals that assist people in working with computer systems. **(10)**

Software piracy. The unauthorized copying or use of computer programs. **(522)**

Solid-font mechanism. The printing element on a printer, such as a daisywheel printer, that produces solid characters. Contrast with dot-matrix mechanism. **(171)**

Sorting. The process of arranging data in a specified order. **(53)**

Source data automation. A term that refers to making data available in machine-readable form at the time they are collected. **(181)**

Source module. The original form in which a program is entered into an input device by a user or programmer, prior to being translated into machine language. Also called *source program.* **(253)**

Spelling checker. A program that is often used adjunctively with a word processor to check for misspelled words. **(363)**

Spooling program. A program that temporarily stages input or output in secondary memory to expedite processing. **(256)**

Star network. A network that consists of a host device that is connected directly to several other devices in a point-to-point fashion. **(220)**

Start/stop symbol. A flowcharting symbol used to begin and terminate a flowchart. **(291)**

Status area. See Control panel. **(367)**

Storage. Pertaining to memory areas that hold programs and data in machine-readable form. **(5)**

Storage register. A register that temporarily stores data that have been retrieved from primary memory prior to processing. **(97)**

Streaming tape. See Cartridge tape. (125)

Structure chart. A program design tool that shows the hierarchical relationship between program modules. It looks very similar to the common organization chart. **(307)**

Structured program flowchart. A flowchart embodying the principles of structured programming. **(301)**

Structured programming. An approach to program design that uses a restricted set of program control structures, the principle of top-down design, and numerous other design methodologies. **(277, 298)**

Structured walkthrough. A formal program development practice in which the work of a systems analyst or programmer is constructively reviewed by peers. **(281)**

Summarizing. The process of reducing a mass of data to a manageable form. **(50)**

Supercomputer. The fastest type of mainframe computer. Typically supercomputers are found in engineering or scientific research environments. **(21)**

Supermicrocomputer. Refers to a desk-top microcomputer system that can accommodate two or more users concurrently. **(416)**

Supervisor. The central program in an operating system. The supervisor has the ability to invoke other operating system programs to perform various system tasks. **(243)**

Support equipment. All the machines that make it possible to get data and programs into the CPU, get processed information out, and store data and programs for ready access to the CPU. **(5, 36)**

Surge suppression. The act of protecting a microcomputer system from random electric power spikes. (422)

Switched line. A communications line that feeds into a switching center, enabling it to reach virtually any destination in the network by means of a telephone number. **(215)**

Synchronous transmission. The transmission of data over a line a block of characters at a time. Contrast with asynchronous transmission. **(224)**

System. A collection of elements and procedures that interact to accomplish a goal. **(472)**

System acquisition. The phase of the systems development process in which equipment, software, or services are acquired from vendors. **(485)**

System board. A board that contains the computer and its primary memory. Sometimes called a *motherboard*. **(114)**

System design. The phase of the systems development process that formally establishes the parts of a new system and the relationships among those parts. **(482)**

System flowchart. A systems development tool that shows how the physical parts of a system relate to one another. Contrast with program flowchart. **(479)**

System implementation. The phase of systems development that encompasses activities related to making the computer system operational and successful once it is delivered by the vendor. **(487)**

System librarian. The person in the computer operations area who is responsible for managing data files and programs stored offline on tapes, disks, microfilm, and other types of storage media. **(498)**

System unit. The hardware unit that houses the computer and its primary memory, as well as a number of other devices such as boards and circuitry. **(36, 416)**

Systems analysis. The phase of the systems development process in which a problem area is thoroughly examined to determine what should be done. **(477)**

Systems analyst. A person who studies systems in an organization in order to determine what actions need to be taken and how these actions may best be achieved with computer resources. **(270, 474, 499)**

Systems development. The process of studying a problem area in an existing system, designing a solution, acquiring the resources necessary to support the solution, and implementing the solution. **(472)**

Systems development cycle. The cycle consisting of the five phases of systems development. **(475)**

Systems development life cycle. See Systems development cycle. **(475)**

Systems programmer. A programmer who codes systems software. Contrast with applications programmer. **(498)**

Systems software. Computer programs—such as the operating system, language translators, and utility programs—that do background tasks for users and programmers. Contrast with applications software. **(50, 240)**

T

Tape unit. A secondary storage device on which magnetic tapes are mounted. **(125)**

Telecommuting. The substitution of teleprocessing at home for the commute to work. **(456)**

Teleprinter terminal. A low-speed printer containing a keyboard. **(178)**

Teleprocessing. Teleprocessing takes place when two or more machines in a computer system are transmitting data over a long distance and data are being processed somewhere in the system. **(204)**

Template. A prelabeled onscreen form that requires the operator to fill in only a limited number of input values. **(371, 389)**

Terminal. Technically speaking, any device that is not a host device is a terminal. **(220)**

Terrestrial microwave station. A ground station that receives microwave signals, amplifies them, and passes them on. **(209)**

Text editor. A utility program that enables an operator to manipulate text in a file. **(259)**

Third generation. The third era of commercial computers, from 1965 to 1970, which was characterized by integrated circuit technology. **(80)**

Time-sharing. Interactive processing in which the computer is shared by several users at, more or less, the same time. The computer system interleaves the processing of the programs so it appears to each user that he or she has exclusive use of the computer. **(249)**

Top-down design. A structured design tool that subdivides a program or system into well-defined modules, organized in a hierarchy, which are developed from the top of the hierarchy down to the lowest level. **(301)**

Touch screen device. A display device that can be activated by touching a finger to the screen. **(168)**

Track. A path on an input/output medium on which data are recorded. **(126)**

Trackball. A cursor-movement device that consists of a sphere resting on rollers, with only the top of the sphere exposed outside its case. **(168)**

Trailer record. See Sentinel record. (294)

Transaction file. A file of occurrences—such as customer payments and purchases—that have taken place over a period of time. (47)

Transaction processing. Pertaining to accounting systems that manage an organization's day-to-day dealings—or transactions—with clients. Two examples are bank teller systems and airline reservation systems. (445)

Transistor. A circuit device that dominated second-generation computers. **(75)**

Twisted-wire pairs. A communications medium that consists of pairs of wires, twisted together, and bound into a cable. The telephone system consists mainly of twisted-wire cabling. **(207)**

U

Unconditional branch. An instruction that causes the computer to execute a specific statement other than the one that immediately follows in the normal sequence. **(294)**

UNIVAC I. The first commercial electronic digital computer. **(73)**

Universal product code (UPC). The bar code that is prominently displayed on the packaging of almost all supermarket goods, identifying the product and manufacturer. A variety of optical scanning devices may be used to read the codes. **(184)**

UPC. See Universal product code. **(184)**

Updating. The process of bringing something up to date by making corrections, adding new data, and so forth. **(56)**

Upward compatible. A computer system that can do everything that a smaller model in the line or the previous model can do, plus some additional tasks. (79)

User. A person who needs the services of a computer system. **(10)**

Utility program. A program used to perform some frequently encountered operation in a computer system. **(255)**

V

Vacuum tube. The circuit device that dominated first-generation computers. **(73)**

Value. In spreadsheet programs a cell entry that can be manipulated mathematically. Contrast with label. **(368)**

Vendor rating system. An objective point-scoring procedure for evaluating competing vendors of computer products or services. **(485)**

Verifier. A device used to detect keying errors by having the operator rekey data. (181)

Very-high-level language. A problem-specific language that is generally much easier to learn and use than conventional high-level languages such as BASIC, FORTRAN, COBOL, and Pascal. **(324)**

Very-large-scale-integration (VLSI). The process of placing a very large number of integrated circuits (usually over 1000) on a single silicon chip. (83)

Vice president of information systems. The person in an organization who oversees routine data processing and information systems activities as well as activities in other computer-related areas. Also often called the chief information officer (CIO). **(500)**

Video teleconferencing. Pertaining to conferences that are held by people at different sites, who see each other on video terminals. **(456)**

Videotex. A computer system that provides picture information, for users to inspect on a display screen, of things such as goods to buy or places at which to dine. (145)

Virtual storage. An area on disk where programs are "cut up" into manageable pieces and staged as they are processed. While the computer is processing a program, it fetches the pieces of it that are needed from virtual storage and places them into main memory. **(249)**

VLSI. See Very-large-scale integration. (83)

Voice-grade transmission. Medium-speed transmission characterized by the rates of speed available over ordinary telephone lines. **(211)**

Voice-input device. A device capable of recognizing the human voice. **(194)**

Voice-output device. A device that enables the computer system to produce spoken output. **(197)**

Volatile storage. Storage that loses its contents when the power is shut off. (417)

W

Wideband transmission. High-speed transmission characterized by the rates of speed available over coaxial cable, fiber optic cable, and microwave. **(211)**

Winchester disk. A sealed data module that contains a disk, access arms, and read/write heads. **(140, 419)**

Window. Refers to either (1) using the display screen as a "peek hole" to inspect contiguous portions of a large worksheet or (2) dividing the display screen up into independent boxes of information. **(259)**

Window area. In spreadsheet software the portion of the screen that contains the window onto the worksheet. Also called the worksheet area. **(367)**

Windowing software. Software that enables a user to assemble independent boxes of information on the screen at the same time. **(259)**

Word. A group of bits or characters that are treated by the computer system as an entity and are capable of being stored in a single memory location. **(113, 416)**

Word processing. The use of computer technology to create, manipulate, and print text material such as letters, legal contracts, and manuscripts. **(348, 455)**

Worksheet. In spreadsheet software the grid that contains the actual labels and values. **(365)**

Worksheet area. See Window area. **(367)**

Answers to Fill-in and Matching Review Questions

Chapter 1

Fill-in Questions
1. central processing unit
2. primary, internal, or main
3. data
4. software
5. secondary, external, or auxiliary
6. hardware
7. program
8. computer system

Matching Questions
1. e 2. f 3. a 4. c 5. b 6. d

Chapter 2

Fill-in Questions
1. input/output medium
2. auxiliary
3. diskette
4. online
5. applications
6. systems
7. field
8. file

Matching Questions
1. b 2. f 3. c 4. e 5. a 6. d

Chapter 3

Fill-in Questions
1. ENIAC
2. Pascaline
3. difference engine
4. Mark I
5. ABC
6. UNIVAC
7. Digital Equipment
8. IBM

Matching Questions
1. h 2. e 3. f 4. g 5. a 6. c 7. d
8. b

Chapter 4

Fill-in Questions
1. millisecond
2. microsecond
3. nanosecond
4. picosecond
5. kilobyte
6. megabyte
7. gigabyte

Matching Questions
1. b 2. d 3. g 4. e 5. h 6. a 7. f
8. c

Chapter 5

Fill-in Questions
1. logical, physical
2. disk pack
3. tracks
4. file-protection ring
5. cylinder
6. rotational delay
7. Winchester
8. mass storage unit

Matching Questions
1. d 2. a 3. c 4. f 5. e 6. b

Chapter 6

Fill-in Questions
1. monitors, display terminals
2. pixels
3. cursor
4. monochrome
5. near-letter-quality

6. daisywheel
7. teleprinter
8. flatbed, drum

Matching Questions

1. e 2. f 3. g 4. b 5. d 6. a 7. h
8. c

Chapter 7

Fill-in Questions

1. twisted-wire pairs
2. coaxial cable
3. digital
4. fiber optic cable
5. modem
6. synchronous
7. common carriers
8. asynchronous
9. dedicated
10. star

Matching Questions

1. d 2. e 3. b 4. a 5. c 6. f

Chapter 8

Fill-in Questions

1. systems
2. operating system
3. multiprogramming
4. time-sharing
5. multiprocessing
6. language translator
7. utility

Matching Questions

1. e 2. d 3. a 4. c 5. g 6. b 7. f

Chapter 9

Fill-in Questions

1. systems analysts
2. maintenance programmers
3. coding
4. structured walkthrough
5. debugging
6. desk check

Matching Questions

1. h 2. c 3. e 4. b 5. f 6. g 7. d
8. a

Chapter 10

Fill-in Questions

1. flowchart
2. conditional
3. unconditional
4. initializing
5. top-down
6. pseudocode
7. structure charts, HIPO charts
8. decision tables

Matching Questions

1. d 2. f 3. a 4. e 5. b 6. c

Chapter 11

Fill-in Questions

1. BASIC
2. FORTRAN
3. COBOL
4. Pascal
5. PL/1
6. Ada
7. C
8. Logo

Matching Questions

1. g 2. a 3. c 4. d 5. e 6. f 7. b

Chapter 12

Fill-in Questions

1. wordwrap
2. proportional spacing
3. window, worksheet
4. cursor, cell pointer (or highlight)
5. absolute, relative
6. template

Matching Questions

1. e 2. b 3. a 4. f 5. c 6. d

Chapter 13

Fill-in Questions
1. file managers, database management systems
2. template
3. database
4. hierarchical, network, relational
5. database administrator
6. concurrent

Matching Questions
1. b 2. e 3. a 4. d 5. f 6. c

Chapter 14

Fill-in Questions
1. random-access memory
2. read-only memory
3. microprocessor
4. nonvolatile
5. operating systems
6. modem
7. surge suppression
8. multifunction

Matching Questions
1. d 2. e 3. c 4. b 5. a 6. h 7. g
8. f

Chapter 15

Fill-in Questions
1. accounts payable
2. accounts receivable
3. general ledger
4. computer-aided design
5. electronic mail
6. video teleconferencing
7. robotics

Matching Questions
1. c 2. a 3. f 4. e 5. d 6. b

Chapter 16

Fill-in Questions
1. steering
2. systems analyst
3. management
4. synthesis
5. design
6. tangible
7. vendor rating
8. benchmark test

Matching Questions
1. b 2. d 3. e 4. c 5. a

Chapter 17

Fill-in Questions
1. data-entry operators
2. computer operators
3. system librarians
4. computer operations managers
5. systems programmers
6. applications programmers
7. systems analysts
8. data processing director

Matching Questions
1. c 2. a 3. b 4. d

Chapter 18

Fill-in Questions
1. cyberphobia
2. ergonomics
3. salami
4. computer ethics
5. piracy
6. hacking
7. Fair Credit Reporting
8. Education Privacy

Credits

TEXT PHOTOGRAPHS

Fig. 18-6 Rolm Corporation
Fig. 18-7 Cranston/Csuri Productions, Inc., Columbus, Ohio
Fig. 18-8 Roland
box on p. 535 Evans & Sutherland

Fig. 18-9 Apple Computer, Inc.
Appendix A, opposite p. A-1 AT&T Bell Laboratories
Appendix B, opposite p. B-1 Charles S. Parker

THE WINDOWS

Window 1

1, 9 Genigraphics Corporation
2, 16 Lightspeed; Artist: Mary Anne Lloyd
3 Produced by Ken Braswell on an AVL Starburst
4 "Dodgers"—sports graphic created on the Aurora/125 by artist Ron Lang for KRON-TV, San Francisco, Calif.
5 Quantel
6, 7 Doyle Puppo Design Associates
8, 14 Lightspeed; Artist: Judy Atwood
10, 13, 19 Sperry Information Systems Group
11 Apple Computer, Inc.
12 NCR Corporation
15 Harris Corporation
17 Hewlett-Packard Company
18 Cincinnati Milacron
20 Buick Motor Division
21 Roland
22 Axlon, Inc., Sunnyvale, Calif.
23, 24 Teitzell Film Incorporated
25 Weather map created by artist Robin Stelling on the Aurora/125 for Aurora Systems
26 Dubner Computer Systems, Inc.
27–29 This series of holiday IDs was created on the Aurora/125 by artist Ron Lang for KRON-TV, San Francisco, Calif.

Window 2

1 Harris Corporation
2, 3, 8 Commodore Business Machines, Inc.
4, 9, 11 Intel Corporation
5 Digital Equipment Corporation
6 National Semiconductor
7 AT&T Bell Laboratories
10 McDonnell Douglas Information Systems
12 AT&T

Window 3

1, 2 Quantel
3, 4 Lightspeed; Artist: Mary Anne Lloyd
5 Lightspeed; Artist: Tyler Peppel
6, 7 Genigraphics Corporation
8, 18, 19 Artronics, Incorporated; Artist: Scott Lewczak
9 Cornell University, Program of Computer Graphics; Artists: Hank Weghorst, Gary Hooper, Donald Greenberg
10 Lightspeed; Artist: Olga Antinova
11 Cranston/Csuri Productions, Inc., Columbus, Ohio
12 "Mt. Fuji"—created on the Aurora/125 by artist Damon Rarey for Aurora Systems
13, 14 Robert Bosch Corporation
15 Dubner Computer Systems, Inc.
16 Created on the Aurora/125 by artist Damon Rarey for Aurora Systems
17 Still from animated piece created on the Aurora/125 by artist Lee Marrs
20–22 Artist: James Dowlen, Time Arts Inc., © 1985
23 Produced by Ken Braswell on an AVL Starburst

Window 4

1 Tektronix, Inc.
2 Quantel
3 Artist: James Dowlen, Time Arts Inc., © 1985
4, 15, 16 SAS Institute, Inc.
5 Produced by Ken Braswell on an AVL Starburst
6 Via Video
7, 13, 14 ISSCO
8 Versatec, A Xerox Company

9–12   Genigraphics Corporation
17–19   Decision Resources, Inc.

Window 5
1, 11   Hewlett-Packard Company
2, 3   International Busines Machines Corporation
4–6, 23, 24   Apple Computer, Inc.
7   Texas Instruments, Inc.
8, 9   Commodore Business Machines, Inc.
10   AT&T
12   Atari
13   Kaypro Corporation
14, 16   Quadram Corporation
15   Houston Instrument
17, 18   Curtis Manufacturing Company, Inc., Peterborough, N.H.
19, 20   Tess Data Systems, Inc.
21   Lotus Development Corporation
22   Digital Research Inc.
25   Eastman Kodak Company

Window 6
1, 15   Apollo Computer Inc.
2   Lexidata Corporation
3   Doyle Puppo Design Associates
4–6   Quantel
7, 8, 12   Robert Bosch Corporation
9–10, 13   Via Video; Artist: Gail Blumberg

11   Via Video; Artist: Leslie Kuhn
14   Alias Research Corporation
16   Evans & Sutherland
17   "Kaiser Pass" by Bob Melvin, Copyright Number Nine Computer Corporation
18–21   Lightspeed; Artist: Judy Atwood

Window 7
1   Hewlett-Packard Company
2–5   "Entertainment Tonight" produced for Marks Communications, Creative Director: Harry Marks; Animator: Carl Rosendahl, Pacific Data Images
6–8   Teitzell Film Incorporated
9, 10   Apple Computer, Inc.
11, 13   International Business Machines Corporation
12   Cranston/Csuri Productions, Inc., Columbus, Ohio
14   Harris Corporation
15   Created by artist Robin Stelling on the Aurora/125 for Aurora Systems
16–18   Evans & Sutherland
19–21   Evans & Sutherland, Daimler Benz
22, 24–26   Doyle Puppo Design Associates
23   "The Other Apple"—News graphic created on the Aurora/125 by artist Robin Stelling for KPIX-TV, San Francisco, Calif.

TRADEMARKS

Apple, Apple II, Apple IIc, and Apple IIe are registered trademarks of Apple Computer, Inc. Macintosh is a trademark licensed to Apple Computer, Inc. Ashton-Tate, dBASE, dBASE II, dBASE III, dBASE III Plus, Framework, and Multimate are registered trademarks of Ashton-Tate. Atari 520 ST is a registered trademark of Atari, Inc. AT&T, AT&T PC 6300, and AT&T Unix PC are registered trademarks of AT&T. Burroughs is a registered trademark of Burroughs Corporation. Commodore Amiga, Commodore 64, Commodore 128, and VIC-20 are registered trademarks of Commodore Business Machines, Inc. Compaq, Compaq DeskPro 286, Compaq Plus, and Compaq Portable Computer are registered trademarks of Compaq Computer Corporation. Control Data is a registered trademark of Control Data Corporation. CP/M and GEM Paint are registered trademarks of Digital Research, Inc. Cray is a registered trademark of Cray Research, Inc. Data General is a registered trademark of Data General Corporation. DEC is a registered trademark of Digital Equipment Corporation. VAX is a trademark of Digital Equipment Corporation. Honeywell is a registered trademark of Honeywell, Inc. HP 150 is a registered trademark of Hewlett-Packard Company. IBM, IBM PC, IBM PC/XT, IBM PC AT, and PC-DOS are registered trademarks of International Business Machines Corporation. Intel, Intel 8048, Intel 8086, Intel 8087, Intel 8088, Intel 80286, and Intel 80386 are registered trademarks of Intel Corporation. Kaypro is a registered trademark of Kaypro Corporation. KnowledgeMan is a registered trademark of Micro Data Base Systems, Inc. Lotus and 1-2-3 are registered trademarks of Lotus Development Corporation. Jazz and Symphony are trademarks of Lotus Development Corporation. Microsoft, Microsoft Word, MS-DOS, Multiplan, and Xenix are registered trademarks of Microsoft Corporation. MOS Technology 6502 and MOS Technology 65C02 are registered trademarks of MOS Technology Corporation. Motorola 68000 is a registered trademark of Motorola Corporation. NCR is a registered trademark of NCR Corporation. Quolor is a trademark of Lightspeed. Qume is a registered trademark of ITT Qume. Starburst is a registered trademark of AVL, Inc. Texas Instruments Business Pro and Texas Instruments Professional Computer are registered trademarks of Texas Instruments, Inc. Tandy 1000, Tandy 3000, and TRS-80 are registered trademarks of Tandy Corporation. Univac is a registered trademark of Sperry Corporation. Unix is a trademark of AT&T Bell Laboratories. VisiCalc is a registered trademark of Visi-Corp. Wang PC is a registered trademark of Wang Laboratories, Inc. Zenith Z-150 is a registered trademark of Zenith Data Systems. Zilog Z-80 and Zilog Z-80A are registered trademarks of Zilog.

Index